GERMANY UNIFIED AND EUROPE TRANSFORMED

Germany Unified and Europe Transformed

A STUDY IN STATECRAFT

WITH A NEW PREFACE

Philip Zelikow

Condoleezza Rice

Harvard University Press
Cambridge, Massachusetts
London, England

Copyright © 1995, 1997 by the President and Fellows of Harvard College
All rights reserved
Printed in the United States of America
Sixth printing, 2002

First Harvard University Press paperback edition, 1997

Library of Congress Cataloging-in-Publication Data

Zelikow, Philip, 1954–
    Germany unified and Europe transformed : a study in statecraft / Philip Zelikow,
    Condoleezza Rice.
        p.   cm.
    Includes bibliographical references and index.
    ISBN 0-674-35324-2 (cloth)
    ISBN 0-674-35325-0 (pbk.)
    1. Germany—History—Unification, 1990. 2. Germany—Politics and government—1990–
    3. Europe—Politics and government—1989– 4. European federation. 5. Germany—Relations—
    Europe. 6. Europe—Relations—Germany. I. Rice, Condoleezza, 1954– . II. Title.
DD290.29.Z45 1995
943.087′9—dc20
95-12187

Contents

Preface, 1997

Over the past year, many friends and scholars have engaged us in discussions of our book. Through reviews, seminars, and letters we have benefited from questions about what we intended, what we did not say, and what we might have written instead.

Many people have asked us about the knotty problem of whom to credit with ending the Cold War peacefully. Credit should be awarded, in abundance, to those who contributed to "a turning point in the more than seventy-year history of antidemocratic and totalitarian systems that emerged after World War I."[1] Yet some prefer to rise above particular human choices and focus instead on anonymous crowds or abstract historical forces, such as the rise of freedom, the information age, and many other candidate "big causes."

Many factors, including the hopes of individuals, contributed to the events that unfolded in 1989 and beyond. We acknowledge them. Our story is placed in a well-defined setting already shaped by the operation of large-scale historical forces. In that setting some felt confident, others frustrated, and still others both hopeful and uneasy. Yet given these underlying circumstances, many outcomes were possible. The former Soviet foreign minister and ambassador to the United States, Alexander Bessmertnykh, stated at a recent conference that "the story of reunification seems simple after you've heard what everybody has to say about it. In fact, it was not that simple; it was not that naive; and it was not that placid. There were a lot of nerve-wracking situations in Moscow."[2] And not only Moscow.

Some recent books put forward particular Germans, Americans, or Soviets as winners of the prize for having made this difference in the ending of the Cold War. However diverting, such a contest tends to shed more heat than light. We are more interested in the interaction of perceptions and choices from several governments. Though some individuals had more influence than others, we found the spotlight shifting from person to person, country to country, at different times or on different issues. Recent events suggest, however, that one person's role is receding into history quickly and unfairly: Mikhail Gorbachev's receiving 1 percent of the vote in the 1996 Russian presidential election was just a footnote as we celebrated the country's first democratic election. As time passes, it is very important that history never forget how this man of great strengths and equally great weaknesses contributed significantly to the ending of the Cold War.

We would like to offer another way of thinking about the challenge of assigning "credit" to one person or another, or to one or another person's favorite cause. The following might be thought of as a map to causal variables in the unification of Germany.

Dependent, or outcome, variables:

- *Unification and its timing.* The two German states are unified into one before the FRG elections at the end of 1990.
- *The fundamental nature of the new German state.* Unification occurs via Article 23 of the West German constitution, destroying the GDR and making the new state an expanded FRG without any fundamental changes in the system of government or principles for the organization of society.
- *The political alignment of the new German state.* The united Germany is a full member of the North Atlantic Alliance, with all German territory protected by NATO, all German forces remaining integrated within NATO's multinational military command, and without placing unique legal limits on German forces.
- *Asymmetrical treatment of NATO and Soviet forces.* All Soviet forces leave Germany; Western forces stay, including U.S. nuclear forces.

Explanatory, or independent, variables, which must meet three criteria:

a. but for the specified content of the variable (that is, in a counterfactual condition with this variable being absent), the content of one or another dependent, or outcome, variable would have been materially different;
b. the above-mentioned counterfactual condition must be reasonable, in that there was a genuine possibility of the variable being absent; and
c. the causal variable is independent, in that the decisive content of the variable was indeterminate even after the contents of preexisting (but not simultaneous) variables were established.

At least thirteen variables appear to meet these criteria:

1. The USSR and the GDR divide sharply and publicly on the need for and direction of reform communism (1988–1989).
2. Hungarian decisions on borders are made and misunderstood, and then Hungary reverses its policy toward Romanian and East German refugees (May–September 1989).
3. East Germans decide against the "Chinese solution" for domestic protest and choose, with Soviet backing, the reform communist government of Krenz (October 1989).
4. Responding erratically to a surge in domestic unrest, the Krenz government's policies culminate in the unplanned opening of the Berlin Wall (October–November 1989).
5. Kohl, with Bush's encouragement, reverts from the Ostpolitik paradigm of "Wandel durch Annäherung" (change through rapprochement) back to the Adenauer paradigm of "Wandel durch Kraft" (change through strength); Kohl destabilizes the East German governments of Krenz/Modrow, spurring popular contemplation of unification; the United States helps deflect international attempts to curb Kohl and restrain popular expectations in the GDR (October–December 1989).
6. Kohl spurns confederative negotiations with Modrow and the "Roundtable," and, with U.S. backing, decides to seek direct economic and political annexation of eastern Germany (January–February 1990).
7. The United States chooses maximal objectives for unifying Germany in NATO and the Two Plus Four plan for negotiating international aspects of unification (January–February 1990).
8. Kohl's agenda for rapid unification, propelled by indicators that it is internationally viable, produces a surprising electoral victory for his cause in the GDR election (March 1990).
9. Soviet diplomatic reactions to German developments are ineffective as Two Plus Four activity is deliberately delayed and constrained and the US-FRG rallies the West behind common objectives for unification (February–May 1990).
10. The FRG offers limited financial aid to the USSR and spurs positive but inconclusive multilateral consideration of a much larger assistance package (January, May–July 1990).
11. The United States and the FRG shape and deliver commitments on German armed forces and significant change in NATO's political and military stance that nevertheless remain consistent with preexisting US-FRG objectives (June–July 1990).

12. Gorbachev makes a series of connected decisions: he avoids an invasion of Lithuania, begins to abandon structures of collective leadership, and starts changing his stance on the German question during and after the Washington summit. Yet he successfully fends off challenges at the Twenty-third Soviet Communist Party Congress (May–July 1990).

13. Complex political-military negotiations of linked political and economic agreements, consistent with preexisting US-FRG objectives, are accomplished among Two Plus Four states and specifically among the USSR, Germany, and the United States (July–September 1990).

Our narrative attempts to reconstruct the intricate details of each of these variables, which are themselves clusters of choices and interactions.

We have also been asked repeatedly what lessons can be drawn from such a complex story. Our opinions differ. To Zelikow, the story shows what kinds of government actions and consequences are possible. He is skeptical, though, about efforts to turn the kind of comprehension that comes from such explanatory knowledge into mind-closing axioms. To Rice, there are lessons here in statecraft that can guide policymakers of the future. This episode reminds policymakers to expect the unexpected (the East German exodus in the summer of 1989), to choose goals that are optimal, even if they seem at the time politically infeasible (Germany fully integrated into NATO despite Soviet objections); and that the government that knows what it wants has a reasonable chance of getting it (as Washington and Bonn did and Moscow did not).

Important new sources on the events of 1989 and 1990 have appeared since our book was first published. We do not believe, however, that these sources oblige us to amend our narrative, and several provide reinforcement of some key details.

Scholars now have wider access to the archives of the former East German government. Some fruits of this access are apparent in a new history of East German disintegration and reconstruction by Charles Maier. New sources also reveal fascinating points for comparison, especially in the linkages of East-West diplomacy and domestic upheaval, between the failed revolt of 1953 and the successful revolution of 1989.[3]

The most important new source is Helmut Kohl's account of German unification. For this memoir, two journalists interviewed him many times, were shown a few documents, and then stitched Kohl's recollections together.[4] The result is a book that is solid and highly useful. It confirms or reinforces the interpretations offered in our book, both about general issues and on key details. Overall the book is marked by the same clarity about basic principles that marked Kohl's policies at the time. The account, by this former history student, is soaked in historical memories and anecdotes that surface in almost every important meeting Kohl recounts. Where we have independent evidence about the episodes being described, Kohl is truthful. He prefers to omit some awkward episodes and problematical policy details. He draws a curtain over the actual content of his discussions with colleagues in the government, especially the details of his clashes with his coalition partner and foreign minister, Hans-Dietrich Genscher.[5]

The memoir reaffirms how deeply ingrained were the convictions Kohl had formed as a young supporter of West Germany's first postwar chancellor, Konrad Adenauer. By the 1980s he was dismayed by how many people had given up on unity: "The times had too powerful an effect, too much resignation, and also—one must say it—betrayal of the inherited path [Verrat ihre Spuren hinterlassen]." He reveals that he was distracted by internal political battles and by prostate problems during the refugee crisis of August and September 1989 (and the near-crash of the American-piloted passenger aircraft in which he was flying on August 22). As events opened the door for movement toward reunification, Kohl describes how on the one hand he constantly assured every foreign leader (except Bush) that he did not want any escalation of the unrest in East Germany, and how, on the other hand, even before the Berlin Wall opened, he had adopted the view that "cosmetic corrections [in the GDR] weren't enough. We didn't want to stabilize an intolerable situation." So he insisted on revolutionary change as a precondition to any aid for the new reform communists. Kohl describes these apparently contradictory positions without acknowledging any inconsistency. His is not a very analytical book. He is quite open, however, about his constant wish to take the initiative away from the East Germans and not help the new government of Hans Modrow. Even when pressure to help the former dissidents became intense, Kohl felt that it was "completely absurd to aid this regime several weeks before the first democratic election." It was an election Kohl wanted to win (through his surrogates).[6]

Kohl reveals his sensitivity to the politics of pursuing NATO membership for a united Germany. He says that he deliberately downplayed the NATO issue in his November 1989 "ten-point plan" for unity to keep from aggravating the already hostile reaction from the Kremlin. Kohl understood well how, after this initiative, George Bush "made it clear to our partners in NATO that the United States supported my policy. [Bush's] calculation was to make himself a spokesman for the German side and in return to secure our firm assurance that we would stick strongly by membership of a united Germany in NATO." Yet in early 1990, after Modrow and Gorbachev arrived at their common approach on the unity issue, Kohl says he feared that, "had Gorbachev now pushed the offer of a quick reunification against NATO withdrawal and neutrality, he could have grabbed wide support for this among the people of both German states. The resulting pressure on the policy would have had fatal consequences."[7]

Kohl is especially helpful in detailing his effective efforts to contain French unease and manage his long-standing relationship with a deeply ambivalent François Mitterrand. At one point Kohl became frustrated at the revival of French-Polish geopolitical cooperation, which he thought of as the revival of the "little entente" practiced against Germany during the 1920s. When one Polish visitor described how the Polish prime minister had told him that one must play ping-pong between Warsaw and Paris, over the German net, Kohl exclaimed, "That old game! I laughed at this then and said to him, 'Naturally you can do that. Certainly we can all repeat the same stupid mistakes we made back then.'" Kohl had little use for the French foreign minister, Roland Dumas, but he thought that in Mitterrand's breast "two hearts were beating," each pulling the French leader in a different direction.[8] For the Americans, Bush and Baker in particular, Kohl has nothing but praise.[9]

The Federal Republic of Germany's former foreign minister, Hans-Dietrich Genscher, has published a massive memoir.[10] Though he offers a strong chapter on the events of early 1989, Genscher's lengthy treatment of the process of German unification has many omissions (especially about the formation of his government's policies), some useful details, and is short on candor. We would rather not comment on each of his claims to have been prescient, to have originated all key concepts, and to have seen every subsequent event unfold in accordance with his plans. Instead, we simply note that opaque policy phrases (such as "cooperative security structures") are put forward and then interpreted to suit the preferred meaning of the moment— then as minister, now as memoirist. To counter this pattern, the interested reader can compare the accounts of particular episodes presented in our book (and others), including the endnotes, and examine the relevant details and meanings of the time.[11] Unfortunately, the resulting habit of wariness can divert attention from the apparent sincerity and importance of Genscher's genuine convictions on the national question and Germany's alignment with the West, principles that demonstrate why his coalition with Chancellor Kohl endured as long and successfully as it did.

President Bush and his national security adviser, Brent Scowcroft, are preparing a book that will recount some of their experiences in detail. Their work will not offer many surprises on the German story to readers of this book, but it may be the most candid memoir ever written by an American president. Thought processes and calculations are opened fully, with the authors acknowledging uncertainties and mistakes as well as presenting insights. We learned that, until December 1989, Scowcroft was more hesitant about German unity than we on his staff had realized. Nevertheless, Scowcroft always forwarded his staff's analyses to the president, even if his own advice sometimes differed from them. The pivotal importance and firmness of Bush's personal judgments stand out more clearly than ever, as does the fact that Bush did not also receive more cautionary advice from his secretary of state, James Baker.

Memoirs have also been published by Baker (with Thomas DeFrank), by President Bush's deputy national security adviser (later director of Central Intelligence), Robert Gates, by the Bush administration's ambassador to the Soviet Union, Jack Matlock, and by one of our National Security Council staff colleagues, Robert Hutchings.[12] None presents significant new material on the issues handled in this book. Baker's account is obviously mandatory reading for researchers. Though he is selective in what he covers and has sanded down many sharp edges, the material Baker gave DeFrank is frequently candid and often reconstructs the decision-making process behind a policy, and the factual assertions are quite reliable. Matlock provides much useful information, especially about some Soviet-American exchanges and about the vital and poorly understood crisis over Lithuania (and other nations in the Soviet empire). Matlock's work is more noteworthy, however, for his observations of the Soviet scene than for its reconstruction of the details of either Soviet or American foreign policy toward Europe in 1989 and 1990. The Gates memoir is an exceptional work. Though he covers too wide a period to treat the issues of this book in depth, Gates provides details about certain White House meetings and also offers new evidence confirming how serious the KGB's discontent with Gorbachev's policies had become by February 1990.[13] Hutchings leavens his memoir with considerable scholarship to provide a broad portrait of American policy toward Europe during the Bush administration.

Gorbachev has also published a 1,200-page volume of memoirs.[14] This valuable work, like Genscher's, has many omissions, as on uncomfortable topics such as the secret discussions of massive multilateral assistance with Kohl and Bush during the spring of 1990. The book does contain many verbatim excerpts from the original records of Gorbachev's meetings, and it is a serious reflection of his thought. In his forthcoming book, Gorbachev's and Shevardnadze's long-time English-speaking interpreter, Pavel Palazchenko, will add even more detail about the meetings between U.S. and Soviet leaders.[15]

The one story that we wish we had known better before our book was published was that of François Mitterrand and French diplomacy. Mitterrand's estate has posthumously published reminiscences about his attitude toward the Germans.[16] More important new evidence supports the much more ambivalent portrait offered in our book. One of Mitterrand's closest advisers, Jacques Attali, has published a third volume of what he claims are excerpts from his diaries, this time covering the period from 1988 to 1991.[17] The publication of this volume caused a stir in France and reportedly kept Attali from being invited to Mitterrand's funeral. Throughout the book significant new evidence is presented about the real content of French bilateral and EC discussions at the highest level, thereby providing confirmation of hypotheses advanced in this book about the beliefs at various times of Gorbachev and Thatcher, as well as of Mitterrand himself.

Attali's diaries show Bush and Mitterrand disagreeing about German unification as early as their Kennebunkport meeting in May 1989, with Bush saying, "It can be done," and Mitterrand answering that a popular call for reunification of Germany was one of "only two possible causes of war in Europe" (the other being German acquisition of nuclear weapons). Thatcher had claimed in her memoirs that Mitterrand tended to agree with her fears about German unification. Attali's diaries back her account. In December 1989, "1913" was always on Mitterrand's mind, and he had warned Genscher that Bonn was about to re-create the pre–World War I Triple Alliance of France, Britain, and Russia, again rallied against Germany. Using another analogy, he complained to Thatcher, "We find ourselves in the same situation as the leaders in France and Britain before the war, who didn't react to anything. We can't repeat Munich!" Mitterrand's private reaction to the opening of the Berlin Wall was that "these people are tinkering with a world war." A month earlier he had confided to Attali that "those who speak of German unification don't understand anything. The Soviet Union will never accept it. It would be the death of the Warsaw Pact: Can you imagine it? And the GDR, it's Prussia. It would never want to fall under the control of Bavaria." Furious in February 1990 that "Gorbachev tells me he'll be firm, and then gives up on everything!" Mitterrand flew to Moscow in May expecting Gorbachev to seek his help in resisting German unification. "I'd enjoy doing it if I thought he would. But why clash with Kohl if Gorbachev will only drop me three days later? I'd be totally isolated." Nevertheless, Mitterrand, knowing he was breaking from the position of his allies, privately proposed to Gorbachev that a united Germany remain in NATO but withdraw from its integrated organization.[18] By that time, however, such ideas faced firm opposition from the United States, West Germany, and Britain.

The new material that has surfaced since this book first appeared highlights the uncertainty, exultation, and fear surrounding the historic months in 1989 and 1990 that changed the future of Europe and the world. As time passes, readers must make a conscious effort to recapture the clamor and detail of this dramatic period of history. We hope our book will continue to help them do it.

Notes

1. Karl Dietrich Bracher, *Turning Points in Modern Times: Essays on German and European History,* tr. Thomas Dunlap (Cambridge, Mass.: Harvard University Press, 1995), p. 21. Bracher's own macro-level distribution of credit highlights two preconditions: "the choice to confront Soviet totalitarianism and the basic striving for freedom and a Western living standard within the East bloc." As to catalysts, "What made the breakthrough possible was Gorbachev's and Shevardnadze's understanding of what was necessary and inevitable, along with the role played by personalities (in the West, Reagan and Bush, Schmidt and Kohl)." Ibid., p. 24.

2. Bessmertnykh made his comments at a March 1996 conference of former Soviet and American officials entitled "The End of the Cold War," hosted at Princeton University by Don Oberdorfer and Fred Greenstein. The proceedings are now being edited by William Wohlforth for publication.

3. See Charles S. Maier, *Dissolution: East Germany from the Crisis of Communism to the Trials of Unity* (Princeton: Princeton University Press, 1997). On 1953, the work cited in the original edition by Christian Ostermann, James Richter, and Hope Harrison has been usefully supplemented by Christian F. Ostermann, "'Keeping the Pot Simmering': The United States and the East German Uprising of 1953," *German Studies Review* 19 (February 1996): 61–90; and Gerhard Wettig, "Die beginnende Umorientierung der sowjetischen Deutschland-Politik im Früjahr und Sommer 1953," *Deutschland Archiv* 28 (May 1995): 495–507.

4. Helmut Kohl, *Ich Wollte Deutschlands Einheit,* ed. Kai Diekmann and Ralf Georg Reuth (Berlin: Propyläen, 1996).

5. Kohl says nothing, for example, about the Genscher-Stoltenberg dispute over the extension of NATO to the former territory of the GDR, and how he reversed his position the next week during his meeting with Bush at Camp David. There are various other omissions at this level of detail. Also, in describing what we know were several difficult exchanges with Genscher about the Polish border question, or the NATO position, or whether to decouple the internal and external aspects of unification, Kohl is cryptic or just describes his own position, without ever detailing the to-and-fro. Yet he describes his confontations with rivals in his own party, as with Heiner Geißler in September 1989, with apparent relish.

6. For the quotations see Kohl, *Ich Wollte Deutschlands Einheit,* pp. 33, 117, 258.

7. Ibid., pp. 189, 254.

8. Ibid., pp. 324, 198.

9. Kohl's warm feelings toward Bush are well known, but here the chancellor offers a striking compliment to Baker, whom he repeatedly calls "brilliant," adding that Baker "had the stuff there to be President himself. George Bush probably would not have achieved so much if Jim Baker had not been standing at his side." Ibid., p. 364.

10. Hans-Dietrich Genscher, *Erinnerungen* (Berlin: Siedler Verlag, 1995).

11. For example, Gunther Hellmann, "Der Präsident, der Kanzler, sein Aussenminister und die Vereinigung, oder: Staatkunst als Heuernte," *Politische Vierteljahresschrift* 37 (June 1996): 357–363; Elke Bruck and Peter M. Wagner, "Die deutsche Einheit und ich," *Zeitschrift für Politik* 43 (Hefte 2, 1996): 208–224. Wagner, with Bruck and Felix Lutz, is associated with the "Forschungsgruppe Deutschland," a research center, currently based in Munich, that has achieved access to some significant West German archival materials.

12. James A. Baker, III, with Thomas M. DeFrank, *The Politics of Diplomacy: Revolution, War, and Peace, 1989–1992* (New York: G. P. Putnam's Sons, 1995); Robert M. Gates, *From the Shadows: The Ultimate Insider's Story of Five Presidents and How They Won the Cold War* (New York: Simon & Schuster, 1996); Jack F. Matlock, Jr., *Autopsy on an Empire: The American Ambassador's Account of the Collapse of the Soviet Union* (New York: Random House, 1995); Robert J. Hutchings, *American Diplomacy and the End of the Cold War: An Insider's Account of U.S. Policy in Europe, 1989–1992* (Washington, D.C.: Wilson Center Press and Johns Hopkins University Press, 1997).

13. The much longer manuscript of the Gates book, before it was pared down for publication by a commercial press, is available for research, both through the CIA Historian's Office and at Harvard University.

14. Michail Gorbatschow, *Erinnerungen*, tr. Igor P. Gorodetzki (Berlin: Siedler Verlag, 1995).

15. Pavel Palazchenko, *Assignment Gorbachev and Shevardnadze: A Memoir of the Last Years of the Soviet Union, 1985–1991* (University Park: Penn State Press, 1997). The English translation of Gorbachev's memoir is hundreds of pages shorter. We therefore assume that the German-language edition is more exhaustive. A recent doctoral dissertation at the University of Bonn, by Rafael Biermann, provides a valuable and detailed reconstruction of Soviet policy toward Germany during the years of revolution. The fine articles by Hannes Adomeit cited in the original edition are being enlarged into a full-scale analysis of contemporary Soviet-German relations.

16. François Mitterrand, *De l'Allemagne, de la France* (Paris: Editions O. Jacob, 1996).

17. Jacques Attali, *Verbatim: Tome 3, Chronique des années 1988–1991* (Paris: Fayard, 1995). Attali's diaries undoubtedly reflect his own selective recall or distillation of events, even as they were happening. Yet where we have evidence to cross-check specific assertions of fact, as with Mitterrand's meeting with Gorbachev in Kiev or his talks with Bush, Attali's notes appear to be substantially accurate. As a further safeguard, the material we use from the book in this preface quotes expressions Mitterrand voiced over and over, on various occasions described in the diaries.

18. For the quotations see ibid., pp. 241, 369, 337, 313, 416, and 495.

Preface to the 1995 Edition

"For decades a thick closed blanket of clouds obscured the star of German unity," Germany's former foreign minister Hans-Dietrich Genscher recalled. "Then for a short time the blanket of clouds parted, allowed the star to become visible, and we grabbed for it." "Grabbed" is a good word for what happened. It captures the sense of a frantic lunge in 1989 and 1990, what the British scholar Timothy Garton Ash has called a "hurtling and hurling together, sanctioned by great-power negotiations." It was, he wrote, a time when "more happened in ten months than usually does in ten years."[1]

Opinions may vary about the result. A renowned German commentator has called the outcome "the greatest triumph of diplomacy in the postwar era." A former Soviet foreign minister has called it "one of the most hated developments in the history of Soviet foreign policy and it will remain so for decades."[2] Although now the outcome may seem almost preordained, those closest to the events—whether former Soviet foreign minister Eduard Shevardnadze or political figures from East and West Germany—still marvel that this tumult did not lead to a "bloodbath," a war, or at least a new phase of cold war.[3]

The main purpose of this book is to tell the story of this extraordinary episode in modern diplomacy. This is, above all, a diplomatic history. Both authors were involved in the events as members of President George Bush's National Security Council staff: Philip Zelikow was a career diplomat detailed to the White House; Condoleezza Rice was on leave from her professorship at Stanford University. The book originated as an internal historical study which a senior State Department official, Robert Zoellick, invited Zelikow to write as he was leaving the government to accept a faculty appointment at Harvard University. After securing promises of unlimited access to all relevant documents at both the State Department and the White House, as well as access to relevant intelligence documents, Zelikow agreed and began work. But as the project took shape, it became clear that the story could not be told properly just from the perspective of the United States.

Historians have rightly criticized works that dwell too much on the perspective of one or another country, neglecting what others were doing or thinking, forgetting that diplomacy is really the interplay of several different sets of beliefs and actions. None of the many books published so far on German unification has tried, for example, to tell the German story *and* the Soviet story *and* the American story, and then study how they interacted to produce the results all could see. That is the task we set for ourselves.

To do this we complemented research in the American archives with a careful study of all materials available in German and Russian. We consulted papers that became available from the East German state archives and some significant archival materials available for the Soviet Union, including papers prepared for meetings of the Politburo and policy guidance prepared for Shevardnadze. We also talked to key decision makers in a number of countries; some of them commented on our draft, and we have constantly cross-checked recollections and published accounts against the available documentary evidence.

We made another decision about this book: we have cited all of our sources. It is not unusual for former officials to consult government records in preparing an account of their experiences, but it is unprecedented for them to cite these records just as a professional historian would. Most of the American records we have cited remain classified and unavailable to the public. We were able to cite them because the citations themselves revealed no secrets. Yet, with these American records, we faced a dilemma. Scholars will not be able to check some of our uses of still-classified government documents. They must, for a time, take on faith that we have used our evidence properly. This is a fair and appropriate concern. But the other side of the dilemma is that by failing to include any citations, we would have frustrated still more scholars who would never know what sources we had used. We decided that this latter concern was more important, for several reasons.

A surprisingly large proportion of our assertions can be checked, directly or indirectly, against published accounts and unclassified documents. This point should be apparent from a careful look at our citations. Also, our notes can convey our inside understanding of what the documents mean, who prepared them, which ones mattered and which did not. Furthermore, problems of privileged access to source material are not unique to former government officials. Often papers or materials held by private persons are available only to certain people or with special restrictions. Here we were fortunate in being able to use documents that belong to the American people and will eventually be made available to the public. So we have cited our sources as carefully as possible. Although the American archival material is not yet catalogued in the Bush Library or the National Archives, the citations are complete enough to enable scholars to find the cited documents once the cataloguing is done. Finally, at our request, the National Security Archive has also filed a massive request under the Freedom of Information Act to expedite the declassification of as much material as possible. The archive will make this material available to scholars. All material that can be declassified, including unclassified but hard-to-obtain public affairs material (transcripts of State Department press briefings, for example), will also join the collections of papers scrupulously maintained by the Archival Library of the Hoover Institution on War, Revolution, and Peace at Stanford University.

We were involved in the events we describe. We had, and still have, opinions about them. This is natural; indeed, even scholars who experience events vicariously can become just as opinionated about them. As former officials we were also obliged by law to let the government make sure we had not abused our special knowledge to reveal secrets that are still important to the security of the United States. (This was not a problem.) But from the start we have been absolutely free to tell the story any way we chose. No one, on any occasion, has even attempted to tilt or shape our story, except in telling us his or her side of it.

In preparing this book we have received help and advice from many quarters. For financial support in performing some of the research, we are grateful to the Carnegie Corporation of New York, Harvard University's Program for the Study of Germany and Europe, and Stanford University's Center for International Security and Arms Control. We are also especially thankful for the encouragement and advice we received at key points from Robert Zoellick, Robert Blackwill, Coit Blacker, and Ernest May. The research and production of this book was aided by Stanford's Center for International Security and Arms Control and the talents of Yvonne Brown, Brian Davenport, Kiron Skinner, John Fowler, Chris Fleishner, Artur Khachikian, Elizabeth Ewing, Matthew Bencke, and Deborah Schneider. We have received many useful comments from the scholars who reviewed the manuscript anonymously for Harvard University Press, and from Alexander Abashkiri, Donald Abenheim, Hannes Adomeit, Alexandra Bezymenskaia, Maxim Bratersky, Gerhard Casper, Gordon Craig, David Holloway, Karl Kaiser, Felix Philipp Lutz, Elizabeth Pond, Alfred Rubin, W. R. Smyser, Marc Trachtenberg, and Peter Wagner. We also wish to acknowledge the encouragement and support of our editor, Aïda Donald, and the patience and creativity of our copy editor, Amanda Heller.

Introduction: Solving the German Problem

NEAR THE END of the day on June 5, 1945, some of the generals who had masterminded the defeat of Germany gathered in the devastated city of Berlin. There was great commotion but little ceremony. General of the Army Dwight Eisenhower, Marshal Georgi Zhukov, Field Marshal Bernard Montgomery, and Général d'Armée De Lattre de Tassigny signed a document announcing what was already well known: the "Four Powers" now ruled Germany, and Germany had become "subject to such requirements as may now or hereafter be imposed upon her."[1]

On Wednesday, September 12, 1990, the foreign ministers of the Four Powers gave up the rights their armies had won in 1945. This time the Germans—East and West—sat with them. Again the arrangements were simple and unremarkable.[2] Held in the lobby of the Communist party's Oktyabrskaya Hotel rather than the palaces of the Kremlin, the ceremony reinforced a sense of anticlimax. The victors of World War II relinquished their rights and responsibilities toward Germany with less diplomatic fanfare than had been afforded scores of trade and arms control treaties during the Cold War.

Global attention was focused a continent away on Baghdad and Kuwait, where Operation Desert Shield would soon give way to Desert Storm. When President George Bush met with Soviet President Mikhail Sergeyevich Gorbachev on September 1 at Helsinki, less than two weeks before the German settlement became final, the subject was not even on the agenda. Only one head of state was present at the Oktyabrskaia. During the signing Gorbachev stood behind the others, well hidden in the throng of middle-level officials and aides and not very far from white-gloved hotel waiters preparing to pour champagne. The Soviet president's face was still—devoid of emotion. Suddenly the West German foreign minister noticed him and pulled him forward. Now Gorbachev flashed his famous smile and extended a hearty handshake to Hans-Dietrich Genscher, soon to be foreign minister of a united Germany. The other ministers followed suit and drank a toast to the resolution of the "German question."

It was in this fashion that the international community closed the book on the partition of Germany. Although this forty-five-year-old problem had been central to the division of Europe, the solution came quickly. The procedure for negotiating the final settlement had been agreed on only seven months earlier. The German question was resolved so smoothly and amiably that it is easy to impute a kind of inevitability to the outcome. But nothing in political history is preordained.

For weeks after the Berlin Wall fell on the night of November 9–10, 1989, even those who dared think about unification laid out timetables in years, not months. There were two German states with different systems of government and international alignments. How could East and West Germany become one when they belonged to opposing military alliances and hosted hundreds of thousands of foreign troops from different sides of the East-West divide? The unification of Germany seemed to be fraught with dangers. Most West Germans were resigned to the division of their country and thankful for the prosperity they enjoyed. Many East Germans, including dissidents who led protests against communist rule, wanted to preserve socialist values. Intellectuals in both Germanys feared the rise of a new German nationalism.

The United States had to worry that a united Germany might turn its back on the forty-year-old North Atlantic alliance, threatening America's place in Europe's future. Britain and France, still bearing searing memories of war, were quite happy to proceed with the integration of Europe's western half with a divided and more manageable Germany at its core. But no state had more to lose in the endgame of the Cold War than the Soviet Union. A divided Germany lay at the very heart of the Soviet security system. The best troops of the Soviet armed forces were deployed in Germany. The German Democratic Republic was Moscow's most important trading partner and had long been its most loyal ally. It was widely (though wrongly) believed that the GDR was the most prosperous and efficient Eastern bloc state, proof positive that the communist system could work.

The division of Germany meant something more to the Kremlin: it was the most visible spoil of war—retribution for Germany's vicious effort to destroy the Soviet state in the Second World War. Everywhere in the GDR stilted monuments to the glory of the Soviet people and the Red Army commemorated Moscow's victory over Hitler's powerful forces. Because it was the last time—perhaps the only time—in its history that the Soviet Communist party and the Soviet people were freely united against anything, the memory of victory in World War II was the party's favorite talisman against political decline.

The six states that would determine Germany's future—the Federal Republic of Germany, the German Democratic Republic, France, Britain, the United States, and the Soviet Union—were thus locked into a web of arrangements developed to make the division of Germany workable. Despite the occasional almost ceremonial references to a unified Germany, the international system had grown quite satisfied with the status quo. In a year it was all gone. International history provides few examples of so rapid a conclusion to any negotiation, let alone one of this importance.

This book recounts how the practical obstacles as well as the deep-seated fears about German unification were overcome. It is the story of the end of Germany's division, and with it the end of the Cold War.

~ 1

When Did the Cold War End?

THE PARTITION of Germany cast a shadow over European politics for more than forty years. A divided Germany was the main front of a quiescent but ever dangerous military confrontation, the wall between two ways of life, and a fundamental barrier to political reconciliation in Europe. When this division ended, the terms of German unification were definitive. There was no coming together of the two systems. A free and prosperous Federal Republic of Germany absorbed the constituent parts of the failed German Democratic Republic. Soon after, the Soviet bloc, and indeed the Soviet Union itself, lay in ruins.

Gorbachev's Vision

The great irony is that the Cold War could not have ended without a fundamental change in Soviet policy. Students of this period will long debate why the Soviet Union pursued a new course, as well as the role of the United States and other countries, but none can deny a central place in the story of the Cold War's end to Mikhail Gorbachev and the "new thinkers" who took power in Moscow in 1985.

One is even tempted to see the outcome as somehow inevitable and inexorable—a natural outgrowth of a fundamental change in the way Moscow dealt with the rest of the world. This is typical of what the English historian Herbert Butterfield has called the "whig interpretation of history." What Butterfield meant, writing more than sixty years ago, was that historians all too often array the past before us with almost godlike powers, placing events into an order that seems to march logically from where we were to where we are, interpreting the past through the eyes of the present. "The total result of this method," writes Butterfield, "is to impose a certain form upon the whole historical story, and to produce a scheme of general history which is bound to converge beautifully upon the present," preferably demonstrating "an obvious principle of progress."[1]

It is easy to fall into a "whig" interpretation of the end of the Cold War. Gorbachev's "new thinking" was crucial, providing as it did the initial conditions for the events that unfolded and for a while pushing the process along. Yet it is wrong to say, as some have done, that Gorbachev intended to end the division of Europe and succeeded.[2]

Gorbachev did want to "end the Cold War" and create a "common European home." He used those phrases. But he attributed a particular meaning to them. Events did not turn out in accordance with his plans. The "whig" historian, writes Butterfield, "too easily refers changes and achievements to this party or that personage, reading the issue as a purpose that has been attained, when very often it is a purpose that has been marred."[3] So it was with the purpose of Gorbachev's "new thinking." Internal change was Gorbachev's main concern. Changes in foreign policy were intended to help perestroika succeed. Yet in domestic affairs Gorbachev did not really seem to know where he was going.[4] He knew that the status quo was unacceptable. It was characteristic of him to keep trying to move forward, zigging and zagging, compromising at times, always the master of tactics, but unsure about his precise destination.

In foreign policy, though, Gorbachev was thought to be resolute. He seemed to know what he wanted: to end the Cold War, encourage the rise of legitimate reformers in Eastern Europe through a policy of noninterference in their affairs, and reintegrate the Soviet Union into the international system as a trusted partner. In this view he moved smartly forward, pursuing this agenda from 1985 until 1990, when events slipped out of his control.

Gorbachev foresaw the Soviet Union taking its place in a "common European home," in which capitalist, socialist, and communist countries existed on a seamless continuum—not in two hostile camps. The states of Europe would trade and work together despite their different forms of governance. The Soviet Union would be not just tolerated because its military power was feared but accepted as the heir to Russia's historical ties to Europe. Gorbachev believed that reform in Eastern Europe would produce "little Gorbachevs" who would make socialist rule viable just as he was making socialism viable in the USSR. He believed that when the division of Europe was overcome in this way, it would be on the basis of "human values" that the Soviet Union had helped to define. He believed that a pan-European security system would replace both NATO and the Warsaw Pact. He believed, in short, that Europe, with the Soviet Union as an integral and organic part, would be a new continent—not Western, not Eastern, but a "common home."

The operational implications of the Gorbachev vision were imprecise, allowing others to fill in the concrete terms. Gorbachev fully intended to maintain, even enhance, the Soviet Union's status as a superpower. Thus, elements of rivalry and competition with the West existed side by side with the vision of the new Europe. On any given day Gorbachev was driven to devise a new way of overcoming the latest opposition of those on the left or the right who did not share his goals.

This is not to detract from the tremendous importance of the "new thinking" or to underestimate how radical it truly was. People sometimes abandon long-held views and make nonlinear leaps of imagination. Such leaps are especially hard for political leaders, whose beliefs are among the sources of their power, reflected in institutions, the bases of their authority and their legitimacy. Not surprisingly, these leaps rarely take place when things are going well. Rather, they often occur in response to crises, when the old ideas have failed and "everything is rotten."[5]

Gorbachev's "new thinking" was a reaction to a system in crisis. The problem was a structural one: the centralized, isolated, and heavily militarized character of the economy, which had its origins in the late 1920s. This system had worked well for industrialization, but the world had passed it by as more decentralized economies, encouraging innovation from below, made rapid technological progress. The Soviet leaders had known for some time that the system was not working and were looking desperately for a way out. Radical new ideas were discussed in academic circles, but they were too unorthodox for the men in power. It is in this sense that Gorbachev is truly a remarkable historical figure. He understood his options differently and somehow saw a link that successive Soviet leaders had failed to see: Soviet domestic problems were inextricably bound up in an international policy guided by definitions of national interest that had changed little since the rule of Josef Stalin.

The Soviet economy was faltering, in part, because it was isolated from the world economy. Gorbachev's knowledge of the international economy and its key institutions was limited. He sometimes seemed to define participation in the world economy simply as membership in the General Agreement on Tariffs and Trade (GATT), the International Monetary Fund (IMF), or the Group of Seven leading industrialized countries (G-7). He did not understand the changes that were needed in the Soviet economy or their implications for Soviet society. But he seemed to grasp one key point: the Soviet Union could not end its economic and political isolation without a fundamental shift in the foreign policies that had made it a pariah within the international system.

In days past the Soviet Union had taken pride in being a pariah—neither an accomplice to nor a victim of global capitalism's exploitation of the world. This is how Soviet leaders understood Marxist-Leninist ideology. And ideology mattered, not as a blueprint for action but in defining the range of the possible.[6] Soviet policy from the time of Josef Stalin had been ideological in precisely this way. It had one central tenet—that the long-term interests of the Soviet Union could not be reconciled with those of an international economic and political order dominated by capitalist democracies. The world had to be divided until the day when socialism would triumph. Marxism was at once both the foundation for the internal organization of the Soviet Union and the basis of its place in the world.

Successive Soviet leaders believed that the West would ultimately try to destroy socialism either by war or, after nuclear weapons seemed to rule this out, by subversion. Stalin structured the Soviet Union as a country that would go it alone until a "ring of socialist brother states" could provide additional resources and security.[7] He made it absolutely clear that the survival and prosperity of the Soviet Union was the first priority for any good communist. The policy demanded self-sufficiency for the economy and provided insulation from an international economic order that the Soviets feared. The system successfully made maximum use of the resources of its multinational empire to support Moscow's goals and prepare the Soviet state for World War II. But this isolation from the world economy, almost from the Soviet Union's inception, doomed Moscow to live with its peculiar economic structure.[8]

After the war Stalin's hopes for "a ring of socialist brother states" were realized. Soviet leaders tried, sometimes imperfectly, to harness Eastern Europe's economic power toward the goal of building a stronger Soviet Union. This was done principally through the Council for Mutual Economic Assistance (CMEA), an institution created to coordinate the administration of the socialist economies—a mandatory function in a system where trade relations could not be regulated by the market or the value of convertible currencies.[9] So the Soviet leaders continued to build this countersystem, which isolated them further from the economic and political order dominated by the West.

The Western policy of containment deepened Soviet isolation. East-West trade was constrained, and the West formed an organization, COCOM (Co-ordinating Committee for East-West Trade), to coordinate limits on the export of militarily useful technologies to the Eastern bloc. The COCOM members argued constantly about what exports to control, but the net effect of the system was to help push the Soviet economy further and further away from cutting edge technologies, stunting not only Moscow's military economy but civilian development as well.[10]

By the 1970s the myth of an "alternative" system was beginning to break down. The Soviet Union was increasingly dependent on imported grain and foreign technology. Some East European states did all that they could to make the boundaries between their own economies and the West more permeable, and occasionally—as with Poland's membership in the IMF—they succeeded. But the Soviet Union never abandoned hope that its own alliance institutions could be revitalized to meet modern economic challenges. Thus, the Soviets fiddled endlessly with CMEA, trying to rationalize trade among the states without converting Eastern currencies. But CMEA remained a closed system, sustained by the exchange of shoddy products that had little value on the world market.

Tactical adjustments were needed, and in the 1970s détente provided the ideal framework for cooperation with the West. Moscow, at the height of its power, thought that it was strong enough to make that accommodation on equal footing. There was little to fear and much to gain. The Kremlin believed that the "correlation of forces,"[11] a kind of rough measure of the progress of socialism, was moving in the Soviet Union's favor.

The West read détente as a means by which to ensnare the Soviet Union in a "web of interdependence" that would give Moscow a stake in the international system and regulate Soviet behavior.[12] But Moscow's stake was very limited. The Soviet leadership wanted to avoid a suicidal war at all costs, acquire economic and technological help from the West, and enjoy the diplomatic and symbolic benefits of superpower status.[13] Moscow was the equal of the United States in military terms. Nuclear equality or parity was the Soviet Union's best insurance that its "alternative" international system was secure. From this perspective détente was a triumph for the socialist alternative, not an accommodation. Leonid Brezhnev spoke proudly of how the West had come to terms with Soviet power and of Moscow's ability to defend not just its own interests but those of the entire socialist world.[14]

But it was not long before the West was thoroughly frustrated with the Soviet government's conduct. Moscow's active policy in the third world, culminating in the 1979 invasion of Afghanistan, led observers to accuse the Soviets of violating the rules of cooperation. Moscow, of course, understood those rules differently.[15] The Carter administration found itself on the defensive as it became apparent that the Soviet Union had undertaken an enormous buildup of its conventional forces. Although debates about the size of the overall military buildup will probably never be resolved—figures range from 12–18 percent to 25–30 percent of some imaginary "real" Soviet gross national product—one expert, David Holloway, perhaps put it best when he told his colleagues, "I am agnostic about how much. Suffice it to say it was a lot."[16]

In the face of that challenge, the United States turned to a strategy that tried to leverage American technology against Soviet brute strength and numbers: the creation of precision-guided munitions and new weapons systems that depended on sophisticated technology Moscow could not hope to match.[17] At the end of his term President Jimmy Carter requested the sharpest increase in U.S. defense spending since the height of the Vietnam war.

For Ronald Reagan even that was not enough. He believed that the West had been soft on communism and had paid dearly for it as Soviet power and influence spread across the globe. He came to office determined to confront and convert his foe. Reagan's confrontational style was evident in the way he thought and talked about nuclear weapons. Convinced that the Soviets believed nuclear war to be winnable, he redirected American nuclear strategy toward "warfighting" as the basis of deterrence. In doing so he frightened many Europeans and made many Americans uneasy, particularly when his secretary of state (and former NATO commanding general), Alexander Haig, spoke about a "demonstration nuclear shot" to convince Moscow of Western resolve should war break out.[18]

That style was evident in arms control, too, which the Reagan administration was certain had codified Western weakness and Soviet strength. Reagan assumed an all-or-nothing negotiating stance, insisting on a "zero option" for U.S. and Soviet intermediate-range nuclear forces in Europe. He made clear that the United States would deploy its own nuclear missile forces in five NATO countries if Moscow did not remove every single one of the more than four hundred SS-20 intermediate-range missiles that appeared to pose a distinct new threat to Western Europe. The deployment of the U.S. missiles was to begin in 1983.

The Soviet government used every available political and diplomatic asset to prevent the deployment of the American missiles. Relations with the United States were tense. Popular movements protesting the deployments were given support. The West German election of 1983 became a testing ground for the political strength of the opposing sides. But the United States and its Western allies stood firm and refused to compromise. Helmut Kohl, who backed up the United States, won the 1983 election. The deployment began on schedule in December 1983. Although it was four years before Moscow accepted Reagan's "zero option," NATO had taken the Soviet Union's best shot at derailing Western policy and won. The failure of that confrontational approach had a lasting effect on the Soviets' thinking about their policy toward Western Europe, discouraging, as Gorbachev later acknowledged, faith in a purely military approach to Soviet security problems.[19]

Reagan's hard line was evident in other aspects of the policy as well.

Moscow needed to be compelled, Reagan and his advisers believed, to pull back across the globe. The United States supported these policies with large increases in military spending. In 1983 Reagan opened a new high technology front with the decision to pursue the Strategic Defense Initiative (SDI), promising that space-based defenses could shield the United States from a nuclear attack. Even though most scientists doubted its plausibility as a "defensive shield against nuclear weapons," Soviet leaders—particularly military leaders—took the challenge very seriously indeed.[20]

The American emphasis on new military technology went well beyond SDI. Most important, it seemed to threaten the Soviets' greatest asset, their conventional forces. Already worried about the emphasis on "smart" munitions, Soviet generals argued that the real impact of SDI would be to harness the sophisticated technology of the West, such as lasers, optics, and real-time information processing, to render Moscow's vast conventional forces obsolete. American high-performance aircraft married to smart weapons and computer-aided guidance became the Soviet General Staff's worst nightmare. Chief of the General Staff Marshal Nikolai Ogarkov railed against these "reconnaissance strike complexes."[21]

The challenge to Soviet military technology crystallized the key structural problem in the Soviet economy. The problem was not just to build a better tank or an atom bomb. The Soviet Union had been very good at that, using its command economy to direct resources toward feats of engineering and industrial production. This time the Soviet Union faced not just a new military weapon but integrated weapons systems that drew on a variety of technological innovations.[22] Soviet military leaders were the first to realize the significance of this challenge. Ogarkov did not simply call for more money. He wanted the Soviet Union to confront the challenge head-on, pouring massive resources into a race for technological sophistication in weaponry, which the Soviet Union was bound to lose.

The worries of the professional officers had to concern the political leaders of the Soviet Union. Military strength had first claim on the country's resources and on its finest human and physical assets. It is no accident that military parades became more grandiose as the Soviet Union's internal decline accelerated. Military power was a source of pride, the country's best and brightest achievement. But in the last year of his life, Leonid Brezhnev began to send signals that he was not so sure that the Soviet Union could or should try to meet the demands of a new arms race.

As Moscow's economic, political, and military difficulties mounted against the Western challenge, a succession of geriatric Soviet leaders—Brezhnev, Yuri Andropov, Konstantin Chernenko—seemed unsure about what to do. They constructed arguments explaining why the West's assault would have to fail. Some said that the hardening Western policies were evidence of a deepening crisis in capitalism.[23] The Kremlin tried to play the "peace card," with worn-out initiatives to demonstrate that the Soviet Union was indeed the guardian of international stability. But the Soviets clung to their leadership of a socialist alternative and hoped that Reagan and his ilk would just pass from the scene.

One option would have been for the USSR to settle into a grim effort to harness the best that the command economy could produce and confront the West yet again. The economy might have sputtered along as in the past. Or the Soviet government could have declined to participate in a new arms race, holding on to existing gains and simply ignoring the U.S. military buildup. But what the Soviet leaders believed they faced was a deterioration in their position, not a continuation of the status quo.

In fact, the Soviet leadership appears to have rejected both of these options before Gorbachev was chosen to take control of the party, and the country, in March 1985. Andrei Gromyko, the foreign minister, had successfully engineered a return to the bargaining table with the resumption of the Strategic Arms Reduction (START) talks in the fall of 1984. With Reagan's reelection appearing certain and Reagan himself describing hopes for a more conciliatory direction in East-West relations, the Soviets may have thought that détente was back on track.

But Gorbachev decided that such minor adjustments in policy were not enough. Muted calls to change fundamentally the Soviet Union's relation to the West had filled the halls of Soviet academic institutes and the pages of scholarly journals for years. Now there was a Soviet leader who was prepared to explore the possibilities. Gorbachev had few preconceived notions about foreign policy and had spent almost no time traveling in the West. This son of an agricultural worker from Russia's Caucasus region was a child during the Second World War, when his home was occupied for four months by German troops during the high tide of German conquest in 1942. But the German occupation of his region was relatively benign. Instead it was the Stalinist deportations following the retreat of the Germans that left searing memories for the young man. Gorbachev's family had suffered hardship and hunger as a result of Stalin's collectivization of agriculture, and his paternal grandfather had been sent to Siberia by Stalin's secret police.[24]

Gorbachev's rise through the party ranks was rapid yet unremarkable. His reputation for unpretentious competence, and a direct no-nonsense style attracted powerful patrons in Moscow, particularly Yuri Andropov. But his biography reads like those of scores of other party apparatchiks of the period. There was little in his background to suggest that this general secretary of the Communist party would be so unlike his predecessors. It did not take long for his distinctive personality to emerge, however. He had an attractive demeanor, and displayed obvious intelligence and courage. In 1989 he was fifty-eight years old. His alert, flashing, and intense eyes were the physical attribute that stood out most, contrasting as they did with his rather squat stature. He greeted people warmly and always with a broad smile. But Gorbachev could turn steely in direct exchanges, speaking from notes that he himself had prepared by hand. He could make off-the-cuff remarks that took his counterparts by surprise. When president-elect George Bush, in his first meeting with Gorbachev, asked what the Soviet Union would be like in three, four, or five years, Gorbachev responded with a quip: "Even Jesus Christ couldn't answer that question!"[25] Yet he rarely seemed truly candid. Rather, he was self-aware at all times, projecting different sides of his persona—sometimes within a matter of minutes—for a presumably calculated effect.

Unlike his counterparts in Washington and Bonn, Gorbachev did not have a national security staff of his own. A suspicious Josef Stalin had destroyed his personal staff out of fear that they knew too much. That tradition survived him, and general secretaries were, from that time on, dependent for assistance on the secretive party apparatus and, in foreign policy, on the staff of the international department of the party's Central Committee. When Gorbachev took power it was as the leader of the party, served by party staff. There was no "presidency" or "presidential staff" then; that came later.

Over time Gorbachev began to build a personal staff. But he was difficult to help, according to those who worked for him, given to placing his own phone calls from his dacha and organizing his own calendar. Western officials found the Kremlin apparatus somewhat chaotic, having difficulty even in small matters, such as knowing how to locate Gorbachev for a phone call. Yet Gorbachev began to rely increasingly on a few advisers who worked directly for him. On Europe and Germany his advisers were drawn from a stable of Central Committee and Foreign Ministry experts and a few close aides chosen not only for their substantive specialties but also for their loyalty.[26]

Alexander Yakovlev, a veteran diplomat and party ideologue known for his unconventional thinking, was one such adviser. Yakovlev had been ambassador to Canada when Gorbachev recalled him to Moscow, soon put him in charge of the Central Committee's international department, and eventually elevated him to membership in the Politburo. Yakovlev had a reputation for harboring anti-American sentiments, but the most important thing about him was his commitment to the "new thinking." He was, in fact, its intellectual father and a principal architect of this new way of defining Soviet national interests.

Gorbachev's closest personal aide was Anatoly Chernyayev, a veteran party theorist and top foreign policy adviser who had served as a propagandist in the international department of the party's Central Committee. Chernyayev, sixty-nine years old in 1989, was rarely far from Gorbachev's side. He was the note taker at almost all of Gorbachev's private meetings with foreign leaders and was the man most often designated by Gorbachev as his point of contact for U.S. officials.

Gorbachev depended, too, on Marshal of the Soviet Union Sergei Akhromeyev, a veteran of the siege of Leningrad, chief of the General Staff until 1988, and a respected military professional. Though more conservative than Gorbachev's "new thinkers," Akhromeyev was an independent thinker on military matters who at times found himself at odds with Chief of the General Staff Mikhail Moiseyev and Minister of Defense Dmitri Yazov.

But by far the most important man in Gorbachev's entourage was, like him, an outsider with no foreign policy expertise. Eduard Shevardnadze, the foreign minister, had been too young to serve in World War II, but his elder brother was killed defending Brest-Litovsk in the first days of the German invasion. Shevardnadze reflected later that "the war with fascism became a personal battle for me" and "the victory in that war became the victory of communism." The war, he wrote, "formed my convictions and purpose in life."[27] Yet Shevardnadze grew up in Georgia, closer to Iran than to Germany, and never seemed to share the deep anti-German feelings sometimes found among Russians scarred by the war.

Shevardnadze rose through the ranks of the party in Georgia to leadership of the republic. He first met Gorbachev during the 1950s, and the two became friends. Shevardnadze had replaced a notorious party boss in the freewheeling Georgian republic and in the 1970s acquired a reputation for vigilance in stamping out official corruption. In many ways he was much like Gorbachev. When the new general secretary needed to bring fresh air to Soviet foreign policy, he called on Shevardnadze, who described the July 1985 invitation as "the greatest surprise of my life."[28]

Shevardnadze replaced Andrei Gromyko, a rigid figure of the past who had been involved in Soviet diplomacy since the time of Stalin. Shevardnadze spoke Russian with a Georgian accent and, free from the habits of Soviet-style diplomacy, brought a sharp change in perspective and style. He was admired by younger diplomats for his energy, honesty, and openness. In 1989 a book listing the hundreds of diplomats slaughtered as spies during the great purges in 1937 was installed in the front hall of the Moscow Foreign Ministry building as a memorial to victims of the terror. That was the kind of ministry Shevardnadze tried to run, an institution willing to look history square in the eye, discard the past, and turn to the future with hope and, sometimes, resignation. In that sense he was a true believer in the "new thinking," if less a tactician than Gorbachev, habitually candid, even emotional in trying to solve problems.

Shevardnadze relied, in turn, on a few close advisers. Sergei Tarasenko, head of the ministry's General Secretariat, was his constant companion. Although the fifty-two-year-old Tarasenko was a career diplomat, with a background as an expert on the Middle East and on the United States, he seemed to hold no views that could be associated with the old regime. His intellectual passion was the politics of the Middle East, where he had served, not of Europe, but he worked on whatever problems concerned Shevardnadze.

Tarasenko found himself in frequent tugs-of-war with the experts on Germany. Among them was Yuly Kvitsinsky, ambassador to West Germany in 1989, then appointed during the spring of 1990 as Shevardnadze's deputy handling European issues. A former arms control negotiator best known in the West for his "walk in the woods" with Paul Nitze during the negotiations on nuclear missiles in Europe, Kvitsinsky was competent but inclined to polemics. Though a wide-ranging, often skeptical thinker, Kvitsinsky supported the fundamental postwar Soviet position on the German question.[29]

More conservative was Alexander Bondarenko, chief of the Foreign Ministry's Third European Department, which included the Federal Republic of Germany. A decorated veteran of World War II, Bondarenko, sixty-seven years old in 1989, embodied the sentiments of an older generation. He had headed the German desk and been a member of the Foreign Ministry's collegium of senior diplomats for nearly twenty years. Although Bondarenko could not have been further from the "new thinking" on Germany, Shevardnadze admired and listened to him.[30]

Outside the Foreign Ministry the main rival source of advice on policy matters was the staff of the international department of the party's Central Committee. Traditionally the Central Committee staff could be quite influential as the in-house source of advice for the general secretary, the effective head of the government, and also because the party and its organs had long provided ideological and practical guidance for the more traditional institutions of government. The Central Committee staff's international department also had primacy in dealings with top party officials in the allied countries of Eastern Europe as well as with other foreign communists.[31]

In 1988 Gorbachev completely restructured the Central Committee bureaucracy. Yakovlev, now a member of the Politburo, supervised the international department, headed by Valentin Falin, perhaps the Soviet Union's leading expert on Germany. Falin had been the Soviet ambassador to West Germany from 1971 to 1978, forming close ties to the then-ruling West German Social Democratic party (in German, SPD). He supported close relations with Germany but understood clearly that Ostpolitik was meant to seal postwar realities in place. Falin in turn was assisted by Nikolai Portugalov, an expert on Germany who was acquainted with Kohl's top foreign policy adviser, Horst Teltschik.[32]

It did not take Gorbachev and his new team long to launch Soviet foreign policy in a different direction, at first through energy and charm, attributes that their predecessors had certainly lacked. The old themes were still evident, casting the Soviet Union as the defender of world peace. But Gorbachev soon gave new meaning to his rhetoric about the impermissibility of war in the nuclear age.[33] Within two years Gorbachev and his advisers had redefined the operational aspects of Soviet military doctrine. They admitted that the Soviet military offensive presence in Europe was so large that it had become an impediment to good relations. Nuclear weapons had made all war unwinnable. Now it was possible to talk about large reductions in Soviet forces, both conventional and nuclear, reductions that might even be asymmetrical—that is, requiring deeper cuts in Soviet forces than in those of the West.[34] The shift culminated in the signing of the Intermediate-Range Nuclear Forces (INF) treaty at the end of 1987, committing both sides to eliminate these weapon systems and requiring the Soviet Union to give up four warheads for each one eliminated by the United States.

Yet the effort to defuse the military confrontation in Europe was just one aspect of Gorbachev's redefinition of Soviet national interests. It is possible to imagine other Soviet leaders pursuing a radical arms control policy to stabilize the military competition against the Americans. What was truly extraordinary was Gorbachev's goal of integrating the Soviet Union into a new Europe. This required a fundamental reevaluation of relations with Eastern Europe. Most startling of all, it moved the "new thinkers" to renounce the class basis of international relations which lay at the very heart of Marxist thought.

This turning point in the "new thinking" apparently came during late 1987 and in 1988, before and after a historic conference of the Soviet Communist party in the summer of 1988. At this party conference Gorbachev accelerated the course of domestic renewal, perestroika. Gorbachev's historic speech to the United Nations General Assembly in December 1988 appears in retrospect to have been the culmination of a reevaluation of Soviet foreign policy and formulation of a new policy for Europe. In his speech Gorbachev announced a unilateral reduction of five hundred thousand in the strength of the Soviet Union's front-line forces as well as measures to reduce the offensive character of the Soviet military presence in Europe. That was the headline. But there was a more fundamental point: his announcement that other socialist countries—the countries of Eastern Europe—would be permitted to find their own path without interference from the Soviet Union.

These military and political initiatives were linked inextricably in Gorbachev's mind. His aide Chernyayev has described the preparation of the speech in great detail and has lamented the widespread failure—even in the Soviet Union—to appreciate fully its ideological significance. It was not the first time that, from the Soviet point of view, the West had missed the point.[35] The Soviets had tried to get Reagan's attention at the June 1988 summit in Moscow with a declaration on the mutuality of interests between states in an interdependent world and the principle of noninterference in the affairs of others. It is not hard to see why Reagan's advisers had viewed the statement as a set of slogans, not unlike those adopted during the period of détente for which Reagan had criticized his predecessors. The Reagan administration was focused on incremental steps to advance its own four-part agenda: human rights, arms control, bilateral relations, and regional security.

Gorbachev, however, was trying to convey a theoretical and philosophical message that, in his world, carried enormous significance. His December 1988 UN speech emphasized what he had been saying for months: Eastern Europe was free to go its own way, leaving no ideological barriers to one demilitarized Europe, tied together by interdependence and common values. When he first took office in 1985 Gorbachev had been cautious, adopting a conservative line with Eastern Europe, and stressing the importance of the world socialist system at party congresses in East Berlin and in Poland. He warned the Poles to be wary of "traps" in their attempts to seek more trade with the West. He derided market-style economic reform. "Some of you," he said, "look at the market as a lifesaver for your economies. But, comrades, you should not think about lifesavers but about the ship, and the ship is socialism."[36]

As perestroika progressed in the Soviet Union itself, though, this policy fell out of step with Gorbachev's domestic course. The Soviet Union began to reevaluate its approach to Eastern Europe. In November 1987, commemorating the seventieth anniversary of the Bolshevik revolution, Gorbachev declared that "national and social differences" in the "world of socialism" were "good and useful."[37] He was ready to count on reformist communist leaders like himself to scuttle the harshest aspects of the Stalinist system without destroying its Leninist foundation.

What was this irreducible "Leninist" foundation? Gorbachev was struggling to decide what was essential to Leninist ideology both at home and abroad. Sensing, perhaps, that perestroika was without firm ideological moorings, he sought to redefine the guiding ideology to keep pace with his vision. He asked working groups—headed by key aides such as Yakovlev and Chernyayev—to examine thoroughly the relationship of Leninism to perestroika in preparation for the party conference. Chernyayev describes Gorbachev in this period (late 1987 and the first half of 1988) reading papers that had been written for Lenin, histories of Marxist thought, and the writings of the "old Bolsheviks," most of whom had been executed by Stalin.[38]

Apparently Gorbachev took two lessons from his studies. First, there were many roads to socialism, and it was permissible to be guided by the historical conditions encountered in a given place or time. Second, there was nothing in Lenin that prevented one from adapting socialism to radically different circumstances, especially circumstances that Lenin himself had not foreseen. Failing to find specific blessings for his radical course, Gorbachev settled for Lenin's vague endorsement of the need to be guided by practice.[39]

The foreign policy implications of those findings soon became clear.[40] Gorbachev had said that every socialist country could go its own way and concluded that there was nothing "un-Leninist" about that. If one could simply be guided by practice, it was easy to admit that the world was very different than in Lenin's day. Thus, Yakovlev and Shevardnadze were able to take dead aim at proletarian internationalism as an outmoded basis for foreign policy. They focused on the revolution in technology and communications, the borderless nature of environmental problems, and a host of other reasons why global interdependence was now the dominant factor in international life.[41] Months before the United Nations speech, Yakovlev had declared that "class struggle" had lost its meaning in the international politics of an interdependent world. Shevardnadze elaborated at a "scientific-practical conference" of the Foreign Ministry, saying that class interests had given way to the interests of one interdependent world.[42] These developments led Yegor Ligachev, one of the last old-style theoreticians remaining on the governing Politburo after the 1988 party conference, to appeal for reaffirmation of the fundamental nature of class struggle in Soviet international life.[43]

But Gorbachev and his advisers did not agree. The Soviet Union would be a member of a common European home. As Gorbachev would tell the Council of Europe in July 1989: "It is not enough now simply to state that European states share a common fate and are interdependent . . . The idea of European unity must be collectively rethought, in a process of creative collaboration among all nations—large, medium, and small."[44] Two different social systems would exist side by side in this common home, with the differences overcome by shared human values. Gorbachev continued to talk about European socialism and Soviet communism as if they were cousins.[45] There was no reason why class struggle had to shape the international system.

In articulating this vision Gorbachev changed the very foundation of Soviet foreign policy. Was it possible to think of Marxism as a set of principles for the internal socioeconomic organization of states and say that this had no implications for international relations? After all, when asked if he was a Leninist, Gorbachev always answered yes, forcefully and without hesitation. He did not accept Western notions of private property, and he once told George Bush that he simply rejected the idea of people working for other people as a form of exploitation. But he saw no contradiction between that Leninist basis for the Soviet state and a set of common international values. That made him unlike all of his predecessors and unlike Marx himself.

The insistence on common values was absolutely fundamental to the "new thinking." When Bush met with Gorbachev at Malta toward the end of 1989, the president asserted that the division of Europe could be overcome only on the basis of "Western values." Gorbachev took that opportunity to rail against this formulation, which he had "heard many times." He proceeded to lecture the American president for almost twenty minutes. "We share the values of democracy, individual liberty, and freedom," he declared. A beleaguered Bush tried to respond, but then Yakovlev and Shevardnadze joined in the argument. Rather than argue about the place of ideals such as democracy and individual liberty in Russian or Soviet history, Secretary of State James Baker asked if it would be more acceptable just to characterize these ideals as "democratic values." The Soviets settled down and agreed.[46]

By 1989 the Soviets had abandoned the old notion of the "socialist alternative."[47] They were ready to be integrated into the international system rather than isolated from it. They intended to join a transformed Europe on full and equal terms. What did all this mean for the Cold War? It obviously meant new chances for easing the U.S.-Soviet military rivalry. It meant that the Soviet Union no longer felt a special obligation to support fraternal socialist movements in the third world or to prop up regimes that would at least ally themselves with the socialist camp. In Europe it meant that Moscow would want friendlier political and economic relations and arms control talks to reduce concerns about the armed forces deployed by the opposing alliances, NATO and the Warsaw Pact.

By 1988 the United States appeared to be defining an end to the Cold War as the achievement of three general goals:

1. Stabilize and reduce any danger from U.S.-Soviet rivalry in the development and deployment of nuclear forces.

2. Defuse and ameliorate any major areas of tension in the U.S.-Soviet competition for influence or advantage in the third world.
3. Persuade Moscow to move toward respect for the fundamental human rights of its citizens as a basis for full Soviet participation in the international community.

By these standards the results at the end of 1988 seemed impressive. The Reagan administration and its allies believed that the 1987 signing of the INF treaty and progress on a START treaty were accomplishing the first goal. They had finally persuaded Moscow to accept on-site inspection as a basis for verifying arms control. Soviet withdrawal from Afghanistan and negotiated settlements in southern Africa were signs that the second goal was moving toward fulfillment. There had also been substantial though still uneven progress in the USSR's recognition of human rights. Hence, the most warlike of cold warriors, British Prime Minister Margaret Thatcher, could declare publicly in November 1988, "We're not in a Cold War now." The American Secretary of State, George Shultz, also judged in retrospect that at the end of 1988 the Cold War "was all over but the shouting."[48]

But what of overcoming the division of Europe? In 1982 President Reagan had told the British Parliament that his goal was to lead a "crusade for freedom" that would end only when it left "Marxism-Leninism on the ash heap of history."[49] Reagan also used the annual occasion of "Captive Nations Week" to launch rhetorical missiles against communist control and Soviet influence over the states of Eastern Europe, including the Baltic republics of the Soviet Union. His vice president, George Bush, appeared particularly convinced, delivering a provocative 1983 speech that denounced the postwar division of Europe.[50] Yet with one major exception Reagan's policies did not act on this rhetoric, though the Soviets worried openly that they might. The major exception was Poland.

After the Polish military declared martial law in December 1980 and seized control of the country in order to curb widening unrest led by the Solidarity movement, Reagan cooperated with an odd assortment of Solidarity's supporters, including the AFL-CIO and the Vatican, in a covert policy to keep its leader, Lech Walesa, and the independent trade union movement alive. The policy was a stunning success, and it contributed to Solidarity's reemergence as a popular force in 1988. But when George Bush sought to travel to Poland in 1987 to pursue talks about legalizing Solidarity, the State Department experts, worried that a Bush trip might stir up controversy, opposed it until they were overruled at the last minute by Deputy Secretary of State John Whitehead.[51]

In general, though, the Reagan administration avoided direct clashes with the Soviet government over the political division of Europe. Reagan did give a memorable 1987 speech in Berlin, standing at the Brandenburg Gate and challenging Gorbachev to "open this gate" and "tear down this wall!" It was a speechwriter who had come up with these words, not the foreign policy professionals. The policies for following up these statements were no more than mild efforts to regularize the existing Four Power controls over a divided Berlin. American diplomats did not consider the matter part of the real policy agenda; Shultz does not discuss the issue in his detailed memoirs. As former German chancellor Willy Brandt later wrote, Reagan may have "publicly called on Gorbachev to get rid of the Wall. But in negotiations with the Russians he set other priorities and certainly did not put in question the division of Germany."[52]

None of this is meant to suggest that Reagan, Shultz, and Thatcher did not care about the division of Europe and Germany. They did. But the postwar realities seemed fixed, and they sought a renewal of détente—this time a genuine and lasting détente—as the best way to moderate the effects of Europe's tragic division. They were succeeding, too. Shultz left office in January 1989 worried mainly that his successors in the Bush administration "did not understand or accept that the cold war was over."[53]

When the Bush administration came to power, it was cautious about Gorbachev's motives. U.S. officials saw the old constraints vanishing but wondered whether the positive trends would continue. "Once you say the Cold War is over," the new national security adviser, Brent Scowcroft, later recalled, "you can never take it back. You can only say it once." Once the words were spoken, it would be hard to hold back massive reductions in defense spending. Scowcroft, like others in the administration, simply did not feel sure enough that the changes in the Soviet Union were irrevocable or had affected Soviet military posture in any fundamental way.[54]

As a result, the Bush administration started out slowly. The new team wanted to set a new course. Bush's advisers believed that Reagan had gone too far to discredit reliance on nuclear weapons in Western defense. They set out to rehabilitate nuclear deterrence and refocus policy toward reducing Soviet conventional forces. Without exception, the top officials on the new Bush national security team were veterans of government service, picked more for their personal and professional qualities than for their ideological convictions. If there was a philosophical coloration, it combined a kind of pragmatic internationalism—belief in the essential verities of postwar American policy and institutions—with a suspicion of both the multilateralist impulses of the Carter administration and the unilateralism of Ronald Reagan.

George Bush himself was both interested and experienced in foreign policy. Raised in an affluent New England family close to the world of establishment

Republican politics, he was strongly influenced by his service in the Pacific theater as a young navy pilot during World War II and by more than a decade as an oil man in the desolate fields of West Texas, a young wife and children in tow. After returning to the political world in the early 1960s, Bush became the consummate insider, eventually capping twenty-five years in and out of public office with eight years of loyal service as Reagan's vice president. He had served as ambassador to the United Nations, as emissary to China, and as director of the CIA.

As a person Bush was restless but unassuming, at once both relaxed and reserved. He was gracious, an easy man with whom to talk, displaying constant attention to small acts of courtesy. He tended to listen carefully, asking few questions and rarely talking at length, seldom using personal anecdotes as Reagan did. He tended to make his points in a self-deprecating way. After being complimented by a foreign leader, Bush answered, characteristically, by quoting Yogi Berra, who once said he had won a game only because "I didn't make the wrong mistakes."[55]

Yet Bush rarely said anything in private encounters that he did not mean to say. His style with foreign leaders bordered on the indirect, but sooner or later he would make his point. His managerial style was equally disciplined. He would discuss issues individually with top subordinates, clearly conveying the principles he cared about. But he would almost never visibly intervene in subcabinet or even some cabinet-level policy discussions. Instead, he was constantly informed about daily developments, usually through Scowcroft and the deputy national security adviser, Robert Gates. Bush would frequently call them for answers to questions about minor facts, news reports, or events that interested him or, on occasion, personally type out notes to other members of his staff.

Bush gathered around him people who shared his penchant for low-key rhetoric and careful attention to details and consequences of action. He also chose those who could get along and keep their egos in check. That done, he consciously delegated day-to-day foreign policy management to those subordinates—James Baker, Brent Scowcroft, Defense Secretary Dick Cheney, and General Colin Powell, chairman of the Joint Chiefs of Staff.

James Baker, secretary of state, had been one of Bush's closest friends for more than twenty-five years. Yet Baker carefully separated two George Bushes in his mind, one the longtime friend and the other the person Baker would address even in small meetings as "Mr. President." Baker, a member of one of Houston's most prominent families, had been schooled on the East Coast, studying history at Princeton, where he wrote his junior thesis on the Kerensky government of 1917 and his senior thesis on the British Labour party. He then returned home to study and practice law. A Marine Corps veteran,

Baker had first served in the Commerce Department in the 1970s before playing a leading part in managing first Bush's then Reagan's presidential campaigns in 1980. A successful White House chief of staff and later secretary of the Treasury in the Reagan administration, Baker was a man whose soft Texas drawl masked his intensity. He was precise in his interactions with foreign leaders, having decided in advance how he wanted each encounter to end.

Baker complemented Bush well, connecting the president's general convictions to operational concerns. Baker's objectives could be very ambitious, but they were always tied to a notion of how these goals were to be achieved. These qualities, together with an instinct for getting to the heart of a problem and visualizing what a solution might entail, made him a highly effective secretary of state.

Scowcroft was the first national security adviser to hold the job twice, having served President Gerald Ford in the same role. He had made his way through the ranks of the U.S. Air Force to lieutenant general, serving on the ground after being injured in a crash early in his career. His formative period as a strategist had been on Henry Kissinger's National Security Council (NSC) staff. Scowcroft was known for his writings on nuclear policy and arms control and had strong views about those issues. He had also served in Yugoslavia as a military attaché and worried often about the danger of conflict in Eastern and Central Europe. But Scowcroft's most important contribution in 1989 may have been the organization and conduct of the national security decision-making process. Never a competitor for the limelight himself, he was hardworking, discreet, and cautious, insisting that internal squabbles not mar the conduct of American foreign policy. Scowcroft had served most recently as a member of the Tower Commission, investigating the role of the NSC in the Iran-Contra affair. His already strong views that the NSC staff should not become involved in the implementation of U.S. foreign policy was reinforced by close examination of Oliver North's adventures.

A kind of informal division of labor arose between Scowcroft and Baker. It was Scowcroft's job to make the government work, using his staff in policy development and engaging Baker, Cheney, and Powell until a coherent and shared policy direction emerged. He also stayed close to the president, constantly checking to make certain that Bush was comfortable with that direction and fully prepared to deal with other heads of state in carrying it out. Bush in turn truly trusted and relied heavily on Scowcroft. Although Scowcroft often met with foreign officials, it was Baker who carried policy into the international arena.

Baker and Scowcroft, in turn, gathered around them a tight circle of subordinates who shared their objectives and suited their personal styles.

When it came to German unification, that circle narrowed even further to just a few key aides. Scowcroft relied heavily on Robert Gates, a career intelligence analyst who had been the deputy director of the CIA in the second Reagan administration. Gates was the perfect alter ego for Scowcroft. He was well organized, determined that the policy-making process run in a highly disciplined manner, and extremely skilled at the day-to-day operations of government. Gates, generally more conservative than others in the administration regarding the Soviet Union, ran the deputies committee of top subcabinet officials so efficiently that full meetings of the National Security Council were rarely needed to clarify issues before they were presented to President Bush.

The most senior among Baker's aides was Robert Zoellick. Zoellick was the gatekeeper to Baker and was chosen by him to be the top subcabinet official on German unification. Raised in the Midwest, near Chicago, Zoellick had earned joint degrees from Harvard's Law School and Kennedy School of Government. Brought into the government by Richard Darman, he then impressed Baker, who took Zoellick with him to the Treasury, made him the issues coordinator for Bush's 1988 campaign, and placed him by his side at the State Department with the formal title of counselor. Zoellick was then thirty-five years old. Dennis Ross, director of policy planning and a specialist on Soviet foreign policy and the Middle East, was Zoellick's partner in advising Baker. He had served in the Pentagon and in the National Security Council during the Reagan administration, leaving the government at one point to take up an academic post at the University of California at Berkeley. Zoellick and Ross were close companions intellectually and professionally, conceptualizing overall strategies.

Though it was outside Baker's "inner circle," the leadership of the State Department's European bureau played an important part in managing American diplomacy toward Germany. From the summer of 1989 onward, the bureau was headed by Raymond Seitz and his deputy, James Dobbins. Seitz was a diplomat's diplomat, a man in whom grace and wit were joined to a keen, careful mind. Dobbins had recently been deputy chief of mission in Bonn, knew Germany well, and, though more acerbic than Seitz, had one of the quickest analytical minds in the foreign service.

Bitter rivalries between the State Department and the National Security Council staff had been a standard feature of Washington politics since the 1960s. But Scowcroft and Baker placed a premium on cooperation. Disputes arose but were always quickly contained, and the key aides to Baker forged close working relationships with members of the NSC staff. The most important of these were the ties between Zoellick and Robert Blackwill, a strong-willed strategist appointed as Scowcroft's senior director for European and Soviet affairs. Although he was teaching at Harvard's Kennedy School of Government at the time he joined the Bush administration, Blackwill had been a career foreign service officer who had worked for both Henry Kissinger and Zbigniew Brzezinski, Carter's national security adviser. He had also served as ambassador to the Vienna arms control negotiations on conventional forces in Europe. Yet Blackwill's energetic operating style was far from typical for a professional diplomat. Blackwill in turn brought Philip Zelikow, a career diplomat and lawyer who had worked for him in Vienna, to the NSC to manage European policy. The council's top Soviet expert, Condoleezza Rice, was recruited by Scowcroft from Stanford University. She had known Dennis Ross during his tenure at Berkeley, which made their working relationship on Soviet affairs an easy one. These three members of the Directorate for European and Soviet Affairs, led by Blackwill, were Scowcroft's principal aides on German unification and European security issues.

Bush Takes the Reins

The new administration emerged from the transition with potentially ambitious objectives but still inchoate policy prescriptions. Within about four months George Bush became the first Western leader to say plainly that the Cold War would not be over until the division of Europe had ended and Europe was "whole and free." This was a powerful philosophical argument. It held that the Cold War could end only where it had begun—in Central and Eastern Europe, and above all Germany. Before taking office Bush had told his advisers, "We should dream big dreams." Scowcroft put it clearly: "We thought we should change our sights from managing the Cold War on the ground in Europe and stabilizing the situation to look beyond, to resolution of the basic issues."[56] But how and how fast? These were the questions for a cautious president and his essentially conservative senior advisers, who wanted to make the most of this historic chance but to avoid "doing something stupid." Baker and his staff wished to pursue opportunities for democracy in Eastern Europe but were concentrating in the first weeks on Nicaragua and negotiation of a Central American settlement.[57]

A much-publicized series of formal policy reviews was launched to consider the implications of the new political situation for U.S. relations with the Soviet Union: National Security Review (NSR-3), Eastern Europe (NSR-4), and Western Europe (NSR-5). As these churned on, both Soviet and West European leaders joined the American media in a chorus of impatient criticism, public and private.[58]

Yet it was the march of events, not the deliberations of the new admin-istration, that forced the emergence of a different, albeit somewhat fragmen-tary approach in the spring of 1989. The Polish communist government, facing enormous economic difficulties, held "roundtable" talks with repre-sentatives of the still outlawed trade union Solidarity as participants. As the talks drew to a close, the NSC staff and the State Department combined to overcome Treasury objections and win President Bush's agreement to the promise of economic assistance as a reward for Polish reform. Bush wanted to be careful not to encourage popular unrest in Eastern Europe that might provoke a negative Soviet reaction; he did not want to repeat the tragedy of Hungary in 1956, when inflammatory U.S. rhetoric contributed to an uprising which was then bloodily crushed as the Americans stood by, unable to help.[59] Now, having waited for the day when Poland lifted the ban against Solidarity's revival, Bush spoke out on April 17, 1989, promising that his offer of aid was only a first step. "Help from the West will come in concert with liberalization," he declared. "The West can now be bold in proposing a vision of the European future."[60] This policy would later expand and become a coordinated effort by twenty-four countries (G-24) to send economic assistance to Poland, Hungary, and, within a few months, the rest of Eastern Europe.

Still, the steady drumbeat of criticism continued, and the president's im-patience began to grow. In response the NSC and White House staffs began to look for ways to demonstrate American leadership. Still lacking, in March 1989, any significant policy initiatives to use in launching such a diplomatic offensive, the White House had decided to create action-forcing events, including presidential trips and speeches that would oblige the government to develop policies. Thus, Scowcroft, Blackwill, and top State Department officials mapped out a plan for two major European trips by the president in 1989. The first, in the late spring, would be to Western Europe, and would include a NATO summit to celebrate the fortieth anniversary of the alliance and consider its future. The second, in the summer, would concentrate on Eastern Europe, and would culminate in the G-7 economic summit, to be held that year in Paris. The White House also decided to use the president's upcoming commencement speeches in May and June to deploy ideas about the direction of policy.

As plans for the trip and the speeches progressed, the policy review on Western Europe, NSR-5, also dragged on, producing a paper for interagency review in March 1989. The paper was prepared by the Policy Coordinating Committee for Europe, then chaired by the outgoing assistant secretary of state Rozanne Ridgway. Ridgway, a career diplomat and former ambassador to East Germany, had served for six years as Shultz's chief aide, helping him manage the turn in U.S.-Soviet relations. During this NSR-5 review the first differences emerged in Washington over policy toward Germany. On the NSC staff both Blackwill and Zelikow began to argue that U.S. policy had to tackle the German question anew if the Cold War was to enter a final phase. But they could not persuade the career staff at the State Department in late February and early March. Ridgway, for instance, believed that the existing situation was stable and a source of peace. She understood recent relations with Germany better than Zelikow did, and judged that renewed debate about the German question would be both premature and unwise. Robert Zoellick later recalled that when, in early 1989, he had asked a visiting West German general about German attitudes toward unification, Ridgway sharply observed that unification was "the subject that all Americans are interested in and no German cares about."[61]

The final version of the NSR-5 policy paper, as prepared by the State Department, reflected Ridgway's views, which were the dominant opinion among the European experts at State. In especially strong language for a bureaucratic document, the paper warned that "the issue of German re-unification is never far below the surface. However, the Germans themselves do not wish to increase the salience of this issue at this time. Nor do the other Europeans. There is no more inflammatory and divisive issue, and it serves no U.S. interest for us to take the initiative to raise it."[62] This paper was reviewed at a meeting of the NSC deputies committee, the top level of subcabinet officials, on March 20. Both the deputy director of the CIA and the deputy chairman of the Joint Chiefs of Staff urged that more attention be given to U.S. policy on German reunification. But there the issue was left.[63]

Neither did the reviews do much to help coalesce the Bush administration's policy on the Soviet Union. In frustration with the review of policy toward Moscow, Scowcroft called Blackwill and Rice into his office late one evening in March. "This is going nowhere," he said. "See if you can write something that has more bite." Rice and Blackwill then drafted an alternate national security directive. The paper laid out a case that containment had been a success but not an end in itself: it was time to move "beyond containment to the integration of the Soviet Union into the international system." The paper went on to lay out a series of conditions for the Soviet Union's entry into the international system.

That document became the centerpiece of the president's first commencement speech of the season, the address at Texas A&M on May 17. The speech itself was met with a yawn, but "beyond containment" became a catchphrase to describe the Bush approach toward the Soviet Union. Bush liked the notion and referred to his policy in that way. Actually, "beyond containment" relied on the Soviet Union to continue to make concessions at a time when it was really the United States that was on the defensive. But Moscow rather liked the idea. By accident, not by design, the speech resonated with a central tenet of the "new thinking": that an end to the Soviet Union's isolation from the international system was now possible.

The policy reviews churned on to a conclusion. Baker's closest advisers, such as Zoellick and Ross, had paid little attention to the review process, considering it largely a waste of time. Scowcroft, Gates, and Blackwill knew that they would not produce the initiatives needed for Bush's trips and scheduled speeches. By March 1989 Scowcroft was considering a major announcement. Intent on getting Soviet troops out of Eastern Europe, he suggested the withdrawal of all U.S. and Soviet troops from Europe. Blackwill dissuaded him from pursuing the proposal by emphasizing the symbolic power of the U.S. troop presence in assuring Europeans of the American commitment to their defense.[64] Scowcroft demurred but continued to cast about for some idea that would attack the basic Soviet military position in Central and Eastern Europe.

Scowcroft's old mentor, Henry Kissinger, had proposed an analogous approach: a U.S.-Soviet dialogue about *mutual* restraint in Eastern Europe, to "give the Soviets security guarantees (widely defined) while permitting the peoples of Eastern Europe to choose their own political future" and "conceive a drastic reduction of all outside forces in Europe—including those of the U.S.—that might revolutionize present concepts of security." Such a negotiation needed a confidential envoy, Kissinger had explained. In Moscow to deliver a courteous letter of greeting from the new president, Kissinger discussed his ideas with Yakovlev and then with Gorbachev. The Soviets were receptive. Kissinger then reported back to Bush, Baker, and Scowcroft on January 28. There is no evidence that Bush liked the idea of such a deal. At the State Department Ridgway and her deputy, Thomas Simons, told Baker that Kissinger's idea was dangerous. Baker, heeding Ross's advice, liked the idea of a discussion with the Soviets about democracy in Eastern Europe but also thought that Kissinger should not be part of such a dialogue. Neither Baker's staff nor the NSC staff (possibly excepting Scowcroft) had any sympathy with the substance of Kissinger's suggested bargain. Preferring a trade of Soviet tolerance in Eastern Europe for U.S. willingness not to exploit such a new environment to threaten Moscow, Baker deliberately quashed Kissinger's initiative in a press interview warning against any "signal that somehow we are getting together with the Soviet Union and carving up Eastern Europe."[65]

The NSC staff set forth its own policy ideas for Europe and the NATO summit in a March 1989 memo written by Zelikow and Blackwill, which, on March 20, Scowcroft sent to President Bush. The memo opened by declaring: "Today, the top priority for American foreign policy in Europe should be the fate of the Federal Republic of Germany." Bush was advised to "help keep Kohl in power" because his "government is now lagging in the polls behind an opposition that, as currently constituted, has too little regard either for nuclear deterrence or for conventional defense." Scowcroft recommended that the goal of U.S. policy in Europe should be to overcome the division of the continent through acceptance of common democratic values.[66] This concept of a "commonwealth of free nations" was offered as an alternative to Gorbachev's call on Europeans to build a "common European home."[67]

More controversial, though, was the suggestion that followed. Scowcroft's memo stated: "Even if we make strides in overcoming the division of Europe through greater openness and pluralism, we cannot have a vision for Europe's future that does not include an approach to the 'German question.' Here we cannot promise immediate political reunification, but we should offer some promise of change, of movement . . . Although virtually no West German expects German reunification to happen in this century, there is no German of any age who does not dream of it in his soul." The memo went on: "The formal Allied position has long been that we want the German people to regain their unity through self-determination. I think we can, working with Bonn, improve on this formula, make it more pointed, and send a clear signal to the Germans that we are ready to do more if the political climate allows it." Bush was reminded that, "amidst all the enthusiasm about 'glasnost,' it is sobering to remember that, in February 1989, East German border guards again shot down and killed a youth for trying to cross the Wall."[68]

The proposed rhetoric was not radical. The U.S. government was already formally on record in support of the peaceful and democratic reunification of Germany. But Bush was urged to put this goal back on the active political agenda. The president had thus been thinking about the issue of German reunification when *Washington Times* editor Arnaud de Borchgrave raised the topic with him in a May interview. Bush declared that he would "love to see" Germany reunified, adding, "Anybody who looks back over his shoulder and then looks at the present and sees a country ripped asunder by division, a people ripped asunder by political division, should say: 'If you can get reunification on a proper basis, fine.'"

Bush describes himself as "less of a Europeanist, not dominated by history." When then–Vice President Bush had visited the German city of Krefeld in June 1983, at the height of the mass demonstrations against INF missile deployment, the new FRG chancellor, Helmut Kohl, had taken time to get to know the American. Bush recalled demonstrators slinging rocks at his car without any security counteraction ("Our Secret Service would have shot them!") and sitting in a garage with Kohl waiting for a route to clear. This, he remembered, was a society willing to pay the price for free speech. Though the first to admit he was not clairvoyant and "can't claim to have understood everything that would happen in Europe from Day One," Bush had concluded that Germany was a solid democracy that had done penance for its sins and that "at some point you should let a guy up."[69]

A few days before the de Borchgrave interview, Blackwill had written another memorandum for Bush on dealing with the West Germans. Blackwill urged again that the United States adopt this issue anew. In the context of renewed nuclear debates in NATO between Washington and Bonn, Blackwill argued that if the Western allies identified their interests more closely with Germany's national aspirations, it would be easier to persuade the German people to reciprocate by continuing to identify their nation's future with the Western alliance. Separately Zoellick was advising a receptive Baker "to get ahead of the curve" on the issue of German unification or Gorbachev "might grab it first" (a mistaken exaggeration of Soviet flexibility on this subject).[70]

The time for rhetorical flourishes devoid of substantive initiatives had clearly come and gone. Administration officials were increasingly uneasy about the continuing perception of the president as slow to react to the historical moment. Gorbachev, by contrast, seemed to garner headlines daily with some new gesture of openness.

The primary source of tension with West Germany and within the NATO alliance was the dispute over the modernization of short-range nuclear forces (Lance). Rather than confront this problem head-on, the administration decided to move on another front—the conventional military balance in Europe. The United States planned to launch ambitious objectives and a fast timetable for concluding a treaty that would drastically reduce the size of conventional forces in Europe and push for an especially significant reduction of Soviet military power west of the Urals. The Bush administration, particularly Scowcroft and his staff, had concluded that the conventional military balance had not received as much attention as the U.S.-Soviet strategic nuclear balance. They would give conventional arms control in Europe much more attention since they believed that the hundreds of thousands of Soviet troops and thousands of Soviet tanks in Central and Eastern Europe were, more than any other factor, the fundamental source of Europe's insecurity.[71]

Scowcroft received crucial support for the idea when Baker returned from his first trip to Moscow in May 1989. This was the secretary of state's first major encounter with the Soviet leadership, and he had felt himself to be on the defensive throughout his trip and was annoyed by some of the showier but militarily meaningless arms control gestures coming from Moscow. When he met with Gorbachev, the Soviet leader opened by stressing the reality of perestroika and pushing for greater effort in arms control. There was a pointed discussion of the planned NATO modernization of short-range nuclear forces, but also a preview of a more meaningful upcoming move in the conventional arms control talks.[72]

Baker came home convinced that Gorbachev might really be serious and sincere. He was also certain that the United States had to take the initiative, had to "define George Bush as the leader of the alliance." Baker met with Bush and Scowcroft on May 17 and joined Scowcroft in rallying support behind a major conventional arms control initiative, prepared during the second half of May. The Pentagon had done some of the analysis to support these plans during the policy reviews, but military leaders were hesitant about going forward with dramatic new conventional arms control ideas, with objections voiced by then-JCS chairman Admiral William Crowe. Bush, however, had made up his mind. "I want this [more radical proposal] done," he said at a meeting of his top advisers. "Don't keep telling me why it can't be done. Tell me how it can be done." The NSC staff prepared the new proposal. Deputy Secretary of State Lawrence Eagleburger and Scowcroft's deputy Gates traveled secretly to Europe to persuade Margaret Thatcher, French president François Mitterrand, and Chancellor Helmut Kohl of West Germany to support the idea.[73]

Decisions were also made about the broad rhetorical themes to be developed during the NATO summit and Bush's related visits to Italy, West Germany, and Great Britain. Bush decided that he would link the end of the Cold War explicitly to an end of the division of Europe, and that he would hint at the implications of overcoming Europe's division for Germany's future.

The NATO summit on May 29–30 turned out to be a major success for the United States, for West Germany, and for Bush personally. The vexing issue of nuclear modernization was adroitly put aside after a negotiation in which Baker and Zoellick both played key roles. Chancellor Kohl and Foreign Minister Hans-Dietrich Genscher were quite satisfied with the outcome. Bush's conventional arms control initiative came as a complete surprise to the gathered journalists and was approved by NATO with enthusiasm. The episode had a dramatic and positive effect on the perception of Bush within Europe and, indeed, on Bush's confidence in his own handling of foreign affairs. He tended to rely thereafter on the improvised and secretive policy-making processes which had contributed to this success. A bit bemused by the acclaim that greeted the summit outcome, Bush reminded reporters three days later, "I'm the same guy I was four days ago."[74]

Bush used his postsummit press conference to deploy his new theme for Europe. He told those assembled that "our overall aim is to overcome the division of Europe and to forge a unity based on Western values."[75] The next day Bush traveled to Germany. He delivered a major address in the Rhein-goldhalle in Mainz, the Rheinland-Pfalz capital, where Kohl had risen to national prominence. The West's goal now, Bush proclaimed, was to "let Europe be whole and free. To the founders of the Alliance, this aspiration was a distant dream, and now it's the new mission of NATO." Bush then made explicit his definition of the end of the Cold War: "The Cold War began with the division of Europe. It can only end when Europe is whole. Today it is this very concept of a divided Europe that is under siege." Alluding to Gorbachev, Bush observed that "there cannot be a common European home until all within it are free to move from room to room." He called for the Iron Curtain to come down: "Let Berlin be next."[76]

Having introduced the volatile language of unity to his German audience, Bush then became more restrained in his speech. "We seek self-determination for all of Germany and all of Eastern Europe," he declared. More radical phrases referring directly to German unification had appeared in an earlier draft, but Scowcroft had removed them in part because he feared that Bush might be getting ahead of Chancellor Kohl's own statements about the national question. During Bush's visit, on a boat trip down the Rhine, Scowcroft raised the unification issue directly with Defense Minister Gerhard Stoltenberg, of Kohl's Christian Democratic Union (CDU) party. Stoltenberg was polite. The United States, he said, should keep raising this question in a calm, logical way, setting an agenda for change.[77]

Bush went on in his Mainz address to propose that the pan-European political organization, the Conference on Security and Cooperation in Europe (CSCE), could do more to promote pluralism and set guidelines for holding free elections in Eastern Europe.[78] The speech welcomed Germans as America's "partners in leadership." Bush's remarks delighted many Germans, who were quick to infer that Bush hoped the seemingly frozen German question would soon begin to thaw.[79] There is no doubt that the president grasped the significance of the new concepts and was not just parroting words drafted by aides. *Washington Post* reporters talking to Bush on the final stop of his trip in London were struck by his emphasis on the potential for change in Eastern Europe. Although the region was relatively quiet at the moment—a week before the Polish parliamentary election and shortly before other states in the region would experience serious unrest—Bush called Eastern Europe "the most exciting area for change in the world." According to one journalist, he "came back to [Eastern Europe] time and again in response to questions on other subjects." What did "beyond containment" mean? the reporters asked. Bush answered: "It means a united Europe. It means a Europe without as many artificial boundaries."[80]

The events in May 1989 thus set the tone for much closer U.S.–West German cooperation, including between Baker, Genscher, and their staffs.[81] That done, American officials could watch the unfolding events assured of a solid foundation for relations with Bonn. Two weeks later they could also watch, without alarm, Gorbachev's triumphal visit to West Germany.

Gorbachev's Turn

Gorbachev arrived in West Germany in June 1989 and received a hero's welcome. Soviet–West German relations had been transformed since the confrontational years of the early and mid-1980s, when Moscow was using all its political strength to stop the deployment of new NATO nuclear missiles into Germany. That battle was over; the INF treaty had been signed. The Soviet government reassessed the situation and began to receive top officials of the Federal Republic of Germany, including President Richard von Weizsäcker in 1987 and Kohl himself in 1988.[82]

There is evidence that both Gorbachev and Shevardnadze alluded to the possible unification of Germany before 1989. An outspoken but tolerated expert at one of the Soviet foreign policy institutes, Vyacheslav Dashichev, argued in 1987 that Moscow should be willing to accept a united Germany as part of a more cooperative relationship with the West.[83]

But what did these Soviet leaders really have in mind at the time? When FRG president von Weizsäcker repeated his 1985 position that unity of the German nation should be accepted but understood in human terms and not in a territorial sense, Gorbachev replied that he was not inclined to theorize on concepts such as the German nation. The current reality was two German states, but "history would decide what would happen in a hundred years." Von Weizsäcker recalled to Timothy Garton Ash that he interjected, "or perhaps fifty?" and Gorbachev indicated his assent. Chernyayev, who was present, recalled that Gorbachev explained at length the importance of the ties East Germany had developed with other states, "ties that cannot be broken." Gorbachev had also told the West German president that East and West Germany should try to strengthen and deepen the ties between the two states (gosudartsv'). Chernyayev comments that this was all theoretical; Gorbachev just "did not rule out" the possibility of German union.[84]

Gorbachev's own published views in his 1987 book *Perestroika* also suggest that he thought of German unification as a distant theoretical possibility. Referring to the discussion with von Weizsäcker, he writes, it must be said "quite plainly" that "statements about the revival of 'German unity' are far from being 'Realpolitik,' to use the German expression. It has given the FRG nothing in the past forty years." As for Reagan's call to open the Berlin Wall, Gorbachev writes that Reagan and other Western leaders "cannot actually offer anything realistic to the FRG as regards the so-called German issue . . . For the time being, one should proceed from the existing realities and not engage in incendiary speculations."[85]

There is clearly no evidence that the Soviet government sought to use the momentum of their new policies to bring the German states together as one. Dashichev himself says that his views were roundly rejected by the entire Soviet foreign policy establishment. Even this maverick called only for the possibility of confederation or even unification in the very long term, after both German states had withdrawn from their alliances and East-West conflicts had dissolved. One scholar who studied the subject, Michael Sodaro, justifiably concludes that "before the dramatic developments of late 1989 it was by no means certain that the Gorbachev leadership had come to any specific decision to modify the decades-old Soviet position on either the division of Germany or the division of Berlin. Ambiguities and reservations abounded in public discussions of these issues."[86]

During Kohl's visit to Moscow in October 1988 he spoke publicly, as he always did, about his hopes for the ultimate unity of the German nation.[87] Gorbachev, Chernyayev, and Valentin Falin conferred about whether Gorbachev should tell Kohl that this sort of talk was unacceptable. Gorbachev even asked Falin to draft talking points that "will not be forgotten." At the meeting, however, Gorbachev did not use this material, because Kohl did not raise the subject of unification.[88] Publicly Gorbachev repeated that history had divided Germany and that any attempt to change the situation with "unrealistic policies" would be "unpredictable and even dangerous."[89]

West German and Soviet perspectives thus seemed to converge when Gorbachev received his tumultuous, even euphoric, reception in West Germany during June 1989. Gorbachev and Kohl could agree that the history of the German nation might take its course. Gorbachev and Kohl could also agree that they did not need to devise common policies that would give history a push. Kohl, for example, told an interviewer years later that he and Gorbachev had a long private conversation overlooking the Rhine. Then, according to Kohl, Gorbachev asked whether he could rely on West German economic help if he ever urgently needed it. Kohl said yes. This, Kohl rosily remembered, was "the decisive moment" on the road to German unity.[90]

Neither Gorbachev nor Kohl's adviser, Horst Teltschik, remembers such a discussion. There is no evidence that Gorbachev thought he had made any substantive concession on the issue of German unity during his Bonn visit.[91] Numerous West German–Soviet joint ventures were announced, and trade between the two states increased rapidly in 1989.[92]

The Bonn declaration issued by the two heads of government announced that henceforth the Soviet Union would join West Germany in seeking to overcome the division of Europe. They would do this by "working on concepts." The "concepts" would examine how this goal could be achieved through the "building up of a Europe of peace and cooperation—of a European peace order or of a common European home—in which the USA and Canada also have a place." There were few specifics. The Soviet government could show tolerance for the existing order by agreeing officially to call the FRG the Federal Republic of Germany rather than the German Federal Republic.[93] The declaration mentioned the need to respect, among other human rights, the "right of peoples to self-determination," but stressed that "continuing differences in values and in political and social orders are no hindrance to future-shaping policy across the system-frontiers *(Systemgrenzen).*"[94] But the postwar realities were just that—realities.

The West Germans did not contest Soviet pronouncements about the real state of the world. In the spring of 1988 leaders of the largest West German political party, the conservative Christian Democratic Union (CDU), almost amended their formal party platform to set aside, as one of them put it, "the old continuing assumption that the German question [had] to be on the agenda." Kohl's two top advisers on these issues in the Chancellery, Wolfgang Schäuble and Horst Teltschik, and the minister of intra-German affairs, Dorothee Wilms, had all supported the push for change in the CDU platform.[95]

In February 1989 the head of the West German Chancellery, Wolfgang Schäuble, talked about the old hopes "that the unity of Germany could be achieved through the reunification of both German states in the not-too-distant future." But, he said, "we know today that these hopes were illusory." It was clear by 1961 at the latest that for the time being there was "no way to overcome the German division." What was left must primarily be the preservation of the "substance of the nation," the "commonality of the Germans," which meant keeping open the "communication between the people." As late as July 1989 Horst Teltschik, Kohl's foreign policy adviser, repeated the point FRG president von Weizsäcker had made years earlier, namely, that "for us, the German question is not primarily a matter of seeking a territorial solution."[96] West German officials hoped that the GDR might begin a process of internal reform, like that in Poland or Hungary, and believed that such reform might be "easier if the GDR was not challenged by the question of territorial unification." Once the East Germans had democratic rights, anything might be possible. But the priority was not unification, it was human rights for East Germans.[97]

The new U.S. ambassador to West Germany, Vernon Walters, a retired army lieutenant general and special envoy to many trouble spots over nearly fifty years of government service, had a deep sense that unification might be coming. But when he confided this view to West German officials in April 1989, he was greeted with polite chuckles.[98] In fact, the West German government was not fully prepared to take on Bush's May hints of support for unification. Teltschik recalled later that the United States "was far ahead of the Germans at this time" on the issue of unification.[99] The West Germans, being realistic, felt that they already had what they wanted—excellent relations with the reformist leadership of the Soviet Union and a continued strong allegiance to their Western values and Western allies.

Unhappiness in East Germany

As Gorbachev sought to renew socialism in the Soviet Union, he looked to communist leaders in Eastern Europe to follow his example. He believed that socialism had put down deep roots and could weather the turbulence of reform.[100] So it is no surprise that Gorbachev himself had no particular sympathy for Erich Honecker, chairman of the East German Communist party, and his hard-line comrades in the government. As early as 1985, at the funeral of Konstantin Chernenko, he had told East German party officials that kindergarten was over; no one would lead them by the hand. They were responsible to their own people. The relations between Gorbachev and Honecker went downhill from there. Hannes Adomeit, who studied both published statements and the East German archives, writes, "As time went by, cutting remarks and cryptic allusions became the order of the day; open controversy and argument that might have cleared the air disappeared from the discourse."[101]

But Gorbachev did not want to destroy the East German state; he wanted to reform it. Honecker traveled to Moscow two weeks after Gorbachev left Bonn and was personally reassured. Chernyayev confirms that Gorbachev adhered to traditional principles in his June 1989 talks with Honecker.[102]

But decades of communist rule and indoctrination had engendered widespread hatred for the system throughout Eastern Europe. As the Polish people were allowed to reenter politics through the April 1989 legalization of Solidarity, it became clear that old-style communism was in real jeopardy in at least some countries, and that Moscow would not intervene to save it. In earlier years mass protests would have been crushed by indigenous security forces, confident that Soviet troops would back them up if needed. Now East European communists were face to face with their own people. Gorbachev and the Soviet government were insisting by the end of 1988 that the "Brezhnev doctrine" was dead. Still, no one could know how Moscow would respond if socialism itself was challenged. After all, it was one thing to talk about different roads to socialism, quite another to confront the prospect that the roads might lead to the *end* of socialism. That Rubicon was yet to be crossed.

In early 1989 few if any observers thought that this was a problem for the East German state. The German Democratic Republic did not seem to be threatened by serious instability. Indeed, it seemed the most solid of the East European states. It had only once—briefly in 1953—experienced the kind of upheaval that had tormented communist leaders in Poland, Hungary, and Czechoslovakia. David Childs, one of the leading Western experts on the GDR, in the standard English text on the country, could judge in 1988 that East Germany "is apparently one of the world's most stable regimes."[103]

Bolstered by relatively greater affluence than his country's Eastern European neighbors enjoyed and a fantastically elaborate system of internal controls, East Germany's longtime leader Erich Honecker seemed secure in his position. His government had long dealt with dissent through a mixture of brutal repression, forced emigration, and the vent of allowing occasional, limited travel to the West for a substantial part of the population. An English observer, Timothy Garton Ash, visited the GDR in July 1989 and noted firsthand the deep pessimism of opposition activists. Officials would say that the situation was "very complicated" and shake their heads but "the State Security Service—the 'Stasi'—still seemed all-powerful, the population at large not prepared to risk its modest prosperity. Above all, the ranks of the opposition had been continuously thinned by emigration to West Germany." A friend complained to Garton Ash that soon "there'll be nobody left in this country but a mass of stupid philistines and a few crazy idealists."[104]

Western observers had long guessed or sensed that many East Germans probably despised and even hated the regime, but this bitterness had seemed to lapse into passive, cynical resignation. A tiny number of citizens were openly critical of the regime: representatives of the counterculture such as the leaders of peace, feminist, and ecological groups; a few figures in East Germany's literary establishment; and a handful of dissident Marxist intellectuals. These individuals could find some shelter for their activities in

Protestant churches, which had secured an uneasy independence from direct state control. Yet these dissenters remained a fringe element in East German society. Demonstrators had been swiftly and severely punished in 1987 and 1988, and again in March 1989 a small demonstration of about sixty church-goers in Leipzig was suppressed by security forces. The East German security chief, Erich Mielke, having been in the business of arresting or killing opponents of communism for more than half a century, assured his government colleagues that only the presence of Western media had inspired the demonstrators to act.[105]

If there was a threat to the regime in East Berlin, it appeared to come from reformist elements *within* the ruling Socialist Unity party (SED). These reformers, such as Dresden party chief Hans Modrow, seemed ready to take their cue from Gorbachev and begin their own East German perestroika. But the GDR's rulers held fast through the spring and summer of 1989, determined to isolate themselves from the turmoil gripping the rest of the Soviet bloc. In the inner councils of the East German Politbüro "the issue of Gorbachev was taboo." To outsiders the line, as one member of the Politbüro remarked to reporters, was that just because "your neighbor renewed the wallpaper in his flat, would you feel obliged to do the same?"[106]

In the winter of 1988–89 the regime tried to quarantine itself against the perestroika virus. The government banned importation of the more heretical Soviet journals. Honecker held a summit with Nicolae Ceauşescu, Romania's dictator and a kindred spirit. The Poles were planning genuinely free elections. Hungary was well along the same road. But the East German government had its own election plans. In May the SED followed its usual practice of rigged local elections and announced it had earned the support of 98.85 percent of the electorate. Protests from activists and church poll watchers were ignored.[107]

The contrast between this behavior and the thawing climate for political reform in Moscow, Warsaw, and Budapest was jarring to many East Germans. It sharpened their sense of injustice enough to widen the usually small circle of popular unrest. But the police made more arrests and increased their harassment of the churches. In June the East German parliament applauded Beijing's bloody crackdown on dissidents in Tiananmen Square, and the Politbüro pointedly criticized Hans Modrow. In August 1989 the well-informed East German security police privately warned party leaders that membership in dissident groups had grown, but the total number of people involved was estimated at only 2,500 in a population of 16 million.[108]

Even if the East German government seemed invincible, it was not at ease. The theoretical implications of Gorbachev's new policies were profoundly unsettling. Otto Reinhold, a top social scientist in the East German Communist party, posed the dilemma for his country: "What right to exist would a capitalist GDR have alongside a capitalist Federal Republic? In other words, what justification would there be for two German states once ideology no longer separated them?"[109] But that was hardly Moscow's worry in the spring of 1989. For the Kremlin the danger seemed to be the recalcitrance of Honecker, and the distance between Moscow and East Berlin was growing. Change had to come to East Germany because the old and sick Honecker was clearly not up to the tasks he faced.

The larger implications of the East German problem were not yet apparent. But what was happening in Eastern Europe and the GDR was only the beginning of a very rocky ride. Soon it would become clear that socialism could be defended only to the extent that capitalism could be attacked. The Cold War was rooted in that conflict, and it in turn sustained the socialist myth at home and abroad. Class struggle was at the root of the myth that, together with Moscow's coercive power, held the Soviet bloc intact. It was the rationale by which Eastern European leaders oppressed their people, confident that the Soviet army would help if things got out of hand. It was the logic for continued sacrifice of the Soviet people to an economy perpetually on war footing. And it was the glue that held a hundred nationalities together in what, without it, was nothing more than an empire waiting to collapse.

Leaders from Stalin to Chernenko had never dreamed of abandoning the philosophical foundation of the Soviet state and its place in the world in order to accept integration into a Western-dominated international political and economic system. They worked desperately to sustain a "socialist alternative" because to abandon it, they believed, would be suicidal for the Soviet state itself. Until the fall of 1989 Gorbachev had no reason to think that they were right. But he would soon confront the full consequences of his ideas and learn that there was something to his predecessors' concerns.

~ 2

Revisiting the German Question

WE ALL TEND TO assume that great changes must have great causes. To think otherwise seems to offend some innate sense of proportion. Writing 150 years ago, Alexis de Tocqueville speculated about the February 1848 overthrow of France's monarchy, a sudden but relatively peaceful revolution that, like the downfall of communism in East Germany, left the victors "as astonished at their triumph as were the vanquished at their defeat." His solution was to combine general causes with particular events, writing that the revolution in France, "in common with all other great events of this class, sprang from general causes impregnated, if I am permitted the expression, by accidents." And although Tocqueville referred to "accidents," he perceptively observed that these were really "that tangle of secondary causes which we call chance, for want of the knowledge how to unravel it."[1]

The leaders who now faced the reemergence of the German question had been taken by surprise. Everyone knew that the earlier struggle had ended in stalemate, not agreement. In that sense Germany's future had never been settled. But not one of the leaders involved had expected to be faced with the problem. They had inherited Four Power "rights and responsibilities" toward Germany that now existed completely outside the context in which they had been won. A stable, democratic, and powerful West German state was an anchor in the Western alliance, not a defeated enemy. For its part the Soviet Union was led by a reformer desperate to rescue his country from internal decay and international isolation, not by a victorious and ruthless dictator determined to consolidate socialist wartime gains.

In 1989 a "tangle of secondary causes" brought these contradictions to the surface. Then the delicate task was to finish the work of 1945 forty-five years later, in the context of all that had happened in between. Unsettled borders, the right of Germans to determine their own destiny, the political and military alignment of a new Germany, Germany's place in a unified Europe: these were not new issues. The historical legacy was there, more like a negative than an original photograph, but just clear enough to remind viewers of the problems and fears attending the question of German unity.

Germany had long been a problem for the international system. Prior to Napoleon the area we now call Germany was a collection of over 350 states and cities loosely affiliated in the Holy Roman Empire. Napoleon reduced the number of states to thirty-nine and combined sixteen of them in a confederation. The German Confederation survived Napoleon's downfall but still included numerous states divided by customs barriers, different currencies, different religions, and different ruling families. The great powers of 1815 thought of the German Confederation as a device to keep Germany weak and divided, an outcome that suited all of them.

In the 1840s and 1850s, however, the idea of national unification commanded growing support as a way to achieve political reform. The hope was that a central democratic government would take the place of local princelings. In the new age of industry and commerce, national unification also looked like a path to prosperity, as merchants were encouraged by the benefits of an 1834 customs union that removed many of the barriers to intra-German trade. In 1848 revolutions against the governments of the German Confederation converged on a common agenda: unification through election of a national assembly for all Germany. The moment passed, however, amid quarrels over the form of unification and the design of this united Germany. For a time liberal unification had seemed inevitable, but it was not. By the summer of 1849 the princes had been restored. The kingdom of Prussia, guided by Otto von Bismarck, seized its opportunity in the 1860s to become the vehicle of unification, forging a German Empire in successive wars with Denmark, Austria, and France. The new empire was proclaimed on the field of victory, in the Hall of Mirrors of the Palace of Versailles outside Paris on January 18, 1871.

None of the other great powers of Europe was pleased by the addition of this newcomer to their ranks. Bismarck's efforts were unquestionably aided by the fact that, during the 1860s, British diplomacy was passive or distracted; the French had annoyed their potential friends; the Austrians were beginning their long decline; and the Russian court disliked the other powers even more than they disliked the Prussians. But thirty years after the creation of the German Empire, France and Russia had already concluded a military alliance against it, and the British were beginning to think of Germany as their principal rival on the Continent. The German Empire was blamed for deaths of millions in the First World War. Then a new German empire led by Hitler plunged Europe into an even more horrifying bloodbath. "After Hitler," Fritz Stern wrote, "nothing is quite the same—not in the world of the mind nor in the world of politics; not in Europe and not outside it."[2] The Nazi onslaught forever changed the image of Germany and Germans for the world. The historian Gerhard Weinberg has observed:

> At the beginning of the century, the German Emperor William II had held up the Huns to his nation as the people they should emulate. The German governor general in World War II occupied Poland proudly proclaimed the intent of naming his province after the Vandals instead. A new dark age was to descend upon the earth, wrecking the existing features of civilization . . . Only this time the destruction was to be more complete and the instruments of continued repression were certain to be more sophisticated.[3]

Hitler's plans for subjugation of much of the world and the notion that a modern government of a highly educated population should endeavor systematically to murder an entire people, the Jews, staggered the imagination. The Germans thus emerged from the Second World War indelibly stained by crimes that strained human comprehension. Their one hope of redeeming national pride was that, as Elie Wiesel once told a German audience, "Challenged by memory, you could move forward."[4]

In the wake of World War II, Europe's leaders developed new nightmares about what might replace a divided Germany. For the Soviet Union that vision was of a reunified and militarized Germany, allied with the West and bent again on the destruction of the USSR. East Germany became the outer armor of the socialist international order's protective shield against the West—against not only its sophisticated armies but its seductive ideas and lifestyle as well. The West had its own fears. Its darkest forebodings were of a new Rapallo, the 1922 treaty that a defeated Germany had signed with Lenin's outcast Soviet Union.[5] In this vision a united Germany, lacking Western moorings, leaned eastward, tilting Europe's balance of power toward Moscow.

When and if the two sides looked beyond their nightmares to a more positive outcome, they confronted the immutable fact that no "united Germany" would serve everyone's interests: Europe's ideological division saw to that. It was simpler to accept the judgment of history and assume that Germany's division was not so fragile after all. Perhaps the period of unification from 1871 to 1945 had been the real aberration. Every now and then— usually at an academic conference or in the rhetorical flourish of a presidential speech—someone would raise the German question. But precisely because prophecies of a reunited Germany seemed so worrying, leaders on both sides of the East-West divide worked even harder to strengthen the respective foundations of the two German states. They thought they were succeeding.

Territorial Questions and the Polish Border

As World War II drew to a close, none of the victorious powers knew precisely what should happen to Germany. They understood that their armies would occupy and govern it for a time, and that during this occupation some sort of peace treaty would be carefully prepared and then concluded with some sort of reconstituted German political authority. But there was little to guide them beyond that dim image. In May 1945 there was no German state to serve as a foundation for reconstruction. The old one had been smashed, and the weary victors were not urgently interested in figuring out how to create a new one. By the time governments began to concentrate on the creation of a new Germany, their ability to work together on even minor matters—never solid to begin with—had all but disappeared. The question of how to establish a new German state was already obscured and partly prejudged by the early quarrels over the postwar military administration of a ruined and dismembered country.

During the war the Americans and the British had toyed with the idea of dismembering a defeated Germany, but now they were not sure whether they should do it. The Soviet Union leaned toward holding the country together as an object for Soviet and communist influence.[6] But the Soviet Union had one clear, immediate goal. Moscow wanted more territory for the USSR so as to expand the Soviet frontier westward. Stalin had tried to get this security buffer by bargaining with Hitler—the infamous Molotov-Ribbentrop pact that divided up Poland in 1939. At the end of the war the Soviet Union occupied about half of Germany as it had existed in 1937, before Adolf Hitler began annexing new territory. Stalin divided this half into two parts, so that about a quarter of prewar Germany remained under Soviet military rule. The remaining quarter Stalin incorporated directly into the Soviet Union and Poland, annexing about half of what had been east Prussia as well as the old German city of Königsberg, which the Soviets renamed Kaliningrad. This Stalin accomplished with American and British acquiescence.

Without waiting for formal British and American consent, the Soviets simply gave the remaining German territory east of the Oder and western Neisse rivers to the new communist rulers of Poland, including the provinces of Lower Silesia which had been inhabited by German speakers for centuries. This was meant as compensation for the loss of those parts of Poland marked for absorption into the USSR. Stalin made the territory Polish by expelling all the Germans who had not yet been killed or starved to death. As he bluntly told the British foreign minister Ernest Bevin, there was no need for the British to worry about this region because "there were not many Germans left in the territories which had been taken from Germany."[7]

The United States and Great Britain told the Soviets they could not agree to Polish annexation of this Soviet-occupied portion of Germany. But they reluctantly went along with provisional Polish administration of this territory with the understanding that "the final delimitation of the western frontier of Poland should await the peace settlement."[8] No peace conference was ever convened. Final delineation of a border between Germany and Poland thus became one of the responsibilities that the Four Powers, which had declared their "supreme authority with respect to Germany" (the United States, the Soviet Union, Great Britain, and France), had to discharge before a unified Germany could be reestablished.[9]

Ideology Takes Over

This practice of putting questions of Germany's political future off to another day continued in the years to come. At Potsdam the Americans, British, and Soviets agreed to work on a draft peace treaty that they would present to the Germans. A Council of Foreign Ministers (CFM) was designated as the forum in which to work out the terms. While the CFM worked on the treaty, the occupiers would work together in administering Germany through an Allied Control Council made up of their military governors.

This Four Power cooperation would have been difficult under the best of circumstances. But with the victors indecisive about the shape of a future German state and squabbling about how the occupation should be run, the task became impossible. Meanwhile, as the official historian of the American military government later wrote, "for about a year following the German capitulation it was virtually impossible to get the White House to give attention to policy matters relating to Germany," its lack of attention mirroring the "almost complete indifference on the part of the American people or of American political leaders to the problem of the occupation of Germany."[10]

Washington and Moscow were slowly assuming leadership of the two poles of the new international order. The Soviets' behavior toward Germany contributed to the growing U.S. pessimism about the possibilities for postwar cooperation. In the summer of 1946 a consensus began to emerge within the Truman administration which interpreted Soviet actions in Germany and elsewhere as part of an opportunistic plan to bring about communist control throughout Europe and the world. U.S. officials feared communist political subversion rather than a Soviet military attack, given the political unrest arising from the poverty and widespread shortages of vital resources afflicting the Continent.

The British government needed no convincing about the Soviet threat. Officials in London had been wary of the Soviet danger since the end of the war and thought the Americans were slow to see it. The British, like the Americans, also worried about economic chaos and even mass starvation in Germany. The British Joint Planning Staff anticipated a complete breakdown of law and order in the British zone of occupation if food rations were cut again. Both governments now recognized that their national interests plainly required German economic recovery, even if this preference cut against the Potsdam mandate to seek Four Power cooperation with the Soviets.

The problem, as Secretary of State James Byrnes put it, was that the Allied Control Council was "neither governing Germany nor allowing Germany to govern itself." Now the United States sought the "maximum possible" economic unification to allow Germany to achieve self-sustaining economic recovery. Byrnes also announced in September 1946 that the Germans should "now be given primary responsibility for the running of their own affairs," with "proper safeguards." Furthermore, he reassured the Germans and America's allies that "as long as there is any occupation army in Germany [i.e., Soviet forces], American armed forces will be part of that occupation army."[11]

Byrnes's successor, General George Marshall, was not yet ready to abandon the strategy of Four Power cooperation in economic administration. As he journeyed to the next CFM meeting, held in Moscow during March and April 1947, Marshall intended to propose a plan to ensure German economic recovery while renewing the American proposal for a treaty guaranteeing complete German disarmament for at least twenty-five years. The Soviets, though, were interested only in a deal that would take immediate reparations out of Germany's paltry current industrial production. Having uprooted at least a third of all the capital equipment they had found in their zone by the spring of 1946, the Russians ceased the plundering of their own zone. At this point they wanted to win reparations from western Germany.

Marshall reluctantly came around to the view that the Soviets would not allow any solution that would let the Western portion of occupied Germany become economically viable. Thus, emergency relief sent by the United States to Germany would effectively be subsidizing the shipment of German economic production to the USSR. Marshall advised Truman that "we cannot accept a unified Germany under a procedure which in effect would mean that the American people would pay reparations to an ally." Marshall was, in the words of his biographer, "the last of the top Americans to abandon hope of being able to negotiate with the Russians."[12]

It seems odd in retrospect that the Soviets rejected Marshall's offer of complete German disarmament and some reparations. Michael Howard has observed that "one of the most remarkable aspects of this whole period is the astonishing *stupidity* of Soviet policy. All the cards were in the Soviet hands if they had only cared to play them. What is more, their opponents were playing with marked cards" because of Soviet espionage.[13] Yet Soviet policy can also be explained by reference to Stalin's implacably hostile, even paranoid view of the international system. Stalin had considered World War II and the wartime Grand Alliance to be only the first phase in the coming war between capitalism and communism. In this view the capitalist states would fight among themselves for supremacy and then turn their fire on the Soviet Union. This was at least one reason why Stalin thought he could make a deal with Hitler in 1939 and stay on the sidelines during the first phase of the cataclysm. The German attack on the USSR exploded that illusion.[14]

Fear of a new world war receded temporarily in the flush of the victory over Nazism. But from late 1946 until 1948, the xenophobe Andrei Zhdanov dominated Soviet thought about the international system. As one historian admits, less is known "about what went on in the Soviet Union during this period of the cold war than during any other period of Soviet history."[15] What is clear is that Moscow pressed harder to weaken Western European governments reeling from the devastation of World War II. In May 1947, for example, the French communists resigned from the coalition government and called for general strikes in order to destabilize the Fourth Republic. These aggressive policies went hand in hand with new economic analyses in Moscow predicting that capitalism was about to experience a major economic crisis and was thus vulnerable.

Preparing for a new world war, Stalin was determined to solidify the Soviet Union's gains and cautious about any offer from the West that diminished his control over Germany's future—or at least that part of Germany under Soviet occupation. According to a Russian historian with access to relevant archives, Stalin and his advisers would have seen any American compromise or accommodation as "merely a tactical maneuver" in the West's supposed plan for war.[16]

The Americans returned from Moscow determined to join Britain in proceeding with separate economic administration of the Anglo-American zones of occupation, bypassing the uncooperative French and Soviets. The State Department then developed the Marshall Plan initiative for a comprehensive European Recovery Program. Both the Americans and the British sought to allow the Germans to participate in the use of Marshall Plan aid. The Germans organized an economic council to take responsibility for economic administration in the "Bizone." The council, which met for the first time in June 1947, prefigured the future West German government.

The American decision to announce the Marshall Plan reflected a basic judgment about U.S. national interests, a decision that far greater commitments of U.S. resources were justified in the cause of European renewal. The Soviet Union rejected the offer to join the Marshall Plan, refusing to accept terms and conditions that to Stalin must have seemed aimed at destroying socialism in the Soviet Union itself. Stalin insisted that the Eastern European governments subject to his influence also refuse to participate.

The ideological dimensions of the German problem were now set. The West would rebuild the part of Europe—including Germany—that it controlled. The Soviet Union was left to treat the other half in accordance with its own wishes. The Soviets tried to influence the political reorganization of western as well as eastern Germany in what Stalin confided to an East German communist were his plans for "zigzag—opportunistic—policies toward socialism" rather than "direct attacks."[17] But the West was no longer interested. Four Power cooperation in running Germany formally ended when the Soviets walked out of the Allied Control Council in March 1948. Germany's fate was now in the hands of two separate and irreconcilably hostile blocs.

German Self-Determination and the Issue of Trust

The arguments over Four Power administration, even if they were shadowed by the growing hostility between the Western countries and the USSR, were still largely arguments about Germany itself. Once Germany became an open theater of East-West confrontation, issues relating to Germany were just factors calculated in a wider contest for Europe, if not the world. British, French, and Soviet policies were clear. All three of these countries were firmly convinced that a united Germany could not come into existence unless: (1) it did not align itself with the opposing side in the East-West split; and (2) it did not grow again into a powerful and dangerous force in Central Europe, repeating the experience of the two world wars. If these conditions meant that there would be no united Germany, then so be it. Europeans, particularly the French, believed that any revival of German power had to go hand in hand with European structures that would keep the German state from endangering France. Indeed, some leading figures in all three governments welcomed the dilution of German power through division into at least two separate states.

The German question was really three questions in one, which all the governments faced in the years between 1948 and 1955:

1. Do we trust the Germans enough to let them become unified again?
2. Do we trust the Germans enough to let them freely determine their own political-military alignment?
3. Do we trust the Germans enough to feel confident that their national aspirations will not threaten European peace?

At any time between 1948 and 1955, the French, British, and Soviet governments would probably have answered all three of these questions with a firm no. But the American response would have been harder to predict. There were genuine internal debates about these questions in the United States. In West Germany the questions prompted wrenching self-examination as the Germans wondered both in private and in public whether they could even trust themselves.

Wolfram Hanrieder has referred to American policy in these years as one of "double containment: the containment of the Soviet Union at arm's length, and of West Germany with an embrace."[18] It is a fair description. But by embracing the West Germans, the Americans hoped to build mutual trust. By 1955, and perhaps even as early as 1950 or 1952, dominant figures in the U.S. government were increasingly ready (though not without some anxiety) to give positive answers to these questions of trust. In part this was because of the decisively pro-Western orientation of the West German government's first chancellor, Konrad Adenauer, and in part it was because the West Germans and the Americans had triumphed together in overcoming the 1948–49 Soviet attempt to blockade access to the western half of Berlin. Partly, too, it was because the West Germans took the further step, between 1950 and 1955, of standing up to the burdens of both political and military alignment with the Western powers.

Kennan's "Program A"

In 1948 the British and the French took the first steps toward concluding new alliances that would ease their fears about both Soviet and German power. The British government sponsored the creation of a Western Union, a regional mutual defense treaty that would include France, Belgium, the Netherlands, and Luxembourg. In the spring of 1948, after the Communist party had seized power in Czechoslovakia in February, American leaders pledged that they would join in providing some form of military reassurance to Western Europe if the Republican Congress could be persuaded to agree. The eventual result was the North Atlantic treaty establishing the NATO alliance, signed in Washington in April 1949.

The previous summer, during the Berlin blockade, the State Department's policy planning staff and its director, George Kennan, suggested that the United States make a last effort to win agreement to a unified Germany. Kennan was chairing an NSC subcommittee charged with considering Germany's future relations with its European neighbors. He suggested that the Four Powers relinquish control of Germany, withdraw in phases from almost all of the country, and hold all-German elections. Limited quadripartite (i.e., Four Power) garrisons would remain in place only to ensure the demilitarization of Germany.[19]

This represented a turnabout in Kennan's own thinking. For years he had thought the idea of a Germany run jointly with the Russians was "a chimera"; but until 1948 his conclusion was that "we have no choice but to lead our section of Germany—the section of which we and the British have accepted responsibility—to a form of independence so prosperous, so secure, so superior, that the East cannot threaten it."[20] Now, in 1948, Kennan decided that letting the Germans choose their own destiny free of Four Power control was less risky than proceeding with the status quo, which meant a permanent Soviet military presence in the heart of Europe amid an unstable division of the German nation. The West German government, he feared, would "become the spokesman of a resentful and defiant nationalism."[21]

The remainder of the State Department disagreed with Kennan, believing that Germany could not yet be trusted with self-government. European division chief John Hickerson told Kennan that it "would be highly dangerous to agree to unite Germany along the lines you propose until Western Europe is stronger, both economically and military." But Secretary of State Marshall was intrigued and urged Kennan to pursue his idea further, getting advice from outside consultants.[22] Kennan and the policy planning staff convened a working group to refine "Program A." Backed by a prestigious group of outside consultants, Kennan presented it to Marshall in November 1948 as a contingency plan should the United States decide to "reveal plainly the terms on which we would be prepared to consent to the establishment of a German government for all of Germany and to the withdrawal of forces from most of Germany." Opposition to the plan remained strong, and acting secretary Robert Lovett, in Marshall's absence, informed Kennan that the proposal should be reconsidered.[23]

Kennan's plan suddenly got a new hearing when Dean Acheson replaced Marshall as Secretary of State and Truman began his second term of office in January 1949. Kennan resubmitted "Program A" to Acheson, knowing that the new secretary had been one of the consultants who had endorsed it the previous year. Acheson warned the British and French ministers in Washington completing work on the North Atlantic treaty that the United States was preparing a new model for the treatment of Germany as a whole, "dim as that prospect might seem." He recalled later that his foreign counterparts found this revelation "sobering."[24]

Acheson chaired a lengthy discussion of Kennan's plan on April 18, 1949. Opinion was split into two camps. There were those who believed that the division of Germany should be maintained for a long time so that West Germany would remain weak and dependent on its Western neighbors. The other view was that U.S. interests would be best served if the division of Germany ended as soon as possible, provided the division of Europe could be ended at the same time. This would involve the withdrawal of the Red Army back toward the Soviet Union as most of the modest number of American occupation troops also withdrew.

The British heard about "Program A" and were appalled at the thought that the United States might withdraw its troops from Germany. Ernest Bevin wrote Acheson that West Germany's leaders would also be gravely concerned about any arrangement for Germany as a whole that might leave the Germans at the mercy of the Soviet-organized police in the Eastern zones and the communists in the Western zones. These leaders, according to Bevin, opposed withdrawal of Western occupying troops until a proper democratic state was well established and the danger from the East had abated.[25]

Acheson was undaunted and remained sympathetic to Kennan's initiative. As he prepared to leave for a new CFM meeting with the British, French, and Soviets, Acheson urged Bevin to study the idea of regrouping occupation troops and moving the Russians eastward. But the day after he sent his reply to Bevin, the ideas contained in Kennan's "Program A" were leaked to the press, probably by one of its enemies within the U.S. government. The news story discomfited top officials, who were not yet ready to defend the policy.

It also permitted opposition in the U.S defense establishment to coalesce quickly. The American commander in Europe and military governor of the American zone, General Lucius Clay, as well as Secretary of Defense Louis Johnson and the Joint Chiefs of Staff all threw their weight against the proposal. Acheson gave up. He had come to conclude that "there would be fewer and less painful difficulties by going ahead with the Western German government than by attempting to unite Germany first." The British and the French were duly reassured.[26]

Years later Paul Nitze claimed that Acheson was still so tempted by "Program A" that he asked his close aide Charles Bohlen to sound out the Soviets informally for any interest in a general withdrawal of all occupation forces. Bohlen met with the Soviet military governor in eastern Germany, General Vasily Chuikov. Chuikov reportedly said: "The Germans hate us. It is necessary that we maintain our forces in Germany." That, according to Nitze, "put an end to any further discussion of Plan A." In fact, Acheson kept toying with ideas for reciprocal withdrawals of both American and Soviet troops from Germany as late as 1951, after the outbreak of the Korean War.[27]

The United States, Britain, and France proceeded with the creation of a West German state, the Federal Republic of Germany, with its capital in Bonn. Both the West and the East kept their occupation forces in place. The U.S. government had considered trusting the Germans to choose their destiny free from the influence of foreign occupation forces. But many in Germany feared that the coercive Soviet presence would always be there; the Red Army would never be an ocean away. Future German choices would be made with foreign armies stationed throughout Germany.

A "Temporary" State on Western Soil

The West proceeded with the establishment of the new Federal Republic. Its constitution, seen as an interim document and thus modestly called a Basic Law, was adopted on May 8, 1949. The next month the Western allies agreed to replace their military governors with High Commissioners.

The United States pressured Britain and France to join in creating the conditions for German prosperity and self-government. In turn, the British and the French insisted on an American guarantee to protect them against both the immediate military threat of the Soviet Union and some future revival of German military power. As we have seen, that promise was fulfilled with the signing of the North Atlantic treaty. It was no coincidence that final agreement to do away with the military governments in western Germany was reached only after the treaty had been concluded.

The Federal Republic of Germany was created as a state in the international legal order, with authority to make law without outside approval and to act independently in international affairs. Nonetheless, the occupying powers reserved for themselves the ultimate control over Germany's future that they had assumed in 1945. In 1952 the new German state signed a treaty governing its relations with the United States, Britain, and France, agreeing that "in view of the international situation, which has so far prevented the reunification of Germany and the conclusion of a peace settlement, the Three Powers retain the rights and the responsibilities . . . relating to Berlin and to Germany as a whole, including the reunification of Germany and a peace settlement." Article 7 of the same treaty added that all the signatory countries would seek "a peace settlement for the whole of Germany, freely negotiated between Germany and her former enemies, which should lay the foundation for a lasting peace. They further agree that the final determination of the boundaries of Germany must await such a settlement. Pending the peace settlement, the Signatory States will cooperate to achieve, by peaceful means, their common aim of a reunified Germany enjoying a liberal-democratic constitution, like that of the Federal Republic, and integrated within the European community." An essential point was that the prewar entity called Germany continued to exist as a state that had passed under Four Power military control with the Allied conquest in 1945. Berlin remained under direct Four Power control after the creation of the Federal Republic. Finally, the sovereignty of the FRG was subject to limitations stemming from the direct Four Power position in Berlin and the Powers' vestigial responsibility "relating to Berlin and to Germany as a whole, including the reunification of Germany and a peace settlement."[28]

This complicated legal situation meant that the FRG was, in fact, an interim state whose final structure and boundaries would be determined in a "peace settlement." The Four Powers remained legally indispensable to the reestablishment and determination, someday, of the boundaries of "Germany as a whole."

Soviet views of Four Power rights varied over the years but tended to differ from the Western position. The Soviets frequently argued that Germany as such had ceased to exist; two new states had replaced it. They therefore asserted that the "state" they had created out of their own occupation zone, the German Democratic Republic, was fully sovereign both in its own territory and in East Berlin, subject of course to the limits on state authority implicit in the international legal order and the GDR's separate constitutional obligations to the USSR.

These legal issues arose from time to time in the years between 1945 and 1989. The status of Berlin drew particular attention. Over time agreements grew up that strictly regulated the most minute details of movement of heads of state, populations, land vehicles, and air traffic. Yet the central question of how Germany could become whole again seemed of little importance until a new generation of international legal officers in the affected countries were suddenly asked to untangle the thicket surrounding Four Power rights and responsibilities for the disposition of Germany as a whole in 1989.

The far more pressing problem in 1949 was how the West Germans would govern themselves. The results were immediately reassuring to the West. The West Germans adopted a constitution, the Basic Law, that provided a durable grounding for democratic governance. The voters also gave a slim plurality to Adenauer's Christian Democratic party (CDU), and the newly elected Bundestag chose the seventy-three-year-old Adenauer as the FRG's first chancellor with a majority of one vote. The election of Adenauer, who remained chancellor for the next fourteen years, was crucial. He was a strong defender of market-oriented economic philosophies, which were challenged even within his own party. His sense of national priorities placed alignment with and reassurance of the West ahead of the unification of the German nation. In both these respects Adenauer differed from his political opponents.

Doubtful that it could obtain a unified Germany on terms acceptable both to the West (including the FRG) and to the Soviet Union, the United States strongly supported Adenauer's pro-Western political and economic course. The greatest threat to Adenauer seemed to be the continued yearning for unity shared by many Germans and championed by the Social Democrat (SPD) opposition. The strong West German SPD, led by Kurt Schumacher, called for Germany to remain free of close ties to a capitalist West that wanted to keep Germany down. Schumacher was a courageous opponent of Nazism and communism and a legitimate rival to Adenauer for popular esteem. The SPD urged the Germans to concentrate not on forming ties to the West but on finding common ground with the socialist East.

The West had to work harder to convince the German people that a pro-Western alignment was consistent with the goal of national unity. Thus, when the Soviet Union somewhat cynically called for a withdrawal of occupation forces and immediate unification, John McCloy, the newly appointed U.S. High Commissioner for Germany, asked for permission to counter this propaganda by proposing an offer of free all-German elections to select an assembly that would prepare a new all-German constitution. The East would not be asked to accept West Germany's constitution first. The State Department approved, agreeing that the United States needed to "seize the initiative" from the Soviet Union. McCloy's proposal was launched in February 1950.[29]

McCloy's immediate goal in stressing free German self-determination in this way was to win the propaganda war with the Soviet Union, to give the West a way to play the "national card" in battling for German public approval. But in doing so he set the longer-term orientation for U.S. policy, one that resonated well when the "national question" returned to the agenda in 1989. McCloy described four broad aims: (1) convert West Germany into the positive pole of attraction with respect to German unification; (2) enlist the psychological support of the German people against Soviet objectives; (3) convince them of the advantages of association with the West; and (4) persuade them that integration with the West did not mean they were giving up on their brethren in the Soviet zone.[30]

Adenauer was cautious at first but then publicly welcomed McCloy's initiative in March 1950. The FRG developed procedures for elections to choose a National Assembly that would draft this new constitution for Germany. But the Soviets and their East German clients backtracked immediately, insisting on numerous preconditions before all-German elections could be held.

The Problem of German Security and Western Alignment

The West had succeeded in bolstering Adenauer's pro-Western orientation with the McCloy initiative. The High Commissioner now suggested that it was time to go further and consider the involvement of the FRG in Western security institutions. But in early 1950 there was little serious discussion of allowing Germany to rearm anytime soon. NATO itself was still just a concept in a treaty, not a full-fledged military organization deploying major combat forces. The outbreak of the Korean War changed the situation. The Soviet-sponsored North Korean invasion of South Korea alarmed officials concerned about the security of the new West German state and galvanized plans for some kind of German contribution to Western defense. By the autumn of 1950 the Allies had agreed that West Germany should be rearmed somehow and accepted as a member of NATO. The United States cemented the consensus with its own historic decision to deploy substantial combat forces in Germany to help deter the threat of aggression.

Western plans were modest. The German contribution was envisioned as part of a multinational army in a proposed European Defense Community (EDC). But this was enough to spur Stalin to deploy an important new policy initiative. In the spring of 1952 the Soviet government dispatched a diplomatic note that supported convening a German peace conference, with participation of an all-German government "expressing the will of the German people." Reversing Moscow's prior opposition to German national rearmament, the note promised that a unified Germany could enjoy full democratic rights. But Germany would be required to renounce participation in any military alliance directed against the Soviet Union. In addition, all foreign forces and bases would have to be withdrawn.[31]

None of the Western powers was certain what to make of the Soviet offer, though they thought it was probably intended to derail any German rearmament within the planned EDC. East German communist leaders apparently shared this cynical view of Stalin's move and were not at all worried that unification would threaten their hold on power. Historians today still debate whether Stalin was so concerned about a rearmed Germany that he was genuinely willing to trade unification for neutrality. But at the time, in West Germany, McCloy feared that Stalin's note would appeal "to everybody—the Nazis, the Generals, the Neutralists, the Ruhr Industrialists, the Unificationists, and the do-gooders."[32]

Adenauer, however, was firm. He would not compromise West German integration into Western institutions in order to chase a mirage of unification. The Western reply took the note at face value but focused on the mechanism for the election of a new German government—a UN commission that had been created for just that purpose. The reply also stressed the right of Germany "to enter into associations compatible with the principles and purpose of the U.N." (i.e., membership in the NATO alliance).[33] One West German historian, Rolf Steininger, later condemned Adenauer for sacrificing the East German people on the altar of integration with the West. He warned in 1985 that history might "repeat itself," that a West German government would "one day find itself in a situation similar to that in which Adenauer found himself in 1952." Then "we shall see what decision will be made."[34] Steininger turned out to be right: the West Germans did get another chance to revisit Adenauer's choice.

Western governments were nervous about how to respond to Stalin's gambit. Some Americans wondered if the Germans could be trusted enough to risk the outcome of free elections. Would they choose alignment with the West even over unification? After some debate State Department officials privately agreed that they had to trust the Germans, that "if the Soviet Union is genuinely prepared to permit free elections and the consequent establishment of a unified Germany, we are prepared to let the ultimate all-German government decide whether it wishes to continue its adherence" to the program of integration with the West.[35] But the Soviets never presented the Germans with the stark choice between unity and Western integration. Moscow balked at setting up procedures that might allow genuinely free elections. Rather than hold the elections under UN supervision, the Soviet Union proposed to give the East German regime veto power over any procedures for organizing all-German elections, a plan that Adenauer and the West German government rejected.

In both tone and substance the Soviets' next note degenerated into public posturing. Their answer struck Kennan as "one that had been prepared by hacks supplied only with grudging, cryptic and guarded instructions and told to make [the] best of it."[36] The exchanges finally concluded with an American note in September 1952 wholly devoted to the problem of how to organize fair and free all-German elections. The Soviets did not reply.

Onward with Two German States

From that time forward the West concentrated almost exclusively on building the FRG and integrating it fully into Western political, military, and economic institutions. The West continued to call publicly for all-German elections while in private remaining anxious about what such elections might yield. Yet the new administration in Washington, led by Dwight Eisenhower, clearly placed a good deal of confidence in the West German people and in Adenauer personally. The United States actively encouraged the 1953 upheavals in East Germany, pulling back as the Eisenhower administration realized that these actions, though effective, would make a Soviet retreat from Germany less likely. Eisenhower and his secretary of state, John Foster Dulles, hoped that after Stalin's death the Soviet leaders could be persuaded to let the Germans choose their destiny now that they were being safely integrated into Western Europe.[37]

But the times had changed dramatically, and the Eisenhower proposition was never tested. The death of Stalin brought one last Soviet flirtation with the German question. The loathsome chief of Stalin's secret police, Lavrenti Beria, made a bid to succeed the dictator. He promised to give the USSR more room to maneuver in European politics by offering to reevaluate the future of socialism in East Germany in exchange for a unified and "peaceful" Germany. The meaning of the fleeting proposal was never made clear since Beria lost out on the succession and was put to death by the victors. Beria's stance on Germany became part of the propaganda explanation for his execution. As a result, succeeding generations of Soviet diplomats all knew how Beria had flirted with a radically new position on Germany and then been shot for it.[38]

Although the years after Stalin's death brought a thaw in East-West diplomacy, the German question was now far too complicated for quick resolution.

The EDC was rejected by the French National Assembly, but German rearmament went ahead, now in the form of a national army embedded entirely in NATO and subject to limitations specified in the 1954 treaties that brought the FRG into the alliance. Both the United States and Britain cemented their commitment to keep large combat forces deployed in West Germany.

The heads of government of the Four Powers met at Geneva in July 1955 for the first time since the Potsdam conference ten years earlier. The West's position remained unchanged: reunification should be sought through free all-German elections. With Germany in NATO, Eisenhower's secretary of state, John Foster Dulles, was quite prepared to accept all-German elections, even to the point of thinking right after Geneva that "we might get a unification in the next two years." But the Soviet Union dropped all pretenses of defending German unity and argued that Germany could be unified only after the confrontation between the two alliances had been erased by the creation of an all-European collective security system.[39] In this way the German question became secondary to general issues of European security. There it remained to be resurrected—someday—when the military confrontation in Europe eased.

Serious discussion of unification faded after 1955, and the international community and the Germans began to reconcile themselves to Germany's division. The East-West confrontation had grown into a global thermonuclear standoff on a scale that seemed to eclipse the old disputes about the governance of Germany. The West strengthened NATO and began contemplating further economic integration within Western Europe. The Treaty of Rome, creating the Common Market, eventually known as the European Community, was signed in 1957.

The Soviet Union had moved on to a new strategy toward Eastern Europe and evinced little interest in the German question. Nikita Khrushchev was more concerned about strengthening the socialist world, placing Soviet relations with Eastern Europe on a firm institutional basis, and turning away from Stalin's reliance on brute force and personal diktat. The Soviet Union would not let things get out of hand, as it showed by crushing the East German workers' uprising in 1953 and the Hungarian rebellion in 1956. But Khrushchev believed that Soviet power in Eastern Europe was now stable, and he sought to strengthen his own legitimacy as leader of the "socialist international order" while extending its frontiers beyond the boundaries of Europe. The Soviet Union worked on building institutions parallel to those of the West—the Warsaw Pact, a stronger Council for Mutual Economic Assistance (CMEA)—and strengthening East European armies that at least wore national uniforms, not pale copies of those of the Soviet military as

Stalin had required. A socialist Germany standing in contradistinction to the capitalist one served Khrushchev's interests very well.

Konrad Adenauer had been as anxious as some Western officials about whether the Germans could be trusted to determine their own future. But as the opposition Social Democratic party began reconciling itself to Germany's continued division, Adenauer worried more and more that the hardening East-West conflict would doom unification for good. He feared the West might put aside its commitment to unification in order to ease tensions with the Soviet Union.

Meanwhile, in East Germany, the government of the German Democratic Republic had different worries. Unification was anathema. Instead it sought legitimacy as a separate state, striving for international recognition and clear sovereign control over all of eastern Germany, including Berlin. On those terms the German question would be settled favorably from East Berlin's point of view. Here the Soviet and East German governments found common ground. Four Power control over Berlin was a constant reminder of the occupation and of the fact that the division of Germany remained an open issue. In 1958 the Soviet government triggered the second Berlin crisis by saying, in effect, the German question is settled. Four Power rights are an anachronism. We will give them up and sign a peace treaty with the GDR, turning over to the East Germans this vestigial pocket of the wartime occupation—Berlin. In 1958 the Soviet government formally declared that all Four Power rights, including Allied rights in Berlin, would become "null and void."[40]

The West Germans knew that this was a crucial test of the West's commitment to Berlin and to keeping open the German question. Eisenhower and Dulles took a tough stand: they were clearly ready to risk general war in support of Adenauer and the Western position in Berlin. Yet the West Germans were well aware of the pressures that might seal the partition of their country, and they feared growing diplomatic isolation. Bonn's response was to try to link the defense of Berlin to a continued commitment to Germany's eventual unification. The West did not cave in, though the ensuing crisis lasted for five years, from 1958 through 1962, highlighted by the 1961 construction of the Berlin Wall and culminating at the time of the Cuban missile crisis. The promise to defend West Berlin was kept. But the active linkage between the defense of West Berlin and the commitment to one Germany frayed and unification moved further into the background.

After the Berlin crisis the Kennedy administration, despite the famous speech at the wall in which the president proclaimed that he too was "a Berliner," acknowledged that the question of unification should be removed from the active diplomatic agenda. In November 1961 John F. Kennedy publicly conceded, "Now we recognize that today the Soviet Union does not intend to permit reunification, and that as long as the Soviet Union has that policy, Germany will not be reunified." Nikita Khrushchev triumphantly agreed, noting that he had forced the young American president to "swallow a bitter pill."[41] But the pill was far more distasteful to Adenauer. The old chancellor was angry at the new president who seemed so ready to accept Germany's division. "The Americans are no longer the Americans they were years ago," he told one of his advisers. "They want an understanding, and the only way to get that is at the expense of the Germans." Kennedy, in turn, considered the old man a relic of the Cold War.[42]

Adenauer's successors judged that it was the Germans who must bend. Social Democratic chancellor Willy Brandt liberated himself from the "Grand Coalition" with the Christian Democratic Union (CDU), forming instead a government with the liberal, centrist Free Democrats (FDP). He then embarked on a new policy of Ostpolitik that sought "change through rapprochement," recognizing the postwar status quo and accepting both the existence of two German states and the territorial changes of 1945.[43] Brandt honored the goal of German unity but admitted, "I must confess that I have stopped speaking about reunification." He accepted the original Eastern view that unification should take a back seat to the relaxation of broader East-West tensions. Brandt won East German acceptance for the formula "two states within one German nation," and the two Germanys signed a treaty recognizing each other in December 1972. The FRG also signed treaties with Poland and the Soviet Union, recognizing the existing European borders as "inviolable."[44]

The new treaties were layered on top of the existing West German Basic Law and the still extant Four Power rights and responsibilities dating from World War II. The West German government held to the position that it could not take on obligations on behalf of a unified Germany; that would have to await all-German elections. The United States led the way in "regularizing" the status of Berlin through the Quadripartite Agreement with the Soviet Union. Henry Kissinger had for many years thought the German question secondary to the overall management of the U.S. relationship with the Soviet Union. Thus, for the United States détente and a modus vivendi with the Soviets on Germany went hand in hand.[45]

The ratification of the postwar status quo had long been a Soviet priority, and the overall thrust of Ostpolitik was congenial to those aims. But the East Germans were unhappy, wanting to keep open their claim to all of Berlin. The Soviet Union would hear nothing of it. Moscow was more concerned with American acquiescence in the USSR's equal status as a superpower than with archaic East German claims about the post–World War II order. Moscow thus helped engineer the overthrow of Walter Ulbricht, a staunch opponent of better relations with West Germany, and replaced him with the more pliant Erich Honecker, who echoed the Soviet view that the two German states should just learn to live with each other.

The Quadripartite Agreement (QA) solidified and stabilized the postwar status quo for Berlin. The Western allies agreed that Berlin would not be considered a constituent part of the Federal Republic and would not be governed directly by Bonn. New limits were placed on West German political activities in the city. The parties also agreed that this situation should not be changed unilaterally by any signatory. The Soviets in turn accepted responsibility for guaranteeing Western access to Berlin. Practical measures for ground access and inter-German administrative arrangements were put in place.

Although the QA acknowledged continuing differences in the legal positions of the parties, it served principally to help cement the partition of Germany. The Soviets and East Germans were thus justifiably proud of the regime. And in truth it was a breakthrough for the beleaguered citizens of both East and West Berlin, weary after years of trying to live and work in a divided city. The rules and the certainty they brought helped make daily life easier.

The old battle lines over German unification were revisited during the negotiation of the Helsinki Final Act in 1974–75. The Helsinki negotiations finally gave the Soviet Union the grand European security conference it had sought since 1955. The Soviets wanted a firmer recognition of the postwar status quo and hoped to build up a pan-European collective security regime that might tempt Western countries away from NATO. The Warsaw Pact's founding document had promised that the Eastern military alliance was open to any European state and that the pact would formally go out of existence when an all-European security system made opposing alliances unnecessary.

The Helsinki Final Act repeated the formulation used in the 1970 Soviet–West German treaty, that existing European frontiers were "inviolable." The West German government of Helmut Schmidt, concerned about conservatives at home, bargained hard to keep open a theoretical possibility of unification. The thirty-five participating states agreed that "their frontiers can be changed in accordance with international law, by peaceful means and by agreement." Residual Four Power rights were also protected by the customary provision that "the present Declaration does not affect" the signatories' other "rights and obligations."[46]

Fifteen years later the language of the Helsinki Act would become quite important. The Soviet government had signed a document that theoretically permitted the peaceful unification of Germany, though that seemed an academic point in the world of 1975. In addition, the document respected each state's "right to belong or not to belong to international organizations, to be or not to be a party to bilateral or multilateral treaties including the right to be or not to be a party to treaties of alliance; they also have the right to neutrality."[47] The Helsinki Final Act did nothing, however, to affect the assumptions underpinning Ostpolitik. The act came to stand for acceptance of the postwar borders and the de facto settlement imposed by the victors. The West Germans believed that they had to accept the status quo in order to change it someday. As the years passed, the West German timetable for affecting the biggest change of all—German unity—seemed to be measured on a time scale more familiar to geologists than to politicians.

In the 1970s and 1980s West German conceptions of how unity might actually come to pass involved "normalization" of all relations or else foresaw a "coming together of the European people." The term *unity* itself was freed from its traditional political meaning. As FRG president Richard von Weizsäcker put it in 1985: "The subject of unity confronting us today primarily relates to the whole of Europe. It no longer revolves around national frontiers and territories. It is not a matter of shifting frontiers, but of depriving them of their divisive impact on people."[48]

This notion of unification as a matter of culture and human contacts, not of territory, deserves elaboration. Writing in 1989, Wolfram Hanrieder eloquently summarized the widely shared critique of the old CDU policies of the early 1960s: "By clinging to the territoriality of the German question, Bonn was fundamentally at odds with developments in Europe . . . It was precisely the general acceptance in both parts of Europe of the territorial status quo that was the irreducible precondition for political change."[49]

By the mid-1980s this new wisdom commanded broad bipartisan support in West Germany. When the Christian Democrats regained the chancellorship in 1982, Helmut Kohl felt grudgingly obliged to adopt the legacy of Ostpolitik as his own. This continuity was reinforced as Kohl inherited Helmut Schmidt's foreign minister, Hans-Dietrich Genscher.

The relationship with East Germany evolved, too, as a necessary part of Ostpolitik. The West Germans wanted to persuade the GDR to do good things (treat their citizens better, let them travel). This meant that the East German government needed to be reassured and stabilized. Such an approach was very unlike the American view of the East Germans. Timothy Garton Ash has characterized the competing views this way: "The governing metaphor of [the American policy of] differentiation was that of 'carrots and sticks.' East European rulers were thus considered to be, at heart, donkeys. In the behavioural psychology of the German idea of détente, by contrast, East European rulers would appear to be, at heart, rabbits. The rabbit will freeze if you fix him in your headlights. If you frighten him too much, he may even bite. But speak to him gently, offer him carrots—above all, lots of carrots— and he will relax, loosen his grip."[50]

In truth, neither approach achieved very much inside East Germany. West Germany helped to sustain a communist government that grew more hard- line in the late 1980s even as Soviet policy, at home and abroad, moved toward fundamental reform. West German money helped the East German govern- ment avert economic and political unrest and maintain one of the most centralized and oppressive political systems in the Eastern bloc. West Ger- many's effort to reassure the East Germans produced no noticeable move- ment in the GDR leading toward eventual unity. Instead it tended to reinforce the conventional wisdom that territorial unification was out of the question.[51]

This hard judgment of West East German détente should be tempered, though, by two considerations. First, there were the humanitarian benefits for some East Germans. Second, there was the well-hidden but growing economic dependence of the seemingly robust East German "consumer com- munism" on West German cash, as well as on Soviet commodities provided at subsidized prices. Chapters 3 and 4 will show how Kohl used this economic leverage as a weapon to force revolutionary political and economic change from the unsettled GDR of late 1989.

The West German strategy of reassurance also paid dividends in Bonn's relations with the Soviet Union. Years of West German cooperation clearly softened Soviet attitudes about the FRG and built up a reservoir of trust, at least among some Soviet officials, toward both the Federal Republic and the Germans as a new nation that had genuinely broken with its past. These benefits from the Ostpolitik with Moscow helped slightly more relaxed atti- tudes about Germany to take root when Gorbachev turned close attention to German issues in 1987. But the Soviets, under Gorbachev as under Brezh- nev, continued to regulate tightly the quality of relations between the two German states. The net result was that the prospects for unification became distant, almost unthinkable. "All fruitless discussion about how open the German question is should be ended," Willy Brandt advised his countrymen in 1984. "It doesn't bring us anything."[52]

In 1987, for the first time, the East German head of state was given a red carpet welcome to the Federal Republic. Erich Honecker was wined and dined in Villa Hügel, the ancestral mansion of the Krupp family, and feted in

Munich by the archconservative premier of Bavaria, Franz-Josef Strauss. By 1988 Manfred Rommel, the CDU mayor of Stuttgart, aroused no controversy when he told a journalist that "the idea of reunification is completely hopeless."[53] Helmut Schmidt spoke of unity as a question for the century to come, noting that he had not used the term "reunification" in public life for over thirty years.

Thus, there was a radical new leader of the weakened Soviet state. Europe's ideological division was breaking down, and with it the Cold War. But few could see that the inherently unstable division of Germany was threatened too. East-West rapprochement seemed founded on acceptance of Germany's division. The structural flaws in this foundation had been forgotten or discounted by those busily engaged in building upon it.

Helmut Kohl clearly did not think that he would have to revisit the old issues of Potsdam or dust off the records of the CFM conferences held after World War II. Kohl always stubbornly insisted, privately as well as publicly, that the German question remained open. But when asked in October 1988, after visiting Moscow, whether the new reformist Soviet leader, Mikhail Gorbachev, might someday offer unity to the Germans, Kohl was scornful. "I do not write futuristic novels like [H.G.] Wells," he replied. "What you ask now, that is in the realm of fantasy."

~ 3

The Fall of Ostpolitik and the Berlin Wall

IN THE SPRING OF 1989 there was no reason to believe that German unification was about to make its way back onto the international agenda. There was certainly little evidence to suggest that the Germans themselves wished to pursue the matter. An April 1989 poll showed that nearly half of all West Germans thought that their country should give up the pretense of even *wanting* to unify the two Germanys.[1] The East Germans were not asked.

That summer Hungary, a popular Eastern bloc travel destination, had tempted East Germans with a widely publicized announcement in May that borders to Austria, and thus the West, were now open. The Hungarians had not expected ordinary East Germans to take them up on their invitation. They had opened the borders since almost all Hungarians were now permitted to travel freely to Austria. Miklos Nemeth, the new prime minister, who took office in March 1989, was an admirer of Gorbachev's; he thought the old barbed wire border was a "gruesome anachronism." The Hungarian leaders considered the act a nice symbolic gesture but with little practical effect. The Hungarian and East German authorities, suspecting that some East Germans might misunderstand the gesture, had already agreed that only East Germans with valid GDR exit stamps in their passports would be allowed to cross the "open border." East Germans trying to cross the Hungarian border illegally would continue to be arrested and sent back to the GDR. About forty such cases had been handled the previous year.[2]

What actually began to happen, however, was that East German travelers, principally in Hungary but in other East European countries as well, would attempt to leave and then, rebuffed, would seek refuge in West German embassies. By the end of June a handful of frustrated East German tourists were refusing to leave the West German embassy in Budapest; a few sit-ins also occurred at FRG diplomatic posts in Warsaw, Prague, and East Berlin. As the summer wore on, many of the mostly young people making their way to Hungary were not vacationers trying to break out on impulse but individuals and families who had planned their trip with the intention of crossing to the West. The East German leaders grasped this fact with growing alarm, remembering the terrible days before they had built the Berlin Wall and closed off the border to West Germany. One Politbüro member, Günter Schabowski, later recalled how "this unspeakable and unbearable manifestation of desertion" had created a spontaneous, if usually unspoken, sense of "concern and malaise."[3]

This revelation of hidden discontent among the East German people galvanized the fringe opposition groups to begin organizing in larger numbers. By late summer, as the refugee crisis worsened and the Honecker regime's impotence became more evident, the opposition groups finally began to gain a broader popular following.[4] At the beginning of August the U.S. embassy in East Berlin, led by Ambassador Richard Barkley, alerted Washington that the growing refugee problem had become "a silent crisis" for the GDR. But the embassy found it "hard to conceive" that this silent crisis would produce severe international tensions. Barkley and his staff instead advised that the draining away of valuable East German workers might finally force changes in the aging leadership and open the way to Gorbachev-style domestic reform.[5] In Washington the State Department agreed that no new policies were needed.[6] Dennis Ross, head of the State Department's policy planning staff, urged Secretary of State Baker to initiate a long-range dialogue with the West Germans about change in the GDR. Yet he argued that this should be done "without igniting instability or dangerous talk of reunification."[7]

The East German leaders seemed uninterested in following Gorbachev's example. Instead, East Germany fell back on old complaints that Bonn was responsible for provoking unrest and was trying to deceive the good citizens of the GDR into thinking that capitalist West Germany was the "land of milk and honey."[8] By mid-August the West German mission in East Berlin held more than a hundred asylum seekers and was closed to the public. More than 150 were in the FRG embassy in Budapest by August 11, with hundreds more arriving each week.[9] Erich Honecker and the East German government continued to rail against the FRG while trying all the time—more desperately with each passing day—to persuade their citizens to return home.

The Subversion of Ostpolitik

Although Hungary had opened its border to Austria, it was still required by a 1968 agreement with the GDR to detain East Germans and prevent them from transiting through Hungary to the West. As more and more East Germans went to Hungary to try to escape to the West, some dodged the police and succeeded in making their way across the border to Austria, others showed up at the West German embassy and asked for asylum, and still more were detained by Hungarian authorities. The Hungarians returned hundreds of them to the GDR as required. But the numbers were growing.

The Hungarians were uncertain about how to proceed. Although their agreement with the GDR required them to send the East Germans back home, the West German government had asked the Hungarians to stay their hand. The government in Budapest had another factor to consider, usually overlooked in accounts of the refugee crisis. It was not just East Germans who were trying to cross to Austria. There were also thousands of Romanian refugees attempting to take advantage of the open border they had heard of in order to get to Austria and the West. For different reasons, rooted in historic enmity with the Romanian government in general and its Stalinist dictator, Nicolae Ceaușescu, in particular, the Hungarians had already decided they would not send the Romanians back. How could they return East Germans to East Germany if they would not send Romanians back to Romania? The Hungarians, still under communist rule but in the midst of a transition to democratic government, paused.[10] On August 9 Hungary stopped enforcing the return of GDR citizens. Their border authorities kept turning back thousands of East Germans trying to cross into Austria, but hundreds were slipping through the net each week. News of the Hungarians' leniency encouraged even more East Germans to make the attempt.[11]

The West Germans were not trying to provoke a crisis. Ostpolitik dictated that they should not seek momentary advantage at the expense of lasting good relations between the two Germanys. Even the specific problem of East Germans seeking asylum as a way to get to the West was not a new one for Bonn. The way such problems had been dealt with in the past was that West German officials had persuaded the asylum seekers to go back to the GDR and seek legal permission to emigrate with some guarantee of protection against reprisals. Then Bonn would work behind the scenes to smooth their ultimate departure from the GDR, usually after money changed hands between the two governments. The real solution to the problem, Bonn would argue, was for the GDR to adopt simpler and more predictable travel regulations.[12]

At the beginning of August the West Germans adopted this same line in dealing with the latest surge in asylum requests. The head of Helmut Kohl's Chancellery, Rudolf Seiters, publicly appealed to would-be refugees to stay in the GDR, or at least not try to hide out in various embassies in Eastern Europe. He pointed out that 46,000 GDR citizens had been able to emigrate legally in just the first seven months of 1989. He counseled others who wished to leave to follow the legal channels available in East Germany.[13] On August 18 Kohl told reporters that both he and Honecker wanted to "continue a policy of good sense."[14] Yet the old repertory of Ostpolitik-style measures did not check the East German exodus. Even worse, the scenes of East German families struggling to come West were featured every day in West German newspapers. The government could not by law forcibly repatriate East Germans seeking to live in the FRG.[15]

Gradually throughout August, then, the Kohl government seemed to be changing the objectives governing its approach to East German emigration. The old objectives could be summarized this way:

1. Reassure the East German government of the FRG's good intentions.
2. Encourage legal emigration of East Germans and GDR adoption of more liberal travel policies to ease the pressure.
3. Where obliged to do so, admit East German refugees.

But during August and September Bonn slowly found itself taking steps that seemed to reflect movement toward a different set of policy objectives. These steps were the following:

1. Help East Germans reach the West, even in defiance of East German laws.
2. Press the GDR to solve problem with more far-reaching reform of travel laws, as well as political and economic reforms.
3. Try to avoid publicly embarrassing or provoking the government of the GDR.

Such objectives represented a turning away from the spirit of Ostpolitik. The defenders of Ostpolitik noticed the apparent shift in policy. On August 15 Horst Ehmke, the deputy chairman of the opposition Social Democratic party, attacked the government for having aggravated the crisis by welcoming the refugees. Throughout the summer of 1989 West German intellectuals had actually been vigorously debating whether to renounce finally and formally even the nominal goal of seeking the unification of the two German states. A cover story in *Der Spiegel*, the most widely read news weekly in the country, asked sharply why the government had not closed its embassies to asylum seekers even sooner.[16]

These new objectives were evolving in reaction to events rather than from some deliberate decision to move in a new direction. The West German Foreign Ministry was "absolutely taken by surprise." Kohl's adviser Horst Teltschik recalled later that the West German strategy was not new; as a humanitarian gesture the FRG had been offering financial support to East Berlin if Honecker would clear the way for refugees to leave Hungary. Kohl wrote to Honecker in August assuring him that his only wish was for the East German refugees to find a worthwhile life back in the German Democratic Republic.[17]

It was Hungary that first made a clean break from the policies of the past. A month after the symbolic border opening, the Hungarian government changed. Miklos Nemeth remained prime minister but now shared power with other reformers who were openly dedicated to preparing the way for free multiparty elections. Nemeth believed that Gorbachev had given a green light for such multiparty elections when he had talked at length with the Soviet leader in March.[18]

Budapest had always maintained somewhat chilly relations with the GDR, even during the well-ordered days of Brezhnevism. Now, in the middle of August 1989, the government of Prime Minister Nemeth was polishing its reformist credentials, seeking Western help, and preparing for elections. It felt little obligation to its fraternal comrades in the GDR. Nemeth recalls that at a key meeting with a few ministers in mid-August, he and Foreign Minister Gyula Horn admitted that they would not want to live in the GDR either. But they were not sure what to do. An East German citizen was shot by nervous Hungarian border guards on August 21 as thousands of East Germans were beginning to fill Hungarian detention camps. Nemeth's Hungary did not want to be presented to the world as the guardians of Honecker's borders.[19]

Caught squarely between its communist past and its democratic future, Hungary chose the future. On August 25 Nemeth and Horn opened secret discussions with Kohl and Genscher at Schloss Gymnich in West Germany. Genscher, convalescing from his second heart attack, left his bed to attend the meeting. The Hungarians informed Kohl and Genscher that they would stop returning East Germans to the GDR and would eventually allow them to travel to the West. Although it was reported that the West German leaders promised in return to extend credits of at least DM 500 million to support the Hungarian economy, those present at the meeting heatedly deny this claim.[20]

A week later Horn went to East Berlin and broke the bad news to the GDR's foreign minister, Oskar Fischer. According to Horn, Fischer sputtered, "That is treason! Are you aware that you are leaving the GDR in the lurch and joining the other side! This will have grave consequences for you!" Unmoved, the Hungarians formally annulled their pact with the GDR on September 10 and, yielding before waves of refugees, opened their Austrian border to East Germans. The Hungarian government claimed that interstate treaties could not be allowed to override international commitments to human rights.[21] By the end of September forty thousand more East Germans had fled to the West through Hungary.

Moscow Watches Tensely

The furious East Germans launched a tirade against the Hungarians, but the decision did not have the threatened "grave consequences" for Budapest. If the East Germans expected Moscow's help in pressuring Hungary, they were disappointed. Officials in Moscow were largely silent about the crisis, not reacting to cables from their embassy in East Berlin, and almost giving the appearance of uninterest. But Soviet officials were interested; they were just unsure what to do. The Soviet response to this first crisis besetting the East German government deserves a closer look because it establishes a pattern that persisted well into September, even as the refugee situation began to cause domestic unrest within the GDR. As we have seen, Gorbachev wanted change throughout the socialist world, including the GDR. He said so directly to Honecker when the two men talked privately and at length after his return from his triumphant trip to Bonn. Gorbachev explained frankly to Honecker that the USSR was changing. Not all of the changes were pleasant, either for him or for the GDR, but there was no other way. "This is the destiny of the Soviet Union," he said, "but not only its destiny; it is also our common destiny."[22]

Yet Gorbachev noted that he had privately told Kohl that any change had to respect the historic "realities." Kohl, Gorbachev confided, had asked about Soviet relations with Honecker, and Gorbachev had replied that the USSR was only now taking steps that the GDR had undertaken ten or fifteen years earlier. The USSR was even studying some of the ways the GDR approached problems of social welfare. Gorbachev stressed to Honecker that he had warned the West Germans that the West would be making "a big mistake" if it should try to use the transitions in Poland and Hungary for "a destabilization of the situation." If that happened, he said now, "the entire movement toward a peaceful period [*Friedensperiode*] in East-West relations would be threatened." Gorbachev also told Honecker that Kohl shared this opinion "in principle," that he had drawn a "clear line" for the West Germans, and so they knew that if they "meddled now" in the socialist transition, the situation could "fall back to the worst times of the cold war."[23]

So how did the Soviet government react to East German accusations that West Germany was now "meddling"? The evidence is spotty. In early September Genscher complained to Lawrence Eagleburger that the Soviets were obstructing his efforts to get East Germans returned from Hungary.[24] When the Hungarians were ready to strike a deal with Bonn, they apparently dropped pointed hints to diplomats at the Soviet embassy in Budapest, but Nemeth did not want to force Gorbachev to make a formal decision about Hungary's actions. Instead, the Hungarians found it easier just to equate silence with consent.[25] Sergei Tarasenko, working at Shevardnadze's side, does not remember getting any advance notice of the Hungarian border decision.[26]

The Soviet leadership seems to have preferred to distance itself from the issue, treating it as a matter to be worked out by Hungary, the FRG, and the GDR. Although some newspaper commentaries in August echoed East German denunciations, adding the charge that Bush was provoking unrest by saying that residents of Gorbachev's "common European home" ought to be free to move from room to room,[27] other media presentations were sympathetic to Hungary's hard choices.[28]

Above all, however, the Soviet leaders were distracted by even more pressing problems in August and September 1989. Poland was in the midst of another government crisis, in both the political and the economic spheres. In response to deepening economic woes, the Polish government had tried to cut budgets by slashing food subsidies and state-paid wages. Panic buying set off a spiral of inflation. As prices jumped, strikes followed throughout the country, some of them violent. Poland badly needed a functioning government. But the carefully crafted rules for forming a new government which had been agreed on by the roundtable in April had now been overtaken by events. The June elections had dealt communist candidates a stunning defeat, with few of them receiving the 50 percent of the vote they required to be seated in the legislature. This had led to Solidarity's taking virtual control of both houses of the Sejm, the Polish parliament, an unexpected development. Solidarity and the communists had thought Solidarity would remain an opposition party.

Poland's ruler, General Wojciech Jaruzelski, tried to form a government from within the ranks of the Communist party. He appointed former interior minister Stanislav Kieszcak as prime minister. But the electoral collapse of the communists gave his government little hope of addressing the economic crisis. Having failed to form a government acceptable to the Sejm, Kieszcak resigned on August 19. After several days of intense speculation, Jaruzelski turned to a longtime member of Solidarity, Tadeusz Mazowiecki, to lead a new effort to form a government. The Polish Communist party was clearly worried that it might be left out of the government altogether. For the first time Gorbachev and the Soviet leaders faced the real possibility that a different path to socialism might result in a government that threw out the socialists. Polish Communist party chief Mieczyslaw Rakowski tried obliquely to play the "Soviet card," noting that a grand coalition was needed in order to "dispel fears of allies and partners abroad."[29] On August 21 Rakowski declared that the party had "entered a period of open struggle for power and [was] threatened by a breach of agreements signed at the 'round table.'" He went on: "The situation is dangerous, but this is not the time to give up. The party should not commit suicide." In Moscow *Pravda* echoed Rakowski's warning, calling the situation in Poland "dangerously aggravated."[30]

The Soviet Union had followed the crisis quietly, issuing a Foreign Ministry statement on August 16 that said: "The Soviet Union is vitally interested in what happens in a neighboring friendly country which is a member of the Warsaw Pact . . . but [the Soviet Union] has no intention of interfering."[31] But as the crisis intensified, so did Soviet concern. By this time the press was filled with coverage of the crisis and reminders of the Soviet Union's stake in Poland's future.

Gorbachev himself became involved on August 24. He called Rakowski. Although the press simply reported that Gorbachev had "expressed confidence that the PZPR [Polish United Workers party] would successfully resolve its existing situation in Poland's social and political interests,"[32] it appears that Gorbachev may have pressured the new Polish government to include communists in key posts.[33] Two days later, on August 26, KGB chairman Vladimir Kryuchkov went to Warsaw for consultations with the new prime minister and the communist leadership. Shortly thereafter Mazowiecki announced what the Soviets wanted to hear most: that communists would retain the defense and interior ministry portfolios and Poland would remain in the Warsaw Pact. With these compromises Gorbachev had acceded to a major development: establishment of the first noncommunist government in Eastern Europe.

The entire Soviet Politburo felt obliged to follow the events in Poland closely throughout 1989 and early 1990. Poland's membership in the Warsaw Pact and Soviet concerns about the activities of Solidarity with "independent" organizations in the rest of Eastern Europe, particularly the GDR, dominated the conversations among the leadership. The Politburo met on September 28 to review a lengthy set of recommendations for policy toward Poland, even as the refugee crisis in East Germany was reaching its peak.[34] In addition, the Soviet government was also distracted by the first popular protests in Czechoslovakia, spurred by the anniversary of the 1968 Soviet-led invasion of that country. The Czech leadership cracked down hard against the few hundred demonstrators who took to the streets on the August 21 anniversary, but it was now clear that Czechoslovakia too was being affected by the spreading turmoil in the Eastern bloc.

Major problems were surfacing even within the borders of the Soviet Union. Ethnic Russians staged strikes in Estonia to protest the Estonian government's efforts to redefine Estonian citizenship within the Soviet Union. The Estonians, joined by Latvians and Lithuanians, turned out in staggering numbers to protest Stalin's forcible annexation of their countries in 1940, commemorating the occasion of the fiftieth anniversary of the signing of the infamous Molotov-Ribbentrop pact between Nazi Germany and the Soviet Union, an agreement that had partitioned Poland and allowed the Soviet Union to extinguish the independence of the Baltic republics.

In the southern USSR there were more strikes, this time over the struggle between the Armenian and Azerbaijani republics over control of Nagorno-Karabakh. There was unrest in the Moldavian republic, bordering Romania. And at the end of August a wave of ethnic violence swept over the Abkhaz region of the Georgian republic, provoking a crackdown by security forces there. Nationalist demonstrators demanded independence for Ukraine. The Soviet leadership was preoccupied by nationality issues. In September Gorbachev called a special party plenum (a full meeting of the Central Committee) to deal with this subject. The session, held September 19–20, led to personnel shakeups, including the replacement of the longtime party chief in Ukraine.

Thus, as serious as the GDR's problems were, they were overshadowed for a time by the crises of the moment in Poland and the Soviet Union itself. In late September the Soviet government began paying closer attention to the refugee situation and the stirrings of unrest in the GDR. At that point some in the Soviet Foreign Ministry thought that the refugee crisis might not be all bad, that it might spur Honecker to adopt a reform program. In discussions with the GDR foreign minister, sixty-six-year-old Oskar Fischer, Shevardnadze encouraged more open travel policies and an agreement with

West Germany on orderly population transfer. He thought that by allowing large numbers of refugees to leave, the GDR might actually ease the pressure on its economy. Shevardnadze even told Fischer that the GDR could appoint a commission to overhaul travel policies and use the opportunity to make other reforms as well. This would allow the East Germans to engage opposition forces (such as they were) and strengthen their popularity by proving that the communist government could lead the forces for change.[35] It is hard to imagine Fischer and Honecker as agents of change, but the Soviet Foreign Ministry thought that the refugee crisis might have been just what was needed—frightening enough to get the East Germans' attention but not dangerous enough to cause the government's total collapse.

Shevardnadze was also paying closer attention to West Germany's behavior. He wanted Bonn to do what Ostpolitik required: help stabilize political conditions in the GDR. In New York at the end of September for the UN General Assembly session, Shevardnadze met with Genscher and outlined the same ideas about liberalized travel that he had suggested to Fischer. Genscher, according to Tarasenko, assured Shevardnadze that the FRG would make no effort to undermine the stability of the GDR. But they did not negotiate any detailed ideas about what should be done.[36]

A more conservative member of the Soviet Politburo, Yegor Ligachev, offered stronger support for the GDR. Traveling to East Berlin to discuss agricultural issues (the portfolio to which he had been sidelined in 1988), Ligachev spoke out in support of the USSR's "forty years of indestructible friendship" with East Germany and went on to say that Gorbachev and the USSR condemned the provocative FRG campaign against the GDR. Having invoked Gorbachev's name for this statement, without the general secretary's knowledge or permission, Ligachev went on to announce that Gorbachev would visit East Berlin for the October celebrations commemorating the fortieth anniversary of the GDR's creation as a state.[37] Gorbachev had actually been reluctant to attend the celebration and thus appear to be aligning himself with Honecker. The next day a Soviet Foreign Ministry spokesman cautiously termed the visit "perfectly possible" and said that a delegation "at the highest level" had not been ruled out. The Kremlin was soon obliged to confirm that Gorbachev would indeed attend the festivities in East Berlin.[38]

The Soviet leadership was in a quandary. The GDR had to be supported, but Honecker was perceived as a burden. The FRG had to be warned to show restraint, but without threatening warmer relations with Bonn. It must have galled the Honecker regime, for instance, to see "normal" contacts continuing unabated between all levels of Soviet officials and their FRG counterparts, even as *Pravda* and TASS railed against the subversion of the GDR by the

West. Even military contacts between the FRG and the Soviet Union were unaffected. Looking for signs of support from Moscow, East German officials must have been annoyed to see *Krasnaia zvezda*, the Soviet army newspaper, welcoming the anticipated mid-October visit of the West German warship *Rommel* and celebrating improving FRG-Soviet ties.[39]

At the same time, though, Soviet officials were anxious to head off any West German attempt to take advantage of the unsettled East German situation. The East German government had begun cutting off travel to Hungary, and by mid-September the stream of East Germans seeking to go West had been diverted to Czechoslovakia, with most winding up at the West German embassy in Prague. The embassy had been officially closed for weeks, but the refugees simply climbed over the fences into the embassy grounds.

So, as the refugee crisis put pressure on the GDR, the Soviet Union became increasingly uneasy. When Prime Minister Thatcher stopped in Moscow in September, President Bush had asked her to pass along to Gorbachev his belief that change in Eastern Europe should not be seen as a threat to Soviet security. Thatcher communicated this assurance, but Gorbachev was skeptical. Perhaps with the Polish compromise in mind, Gorbachev warned Thatcher that Soviet security interests included keeping the Warsaw Pact intact.[40]

The mixed, sometimes sympathetic tone of Soviet press commentary on the East German refugee problem in August changed during September as the crisis continued and spread to Czechoslovakia. The Soviet media denounced FRG "propaganda campaigns" against the GDR and warned against talk of upsetting the postwar status quo.[41] Remarkably, the Politburo itself took the time to review and approve this press comment on West German behavior. Moscow was especially angered by the tone of the Christian Democratic Union party conference held in Bremen on September 11. There some delegates had spoken out about the restoration of Germany within its borders of 1937. The Soviet ambassador in Bonn, Yuli Kvitsinsky, cabled back that Kohl had done nothing to suppress such dangerous talk. He had said instead that it was a time to celebrate the "realization of this vision" in which all Germans could enjoy "freedom and unity." Although Kohl was vague on specifics, he invited his audience to observe the beginning of a historic process. Kvitsinsky believed that the Soviet government ought to fire a diplomatic warning shot.[42]

The Soviets confided their concerns about the West Germans' behavior to the Americans. Shevardnadze raised Soviet anxieties when he arrived in the United States to join James Baker for extended talks in the magnificent setting of Jackson Hole, Wyoming. During the flight from Washington to Jackson

Hole, in the midst of a long talk about domestic conditions in the USSR and developments in Eastern Europe, Shevardnadze drew Baker's attention to the CDU party conference, saying that he found Kohl's remarks there "very similar to statements made by German leaders in the 1930s." Baker replied that the United States supported self-determination, not instability. Yet the Americans did want Eastern Europe to be part of a Europe whole and free, its divisions ended in a peaceful fashion. He thought that was also the FRG's view. Shevardnadze acknowledged that his government had supported the concept of a "common European home." Still, it was important to respect existing realities. Rather than respond to this assertion, Secretary Baker turned the discussion to the need for perestroika in the GDR, and the exchange on Germany tailed off in friendly argument about the gravity of the internal crisis facing East Germany.[43]

Five days later, on September 26, Shevardnadze publicized Soviet worries in his speech to the UN General Assembly. Officials in Moscow, including Valentin Falin, drafted new, more pointed language on Germany, which was sent to the Soviet mission in New York for insertion into the speech. Shevardnadze delivered an extended criticism of forms of nationalism "where the national idea is being opposed to the common interest." Although some of this critique could be explained as a defense of Moscow's nationalities policy, Shevardnadze was plainly referring to Germany when he said, "It is to be deplored that fifty years after World War II some politicians have begun to forget its lessons." The Soviet foreign minister then delivered a warning: "Now that the forces of revanchism are again becoming active and are seeking to revise and destroy the postwar realities in Europe, it is our duty to warn those who, willingly or unwillingly, encourage those forces. The revanchist movement is dangerous and hostile to the march of peace to which President Bush referred here yesterday."[44]

The Soviets were trying, belatedly, to define more precise limits to their tolerance. But there was a fundamental contradiction between their "hands-off" policy toward Eastern Europe and the desire to forestall an attack on the postwar order for Germany. As a result, Soviet policy seemed to vacillate between shrill press commentary and efforts to demonstrate that the relationship with the FRG was on an even keel.

After his speech Shevardnadze quietly asked Hungarian foreign minister Horn, "How many citizens of the GDR do you think want to flee to the FRG?" Horn answered that no one could know exactly, perhaps 1 or 2 million. Shevardnadze said that he thought they should just be allowed to go because they could not be stopped by force.[45] The Soviet foreign minister did not seem to see any inconsistency between his resignation to the GDR's circumstances and the warning he had just delivered that "postwar realities" could not be revised.

In Prague thousands of East Germans were scaling the walls into the West German embassy. The East Germans tried the old approach again, promising their people that if they came home, they would be allowed to emigrate legally. This method worked for the first 250, but by late September over five thousand people had crowded into the muddy grounds of the embassy. The FRG now had little choice. It could not force them to go back to the GDR. Promises of legal emigration had failed. Bonn's ambassador in Prague cabled Bonn that a "critical limit" had been reached for providing basic sanitary measures, a matter picked up in both the East German and the Soviet press to embarrass Bonn. Genscher had to persuade the Czech government to let the refugees leave.[46] The Prague government was now alarmed by the sight of so many people trying to run to freedom, fearing the effect the spectacle might have on the reawakening Czech dissident movement.

When foreign ministers gathered in New York for the UN General Assembly meeting, Genscher worked in a frenzy to break the impasse. East German foreign minister Oskar Fischer grudgingly conceded on the night of September 28 that the GDR might let the refugees pass on trains through East German territory to the West. Genscher pressed Fischer to win agreement from East Berlin.

Alarming messages were reaching Genscher from Bonn, warning of the real danger of a catastrophe at the embassy, including a possible fire or structural collapse. Genscher immediately asked for an emergency meeting with Shevardnadze. Lights flashing, a New York City police car rushed him to the Soviet mission, where he urged Shevardnadze to weigh in with the Czechs. Shevardnadze, touched by the plight of the five hundred children encamped at the embassy, promised his support. Genscher then sought out the Czech foreign minister, who claimed that his government had no responsibility for the mess. Meeting with his Western colleagues at a dinner of G-7 ministers, Genscher urged his French counterpart, Roland Dumas, to join him in pressuring the Czechs. Baker came up and asked, "Hans-Dietrich, what can I do for you?" He was asked to use his influence with the Czechs and to keep giving refuge to East Germans in the U.S. embassy in Prague. "They can stay," Baker promptly replied. It was, Genscher recalled, "a memorable moment." The next day the East Germans passed the word that they had agreed to the arrangement worked out between Genscher and Fischer. Genscher flew back to Bonn and then, joined by Chancellery minister Rudolf Seiters, flew on to Prague, where, after speaking to the refugees, the two men dramatically arranged for sealed trains to bring the refugees West.[47]

On October 1 the East German government declared defiantly that those who had fled had "removed themselves from our society" and so "no tears need be shed." On October 2 TASS welcomed the GDR decision to "allow emigration." Falin, in an interview with *Die Welt,* also praised the GDR's decision.[48] But relations between the Honecker government and Bonn would never recover from the refugee episode. The GDR, for its part, was furious that Genscher had "taken personal credit" for the "expulsion twenty-four hours ago of former GDR citizens." East Berlin said that the GDR had made a "humanitarian decision" and accused the FRG of continuing its provocation in hopes that the GDR would crumble.[49] How could this West German behavior be consistent with Ostpolitik?

Kohl Explores New Possibilities

In Bonn, policy-making on the German question was dominated by a small number of key personalities. The list begins with the chancellor, Helmut Kohl. Kohl, fifty-nine years old in 1989, had led the Federal Republic since 1982. He came to political maturity under the shadow of the Rhineland's great states-man Konrad Adenauer. Kohl's family had voted for Adenauer's Catholic Center party, and Adenauer's picture sat prominently on Kohl's desk when Kohl became minister-president of Rhineland-Palatinate.

Kohl had been politically active in the Christian Democratic Union since the age of seventeen, giving campaign speeches as early as 1949, when he was only nineteen. During these formative years, first in CDU youth groups and then in the CDU itself, Kohl undoubtedly internalized and had often de-fended Adenauer's vision for solving the German question by "change through strength." Kohl spent decades defending the public version of this policy, which treated East Germany as a false, illegitimate state, viewed the Americans and the French as Germany's closest friends, and stressed the link between European integration and German reunification.[50] Kohl was the first chancellor of the FRG who had not been of military age or older during the Second World War. He instead represented the first postwar generation, which remembered both the pain of German division and the Berlin airlift as formative experiences. Kohl's wife came from a family of refugees from Germany's lost eastern territory. Kohl's generation, especially in the Rhineland, has been inclined to be strongly pro-American and friendly to-ward France.[51]

Never known as a charismatic speaker or party visionary, never the ideo-logical standard-bearer, Kohl has been underestimated throughout his career.

Two characteristics have consistently brought him political success against the odds. The first is consummate mastery of CDU party politics and shrewd political judgment. Kohl's instincts were almost always for the middle ground on an issue even before others could discern what the middle ground might be. By the time they found it, Kohl would already be standing there. The second characteristic involves Kohl's personal style, which is more distinctive than his ideology. He projects a solid common touch which connects with the beliefs of many ordinary people. Rarely conveying even the veneer of cosmopolitan sophistication, Kohl instead reveals, in private as well as in public, a dedication to traditional family values and a deeply felt but often defensive pride in his German nation. This pride and defensiveness can emerge at the slightest provocation, with Kohl, who had earned a doctorate in history, usually seizing a historical analogy to illustrate his point, a habit that could sometimes give offense (as when, in 1986, he compared Gorbachev's public relations with those of Nazi propaganda minister Josef Goebbels).

Kohl was like Bush in the sense that underlying principles or convictions were more important to him than the particulars of policy disputes. He was entirely comfortable in leading the conservative *Tendenzwende* (an intellectual "change in the trend") during the 1980s at the time of the Euromissile debate, declaring that East and West were not equivalent systems, and firmly aligning himself and West Germany with Western institutions such as NATO. Kohl's children attended colleges in the United States.[52]

Yet in his political career Kohl has often trimmed his principles to suit what seemed to be possible. Having denounced Ostpolitik for years, he accepted its legacy when he became chancellor because he knew that most West Germans associated it with the SPD coalition's superior reputation for managing foreign policy. He also knew that he would be keeping his predecessor's foreign minister, Hans-Dietrich Genscher, since the Free Democratic party (FDP) was now *his* coalition partner.

Kohl's closest aide for foreign policy was Horst Teltschik. The entire Chancellery was headed by Rudolf Seiters. Seiters was a key adviser on the range of domestic and foreign issues related to the German question, but there was no doubt that Teltschik, forty-nine years old in 1989, was Kohl's principal adviser on international affairs. With Genscher and the Foreign Ministry barred from both the "domestic" inter-German unity negotiations with the GDR and some of the key high-level diplomacy, Kohl became the central figure for the FRG. Teltschik was his main diplomatic aide. Interior minister Wolfgang Schäuble handled the negotiations on internal German issues.[53]

Teltschik had suffered personally from Germany's defeat and division, fleeing to Bavaria at the age of six with his family, refugees from Czechoslovakia's Sudetenland. The family had a difficult time building a new life. But Teltschik earned an officer's commission in his Bundeswehr service and then built an academic career as a political scientist. His dissertation, for Richard Löwenthal, was on the interdependence between the GDR and the Soviet Union. He spoke both Russian and English. Teltschik had begun looking for ways to influence policy early in his career and in 1972 began working for a little-known regional politician named Helmut Kohl. He stayed with Kohl through electoral ups and downs until, in 1982, he became the new chancellor's chief foreign and security policy adviser. In the Chancellery Teltschik was generally considered the "ace," with his acute analytical ability and first-class political instincts.[54]

Neither Teltschik's influence nor his brashness won him any friends at the Foreign Ministry, where Genscher had become an institution, and a powerful one. As foreign minister for an unprecedented eighteen years (1974–1992), Genscher was one of the most enduring and popular figures on the West German political scene. He grew to adulthood during the Hitler period and the Second World War. Genscher joined the Hitler Youth in 1937 when he was ten years old and, as a youth of sixteen, served in Luftwaffe auxiliary air defense batteries, then in a military construction unit. He was taken prisoner by American forces as the war ended. After his release Genscher rejoined his mother in their hometown of Halle, which fell within the Soviet zone of occupation.

After the war Genscher returned to his study of the law, but found the prospect of life under communism increasingly unbearable. In 1952, after living for seven years under communist rule, Genscher—still a young man of twenty-five—decided to flee to the West. He settled into FDP politics in Bremen, then Bonn. This liberal party was known for its libertarian ideology and its rejection of communism, socialism (the SPD), and clericalism (the CDU). Witty and shrewd, Genscher entered the Bundestag and rose to become interior minister in 1969, then foreign minister in the 1974 coalition formed by SPD chancellor Helmut Schmidt.

As the SPD turned leftward in the early 1980s, Genscher—firmly pro-Western—helped lead the FDP breakup of the government. Then, as foreign minister under Kohl, he carved out a niche as the centrist spokesman for dialogue and negotiation with the East. But Genscher, whose wife's family had also fled Germany's former eastern territory, shared Kohl's deep convictions about Germany's larger national identity. Still, Genscher positioned himself as a bridge between East and West. This stance was popular as was Genscher's energetic globetrotting style. By 1989 he had come to personify

German foreign policy to an entire generation that could barely remember a time when he did not hold the post.

Genscher relied on two key aides in handling German unification issues. First among them was Frank Elbe, chief of Genscher's private office. In addition to being head of Genscher's personal staff, he was probably closest to being a confidant of the minister. A fluent English-speaker who dealt easily with Americans, Elbe was a younger and more flamboyant diplomat than many of his high-ranking peers in the ministry. The other key adviser to Genscher, representing the institutional advice and abilities of the Foreign Ministry, was Dieter Kastrup, the ministry's political director. Kastrup was a career diplomat responsible for East-West relations and relations between the two Germanys. Though not known as an intellectual, Kastrup was renowned for his cool analytical ability and professionalism. Patient and attentive to nuance, he was a Westphalian who had grown up in Bielefeld, studied at the European Community in Brussels, and joined the diplomatic service in 1965. He spent many years managing the day-to-day requirements of Ostpolitik with both the Soviets and the East Germans. Genscher made Kastrup the key subcabinet negotiator in all the most important talks during 1990. Kastrup was considered steady and reliable, earning the trust of his colleagues for, as one of them put it, "pulling his plow and carving absolutely straight furrows."[55]

At the beginning of October 1989, the predominant West German attitude toward East Germany's refugee crisis was that it was an emotional episode that would force overdue political and economic reforms on the GDR's sick and aging leaders. (Honecker had been hospitalized for a gallbladder condition during much of August and September.) Reform in the GDR was the goal; unification was still a mirage.[56]

But Kohl did not want to do what Ostpolitik required. Now that the GDR was in trouble, his emotions welled up at the sight of thousands of East Germans trying to come West. That was not all. In September 1989 Kohl knew that he had an election coming up the next year, and it was an election many observers expected the CDU to lose. The Christian Democrats were so anxious that Kohl found himself facing significant challenges to his leadership within his own party. At the CDU congress in Bremen in September, 147 out of 738 delegates voted publicly against Kohl's reelection as chairman, his worst tally since he had first been chosen to lead the party in 1973.[57]

Kohl began to test the limits of the possible. On August 22 he announced publicly that the German question was "back on the international agenda." Theo Waigel, head of the more conservative CSU party, based in Bavaria, promised to revive the issue of German unification. Discarding the Ostpolitik compass and distinguishing himself from his political foes, Kohl began to fall back on the vocabulary of another time and another leader. When Kohl told his CDU colleagues in Bremen that the end of communism was coming and declared that the "idea of one Germany" was closer than ever, the Soviet press was not far off the mark in angrily commenting, "According to this concept, the European Community countries must also be harnessed to the old ideas of Adenauer." The commentary specifically attacked Kohl's suggestion that somehow the Kohl-Gorbachev declaration signed in Bonn during June was different from the old path of Ostpolitik laid down in the 1970 Moscow treaty signed by Willy Brandt and Leonid Brezhnev.[58] Gorbachev himself soon castigated the "rewriting of the Bonn document by some parties."[59]

Gaps were opening within Kohl's governing coalition. Unlike Kohl, Genscher wanted to dampen public speculation about reunification. He made no mention of the broader national implications of the refugee issue when he met with U.S. deputy secretary of state Eagleburger in early September and again when he met with Baker on September 26.[60] On September 25 *Der Spiegel* published a lengthy interview with Genscher in which the foreign minister declared that the FRG should stay on course with its traditional intra-German policy and should urge the GDR to reform itself as the Soviet Union was doing. "There is neither a socialist German nation nor a capitalist German nation . . . The word 'reunification' was coined in the period of a Europe of nation states," Genscher said. "I speak of German unity before the United Nations year after year, but embedded in the development of Europe."[61]

But Kohl was hearing more supportive words from the United States. As the refugee crisis heated up, the American news media commented on the possibility of unification, mostly negatively. Bush, of course, had already given a sign of his views in his "Europe whole and free" speech at the end of May. On September 7 Eagleburger told Seiters that "one thing needed to be clear about U.S. policy: although it does not make much sense for the U.S. to talk a lot about the subject of reunification, when President Bush says that he favors reunification, he means it. The U.S. private position on reunification is the same as our public one—we favor it."[62] Bush soon found the opportunity to reiterate this public position.[63]

The United States had played little part in the diplomacy surrounding the refugee crisis in August and September. The White House was preoccupied with political events in Poland and the development of an economic aid package for Poland and Hungary. Baker and his staff were concentrating on the improvement of U.S.-Soviet relations and the Jackson Hole meeting with Shevardnadze. The East German crisis was seen as a challenge to the GDR's communist leadership, not as a threat to the viability of the state itself. The issue of unification was rarely mentioned.[64]

On the morning of September 18 columns appeared in the *Washington Post* and the *Wall Street Journal* discussing German unification. The *Post* piece, by Jim Hoagland, had perceptively called attention to the fact that Ostpolitik was "no longer a credible alternative to reunification for Germans behind the Wall." With the question in the air, a reporter later that day asked Bush, during a presidential stop in Helena, Montana, whether the reunification of Germany would be stabilizing or destabilizing. Bush chose to give a direct answer: "I would think it's a matter for the Germans to decide. But put it this way: if that was worked out between the Germanys, I do not think we should view that as bad for Western interests. I think there has been a dramatic change in post-World War II Germany. And so, I don't fear it . . . There is in some quarters a feeling—well, a reunified Germany would be detrimental to the peace of Europe, of Western Europe, some way; and I don't accept that at all, simply don't."[65]

Bush continued to raise the question of unification. When the president met with CSU chairman Theo Waigel in Washington on September 26, he opened the discussion by asking how Waigel was handling the reunification issue. Waigel thanked Bush for his support. Yet even the conservative Waigel still couched his vision of unification only in the misty future when there would be a general transformation of European politics. The current contest, he thought, would yield "an opportunity to end the division of Germany within the context of a European peace order and self-determination for all people."[66]

The East German Political Crisis Comes Home

When the East German government closed its border with Czechoslovakia and Genscher led the Prague asylum seekers to the West, the refugee crisis seemed to be over; the critical leak appeared to have been plugged. But the refugee crisis had stimulated an outpouring of domestic dissent. The refugee crisis and the reformist movements in the Soviet Union, Poland, and Hungary all encouraged groups of protesters to take to the streets in late September and early October. The travel issue catalyzed the demand for internal reform. According to one historian these demonstrators aimed not "to destroy the GDR but to democratize it. For the democratic revolutionaries the *Ausreisewelle* [mass exodus] merely provided the context in which the regime betrayed its popular legitimacy."[67] The East German regime, headed by a sick and aging leader, could not decide how to meet this first wave of protesters. The regime was restrained in dealing with them between September 25 and October 3.

Once others saw that protesters could demonstrate without severe repercussions, however, a point was quickly reached at which first large numbers of young people, then workers, joined the protests, more and more confident that the regime could not punish all of them. Tougher measures were used against protesters who gathered as the trains carrying refugees from Prague passed through Dresden en route to the FRG. The border with Czechoslovakia was closed on October 3.

The crucial decisions about how to deal with the demonstrators came between October 4 and 9. Episodic police brutality angered demonstrators without deterring them. A massive demonstration in Leipzig on October 9 was a pivotal confrontation. Robert Darnton, a historian living in East Germany at the time, recalled that the immensely powerful East German secret police, the Stasi, were poised eight thousand strong, together with the regular People's Police and a special party militia, the Betriebskampfgruppen, for action against the demonstrators. "Everyone present at that demonstration was convinced that the government had prepared to commit something comparable to China's Tiananmen Square massacre," he wrote. Yet, at the last minute, the troops withdrew. The communist officials in Leipzig had been unable to get any final guidance from their leaders in East Berlin, who were too paralyzed by indecision to order a violent "Chinese solution."[68]

The ruling party's will was undermined by self-doubt and widespread internal frustration with the stagnant leadership headed by Honecker. Most of the party leaders did not see a choice between repression and losing the GDR; the dissidents among them (like the Soviet officials) instead just saw a choice between repression and losing an aging, out-of-touch Erich Honecker. The government certainly had the means to carry out a "Chinese solution." The East German security establishment was well prepared for a violent countrywide suppression of dissent, even to the point of shooting demonstrators and imprisoning thousands. The ancient security minister, Erich Mielke, had given general orders for "offensive measures to thwart and break up conspiratorial assembly." The Stasi had developed extraordinarily elaborate and quite serious plans for such a crackdown and might well have succeeded in crushing dissent.[69] But Honecker apparently balked at the brink of ordering such a violent crackdown, and some of his colleagues appear to have judged at the eleventh hour that the situation might be manageable if only Honecker were replaced.

During this pivotal period in early October the most important outside influence on the East German government was the Soviet Union. Controversy persists about the exact role the Soviets played in Honecker's downfall. Some authors have argued that the USSR actively plotted with East German reformists to unseat Honecker and that the Soviets kept the East German security services from implementing the "Chinese solution." According to these theories, the KGB worked closely with its old comrade Markus Wolf, the brilliant spymaster of East German foreign intelligence from 1958 to 1987, who had positioned himself publicly as a prominent supporter of Gorbachev-style reforms.[70]

There is no doubt that Soviet officials had little regard for Honecker. In the era of perestroika Soviet analysts were not inclined to excuse the "political sterility" of his regime. Many East German officials were undoubtedly aware of this Soviet scorn.[71] Yet Soviet policy throughout October remained essentially passive. Why?

One reason was that Moscow was anxious about the talk of unification coming out of West Germany—and the United States. The Soviet Union felt obliged to shore up the East German state as a shield, albeit a flimsy one, against such speculation. So Gorbachev reluctantly decided to go to East Berlin for the fortieth anniversary celebration. He did decide to scale back the size of his delegation and the scope of his program while in the GDR. Soviet commentators might refer to the need for reform in the GDR, but on balance the Soviets tried to be positive. Their press was filled with odes to East German economic and social development, and Honecker was afforded ample space in *Pravda* to trumpet his country's achievements.[72]

When Gorbachev finally arrived in East Berlin, he participated in a stiffly staged "celebration," complete with a conversation with East German children and a visit to the tomb of the unknown Soviet soldier, "the liberator."[73] Gorbachev was guarded in his public remarks, too, saying that every country had to find its own route to renewal. His speech was sprinkled liberally with references to the importance of the GDR as an ally, to its role in ensuring the peace, and to its important contributions to the development of socialism. Yet Gorbachev did not openly criticize the FRG. Instead he defended the "new thinking" in Europe, saying that this policy had yielded many positive results. Then, in an odd reference, he chose to quote from the Russian poet Fedor Tyutchev, who had commented on Bismarck's nineteenth-century efforts to unify Germany in the forge of war, of "blood and iron," writing:

> The oracle of our times has proclaimed unity,
> Which can be forged only with iron and blood,
> But we try to forge it with love,
> Then we shall see which is more lasting.

Though a nice quotation, it was certainly a strange way for the leader of the Soviet Union to warn the FRG to respect the "postwar realities."[74]

During his trip Gorbachev met with Honecker and the entire East German Politbüro. The East German notes of these meetings make it clear that while Gorbachev's tone was supportive, he offered two clear messages: first, that delay in taking hard decisions would only make them more painful; and second, that the USSR would not interfere in East Germany's domestic policies. The Soviet Union had chosen its path to reform, facing difficult choices along the way; others would have to make their own decisions. Honecker repeatedly criticized Kohl to Gorbachev and attacked the way Kohl was tying West German economic aid to political reform in East Germany. Honecker said that Kohl's position had to be "massively rejected," but Gorbachev made no particular reply. Although Gorbachev is widely believed to have ominously warned the GDR Politbüro that "life punishes those who fall behind," his actual words were not quite so menacing. In fact, as Gorbachev later confided to Egon Krenz, he had actually just been talking of his own experience. Gorbachev did say, in a separate remark, "Our experiences and the experiences of Poland and Hungary have convinced us: if a party does not respond to life, it is condemned." But above all Gorbachev stressed the importance of East Germany to the socialist community.[75]

Soviet policy was to encourage Gorbachev-style reform but not to interfere directly in the GDR's internal decisions. On the eve of the crucial October 9 demonstration in Leipzig, a worried Krenz phoned Soviet ambassador Vyacheslav Kochemasov. According to Kochemasov, Krenz said that Honecker has asked him to fly with leaders of the security ministry and army to Leipzig, take charge, and carry out the "necessary measures." Kochemasov told him: "As I understand it, the most important thing is to avoid bloodshed. Therefore my categorical advice is: In no case use repressive measures, certainly not the army." Krenz agreed that this would be unthinkable. Kochemasov thought that Krenz had already made up his mind but wanted to be sure that the Soviet embassy would back him if he refused to carry out Honecker's orders. Kochemasov, acting on his own authority, also told the Soviet military commander in East Germany to keep his forces clear of the unrest in Leipzig, instructions that were confirmed the next day by Moscow.[76]

Honecker had visibly lost Soviet protection. Noninterference itself was a notable change from the way Moscow usually did business in East Berlin. But the Soviets did not actively work to overthrow Honecker. They would have been happy to cooperate with any GDR leader who could take the necessary steps to regain control of the situation. Krenz, who succeeded Honecker, did not believe that Gorbachev's visit to East Berlin had much effect on the plans to topple the old party chairman. But just before Honecker's removal, Krenz did send a top party official to Moscow to inform the Soviets what was about to happen. According to Krenz, Gorbachev told the emissary that he wished the plotters great success. Chernyayev remembers that Gorbachev simply decided not to get involved.[77]

Igor Maximychev, Kochemasov's deputy at the Soviet embassy in East Berlin, was a perceptive observer of these events. For him a central question is why the Soviet Union, "whose influence in the GDR was decisive, did nothing (except for fruitless attempts by Gorbachev to 'sell' the advantages of perestroika to Honecker) to lift, at least a little, the lid of a cauldron in which pressure was close to the critical mark." Maximychev offers two answers: first, that Soviet officials were so accustomed to equating the "will of the party" with the "will of the people" that they could not adequately grasp the potential for popular overthrow of a socialist government. Second, he points out that the Soviet government was itself unable to resolve the dilemmas about how to deal with the East German crisis. His explanation is worth quoting at length:

> All suggestions about giving expression to our disapproval of the suicidal line of the East German leadership were rejected on the logical ground that the situation in the republic was entirely the responsibility of its German leaders and that to impose anything upon them would mean taking over that responsibility with all that this implied. In less official terms, the refusal to influence Honecker was explained by claiming that to ensure the success of perestroika, we needed stability in the "socialist community" and one of its key pillars, the GDR. And unofficially it was said that Honecker knew the situation in the GDR better than anybody else and would do his best to prevent an explosion on which his own destiny hinged.[78]

Chernyayev later wrote that Gorbachev preferred just to discuss his own experiences with perestroika and leave other socialist leaders to deduce what was relevant to them from the analogy.[79]

In the last week before Honecker's overthrow, East German Politbüro members Egon Krenz and Günter Schabowski first drafted an "appeal to the people" promising reform. On October 10 and 11 the Politbüro debated the domestic situation at length. Honecker thought that radical change carried with it greater risks than attempts to defend the status quo. The proposal for the "appeal" was adopted, but its elements were buried under a "thick layer of the usual verbiage."[80]

Once the ruling Socialist Unity party turned away from the "Chinese solution," Honecker's position predictably became untenable. He was replaced on October 17 by a faction within the East German Politbüro, headed by Krenz. The new leaders intended to follow what they thought was Gorbachev's model for accommodating the demands of the people to sustain socialist rule.[81]

Krenz and Gorbachev Devise a Plan

By October 18 Egon Krenz was hoping to become East Germany's Gorbachev. Those East Germans who had fled to the West were welcomed back and promised there would be no reprisals. Krenz and his Politbüro colleague Günter Schabowski wanted to display "an SED with a human face," but they did not know how. Instead, Krenz would read long, turgid Central Committee speeches on television. They found it difficult to stay ahead of escalating mass public protest demands.

The opposition was calling for a full-fledged political and economic reform program, including a far broader housecleaning of the "old guard" in the Politbüro, free elections with no guarantee of communist monopoly on power, and a reconsideration of restrictions on travel to the West (including the matter of the Berlin Wall).[82] Still, Helmut Kohl courteously telephoned Krenz, wished him success, and promised him—sincerely or not—that he, Kohl, was interested in seeing "calm, sensible" developments.[83]

Opinions in the West differed about whether Krenz could take charge and restore the stability and credibility of the government. Estimates reaching Washington in late October and early November varied on whether he could even manage his internal crisis. Ambassador Barkley and his staff thought Krenz might well succeed.[84] The Soviet government, for its part, threw its full weight behind Krenz as the man to restore stability to the GDR. The Soviet press was filled with stories about Krenz's reform activities—meetings with workers, protesters, church leaders, and the like. Krenz soon made the requisite trip to Moscow for consultations, arriving on October 31, and met with Gorbachev the next day.

This was an absolutely crucial meeting for Krenz and for the GDR. Gorbachev now gave his full attention to German issues. He finally had an East German leader he could talk with openly, and he prepared intensively for lengthy, detailed talks, and with specific recommendations in mind. Gorbachev and Krenz met, speaking in Russian without interpreters present and with only two other people in the room, the note takers for either side. What ensued was an extraordinarily candid and revealing discussion, documented by the practically verbatim East German notes.[85]

Gorbachev remarked that all the world could see how quickly Krenz's SED was making changes, which was just what was needed to stay ahead of events.

He urged Krenz not to be frightened by the complicated problems he faced. Perestroika, he said, was not yet finished, even in the Soviet Union: "The horse is saddled, but the ride's not yet perfect." Krenz and Gorbachev talked about how much they had liked Honecker, but then commented at length on his mistakes. "Comrade Honecker," Gorbachev remarked, "obviously maintained he was number one in socialism, if not in the world. He couldn't see any more what was really happening."

Krenz was deferential. One of the worst problems, he said, was that people could no longer see the GDR and the Soviet Union standing shoulder to shoulder as in the old days. After more discussion of personalities (Krenz recounted that Honecker once told him to fire reform communist leader Hans Modrow, but Krenz had managed to let him off with only a reprimand), they turned to business. Gorbachev said that he was aware of the true economic condition of the GDR. Although East Germany had many advantages over the USSR, he knew that production figures had long been exaggerated. Krenz heard Gorbachev out and then gave him a shock. He declared that the stability of the country was threatened by its lack of foreign exchange. The GDR owed the West $26.5 billion as of the end of 1989 and had a current account deficit for 1989 of $12.1 billion. The note taker recorded: "Astonished, Comrade Gorbachev asked whether these numbers are exact. He had not imagined the situation was so precarious."

There was no mistake. In fact, Krenz explained that just to pay the interest on the GDR's foreign debts would require $4.5 billion, or about 62 percent of all the foreign currency earned by the country's exports. East Germany had been living well beyond its means, starting in the early 1970s. If the GDR based its standard of living only on its own output, then the living standard would immediately drop by 30 percent. Krenz needed to get financial credits. He had considered going to the International Monetary Fund, but thought that giving the Western-dominated IMF an influence over the economy would create an extremely difficult political situation.

Gorbachev advised Krenz to tell the East German people the truth, that they had been living beyond their means. The Soviet Union would supply vital raw materials. The GDR would also have to continue a "principled and flexible" policy toward West Germany. "Naturally," Gorbachev remarked, "one must handle things so that decisions will be made in Berlin and not in Bonn." Krenz understood. For him the first priority in helping his country's economy was to achieve closer economic cooperation with the USSR, which meant a more carefully coordinated division of economic tasks in the combined central planning of the two governments so that his economy would be assigned a greater role within the socialist bloc. After all, Krenz said, "the

GDR is in a certain sense the child of the Soviet Union, and one must acknowledge paternity for his children." Gorbachev agreed.

Obviously the danger was that the West might exploit the East German economic weakness to push for German unification. But Gorbachev felt confident that other leaders would oppose such a move. He recounted a conversation between Alexander Yakovlev and Zbigniew Brzezinski, national security adviser under President Carter. They had discussed whether they could imagine the reunification of Germany becoming a reality. According to Gorbachev, Brzezinski had stressed that unification could make "everything" break down.

Gorbachev said he was glad that Krenz had raised the issue of unification. Up until this point the USSR and the other socialist countries had followed the right course, he said, in recognizing the existence of two German states. Western leaders agreed, too. In recent conversations with Margaret Thatcher, François Mitterrand, Jaruzelski, and Italian prime minister Giulio Andreotti, "it was made clear," Gorbachev noted, "that all these politicians started from the preservation of the realities of the postwar period, including the existence of two German states. All of them will consider raising the question of the unity of Germany as extremely explosive. They also did not want to disrupt NATO and the Warsaw Pact and wanted Poland and Hungary to stay in the Warsaw Pact."

The Americans were more troubling. They used to have a position like that of the Europeans. But "currently there is a good deal of discussion in their alliance with the FRG," said Gorbachev. "One sympathizes in words with FRG concerns about the divided Germany. In the USA there had recently been some nuances that needed to be investigated further." Gorbachev's aide at the meeting, Georgi Shakhnazarov, interjected that the Americans' remarks were probably just for their own public. Gorbachev agreed with this. In practice, he said reassuringly, the Americans were sticking by their "old line."

Gorbachev then added another argument against unification. Willy Brandt had declared, he said, that the disappearance of the GDR would be a shocking defeat for social democracy, if one considers the GDR an enormous achievement of socialism. "If he [Brandt] puts aside communism, then he considers social democracy as a branch of the workers' movement and holds on to the socialist ideal," Gorbachev said. Egon Bahr of the Social Democrats had often made the same point. The bottom line, Gorbachev concluded, was that for the socialist countries it was best to emphasize that the current situation was the result of history. No one would try to block human contacts between the German states, if such contacts were appropriately regulated. But Gorbachev wanted to be sure that relations between the FRG and the GDR were managed according to three principles.

First, since relations between the GDR, the FRG, and the Soviet Union were a triangle, management of their relations had to be better coordinated. There should be no secrets between Berlin and Moscow. And it would be useless for East Germany to try to keep any of its relations with West Germany secret from Moscow, for the Soviet Union, Gorbachev said, knew from "other sources" how relations were developing between the GDR and the FRG. Indeed, he added in an aside, the USSR "similarly knew after three days what was being considered in the National Security Council of the USA." The United States also had good information about developments in the Soviet Union, or once did. In any case, Gorbachev suggested that there should be a common office to coordinate GDR and Soviet relations with the FRG. There used to be an office, staffed jointly by Soviet and East German officials, that managed relations with West Germany. This office should be revived. Krenz agreed. Gorbachev then suggested that Krenz get the approval of his Politbüro or a "smaller circle."

Second, Moscow would tighten its relations with Bonn. Since Moscow and East Berlin would be managing their relations with West Germany together, the GDR would benefit by being closely tied to Moscow. Gorbachev then explained how Moscow could manipulate the West Germans. Bonn believed that the Soviets would help with reunification. The West Germans always said that the key to that process was in Moscow. The Americans said so too, though for them this was a very comforting evasion: the Americans told the West Germans how much they supported reunification but then said the key was in Moscow. This left Moscow playing the bad guy, "Black Peter." The Americans were not happy to see Bonn and Moscow move closer together in politics and economics, Gorbachev said, but in practical terms not much of this progress had happened yet. There was no use in rushing the FRG, because its representatives took their time. But, Gorbachev warned, as the GDR improved its relations with the FRG as part of the FRG-GDR-USSR triangle, the East Germans would have to be careful not to give their ideological enemies any positions that they could use to seize the advantage. Here he implicitly revealed how Moscow might both support and regulate the relations between the two Germanys. He linked the Soviets' supplying the GDR with vital raw materials to careful regulation of East Germany's relations with the FRG so that the East Germans would not fall into the "embrace" of the West Germans.

Third, the GDR would have to develop good relations with other countries in addition to the FRG. In other words, the GDR should try to get economic aid from other countries—not just from the Soviet Union. The USSR could do little to help, but it could assist the GDR in getting aid from the West. Gorbachev noted that Hungary and Poland were already very actively engaged in this area.

Gorbachev believed that these measures would work. There was no reason, he said, to go along presuming that the East's position on the German question would be relaxed. Current realities had to be taken into account. "That is the most important thing," he said. If rapprochement in Europe went on for "several decades," with an integration process unimpeded by differences in social systems, with new cultural developments and exchanges of all kinds of goods, then possibly someday the question of unification might come up. But, he added, "today this is no problem of actual policy. In actual policy the current line had to be continued." Krenz concurred, but noted the disturbing trend toward "de-ideologizing" the relations between the two German states. In what appears to have been a careful indirect jab at Gorbachev, Krenz reminded the Soviet leader that "de-ideologizing state relations would in this case mean a renunciation of the defense of socialism."

Gorbachev then changed the subject to the issue of travel. The time was ripe to find some formula for dealing with the refugee issue. The national question was becoming dominant in West German politics. There were people in the government parties, Gorbachev said, who wanted to get rid of Kohl, so Kohl had climbed on the nationalist horse. There was wild speculation about the issue of reunification.

Krenz explained that he had already worked out a program for handling refugees. First, the GDR would stop shooting people attempting to cross at the border. Second, the draft of a new travel law, which was being considered and might be ready for parliamentary approval before Christmas, would make almost all East Germans eligible for a passport and exit visas valid for all countries. Third, the unfortunate necessity was that people would be allowed to travel but not to take money with them; the foreign exchange problem made it impossible to supply travelers with sufficient currency.

Gorbachev was pleased with these proposals. He promised to inform all statesmen that the GDR was making necessary changes, and that Soviet ambassadors would support the East German efforts. Krenz then commented that he had spoken on the phone with Kohl and that they had had a cordial discussion. Gorbachev offered a bit of advice about Kohl. Helmut Kohl, he said, was no intellectual light but a petty bourgeois ("Kleinbürger"). This description was the best way to understand him. Yet Kohl was a shrewd, hard-nosed politician. Gorbachev thought that this same combination of qualities explained how Ronald Reagan had stayed popular for so long.

Krenz then turned to his domestic plans. He warned that he would be pushed by some in his country to adopt free market reforms. But the answers to the GDR's economic problems had to be found in socialism, not in the free market. There would also be pressure for democracy. Krenz was willing to work on a new election law and allow expanded press freedoms. But the question of the Communist party's dominance, "the leading role of the party under new conditions," would have to be discussed. His approach would be to encourage greater self-criticism within the party to avoid "subjectivism." He would also consider term limits on party leaders. That was all. Krenz and Gorbachev then reviewed "cadre questions" such as who should stay in high office when the party convened for its plenum in the coming week. Krenz presented his choices for Gorbachev's consideration, and Gorbachev indicated a couple of his preferences.

Finally the two men turned to the issue of public demonstrations. Krenz promised that these would be handled peacefully, though he did make the point, interesting in light of what was to occur a week later, that his government was adopting security measures to ensure that demonstrations in Berlin did not turn into a mass rush of the wall. That would be a bad thing, and the police, as well as "certain elements," would be prepared to stop it. Such a development, he thought, was quite improbable. Still, one had to be prepared.

In all, Krenz and Gorbachev had agreed on a detailed plan of action. Gorbachev had taken an active hand in suggesting how the East Germans should manage their affairs and had shown a calculating, disciplined side of his public personality that Westerners almost never saw. The refugee crisis was closed. There was a common understanding that travel laws would be revised to let East Germans travel (without money) to the West; after all, East Germany had survived a more open border in the 1950s. Yet the Soviets could not overcome a sense of unease. Chernyayev remembers that as the plane carrying Krenz and his entourage took off from Moscow, several Soviet officials joked darkly, "There goes the committee for the dissolution of the GDR."[86]

Kohl's behavior was obviously a crucial variable in determining the success of the Krenz-Gorbachev plan. The two socialist leaders were plainly counting on Kohl to pursue an Ostpolitik-style policy. This would mean that West Germany could be expected to allay East German fears about West German intentions; work to improve conditions for East German citizens—especially with regard to travel—so that there would be no further exodus; reassure the Soviets; grant economic assistance in order to stabilize the GDR; and press for measured reform. The West Germans would probably think that there was a very good chance that, with a little financial encouragement, Krenz would follow the Polish or Hungarian road. Socialism might survive, but reform would be under way in a more orderly fashion. That was the policy Gorbachev and Krenz were counting on the FRG to adopt. But at this critical juncture Kohl changed the course of German politics. We have already seen that in August and September Kohl could not resist the urge to attack the old verities of Ostpolitik—stimulating popular unrest in the GDR and making his own none too subtle references to the possibility of unification. Now, even as Krenz and Gorbachev had arrived at a plan that hinged on their relations with the FRG, Kohl was preparing to move even more decisively to abandon the last remnants of Ostpolitik.

The Rhetoric Escalates in Bonn and Washington

The West Germans faced a difficult problem. They had operational choices to make in deciding whether to help the Krenz government stabilize conditions in the GDR. Under Ostpolitik the assumption had been that fostering such stability and reassurance of East German leaders was the only feasible path to incremental change. But events in August and September had forced some West Germans to reevaluate this assumption. The differing West German reactions to this challenge became clearer in September and October. Although Baker, in a note to Bush calling attention to the unrest in East Germany, said that West German leaders were uniting to encourage stability and reform within East Germany,[87] it soon became obvious that Kohl was stepping outside the old Ostpolitik consensus.

West German officials were worried about the difficulty of absorbing so many arriving East Germans. Kohl, however, had led his coalition to a firm position welcoming the immigrants and denying economic aid to the East German regime until it adopted fundamental political reforms. Just when Krenz desperately needed help in order to stabilize his country, Kohl was prepared to deny this help unless Krenz overturned the existing system.

Kohl cared deeply about foreign reactions to his conduct. American diplomats in Bonn reminded Washington that other countries' attitudes on the issue of German unity were the critical determinant of West German policy: "West Germans know in their heart of hearts that reunification can only come about when the FRG's European allies and the Soviet Union not only go along with the process of reunification, but also actively support it. West German leaders do not believe that is yet the case."[88] Kohl was attentive to foreign reaction not just because of diplomatic calculations but also because foreign reactions reverberated in West German domestic politics. Consciousness of West Germany's special historical responsibility had conditioned the West German public to be extraordinarily sensitive to perceptions of world opinion. International disapproval could be a big vote-getter for Kohl's political opponents. So while keeping a weather eye on foreign reaction, especially in Washington and Paris, Kohl was moving.

The overthrow of Ostpolitik would not begin with a push for unification. First, the GDR would be pressured to abandon socialism and accept real democracy. Naturally, if East Germany lost socialism, it would lose the main principled justification for its existence as a separate state. So as communism came under attack, West Germans—like so many others in the West—naturally speculated about the possibility of German reunification. Still, as the American embassy in Bonn advised Washington in late October, although the idea was on everyone's mind, "virtually no one believes reunification is the first order of business on the German-German agenda."[89] The West German Social Democratic party emphasized the need for internal reform of the GDR and therefore attacked any hints from the Christian Democrats about reunification. Some factions of the SPD went further and denounced even the desire to unify the two German states in the first place.[90]

Kohl's foreign policy adviser Horst Teltschik recalled later that government policy at the time leaned not toward "a goal of territorial unification" but toward the "struggle for political changes in the GDR—economic reforms and movement toward democracy."[91] It is possible, however, that Teltschik, a young political scientist and Soviet expert, did not realize that Kohl's latent convictions were slowly but steadily coming to the surface. President Bush's September 18 comments at his Montana news conference in support of reunification had received wide press coverage in the FRG and could only have reinforced Kohl's instincts. Even Gorbachev had begun to worry about the "nuances" coming from President Bush. There were more to come.

Brent Scowcroft was concerned that Bush's pronouncements about unification seemed to be getting ahead of what the Germans themselves were prepared to say. Baker was also explicitly endorsing the possibility of German unification in his public statements.[92] Scheduled to deliver a major speech on U.S.-Soviet relations, Scowcroft asked Baker to use the word "reconciliation" instead of "reunification." Baker agreed. The press, to his chagrin, then seized on the new wording as evidence of American retreat.[93]

Kohl, needing more international support, called Bush on October 23 to ask for help. The chancellor was annoyed by media opinion, which he believed had portrayed the Germans as more concerned about maintaining good ties with the East than with the West because they saw the Soviets as the key to unification. Calling this nonsense, Kohl said he would tell everyone that the changes in Europe stemmed from Western strength, both a strong NATO and a strong EC. Then Kohl made his pitch: Could Bush publicly stress Western solidarity as the key to continued change in the East? (This was, of course, Adenauer's classic argument in defense of his policy of integrating the FRG into Western institutions.) Bush, noting the spate of stories predicting that German reunification would result in a neutralist Germany and a threat to Western security, promised, "We do not believe that." Of course, Bush added, the United States was trying to react carefully to change in the GDR. But he thought that Kohl was doing a fine job, and he, Bush, would find a way to signal how important U.S. relations with West Germany were, "especially when we see some of these mischievous stories around."[94]

Bush did not wait long to keep his promise. The next day he gave an interview to *New York Times* reporter R. W. Apple. Referring to Chancellor Kohl's phone call, the president told Apple that he expected major changes in Germany's status. Then he said, "I don't share the concern that some European countries have about a reunified Germany." He believed that "Germany's commitment to and recognition of the Alliance is unshakable," and stressed that "there's a lot written on the fear of reunification that I personally don't share." Bush would not tell the Germans what they should do: "I don't think we ought to be out pushing the concept of reunification, or setting timetables, or coming from across the Atlantic over here making a lot of pronouncements on this subject. It takes time. It takes a prudent evolution. It takes work between [the East and West Germans]. And understanding between the French and the Germans, and the Brits and the Germans on all this. But the subject is so much more front and center because of the rapid changes that are taking place in East Germany."[95] With this interview Bush showed sympathy for European concerns. But by taking the high road and reiterating support for German aspirations, he made it very difficult politically for any Western European leaders to give public voice to their private doubts and fears.

News of the interview, carried on the front page of the *New York Times*, soon reverberated across the Atlantic. The day it was published undersecretary of state Robert Kimmitt was hosting a lunch for key political directors from states of the European Community. France's political director, Bertrand Dufourcq, asked Kimmitt about America's position on developments in

Germany. "That is easy to answer," Kimmitt replied, directing him to the front-page interview.[96]

West German officials welcomed Bush's position. Other Europeans reacted anxiously. Conor Cruise O'Brien spoke for many in Western Europe when he wrote in the *Times* of London that Bush's remarks were "more like a declaration than a reaffirmation. Until recently, U.S. support for reunification has been vague and theoretical." Now Bush had given "a warning to Britain and France that the U.S. would oppose efforts on their part to put obstacles in the way of reunification," and "its significance should not be under-estimated."[97]

Scowcroft had been trying to restrain American commentary on unification to keep Bush from getting ahead of German opinion. Now he gave up. Bush had settled the issue once and for all.[98] Despite the generally negative tone of American editorial commentary about the prospect of German unification,[99] Baker too discarded the theme of reconciliation and moved back to straightforward acceptance of Germany's possible unification.[100]

With the United States behind him, Kohl soon tested the political waters again to see what was possible. On November 8, speaking to the Bundestag, he stressed two key points. First, he promised West German financial aid for the GDR only if it undertook "thoroughgoing" *political*, not just economic, reform, which would entail the Communist party's giving up its "power monopoly," allowing the formation of independent political parties, and ensuring "binding free elections." This was the political condition Krenz had privately told Gorbachev he could not accept.

Second, Kohl referred more openly to the possibility of German unification. He noted President Bush's October 24 statement with appreciation (as well as Mitterrand's more cautious November 3 endorsement, described in more detail in the next section). The key, Kohl said, was "free self-determination." He went on: "Our fellow Germans do not need lectures—from anybody. They themselves know best what they want. And I am sure: if they get an opportunity, they will decide in favor of unity." After quoting, significantly, Konrad Adenauer ("We strive for both—for a free and united Germany in a free and united Europe"), Kohl concluded: "We have less reason than ever to be resigned to the long-term division of Germany into two states."[101]

With these words Kohl applied maximum pressure on the GDR, making it clear that Bonn—not Berlin and not Moscow—would decide when political reform in the East was sufficient to warrant the FRG's largesse. It was a fair guess that the East German leadership in its weakened state could not withstand the turmoil and might give way to democratic forces and free elections. If this was not Adenauer's policy of "change through strength," it was a very close approximation.

Unease in London and Paris

As Western governments reflected on whether the unification of Germany truly was in their national interest, one such government was already forming a view sharply at odds with that of the United States. It was the government of America's closest ally in the world, Great Britain. Even during the early postwar years the British had never felt strongly committed to the goal of unification. In 1946 and 1947, as we have seen, London had supplied both ideas and energy to plans for the separate development of a western German entity. The British were not eager to see any new concentration of power on the European continent, whether from the Soviet Union or from Germany. In 1989 former prime minister Edward Heath spoke for many in his reported comment that "naturally we expressed our support of German reunification, because we knew it would never happen."[102]

One person who shared Heath's views, though she agreed with him on little else, was Britain's current prime minister, Margaret Thatcher. She began expressing her anxieties to foreign leaders in September 1989, though she did not confide her fears to President Bush, whose pro-German stance was already becoming all too clear. Instead she discussed her worries with a statesman she thought would be more sympathetic: Mikhail Gorbachev.

Stopping in Moscow on the way back from a visit to Japan, Thatcher raised the subject of Germany with the Soviet leader. She later recalled: "I explained to him that although NATO had traditionally made statements supporting Germany's aspiration to be reunited, in practice we were rather apprehensive." Another Western leader agreed with her, she said. (Here she was referring, though she did not tell Gorbachev, to a meeting of the minds she thought she had reached on this matter with President Mitterrand of France.) Thatcher was reassured by what she heard from Gorbachev. He did not want German reunification either. This, she has written, "reinforced me in my resolve to slow up the already heady pace of developments." Like Gorbachev, she supported democratic reform in East Germany, of course; but to her unification was a separate question, one "on which the wishes and interests of Germany's neighbours and other powers must be fully taken into account." At that time she thought the West Germans accepted this reality.[103]

Britain's Foreign Office was also thinking about Germany, but was far more circumspect in its views. The office was itself going through some turmoil as John Major's brief and ill-starred stint as foreign secretary was about to give way to the long tenure of his successor, Douglas Hurd. Yet its staff prepared an extensive analysis of the German question in late October. This Foreign Office paper noted that previous British governments had tended to refer to the goal of self-determination rather than to reunification, implying that the German nation might recover its unity by something other than full re-unification of a German state (a position analogous to the one being recommended by the Department of State's policy planning staff in Washington). The British had therefore instantly noted Secretary Baker's careful (though short-lived) use of the term "reconciliation" rather than "reunification" in his October 16 speech. On the substantive question of reunification, the Foreign Office was doubtful that all the obstacles to such a development could be overcome. The paper maintained that the GDR could well go on as a separate state even if its communist rationale were overthrown. Yet the Foreign Office advised that it was best not to risk alienating the Germans by openly dis-couraging reunification. Better stick to the careful phrasings of the past, the paper suggested.[104]

Although Thatcher was correct in believing that France shared her worries about the possibility of German unification, she was mistaken if she thought she could rely on Mitterrand as a diplomatic ally. To be sure, a powerful united German state evoked obvious historical anxieties for a country that had been invaded three times by such a state in little over a hundred years. The possibility of German unification would also call into question France's relative stature within European politics and the European Community. These French concerns were muted, however, by President Mitterrand's per-sonal conviction that Franco-German cooperation should continue to be at the center of French policy in Europe. Stanley Hoffmann has commented perceptively that Mitterrand was "better at driving on old tracks, or at moving them just a shade, than at setting new ones in new directions." His style was to proceed "by small touches, oblique statements, contradictory advances and retreats." The "earthquake of 1989–90 upset his expectations and calculations; he had to improvise, and it showed." So Mitterrand's position was anything but clear. Yet, just by not taking a clear stand *against* what Kohl was saying, Mitterrand found himself showing more tolerance for German aspirations to unity than was evident anywhere else in the top echelons of France's ruling Socialist party.[105]

After meeting with Chancellor Kohl at the beginning of November, Mit-terrand went public with a lengthy prepared statement on the possibility of German reunification in a November 3 joint press conference. The remarks are typical of Mitterrand. He noted the importance of peaceful change and the need to deal with the legal issues involved. But, he said, "what counts is what the Germans want to do . . . And where does the German Democratic Republic stand in all this? . . . Is there even a question of reunification in those circles? I shall wait for the facts before completing a report."

Still, Mitterrand professed that he was "not alarmed" by the idea of re-unification. "History is there," he said. "I take it as it is. I do think concern over reunification is justified for Germans. If this is what they want and they can bring it off, France will adjust its policy so as to be able to act for the best in Europe's interest and in its own interest . . . The answer is simple: insofar as Eastern Europe is evolving, Western Europe must itself grow stronger, strengthen its structures and define its policies." These elliptical remarks were deemed at the time to be quite tolerant, even though Mitterrand also added: "Reunification poses so many problems that I shall make up my mind as the events occur."[106]

The Wall Comes Tumbling Down

Events did occur, and at an extraordinary pace. As the new East German government prepared to announce its reform program at the party plenum, ordinary citizens poured into the streets to voice pent-up dissatisfaction with decades of hardship and repression. The daily public protests were capped by the rally of an estimated 500,000 in East Berlin on November 4.

Krenz replaced part of the ruling Politbüro on the eve of the Berlin demonstration. The Socialist Unity party plenum reorganized the government and vaulted Hans Modrow, a reformer within the SED exiled as party boss in Dresden, into the Politbüro. Promises were made to legalize the New Forum and other opposition parties. The U.S. embassy in East Berlin reported to Washington that the plenum had demonstrated "a significant shift toward potentially credible reform, primarily because of the dramatic rise of Mo-drow."[107]

The Soviet Union certainly felt better about Modrow than about Krenz, having long harbored a friendly interest in the Dresden chief's future.[108] Now that reformist communists such as Schabowski and Modrow were coming to the fore, the USSR felt even more strongly committed to backing a new leadership which, the Soviets hoped, could stabilize the situation. On November 6 Gorbachev telephoned Ambassador Kochemasov in East Germany and told him emphatically, "Our people will never forgive us if we lose the GDR."[109]

The reorganized East German government quickly came face-to-face again with the problem of travel restrictions. On November 4 the GDR had begun allowing East Germans to travel to the FRG through Czechoslovakia. Once again tens of thousands of East Germans crowded the roads into Czechoslovakia, trying to make their way west. Once again the West German embassy grounds in Prague began filling with refugees. Krenz had promised Gorbachev that he would allow almost all East German citizens to travel, so long as they took no money with them, and Gorbachev had posed no objection.[110] But the Soviet bureaucracy apparently did not know about this secret conversation. The USSR embassy in East Berlin, hearing that a new travel law was being prepared, asked Moscow what to do. Shevardnadze's top deputy, Anatoly Kovalyov, phoned Kochemasov to tell him to leave the East Germans alone and treat the travel laws as a GDR decision. Kochemasov insisted on receiving a written instruction to this effect. After a few days the cable arrived, duly stating that the travel law was "an internal responsibility of the GDR."[111]

The East Germans delegated the task of preparing the new travel law to Erich Mielke, the former security chief, who had been forced out of the government and the Politbüro. In the new draft, completed in the week after Krenz returned from Moscow, procedures for issuing passports and exit visas were streamlined. The text of the law was hastily drafted, the Soviets were later told, by two Stasi colonels and two departmental chiefs from the Interior Ministry. The draft extended the new liberal rules to all trips, even short private ones, and to all of the GDR's frontiers, including those in Berlin. No senior official on the East German side fully grasped that, in theory, the law would apply to the Berlin Wall, a border and a city under Four Power supervision. The East Germans had not yet consulted Soviet officials, who might have caught the error. The poorly drafted text read: "Requests for private trips abroad may be submitted from now on even in the absence of special prerequisites." There was certainly no intention to authorize trips abroad without prior processing of an exit visa. But the draft was submitted to the 213 members of the SED Central Committee present for the party plenum, and no one objected.[112]

The Central Committee blessed the draft on November 9. Krenz then gave a copy to Schabowski, who had been holding daily press conferences on the activities of the SED party plenum. Krenz was busy with other matters. He was planning the day's major announcement: the decision to call a special party conference in December that would transform the leadership of the GDR. One of the notes to the document promised that the new travel regulations would be announced the next day, November 10, *after* exact instructions on how to implement the law had been circulated to East

German security authorities throughout the country. Krenz had told Gorbachev that he would submit the new law to the legislature before Christmas.

Schabowski overlooked this detail and read the new law near the end of his hour-long press conference. Reading and extemporizing, Schabowski said that interim travel regulations had been prepared which would allow anyone to apply for private travel, that permission would be forthcoming in short order, and that the police had been told to issue visas for permanent emigration "immediately," without application. The new law, he said, would take effect immediately. Then, just after 7:00 in the evening, Schabowski drove home.

Those watching the press conference were seized with curiosity. But the exact text of the draft was not available, so the journalists reported their interpretations of the law, garbling the language and creating a public sensation during the night of November 9–10. Confused diplomats and West German officials were trying to figure out what Schabowski had meant. During Schabowski's press conference the West German mission's press representative—clearly more aware of the import of the announcement than Schabowski himself—had been seen to grasp his head, moan, and dash from the room to sound the alarm. Officials in Bonn, including the intelligence service, were taken by surprise.[113] Rumors spread that all travel restrictions were being dropped, including exit visa requirements. Thousands of people began massing near the Berlin Wall. They asked border guards about the new regulations, but the guards had no information and no guidance to offer.

As the night wore on, huge numbers of people crowded at the wall. The guards at their checkpoints still had not received their instructions. They did not know what to do and were uncertain about their legal duty. Security forces might have been able to handle a planned demonstration, but this was not a demonstration. With hordes of people forcing the guards to give way or shoot the confused and milling throng, local guard commanders gave way. The bewildered interior minister ratified what his guard commanders had already decided. Crowds streamed through into West Berlin. The wall had been opened. November 10 became a holiday in Berlin as masses of East Germans joined their Western brethren in a tumultuous, euphoric celebration.

Krenz immediately put the best face on events and pretended that the opening of the wall had been intentional. That was true in substance. But it was not supposed to happen the way it did. Actually the government had been so disorganized that it took months before Schabowski himself was able to piece together just what had happened that night. Krenz had phoned the Soviet ambassador in the morning of November 10, and Kochemasov had told him that the Soviets were confused about what was happening and were angry that he, Krenz, was being so indecisive. But, Krenz replied, we were planning to open the borders in any case, as your side knew. But not this way, Kochemasov answered, and on the FRG-GDR frontier, not in Berlin. Matters in Berlin affect the interests of the Four Powers. Well, replied Krenz, this is now a theoretical question.[114]

The truth of the matter is that the hapless East German government had opened the Berlin Wall by mistake. In one of the most colossal administrative errors in the long, checkered history of public bureaucracy, the Krenz government abdicated responsibility for the most important decision in its history to the people in the street. The enormous facade of government authority had been devastated. Robert Darnton observed a week later that "in East Berlin especially, the idea has spread that in conquering the Wall the people seized power."[115] The people never let the government have its power back again. It was a mortal blow to the communist regime.

Schabowski was not worried, however. He was just glad that the government had finally done something popular. "We hadn't a clue that the opening of the wall was the beginning of the end of the Republic," he said. "On the contrary, we expected a stabilization process." But years of insulation from the feelings of ordinary people had left East Germany's leaders with no instincts for how they should seize this historic moment. In the next few days not a single leader of the GDR appeared at the wall. But every leading figure in the Federal Republic of Germany showed up there. They came to speak both to West Germans and to the new leaders of East Germany—the common people.[116]

～ 4

The Goal Becomes Unification

HELMUT KOHL first heard about Günter Schabowski's press conference while sitting in a guest house in Warsaw. Kohl, too, was taken by surprise. Of course, the situation in the GDR had been on his mind. Just the day before he had delivered a speech to the Bundestag demanding radical political reform in East Germany as the price for West German economic aid. And he had expressed confidence that, given the chance, East Germans would choose unity. But it was characteristic of the tumultuous times that the West German chancellor had moved on quickly to yet another historic event, his first state visit to Poland, to praise that country's movement toward democracy and to celebrate German-Polish reconciliation. Now there was this news from Berlin. Did it mean the wall was opening?[1]

There was no time for analysis. Kohl and Foreign Minister Hans-Dietrich Genscher were off to the welcoming state dinner, to be hosted amid the faded elegance of the Palais Radziwill by the new Polish prime minister, Tadeusz Mazowiecki. The dinner conversation was dominated by the news from Berlin. Poland's own symbol of democracy, Solidarity leader Lech Walesa, could not believe the East German government would just open the wall. Walesa thought that Egon Krenz was not ready to handle the democratic reform the people would demand if the wall came down. It might take another week or two, he thought. But what then? The situation in the GDR was so dangerous. Walesa was worried that the country could be overtaken by revolutionary chaos. He repeated those concerns to Genscher and Horst Teltschik the next morning. Things were happening so quickly, and Walesa feared that Poland "would pay the price for it."[2]

As events unfolded throughout the evening, Kohl and his party realized that they had to cut short their visit to Poland and go to Berlin as quickly as possible. But the chancellor could not get there directly. Under Four Power rules, West German aircraft were not permitted to fly directly from Poland to Berlin. The American ambassador, Vernon Walters, arranged for a U.S. military plane to meet the chancellor in Hamburg. Kohl left Poland, changed planes, and—in an act thick with symbolism that no one seemed to notice at the time—the Americans flew the West German chancellor to Berlin.[3]

On the podium in Berlin that November day, facing jubilant crowds, SPD senior statesman Willy Brandt, who had been mayor of Berlin when the wall was erected, celebrated its downfall and an end to the "unnatural division of Germany." Genscher, already worried about the attitudes of Germany's neighbors, said that no one "should be fearful if the doors between West and East opened" or if "freedom and democracy will become a reality in the GDR."

Moments before Kohl began his remarks, Teltschik had spoken to the Soviet ambassador in Bonn, Yuli Kvitsinsky. Kvitsinsky conveyed an urgent message from Gorbachev angrily warning against destabilizing the GDR with talk of unification and asking Kohl to calm the people and head off "chaos." Teltschik barely had time to pass this message to Kohl before the chancellor addressed the crowd. Kohl did not respond directly to Gorbachev's prompting. Instead he emphasized the German right to "self-determination" and thanked the Western allies for their support and solidarity. He also thanked Gorbachev for having recognized the right to self-determination. Then Kohl became more expressive: "We demand this right for all in Europe. We demand it for all Germans." Claiming that the road ahead led to "unity and right and freedom," Kohl, now filled with emotion, quoted the FRG national anthem and declared: "A free German fatherland lives! A free, united Europe lives!"[4]

The opening of the Berlin Wall was as electrifying and emotional an event as the world had seen in many years. Although the wall's collapse immediately called into question the postwar order and Germany's future, those were hardly the concerns that dominated the moment. Rather, there were, first and foremost, the scenes of Germany overcoming its division in the most human of terms as families were reunited after years of separation. There were the expressions of giddy East German citizens encountering the casual prosperity most West Germans took for granted, the bewildering array of material goods that had been nothing more than images on West German television. And there were the feelings of nationhood that welled up in Germans on both sides of the divide—among people who had assumed that those emotions were long dead and properly buried. In one such response the Federal Bundestag broke spontaneously into the national anthem upon learning that the wall had opened.

About 9 million East Germans visited the West during that first week, a majority of the entire country's population. They were welcomed as brothers and sisters by those in the West. The whole German nation enjoyed days of wild celebration. Almost all the Eastern visitors returned to their homes, but some were biding their time, waiting to see what would develop. No one— neither ordinary citizens nor heads of state—knew what would or should happen next.

Years after the event it is easy to assume that the popular pressure for unity was immediate, predictable, and irresistible. But it was not. Even after the first popular voices for unification were heard nearly two weeks later on November 19 in Leipzig, many East Germans still thought that the GDR should remain a separate sovereign state. Even those who favored the idea of eventual unification wanted to retain "socialism."[5]

That is not to say that the communists were popular. The party's rank and file wanted change. On November 11 an American diplomat on the scene noted: "The SED is far from a 2-million-plus bulwark for Krenz. Its total control of society is shattered beyond recovery, and its disgruntled member-ship may be the greater immediate threat to his position."[6] The way the wall had opened had robbed the Krenz government of any credit for the deed. East Germans wanted more prosperity and even greater freedom. Still, the leaders of street protests against the GDR regime did not yet want unification. Bärbel Bohley, a founder of the protest movement New Forum, was angry at the way the government had opened the wall. East German dissidents wanted a better socialism in a separate German state, one that rejected the material-ism and exploitation of the West.[7]

The political counselor at the American embassy in East Berlin, an astute judge of the East German public temper, described matters well in an opinion piece he drafted on November 12 to help Americans understand what was happening. What do the reformers want? "Essentially the democratic, human rights standards of the Helsinki Final Act." Are the communists doomed? "Not necessarily." Through Gorbachev-style reforms they might renew their hold on power. Were there alternatives to the communists? "Of course, but each has problems." Above all, will Germany reunite? That was the wrong question. "The current insistence is on self-determination, not reunification. They are not necessarily equivalent."[8]

Helmut Kohl did not focus immediately on unification either. After flying back to Bonn in the early evening of November 10, Kohl spoke on the telephone with Margaret Thatcher. She had publicly welcomed this "great day for freedom." Privately she wanted to know what Kohl planned to do next. She hoped to convene a special summit of European Community leaders to consult about the future. She urged Kohl to confer soon with Gorbachev. Kohl then phoned President Bush. Bush had first heard the news about the new East German travel laws during the afternoon of November 9. Coincidentally, there had been a special intelligence briefing for the president the day before about the quickening pace of reform in East-Central Europe and the possibility of more radical developments in East Germany. The lead briefer had begun his presentation by saying that events were moving so fast that he had torn up his notes three times on his way to the White House.[9]

Reporters gathered in the Oval Office that same day to hear Bush's reaction to the first news about the East German travel laws. The president was extremely guarded, saying only, "I am very pleased with this development." Was this the end of the Iron Curtain? one reporter asked. "Well," he answered, "I don't think any single event is the end of what you might call the Iron Curtain." Had he ever imagined that this would happen? "No, I didn't foresee it, but imagining it? Yes." Asked why he did not sound more elated, Bush replied, "I am not an emotional kind of guy . . . I'm very pleased." Bush was instantly criticized by legislators and journalists and widely satirized for his underwhelming, even rambling reaction to such a momentous occasion. Some thought he should have rushed to Berlin to celebrate the victory of freedom. Bush was annoyed by this criticism. He had made a deliberate choice not to humiliate the Soviets by gloating. "I won't beat on my chest and dance on the wall" was the way he put it. At the time Bush talked to the reporters, though, his main problem was lack of information. No one knew precisely what Schabowski's press conference meant.[10]

Bush could have avoided the criticism had he made an eloquent—if anodyne—statement the following day, after it became clear that the wall had been opened. The idea was never considered. This was characteristic of Bush and his national security staff—often well reasoned on substance but inattentive to the ceremonial dimension of the presidency. Yet Bush was attentive to his diplomatic duties in the face of these changes. In a phone call he congratulated Kohl. The grateful chancellor said that this historic moment could not have happened without the support of the United States. But Bush's attention was concentrated on the Soviets. He would be holding his first summit meeting with Gorbachev in less than a month, in Malta. The two leaders agreed to consult intensively with each other before Bush met with the Soviet leader.[11]

Later that night, an hour before midnight, Kohl gathered his closest aides together for a talk. It had been a long day since they had first awakened that morning in Warsaw. Kohl's interior minister, Wolfgang Schäuble, thought that the East German refugee problem would now subside and that West German public sympathy for the refugees would also diminish since they no longer appeared to be victims of Germany's division. New issues loomed. The East German government would be pushing hard for West German money to help stabilize the country. Kohl would talk the next day to Krenz. The chancellor needed to decide whether and how to reward Krenz's government for opening the wall. No one discussed unification. In that room, as in many others in capitals across Europe, the subject just hung in the air.[12]

As the group was talking, Teltschik had to break away to take a phone call from General Scowcroft in Washington. Scowcroft had news. Gorbachev had sent a message to Washington. The Soviets wanted to call an immediate Four Power meeting to prevent a "chaotic situation" from emerging, with "unforeseeable consequences." Similar messages had gone to Thatcher and Mitterrand.[13] As celebrations continued in Berlin, euphoria in Bonn, Washington, Paris, and London was giving way to hard calculations about what was to come. There were certainly no celebrations in Moscow.

First Moves

The events in Berlin left Soviet leaders struggling to gain their footing in the soft mud beneath their Eastern European policy. Ironically, the deliberate opening of the powerfully symbolic Berlin Wall could have been the crowning display for Gorbachev's "new thinking," the grandest of initiatives from a man already known for his mastery of the diplomatic game. After all, Gorbachev had encouraged the replacement of orthodox leaders by the strongest advocates of reform within the Eastern European Communist parties. The Soviet Union had renounced the Brezhnev doctrine, and the world breathed a sigh of relief when Moscow held to that promise in the face of events in Poland during the spring and summer of 1989. Gorbachev and Shevardnadze had long advocated looser travel laws in the GDR as a first step toward a more humane and respectable East German regime. Like many in East Berlin, they thought that a reformed but still socialist East Germany could survive without imprisoning its citizens.

Moscow never got the chance to deliver the grand gesture. The wall was not removed, it was overrun. That would soon become a metaphor for Soviet policy in Eastern Europe and Germany. The Gorbachev of November had to be a less confident man than the one who had paraded triumphantly through

Bonn in June. The Soviets' gamble that the pace of reform would be deliberate and its direction predictable had not paid off in Poland, in Hungary, and now in the GDR. Soviet policy in Europe was coming apart.

Not surprisingly, then, the first reaction from Moscow was one of barely disguised panic. As we have noted, on November 10 Gorbachev had sent warning letters to Western leaders. He told George Bush that he was worried about the potential for civil disturbance in Berlin ("a chaotic situation may emerge with unforeseeable consequences"). Gorbachev then warned bluntly of the "political extremism" the Soviets saw in West Germany. He could live with reform in East Germany. But "when statements are made in the FRG designed to stir up emotions, in the spirit of implacable rejection of the postwar realities, that is, the existence of two German states, then such manifestations of political extremism can only be seen as aimed at undermining the current dynamic processes of democratization and renewal of all aspects of the society's life. And, looking ahead, this can bring about a destabilization of the situation not only in Central Europe, but on a larger scale." November 10 was a holiday in Washington, and this ominous message had been delivered to Robert Gates and Condoleezza Rice by a Soviet emissary. Gates and Rice found the Soviet message worrying—at once both insecure and threatening. Gates called Scowcroft at home, suggesting that he alert the Germans. It was then that Scowcroft phoned Teltschik, pulling him out of the late-night session with Kohl. Gorbachev had also sent a message to Kohl, but it had not included the proposal for Four Power talks. Scowcroft and Teltschik quickly agreed that the Soviet demand for talks should be rejected. The West German cabinet had decided just days earlier to resist any Four Power contacts "over the heads of the Germans."[14]

The White House did not reply immediately to Gorbachev. Instead, Washington worked to ensure that the Americans, the British, the French, and the FRG agreed on a common approach. This was the first but certainly not the last time that the Americans assumed the role of orchestrating a unified Western response to events in Germany. Baker emphasized caution in his phone conversations that day. He told West German foreign minister Genscher that free travel was a long way from reunification, and he advised Genscher that it might be premature to address the subject of reunification right away. Genscher answered, obliquely, that there would have to be free elections in the GDR, and a free and democratic country could never be a threat to its neighbors. Like Scowcroft and Teltschik, Baker and Genscher also agreed that a Four Power conference on Germany was a bad idea.[15]

The American secretary of state called British foreign secretary Douglas Hurd the next day, November 11, and recounted his talk with Genscher. The two agreed that reunification was still some distance away. Baker told Hurd that he had asked Genscher not to jump to premature conclusions on reunification and Genscher had concurred, instead stressing the FRG's ties to the West. Hurd agreed on the need to follow a cautious public line.[16]

The United States proposed a reply to Gorbachev that ignored his warnings but welcomed his public support for the East German decision to open the wall. The answer would agree that maintaining public order was important yet express confidence that West Germany was committed to a stable, step-by-step process of change. The Western allies concurred, and President Bush dispatched a reply along these lines on November 17. Only Thatcher's reply went further to show how much she sympathized with Gorbachev's fears. "I agree with you," she wrote to the Soviet leader, "that the speed with which these changes are taking place carries its own risks of instability." She urged the need to take "a measured view of the way ahead."[17]

Soviet press spokesman Gennady Gerasimov told reporters that Bush had handled the opening of the wall like "a real statesman," but warned the Germans about "recarving the boundaries of postwar Europe." East Germany, he said, must remain a "strategic ally" of the Soviet Union. Still angry about Kohl's Bundestag speech of November 8, which Shevardnadze singled out for criticism when he spoke to Genscher on November 11, the Soviet Union seemed ready to adopt a firm stand in its dealings with the FRG.[18]

But when Kohl and Gorbachev spoke on November 11, their tone was calm. Kohl was reassuring. The East German people should stay home, he said. He wished "for no destabilization of the situation in the GDR." He remained ready to help Gorbachev with his economic reforms. Gorbachev said that the changes in Eastern Europe were occurring faster than he had anticipated. The GDR needed more time to adopt the necessary reforms. Every action must now be "carefully thought out." This was a turning point, he said: "We cannot allow clumsy actions to endanger this turn or, worse, to push events toward an indescribable path, a path to chaos." Gorbachev asked Kohl to use his authority, his political weight, and all his influence to hold matters within a framework that would allow adequate time to deal with events. Kohl replied that his entire government agreed, and he reassured Gorbachev that he too felt a "strong feeling of responsibility" for the historic consequences of his actions.[19]

Kohl and Teltschik were delighted with this phone call after the very ominous message from the Soviet leader the previous day. Gorbachev had not criticized West German rhetoric or mentioned his proposal of the day before for Four Power talks. "No threat, no warning, only the request to show caution," Teltschik noted in his diary.[20] Other Soviet officials, however, did continue to use tough rhetoric about German behavior. The French foreign minister, Roland Dumas, was the first Western minister to arrive in Moscow after the wall came down. The public Soviet account of his visit stressed that Shevardnadze had told Dumas of his "great concern" about efforts to put German reunification "on the plane of present-day policy." This was nothing less than a challenge to "the territorial and political make-up of the continent as a whole." Chancellery officials were instantly told about these comments, recognized them as an "unmistakable warning," and then discounted them because, after all, they had received a different impression of the Soviet tone directly from Gorbachev himself.[21]

Gorbachev's adviser Chernyayev believed that at this point Gorbachev was still counting on a transitional period during which a profound perestroika could revive the fortunes of the GDR. He feared the results of an uncontrolled rush to German reunification. Nonetheless, Gorbachev had chosen not to convey that sense of alarm to Kohl.[22] Perhaps Gorbachev had wanted to send a strong message through other channels while adopting a more amiable tone—hints rather than warnings—in a person-to-person conversation with Kohl. The Soviet leader may also have thought that Kohl was genuinely trying to reassure him, and that Kohl's reassurances could be accepted at face value. Whatever Gorbachev's real intentions, Kohl and Teltschik chose to adopt the most benign possible interpretation, thinking that the Soviet leader was more tolerant in private than his government appeared in public. This muffled any effect on Bonn of all the other signals Soviet diplomacy was trying to convey.

The confused messages from Moscow—one day anxious, the next calm, tough with one set of officials and flexible with another—set a pattern to be repeated again and again in the months to come. One senses that after the Berlin Wall fell, Moscow began to temporize rather than to elaborate a strategy that contained a bottom line. That, in turn, left it to others to set the agenda, exploiting the appearance of Soviet indecision.

Bonn and East Berlin Seize the Initiative

The East German leaders were in the unenviable position of needing Bonn's comprehensive aid in order to sustain current living standards. And yet the FRG's demands for political change threatened the vitality of the communist state itself. Still, the battered East German leadership spoke up for the nation's right to exist. In a November 11 call Krenz told Kohl that reunification was not even on the agenda. Kohl could not let that pass. The chancellor said that he stood by the commitment to eventual unification in the FRG's Basic Law, but agreed that other questions now took precedence.[23]

Privately Kohl had already decided how he would handle Krenz's pleas for aid. He would stand by the position he had taken in his November 8 speech. Massive economic aid to East Berlin would be conditioned on revolutionary political change: genuinely free elections in the GDR, the Communist party's surrender of its monopoly on power, and the creation of new independent political parties. As for unification, Kohl would insist on self-determination for East Germans while stating his belief that, given a free choice, East Germans would choose unification. Kohl knew that Bush would back him. Gorbachev's apparent retreat from his tough language of November 10 emboldened Kohl to believe that there were no limits to reform in the GDR so long as specific Soviet security interests were respected.[24]

So Kohl announced to the Bundestag on November 16 that the FRG was ready to offer a "completely new dimension of aid and cooperation" if the GDR enacted a long list of radical political and economic changes, from free elections to a free press and free markets. On the national question Kohl emphasized, "We are still far from our goal: the right of all Germans to self-determination is not yet realized"; the provisions of the Basic Law calling for the "unity and freedom of the Germans" had not yet been fulfilled. The people of the GDR must decide for themselves which path to the future they wanted to take: "They themselves know best what they want. That also applies to the question of German unity, the question of reunification." Any decision the East German people made in free self-determination should obviously be respected.[25]

The East German leaders were indeed making new choices. Their first, on November 13, was to change the government. With the Socialist Unity party plenum concluded, its policy proposals were presented to the Volkskammer. But the East German parliament was no longer simply a rubber stamp for the ruling party's preferences. The one credible reform figure in the SED was Hans Modrow, the party secretary from Dresden who had been chastised in early 1989 for supporting Gorbachev-style perestroika. The Volkskammer selected Modrow as prime minister, to run the government while Krenz continued as general secretary of the party, chairman of the council of ministers, and head of state. The unassuming and straightforward Modrow formed a government with several new faces, including some from outside the SED, and he initially garnered wide public support. As one expert noted, "Both Eastern citizens and Western media considered him the most hopeful leader of the successor generation."[26]

Modrow announced his program on November 17. He detailed specific reforms in areas from politics to education to environmental improvement. Dissident leaders welcomed his initiatives. Modrow also offered a vision for progress on the national question, posing an East German alternative to

Kohl's statement the day before. Political reform, he explained, would establish the legitimacy of the GDR as "a socialist state, a sovereign German state." Not just with words but with a new reality in daily life would the GDR reject the "unrealistic as well as dangerous speculation about a reunification." The two German states could have a "cooperative coexistence" on all questions, from peace and armaments to culture and tourism, cemented by a "treaty community" *(Vertragsgemeinschaft)* building on past agreements and hopes for a "common European home."[27] Ruling out unification, Modrow offered instead a relationship between the two German states not unlike that between members of the European Community.

The Meaning of "Self-Determination"

It was hard to argue, at least in public, with West German claims that all Germans had a right to "self-determination." States were bound by their assent to that principle in the Helsinki Final Act of 1975 and the general view that some right of self-determination was clearly extended to member states of the United Nations by the UN charter.[28] Kohl had also adopted a relatively narrow interpretation of this principle. He did not argue that the German people as a whole could determine the GDR's fate. He asserted only that East Germans should decide their own future, and West Germany was obliged to respect their decision.[29] The Soviets could, and did, argue that an FRG or GDR decision for unification was qualified by various agreements, that these countries had voluntarily limited their sovereign rights. But Moscow and East Berlin could not argue directly that the East Germans had no right to self-determination, nor could they claim that this right did not extend to the form of government. Thus, international norms and agreements strongly influenced the vocabulary and shape of the emerging debate over Germany's unification. But there were still many possible interpretations of "self-determination" and great uncertainty about what was politically possible. East Berlin and Bonn had placed radically different images of the German future on the table. The next ten days saw frantic efforts to define for the German people just what was possible and what was not.

In mid-November the tide seemed to be turning against Helmut Kohl and his gamble that self-determination would mean unification. Modrow's option for the coming together of the two German states smartly pushed unification aside. For the first time there was a voice in East Berlin to counter Kohl's vision for Germany.

There were popular stirrings over unity in the East, but they were still weak.

On November 19 a few Leipzig demonstrators began changing the slogan "Wir sind das Volk" (We are the people) to "Wir sind ein Volk" (We are one people). So East Berlin stepped up the pressure to convince the East German people that the path of unity was not open. According to one observer, "Western interviews with demonstrators and various opinion polls . . . had indicated strong support for preserving the GDR as a separate state."[30] Leading East German intellectuals were quite strongly opposed to unification and were able to rally strong and vocal public backing for this view within both East and West Germany.[31]

But Kohl did not want to see unity pushed off the table. He wanted the East German people to believe that it might be allowed. He was convinced that if the East Germans thought that unity was really possible, not just a mirage, they would rally to this standard. The crucial task was to keep the option alive against growing pressure from world and domestic opinion. Immediately after hearing the details of Modrow's call for a "treaty community," Chancellor Kohl decided to call President Bush.

Bush was well prepared for the call. In the preceding week the U.S. government had considered how to express its policy toward change in the GDR and the possibility of unification. Both Bush and Baker had been advised to choose a passive policy for the moment, one that mirrored Kohl's support for self-determination which might lead to unity but was stated mildly enough not to alarm the anxious Soviets any further. The Americans had already decided to reject Gorbachev's proposal for Four Power intervention.[32]

Reaching Bush on the phone, Kohl explained what he was saying to the East Germans and to the Soviets. He had told the East Germans that any aid would be conditioned on far-reaching political reform, including free elections, freedom of the press, and free trade unions, and he had told Gorbachev that the FRG would do nothing to destabilize the GDR. Nonetheless, if the GDR did not undertake reforms as in Poland or Hungary, it was Kohl's belief that the new government was likely to fail. Although Kohl's promise to Gorbachev may have seemed disingenuous, Bush liked his position. He assured the chancellor that the United States would be restrained in its public comments about Germany's future. His greatest worry was that American gloating might upset the fragile Soviet or East German tolerance for fundamental reform. The euphoric excitement in the United States, he said, ran the risk of triggering unforeseeable reactions in the USSR or the GDR which could prove dangerous. "We will not be making exhortations about unification or setting any timetables. We will not exacerbate the problem by having the President of the United States posturing on the Berlin Wall," he promised

Kohl. The two leaders then arranged for more discussions before and after Bush's meeting with Gorbachev in Malta. Bush said that he had never needed Kohl's input more than he needed it now, in preparation for this summit.[33]

François Mitterrand and Margaret Thatcher were not as relaxed about developments in Germany. The French president invited all twelve heads of government of the European Community to a special meeting in Paris on November 18 to consider the German situation. In her memoirs Thatcher recalls that Kohl's own statements had prompted this hastily arranged European summit session. In private she was hearing that Genscher was offering reassurances to Hurd that Germans wanted to avoid talk of reunification.

Mitterrand opened the Paris discussion by posing questions to Kohl about his intentions, including the future of Europe's borders. Kohl spoke for forty minutes. He repeated his publicly stated themes, emphasizing respect for self-determination but finding no need to discuss borders. Thatcher then detailed her concerns. Any talk of border changes or German reunification would undermine Gorbachev and open up a Pandora's box of territorial claims. "I said," she wrote later, "that we must keep both NATO and the Warsaw Pact intact to create a background of stability." Kohl voiced no reservations and in fact did not speak of unification at all. His theme was one of reassurance. In private, of course, Kohl's advisers were carefully noting the differences in the way foreign governments had reacted to the opening of the Berlin Wall. The Americans were obviously most positive, the French seemed friendly but reserved, and the British and Dutch were cold.[34]

In fact, the American attitude was beginning to crystallize. The regular bureaucracy was cautious, counseling support for German national aspirations but concluding that "at the moment neither the people of the GDR nor the government of the FRG is talking about reunification . . . The emphasis has been on democratization, and this is where we should keep our emphasis as well."[35] Baker himself, however, was attracted to the specific guidelines on unification proposed in a paper prepared by Dennis Ross and Francis Fukuyama of his policy planning staff emphasizing the "four principles which should frame our policy." They were: (1) the United States should support true German self-determination without endorsing any specific outcome; (2) unification must be consistent with Germany's membership in NATO and the EC; (3) moves toward unity should be gradual, peaceful, and step by step; and (4) on the issue of postwar borders, all should respect "the principles adopted in the Helsinki Final Act recognizing the inviolability of frontiers in Europe, and allowing for the possibility of peaceful change."[36]

Baker did not want to get into a detailed discussion of what these principles might mean when Foreign Minister Genscher visited Washington on November 20. Genscher was downplaying the unification issue. He emphasized that unity was a process evolving within the framework of general change in European politics, including the FRG's ties to the EC, NATO's posture toward the Soviet Union, and East-West relations. It was President Bush who raised the subject of unification with Genscher. The president, saying he backed German self-determination, asked, "Will reunification move faster than any of us think?" Genscher replied that no one could tell. There were many voices being heard in East Germany. The first thing was to establish democracy in the GDR. The FRG would stand by its obligations to NATO and the EC, "but all of this must be done in a way that does not alarm the Soviet Union."[37]

In a separate meeting Scowcroft asked Genscher whether the Soviets might propose negotiating a peace treaty to settle the status and borders of Germany during the upcoming Malta meeting. Genscher doubted it. He did think the Soviet president might suggest a CSCE summit to boost the NATO–Warsaw Pact arms control talks on conventional armed forces in Europe (CFE)—an idea Genscher liked. In any case, Genscher had little use for the idea of any forum dominated by the Four Powers. "We don't want to take our place at the *Katzentisch* [cat's table]," he said. (In the past at Four Power talks the Germans had been off to the side, at the "cat's table.") Also, he said, German issues must be tied to everything else in East-West relations. "Germany's fate should never again be isolated. This would happen if Four Power talks isolated the German national problem from the European problem . . . Together with our friends, we can build a new Europe. We have the winning concept. We should not talk about it too much, but we know things are going our way."[38]

In late November, then, the United States and the FRG were united in their support for German self-determination and the immediate policy objective of encouraging democracy in East Germany. President Bush was comfortable with Bonn's policy and did not press Chancellor Kohl to elaborate his design for Germany's future.

Still, the British and French governments were uneasy. Thatcher's views were already clear, and, characteristically, she made no effort to mute or conceal them. Prime Minister Thatcher first described her country's policy in the aftermath of the opening of the Berlin Wall in a November 13 speech in which she said publicly what she had been writing to Gorbachev privately, that "in East Germany the objective must be to see genuine democracy" and that "would itself be a huge achievement." But "once the demand for reform starts, there is a tendency for it to run very fast. Indeed the very speed of change could put the goal of democracy in jeopardy. Strong emotions have been aroused on all sides by recent events. The need now is to take a measured view of the way ahead." Writing to President Bush a few days later, Thatcher went right to the point: "We must demonstrate that we do not intend to exploit the situation to the detriment of the Soviet Union's security interests. This will involve continuing to make plain our view that the future of the Warsaw Pact, like that of NATO, is a matter for its members to decide without interference from outside; and that German reunification is not a matter to be addressed at present." Thatcher added that she might phone the president to confirm his agreement on these important points, and indeed she did.[39]

During their telephone conversation on November 17 (several hours after Bush had spoken with Kohl), Bush agreed with Thatcher that change should follow a measured pace that would ease Soviet concerns. But Thatcher reiterated her feeling that discussion of German reunification was premature and unwise. "Talk about that here has led to some strong emotions. History here is living history," she said, adding that the West should "respect Gorbachev's wish to keep the Warsaw Pact frontiers." She welcomed Bush's idea for a NATO summit meeting right after the Malta summit meeting with Gorbachev. She thought that an allied discussion of Germany would calm Kohl: "A discussion in a wider forum could really help steady the ship."[40]

The president prepared to discuss Germany at much greater length with Prime Minister Thatcher on November 24, when she was to join him at Camp David for a full day of meetings. Since Thatcher's views were obviously so strong, the NSC staff urged Bush not to be drawn into formulations that supported German self-determination but treated reunification as a distant and unattainable goal. Instead, Scowcroft recommended, "Your position should remain clear: that we are prepared to honor the German people's choices about their future—including a choice for reunification; that we are committed to peaceful change in a stable way; and that we are comfortable with the way Bonn is meeting the challenge posed by recent events." Bush studied this recommendation and noted his agreement.[41]

At Camp David, Prime Minister Thatcher stated that her top priority was to consolidate the movement toward democracy in Eastern Europe.[42] To achieve that goal an environment of stability was essential. That meant preserving NATO, and with it the Warsaw Pact. Germany's fate, she argued, was not just a matter for self-determination. The borders issue, the role of the Four Powers in Berlin, the CSCE position on inviolability of frontiers all widened the problem. She concentrated again on two themes: the significance of the borders issue (pointing out the implications on a map) and the danger to Gorbachev. Reunification would mean Gorbachev is lost. He loses the integrity of the Warsaw Pact. Thatcher urged Bush to focus his attention instead on democratization of the GDR. True, it would be hard to keep the

Germans from unifying if they wanted to, but one could certainly dampen their expectations.

At first Bush did not respond directly to these arguments. He asked the prime minister to put aside East Germany for a moment and consider what would happen if other East European countries wished to leave the Warsaw Pact. Even if that happened, NATO, he thought, must stay in place. Thatcher said the point was that if Europe were destabilized by developments in Germany, democracy might not come to Eastern Europe at all. Bush was noncommittal. As Thatcher later concluded in her memoirs, "The President did not challenge me directly," but "the atmosphere did not improve as a result of our discussions."

The British government was not alone in resisting "premature" discussion of German unification. French leaders were concerned too. But President Mitterrand displayed a more philosophical stance, at least in public, and concentrated on the need to deepen European integration and with it the FRG's ties to the EC. On November 17, the day Bush talked with both Kohl and Thatcher about Germany's future, he also spoke with Mitterrand. Neither leader chose to discuss Germany.[43]

After the special EC summit in Paris on November 18 had produced Kohl's reassuring presentation, the French took no further action to organize European opinion on Germany. But later in November, as East Germans in the street began calling for a united fatherland, French political commentary became more anxious, and Mitterrand's mask of philosophical detachment began to slip. He wrote to Bush on November 27 posing a question that, he said, troubled the EC: How could the community encourage more democracy in East Germany "without provoking a modification of the strategic equilibrium for which the Soviet Union is not ready?" Answering his own question, Mitterrand wrote: "Each of our governments is very aware of the role which the EC can and must play in the definition of a new European equilibrium, as soon as the EC has reinforced its own cohesion." Although the tone was, as usual, oblique, the message came through: the EC must play a critical role, and a radical revision of the postwar status quo must be linked to, if not preceded by, agreement on stronger European integration.

On November 30 Genscher came to Paris. Mitterrand said that he would not stand in the way of German unification, adding, "But I'm asking you: Will Germany continue the process of European unification?" Without a doubt, Genscher assured him, European integration would become even more important. From this point on Mitterrand pursued the strategy of linking the German question to his own agenda for more rapid movement toward new forms of European union. Perhaps reacting to the worried tone of debate in the French senate, Mitterrand announced, without consulting Bonn, that he would visit East Germany in December, before Kohl's own first trip there. Then the French government also announced that Mitterrand would soon meet with Gorbachev in Kiev.[44]

Bush's readiness to accept German unification was apparently not shaken either by European cautions or by the worries repeatedly being voiced in the editorial pages of American newspapers.[45] Talking to foreign journalists on November 21, Bush was asked what he would say to the people of Britain and France who were against German reunification. He replied: "I say to them: That's a matter for the German people to decide. And there are some that worry about it. I understand that Mr. Gorbachev has some understandable constraints, because he looks at borders, he looks at history—he's concerned. But . . . this is 1989. And we can learn from history, but we also can look to the future. And my view is: Let this matter be determined by the people in Germany."[46]

By late November the U.S. government and its key allies were avoiding an open clash over Germany only because they could all agree that they shared a short-term national interest in seeing political reform continue in the GDR. Even Moscow could share that goal. The Soviet government fervently hoped that Modrow would be able to master the situation with a mix of domestic reforms, the allure of a "treaty community" with the FRG, and discouragement about prospects for any other form of unification. But at a critical point, with things finally going reasonably well in East Germany, freewheeling Soviet officials perhaps inadvertently encouraged the Germans to think beyond reform in the GDR and consider the terms for possible unification of the two German states.

The day before Kohl's November 16 Bundestag speech in which he linked aid to political reform in the GDR and pressed the goal of "self-determination," Alexander Yakovlev, traveling in Japan, told the press that the Soviet Union would not be forced into playing the role of the villain. "The U.S., Britain and France do not want reunification of Germany and hope the Soviet Union will forestall such a development," he said. Yet it was the Soviet leaders who were insisting most stridently that postwar realities had to be respected. Modrow, confident of the Soviet stand, had categorically rejected unification in his speech on November 17; and, after Kohl spoke to the Bundestag, heads of the French and German national legislatures heard directly from Gorbachev that "reunification is not on the agenda."[47]

Then, on November 21, Central Committee staff member Nikolai Portugalov met with Horst Teltschik.[48] Portugalov handed Teltschik a handwritten paper. The first part, Teltschik recalled, had an "official character" and had been approved by Falin and Chernyayev. It identified the GDR's renewal with the Soviet Union's own perestroika. The second part of the paper had only been discussed with Falin. It indicated a wide range of issues to be considered before unification could take place, including alliance membership and a German peace treaty. "As you can see," Portugalov said, "we are thinking about all possible alternatives for the German question, even things that were practically unthinkable." He confided that the Soviets might even give a green light to a German confederation.

According to his own account, Teltschik was "electrified" by this news. He immediately began wondering how much further the Soviet leadership might go—obviously further than had previously seemed possible. This "green light" evidently emboldened Teltschik, who was about to begin drafting the speech that would become Kohl's ten-point plan for German unity.

It is far from clear, however, that this was the message Portugalov had meant to deliver with his unofficial remarks. Portugalov himself had publicly denounced unification only a few days earlier as "not liked by any of the neighbors" of the Germans and "incompatible with the geopolitical and geostrategic requirements of stability." Portugalov had even added that, "in the foreseeable future and also in the long run, the two German states will continue to exist as sovereign and equal states." Portugalov had not forgotten these words; he actually referred to this interview in his meeting with Telt-schik. It is hard to avoid the conclusion that both sides to the conversation heard each other selectively. Portugalov had no way of knowing that Teltschik was preparing a major address for the chancellor and might be particularly sensitive to any hint of Soviet flexibility. This rather minor Soviet official's elaborations on his handwritten paper, a paper that had not been seen by any Foreign Ministry officials, offer a reminder why veteran diplomats emphasize precision in written as well as oral expression.

Kohl understood that others, particularly Modrow, were trying to take unification off the political agenda. Faced with an uncertain political land-scape, Kohl decided to seize the initiative and put unification back at the center of the discussion.

A Program to Achieve German Unification

Kohl and his closest advisers secretly decided to prepare a policy program showing how unification could happen. The chancellor's team wanted to "take the offensive." This program, they thought, would accomplish several goals. First, it would fuel the interest in unification that was just beginning to catch fire in the dry kindling of East German unrest and soaring expectations. Second, their program would instantly differentiate Kohl politically from his more cautious opponents, better positioning the unpopular chancellor for elections the following year. Third, the move might decisively counter Modrow's "treaty community" idea, overwhelming it before an international consensus could build up around it and back Kohl into a corner.[49] Modrow's government was already explaining how their "treaty community" could mean some sort of confederation, a broad term that encompassed any close combination of independent states for a common purpose.[50]

Within the Chancellery, Seiters had been worried about the planned references to unification, fearing a harsh Eastern reaction. His hesitance was not surprising. Opinion within West Germany about unification was divided. A week after the wall came down, a poll found that about a quarter of the West German public believed that during the next few years the FRG would remain oriented toward the West, with a separate GDR facing East. Another quarter thought that reunification might be possible. The largest segment, 44 percent, foresaw closer relations between the two states along the lines of the FRG's ties to Austria and Switzerland. Another poll, more encouraging to Teltschik, showed that most West Germans at least supported reunification in principle, and nearly half thought it might be achieved in as little as ten years. Meanwhile, Kohl's likely opponent from the opposition Social Democratic party, Oskar Lafontaine, was commenting that "the conservative right wing" might have "the old national state as its point of orientation." But Lafontaine warned that "this isn't appropriate anymore, and it certainly has nothing to do with the current wishes and feelings of the people of the GDR."[51]

The East German economic situation was continuing to deteriorate. The outflow of emigrants had not stopped. Over 130,000 East German citizens, almost 1 percent of the population, moved to the West in the month of November alone. As the mass of East Germans realized the full extent of their country's problems and considered the obstacles they would face in solving them, they began to see unification with the Federal Republic, a country that already exemplified the virtues of democracy and prosperity, as the clearest answer. As one German newspaper pointed out: "Speakers in Leipzig demanded reunification above all and exclusively because for them existing socialism has collapsed. Because they do not want to sacrifice their lives for five years, not one year, not one month more."[52]

Leaders can shape opinion. They can provide a focal point for confused or uncertain public views by taking a stand. On November 28 Helmut Kohl did just that. He delivered an address to the Bundestag that presented a ten-point program for achieving German unity. The ten points were:

1. Institute measures to facilitate travel between East and West Germany.
2. Expand technological cooperation with the GDR, as in environmental protection, telecommunications, and railroads.
3. Expand economic aid to the GDR on a large scale *if* "a fundamental change of the political and economic system is bindingly resolved and irreversibly started in the GDR." This meant free elections in the GDR with no guarantee of SED monopoly on power, as well as dismantling of centralized economic planning. "We do not want to stabilize conditions that have become untenable," said Kohl.
4. Establish a "treaty community" with the GDR to cooperate institutionally on a variety of common problems.
5. Proceed, after free elections in the GDR, to develop "confederative structures" between the two German states [not a confederation] and, eventually, a federal system for all Germany. The policy of "small steps" to mitigate the consequences of division would be replaced by new forms of cooperation, starting with joint governmental committees and a common parliament. "Nobody knows today what a re-united Germany will ultimately look like," said Kohl. "I am sure that the unity will come if the people in Germany want it."
6. Embed the development of inter-German relations "in the all-European process and in East-West relations."
7. Encourage the EC to open itself to a democratic GDR and "other democratic countries in Central and South-Eastern Europe."
8. Speed up development of the CSCE, perhaps including new institutions for East-West economic cooperation and environmental relations.
9. Support rapid progress in arms control.
10. Strive for a "peace order" to allow German reunification as one state. As for the "particularly difficult" question of "transnational security structures," said Kohl, embedding the German question "in the all-European development and in the East-West relationship" might allow for "an organic development which takes into consideration the interests of all parties concerned and guarantees a peace order in Europe."[53]

With this speech Chancellor Kohl defined a path to German unity, both internationally and within German domestic politics. The initiative, drafted principally by Teltschik, was brilliantly constructed. The speech built on Kohl's November 8 and November 16 positions. It borrowed traditional Ostpolitik rhetoric about the "all-European process" and the sacred "peace order" while actually completing the subversion of old Ostpolitik and returning to "change through strength." It was a step-by-step process, but it marched

straight through Modrow's "treaty community," past the latest "confederation" idea, and onward to reunification, though enveloping this goal within
vague phrases calculated to mollify concerns. Still, the ultimate destination,
reunification, was marked clearly on the map.

Kohl's address started to bridge the vast gulf between the abstract desire
for unification and operational accomplishment of the goal. The East Germans could see that the idea not only was still on the table but was a real
possibility, something they could demand. Kohl's speech gave the emerging
East German public mood a focal point—and a leader. Teltschik exulted in
his diary about the "giant success!" He wrote: "We have achieved our goal.
The Chancellor has taken over the leadership of opinion about the German
question."[54]

In particular, Kohl had outflanked his coalition partner, Hans-Dietrich
Genscher. Genscher had been gathering public praise during November for
his conduct of what seemed to be a very successful foreign policy. This meant
votes for Genscher's small Free Democratic party. In order to secure his own
political coup, Kohl had told no one else in the government about his plans,
including his own foreign minister. To mute reaction to his move, Kohl had
emphasized a gradual process of integration between two German states in
a flexible framework. But his program clearly went far beyond Genscher's
public and diplomatic approach, which had strongly downplayed the significance of unification as an operational objective for policy. Yet Kohl's
ten-point plan was so unassailable that Genscher was obliged to congratulate
Kohl on his "great speech" and stand by the program. The SPD, divided on
how to react, offered qualified support for Kohl's plan.[55]

Fearful of leaks, Kohl had not revealed the contents of his speech to his
Western allies. Anyway, he could hardly tell foreign governments what he
would not tell his own foreign minister. Some of his advisers, including
Rudolf Seiters, thought that springing the move without any warning could
prove to be counterproductive. Teltschik preferred to keep the "surprise
effect," and Kohl backed this view, but with one exception. He ordered that
the text of the speech be sent to President Bush as it was being delivered,
accompanied by a lengthy message explaining what Kohl was trying to do.
Other countries would be briefed afterward by Teltschik, through their ambassadors in Bonn.[56]

In Washington, on November 28, President Bush was receiving another of
his pre-Malta briefings in the Oval Office, this time on the German question
and Berlin. James Dobbins from the State Department reviewed the international situation, remarking that events—especially among the East German
populace—were starting to force the pace of German unification. News of

Kohl's speech had just arrived, and Dobbins recognized it as an important development, putting unification on the policy agenda with a concrete program. Intelligence analysts agreed.[57] Bush seemed relaxed about the prospect that momentum was building toward unification. That same day Robert Zoellick prepared an informal analysis of Kohl's speech for Secretary Baker which was also positive, emphasizing that the speech allowed for a spectrum of possibilities leading eventually to some form of unification.[58]

Chancellor Kohl's November 28 message to President Bush not only reported on his speech but also offered detailed advice on every major topic in East-West relations, looking ahead to Bush's meeting with Gorbachev. The key was Kohl's discussion of "Malta philosophy." Kohl was glad that Bush had clearly "rejected any parallel between Yalta and Malta." Therefore, Kohl argued against any attempts "to contain or channel popular movements." He urged Bush not to let the Malta meeting take on the appearance of being "a status quo summit."

On the specific question of German unification, Kohl first expressed "heartfelt" thanks for Bush's support. He warned that Gorbachev might insist that there should be no change in "the existing borders between East and West" and hoped that Bush would stand by his previous position. Kohl had not tried to achieve "the national goal of the Germans independently." There should be no doubt, he wrote, about the FRG's "unwavering loyalty" to the NATO alliance. Kohl summarized his ten-point program and closed: "Dear George, I would be particularly grateful if in your talks with Mr. Gorbachev you would support the policy expressed in these ten points and emphasize to him that this future-oriented course, not adherence to outmoded taboos, is in the best interests of his country, too."[59]

The same day President Bush received a very different kind of message from the East German president. Krenz urged Bush to agree that the existence of two German states "and their membership in different alliances" were "fundamental" elements of European security. "Nationalism, a revival of Nazi ideas, and the striving for a revision of the results obtained in the wake of the anti-Hitler coalition's victory," Krenz wrote, "are detrimental to achieving a secure peace in Europe."[60] Bush never replied to this message.

U.S. officials immediately recognized that, with his ten-point plan for unity, Kohl had attempted a tremendous gambit. He could be very exposed politically in the FRG, especially if the German public believed that he had triggered an international crisis. The unhappiness of the Soviets was soon evident, despite Kohl's advance consultations with Gorbachev. So officials at the State Department and the NSC staff quickly decided that Washington must energize U.S. policy in order to back Kohl's initiative and shield the chancellor from severe international criticism. They hoped that President Bush, after his Malta meeting with Gorbachev, could rally a Western consensus behind a policy that would stand by Kohl while ensuring that his program met their own criteria for unification. The American officials were worried that Kohl's private affirmation of support for NATO had not been voiced in his speech.

President Bush spoke for half an hour with chancellor Kohl early on the day after his historic speech.[61] Kohl was convinced that more change was coming to the GDR. He expected free elections in East Germany by the autumn of 1990 or the beginning of 1991. Movement toward unification would, he said, be a "long-term process." (Privately, at that time Kohl and his advisers thought they would be lucky to achieve unification within five or ten years.) He did not want to confront the issue of a united Germany's alliance membership. "They will remain in the Pact and we, in NATO."

Kohl was, however, thinking much more concretely about how to get the French to support his plan. He had decided to join with Mitterrand in backing rapid progress toward a new European treaty to establish economic and monetary union (EMU) at an upcoming EC summit (December 8 in Strasbourg), the last such meeting with France in the chair of the EC's governing body, the European Council. Kohl assured Bush, "It is an iron law that there will be no going it alone in German policy." The Germans were fortunate, Kohl commented: "History left us with good cards in our hands. I hope with the cooperation of our American friends we can play them well."

Bush supported Kohl's general approach. Stability was certainly important, and Bush assured Kohl that he had tried "to do nothing that would force a reaction by the USSR . . . We are on the same wavelength. I appreciated your ten points and your exposition on the future of Germany."

Kohl finished the call, saying: "Germans—East and West—are listening very carefully. Every word of sympathy for self-determination and unity is very important now."

Bush was ready to provide those words of sympathy. Talking to reporters later in the day on November 29, Bush discussed his phone conversation with Kohl. "I feel comfortable," he said. "I think we're on track." The reporters asked Bush what he wanted for Europe. Bush replied: "In terms of the 'vision thing,' the aspirations, I spelled it out in little-noted speeches last spring and summer, which I would like everyone to go back and reread. And I'll have a quiz on it [laughter] . . . You'll see in there some of the 'vision thing'—a Europe whole and free. Now that, I think, takes on a little more relevance today, given the changes that have already taken place or that are taking place . . . But in terms of your question, I think a Europe whole and free is less vision and perhaps reality. But how we get there and what that means and when the German question is resolved and all of these things—I can't answer more definitively."[62]

The next day, November 30, President Bush departed for his shipboard meetings in Malta with Gorbachev, which would be followed by a meeting with all heads of government of the NATO alliance. It would be the first U.S.-Soviet summit of Bush's presidency and the first meeting of Western leaders since Kohl's plan had grabbed headlines around the world. The week to come would help determine the fate of Kohl's new "offensive." And Kohl needed help. As some of his advisers had predicted, both the substance of the plan and the lack of consultation had provoked a negative reaction from practically every other country in Europe. French diplomats complained confidentially to German officials about a "surprise attack" and publicly expressed strong reservations about "precipitate" action. Prime Minister Thatcher let Kohl know that she did not believe that unification "was on the agenda."[63]

Moscow was unhappy, too. Just prior to Kohl's speech, Gorbachev and Shevardnadze had met with Canadian prime minister Brian Mulroney, who later told Bush that Germany was the top concern for the Soviet leaders and that they thought the Germans should just forget about reunification. According to the Canadians, Gorbachev, especially irritated, had accused the American ambassador in Bonn of "acting like a German gauleiter" for having publicly voiced his support for unification. The Canadian foreign minister recalled Shevardnadze's saying that most Europeans agreed with the Soviets, since "all of us who were in the war are against revanchism and neo-Nazis." More ominously, Mulroney remembered Gorbachev's remark that "people have died from eating unripened fruit."[64]

The Soviet government was attacking Kohl in public as well as in private. Gorbachev told a group of students: "There are two German states. History saw to that. And this fact is generally accepted by the world community . . . That is the reality, and we must work on the basis of that reality . . . I do not think that the question of the reunification of these states is currently a pressing political question."[65] Moscow's pique carried great risks for Kohl, raising the danger of a genuine crisis. Faced with a confrontational response, Kohl would be blamed—not aided—by his Western European allies. The West German public might quickly deem his stance, and his secrecy in springing the move, to have been dangerously provocative, a damning accusation in West German politics.

The Soviet Union was still counting on Modrow's ability to gain control over conditions in the GDR. But at the end of November some within the

Soviet government thought it a slender reed on which to hang Soviet hopes. The Soviet ambassador to Bonn, Yuli Kvitsinsky, felt that Moscow would need a more dynamic policy—not just vague public statements—in order to protect its relations with the GDR and influence the German future. He cabled home that the continued existence of the GDR was only a question of time. The exodus to the West reminded him of the months before the wall was built in 1961. The East Germans would not stay and work in the East when they could go a hundred or so kilometers west and earn four to six times as much for the same work. Therefore, Kvitsinsky went on to argue, it no longer made sense to try to reject national unity for the Germans. Instead, the GDR and socialism could be preserved by preempting Kohl with the idea of a confederation binding two separate states with different social systems. The initiative should come from the parties in the GDR rather than from Moscow. But there was not much time, he warned, before the chance to move would be lost—only a matter of weeks.[66]

Shevardnadze answered immediately, supporting Kvitsinsky's idea. But then another cable arrived from Moscow, saying that Shevardnadze's initial reply did not reflect the final opinion of the Soviet government. The new instruction characterized Shevardnadze's reply as a sign of Moscow's interest in Kvitsinsky's views, but his proposal was in many respects overly hasty and controversial. Kvitsinsky felt that he was being told he had unduly dramatized the situation. He thought that back in Moscow the attitude was: "One could definitely not talk of the disappearance of the GDR. The Soviet Union will not permit it."[67]

The Malta Summit

The Americans were wondering where Moscow stood. Mulroney's warning seemed to suggest that the Soviets would take a tough line at Malta. Scowcroft gave Bush the NSC staff's best estimate, drafted by Rice. Bush's staff offered four judgments:

1. The Soviets had lost control of their policy toward Eastern Europe. They had not anticipated current developments. They were now reacting to events day by day.
2. The Soviets were opposed to German reunification, which they thought "would rip the heart out of the Soviet security system." Their "worst nightmare" was a reunified Germany allied with NATO. "The Warsaw Pact, having lost its East German anchor, would quickly disintegrate

and the Soviet line of defense would begin at the Ukrainian border."
The gains of World War II, bought so dearly, would be gone.

3. Moscow was now struggling to devise policies to prop up the continued existence of two German states. It would try to work with France and Britain to stabilize the existing situation.

4. There was still no evidence of panic in Moscow on the German issue. If Soviet influence began to deteriorate more rapidly, the USSR might revert to 1950s-style calls for pan-European collective security or negotiation of a German peace treaty.[68]

The CIA prepared a similar analysis, but added that Gorbachev's own views on Germany had betrayed some ambiguity and that Gorbachev might harbor a pragmatic outlook. For a variety of reasons the CIA did not expect Gorbachev to be candid with the president in revealing his real bottom line on Germany. Instead, they expected him to project a concerned but philosophical attitude—especially if his leanings were indeed pragmatic.[69]

Informed by these analyses of likely Soviet attitudes, Blackwill, Rice, and Zelikow worked intensively with Zoellick and Ross to develop a policy for Bush to take to Europe for his meetings with Gorbachev and the NATO summit. The German issue was, of course, only one aspect of a complex U.S.-Soviet agenda, which included the timing of a full-scale summit, the future of perestroika, economic relations, arms control, and regional issues. To avoid leaks, the president's materials were held closely by those five officials and their direct superiors.

As it touched on Germany, the American approach to the Malta summit with Gorbachev and the subsequent Brussels meeting with allied heads of government had three operational objectives. First, the president should avoid alarming the Soviets by stressing the immediate need for democratic reform and self-determination in the GDR. But, as needed, Bush would stand up for the goal of German unity and reject any proposal for a Four Power peace conference. Second, Bush would try to rally allied support for Kohl and his ten-point unity plan while using America's pivotal position with the Germans to cement Bonn's continued support for NATO and a responsible position on borders. Third, he would outline a vision for the general transformation of European politics to accompany the political revolutions in Central Europe.

Meanwhile, Gorbachev was coming up with his own initiatives. En route to Malta he stopped in Italy and announced his major proposal: he restated his hope for a "common European home" of sovereign and economically interdependent nations and called for a summit meeting of leaders of the thirty-five CSCE member countries, to be held in 1990. In this setting Germany's future could be debated as part of a general discussion of European security and politics. An all-European process was important, Gorbachev said, but it had to accept the existence of two German states as a fact of life.[70] The Americans left for Malta somewhat worried that Gorbachev might ask Bush to throw the German question into the most unwieldy European forum imaginable—the CSCE. There it would be debated until the end of the century.

Aboard the *Maxim Gorkii*

American and Soviet leaders arrived in Malta along with one of the Mediterranean's infrequent but violent winter storms. They had intended to meet aboard cruisers of the respective navies. Instead, as the winds howled outside, the talks on Marsaxlokk Bay were confined to the wardroom of a support ship, the Soviet cruise liner *Maxim Gorkii*.[71]

Bush had decided to lay his cards on the table at the very beginning. He knew that Gorbachev still harbored suspicions that he, Bush, did not support perestroika. The president therefore began with a lengthy statement setting out nearly twenty different policy initiatives, ranging from moves in arms control talks to ideas for increased U.S.-Soviet economic cooperation.

Gorbachev replied that he had been looking for a tangible demonstration of American support. "During your presentation, I heard it. I was going to ask you today to go beyond words. But you have done so." Gorbachev stressed his philosophical approach, saying, "The emphasis on confrontation based on our different ideologies is wrong." Gorbachev thought that "strategically and philosophically, the methods of the Cold War were defeated." The Soviet leader knew that some Americans thought Eastern Europe was falling apart, the policies of the Cold War were right, and the United States only needed "to keep its baskets ready to gather the fruit." But he did not think that Bush believed this. Bush assured Gorbachev that, as Europe had changed, "we have not responded with flamboyance or arrogance . . . I have conducted myself in ways not to complicate your life. That's why I have not jumped up and down on the Berlin Wall." Gorbachev said he had noticed that, and appreciated it.

Then the two leaders separated for a more private one-on-one discussion. They turned to the subject of Germany. Gorbachev told Bush he knew that some of West Germany's allies were worried about reunification. He too was worried but, "unlike you and your allies," would state clearly that "there are two German states, this was the decision of history." Referring to their November 11 phone conversation, Gorbachev remarked that Kohl "realizes his responsibility and will adhere by the agreements that we reached in Bonn" in June 1989. Bush promised not to take ill-conceived steps to accelerate the solution of the German question. But even though some Western countries might agree with the Soviet position, they and everyone else "have to think about the time when the notions of FRG and GDR will become a part of history." Bush urged Gorbachev to accept the changes that were under way, with the understanding that the United States would take no rash steps that could have dangerous consequences. Bush promised that he would not "jump on the wall because too much is at stake in the situation." Yes, Gorbachev replied with a laugh, "jumping on the wall is indeed not an occupation for the President."[72]

The subject of Germany came up again at a larger meeting the following day, December 3.[73] The meetings were drawing to a close, and the atmosphere was friendly. Bush's initiatives had made a good impression, as had his receptiveness to Gorbachev's philosophical approach. Gorbachev, in turn, had responded seriously to Bush's concerns on issues such as the need for free elections in Nicaragua and more restraint in Soviet support for Cuba's foreign policy adventures.

Referring to the previous day's one-on-one conversation on Germany, Bush now countered Gorbachev's assertion that the existence of two German states was a fact of history. Bush said that the United States could not be asked to disapprove of German reunification. He knew how sensitive this subject was for Moscow. He had tried to act with restraint. He was also well aware of the Helsinki Final Act language concerning borders. He asked what Gorbachev saw beyond the status quo.

Gorbachev began by emphasizing his acceptance of America's involvement and engagement in Europe. Any other approach, he acknowledged, "would be unrealistic and unconstructive." As for the relations between East and West, that was "an objective process where the countries of Europe will become closer to each other." All Europeans, even Kohl, agreed that "we should do everything within the Helsinki context rather than ruining what has been done," said Gorbachev. Therefore, he proposed a "Helsinki II Summit" to deal with this new phase in a prudent and responsible way. The summit of thirty-five European countries should improve stability and turn the Warsaw Pact and NATO into political rather than military organizations.

Gorbachev then attacked the U.S. view that "the division of Europe should be overcome on the basis of Western values." He warned that if "policy is made on that assumption the situation could become quite messy. You used to make similar accusations against the USSR—the export of revolution," he told the Americans. Instead, as Eastern Europe became more open and democratic and came to respect universal human values, "this opens up the possibility for a tranquil and placid pause." It was "dangerous" to "try to force the issues" to achieve an advantage. Gorbachev offered his own vision of gradual historical change, carefully managed to avoid "a chaotic situation." He was optimistic: "You can tremble and some panic, but if you look at it philosophically—things fall into place. We are dealing with fundamental processes if nations and peoples are involved in the developments—one can't expect it to be smooth."

Bush acknowledged that democratic values are universal, not just "Western." Gorbachev in turn agreed that each country should be able to choose its political, cultural, or economic system. Bush concluded that there was no difference, then, in their support for self-determination. Baker pointed out that the U.S. leaders spoke of Western values in the context of German reunification in order to stress the importance of openness and pluralism, in contrast to the situation in Germany in the 1930s and 1940s. The Soviets—Gorbachev, Shevardnadze, and Yakovlev—repeated their wish not to refer to these common values as Western. "They are our values too," Gorbachev claimed. Secretary Baker then suggested the phrase "democratic values" and Gorbachev, mollified, concurred.

The two leaders then held another short one-on-one discussion. They agreed that the meetings had gone just as they had hoped. There was no mention of Germany. They did, however, discuss the potentially explosive situation in the Baltic republics, and reached a sensitive understanding that the United States would try to give Gorbachev scope to deal politically with the Baltic peoples' demands for independence by not pressing its formal position in support of their goals. In turn, the Americans insisted that he not use force in dealing with the Baltic problem. Gorbachev understood.[74]

The same nonconfrontational tone that had been evident in the meetings was apparent in the friendly press conference given by Bush and Gorbachev at the conclusion of the summit. The two leaders had decided on the spot to hold their press conference jointly. The press conference would send a message to the world about how the Americans and Soviets had handled the issue of Germany and Kohl's proposal. Asked specifically about German unity and Kohl's plan, Bush said that the United States and NATO had a long-standing position, mistakenly adding that "Helsinki spells out a concept of permanent borders." He had made clear, he said, that Washington would act with restraint—"not to go demonstrating on top of the Berlin Wall to show how happy we are about the change. We are happy about the change." The president affirmed that the rapidity of change was a matter for the German people to determine themselves.

Picking up the question, Gorbachev fell back on the "Helsinki process." That process, he said, "summed up the results of the Second World War and consolidated the results of that war. And those are realities." The two German states were a reality. That "was the decision of history." His thesis was that "history itself decides the processes and fates on the European continent and also the fates of those two states." He warned against any "artificial acceleration or prompting" of the processes that are going on in those two countries.[75]

Gorbachev had given the impression, publicly and privately, of being uneasy though not gravely concerned about developments in Germany. None of the hostility Mulroney had seen a week earlier was in evidence. Gorbachev, defender of the USSR, meeting with Mulroney in the heart of the Kremlin, had been replaced by Gorbachev the statesman, philosophical about the historic transformation taking place in the world. Bush, in turn, had soft-pedaled his presentation of the U.S. position on Germany as he noted and took advantage of the low-key Soviet approach.

But Gorbachev's relaxed demeanor convinced the Americans that the Soviet leader was malleable on the German question. As the meetings wrapped up in Malta, Baker and Scowcroft's advisers talked about avoiding any situation in which the Soviet Union might be forced to say no to some concrete proposal on Germany. They reasoned that the Soviet government did not seem to know where it was going, so the West should not try to force Gorbachev to declare a bottom line.

Was that the impression that Gorbachev intended to give? His close aide Chernyayev, who has remained unfailingly faithful to Gorbachev, provides an interesting insight into that question. Commenting generally about Gorbachev's character as a statesman, Chernyayev has remarked on his "renowned tendency to seek compromise, his predilection for bringing about peace everywhere, and hence his calculated readiness to accept what he does not really approve of. When he does this it is because he finds it necessary to pacify his opponent so as to prevent him from drawing undesirable conclusions or doing something wrong and believes that afterwards things will take care of themselves and agreement will be reached." Chernyayev judged that this trait "makes Gorbachev as a person and politician at once strong and weak."[76]

In retrospect, some considered Gorbachev's handling of the issue at Malta to be a fateful error. One of the participants on the Soviet side in Malta, Marshal of the Soviet Union Sergei Akhromeyev, later reflected bitterly that Gorbachev's failure to give a "concrete answer" to the German question must have convinced the West that they would encounter no decisive opposition from the USSR. "G. Bush realized that had a position like this been formed, it would have been expressed by M. Gorbachev in Malta . . . It is hard to doubt that G. Bush informed H. Kohl about this shortly," wrote Akhromeyev. He blamed Gorbachev, and he blamed a Foreign Ministry that "was not ready for a serious discussion" of the issues.[77]

The European Summits

As President Bush flew from Malta to Brussels for his meetings with allied leaders, he faced another formidable task. Having determined that Soviet policy on Germany was still relatively quiescent, he now needed to accomplish the remaining operational objectives for his trip. Most crucial among them was to rally allied support behind Kohl's ten-point plan for unity providing a safe harbor for Kohl while using America's now solid position with the chancellor to link moves toward unification with assurances about Germany's continued commitment to NATO.

Soon after his plane touched down in Brussels, Bush met with Chancellor Kohl. Baker chose not to attend the dinner meeting, deliberately permitting the two heads of state to talk without Genscher (Baker's counterpart) present and thus allowing Kohl to speak more freely.[78] To the Germans, Bush and Scowcroft seemed tired. But Bush launched into a detailed report on the talks in Malta. The American president warned Kohl that Gorbachev thought the chancellor was in too much of a hurry. Kohl said he had reassured Gorbachev that no one wanted events in the GDR to get out of control.

Kohl then thanked Bush for his "calm" reception of the ten-point plan. He promised not to do anything reckless. There was no timetable. The FRG was part of Europe and part of the EC. The chancellor said he always worked carefully with President Mitterrand. Continued integration with the West was a "precondition" for the ten points. After free elections in the GDR, the next step was confederation, but with two independent states. The third phase, federation, lay in the future. It would take years, perhaps as many as five, to reach this goal.

Bush summarized Gorbachev's attitude as one of uncertainty. That, he said, was why "we need a formulation which doesn't scare him, but moves forward." Kohl assured Bush that he did not want Gorbachev to feel cornered. The newspapers were full of nonsense, he said. Kissinger thought the Germanys might come together within two years. That was obviously impossible—the economic imbalance between the two states was too great. But Bush should not misunderstand; the unification question was developing "like a groundswell in the ocean." West European reactions were mixed. "I need a time of quiet development," Kohl remarked, sounding a little drained by the extraordinary events of November.

Both the White House and the Chancellery considered this dinner conversation significant. The Americans found Kohl clearly determined to move forward toward unification. The Germans felt somewhat relieved about the way Gorbachev had approached the unification issue with Bush at Malta. Scowcroft felt sure Kohl now understood that the United States would stand by him, and Scowcroft was right.

The NATO summit meeting of sixteen heads of government, to be held in Brussels on December 4, would consist of two main sessions. In the morning the president would debrief his counterparts on his meetings in Malta. In the afternoon he would offer a general overview of the future of Europe, which Blackwill and Zelikow drafted before the trip. They had started with a paper originally prepared when Blackwill was first flirting with the idea of a landmark joint statement by President Bush and Gorbachev and turned it into a statement of American policy toward Germany and Europe. It included an outline of NATO, CSCE, and the EC as the central institutions for Europe's future. The draft welcomed the possibility of German unification. Scowcroft had circulated the draft to Secretary of Defense Cheney, who had endorsed it with enthusiasm.

On the road, Bush's planned policy statement was significantly revised, principally by Zoellick and Blackwill. The revisions on Germany were especially important. In late November Baker had endorsed four clear guidelines for American policy on German unification which had been put together for him by Dennis Ross and Francis Fukuyama of his policy planning staff. Although the press took little notice, Secretary Baker first publicized an initial version of these four principles in his pre-Malta briefing for the White House press corps in Washington on November 29.[79] During the trip Zoellick suggested that Baker's four principles be inserted into Bush's statement. Blackwill agreed, and the traveling party worked on the language, strengthening its endorsement of German unification. The draft was reviewed and approved by Scowcroft, Baker, and Bush.

President Bush began the afternoon session before the NATO leaders with his policy statement about "the future shape of the new Europe and the new Atlanticism." The alliance, he said, faced great choices in consolidating the peaceful revolution in the East and providing the "architecture for continued peaceful change." The United States and NATO had never accepted the "painful" division of Europe. All had supported German reunification, he said, "and in our view, this goal of German unification should be based on the following principles":

> *First,* self-determination must be pursued without prejudice to its outcome. We should not at this time endorse nor exclude any particular vision of unity. [The earlier State Department addendum saying the outcome must also be acceptable to Germany's neighbors had been dropped.]
>
> *Second,* unification should occur in the context of Germany's continued commitment to NATO and an increasingly integrated European Community, and with due regard for the legal role and responsibilities of the Allied powers.[80]
>
> *Third,* in the interests of general European stability, moves toward unification must be peaceful, gradual, and part of a step-by-step process.
>
> *Lastly,* on the question of borders we should reiterate our support for the principles of the Helsinki Final Act.

Bush added: "An end to the unnatural division of Europe, and of Germany, must proceed in accordance with and be based upon the values that are becoming universal ideals, as all the countries of Europe become part of a commonwealth of free nations. I know my friend Helmut Kohl completely shares this conviction." Then Bush proposed, following up on the "Europe whole and free" rhetoric of his May 1989 trip, that the alliance should make the promotion of greater freedom in the East a basic element of its policy. At the same time, NATO should continue to be the guarantor of stability in this period of historic transition. In this context Bush said: "I pledge today that the United States will maintain significant military forces in Europe as long as our Allies desire our presence as part of a common security effort . . . The U.S. will remain a European power." Bush also praised "intensified" integration of the EC and said that the United States would seek closer ties with the community.[81]

After Bush completed his statement, Chancellor Kohl remarked that no one could have done a better job of summarizing the alliance approach: "The meeting should simply adjourn." After an awkward pause, Italian prime minister Giulio Andreotti asked to continue with his presentation. He warned that self-determination—if taken too far—could get out of hand and cause trouble. Kohl snapped back that Andreotti might not hold the same view if the Tiber divided his country.

The Dutch prime minister, Ruud Lubbers, interrupted the skirmish between the Germans and the Italians to support Bush's approach. Prime Minister Thatcher could not let the matter rest there. She said that she shared Andreotti's concerns and wanted to study Bush's proposal more carefully. But one by one, other allied heads of state supported the general thrust of the Bush approach.[82]

Thatcher felt defeated, both by the American stance on Germany and by Washington's strong support for the further integration of Europe. After the NATO meeting in Brussels, she later wrote: "[I knew there] was nothing I could expect from the Americans as regards slowing down German reunification [and] possibly much I would wish to avoid as regards the drive towards European unity."[83] Kohl and his advisers, by contrast, were elated. The NATO framework would now dominate the treatment of Germany at the EC summit four days later. The world leaders would not derail Kohl's plan. "On the contrary!" Teltschik wrote. "The signal stayed green—caution will be admonished, but the railway switches are all thrown the right way."[84]

Gorbachev Strikes Back

The NATO allies were not the only ones to get the news from Malta. Warsaw Pact heads of government also gathered on December 4 to hear Gorbachev's report.[85] All these states were now ruled by communist "reformers" except for Poland and Romania. Gorbachev praised the Malta summit and President Bush. He said that Bush did not lecture him as Reagan sometimes did, but instead formulated careful positions "slowly, thoughtfully." In Gorbachev's book of his public and private statements, the chapter on Malta is titled "A Historic Breakthrough." Privately, too, Gorbachev felt he could trust Bush.

But Gorbachev was displaying second thoughts about the German issue. According to one participant, he told the East European delegates that both NATO and the Warsaw Pact must be maintained to preserve Europe's security. Kohl's ten-point speech, he said, had gone too far. Gorbachev asked for comments. There were none, except for a bitter tirade from Romania's dictator, Nicolae Ceauşescu, a man whose overthrow and execution by his own people was then only three weeks away. Hans Modrow, in Moscow for the Warsaw Pact meeting, was able to meet with Gorbachev, who told him that the East German's "treaty community" idea was acceptable only if it did not lead to German unification.

Storm clouds were forming around Modrow's once hopeful government. By early December it was clear that the East German people would force their leaders to allow free elections, whatever this choice might mean for the future of socialism in the GDR. On December 1 the Volkskammer voted to revoke the constitutional guarantee of the SED's leading role in politics. The country was rocked by disclosures of top-level corruption. Shortly afterward the entire SED Politbüro, then the full Central Committee, resigned their positions.

The arrests of former top officials began on December 3. They were charged with corruption and abuse of power. Krenz resigned his post as head of state on December 6, leaving Modrow alone at the top. Civil authority began to break down. Some citizens' committees seized public buildings in order to stop secret police destruction of incriminating government records.[86] There were several attacks on East German and then Soviet military installations in the GDR. The Soviet press angrily warned that "attacks on military property would not be tolerated." The situation became so unstable that on December 7 or 8 Soviet military commanders ordered Soviet forces in the GDR to undertake "emergency measures to protect themselves and property."[87]

Ambassador Yuli Kvitsinsky was recalled from Bonn back to Moscow to help prepare a long, highly secret interdepartmental paper on upcoming Soviet negotiations with the government of the GDR. The paper contained his still controversial proposal to persuade the East German government to press the idea of a German confederation as an alternative to unification. Kvitsinsky reminded his colleagues that the paper could be put forward only after it had been formally approved by the Politburo of the USSR. Yakovlev and Falin came to East Berlin, where, on December 8, Modrow's beleaguered party was holding a congress to plan the next steps. The visiting Soviets, Falin in particular, offered their frustrated hosts little beyond philosophical musings about the need for two German states.[88]

On December 5 Gorbachev abruptly dropped his philosophical tone. The appeals to history and to Kohl's "sense of responsibility" were not working. Bush and Kohl had received the impression from Gorbachev that he was not anxious about Germany's future, perhaps because—as Chernyayev noted—Gorbachev liked to avoid confrontation in personal discourse. Now he seemed frustrated and angry that they had misread his message. To Chernyayev, Gorbachev seemed angriest that the West Germans had not consulted him about Kohl's ten points. Yet when he had the chance to tell the American president that directly, he had not done so.

Perhaps there was no single cause for the shift in Gorbachev's mood. The situation in East-Central Europe was continuing to deteriorate. Czechoslovakia, Bulgaria, and Romania were all in the throes of crises. At home, pressures from the republics and from a relentlessly outspoken Boris Yeltsin were building. Now, with the GDR trembling again with internal crises, yet another gamble—this time on Modrow—was on the verge of collapse. The stakes were very high. As the situation worsened in the GDR, Gorbachev had reason to worry that a loss of face on Germany might be the final straw, radically altering the domestic balance of power in Moscow and with it all that he had worked for at home.[89]

Genscher was the first target of the wrath of the now anxious and angry

Soviet leader. In an extraordinary meeting which Chernyayev—who was present—thought went "far beyond the bounds" of Gorbachev's usual discussions with statesmen, Gorbachev treated Genscher like an errant child.[90] He told Genscher at the start that the conversation would be serious and Genscher would not be spared, especially since the two men knew each other well and Gorbachev felt he could be direct. Then Genscher delivered a general presentation about Soviet-German rapprochement. Gorbachev said he could only welcome such comments. But more needed to be said.

This was a test of history, Gorbachev remarked, and he could not understand why Kohl had come out with his ten-point plan. Kohl's demand for revolutionary political change in the GDR as a condition for German assistance outraged him: "One should say this is an ultimatum, a 'diktat.'" The move had been an "absolute surprise" to Gorbachev, who thought that he and the chancellor had reached an understanding in their phone conversation on November 11. "And after that—such a move!"

Or perhaps the chancellor did not need this understanding anymore. "Perhaps," said Gorbachev, "he thinks that his melody, the melody of his march, is already playing and he is already marching to it." This attitude could not be reconciled with the talk of constructing a common European home. Kohl had promised a balanced, responsible policy. But Gorbachev attacked the ten-point plan in detail. These confederation ideas, Gorbachev exclaimed, what did they mean for defense and alliance membership? Would the FRG be in NATO or the Warsaw Pact? "Did you think this all through?" he demanded of Genscher.

Genscher loyally defended the ten-point program, though in fact he had been as surprised by it as Gorbachev was. He pointed to the qualifying language, to the vague assurances, to the goodwill of the German people, who, Genscher said, had learned from their mistakes. It was a proposal, not an ultimatum. Gorbachev would not be assuaged. "Never mind all that," he said. The German chancellor was treating citizens of the GDR as if they were his subjects. Shevardnadze interjected dramatically: "Even Hitler didn't permit himself this." Gorbachev made it clear that Kohl's conditions for helping the GDR amounted to demands for revolutionary change. Genscher tried to explain, but Gorbachev said he was not fooled. This line of thinking from Kohl "was a political blunder." The Soviets "left no doubt" that the GDR must remain an independent state and a member of the Warsaw Pact.

Breaking with what had become a practice of downplaying differences between Western and Soviet leaders, the Soviet press went out of its way to emphasize that Genscher's meetings with Gorbachev, Shevardnadze, and Yakovlev had been "extremely frank."[91]

Gorbachev formally reported on his German policy to the Communist party's Central Committee in a plenum on December 9. "We underscore with all resoluteness," he declared, "that no harm will come to the GDR. It is our strategic ally and a member of the Warsaw Treaty." He harshly attacked Western attempts to "influence the processes underway in socialist countries" and promised to "neutralize attempts at such interference, in particular, in regard to the GDR."[92]

Meeting Gorbachev in Kiev the day after the Soviet president had savaged the West German foreign minister, French president Mitterrand heard firsthand about the Soviets' anger over Bonn's behavior. At the end of November Gorbachev had phoned Mitterrand and reportedly told him that on the day Germany unified, "a Soviet marshal will be sitting in my chair." At their meeting in Kiev Gorbachev began with a philosophical discussion, but Mitterrand replied bluntly, "Today the problem is Germany." Mitterrand emphasized the all-European process. The German component should be a part of all-European politics, "not overrun it." He was not afraid of a unified Germany, but the Four Powers had to safeguard the balance of power in Germany's relationship to Europe.

Mitterrand, like Gorbachev, thought that Kohl was hurrying. He had said so to Genscher on November 30, and Genscher had not seemed to disagree. Gorbachev recounted how he had talked "rudely" to Genscher the day before, criticizing Kohl's plan as a "diktat." Mitterrand expressed his surprise at the tone and pressed Gorbachev for the details. Mitterrand mentioned his plan to visit East Germany and asked if Gorbachev would like to join him there. Though this move would have been seen as a tremendous boost for Modrow, Gorbachev seemed too astonished by the suggestion to reply. Mitterrand asked at one point, "What should we do concretely?" But neither leader had answers to that question, and the meeting ended inconclusively.[93]

With Soviet concerns ringing in his ears, Mitterrand flew back to France to prepare for another EC summit, a meeting of the European Council, which he would chair in Strasbourg on December 8. Mitterrand soon found that the British wanted him to help open up a second front against Kohl's plan. Discouraged by Bush's handling of the NATO summit meeting, Thatcher had still not given up. Her attention turned to Paris. "If there was any hope now of stopping or slowing down reunification," she recalled, "it would only come from an Anglo-French initiative."[94]

Mitterrand and Thatcher had two private meetings in Strasbourg on the margin of the summit. The subject was Germany. Thatcher recalls Mitterrand as being "still more concerned than I was." Mitterrand criticized Kohl's plan and commented disparagingly on the Germans. So what could be done? Mitterrand said that Kohl had already gone well beyond the assurances he had offered EC colleagues in Paris a few weeks earlier. Mitterrand, according to Thatcher, commented that at times of great danger France and Britain had always established special relations. Such a time had come again. But the two leaders could not agree on a plan of action.[95]

At least France could ease its worries by assuring itself that steps toward German unity could be matched by equally large steps toward European union. This was just the approach Jacques Delors, president of the European Commission, had chosen to adopt. On these points Kohl was ready to agree; Mitterrand would be pushing on an open door. So France was able to accomplish its most important operational objectives for the Strasbourg summit of the European Community. Mitterrand won Kohl's support for convening, in late 1990, an intergovernmental conference to amend the Treaty of Rome, which had created the European Community, in order to prepare a new treaty adopting economic and monetary union. In return the EC endorsed Germany's movement toward unification in terms similar to the guidelines proposed by President Bush at the December 4 NATO summit.

Yet the language on Germany was contested. The German negotiators, led by Kastrup, sought unequivocal support for self-determination. The French and the Italians objected that the Germans alone could not determine Germany's future. Genscher thought that the German attitude toward monetary union would be the test for earning Mitterrand's support. Bonn passed the test. After a sometimes heated discussion, the EC heads of government agreed on a single modest paragraph:

> We seek the strengthening of the state of peace in Europe in which the German people will regain its unity through free self-determination [the traditional formula]. This process should take place peacefully and democratically, in full respect of the relevant agreements and treaties and of all the principles defined by the Helsinki Final Act, in a context of dialogue and East-West cooperation. It also has to be placed in the perspective of European integration.[96]

Kohl commented later on the "icy climate" he had encountered among his fellow leaders in Strasbourg. The winds from Moscow were chilly too. The United States had been watching with alarm as pressure was being put on Kohl. He seemed to be isolated on all fronts. Gorbachev may have been calm at Malta, but now he seemed furious. In Bonn, though, Teltschik was still discounting the Soviet worries as nothing but "appeals and warnings." After all, when West Germany had accepted deployment of new U.S. nuclear forces in 1983, "the Soviet leadership had threatened us with war and missiles."[97] Fortunately for Bonn, the Soviet, British, and French governments seemed to have an attitude without a policy.

The top priority for Moscow was to find some diplomatic brake that could slow developments in Germany. Gorbachev's late November proposal for a "Helsinki II," a CSCE summit, was still on the table even though the Soviet leader had failed to press the idea at Malta. From the Soviet perspective such a summit could treat the German problem in the context of broader changes in European political structures, such as the nature of the two alliance systems. Mitterrand had openly backed the Soviet suggestion, and other West European governments were sympathetic, although Genscher showed more interest than Kohl.

The U.S. government seriously considered the Soviet idea for a Helsinki II, but officials disagreed on how to reply. At the State Department both Seitz and Ross urged Baker to "respond more positively to Helsinki II, even press it" as a way to hold the allies together and get others to agree with the ideas for Europe-wide change that President Bush had announced in Brussels. Seitz's specific recommendations were more reserved, however, since he thought that in practice several conditions would have to be met before a CSCE summit could be held, including signature of a CFE (conventional arms control) treaty. Zoellick also thought about preconditions, both for CFE and for winning Europe-wide agreement on norms of democratic governance and principles of free enterprise. To Baker the debate seemed a bit abstract, since even Seitz's conditions, he noted, "would put it [the CSCE summit] in late 91 or 92 at earliest."[98]

The NSC staff vehemently opposed the Helsinki II idea and counseled the president to resist it when he met with Mitterrand in December. Blackwill feared that a CSCE summit would divert attention from CFE. Any 1990 summit, he thought, should just be dedicated to signing the CFE treaty. Otherwise the idea could develop into an "open-ended negotiation about the future of Europe in about the worst multilateral setting one can imagine." Scowcroft agreed. Fortunately for Washington, the issue never came to a head. When he met with Bush in December, Mitterrand did not press the question of a summit. Doubtful of its merits and not under strong compulsion to agree, the Americans remained cautious, and the idea of a CSCE summit to deal with the German question stalled.[99]

In any case, the Soviet Union—rarely able in this period to pursue a policy line for very long—pushed its own idea aside in favor of a different proposal for a Four Power meeting. On December 8, the day before Gorbachev explained his policy to the Central Committee, Moscow proposed a meeting of ambassadors of the Four Powers "within the shortest possible time" in Berlin to address grave concerns about events in the GDR and a possible breakdown of public order there. The Soviets had no trouble getting French and British support. Mitterrand, still in Strasbourg for the EC summit, conferred with colleagues and backed the Soviet proposal for the first meeting of Four Power ambassadors since the conclusion of the Quadripartite Agreement in 1971. Asked if Bonn would be displeased with the Four Power meeting, a senior French official replied, "That is the point of holding it."[100] Although they had rejected the idea at U.S. urging on November 10, a great deal had happened in the interim to increase the unease of the French and British.

The State Department and the White House quickly agreed that the Soviet proposal clashed with U.S. policy, settled since mid-November, against invoking Four Power intervention to regulate German internal developments. Trying to avoid an open breach within the alliance, Washington fashioned a reply to the British and French, proposing that a meeting be held, but only to discuss the allied Berlin initiative (originally offered by Reagan in 1987 and renewed by Bush in May 1989) to enhance Berlin's status as an international city through sports events such as the Olympics, conferences, and student exchanges. As a sovereign country, the Soviet Union would of course be able to talk about whatever it wished.[101] In a break with the tradition of Four Power consultations, the proposal was sent to Bonn as well.

The West Germans, however, did not want a meeting of the World War II victors from which they were formally excluded. "We were furious," Kastrup recalled. Genscher felt "embarrassed." They urged Kohl to treat the idea as totally unacceptable. Still, Bonn finally went along with the American idea for a limited meeting with a limited subject. The Americans just wanted the meeting to be held quickly and with little fuss. Baker was preparing to go to Berlin (on the evening of December 11), and the United States wanted the Four Power affair to be over before he arrived. The December 11 meeting of the four ambassadors took place in the Allied Control Authority building in Berlin's American sector.[102]

It began with a careful U.S. statement about the old Berlin initiative. The Soviet ambassador to East Germany, Vyacheslav Kochemasov, reiterated the now standard line that the existence of the two German states was a reality whose fate could only be determined by history, and proposed institutionalizing regular meetings of the Four Power ambassadors, to be prepared by a "multilateral working group." This would turn the Four Power forum into the regular institution for diplomatic discussions about developments in Germany. The United States managed to achieve Western consensus on the spot to decline this invitation.

Despite the meeting's modest content, the fact that it was held at all angered many West Germans. Ambassador Walters thought that the widely reprinted picture of the four ambassadors of the victorious powers standing together in front of the old Allied command headquarters was "the worst picture of the year." But one of the Soviet officials involved thought that the meeting had been the warning shot which "beyond all doubt, [was] one of the major conditions that enabled the revolution in the GDR to remain bloodless." The Americans had reasoned that the best way to diffuse tensions at that moment was to do something to bring the Soviets down from the ceiling. Moscow needed an outlet for its anxiety. So in fact did Paris and London. The meeting—as uncomfortable as it was for the Germans—served its purpose.

The more important priority for the United States was to keep the path for Kohl open—free of conditions that Moscow, or the French or British for that matter, might attach. In early December the only addendum to Bonn's goals were the principles articulated by Bush, putting Kohl on the record in support of continued German alignment with NATO. As one of Genscher's top advisers put it, "In this way Bush had made Germany's NATO membership an unequivocal prerequisite for the later process of unification, like the solution of the border question with Poland."[103]

A week after the Strasbourg summit, Mitterrand flew to St. Martin in the Caribbean to review developments in Europe in person with President Bush.[104] They discussed the future of Germany at some length. Again Mitterrand tried to find the proper balance. Though not projecting the alarm Thatcher recalls from the Strasbourg summit, Mitterrand was clearly very troubled about developments in Germany. This time he agreed with President Bush that Germany could unify, with "a proper transfer" of power. But the objections of the Soviets, Poles, Czechs, Belgians, Danes, Italians, and others could not be ignored. Mitterrand had told Kohl (the two leaders had just met in Switzerland) that Germany should go no faster than the EC, or the whole thing "will end up in the ditch." Mitterrand repeated that, for him, developments in Germany were linked to developments in NATO and the EC. He could understand what the Germans wanted, and it was hard to stop them. But if Kohl went too fast, he could cause a diplomatic crisis. It would have the wrong effect, complicating East-West relations at a time when the West was winning hands down.

Baker pointed out that the NATO and Strasbourg summits had shown the way to a common position. Mitterrand agreed with Bush, but he was trying to manage the contradictions of the situation. Fast movement could disrupt the equilibrium in Europe and on the frontiers. Like Gorbachev, Mitterrand had been annoyed by Ambassador Walters's speculation that reunification could occur in as little as five years. Bush replied that Walters's view was not official, and was not being repeated. Nevertheless, Mitterrand argued, Walters said it in Germany, and the Germans heard it. We should not encourage more speed, he said. There also needed to be movement on arms control, EC integration, and Euro-American relations. Mitterrand's anxiety seemed to spill over as he went on to say that there had to be a new Europe or Europe would be back where it was in 1913 (an analogy Mitterrand had also used in Kiev), and everything could be lost.

Baker Travels to Berlin and Potsdam

Consequently, as Secretary Baker traveled to Berlin on December 11, he knew that the political environment in Germany was increasingly unstable. Soviet fears were growing, and the narrow Four Power outlet the allies had granted them would not placate Moscow for long. The CIA estimated that a complete political reshaping of East Germany was now certain to occur within months, leading to noncommunist rule and a dramatic intensification of sentiment for reunification. State Department officers reported that the West German parties tended to support Kohl's program, but with significant qualifications. Genscher was going out of his way to reassure the Soviets that their interests would be addressed. In December, even in conservative Bavaria, "an almost universal disquietude about inconceivably rapid developments seems to be gaining the upper hand." If Kohl stumbled, the Federal Republic's commitment to take on the difficult task of moving toward unity might fade.[105]

En route to Berlin, the secretary stopped off in London and heard again from Thatcher about her unhappiness with premature consideration of German unity. In Berlin Baker's first major event was a speech (principally drafted by Zoellick) to the Press Club in the Steigenberger Hotel, which addressed his trip's primary objective: to consolidate a common Western vision of how Europe's political structures could adapt as the Continent's division—and, it was hoped, the division of Germany—came to an end. His speech was titled "A New Europe, a New Atlanticism: Architecture for a New Era."[106]

In Brussels President Bush had already outlined his thoughts on how Europe could "consolidate the fruits of this peaceful revolution and . . . provide the architecture for continued peaceful change." Baker explained in his address that the "new architecture for a new era" must first offer an opportunity for the division of Berlin and of Germany to be overcome through peace and freedom. Second, it should reflect the continued linkage of America's security to Europe's security.

The first element of the new architecture would be a new mission for

Signing of the final settlement for Germany, Moscow, September 12, 1990. Seated from left to right: James A. Baker III; Douglas Hurd; Eduard Shevardnadze; Roland Dumas; Lothar de Maizière; and Hans-Dietrich Genscher. Mikhail Gorbachev can be seen standing behind Dumas, listening to Soviet deputy foreign minister Yuly Kvitsinsky. (Bundesbildstelle Bonn)

Mikhail Gorbachev and George Bush, Camp David, June 1990. From left to right: Baker, Barbara Bush, George Bush, Raisa Gorbachev, Mikhail Gorbachev, Shevardnadze, Brent Scowcroft, and Sergei Akhromeyev. (Bush Presidential Materials Project)

Bush meets with advisers at the White House. From left to right: Scowcroft, Vice President Dan Quayle, Bush, Baker, Robert Gates, and Press Secretary Marlin Fitzwater. (Bush Presidential Materials Project)

Bush and advisers at his summer residence, Kennebunkport, Maine. From left to right: Treasury Secretary Nicholas Brady, Quayle, Philip Zelikow, Bush, Robert Blackwill, Baker, Raymond Seitz, Dick Cheney, Robert Zoellick, and Colin Powell. (Bush Presidential Materials Project)

Baker and Bush at the NATO summit in Brussels, May 1989. (Bush Presidential Materials Project)

Erich Honecker and Helmut Kohl, Bonn, May 1987. (German Information Center)

Commemorating the fifth anniversary of the westward exodus of East German asylum seekers from the FRG embassy in Prague, September 1994. From left to right: Genscher's successor as foreign minister, Klaus Kinkel; Genscher; and Rudolf Seiters. (German Information Center)

Horst Teltschik. (German Information Center)

Wolfgang Schäuble. (German Information Center)

Margaret Thatcher and Bush, Camp David, November 1989. (Bush Presidential Materials Project)

Bush and advisers review talking points for meeting with Gorbachev. From left to right: White House chief of staff John Sununu, Fitzwater (seated against wall), Dennis Ross, Condoleezza Rice, Scowcroft, Baker, and Bush. (Bush Presidential Materials Project)

François Mitterrand and Bush, St. Martin, December 1989.
(Bush Presidential Materials Project)

Hans Modrow and Kohl. (German Information Center)

NATO. In addition to its traditional role of deterrence and defense, the alliance would attend more to nonmilitary aspects of security, specifically including the CFE treaty and arms control verification. The alliance would also need to pay more attention to regional conflicts and the proliferation of weapons of mass destruction. It would consider new Western initiatives, as in the CSCE, to build political and economic ties with the East. NATO's example of a cooperative, not coercive, alliance for common security was important for Europe. Even the interests of the Soviet Union would be served by maintaining a vigorous NATO.

The second element would involve the future development of the European Community. Building on Bush's May 1989 announcement, the United States would renew its support for political as well as economic integration within the community. Baker proposed "a significantly strengthened set of institutional and consultative links" between the United States and the community, as well as expanded EC support for the new democracies of Eastern Europe.

A final element of the new architecture was the CSCE. Baker argued that the CSCE had outgrown the pessimistic view in 1975 that it would only codify the postwar status quo. Instead, the organization had set up standards for human rights and consultation that were already helping to overcome the division of Europe. To go further, Baker proposed new agreements in each of the organization's three "baskets" of issues: security, economic transactions, and human rights.

In the economic basket he offered a new initiative—building on a suggestion Bush had presented to Gorbachev in Malta—to involve the CSCE in setting guidelines for the transition from planned to free market economies. These principles could be agreed on at the CSCE intersessional meeting already scheduled for Bonn in May. In the human rights basket the secretary renewed the idea—first introduced by Bush in his May 1989 Mainz speech— of asking the CSCE to set standards for the conduct of free elections. New Europe-wide rules for democratic governance could become the top priority for the CSCE.

Baker then turned to Germany. He reiterated the four principles the president had stated in Brussels. He told his German audience that "this very positive course will not be easy, nor can it be rushed. It must be peaceful. It must be democratic. And of course, it must respect the legitimate concerns of all the participants in the New Europe."

The repetition of the four principles on German unification now received much wider public notice in Western Europe. The French and British press was positive, while the mainstream West German press, to quote *Die Welt*, commented that the U.S. approach could provide "the decisive support for a newly-forming Europe and especially for German reunification." Even Shevardnadze later told Manfred Wörner that he had carefully noted the step-by-step approach recommended in Baker's speech. Bush had promised American leadership. His policy statement at the NATO summit and Baker's speech were now delivering on that promise.[107]

But the Americans were a little unnerved by what they saw in Berlin. Along the motorcade route campaign slogans had been plastered everywhere by the CDU, which was gathering for a party conference: "One people; one nation!" Meeting with Kohl over breakfast on December 12,[108] Baker pressed Kohl to be more careful in his handling of the Soviets, British, and French. Baker began the conversation by restating the consistent American support for German unification. But surely, he said, Kohl could understand the nervousness of the USSR, Britain, and France.

The German chancellor warned that the West might be embarking on a dangerous path in confronting the German people. The FRG did not want to upset the current equilibrium in the GDR. But the most dangerous gate "on this slalom course" was public opinion, as opposed to the opinions found in the media. The people of the two German states wanted to grow together. They had to be offered a "perspective" on how they might eventually reach their goal. Again, Kohl explained, unification would take a number of years. But now his estimate was three or four years, not five or ten. First there would be "contractual relationships" and then confederal structures—such as joint governmental committees—even before a confederation, which was still short of federation. But people had to be shown "a perspective." Without it, there was a danger of violent frustration in the GDR.

Kohl then informed Secretary Baker, in confidence, that he hoped to see Gorbachev soon. (In fact, the Soviets would stall and refuse to see the German chancellor until early February.) Kohl said that he understood Soviet concerns, which stemmed from the war. It was Kohl's feeling that Gorbachev objected only to making federation the goal of the ten-point plan. Kohl argued that if he had not put forward his plan, the Soviets might have proposed reunification linked to the neutralization of Germany in a reprise of Stalin's ploy in 1952. Such a move, he asserted, had been in the air.

Kohl was glad that the United States did not have the complexes other Europeans had about Germany. Thatcher opposed mentioning unification as a goal, hoping it would go away. The British had won two world wars and lost an empire. Germany had lost twice but was again the premier power in Europe economically. Some thought the prospect of adding another 17 million Germans to this force was a nightmare. Kohl had told Thatcher, shortly after visiting Churchill's grave, that the difference between Kohl and Thatcher was that Kohl lived in the post-Churchill era. Mitterrand, in Kohl's view, was more farsighted than Thatcher. He recognized that the key was to tie Germany to Europe, to the EC. This was why Kohl was ready to push for new European monetary integration even over the objections of the Bundesbank.

Baker replied that Germany's nervous neighbors had to be reassured about Bonn's firm ties to the West. The borders issue was also important. Kohl said that those who were worried about the Oder-Neisse border talked about borders in the plural because they wanted to freeze the inter-German border as well. The FRG had made commitments to Poland on the Oder-Neisse line and would stand by them, even if it still lacked the legal authority to make commitments for "Germany as a whole." In an implicit linkage between flexibility on the inter-German border and the Polish-German border, Kohl believed that if German reunification were on the table tomorrow, there would be no problem for Poland's border. Kohl said that he was being completely open with the Americans. The FRG's relationship with the United States was its most important international tie. He would maintain a step-by-step approach. He knew that Washington had reacted positively to his ten-point plan. He asked repeatedly for continued U.S. understanding and support.

Baker advised that everyone's statements on the German question were being carefully scrutinized and the chancellor would need to take care that his statements were not taken out of context. The secretary was pleased that the chancellor supported a gradual and peaceful strategy which took account of others' concerns. There would be resistance. That was why it was so important for the process to be handled correctly.

Knowing that Kohl believed that the pace of events in the East was quickening, Baker had to decide whether to visit the German Democratic Republic. At the end of November Baker had read a CIA analysis of the changing relationship between the two German states. He studied the paper carefully and came to one clear conclusion: "GDR holds key!"[109] Baker would be the first U.S. secretary of state to visit the GDR, and the political situation there was very unstable, offering much to worry about. Would Baker's trip be read as support for two German states and a rejection of Kohl? On the evening of December 11 Baker conferred with his advisers, with Ambassadors Barkley and Walters, and with Minister Harry Gilmore of the U.S. mission in Berlin. Barkley favored a stop in the GDR; Walters disagreed. Baker decided to go.[110] After consulting first with Kohl and Genscher, he arranged a meeting in Potsdam (not in Berlin), in the GDR, with Modrow and with church leaders who had played such an important part in mobilizing opposition to the old regime. Toward dusk on December 12 the secretary and his party drove across the Glienecke Bridge, scene of spy exchanges in the bitterest days of the Cold War, into Potsdam.

One factor in Baker's decision was his desire to bolster the Modrow government sufficiently so that it could prepare free multiparty elections for the GDR (then planned for May 1990). As Baker began his meeting with Modrow,[111] U.S. officials were startled when there entered the room a man who looked like the former SED leader Egon Krenz, whom Baker would never have agreed to see. They were relieved when he turned out to be a waiter who merely bore an eerie resemblance to Krenz.

Baker, like Kohl, linked any Western economic assistance for the GDR to fundamental political and economic reform. He stressed the importance of genuinely free elections. Modrow pledged his commitment to reform. The church leaders assured Baker that they too counted on Modrow to manage the transition to free elections. The clerics openly described their fears about the future. There was widespread anger about the disclosures of communist corruption and a desire for vengeance against the hated secret police. The danger of violence was real. Furthermore, the churchmen believed that popular desire for unification with the FRG, as the shortest path for matching the material prosperity of the West, was growing. The clergymen did not necessarily sympathize with this mood, but they had to reckon with it nonetheless. Baker noted that the two Germanys could come together economically before moving to political unification. But the Lutheran leaders thought that the people would demand more, and they feared that international conditions would not permit the rapid movement toward unification needed to appease the demands for an accelerated process.

Immediately after his meetings in Potsdam, Secretary Baker traveled on to Brussels, where he met with EC foreign ministers on December 13, principally to discuss the status of economic assistance for Eastern Europe. Most important, on the evening of December 13 he had a working dinner with Foreign Ministers Hurd, Dumas, and Genscher to discuss Berlin and German issues. The ministers responded positively to the themes articulated in Baker's Berlin speech. But the Germans were still angry about the sight of Four Power ambassadors standing together in Berlin. Genscher felt that there should never be another such meeting. Never again should the Germans be left sitting at the "cat's table." Behind the scenes Genscher's advisers had begun to warn of the danger of a new peace treaty "like Versailles." Baker put his hand on Genscher's arm and said, "Hans-Dietrich, we have understood you."[112]

Other European statesmen pursued their own efforts to moderate the quickening pace toward German unity. Mitterrand, completing his energetic round of diplomatic consultations, met with Modrow in East Berlin on December 21 and called for caution, as well as closer GDR ties to Western Europe. Privately one of Mitterrand's advisers warned Teltschik again that Kohl was going too fast in pressing the pace of change.[113]

Nevertheless, as 1989 drew to a close, Helmut Kohl clearly held the reins in determining Germany's future. Bush and Baker had deliberately decided to legitimize Kohl's program, and the United States had succeeded in adding its own objective—Germany's continued membership in NATO, anchoring the FRG firmly to the West. The U.S. diplomatic strategy was intended to calm the Soviets and keep the allies from descending into renewed national hostilities so that Washington's and Bonn's goals could be achieved.

Chancellor Kohl tried to reassure the Soviets. He sent a message to Gorbachev promising not to destabilize the situation in Europe. It was the people, he wrote, who were putting the German question back on the agenda. Any developments would be embedded in all-European structures. He recognized the legitimacy of Soviet security interests. As this message was being delivered, Gorbachev was sending his own letter to Kohl. Its tone was cold. Gorbachev said that the USSR would do all it could to "neutralize" intervention in the GDR's internal affairs. East Germany was a strategic partner of the Soviet Union, and the existence of two German states was a historic fact.[114]

Kohl, as he had told Baker he would, tried to meet with Gorbachev, but the Soviet leader rebuffed him, saying that he did not have time at present. According to several officials, the Soviets were trying once again to reevaluate their policy options.[115] Perhaps Gorbachev was still angry and wanted to keep Kohl waiting. But here Moscow again forfeited a chance to define the agenda. By the time the meeting took place in February, the German Democratic Republic was a walking corpse.

Undaunted by Gorbachev's rebuff, Kohl pressed on with the first steps in his ten-point plan, meeting with Modrow in Dresden on December 19 to begin negotiating new agreements on social, cultural, and economic ties between the two German states. Kohl indicated a readiness to help Modrow stabilize the GDR and listened sympathetically to a request for billions of marks in aid. The leaders announced that they would open the Brandenburg Gate in Berlin as a border crossing and remove the remaining restrictions on cross-border movement in time for Christmas.

The Dresden trip was important for Kohl, bringing home the momentum of East German opinion and providing an opportunity to seize the moment. Addressing cheering crowds in Dresden, Kohl spoke emotionally of the German nation and was met with chants for unification. Kohl had rallied political support for his cause within his party. He had kept his program for unity on the table. And now, as he had hoped, the East German people were rallying to the dream he, Kohl, had told them could come true.

In Washington, even the Americans were beginning to fear that the CDU was acting imprudently. Conceding that Kohl had scored a public relations coup in his visit to East Germany, Secretary Baker advised President Bush that Kohl's activities "may raise again the question with some, however, of whether the Chancellor's domestic political interest is leading him too far, too fast on the issue of unification; he's tapping emotions that will be difficult to manage."[116]

It was clear that the frenzied diplomacy in the month after the opening of the Berlin Wall had dramatically altered the political landscape. Genscher's adviser Frank Elbe captured the change when he recalled that in the middle of November he had told Zoellick that "the tempo of German unification cannot be permitted to endanger the stability of Europe." In early December Elbe was now telling Zoellick, "If German unity *doesn't* come, *that* will endanger the stability of Europe."[117] As pressure mounted in 1990, no one doubted any longer that the two German states would come together as one. The most difficult challenge now was to determine when and how, and to balance these plans against the danger of a new East-West crisis that could plunge Europe back into a cold war.

～ 5

The Process Becomes the Two Plus Four

AT THE START OF December 1989 the Soviet foreign minister, Eduard Shevardnadze, was wondering how to translate Moscow's concerns about German reunification into an international policy. He knew that the Soviet government had lost the initiative. In November his ambassador in Bonn, Yuli Kvitsinsky, had urged him to forge ahead of Kohl and recover the momentum with a plan for a confederal Germany, to be sponsored, of course, by the East Germans. The Soviet government had judged the plan too radical. When the East German government had pressed the idea of a limited confederation, the Soviet government had remained anxious but passive.

So weeks had passed without Kohl's move receiving any clear public rebuff. Kohl's announcement had shrewdly used the language of confederation, but Germans East and West knew that the pole of unification now guided Kohl's compass. In this climate many East Germans were now thinking the unthinkable, speculating about direct unification with West Germany rather than some sort of confederation that would preserve separate East and West German states. The Soviet Union thus faced a very tough decision—whether to fight unification inch by inch or side with German national aspirations, freely accepting some form of unification in order to insist on conditions that would protect the perceived interests of both the East German republic and the USSR.

Shevardnadze was preparing to give a major address to the Political Commission of the European Parliament in Brussels on December 19.[1] Unhappy with the hard-line speech drafted for him by the European Department of the Foreign Ministry, he asked his close aide Sergei Tarasenko to compose more forward-looking remarks. The foreign minister wanted to concede the possibility of unification yet force states to confront the serious issues that would arise. Tarasenko, though no expert on Germany, obliged. But as he set out to prepare the delicately balanced speech, his job was made harder by the stance that Gorbachev had taken on December 9 at the meeting of the CPSU's Central Committee. As we saw in Chapter 4, Gorbachev's angry and inflexible remarks, probably influenced by the views of the top Central Committee international adviser, Valentin Falin, left no doubt that the Soviet Union would fight for the GDR's continued existence and continued acceptance of the "postwar realities."

Gorbachev's firm public position had to be taken into account in preparing Shevardnadze's speech. Shevardnadze could not imply that Moscow accepted German unification. Thus, Tarasenko prepared a draft that focused on the conditions to be attached to unification, appearing to accept the possibility that unification might occur. The draft went back to the European department, where Alexander Bondarenko and his deputy were upset with what they saw. They angrily confronted Tarasenko, telling him that they could not accept the possibility of unification. It could not be discussed this way. "Tell that to the minister," Tarasenko shot back. The officials then took their disagreement to Shevardnadze. Bondarenko insisted that Shevardnadze not go beyond Gorbachev's statement. Shevardnadze retorted that he was a minister, "not a parrot." He could not go to Brussels and speak nonsense. Moscow needed a constructive approach, not just a negative stance of trying to block developments.

His speech was polished, and Shevardnadze departed for the West with his text mostly intact. He did not clear the remarks with the Politburo, nor did he circulate his draft to the Central Committee staff. But Shevardnadze respected Kvitsinsky's knowledge of Germany and shared his draft speech with this seasoned diplomat. Kvitsinsky also thought the Tarasenko draft went too far. He cleverly edited the speech to tilt it away from implicit acceptance of unification and harden the conditions. Shevardnadze received Kvitsinsky's rewrite at the last minute, after he had arrived in Brussels. Tarasenko protested the changes, but Shevardnadze chose to accept them.

The result was that Shevardnadze's speech—the first comprehensive Soviet policy statement on the revival of the German question—was a strange hybrid of old policy and new.[2] The minister seemed to muse indecisively before the world, raising questions but providing no answers to them. The premise of the speech was that German unification was indeed on the agenda: the possibility had to be considered. But then Shevardnadze also appeared to rule out unification while at the same time posing questions about how it could occur. He offered no alternative conception of East Germany's future. The effect was at once puzzling and ominous.

Europe, Shevardnadze said, faced a choice between experiencing a "polarization of forces" or becoming a "polycentric community of peoples and states." If the entire legal structure of Europe were not taken into account, it was possible that one state might "catch some point of detail or other and by pulling it upon [itself], bring about the collapse of the whole structure."

Shevardnadze restated Gorbachev's public stand expressed at the Central Committee plenum, including the warning that any departure from the postwar reality of two German states would threaten "destabilization in Europe." The Soviet Union would, however, support peaceful cooperation between the GDR and the FRG based on respect for the equality and sovereignty of both states. Yet the future progress of such cooperation would be determined by history "within the framework of development of the all-European process," a clear link to parallel progress in the CSCE. This, he said, would clearly be "interstate" cooperation as envisioned in the 1972 treaty between East and West Germany, thus hinting at the Soviets' readiness to support some sort of confederation.

But then, becoming even more strident, Shevardnadze warned that the Helsinki process of pan-European cooperation should not "go to ruin on German soil. That is impermissible." The allied powers had legal rights over Germany, and as if that were not enough, Shevardnadze added frighteningly, the Four Powers "have at their disposal a considerable contingent of armed forces equipped with nuclear weapons on the territory of the GDR and the FRG."

So the postwar realities could not be ignored. These included the postwar borders, and anyone who reopened the "definitive and irreversible" borders of Europe would block further advancement in relations between the GDR and the FRG. "Self-determination" was important, but it did not give "instructions on how and at what times to change the state structure of the GDR." There had been a chance to get a united democratic Germany, Shevardnadze acknowledged, but that time was gone. It had passed after rejection of the Soviet note of 1952 and the FRG decision to join NATO.

Having denounced German unification unequivocally, Shevardnadze then posed seven questions that would have to be addressed by anyone who hoped to restore German unity. They were:

First, where are the political, juridical, and material guarantees that German unity, in the long term, will not create a threat to the national security of other states and to peace in Europe? There is no answer to this question.

Second, will such a hypothetical Germany—if it comes into being—be willing to recognize the existing borders in Europe and renounce any territorial claims whatsoever? As is known, the government of the FRG is avoiding an answer to that question.

Third, what place would this German national formation take in the military-political structures existing on our continent? For one cannot seriously think that the status of the GDR will change radically while the status of the FRG will remain as it was.

Fourth, in the event of German unity taking shape, what will be the real potential of this new formation? What will be its military doctrine and the structure of its armed forces? Will it be prepared to take steps toward demilitarization, to adopt a neutral status and radically restructure its economic and other ties with Eastern Europe as was envisaged in the past?

Fifth, what will be the attitude toward the presence on German soil of Allied troops and to the continued operation of military liaison missions and to the Quadripartite Agreement of 1971?

Sixth, how will the possible creation of such a German formation tie in with the Helsinki process? Will this promote its constructive development in the direction of overcoming the division of Europe, eliminating any discrimination in mutual relations between European states and further movement toward creating unified legal, economic, ecological, cultural, and information zones in Europe?

Seventh, if the German states do in some way express themselves in favor of starting to move toward the unity of the Germans, will they be ready to consider the interests of other European states and, on a collective basis, to seek mutually acceptable solutions for all issues and problems which may arise in this connection, including concluding a European peace settlement?[3]

Looking back in his memoirs, Shevardnadze considered this speech to have been an important breakthrough, one in which he dramatically conceded the possibility of unification in order to recapture the initiative. This may have been the minister's original intention. Yet the speech Shevardnadze actually delivered reflected the dilemmas of Soviet foreign policy without resolving them.[4]

Shevardnadze's warnings went largely unnoticed in a West German press preoccupied with Helmut Kohl's tumultuous visit to Dresden, civil strife in Romania, and the American invasion of Panama. Some in the West German Foreign Ministry found the speech worrying. The Soviets were now publicizing the harsh message they had given privately to Genscher two weeks earlier. But Genscher, meeting with officials, held up an article from the popular newspaper *Bild-Zeitung* which suggested answers to Shevardnadze's questions: that the Germans would not accept neutralization but would consider abolishing both alliances or reducing the American troop presence to a "symbolic contingent" if the Soviets would just say what they wanted. Genscher told the officials, if you want to know our answers to these questions, read this article! Teltschik, at the Chancellery, preferred to see Shevardnadze's questions as an effort to initiate a dialogue on the terms of unification.[5]

Still, the Soviets' open hostility left Kohl exposed to domestic political criticism. His position became more vulnerable as West German politicians called on him to state his acceptance of the postwar border with Poland. The respected president of the republic, Richard von Weizsäcker, urged the government to reaffirm that the border with Poland was inviolable. His CDU colleague Bundestag president Rita Süssmuth also suggested a joint FRG-GDR declaration that would again recognize Poland's western border. Kohl called this proposal "unacceptable," noting that the FRG's position was already clear and that neither the FRG nor the GDR had the legal authority to settle the border question in a more definitive way. The Four Powers had long since reserved the ultimate power to determine the borders of "Germany as a whole." Kohl's position was legally defensible. But many West Germans believed Kohl's argument to be a clever dodge, designed to pander to a few voters who resented the loss of so much historic German territory in 1945 and who might be attracted away from the CDU to far right-wing opposition parties. Kohl was thus attacked for sacrificing international stability on the altar of his domestic political ambitions.[6]

Kohl was also under pressure from the new, more reformist East German government headed by Hans Modrow. The Modrow government was weak but was fighting to broaden its base of popular support. Modrow's government had established a partnership with a "roundtable," created under church auspices, that included more than thirty delegates from every existing political faction. Most of these delegates reflected the views of the dissident elite that had led or helped organize the protests of October and November. These dissidents, like Modrow, opposed unification and pressed instead for reconstruction of the GDR, searching for a "third way" between communism and capitalism. Communist trade union representatives even threatened to stage a general strike if the government moved toward unity with the capitalist West.

The roundtable agreed on a May 1990 date for new parliamentary elections. The members of the roundtable began to act as a surrogate parliament, taking on the still powerful and recalcitrant secret police by publicizing new revelations about the murderous activities of the Stasi. The East German Communist party, the SED, under its new reformist leader Gregor Gysi, changed its name to the Party of Democratic Socialism, or PDS (for a time it was known by the hybrid acronym SED-PDS). For a short time it looked as if the GDR might regain its footing with a new program of reform socialism.

With the date for free elections set, Modrow turned his attention to Bonn and pressed Kohl to make good on his Dresden promise of comprehensive aid. Kohl balked. He refused Modrow's request for an emergency sum of DM 15 billion but stalled by authorizing negotiations on economic aid. Meanwhile, respect was increasing for Modrow's government, and though polls were not wholly reliable, there seemed to be greater support for the East German leader's "treaty community" between the two German states than for unification into one country.[7]

Helmut Kohl was clearly at another crossroads. Conditions in East Germany were unsettled; the Soviets were hostile. He was under fire within his own party and from his coalition partner, Hans-Dietrich Genscher. His plan for unity was on the table, but what was the next step? Talks with Mitterrand at the French president's home in southwest France shed no new light. The momentum toward unity had surely slowed as 1989 came to an end.[8]

The Soviets Push Again for Four Power Intervention

There was anxiety in Washington, too. George Bush's four principles on German unity had shielded Kohl's program from Western attacks while tying it to German membership in NATO. The principles had served their purpose. Now the United States needed a new policy too.

As Robert Blackwill paused to think about next steps, he wondered whether America ought to slow down the process it had helped to accelerate. He was worried about what the Soviets might do. Blackwill and a member of his NSC staff, Robert Hutchings, sent a memorandum to Brent Scowcroft arguing that Gorbachev, alarmed by the threat to the GDR's existence, might call for a German peace conference, perhaps inviting all the World War II combatants.[9] Gorbachev might well persuade other countries to agree, especially if he pleaded privately that his political and even personal survival was at stake. At such a German peace conference, the Soviet leader could then propose that Germany be reunified over a period of years, under conditions of neutrality and substantial demilitarization. The Soviets might propose, for example, that Germany remain in the EC but not in NATO. The East Germans would support the Soviets on the substantive issues, while the British and the French would want to brake moves toward unification. Bonn and Washington would be diplomatically isolated.

The NSC staffers went on to suggest that Kohl would find himself under unbearable pressure to offer the withdrawal of foreign forces and nuclear weapons from Germany in order to win Soviet acquiescence to German unification. He could attempt to replace German NATO membership with various bilateral security guarantees between Germany, America, and other states. Intelligence analysts had earlier given just such an estimate of likely German and European reactions to the dynamics of a possible German peace conference.

Blackwill and Hutchings therefore concluded that, "given the difficulties of managing a peace conference proposal issued by a desperate Gorbachev, our aim should be to insure that such a Soviet initiative never comes to pass." To stave off such a Soviet proposal, the United States might need to use "such influence as we have to slow down artfully the reunification process this year and bring some order and predictability to it—for our sake as well as Gorbachev's."

Scowcroft did not agree. He too was worried about what the Soviets might do. But the die was cast with Kohl, he thought, and Bush's views were clear. The United States would simply have to find another way to handle the Soviet problem.

Moscow was indeed searching desperately for a way to slow down the process of unification. The Soviets settled on a push for Four Power intervention. Shevardnadze sent a message stating that the "Big Four" understood that "a requirement may arise for some parallel or coordinated steps with respect to German affairs." The Four Powers could not be indifferent to the FRG-GDR negotiations on their new "treaty community." Shevardnadze called for Four Power discussion of the developing relations between the FRG and the GDR. He suggested that special envoys or the four ambassadors in Germany take up the task.[10]

The United States promptly informed the FRG about the Soviet proposal. Alarmed, Genscher immediately wrote letters to Baker, Hurd, and Dumas urging the "closest consultation" about a proposal that had such "fundamental significance" for the Germans and East-West relations. Genscher did not need to worry about the American stance. Secretary Baker thought that he and Genscher had agreed a month earlier, in Brussels, to resist Soviet calls for Four Power intervention in German politics. Washington accordingly suggested to its allies that they all answer the Soviet note with an offer to talk about only cultural and commercial contacts in Berlin. The discussions would be conducted by lower-ranking diplomats.

As expected, the British and French wanted to be more receptive to Soviet concerns. But the four Western countries finally agreed to a reply along the lines suggested by the American government.[11] The Western answer to the Soviet proposal temporarily held off the push for direct Four Power regulation of German unification. The West Germans were adamant. In December Genscher had made it clear that he hoped there would be no further meetings of Four Power ambassadors. His political director, Dieter Kastrup, categorically informed his U.S., British, and French counterparts that under no circumstances could the four World War II victors sit down together in the Allied Kommandatura to consider the German political situation. Kastrup was duly assured that there was no intention to form a Four Power directorate that would negotiate over the head of the FRG.[12]

Rebuffed in this first attempt, the Soviets tried again. Protesting the suggestion that West Berliners might finally vote in West German elections, Soviet diplomats in late January called again for Four Power intervention and summoned apparitions from the past. Their note referred to "recently intensified activities of right-wing extremist and neo-Fascist forces in the FRG, GDR, and some other West European countries," and added, "Attempts to play down the significance of the neo-Nazi threat are untenable as they are refuted by the facts." The note called on the United States to join in concerted action against "the increase of 'brown' danger which accompanies the process of rapprochement between the two German states," suggesting action both in the CSCE and through Four Power mechanisms. The State Department was puzzled by the way this note was delivered (by the deputy chief of mission rather than the ambassador) and by the "old-fashioned and almost hysterical language" of the comments. Washington informed Bonn and other allies about this second demarche but decided essentially to ignore it. Still, it was a disturbing glimpse into the Soviet bureaucracy's mental image of developments in Germany.[13]

Through most of January 1990, the United States, along with the FRG, France, and Britain, had hoped for time to devise answers to the hard questions about how German unification might come to pass. There was a delicate balance to maintain. Both Washington and Bonn hoped that Modrow could hold his country together until the elections in May. Although neither Bush nor Kohl wanted to stabilize the communist government, they did not want a sudden collapse. Kohl and his CDU colleagues hoped that the communists would be swept out of office in May and that East Germany's new leaders would take the GDR down a gradual path toward confederation, then federation, as envisioned in Kohl's plan, with unification possibly being achieved as early as 1994 or 1995.

But in the unsettled environment at the end of the Cold War, no policy line seemed to hold for very long. Just weeks before it had seemed that Modrow—forming his roundtable and speaking of market reform—might stabilize the GDR. But in January 1990 conditions in the GDR deteriorated, and policies that had seemed bold in November and December were about to be overtaken by events.

Bonn and Washington Hit the Accelerator

Although Modrow was weathering some of the storm of political criticism following the first wave of disclosures of corruption and Stasi abuses, he was increasingly besieged by grave economic problems, especially the lack of foreign exchange. Krenz had revealed the full extent of this danger to Gorbachev at the beginning of November. With press censorship lifted, the East German people learned what Krenz had told Gorbachev months before: the GDR was an economic Potemkin village and had been living beyond its means for nearly a decade. West German cash had been the lifeblood of the GDR economy, subsidizing the inefficiencies of central planning and paying the bills for Western goods.

Modrow's government had no answer to the economic crisis. He had difficulty staffing key positions and was unable to put together a budget. His program, supervised by economics minister Christa Luft, at first included only a few market elements. It offered little scope for privatization even as state enterprises, starved for subsidies, were starting to go bankrupt.

Tensions grew between the Modrow/roundtable government on the one hand and Kohl's government and the city government in Berlin on the other. Bonn saw that money given to the East German government would be wasted without fundamental market reforms. The East realized that West German demands amounted to the imposition of the Western economic system on East Germany. Accepting these Western demands would crush any hope of finding a "third way" to rebuild the GDR based on reform or on genuinely democratic socialism. Both Modrow and the East Berlin intellectuals who dominated the roundtable thought that Kohl's CDU was looking ahead to using its economic leverage to buy votes for its political opponents, led by the CDU-East party headed by Lothar de Maizière.

Even in the political sphere Modrow's government had not fully satisfied the popular demand for reform. Some old and discredited figures still held high office. The government parroted Moscow's preoccupation with the neo-Nazi threat to justify maintaining the hated secret police apparatus. East Berlin first changed the police name from Stasi to an even more unfortunate acronym, Nasi, then, realizing the error, changed it still again. Tens of thousands of demonstrating citizens stormed and pillaged the central secret police headquarters in East Berlin on January 15. In some areas the East German government simply ceased to function. East Berlin asked the West Berlin municipal authorities to take over the East's garbage collection. By January 16 West German officials who met with Modrow noted that he, and even the CDU-East's de Maizière, were at the edge of "despair."[14]

Many East German citizens were no longer prepared to wait for internal reform. The flow of refugees—including some of the country's most highly skilled young people—reached an average of about two thousand a day in January, and Modrow conceded that many of those who remained were packing their bags. For those who stayed, the road to meaningful internal reform seemed so long that they began to see unification with the FRG as their only salvation. This seemed to be the alternative to the painful reform that the people of Poland and Hungary were enduring.

Kohl's success in making unification seem possible was gnawing away at the stability of Modrow's government. People began to imagine that absorption into the FRG would instantly bring them into a magnificent social welfare system, secure the value of their future earnings, and sweep away the debris of the old, repudiated, even hated communist structure as nothing else could. The widening gap between the attitudes of the public and their political representatives posed a danger of collapse in the GDR, and possibly even violent confrontation, even before the scheduled elections in May.

For weeks West Germany and the United States watched as the gap between their policies and the realities on the ground widened. In January the governments of both countries conducted reviews of their policies. There is no one point at which Bonn decided to discard the gradual approach. This policy envisioned some initial confederal structure, probably involving economic and monetary unity, and coordinated with East German entry into the European Community. But there had to be a viable GDR as the receptacle for a new, reformed, noncommunist state. That possibility was diminishing daily as the East German people grew restless and impatient. Kohl's warning to Baker in December that the push for unity might come from the streets suddenly seemed prescient. Demonstrators, now constantly on the march, often chanted "Deutschland einig Vaterland," Germany united Fatherland.

Modrow himself confessed to Kohl, on the margins of a larger meeting in Davos, Switzerland, that he could no longer rely on some branches of his government to obey his orders. The East German state did not seem to be working anymore. It could not pay its debts. There was a sense that the country was falling apart, a conviction reinforced for Kohl when it was repeated to him by Katherine Graham, the American news magnate, after she had visited Berlin and the GDR.

Kohl had publicly agreed to meet with Modrow in February, to cap another phase of negotiations for the terms of confederation. But Kohl became convinced that he should have nothing to do with Modrow or any other official of the old Communist party. By the time Modrow proposed a draft treaty for confederation, Kohl was no longer interested.

Instead Kohl began preparing to take another risky leap. Seeing the CDU-

East, despite its former status as a puppet party of the communists, as the only available Eastern ally for his own party, and also seeing the coming elections in the East as a preview of those in the West, Kohl started to imagine a direct path to the unification of Germany on his terms. He and Teltschik became convinced that the East German elections should be held soon, earlier than May. The pressures in the GDR were tremendous, and Modrow himself realized that he could not hold the country together until spring. When Modrow and the roundtable advanced the elections from May 6 to March 18, Kohl welcomed the move, although he, like Modrow and the West German SPD, thought that earlier elections would actually favor the communists and the SPD-East since they had the best-known and best-organized parties in the GDR.

Kohl was still speaking of a five-year timetable for unification. When Mitterrand's adviser Jacques Attali called Teltschik on January 29 and, during the conversation, offered a bet that Germany would be united by the end of the year, Teltschik laughed nervously. But, by dropping any effort to negotiate a step-by-step arrangement with Modrow, Kohl had dramatically altered his course. The alternative to a confederal structure negotiated with Modrow's government was a straight line toward unification with no stops in between. And that policy made sense on only one timetable—as fast as the international traffic could bear. When Teltschik met Scowcroft at a conference in Munich on February 3, he discovered that the White House had come to the same conclusion: there should be a direct move, and at the fastest possible pace.[15]

Washington had begun to adjust its course in the second half of January. The bureaucracy was still churning along, trying to think of ways to bolster the stability of Modrow's government. A working-level meeting on January 11 concluded that the United States should prepare an aid program for the GDR following the pattern already set in providing aid to Poland and Hungary. But as soon as top officials learned of the idea of sending U.S. money to Modrow, the idea died.[16]

At the White House, Blackwill was worried, as he told Scowcroft, that "we seem to be proceeding with business as usual—unwieldy . . . extended interagency disputes too small to be seen without the aid of a magnifying glass; routine and episodic exchanges with our Allies, etc. You will know the quality of exchanges on these breathtaking developments in Europe at your breakfast meetings with Baker/Cheney." The United States needed a more ambitious policy. Shaking off the pessimism of late December, Blackwill had concluded that the sooner Germany became unified, the better. There should be a rush toward de facto unification along lines worked out between the United States and the Federal Republic. The international community would be presented with a fait accompli. That might mean the Americans would waive their Four Power rights, but Washington should spare no effort to seize the high ground with the German people as the foremost advocate of their national unity.[17]

Blackwill feared that, if unification were stretched out for years, the Soviets and others would find too many opportunities to trade their acceptance of unity for concessions from Bonn on Germany's NATO membership, its military participation in the alliance, and the presence of American forces and nuclear weapons in Europe. At the moment the Soviets wanted the friendship of the West, and their German policy was cautious, even confused. But Blackwill thought that this window of opportunity would not stay open much longer. The West should move quickly. Western European concerns should also be put aside. Blackwill advised Scowcroft on January 26 that "reunification is coming rapidly, not gradually and step by step, and the process will not await 'an increasingly integrated European Community.'" Baker and his aides had arrived at the same judgment separately.[18]

But what would the Soviets do? Blackwill asked Rice to make the assessment for Scowcroft. She argued that "creeping reunification—because everyone is afraid to talk about terms—is probably not very smart." Of course, Gorbachev would be alarmed if the pace quickened. Rice preferred to try to achieve rapid reunification through a six-power negotiation that would include the two German states. The Soviets would resist a more rapid pace. Yet they were in a difficult position, and Rice thought that the United States should go ahead and hit the accelerator. She made a crucial judgment: "I believe (and this is a hunch and I guess if we did this that I would spend a lot of time in church praying that I was right) that the Soviets would not even threaten the Germans. Within six months, if events continue as they are going, no one would believe them anyway."[19]

Gorbachev and Modrow Develop a New Plan

While the Americans were making guesses about Soviet thinking, the Soviets themselves were trying to decide what to do. But once again, the dizzying pace of change in and around the Soviet Union made it difficult for the leadership to concentrate—even though Germany was arguably the most important foreign policy problem confronting the country. It is hard to imagine life in the Kremlin in early 1990. Soviet leaders must have looked back with nostalgia on the earlier days of perestroika and the "new thinking," when events seemed to follow Gorbachev's baton and the world acclaimed every performance. Now, in this winter of 1990, Vadim Zagladin, an adviser to Gorbachev, greeted Rice at the Kremlin and apologized for being late, saying, "These days are very difficult. I come to work every day to see what new disaster has befallen us."

In December, while he was considering policy toward Germany, Shevard- nadze had been distracted by his anger over the government's cover-up of the facts surrounding the massacre of civilians in his home capital of Tbilisi, in Georgia. He offered his resignation to Gorbachev, who refused to accept it and persuaded Shevardnadze to stay on.

Even larger issues loomed in the Baltic republics of the Soviet Union— Lithuania, Latvia, and Estonia. Once part of the czarist empire, these nations had gained their independence after World War I. In 1940, while Hitler and Stalin were dividing up Eastern Europe, the USSR had forcibly annexed these short-lived republics. (The United States had never recognized these annexa- tions.) The communist leaders of Lithuania were encouraged by Gorbachev's "new thinking" and the turmoil in Europe to take the bold step of formally breaking relations with the central government in Moscow. At the beginning of 1990 the Lithuanian leaders demanded full independence from the USSR. After narrowly heading off demands for immediate use of force against the dissident republic, Gorbachev canceled all his foreign appointments and headed a delegation that flew to the Lithuanian capital, Vilnius, on January 11. The results were inconclusive.

A little more than a week after the talks in Lithuania, new nationalist unrest in Azerbaijan obliged Gorbachev to send defense minister Dmitri Yazov to the scene. Yazov ordered the use of force, and hundreds were killed during fighting in Baku on January 20.

Meanwhile, Soviet policy toward Germany was going nowhere. Gorbachev had stopped calling Ambassador Kochemasov in East Berlin and seemed to have lost interest in daily developments. The periodic pleas for Four Power talks elicited no action. Shevardnadze's December statement had had little lasting effect. A month after his "seven questions" speech Shevardnadze was still musing vaguely about developments in Germany, warning the West but offering few ideas. The Soviets indicated support for a proposal of the new East German communist leaders that all nuclear weapons be removed from Germany and showed interest in their suggestion that all foreign troops leave German soil too. Yet Moscow had no diplomatic plan for pushing these ideas. It was diplomacy backed by the threat of an international crisis, not some overt use of force, that worried the Americans. They understood how the danger of an East-West crisis would transform West Germany's domestic politics. In December Blackwill had feared that Gorbachev might call for a German peace conference. Neither this nor any other threatening initiative had materialized.[20]

This, then, was the setting when Gorbachev convened an extraordinary meeting of advisers to discuss policy toward Germany, on January 26 after he had returned from his talks in Lithuania.[21] Falin had suggested gathering a "crisis staff" to work on Germany. Present in his Kremlin office were Shevardnadze, the prime minister, Nikolai Ryzhkov; Politburo member and Central Committee secretary Alexander Yakovlev, along with Valentin Falin, Rafael Fedorov, and Vladimir Ivashko from the Central Committee's international department; Vladimir Kryuchkov, head of the KGB; and Marshal Sergei Akhromeyev, Anatoly Chernyayev, and Georgi Shakhnazarov from Gorbachev's personal staff. Gorbachev set the tone. We must say quite plainly, he insisted, that all premises are open for discussion except one: there will be no action with our armed forces. Thus began four hours of tense debate.

Chernyayev adopted a radical pro-Western position, urging Gorbachev to align himself directly with West Germany. He was blunt. The Soviet government, he said, should work for a mutual understanding with Kohl's ruling coalition. Chernyayev thought that Kohl was a reliable partner, that firm FRG ties to NATO were a good thing, and that Kohl would link German unification to development of the "all-European process." Gorbachev should just drop the discredited East German government, refusing to see Modrow and, especially, refusing to see the new head of the "reformed" East German communists, Gregor Gysi.

Falin and Fedorov disagreed. They argued that Moscow could not abandon either East Germany or its communists. Fedorov even argued that no one in West Germany really wanted reunification. But what can one do? Gorbachev asked. Every alternative seemed to involve some use of Soviet troops. Falin thought that the Soviets, like the GDR, were now harvesting the fruits of a shortsighted policy. Whatever the Germans might decide, the USSR had every right to insist that its interests be respected. It was wrong, he said, to treat the transformation of East Germany into a NATO sphere fatalistically, as something that was inevitable. Yakovlev had been the Soviet point man on the important constitutional changes taking place in the Soviet Union itself and on Baltic issues. He had been at the margins of Soviet policy toward Germany, but in this instance he backed his deputy, Falin. Yakovlev was for action, not contemplation.

Falin was concerned, too, with how Germany might unify, if indeed it did. He grasped the crucial distinction between direct unification through a West German takeover of East Germany and the quite different notion of a confederation of two equally sovereign states. But, by Chernyayev's own admission, no one in the room knew what Falin was talking about.

Shevardnadze and Ryzhkov took a middle stance. They agreed that the

USSR should try to work with, not block, the path of change in Germany. Kryuchkov, for the KGB, was neutral on policy but reported that the old East German Communist party no longer existed and the state structures of the GDR were falling apart. This group all agreed, as Ryzhkov put it, that "one should not give everything to Kohl." The Soviets should work more closely with those seeking to restrain the West Germans, particularly the British and the French. Beyond this, Shevardnadze was looking for guidance from Gorbachev.

Chernyayev recalls proposing that the Soviet government come forward with the idea of negotiating the unification problems in a "group of six," the Four Powers joined by the two German states. No one appears to have suggested either calling for a German peace conference or pressing hard for the earlier idea of holding a CSCE summit to discuss Germany.

Gorbachev then summed up the conclusions. He tried to see all sides of the issue. All agreed with the idea of the "group of six." The USSR would orient itself more toward Kohl. Gorbachev recognized that, realistically, he would have to deal with the chancellor. He was also more favorably disposed to Kohl in January than he had been in December. He knew that earlier in the month he had pressed Kohl to make good on some of his June 1989 promises by asking the FRG for urgent deliveries of food, especially meat. Kohl had responded. Two weeks after the Soviets made their request, the FRG had finalized plans to deliver about a $100 million worth of food, including more than 100,000 tons of meat.

But Gorbachev also agreed that the East German communists should not be ignored. Both Modrow and Gysi would be invited to Moscow at the end of January. The Soviet Union would try to work more closely with London and Paris. Gorbachev was even willing to consider traveling to both capitals in order to build a common front. The unification of Germany should not bring NATO closer to the Soviet border, he said. A united Germany's membership in NATO was unacceptable. Meanwhile, Akhromeyev was asked to look into possible plans for the withdrawal of Soviet troops from East Germany, a plan that should be linked to the East German proposal for the withdrawal of all foreign forces, Western as well as Soviet, from both the FRG and the GDR.

The Soviet government deployed its new policy in coordination with the East Germans during Modrow's January 30 visit to Moscow.[22] Modrow and his advisers hastily refined their own plan for a confederation of two German states, bound by a treaty that would link them economically and in some spheres of governance while preserving political independence. Eventually it might be possible to imagine both German states transferring sovereign powers to the new confederation. The German right to self-determination would be undisputed. So Modrow could announce a plan for "unification" through confederation.

Modrow found Gorbachev brilliant and open-minded but also indecisive and lacking a deep understanding of economic problems. Locked in a battle with Kohl for the hearts and minds of the East Germans, Modrow wanted Gorbachev to pressure Kohl for the economic aid he thought Kohl had promised. Nonetheless, Gorbachev and Modrow found a common basis for work. Gorbachev thought that Kohl's attempt to destabilize the GDR was a mistake which could have consequences for both the FRG and other nations in Europe. He was hopeful that the East German people would vote on March 18 to keep the GDR. Although the Soviets had not openly endorsed a confederation proposal before, Gorbachev liked Modrow's plan, which dovetailed well with the outcome of the Kremlin's policy review. So for the first time the Soviets were prepared to accept the prospect of some sort of German unification, but based on Modrow's confederation plan.

Gorbachev emphasized Soviet interests in security issues and presumed that a future German confederation would be militarily neutral. He could imagine working with the British and the French to develop a plan for all of Europe in which NATO would be transformed and Germany would be neutralized, all sealed by a German peace treaty. Modrow, with little time to consult others in the roundtable or the government, publicly presented his new plan on February 1. Gorbachev and Shevardnadze repeatedly praised the logic of Modrow's approach, conceded the right of Germans to self-determination, and envisioned gradual moves toward confederation. Their vision of this "rapprochement" of the two German states was consistently linked to a peace treaty, the "all-European process," and a new Germany that was militarily neutral and disarmed. Moscow finally had a coherent policy coordinated with East Berlin.

Gorbachev wrote to Bush, describing Moscow's joint policy with East Berlin and warning darkly: "Unification sentiments are boiling over, which someone is clearly trying to exploit in order to create an uncontrollable situation." The best way to deal with this pressure, according to Gorbachev, was to back Modrow's gradualist plan, which would take external interests into account. "Any haste, leaping over stages, overly categorical conclusions and assessments can only result in a chaos," he wrote. Modrow had also agreed, according to Gorbachev, on the need for Four Power involvement in German affairs to address these issues. Despite the earlier discussions within the Soviet government about a six-power forum, Gorbachev referred only to a Four Power diplomatic process. The situation required "a heightened sense of responsibility."[23]

But Bonn and Washington had come to the conclusion that the route to unification should be fast, not slow. Moreover, just as the Soviets were hoping to strengthen their diplomacy by coordinating their new stance with the British and the French, the prospects for such a coalition were already fading. Margaret Thatcher's final attempt to cement an Anglo-French axis to confront the Germans had failed. Discouraged by the American-led blockage of the Four Power avenue, and having clearly failed to win any support from President Bush during her November talks at Camp David, Thatcher now pinned her hopes on talks with Mitterrand in Paris on January 20.[24] Germany dominated their conversation at the Elysée Palace. Mitterrand was annoyed by the West Germans' behavior. He thought, Thatcher recalled later, that the Germans had the right to self-determination, but they did not have the right to upset the political realities of Europe or make their drive for unity take precedence over everything else.

Still, though Mitterrand agreed with Thatcher's analysis of the problem, he could not imagine what might be done. Thatcher believed that there were a number of diplomatic devices available to slow the process down. But, she said, the trouble was that other governments would not speak out openly about their fears. The meeting ended inconclusively. The two leaders agreed that their foreign and defense ministers should confer about German re-unification and greater potential Franco-British defense cooperation, but, as Thatcher admitted, "little or nothing in practical terms came of these discussions between me and President Mitterrand about the German problem."

The fact is that Bonn and Washington were united in a way that made it nearly impossible politically for other NATO allies to go public with their concerns about unification, much less work to derail the process. Without American backing, almost all diplomatic options for Britain and France seemed quixotic. Mitterrand was also not willing to risk his hopes for the future of the European Community on a gambit with the British to confront Bonn.

Washington Answers Three Questions

Once the U.S. government concluded that unification should happen directly and as quickly as possible, it had to face up to other issues that would arise. Three questions seemed paramount by the end of January.

- How quickly did the United States want German unification to happen, and what outcomes for NATO were acceptable?
- What kind of process should the United States support for managing the external aspects of German unification?

- What kind of military presence should the United States plan to maintain in Europe, and particularly in Germany, in the 1990s, and how should this military presence be reflected in the arms control process?

Blackwill at the NSC staff recommended that the United States and the FRG sketch out a blueprint for the security outcomes from rapid unification. The blueprint placed all of a united Germany in the NATO alliance, even if the former GDR territory was demilitarized. Substantial but reduced U.S. forces would remain stationed in Germany. Current FRG-GDR borders would mark the borders of a united Germany. The Four Powers, the FRG, and a newly elected government in the GDR would eventually meet to bless the substance of a German peace treaty. This treaty would then be presented to the CSCE for its information only.[25]

Blackwill discussed his views with a few top officials at the State Department, including Zoellick. Lower-level officials there had been considering the same issues but were coming to quite different conclusions from those the NSC staff had reached. Members of the policy planning staff thought that the United States might need to yield on the NATO issue. Although a united Germany might be a member of NATO, these officials thought that Washington should consider letting Germany leave the alliance's military organization and should be prepared to negotiate the withdrawal of all U.S. as well as Soviet troops from German soil. Working-level diplomats in the State Department's European bureau harbored a different form of pessimism. They thought that the United States should be ready to negotiate the removal of all nuclear weapons from Germany. They also thought that the Four Powers should stay out of the process and that the CSCE should be allowed to ratify a diplomatic solution. But none of these ideas was actually presented to Baker or to the White House. Instead, at the beginning of February 1990 Blackwill's blueprint remained the most influential articulation within the White House and with Baker and Zoellick of U.S. preferences on the international status of a united Germany.[26]

American preferences could not be forced on Bonn, however. The American government noted that Kohl, when asked in a mid-January press interview whether a reunified Germany would be a member of NATO, replied that it was too early to say. President von Weiszäcker began declaring his hope to embed German unification gradually in a European framework, but he would not be more specific. He, too, had no answer to the NATO problem.[27] So the question was left there for the moment, as the U.S. government pondered what process to propose for the unification of Germany.

The Two Plus Four Is Born

Washington had settled on a policy that supported rapid unification but had not articulated a diplomatic process for carrying it out. At the NSC staff this was deliberate. Scowcroft, Blackwill, Rice, and Zelikow all hoped that the two German states could accomplish de facto unification quickly, before the Soviets and others could muster effective diplomatic resistance. Then, when unification was effectively accomplished, the German states could come together with the Four Powers to bless the outcome. At that point, they hoped, the Soviets would have little choice but to go along.

Over at the State Department, Baker's close advisers Dennis Ross and Robert Zoellick had a different view.[28] To meet Soviet concerns they felt that Moscow would have to be offered the chance to participate in some kind of process that would consider aspects of unification as it was happening, not after it was an accomplished fact. Like the NSC staff, they had rejected both the Four Powers and the CSCE approach. But they had developed an alternative mechanism, called the Two Plus Four Power talks, which they described to Secretary Baker. "Over the next several months," they warned him, "the unification process could accelerate to the point that it overwhelms the careful approach you laid out in your Berlin speech." So they concluded that "we need to shift to 'fast-track' unification sequence." To do this they proposed transforming the Four Power process into a Two Plus Four Power forum.

They knew that the West Germans would resent any appearance of Four Power intervention. Although West German participation ameliorated this concern, Ross and Zoellick wanted to be able to go further and explain clearly that "the US will use Two Plus Four Power talks to bring German unity to fruition." The talks would begin only when a freely elected East German government could participate, after the March 18 elections in the GDR.

Creating a forum was thus not enough. Ross and Zoellick said that the forum must be created alongside acceptance of three "irreducible" conditions: (1) the East German delegates must come from a freely elected government; (2) the two German states must be full participants in "consultations" with the Four Powers about German unity; and, most important, (3) all participating countries must agree publicly that the goal of the talks was to produce a mandate for unity, empowering the two German states to accomplish unification. The two officials thought that Moscow, wanting some diplomatic intervention in the process of German unification, would welcome their Two Plus Four idea "but may have to swallow hard on the conditions for such talks." Yet Ross and Zoellick believed these conditions to be essential if the

West Germans were to be persuaded to agree to Four Power involvement in deciding Germany's future.

After submitting their memo to Secretary Baker, Ross and Zoellick shared their views with Raymond Seitz, the head of the State Department's European bureau. Seitz, after consulting with James Dobbins and another adviser, Brunson McKinley, decided to oppose the proposal. He wrote a note to Baker telling him that "Bob Zoellick and Dennis Ross have sent you a memorandum on Germany with which I disagree."[29]

The European bureau made three basic arguments against the Two Plus Four idea. First, Seitz thought that unification might be happening faster than Europe wanted, but it was not "a stampede." The Germans had a sensible plan for negotiation between the two German states. "Raising an alternative or even complementary mechanism is premature at best," he said. Or, as McKinley put it in separate comments, "Two Plus Four is not a 'fast-track unification sequence'; it is a slow track. Two Plus Zero is the fast track." This was, of course, also the NSC staff's view.

Second, Seitz thought that "a Four-Plus-Two formula will be seen for what it is: A Four Power nose under the German tent." This would alienate the Germans. It would place America as an opponent of German self-determination and would signal distrust of the FRG, jeopardizing U.S. influence, which had—so far—been strong.

Third, Seitz thought that U.S. interests were not served by "inviting the Soviets into an essentially German affair, certainly not at this stage." Limited Four Power involvement should take place on the basis of "a tightly restricted, pre-arranged agenda" and should come at the end of the process rather than the beginning. Instead, the United States needed to strengthen its bilateral efforts with the FRG, and with the Soviets. Agreeable substantive outcomes could probably be worked out with the West Germans. With Bonn the United States should concentrate more on Kohl and the Chancellery and less on Genscher.

Zoellick forwarded this dissent to Baker, arguing that the disagreement was really about how best to manage the Soviets. Zoellick maintained that, without a multilateral forum, the FRG would probably be obliged to work out a private deal with Moscow. That was risky. "If the Germans work out unification with the Soviets," he said, "NATO will be dumped and will become the obstacle." Furthermore, without an ongoing multilateral forum the United States might be left behind, out of the game. Zoellick argued that the "timing of two and four is a legitimate question, but if it only becomes a ratifying device, we'll be ratifying a deal the FRG cuts with the USSR."

At the same time the United States was considering the goals and process for a policy on Germany, it had to balance these thoughts with judgments about the future of American forces in Europe. The problem clearly had a military dimension—deciding what forces would be needed as the tensions of the Cold War subsided. But it also had a diplomatic dimension, since the United States was pushing hard to wrap up a treaty in 1990 regulating all conventional forces in Europe; now it also had to respond to proposals coming from Moscow and East Berlin envisioning the complete withdrawal from the two German states of all foreign forces as well as all nuclear weapons.

In 1989 President Bush had promised to keep substantial U.S. nuclear and conventional forces stationed in Europe. His administration believed strongly that, even if the immediate military threat from the Soviet Union diminished, the United States should maintain a significant military commitment in Europe for the foreseeable future. The administration held this view because the political situation seemed so turbulent and unsettled, because U.S. forces in Europe had become vital to projections of American power in other areas such as the Middle East, and because Soviet military power would inevitably remain large enough to overawe Western Europe if the Americans departed. Every European head of government Bush spoke to wanted U.S. forces to stay in Europe, and to stay in strength. The American troop presence thus also served as the ante to ensure a central place for the United States as a player in European politics. The Bush administration placed a high value on retaining such influence, underscored by Bush's flat statement that the United States was and would remain "a European power."

American officials hoped that the continued military presence on the Continent would be anchored by U.S. forces in the Federal Republic of Germany, then the base for about 80 percent—approximately 250,000—of the more than 300,000 U.S. soldiers and airmen deployed across the Atlantic. But U.S. force plans would adjust as the Warsaw Pact's military potential faded. The administration would submit its five-year defense plan to account for those changes in January. Congress would have its own ideas. There was a real danger that the U.S. troop presence could drop precipitously, leaving the allies uncertain about whether the United States would continue to play its part in guaranteeing Europe's security. The challenge to President Bush was to find a way to plan for a continued strong troop presence in Europe, manage the defense budget, and remain a stable and predictable leader of the NATO alliance.

These were fateful judgments. The Bush administration was determined to maintain crucial features of the NATO system for European security even if the Cold War ended. Germany would continue to rely on NATO for protection; the United States would keep substantial forces in Europe as a token of its commitment. The Germans would thus forgo pursuit of a purely national defense, including development of their own nuclear weapons. The United States would accept the responsibility of being a European power, based on a recognition that America's fate, like it or not, had always been linked to that of Western Europe. The task, then, as the Bush administration saw it, was to reduce the American military commitment without setting in motion a free-fall that might wipe it away.

As part of his May 1989 proposal to energize the conventional arms control talks (CFE), Bush had suggested setting a ceiling on U.S. and Soviet stationed troop strength of no more than 275,000. That would mean about a 10 percent cut in U.S. forces and a withdrawal of more than half of stationed Soviet forces. To respond to the momentous events of late 1989, Bush was presented with three new alternatives. Secretary of Defense Richard Cheney, General Colin Powell of the JCS, and NATO's military chief, U.S. General John Galvin, wanted to hold to the 275,000 figure and not trigger a debate over how far to cut. Scowcroft and his staff thought that the debate could not be avoided, so they wanted Bush to shape it with his own proposal dropping to a floor of 200,000 U.S. troops and codifying this figure in the CFE treaty. Baker wanted to retain 275,000 troops until after CFE was signed, but then promise unilateral cuts down to 200,000.[30]

Bush preferred the NSC staff approach, but he wanted to make sure that no new initiative would get in the way of wrapping up a CFE treaty in 1990. He asked the Pentagon to pick an optimal number for U.S. troop strength close to 200,000. They came up with 195,000 for the Americans and Soviets in Central and Eastern Europe and a grand total of 225,000 for all of Europe by 1994. Such cuts would eliminate about a quarter of American troop strength in Europe and the majority of Soviet deployments in Europe outside the USSR.[31]

Bush first called Kohl, who was completely supportive. Kohl also wanted to come to Washington to talk about Germany directly with the president. A date was set for the following month.[32] Bush got more support from Italian prime minister Giulio Andreotti. Mitterrand, however, was less comfortable with the planned American move.[33] Mitterrand first wanted to know Kohl's reaction. The president said that both Kohl and Andreotti had been very supportive. Mitterrand worried that one reduction after another would lead to German neutrality. Bush assured him that the United States opposed such an outcome. Mitterrand suggested that France might also examine its troop commitment in Germany, but he wanted to be sure that Bush would not confuse any French withdrawals with support for the neutralization of Germany, which he thought was the Soviet objective. Bush understood.

Bush asked if Mitterrand was now more worried than before about German neutrality. Mitterrand replied that, given the present drive to reunification, the great risk was that parliaments elected to support unity might spur a great popular movement in favor of ridding Germany of all foreign troops and nuclear weapons. Mitterrand thought that the American proposal made sense, but he wondered if Kohl's enthusiasm for it might actually be a bit troubling. Mitterrand wanted to make himself very clear: the American plan was feasible only if everyone understood that it was not possible to proceed from the necessary reduction of forces to the idea that there would be no American forces left between the Soviet Union and Western Europe.

Bush finally called Thatcher. She too was concerned about retreating piecemeal from NATO positions without taking full account of the pressures that might accompany German reunification. Her ambassador in Bonn had mentioned Kohl's plan to achieve unity in five years, by the end of 1994. There needed to be a fundamental political and strategic assessment of the situation in Central Europe. The prime minister would be talking to her foreign and defense officials at Chequers about these matters. She proposed a fundamental political assessment "between us as only we can do without it leaking." The president delicately acknowledged that there was a "nuance of difference" between the two leaders on Germany, and that they needed to talk about it. Thatcher remained concerned about the fate of NATO if Germany reunified and favored denuclearizing its territory. The president agreed that the "jury was still out" on the implications of the changes in Europe, but he defended his plans for reducing U.S. troops.[34]

Lawrence Eagleburger and Robert Gates, Bush's secret envoys dispatched to explain the plan to the European leaders, encountered reactions similar to those Bush had already heard directly from them. There was serious tension between the British and the Germans. Mitterrand had no difficulty with the proposal itself, but he restated his concerns about avoiding any neutralization of Germany. Kohl repeated his support for a continued U.S. troop presence in Germany but, worryingly, made little reference to NATO. Within the Chancellery, officials were looking for ways to link a drive toward unification with broader European developments, and Teltschik was pleased about "how Bush and Baker are readying the ground for us."[35]

With consultations among key allies complete, the president sent an explanation of his proposed troop cuts to President Gorbachev on January 31, the day he intended to include the initiative in his State of the Union message to the Congress. In his letter Bush told Gorbachev quite candidly that "the U.S. intends, within this ceiling and with the consent of our allies, to retain a substantial military presence in Europe for the foreseeable future, regardless of the decisions you take about your own forces." Bush then phoned Gorbachev and repeated this message. Gorbachev restated the point to make sure that he had understood it, then he promised to consider Bush's proposal in a constructive spirit.[36]

Thus, by the end of January U.S. officials had developed three lines of policy for Central Europe. First, the White House and the State Department had agreed to encourage the fastest possible achievement of German unification and had established how NATO should figure in the outcome to the process. Second, officials at State had developed a design for a Two Plus Four process to negotiate external aspects of Germany's movement toward unification. It would provide an outlet for those who wanted some forum, but it would involve neither Four Power supervision nor a thirty-five–nation CSCE conference. Also, the participants in the Two Plus Four would have to agree that the process had unification as its goal. Third, Bush had decided what level of troop strength the United States should keep in Europe for years to come and how his decision should be tied to the ongoing arms control talks.

In the first half of February the emerging American policy would be juxtaposed against the new approach that had just been devised by the Soviets, along with the East German government. At the same time, the West Germans were organizing their own thoughts about the next steps on their path to national unity. With so much at stake, diplomacy intensified. The British and German foreign ministers went to Washington; the American secretary of state went to Moscow, followed there by the West German chancellor; and foreign ministers from the NATO and Warsaw Pact countries gathered in Ottawa—all within a span of two weeks.

Baker and Genscher Suggest Strategies

Preparing for the weeks ahead, Secretary Baker sat down and talked through his ideas on policy toward Germany with President Bush. Although there is no written record of the meeting between the two men, Baker's notes show he understood that "Soviet statements [were] now recognizing unification will happen, but making clear the *terms* will be at issue." The big risk was that the Soviets would refuse to allow unification with Germany in NATO. American insistence on Germany's membership in NATO might then be seen as the obstacle to unity, and it would be the Americans, not the Soviets, standing in front of the train. So the Americans had to talk frankly with the West Germans about the need to keep a united Germany in NATO, even if the eastern portion were demilitarized. Baker had in mind a straightforward quid pro quo: the United States would help make unification happen, *if* the West Germans stood with the Americans on the issue of NATO.[37]

Baker began his diplomatic work in Washington, meeting with the new British foreign secretary, Douglas Hurd. Hurd held separate meetings with Baker, Scowcroft, and Bush.[38] All agreed that Germany was the chief issue facing the West. Hurd, who had just visited the GDR, agreed, too, that unification was inevitable and could happen quickly. But Hurd was afraid that the consequences of unification had not yet been thought through. That, he said, was why Prime Minister Thatcher was hesitant to endorse unification: she was "a reluctant unifier. Not against, but reluctant." Hurd thought that Mitterrand shared this reluctance (at least when he met with Thatcher), but was just less willing to say so in public.

What had to be thought through? Hurd ticked off the problems: (1) Germany and the EC, for the community was not ready to take in 16 million new people from a different economic system; (2) NATO, where the problem of unification could pose a serious, even lethal blow to the security system; and (3) the USSR, which had to be handled appropriately.

Everyone agreed on the importance of the NATO issue, but no one had a clear solution for addressing it. Baker then opened a discussion of process. The United States would tell the Soviets that Four Power talks were out. But something else was needed. Hurd agreed. That evening two senior British diplomats, Sir Patrick Wright and Ambassador Antony Acland, invited Blackwill and Zoellick to the British embassy for a further discussion. A few days earlier Thatcher had urged President Bush to set up a discreet channel for bilateral U.S.-U.K. discussions on developments in Central Europe. Hurd had raised the matter, and the channel was now being opened, with the British embassy on one side and Zoellick and Blackwill on the other.

Zoellick told the British about the Two Plus Four idea. The British displayed interest but made no commitment. They, like the French (and Genscher), were all moving toward accepting the Soviet proposal for a CSCE summit. This was clearly envisioned as a forum where events in Germany could be related to the concerns of all European countries. Indeed, Hurd told Baker and Scowcroft that the EC foreign ministers, meeting in Dublin, had just agreed to accept the Soviet idea for a CSCE summit, to be held in 1990.

The United States, however, had crystallized its own thinking about such a thirty-five–nation conference. Baker said that Washington could go along with a CSCE summit only if certain conditions were met. First, there had to be more progress on human rights, such as agreement to the U.S. initiative on principles for holding free elections (perhaps at the Copenhagen meeting of diplomats from CSCE countries in June). Second, any CSCE summit had to be preceded by completion of the CFE treaty. (Since the treaty would effectively eliminate the imbalance of Soviet conventional forces in Europe, erasing the advantage Moscow had enjoyed for decades, the Americans intended to use Soviet interest in the CSCE summit as a lever to secure Soviet agreement to this crucial arms control document.) Scowcroft also warned Hurd that the United States would not let a CSCE summit turn into a German peace conference. Hurd did not argue with him. Scowcroft emphasized that the administration preferred that there be no German peace treaty. Chancellor Kohl supported NATO, but in the atmosphere of a German peace conference he might be vulnerable to acute pressure from Gorbachev and other delegates.

Baker's next step was, in some ways, the most important. Hurd's visit to Washington was followed by a meeting with Hans-Dietrich Genscher, who spoke with Baker on February 2. The West German foreign minister was determined to regain the initiative from Kohl and begin taking charge of the West's diplomatic handling of the German question.

First, Genscher had publicly announced that German unification was indeed inevitable. He advocated early progress to accomplish unity, starting with economic and monetary union. As for the process, Genscher spoke out against any use of postwar Four Power structures to regulate German self-determination. Genscher's January 31 speech at Tutzing, "German Unity in the European Framework," was a major public presentation of his diplomatic strategy for the months and years ahead. Genscher had worked on it for weeks with one or two aides, with little analysis of the substantive issues by his ministry's experts.[39] Genscher thought that after the March 18 elections the FRG and GDR could alone negotiate a "treaty charting the course to German unity in Europe." Germany's position in a future Europe would also be clarified. Existing borders would be respected. Germany would remain a member of the EC and of the Western alliance. "We do not want a united Germany that is neutral," Genscher declared.

Genscher's plan was consistent with the Soviet–East German stance in that it envisioned a treaty setting the course for German unity, implying a gradual step-by-step path toward a new confederation. Genscher differed from the East Germans, however, in standing by NATO. To address GDR concerns about these choices, Genscher proposed that there be "no expansion of NATO territory eastwards." The former GDR would not be incorporated into NATO or NATO's military structures. Indeed, NATO itself, along with the Warsaw Pact, would become "elements" of new "cooperative security structures throughout Europe."

The CSCE would be strengthened, with a new framework to be agreed on at the CSCE summit. That summit would be the key European diplomatic forum for considering the "future structure of Europe," including Mitterrand's suggestion for a European confederation. In his speech Genscher suggested ten different institutions the CSCE could set up, from those governing economic cooperation and "conflict management" to others overseeing the environment, science, law, and human rights. Following these steps, Genscher said, would place the process of German unification in a European framework.

Genscher's idea was comprehensive, but it was unclear how a united Germany would be absorbed into NATO if the alliance would, like allied forces themselves, be limited to the old FRG. NATO and the Warsaw Pact were equated as structures that could turn into a new system as yet undefined. Intelligence reports available to American officials alleged that Genscher saw NATO as continuing only in the short term, and that he was considering announcing new pan-European security ideas later in 1990. Officials in Washington also noted that there was, ominously, no discussion in Genscher's speech of the future of either American nuclear weapons or U.S. or other foreign forces in the new Germany.

Genscher was quite clear, however, about keeping all GDR territory out of the NATO alliance. This territory would, in his view, be both neutralized and demilitarized. "To think," he scoffed to former U.S. Senator Charles Mathias, "that the borders of NATO could be moved 300 kilometers eastward, via German unification, would be an illusion . . . No reasonable person could expect the Soviet Union to accept such an outcome." Genscher was equally categorical in a press interview published on January 28: "Whoever wants the border of NATO to extend to the Oder and Neisse [the GDR-Polish border] is closing the door to a united Germany." Genscher knew that the idea of having Germany only partially included in NATO might seem odd, but to him it "sounded more difficult in theory than it would work out in practice." Meanwhile, Teltschik at the Chancellery was noting privately, "How could [Genscher's idea] be imagined in practice: a united Germany with two-thirds in NATO and a third outside it?"[40]

Genscher acknowledged the arguments against his Tutzing formula. But he was more concerned about the views of the Soviet Union. In fact, he was extremely worried about the Soviet reaction to his plan. Elbe later recalled how "nervous" Genscher was, fearing that even this commitment to NATO was on "thin ice."[41] Genscher, more than any other Western statesman, had seen Soviet wrath firsthand, when he had been dressed down by an angry Gorbachev in early December.

Genscher's thinking also seemed to diverge from the State Department's vision of the appropriate diplomatic process. The Four Powers were barely mentioned. The external aspects of German unity would be determined by the two German states, then blessed at a CSCE summit. While this was consistent with some Soviet views, the top American officials thought that a CSCE summit would inevitably become the outlet for outside states wishing to address the German problem, and that this thirty-five–nation forum, which would include Europe's neutral countries, such as Sweden, Finland, and Cyprus, was the wrong place to try to protect Germany's political and military alignment with the West.[42]

The danger of disagreement between Baker and Genscher, however, had already been headed off before the two men met. Genscher sent Elbe ahead to confer with Zoellick and Ross. The Americans went along with Genscher's Tutzing formula for not extending NATO eastward into the former GDR. Elbe agreed to the Two Plus Four design crafted by Baker's aides, including its key element—express commitment to the outcome of unification. Elbe met Genscher at Dulles Airport and briefed both Genscher and Dieter Kastrup of the Foreign Office while they were riding to the State Department. Genscher was very pleased with the Two Plus Four idea, so long as it was clear that this was "Two Plus Four" (i.e., Germans first) and not "Four Plus Two."[43]

In a relaxed and friendly, jackets-off, two-hour fireside talk with Baker, Genscher outlined his ideas.[44] Baker understood Genscher to say that Germany would remain in NATO, but the Soviets had to be assured that NATO's territorial coverage would not extend to the former GDR. The NATO treaty's defense commitments would not extend to the former GDR. When Baker noted during their subsequent press conference that Genscher supported continued membership for Germany in NATO, Genscher promptly elaborated that he and Secretary Baker "were in full agreement that there is no intention to extend the NATO area of defense and security towards the East."

When journalists pressed Genscher to explain how the Tutzing formula would work, he replied: "Nobody ever spoke about a halfway membership, this way or that. What I said is, there is no intention of extending the NATO area to the East. And I think you should wait for things to further develop . . . That will be the situation at this summit, the CSCE summit."

Baker, for his part, was able to announce Genscher's assent to the U.S.

conditions to be met before there could be a CSCE summit. "Any such summit," he told reporters, "should sign a CFE agreement . . . We are also in agreement that any such summit should involve the inclusion of a right of free elections as an additional human right in the human rights basket of CSCE."

Privately Baker had won assent to the Two Plus Four scheme. He had made the point to Genscher that the CSCE process was not the appropriate place for determining Germany's future or managing Soviet concerns. Nor, the ministers agreed, would it be acceptable for the Four Powers to act alone. Genscher, however, wanted to keep a Two Plus Four proposal under wraps before the March 18 GDR election because he thought that such an announcement might be construed by the Soviets as more pressure from a West bent on intervening in the affairs of the GDR. Baker, meanwhile, intended to use his plan to reassure the Soviets.

Genscher, of course, represented only part of the West German government. Much of West German policy on the unification question was being determined separately by the Chancellery, where a new working group on German policy had been created under the chairmanship of Rudolf Seiters. Genscher had not cleared his Tutzing formula with the Chancellery and the cabinet. In turn, Genscher only found out about Gorbachev's invitation for Kohl to come to Moscow from Baker, not from Kohl.

While Baker was meeting with Genscher, Scowcroft and Blackwill were on their way to Germany to participate in an unofficial conference of security officials and prominent academics. They arrived in a country consumed by the question of unification. Berlin's SPD mayor introduced the latest major proposal for unification on February 3, the day Scowcroft and Blackwill arrived. His nine-point plan provided for the Four Powers to take over all of East Germany for a brief period, followed by unification accompanied by a settlement of the international issues at a summer CSCE summit. Under this scheme for unification, West German domestic laws would be extended eastward, but not West German defense structures or international commitments. The GDR would be demilitarized, and Soviet forces could remain there in numbers matching those of Western forces stationed in the FRG, providing security in the East in concert with enhanced Four Power military liaison missions. These ideas were presented as a third path between Modrow's plan for a neutral Germany and the CDU-CSU proposals for inclusion of the GDR in NATO.[45]

While in Munich, Scowcroft and Blackwill consulted with Teltschik.[46] They learned that Kohl planned to tell Gorbachev that either a mass exodus of East Germans or the unilateral action of the East German parliament could force unification on the FRG very quickly after the March 18 elections. Consistent with the policy line developed in Washington, Teltschik and the White House representatives came to a clear understanding that Washington and Bonn were prepared to cooperate in encouraging a very rapid movement toward unification. Teltschik also revealed that Kohl would tell Gorbachev German neutrality was out of the question. Teltschik added, however, that NATO's plans for modernization of short-range nuclear forces might have to be scrapped. Kohl would take up this matter with Bush at Camp David later in the month. Teltschik was sure that Kohl would want to retain the political initiative in shaping the electoral debate about nuclear weapons in Germany during the upcoming West German campaign.

As for the process of getting to unity, Teltschik was very worried about Four Power intervention. He thought that the Soviets would push hard to slow the pace and that the British and French might be inclined to go along. Scowcroft assured him that President Bush would do nothing to embitter the Germans or weaken Kohl politically. Both men agreed that any CSCE summit should not be turned into an "ersatz" German peace conference. Scowcroft, however, did not present the Two Plus Four alternative because Scowcroft and Blackwill had not yet accepted the idea, and perhaps did not fully understand how far Baker had already gone in launching it.

One point was obvious by early February. The readiness of Gorbachev and Modrow to accept movement toward unity had unleashed expectations for real unification much sooner than had been considered possible. The effect on officials and ordinary citizens was riveting and intoxicating. Kohl's own five-year timetable was now obsolete. Unification could happen, people thought, in a year or two. Enormous expectations were clashing with equally enormous uncertainties. All major participants agreed on the need for a West German economic union of some sort with East Germany; that, after all, could be reconciled with the plans for economic and monetary union among the entire European Community. But Kohl was also thinking privately, the Americans knew, about the explosive idea of publicly discarding the confederation path and contemplating a direct merger of the GDR into the existing FRG. Scowcroft wrote to President Bush that Germany "was like a pressure cooker." It would take America's best efforts, and those of Kohl, "to keep the lid from blowing off in the months ahead."[47]

The locus of diplomatic activity now shifted to Moscow. Baker arrived there in February, immediately followed by Chancellor Kohl. One way or another Gorbachev would have to make his position clear. As Blackwill told Scowcroft, "The Politburo must know that if Kohl leaves the USSR having heard the same ambivalent mush that represents today's Soviet position on

Germany, the Chancellor is likely to conclude he can do as he likes." Blackwill concluded, "In any event, what John J. McCloy called 'The Big Game' of settling the postwar political geography of Europe is underway."[48]

Baker Goes to Moscow

Flying to Moscow, Baker had another chance to audition his Two Plus Four design. Since the American secretary of state used a thirty-year-old Boeing 707 as his official aircraft, the plane—like others of its generation—had to stop in Shannon, Ireland, to refuel during flights to the Continent. So Baker used the stop in Shannon to talk at two o'clock in the morning with the French foreign minister, Roland Dumas, who was in Ireland for an EC meeting.[49] Baker presented the Two Plus Four as a way to handle the external aspects of unification, leaving the internal issues to be worked out by the Germans. Baker thought that the Soviets would need some sort of diplomatic outlet for their anxiety, but Four Power intervention was the wrong answer. Dumas agreed that the Soviets were nervous and needed some outlet. But they were not alone, Dumas added. The British, Dutch, and Poles were nervous too. Dumas did not argue for the CSCE as a forum on Germany, though both Mitterrand and the EC had gone on record in support of a CSCE summit. It might have occurred to him that Two Plus Four, as a more exclusive forum, would give France greater cachet. Dumas, on the whole, seemed more and more taken with the Two Plus Four idea.

Baker then flew on to Prague. He talked about Germany with the onetime dissident playwright, suddenly the new Czech president, Vaclav Havel. The Czechs wanted to dismantle the Warsaw Pact and get Soviet troops out of their country. Havel, who was about to see Modrow, promised Baker he would tell Modrow that Germany could not be neutral, but he also could not imagine a united Germany in NATO. Reporting on these meetings to President Bush, Baker commented, "Ideas are moving fast and furious here—but they aren't reconciled effectively."[50]

The Americans understood the essence of the joint Soviet–East German approach: the philosophical acceptance of unity, the vision of a gradual process leading through a new confederation, the adamant insistence on neutralizing and demilitarizing a united Germany. They also knew that even this stance was considered far too soft by some in the Soviet government. Germany was exhibit A in an attack just launched against Gorbachev from the right wing of the Communist party's Central Committee, and led by Politburo member Yegor Ligachev, who pleaded with the Soviet leader "to prevent a prewar Munich." Or, as Ligachev put it in an emotional confidential letter sent to Gorbachev the next month: "The socialist commonwealth is falling apart, NATO is gaining strength. The German question has become of primary importance."[51]

Shevardnadze was thus exceedingly gloomy when Baker turned to the subject of Germany in a small one-on-one session, including just the two men, two note takers, and interpreters.[52] Baker opened with a careful presentation. German unification, he said, was coming quickly. A process was needed to handle the external aspects, to ensure stability and respect for the interests of others. The process could involve East and West Germany plus the Four Powers—a Two Plus Four mechanism. It would start work once the two Germanys had agreed on internal issues after the March 18 GDR election. Baker argued that a Four Power forum would be unacceptable to the German people, while a CSCE forum would be too unwieldy.

On the ultimate outcome of the process, Baker said that the United States opposed Modrow's proposal for a neutral Germany. He wanted the Soviets to see that a neutral Germany would be more dangerous to Moscow than a Germany in NATO. A neutral Germany would acquire its own nuclear capability, Baker contended. A Germany firmly anchored in a more political NATO would have no need for such a capability.

To ease Soviet concerns, Baker used the formula he had picked up from Genscher and, turning Genscher's "no extension of NATO" language into a more lawyerly formulation, promised that if a united Germany were included in NATO, there would be ironclad guarantees "that NATO's jurisdiction or forces would not move eastward." But U.S. troops would remain in Europe as long as America's allies wanted them there. Baker also pledged that NATO would evolve into a more political and less military-oriented alliance.

Shevardnadze then presented his position. He agreed that unification was arriving faster than anyone had expected—too fast. All of Europe had to change to make unification possible, but those changes were not keeping pace. The Soviets had once supported a unified Germany, but a neutral unified Germany. A united Germany could not be adapted to the alliances as they now existed. The Soviets were alone in expressing reservations about the danger of a massive militarized Germany. They had nothing against unification or self-determination per se. But guarantees were needed, and not just from the CSCE. The Soviets knew well the dangers of war with Germany. (Shevardnadze's brother had been killed by German forces near Brest in 1941.)

In short, Moscow supported Modrow's plan. It was no secret that Modrow had reviewed his ideas with the USSR before presenting them. Shevardnadze liked the fact that Modrow's plan was gradual, it would unfold in phases, and it ran in parallel with the process of strengthening European structures. More arms control and more defensive military doctrines were needed, too. In any case, said Shevardnadze, "unification will happen before we can achieve the next stage of disarmament." He then added, striking a note of impotent regret, "I am afraid that's the case, and I'm not sure of any way to avoid it." Growing even gloomier, Shevardnadze conceded that unification was a fait accompli. He was annoyed that his Foreign Ministry's pleas to invoke Four Power intervention had been rebuffed. He blamed the Americans. Shevardnadze emphasized repeatedly that a unified Germany might be different from the current FRG. History would not forgive a failure to use the Four Power mechanism effectively.

Shevardnadze again urged Four Power negotiations, specifically to discuss a peace treaty. He had suggested a European referendum on unification, but the Germans had rejected it. Shevardnadze declared that he had now "become enemy number one in Germany." He could support unification, but gradually—in phases. There were so many problems to be addressed, including economic ones. The British and the French, he said, privately shared many Soviet concerns. The Modrow plan was best.

Shevardnadze kept returning to his fears of what might eventually happen if Germany again became one country. He was worried about losing the chance for a peaceful nonnuclear world ten years down the road. He was worried about neo-Nazis gaining power in Germany. The German Republikaner party might get as much as 20 percent of the vote. It was a serious force.

Baker asked if the idea of a united neutral Germany that was also demilitarized had been in the Modrow plan. This requirement had been added in Moscow, said Shevardnadze. Modrow feared that if he raised the question of demilitarization, it would be the end of him politically. Baker then made clear that this too was also unacceptable to the United States. A united Germany should not be disarmed. The Soviet Union would still be a major land power, and Germany was entitled to have the means to defend itself. But, Baker added, the American approach would anchor German military power firmly in Western institutions. This might actually be more helpful, even from Moscow's perspective, than just calling for neutrality.

"I realize that might be hard for you to believe," Baker told Shevardnadze. "In effect it suggests that the risk comes not from the United States, which for a long time you've seen as your enemy, but instead it suggests that greater risk could come from a neutral Germany that becomes militaristic." That was why the United States wanted Germany to stay in NATO with a continued

American troop presence. The Two Plus Four mechanism could help negotiate this good outcome, he argued, including an absolute ban on NATO forces in the eastern part of Germany.

Shevardnadze bent a bit. Well, he replied, all options ought to be considered. "After all, the reality is that our action is late, given the way events are moving." Baker then made it clear to Shevardnadze that the Two Plus Four was an American proposal, that he could not guarantee German agreement to it. He had discussed it with Genscher and had heard no objection, but neither had they agreed.

Baker next tried out his presentation in the Kremlin, on Gorbachev himself.[53] Gorbachev for the first time hinted that the Soviets had also been thinking about a "six-power" forum: "I say four plus two; you say two plus four. How do you look at this formula?"

"Two plus four is a better way," Baker answered. It put the German states first.

As he had with Shevardnadze, Baker explained why the United States opposed a neutral Germany but repeated his version of Genscher's formula that, if Germany was part of NATO, "there would be no extension of NATO's jurisdiction for forces of NATO one inch to the east." This was an approach that could be agreed on in the Two Plus Four.

Much to Baker's surprise, Gorbachev's reaction was quite different from Shevardnadze's. There was no handwringing about the historical danger of German militarism. Instead he said, "Basically, I share the course of your thinking." The USSR had to adjust to the new realities: "There is nothing terrifying in the prospect of a unified Germany." He knew that some countries, such as France and Britain, were concerned about who was going to be the major player in Europe. But this was not a Soviet or an American problem: "We are big countries and have our own weight."

The process, in Gorbachev's view, had to be handled properly in order to recognize various sensitivities with tact. Even though earlier in the day Shevardnadze had supported the bureaucracy's stance and renewed the plea for Four Power intervention, Gorbachev now accepted Baker's idea, so similar to the six-power formula that Chernyayev had proposed during the January crisis staff meeting. "So the mechanism of four plus two or two plus four, assuming it relies on an international legal basis, is suitable for the situation," Gorbachev said.

Baker had not forgotten the other half of the Zoellick-Ross design: an explicit understanding that the Two Plus Four participants would not interfere with a German choice for unification. Secretary Baker explained that, to win Germany's support for the Two Plus Four idea, it was essential not to start the Two Plus Four until after March 18, the day when the East Germans would make their choice, "and only after the internal aspects of unification are being discussed by the Germans." It must be clear, he said, that the "internal aspects are for the two Germanys to determine." The Two Plus Four would deal with the external aspects, mainly security concerns and questions such as the status of Berlin. Baker repeated that he had not discussed the Two Plus Four idea with Chancellor Kohl, but he believed that Genscher would go along. Kohl, running for reelection, would be careful not to be seen as "turning over to others the question of unification."

Gorbachev used this reference to German domestic politics to offer a sophisticated portrait of the range of views within West Germany about unification. Some wanted confederation; others wanted a federation. There was division about keeping Germany in NATO. Some favored neutralism. Others spoke up for a confederation wherein both countries would retain their alliance memberships until the current alliances were replaced by new CSCE structures. Most surprising, to Gorbachev, was the position of Willy Brandt, who argued that Germany should proceed to unity without waiting for the CSCE process, letting western Germany remain in NATO and working out a special status for the former GDR. Gorbachev observed that most West Germans thought Brandt had gone too far. It was argued that such German nationalism could provoke resurgent Russian nationalism. Gorbachev believed this to be true.

Gorbachev referred to this "mosaic" of opinion on possible outcomes. Rather than be swept away by emotion, he said, "we shouldn't stop our thinking about how to channel the current events and the unification process. Let's be sure that we recognize realistic forces and take them into account."

Yes, Baker replied, and this is why we need a process to "shape the external aspects of unification in a way that enhances stability."

Coming back to the problem of a united Germany's membership in NATO, Baker asked Gorbachev directly whether he would rather see an independent Germany outside of NATO, with no U.S. forces on German soil, or a united Germany tied to NATO but with assurances "that there would be no extension of NATO's current jurisdiction eastward."

Gorbachev replied that he was still giving thought to these options. "Soon we are going to have a seminar [i.e., a discussion] among our political leadership to talk about all of these options." One thing was clear: "Any extension of the zone of NATO is unacceptable."

"I agree," Baker replied.

Gorbachev added that he could see advantages to having American troops in Germany. Clearly impressed by Baker's argument, Gorbachev acknowledged, "The approach you have outlined is a very possible one. We don't really want to see a replay of Versailles, where the Germans were able to arm themselves . . . The best way to constrain that process is to ensure that Germany is contained within European structures. What you have said to me about your approach and your preference is very realistic. So let's think about that. But don't ask me to give you a bottom line right now."

Secretary Baker's discussion with Gorbachev was extraordinarily significant. Gorbachev had adopted a position on both the process and the substantive outcome of German unification which was different from and more flexible than any that Baker had heard from Shevardnadze or that Seitz had heard at the same time from his counterpart in the Soviet Foreign Ministry or that Rice had heard during the same trip from Vadim Zagladin of the Central Committee or from Sergei Akhromeyev. Only Gorbachev seemed to be truly flexible on the German question.[54]

Baker had also been the first Western statesman to present his version of Genscher's Tutzing formula, calling for no extension of NATO "jurisdiction," directly to Gorbachev. Neither Baker nor the NSC staffers accompanying him (Gates and Rice) had fully appreciated the legal significance of Genscher's formula for the defense obligations (articles 5 and 6) of the North Atlantic Treaty. But after Baker had departed for Europe, other NSC staffers back in Washington (Blackwill and Zelikow) had thought about the question and come up with quite a different position. This White House formulation, unlike Genscher's, held that all of German territory would be in NATO, protected by the alliance. The White House also differed from Genscher in refusing to agree that eastern Germany should be demilitarized. Instead, the NSC staff position promised only that the territory of the former GDR would have a "special military status" within NATO.

While Baker was still in Moscow, he and his advisers received a draft of a letter from Bush to Kohl that contained the new American line. Although the draft did not call attention to the new language, Baker grasped the distinction quickly and agreed with it. He promptly began edging away from the Tutzing formula, which he had just offered to Gorbachev. In Moscow Baker told the press that with a united Germany in NATO, "you will have the GDR as a part of that membership." There would, he said, just need to be "some sort of security guarantees with respect to NATO's forces moving eastward or the jurisdiction of NATO moving eastward" for Germany to be a member of NATO. There might be "some special arrangements within NATO respecting the extension of NATO forces eastward. That's all I meant there."[55]

On balance, American officials were quite satisfied with the results of Baker's discussions with Gorbachev on Germany. They could justifiably believe that they had been given a green light from the leader of the Soviet Union for the policies the United States was developing to deal with the imminent prospect of German unification. Genscher's aide Elbe later credited Baker with providing "decisive help for the German side" by making such a strong case to Gorbachev with all the weight and authority of the leading power of the West.[56] Next the Americans worked to coordinate their diplomatic approach with that of Chancellor Kohl, as he followed Baker into Moscow.

Kohl, the Americans, and Gorbachev

Bush thought that when Kohl encountered Gorbachev, right after Baker's trip to Moscow, the American and the West German positions on the key issues must appear to be absolutely identical. The American president was sensitive to the tremendous personal and political strain Kohl would be under as he went to Moscow. So Bush wanted Kohl to know that Washington backed him. "With Kohl traveling to what may be the most portentous foreign meeting of his life," Scowcroft advised Bush, "I believe you should both give him all the personal support you can and make clear to him our preferences concerning the future of a united Germany."[57]

To accelerate unification and win German support on the vital security questions, the United States government sent two important messages to Chancellor Kohl on February 9–10, one from Bush and one from Baker. In deciding what Bush should say, the White House had two very different draft letters to choose from.[58] One, drafted by the NSC staff, offered unprecedented U.S. backing for Kohl's push toward unity in direct, personal terms and stressed the need to maintain NATO membership, the American troop presence, and nuclear deterrence. The other proposed letter, drafted by the European bureau of the State Department, urged Kohl to reassure the Soviets about Germany's intentions and suggested a new way of handling the NATO problem: the former GDR would be protected not by NATO but by new promises to defend this part of a united Germany which would be given, outside of the NATO treaty, directly to Bonn by the United States, Britain, and France.

Blackwill thought that the State Department draft was too defensive and disagreed with its position on NATO. The United States should fortify Kohl, not urge him to assuage Soviet fears. Blackwill also wondered how the United States could promise entirely new security guarantees for part of Germany before the administration had either analyzed the idea or won the consent of concerned agencies such as the Department of Defense. Scowcroft arranged to have both draft letters sent out to Baker in Moscow to see what he thought about them. Baker and Scowcroft agreed that they preferred the NSC draft. Bush agreed with their recommendation, and the letter was sent directly to Kohl through special White House channels on February 9.

Bush's letter went straight to the point. German unification was coming soon. Still, "these new developments do not alter the complete readiness of the United States to see the fulfillment of the deepest national aspirations of the German people. If events are moving faster than we expected, it just means that our common goal for all these years of German unity will be realized even sooner than we had hoped."

Bush then dealt equally directly with any possible Four Power intervention in German affairs. Yes, America had legal rights over Germany. But these rights could be justified only by the desire to create a peaceful, democratic German state. That had already been accomplished, in Bush's view. "As I see it, no one can doubt the strength and vitality of the Federal Republic's democratic institutions," he wrote. So, "whatever the formal legal role of the Four Powers may be in recognizing the freely expressed will of the German people," Washington would "do nothing that would lead your countrymen to conclude that we will not respect their choice for their nation's future." To be even clearer, Bush expressly pledged, "In no event will we allow the Soviet Union to use the Four Power mechanism as an instrument to try to force you to create the kind of Germany Moscow might want, at the pace Moscow might prefer." Kohl would thus go to Moscow carrying in his pocket an extraordinary written guarantee of American backing, worded in the strongest possible way.

Bush then specified what he considered important, turning to the NATO issue. He said that he "was deeply gratified by your rejection of proposals for neutrality and your firm statement that a unified Germany would stay in the North Atlantic Alliance." Bush felt sure of Kohl's agreement that, although NATO needed to place "more emphasis on its original political role," continued German membership would mean the presence of American troops on German territory backed by a credible nuclear deterrent.[59]

Bush went on to offer his own formula for handling the status of former East German territory in NATO. Blackwill and Zelikow had liked the phrasing used by NATO Secretary General Manfred Wörner in a speech in Hamburg on February 8, in which Wörner had referred to a possible "special military status" for the former territory of East Germany. Blackwill won Scowcroft's agreement to include this formulation in the president's letter. So Bush formally proposed that "a component of a united Germany's membership in the Atlantic Alliance could be a special military status for what is now the territory of the GDR."[60] Bush also explained that he expected this "special military status" for the former GDR to be accompanied by substantial, even total, withdrawals of Soviet troops from Central and Eastern Europe. The "special military status" meant that NATO's defense commitments would extend to all of Germany. Since it would be illogical for Soviet troops to remain in an area defended by NATO, Bush expected them to go home.

This was an important letter both to Bush and to Kohl. A couple of weeks later, when the two men were holding a joint press conference, Kohl said: "I wish to seize this opportunity, Mr. President, to thank you publicly today, and here before the press, that on the eve of my trip to Moscow you sent me a letter which did not only speak about supporting our policy and was not only marked by the habitual friendship but which will be going down in history as an important document of German-American friendship."[61]

President Bush's message to Kohl was complemented by a parallel message to the chancellor from Secretary Baker briefing Kohl on what he might expect to hear from the Soviets.[62] The letter then moved to the heart of Secretary Baker's message: the case for acceptance of a Two Plus Four forum. The internal elements of unification were strictly a German matter, Baker wrote. But everyone agreed that the interests of others were implicated in the external aspects of unification. Four Power intervention was unacceptable. The CSCE was unwieldy. It might "sanction the result of the unification process, but couldn't be a near-term practical mechanism for helping to shape it." The Two Plus Four structure might be the most realistic. It would begin work only after the March 18 elections, after the process on the internal aspects of unification had begun, and only if the Germans accepted it.

On the NATO issue, Baker recounted the question he had posed to Gorbachev about choosing between a unified Germany outside NATO, independent, with no U.S. forces, and a unified Germany, tied to NATO, "with assurances that NATO's jurisdiction would not shift one inch eastward from its present position." (This letter was drafted before Baker had internalized the different stance on NATO elaborated in the Bush letter.) Gorbachev did not appear to be "locked in," Baker noted. The Soviet leader "may well be willing to go along with a sensible approach that gives him some cover or explanation for his actions. I suspect that the combination of a Two Plus Four mechanism and a broader CSCE framework might do that."

Bush and Baker thus provided Kohl with a clear understanding of the backing he could expect from the United States, a statement of the most important American concerns, advance notice of Soviet attitudes, and a recommended framework for managing the external aspects of unification.

The West Germans based their presentations on what Baker told them to expect and found that the Soviet leaders used the same points they had used with the Americans.[63]

Kohl and Genscher met with the Soviet leaders on February 10 and 11.[64] The critical meeting was between Kohl and Gorbachev on February 10, lasting more than two and a half hours. The atmosphere was friendly. Kohl, who had delivered on the Soviet leader's request for food aid earlier during January, did not encounter the angry Gorbachev that Genscher had faced in December. When Kohl detailed the deteriorating political and economic situation in the GDR, Gorbachev made no effort to dispute the dire predictions for the future of the East German state. He did not utter one word of criticism about Kohl or the FRG's policies.

Kohl played heavily on the economic advantages the USSR could derive from a friendly relationship with a united Germany. He noted that the GDR was a principal supplier of manufactured goods to the USSR but was defaulting on its delivery contracts. Rapid unification could provide more reliable delivery of better, cheaper goods. The FRG was willing to negotiate with Moscow on delivery contracts and maintain the close commercial ties between the former GDR and the Soviet Union. In addition, Kohl pointed out that trade with a unified German state could provide the Soviets with access to the EC market.

As he had with Baker, Gorbachev told Kohl that he was prepared to accept the prospect of German unification. It was up to the Germans to decide for themselves whether or not they wanted to unify. It was also up to the Germans to choose their form of government, the pace of unification, and the conditions under which it would occur. Kohl, filled with emotion, assured Gorbachev that nothing but peace would ever rise out of German soil, and silently gestured to Teltschik to make sure he was copying all of this down, word for word. Teltschik was jubilant inside. "That is the breakthrough!" he noted in his diary. Gorbachev repeated these words later in the meeting. There could be no misunderstanding. Gorbachev, however, saw this statement as consistent with the position he had agreed on with Modrow at the end of January.

The two leaders then took up the NATO problem. Kohl said that Germany had to remain in NATO, but he could accept a plan restricting NATO forces (not NATO "jurisdiction") to the former FRG. The East German army could be converted into a paramilitary force similar to the FRG's Bundesgrenzschutz (federal border police). The West Germans were struck by Gorbachev's attitude on the NATO issue. In contrast to Shevardnadze, who had said that a united Germany in NATO was out of the question, Gorbachev did not propose a neutral Germany or demilitarization or even the removal of Western nuclear weapons. As he had with Baker, Gorbachev simply noted the spectrum of possible outcomes and said he needed to think further about the different possibilities. "Again a sensation!" Teltschik noted later. "No demand for a price and no pressure. What a meeting!"

Kohl also said that Soviet troops could remain in the former GDR, perhaps believing that, as a practical matter, the Soviet military would find itself in an untenable position anyway in a united Germany. Gorbachev wanted to know whether current East German subsidies for Soviet forces could be paid in deutsche marks. The FRG had not yet considered that point. Chancellor Kohl and Genscher also tried to reassure the Soviets by promising that a unified Germany would continue to forgo development of nuclear and biological weapons. In addition, Kohl gave explicit assurances to Gorbachev that he would not contest the borders of a united Germany. He was willing formally to agree that Germany's borders would consist only of the territory of the current FRG and GDR, renouncing all claims to former German territories.

When the leaders turned to the question of process, Baker's Two Plus Four plan carried the day. Gorbachev endorsed it, clearly understanding that such a conference would not amount to the Four Powers summoning the two Germanys: it would not be the Four Plus Two. Gorbachev had been persuaded that the CSCE was too unwieldy to be a useful forum for discussing the German question. The West Germans agreed.

Kohl, at Teltschik's urging, portrayed the meeting as a historic event. He wanted the German people to know that the Soviet leader had given him the "green light." Genscher and his aides were appalled. They considered such crowing about a "breakthrough" very risky, fearing that the Soviets would react badly. Gorbachev had been philosophically reconciled to unity in some form ever since he had agreed on a joint position with Modrow at the end of January. It was not clear that there had been decisive moves on substance; certainly Genscher had encountered a more cautious position in his meetings with Shevardnadze. Genscher and his team scorned Teltschik as a foreign policy "amateur."[65]

Indeed, Teltschik had seized as much on the relaxed tone of the meeting as on the substance of Gorbachev's presentation. It helped Kohl politically to dramatize the moment, just as it put Genscher's role in the shade. But it is hard to doubt that Kohl and his advisers genuinely believed this to have been a historic moment. As Genscher and Elbe noted, complexities loomed ahead. But in crowing about the "green light," Kohl had manufactured the momentum to carry his cause to victory in the East German election little more than a month away.

Veteran Soviet officials instantly understood what Kohl was doing. They hastily, and angrily, took pains to contradict Kohl's glowing portrait of the decisions made in Moscow, starting with the more nuanced press reporting of the visit. In Washington, London, and Paris, Soviet ambassadors called on top Foreign Ministry officials to present their written version of the meetings between Kohl and Genscher. According to this "official" version the Germans were free to choose unity, but their decision had to be linked inseparably to "the overall European development," taking into account the interests of others. The Soviets claimed to have "sharply criticized the FRG interference in the election struggle in the GDR, its policy of forcing the pace of developments and heating up emotions around the unification issue." On NATO membership, "the idea that a unified Germany be part of NATO was categorically rejected." As for Genscher's Tutzing formula, the Soviets claimed that their leaders "couldn't understand such a scheme."[66] The Soviet Union tried desperately to show that its policy remained formidable.

But the mask had slipped. Gorbachev had allowed both the Americans and the Germans to leave Moscow believing that he was not willing—or perhaps not able—to offer decisive opposition to their plans. In fact that was true. Gorbachev was not prepared to pressure Kohl to help Modrow because he had apparently decided that Modrow was doomed. This is evident from Gorbachev's dispassionate telephone debriefing of Modrow after Kohl and Baker had left Moscow. Gorbachev mentioned how impressed he was that the Americans and Germans had reached agreement on a common course of action. But when Modrow launched into an impassioned plea for Gorbachev's help in dealing with Kohl, the Soviet leader did not respond. Rather, he said that it was important to maintain a principled course and wished the embattled Modrow success. Perhaps the Soviet leader, with so much crashing down around him, had become resigned to the inevitable and was turning his attention to more pressing matters at home. Chernyayev recalled that around this time Gorbachev believed that with the socialist bloc collapsing, the most important goal was to strengthen perestroika so the Soviet Union would not do the same.[67]

Bonn and Washington were eager to exploit this opportunity but were now worried about Gorbachev's political position at home. It was increasingly clear that Gorbachev himself was the key to the outcome of German unification. From this time forth the United States and the FRG were exceedingly careful to conduct the unification process in a way that would not make the

Soviet Union look like the great loser. Humiliating the Soviet government could boost the right-wing reaction that American officials feared was already gathering strength. Gorbachev was in a delicate position, and the West could not afford to lose him.

The Ottawa Meeting

With the European transformation accelerating, foreign ministers from every NATO and Warsaw Pact country gathered in Ottawa, Canada. The Ottawa meeting had originally been scheduled to begin serious negotiation of an agreement on Open Skies, an initiative first launched by President Eisenhower in 1955 and reintroduced in a broadened multilateral form by President Bush in May 1989 as a way of testing the extent of Soviet commitment to real glasnost, a new openness. That subject for the gathering was now eclipsed, however, by the diplomacy swirling around questions of Germany's and Europe's future.

On Sunday night, February 11, NATO foreign ministers caucused to plan their common approach at the meeting. They wanted to talk about a diplomatic channel in which changes in Europe could be discussed. The European Community, accepting the USSR's view, wanted to rely on a CSCE summit, to be held in Paris. Baker persuaded his colleagues to agree that such a summit should be held only after a CFE treaty reducing and limiting the conventional forces of East and West in Europe was also complete and ready to be signed. The conventional forces agreement was no longer simply an arms control negotiation. Now, with the rapidly changing situation in Europe, it would also speak volumes about the underlying political situation.

The United States had proposed a reduction in the numbers of U.S. and Soviet troops stationed on foreign territory in Europe. In Moscow Gorbachev had agreed, but only if it were modified so that U.S. and Soviet forces would have a common and equal ceiling. Baker and Bush wanted to avert any public perception that U.S. and Soviet troops should be treated alike. It was their belief that the Soviet troops must leave and the American soldiers must stay. So Bush asked Baker to keep pushing for limits that would allow a larger American than Soviet troop presence on foreign soil in Europe.[68]

Seeing the difficulties ahead, Foreign Minister Dumas of France argued that a CSCE summit might need to be held in Paris, regardless of progress on CFE, in order to deal with the German issues. Genscher and Baker presented a united front against this argument. Genscher, amending his earlier view, said that the CSCE summit should not be about Germany. Baker stated unequivocally that the United States would not attend a summit unless a CFE agreement was going to be ready for President Bush's signature.[69]

Baker and Shevardnadze then hammered out a compromise on troops under which both the United States and the Soviet Union would be limited to 195,000 military personnel in Central Europe (defined to include the two Germanys, the Benelux countries, Denmark, Poland, Czechoslovakia, and Hungary). The Americans would have the right to station an additional 30,000 troops elsewhere in Europe (e.g., Great Britain or Italy). The Soviets had no troops stationed in Europe outside the central zone, and they were given no such extra entitlement. The Soviets thus abandoned the insistence on equal ceilings voiced in Moscow, and the outcome was remarkably close to Bush's original terms.[70] The political message was precisely what the United States wanted: American and Soviet troops were not to be treated as parallel.

The next morning, February 12, Baker spoke with Shevardnadze at a breakfast hosted by Prime Minister Brian Mulroney and Foreign Minister Joe Clark of Canada. Shevardnadze was still worried about Germany. He said that 90 percent of the Russian people would vote against the reunification of Germany if they could. Mulroney added, unhelpfully, that he did not see how the EC could accommodate the weight of a united Germany either. Shevardnadze pleaded for changes in Europe's political structures to keep pace. The Soviet conservatives, he added, once "had their Wall, their Honecker, their security guarantees—what's it going to be now? They want to know." On that note the ministers went on to the conference.[71]

Baker used any spare moment between obligatory sessions of the Open Skies plenaries for intensive diplomacy with other foreign ministers, including Shevardnadze, on the German issue. Shevardnadze had had little time to receive instructions from Moscow, and he was clearly nervous. Many of these meetings between ministers were ad hoc, arranged on a few minutes' notice. For example, on February 13 alone Baker met with Shevardnadze on at least five separate occasions, held an equal number of meetings with Genscher, met privately with Hurd and Dumas, took part in two Quad ministerial meetings (with representatives from Britain, West Germany, and France), and led a NATO ministerial caucus. This was in addition to the conference's formal Open Skies activities and previously scheduled bilateral meetings. The job was not just to get agreement on the Two Plus Four as a forum, but to nail down the other half of the design—the public agreement linking this forum to unimpeded unification of Germany.

The United States prepared a joint announcement, which was worked over, word for word, on February 13. The Americans got others to agree that this new forum would discuss only the "external aspects" of unification. The final announcement, released to the press on February 13, stated simply that the foreign ministers of the six countries had agreed that the foreign ministers of the FRG and the GDR would meet with the French, British, Soviet, and American foreign ministers "to discuss external aspects of the establishment of German unity, including the issues of security of the neighboring states. Preliminary discussions at the official level will begin shortly." Now that a process to deal with German unification had been created, the Americans were under pressure to put it into action right away. Genscher and Baker had originally agreed that the new forum would not start work until sometime after the East German elections on March 18, after the internal process of unification between the two Germanys was already launched and under way. Now Ross and Zoellick, drawing on the Ottawa accord, said only that no *ministerial* meeting would occur until after March 18. Meetings of officials could begin "shortly," which meant before the East German elections.[72]

The plan met with intense criticism from other members of the Western alliance who had not known that this forum was being created and felt left out. Dutch foreign minister Hans Van den Broek decried the lack of consultation. After all, the announcement implied that the six would negotiate the concerns of all of Germany's neighbors. But not all of those neighbors were part of the process. Italian foreign minister Gianni De Michelis was equally unhappy. "We have worked together within the Alliance for 40 years," he complained. Luxembourg, Norway, Belgium, Spain, and Canada echoed this dissatisfaction. The situation was particularly embarrassing for the Canadians, who were, after all, hosting the conference. The Americans, British, French, and West Germans all tried to be conciliatory. Baker pledged to consult others about the activities in this new forum. Finally, however, after De Michelis repeated his concerns, Genscher lost his patience. Genscher turned to the Italian and said sharply, "You are not part of the game." In the stunned pause which followed that remark, the Canadian chairman gaveled the meeting to a close.[73]

Baker had more to worry about than unhappy allies. The NSC staff had never reconciled itself to the Two Plus Four plan. Like the State Department's European bureau, Scowcroft and Blackwill thought the idea would simply intervene in and slow down the process of German unification. This would, in turn, defeat the goal of letting unification happen at a pace set by the Germans—preferably as fast as possible. Baker had overruled Seitz and the European bureau.

On February 12, the first day of Ottawa talks, Scowcroft suddenly feared that the Two Plus Four, which he still thought was a subject for consultation, was about to become a reality. Bush wanted to stand by Kohl and not interfere with his plans. Scowcroft conveyed his concerns to Baker, whose advisers thought that Scowcroft's worries were overblown. They mistakenly believed that Scowcroft was the one trying to slow down unification while they were trying to speed it up. Baker had urged Bush that it was necessary to go forward, telling him, "You can't say no to this," and Bush had assented. In any case, Baker knew that Genscher was on board and that Kohl had agreed to the idea with Gorbachev. So Baker asked Genscher to urge Kohl to give Bush a call.

Kohl phoned President Bush on February 13. He first expressed his deep gratitude for the messages he had received from Bush and from Baker before his talks with Gorbachev. He then summarized his discussions with Gorbachev and said that he knew the Two Plus Four idea was being worked out in Ottawa. After the call, however, Bush was still not certain that Kohl had made clear his support for the Two Plus Four idea. So to avoid any chance of misunderstanding, Bush called Kohl back. The chancellor immediately reassured the president: "George, I have a feeling there is a misunderstanding. I'm in agreement with what the foreign ministers are talking about in Ottawa." Kohl was flattered by Bush's care in soliciting his views.[74]

Baker then received the go-ahead from President Bush. But Scowcroft was still unhappy with and unreconciled to the Two Plus Four idea. He and Blackwill believed that the Soviets, the British, and the French now all had a means for slowing down unification. Rice and Blackwill believed that the forum would force Gorbachev to take a stand on German issues, which was just what they thought he was trying to avoid. Scowcroft was troubled, too, because he believed that the idea had not been properly considered within the U.S. government or sufficiently vetted with the NATO allies. He believed that Baker had presented Bush with a fait accompli, and the president had been obliged, with some hesitation, to accept it.[75]

This episode was by far the most serious example of internal disagreement within the U.S. government during the process of German unification. It appears to have turned largely on misunderstandings between the State Department and the White House on how far the concept of the Two Plus Four had progressed. Moreover, Baker, who had used every opportunity to float the idea, found himself with a chance to push it through at Ottawa. Time was of the essence, and the secretary of state went ahead.

In truth, the White House had had substantial notice of Baker's intent to pursue the Two Plus Four idea. Blackwill probably first became aware of this thinking at the time of the talks with Hurd and with Genscher and Elbe at the end of January, if not earlier. The White House had cleared Baker's February 10 letter to Kohl pressing the idea.

Second, neither the White House nor the State Department, though for different reasons, had attempted to place, let alone to force, the Two Plus Four issue into a formal (or even a good informal) decision process leading to the president. Responsibility for securing such a decision rested with both Scowcroft and Baker. In the rush of events there was no opportunity for a timely airing of the different positions.

Third, neither Scowcroft nor Baker fully understood each other's concerns at the time. Ironically, though Scowcroft himself was inclined toward caution, officials in both camps shared the objective of accelerating German unification and thought that the other side wanted the opposite.

But, remarkably, the internal disputes about the Two Plus Four idea never leaked to the press. Personal relationships, though strained, did not break. With the adoption of the Two Plus Four at Ottawa, the NSC staff and the State Department turned quickly to the question of how to make it work.

Taking Stock

Baker had done more in Ottawa than just win agreement to the creation of a mechanism to manage the diplomacy of German unification. The joint announcement also served, symbolically, as public recognition that unification had passed beyond speculation and expectation into the realm of day-to-day planning. Suddenly, Elizabeth Pond observes, "it dawned on the public that German unification was going to come very fast indeed." Kohl was jubilant. Germany, he said, was "jumping with a single leap" toward unification. In Moscow Falin fired a warning: "If the Western alliance sticks with its demand for NATO membership for all of Germany, there won't be any unification."[76]

The U.S. officials knew that they wanted to propose NATO membership for a united Germany. Bush had discussed the problem with Manfred Wörner, a leading conservative political figure in West Germany, former FRG defense minister, and now NATO's able secretary general.[77] The president told Wörner that the German question dominated everything else and made the issue of U.S. force levels, the U.S. role, and the U.S. position in Europe complex. Wörner, agreeing, was adamant about the need to keep a united Germany firmly in the alliance, or else "the old Pandora's box of competition and rivalry in Europe would be reopened." Neutrality was dangerous, for Germany and for Europe. Eventual German acquisition of nuclear weapons was quite possible. A demilitarized Germany was also unacceptable. A neutral or disaffected Germany would be tempted to float freely and bargain with both East and West. The EC and CSCE were all talk. Nothing could replace

NATO as the only stable security structure. It was Bush's "historic task," Wörner argued, to protect the Germans from temptation, save Europe from instability, and safeguard those who had made a new Europe possible. It was the way to assuage the fears of other countries in Western Europe, too.

Both Bush and Wörner felt that Gorbachev would accept the presence of a united Germany in NATO if the United States stood fast. But Bush knew that he would have to work hard to persuade the Soviet leader. Wörner took care to specify that German participation in NATO also had to mean German participation in NATO's military structures. The FRG was the key to the integration of member armies into an alliance military command. Politically this was crucial, for it made European defense a multinational effort rather than a national one, with national rivalries. In addition, Wörner confirmed that his notion of a special military status for the former GDR did not mean demilitarizing eastern Germany. He did not know that Bush's staff had already borrowed this concept and presented it to Kohl as the American government's view.

No one doubted that the road to unification still led through Moscow. The Soviets and East Germans hoped to channel unification into a more gradual process. Their hopes rested on a leftist victory in the March 18 GDR elections, the outcome that most observers expected. Shevardnadze did not believe that he had yielded to faster unification with the adoption of the Two Plus Four framework.[78]

Although it is tempting to think that the Soviet position was hopeless by this time, no senior officials in either Washington or Bonn believed this. They knew that the USSR still had significant leverage over events in Central Europe. Moscow could force the German people to choose between unification and membership in NATO, channeling the surging tide for unity against the supporters of the alliance. Moscow could also force the German people to choose between respecting the Soviets' wishes or precipitating a major international crisis. Right after the Ottawa accord was announced, Falin described matters in the pages of *Der Spiegel*, the most widely read publication in West Germany. How, he was asked, could the Soviets convince Bonn and Washington? He replied:

> I think that life will convince the Americans and the majority in the Bundestag . . . The only correct answer would be not to play the problem down, not to pretend that we are unable to defend [our] interests legally— and not only legally. There is no legal vacuum in Germany. Either the GDR—regardless of which government will be in power there—fulfills its . . . obligations concerning the Warsaw Pact and us, or the Soviet Union's

latent rights [over the GDR and all of Germany] become effective . . . The Germans are intelligent enough to understand that it cannot be in their interest to bring about a confrontation. We do not threaten anyone, but we do not want to be threatened either.[79]

The U.S. government knew that, especially in an election year, Kohl and the West German voters had little stomach for a major international confrontation with Mikhail Gorbachev, a man who had been widely celebrated in the FRG the year before as the revolutionary leader of perestroika.

So the United States, in the days after the Ottawa meeting, faced two great challenges: to flesh out a precise and sustainable position on the external alignment of a united Germany in Europe, including a diplomatic strategy for the Two Plus Four that would protect this position; and to win the acquiescence of a weakened but still dangerous Soviet Union to an abrupt realignment of the European balance of power. The United States intended to consolidate the democratic revolution in Europe, reduce Soviet military power in Eastern Europe, and eliminate the Soviet armed presence in Germany. American forces—though fewer in number—would remain. The harsh truth was that the American goal could be achieved only if the Soviet Union suffered a reversal of fortunes not unlike a catastrophic defeat in a war. The United States had decided to try to achieve the unification of Germany absolutely and unequivocally on Western terms.

Yet American officials wanted the Soviets to accept this result and believe that they retained an appropriate, albeit diminished, role in European affairs. They did not want Moscow to nurture a lasting bitterness that would lead them someday to try to overthrow the European settlement. In the past, whether at the Congress of Vienna (1814–15) or the Congress of Berlin (1878), accommodating the interests of a defeated power was a familiar aspect of balance of power politics. Defeated powers were "compensated" for the loss of valued territory with other, perhaps less valued, land. In this way the victors sought to cushion the blow to the vanquished and protect the settlement. In our more enlightened age such compensation for political losses was not possible. The answer had to be sought in less tangible marks of power and influence. The odds of success seemed long, but the United States set its sights on creating a dignified way for Moscow to accept the unraveling of its presence and its authority in the new Europe.

~ 6

The Design for a New Germany

On the afternoon of February 14, 1990, President Bush walked into the Roosevelt Room of the White House to sign a bill providing aid to the new government of Panama. Before the signing ceremony began, Bush praised the "breakthrough" in Ottawa that would bring about the union of Germany and with it "the objective that I have stressed throughout the first year of my Presidency: a Europe that is whole and free." But Bush also repeatedly referred to the way "things moved quite fast" in Ottawa, the tiniest sign of lingering White House unease over Baker's achievement. A reporter reminded Bush that on February 12 he had rejected a Four Power conference on Germany. What had changed between February 12 and February 13, the day the Two Plus Four accord was announced? Well, Bush answered, Chancellor Kohl had assured him just yesterday that he considered this a sound step. Bush did not distinguish between a Four Power conference and the Two Plus Four mechanism that included the two German states. Instead he finished his answer obliquely, saying: "We're not trying to dictate to anybody over there how it would work; I left that question open. But, yes, it moved very, very fast." The president invited Secretary Baker to add to this answer. Baker declined.[1]

Indeed the process had moved very fast, and there were large blanks still to be filled in. The Americans believed firmly that Germany should stay a member of NATO, that U.S. troops and nuclear weapons would remain in Germany, and that the territory of the former East Germany should have some sort of "special military status" that would permit its integration into NATO.

In the winter of 1990 nothing could be taken for granted about Germany's political future. A conservative such as Henry Kissinger believed that a new

Germany might take the form of a confederation linking the FRG and GDR, with a disarmed eastern portion integrated into NATO. Moreover, such a Germany would accept binding limits on its armed forces, and the Western allies would cut their forces in Germany to a fraction of their former strength. Not only would NATO forces not move eastward, but the alliance would move westward—back to some agreed-upon line east of the Rhine.[2]

But the Americans and the Federal Republic had more ambitious objectives. The FRG had rejected the notion of confederation. Now it was time to devise an alternative plan for unity. In Bonn a new working group on "Deutschlandpolitik" began to meet on January 31, led by the head of the Chancellery, Kohl's chief of staff Rudolf Seiters.[3] The Chancellery working group at the subcabinet level would report, in part, to a new cabinet committee on "German unity."

It was agreed that there should be economic and monetary union between the FRG and the GDR. The Modrow government wanted and needed it, particularly the vast economic support that it would bring; the major West German parties supported it; and the idea seemed to harmonize nicely with the European Community's own plans for creating such a union. The crucial problem was to determine the political arrangements under which that union would take place. Would there still be an autonomous GDR that might even be under communist rule?

Kohl's government concluded that it would instead link economic union to the dismantling of socialism and the creation of a market economy in the GDR. Without that step, as finance minister Theo Waigel explained to the Bundestag, the deutsche mark could not become the de facto currency of the GDR. That, in turn, might be the way to persuade its citizens to stay home. About 340,000 East Germans had arrived in the FRG during 1989, and since the beginning of the new year over two thousand East German resettlers were arriving in the FRG each day. CDU-East leader Lothar de Maizière reportedly believed that another 2.5 or 3 million East Germans were sitting on packed suitcases. Kohl's government thought that the government of the GDR would be crushed by an avalanche of that proportion, which would also swamp West German resources for housing and social programs, and finish Kohl's chances for reelection. If Bonn did not want the East German people "to come to the D-Mark," said Teltschik, "then the D-Mark must go to the [East German] people."[4]

Kohl submitted his proposal for economic and monetary union to his cabinet on February 7, emphasizing that money alone would not be a way out for Modrow's government. There would have to be fundamental reforms, too. He, the CSU leader and finance minister Waigel, and Free Democratic party leader Lambsdorff all agreed that economic union required a common economic order. Thus, the FRG planned to negotiate with the East on completely new federal structures to govern the GDR shortly after the March 18 elections.

Waigel outlined three possible designs for economic and monetary union. The most complex plan envisioned a move toward full currency union after economic reforms were under way. A second option was to establish a fixed exchange rate between the deutsche mark and the East German Ostmark, to be propped up by the Bundesbank. Third and simplest would be immediately to make the deutsche mark the sole legal currency in East Germany as well as the FRG. This dramatic step would require the Bundesbank to take more responsibility for the GDR's monetary policies as East Germany was absorbed into the West German economic system.

The president of the Bundesbank, Karl Otto Pöhl, had been invited to take part in this cabinet meeting. He had no quarrel with Waigel's outline or with the need for monetary union with the GDR. After all, East Germany's foreign exchange reserves were already exhausted. There was no other choice. But despite the magnitude of the East German crisis, the meeting adjourned without a clear decision on Waigel's options. In a background press briefing on February 9, Teltschik derisively commented that the GDR could become "insolvent" within a few days. The next day another CDU official, Lothar Späth, told a reporter that the unconditional economic surrender of the GDR was the only way to prevent imminent financial collapse. After a flurry of headlines Kohl, returning from Moscow, was more diplomatic: the GDR, he said, was not on the verge of bankruptcy. Privately, however, Bonn officials assumed that Modrow would have to agree to Kohl's proposal for quick economic and monetary union of the two Germanys during his visit to Bonn on February 13–14.[5]

The Modrow visit highlighted the gulf between the different notions of economic and monetary union. Modrow was under pressure from the former dissident leaders of the roundtable to protect the East German social welfare system and avoid any quick surrender of "financial sovereignty." Modrow did, of course, want West German money—DM 10 to 15 billion worth. In other words, the East Germans wanted to receive the benefits of monetary union while maintaining their economic autonomy. Modrow arrived in Bonn with seventeen ministers in tow (eight from the roundtable). He presented "the position of the Round Table" but achieved little. Kohl linked massive aid to economic reforms. He promised deutsche marks but insisted on a dominant role for West Germany in setting the monetary policy of the East. The East Germans balked, accusing the West Germans of trying to annex them as

Hitler had annexed Austria in the Anschluss of 1938. The Westerners were offended, and the Easterners were annoyed by what they perceived to be the haughty and peremptory tone of the Western side. The two countries could agree only to ask their negotiators to work on the detailed terms of "currency union and economic community."[6]

Kohl summarized the fast-breaking situation to the Bundestag on February 15. He called attention to the positive meeting with Gorbachev, the "more far-reaching agreements in Ottawa," and the beginning of talks with Modrow on monetary union and economic community. Kohl justly claimed that these developments, taken together, had "qualitatively changed" the situation in Germany.[7]

But Kohl was still exposed to political attacks at home. The stalemate with the GDR was not just bad for Modrow. As more refugees poured in from the East, Kohl's popularity was threatened. He needed to settle on a preferred path to unity, to pick one of Waigel's three options for monetary union, and to think through the route to political union. German officials, like their American counterparts, hoped that the Two Plus Four would lag behind the negotiation of the internal aspects of unification. In the best of all worlds, the Two Plus Four might soon be One Plus Four.[8] Delays in negotiations between the two German states threatened this delicate calculation. The important decisions could no longer be avoided.

Kohl Decides on Takeover, Not Merger

The FRG had to select between the two paths to unification provided in West Germany's constitution, or Basic Law. Under article 146 all-German elections would be held to choose delegates to a national assembly, which would in turn negotiate a new constitution for a unified Germany. This was the same route to unification that had been developed and offered to the East during the Adenauer era, stemming from the McCloy initiative of 1950. It was consistent with the creation of a confederation and assumed that a united Germany would be a new state, with a new constitution and form of government, and a new set of rights and responsibilities in the international system. In short, this was a provision for a merger, with the character of the new entity to be determined by the negotiations in a special national assembly elected for this purpose.

The Basic Law also offered a second possibility. Article 23 permitted "other parts of Germany" simply to join the existing FRG. This article had actually been used for the incorporation of the Saarland in 1957, after France agreed to end its military occupation of the province. This was a provision for a takeover. The GDR would become part of the existing Federal Republic. The constitution, form of government, and rights and responsibilities in the international system of the FRG would remain intact.

From the beginning of February, at the first meetings of the Deutschland-politik working group, Kohl's circle of advisers was drawn to the article 23 option. If the FRG's constitution were opened for renegotiation, pressure for substantial changes in the founding document of the West German state might be irresistible, especially if the East German SPD won the March elections and established primacy in the constitutional assembly. There was simply no way to tell what the outcome might be, particularly given the external pressures now surrounding German unification. Invoking article 23 would also simplify the problem of persuading the European Community to accept East Germany into its ranks, since there would be no need to amend the Treaty of Rome establishing the community.[9]

By the beginning of March, Kohl had begun to state publicly that article 23 was the only acceptable route to unity, and the CDU-backed parties contending for power in East Germany promptly adopted this position.[10] This stand automatically answered Waigel's question from the February 7 cabinet meeting, since a direct West German political takeover would appropriately be preceded by a West German economic takeover. In other words, Waigel's third option was best: making the deutsche mark legal tender in the GDR.

The East Germans understood what was at stake. Invoking article 23 would amount to a virtual annexation of the GDR. Valentin Falin understood this too and had tried to get Moscow to focus on this important question at the time of the January "crisis" meeting. No good could come from the use of article 23 from the point of view of the East German government. Kohl had to rely on the support of the East German people, on a clear mandate from the March 18 elections.

But the conventional wisdom in both the West and the East was that the East German Social Democrats (SPD) would win the March 18 elections. The SPD's prospects in the East seemed good because the East German Länder included areas that had been historic strongholds of SPD electoral strength before the Nazi seizure of power. The West German SPD was also thought to be well ahead of its CDU and FDP rivals in providing money, equipment, campaign advice, and stump speakers for its East German colleagues. The SPD-East, like the SPD-West, wanted monetary union without a West German economic takeover. It was sympathetic to the "confederation" approach to unification and favored article 146 over article 23.

American officials also noted that the SPD-East and SPD-West had issued a joint foreign policy statement announcing that "a future united Germany should belong neither to NATO nor to the Warsaw Pact."[11] This demand for neutrality was a potentially serious problem for Bonn and Washington. Kohl and his advisers did not want to argue with the SPD about foreign policy. The idea of German membership in NATO was not terribly popular. A February 15 poll showed that an astonishing 58 percent of West Germans wanted a united Germany that was neutral, outside both alliances. Many of the pro-NATO officials comforted themselves with the thought that both NATO and the Warsaw Pact would give way to a pan-European collective security organization, perhaps housed within the CSCE. There was wide speculation that Germany would leave NATO's integrated military command and an equally widespread assumption that U.S. nuclear weapons—and possibly all Western troops—would have to leave Germany. Government leaders in the FRG were doing little to quiet such talk.

Defense minister Gerhard Stoltenberg tried to settle the issue of the GDR's future military status in a united Germany.[12] In a new cabinet working group on the foreign and security aspects of unification, Stoltenberg had privately challenged Genscher to explain how the Tutzing formula on NATO "jurisdiction" would allow NATO to protect the new eastern portion of a united Germany. How would Bundeswehr deployments be handled, since the West German army was entirely integrated into NATO's military command? Teltschik chimed in to support Stoltenberg. Genscher, probably annoyed by the challenge to his primacy in foreign policy and certainly worried about Soviet reactions, bluntly replied that only his approach was realistic.

Stoltenberg, thinking or hoping that the Defense Ministry analysis had convinced Genscher, issued a public statement two days later that rejected neutralization of the GDR and stated that all of the territory of a united Germany would be part of NATO. He also rejected demilitarization of the East, asserting that the Bundeswehr could be deployed eastward. He thus broke with Genscher's Tutzing formula and associated himself with the U.S. position. In a concession to Genscher, Stoltenberg promised that the German forces in the former GDR would be detached from NATO's command structure.

Genscher had not been persuaded. He declared publicly that Stoltenberg's "private" view was wrong: NATO territory would not extend eastward; nor would the West German army move into the East, since it was indeed integrated into NATO. Genscher and his ministry fumed at the stance of the Defense Ministry and the Chancellery, a position they viewed as irresponsible and dangerous. The NATO issue was extraordinarily perilous. The Foreign Ministry could see no way to get the Soviets to accept full NATO membership for a united Germany. Nor did Genscher think that it was in Bonn's interest to defy Gorbachev if success meant the reformer's downfall and the end of perestroika. Genscher worried about what would happen if the Soviets played the German card. Would the Germans choose NATO or unity?

Stoltenberg was forced to back down. Angry about the whole dispute, Chancellor Kohl had to intervene. Teltschik advised the chancellor that Stoltenberg was right, that the Soviets had not yet pressed the issue, and it was much too early to make preemptive concessions to them. Unmoved, Kohl supported Genscher. He ordered preparation of a joint declaration by both ministers, negotiated with help from Seiters, which was released on February 19. The statement dropped the notion that NATO "territory" would not extend eastward. But the declaration held that "no formations or institutions of the Western Alliance should be moved forward to the present territory of the GDR," the declaration read. This included "NATO-assigned and non-assigned military forces of the Bundeswehr." The American embassy observed that Kohl had been obliged to go along with a position under which the former East German state would be "not only 'de-NATOed' but demilitarized."

Focused on the East German elections and his dramatic gamble to unify under article 23, Kohl made his top priority solidarity with Genscher. Bush's plea to concede no more than that the former GDR might have a "special military status" had not been heeded.

The Soviets Dig In as Europe Squirms

The Soviet government had established a policy on Germany at the end of January. Although Soviet officials sensed that Gorbachev had not firmly communicated this position to Baker and Kohl, they had not thought the policy had changed. Their job now was to dig trenches and fortify their position. The Soviets clearly hoped that the Two Plus Four mechanism would help. The day after the meetings in Ottawa, Alexander Bondarenko told an American diplomat that unification was more complicated than the Germans realized. The Four Powers would have to take charge of matters. And, he warned, the Soviet public was only beginning to grasp the seriousness of Moscow's situation in Germany. American experts tried to distinguish the position of the midlevel Germanists in the Kremlin from the more progressive beliefs they ascribed to Shevardnadze; the American embassy in Moscow even thought that the old guard might be replaced.[13] In fact, Shevardnadze respected Bondarenko and relied on Kvitsinsky, and the Soviet Foreign Ministry's German working group combined both "old" and "new" thinkers in support of the existing policy.

Flying back from Ottawa, Shevardnadze gave an interview reiterating the Soviet policy line. Gorbachev himself detailed his views on Germany on the front page of *Pravda:* he might accept unification or the fall of Modrow, but he had not accepted a unified Germany in NATO. Perhaps, he suggested, "history has started working in an unexpectedly rapid way." But that was just "one side of the matter." The other side was that unification concerned "not only the Germans." No one must be threatened by unity. There needed to be a peace treaty with Germany, he said. "It is this agreement that can finally determine Germany's status in the European structure in terms of international law." This treaty would maintain the role of both NATO and the Warsaw Pact, since any change in the "military-strategic balance" between these two organizations was "impermissible." He also promised that Moscow was ready to resist any Western effort to dictate terms in the Two Plus Four: "We rule out such a method whereby three or four first come to an arrangement between themselves and then set out their already agreed position before the other participants. This is unacceptable."[14]

Just to rebut any lingering presumption that Moscow had given Kohl a "green light" to do what he wished, the German working group in the Foreign Ministry rallied an extraordinary ministry collegium. Shevardnadze, his deputies, and fourteen other officials issued a rare joint public statement. The collegium declared that the Soviet Union could not accept NATO membership for a united Germany. Shevardnadze's main concern was that, while his government was digging in, the Western countries were keeping events in constant motion. In Ottawa he had complained in a speech to the Canadian Parliament about "politicians . . . who want to play a game of political speed chess with a time limit of five minutes."[15]

Shevardnadze was not the only statesman to resent the game of "political speed chess." François Mitterrand was also struggling to keep pace. As he had from the start, Mitterrand offered ambivalent support for German unity but had been active diplomatically in devising ways—intentionally or not—to slow the pace. He had wanted a CSCE summit, held in Paris, to consider the future of Europe. He had got it, too, though the Americans were determined to keep the question of Germany's future out of a chaotic debate in this large forum. Mitterrand wanted to pursue the most ambitious possible agenda for the European Community. Kohl went along with the plan for another EC summit to talk about Germany and other matters, but balked on a specific push to start negotiating European economic and monetary union.

Mitterrand mused publicly about the disappearance of both alliances within a decade and expressed indifference about West Germany's NATO status. The FRG would do as it pleased, he said. France, after all, had nuclear weapons and Germany did not. "The main thing, for me," he said, "is for Europe to take up its true place in the world again after the self-destruction of two world wars. In short, I expect Europeans to keep in mind, as I do, a paraphrase of that well-known expression, 'Let Europe take care of itself.'"[16]

Mitterrand offered no plan for how Europe would do this if NATO were wrecked, Germany became neutral, or the Americans left. He had a rather vague notion of a European union that might someday have global military power in its own right. Franco-German cooperation was somehow to be the core of this, though with a neutral Germany that arguably would have been difficult to achieve. It was never clear whether the Americans were to be in or out. With events moving rapidly in February 1990, Mitterrand preferred to think of distant horizons, not the compelling issues of the moment.

The Americans were troubled by these trends in France. The French were gloomy, and seemed to think that the Americans were on their way out of Europe. A veteran U.S. diplomat who knew France well and was now on the NSC staff visited Paris and advised his colleagues:

> Gone is the vision of a Europe co-managed by equals in Paris and Bonn, with German economic superiority offset by France's nuclear capability and essential strategic role in the face of a strong Warsaw Pact. But, so far, no clear alternative vision has emerged . . . The most striking impression I derived from my many conversations is the nearly total absence of the US in the mid- and long-term calculations of French policymakers. So convinced do the French seem that the US will rapidly withdraw its forces from Europe that they are thinking, and at times acting, as if we were already gone.[17]

French officials were clearly troubled by the prospect of German power. Months after the event they were still gossiping about the reputed comment of a German government spokesman at a dinner in Paris in late 1989: "Who can contest that Silesia is a German territory?" There was deep suspicion of Germany, and much pessimism about the future. At the end of February a top Quai official told an American counterpart that America and France ought to guard against a situation in which Germany once again would become a "hegemonic" power in Europe. The Two Plus Four, he said, must deal with the Germans "very firmly."[18]

Across the English Channel the British government was also still uncomfortable about developments in Germany. Prime Minister Thatcher continued to express her doubts about German unification, publicly and privately. At the end of January she met at her country house, Chequers, with her key advisers to talk about policy toward Europe. One of the ministers present, the historian Alan Clark, noted in his diary that he had argued for accepting, and exploiting, German reunification "while they still needed our support." Thatcher's own advisers from Number 10, Charles Powell and Percy Cradock, also urged her to be more sympathetic to the Germans. But, Clark wrote, it was "no good. She is determined not to." Clark cornered her later, disturbed that the conversation sounded so much like "the old Appeasement arguments of 1938." He recorded her reply with parenthetical awe: "'Yes,' she said, eyes flashing (she's in incredible form at the moment), 'and I'm not an appeaser.'"[19]

Disillusioned with the weak support she had received from Mitterrand and even Gorbachev, Thatcher took a new tack in a long phone conversation with President Bush just before Bush met with Kohl at Camp David.[20] It was a disagreeable conversation for both parties. Thatcher feared German ambitions. Germany, she said, "will be the Japan of Europe, but worse than Japan." Mitterrand was just as worried, she said, that "the Germans will get in peace what Hitler couldn't get in the war." The two leaders were talking about a "closer Entente Cordiale." But her initiative for Bush was to suggest that Soviet troops be allowed to stay on indefinitely in a united Germany. This would make matters easier for Gorbachev and help restrain the Germans. Genscher, she said, had no problem with this proposal. The Poles, too, would prefer that Soviet troops stay in Germany.

Bush gently told Thatcher that he was uncomfortable with the idea of letting Soviet troops stay in Germany. He was also uncomfortable with the Genscher-Stoltenberg statement implying that Germany might not retain full membership in NATO. Thatcher was less bothered; she thought that the U.S. position might be too extreme for Gorbachev. She also doubted, answering a question from Bush, that Mitterrand would care much about NATO's military arrangements. What Mitterrand cared about was keeping American troops in Europe. Disturbed by Thatcher's vivid portrait of British and French views, Bush suggested that, after he met with Kohl, perhaps he, Thatcher, and Mitterrand ought to get together, as a "triumvirate there to review things at some point."

The unease with the quickening pace of unification was palpable among Germany's Eastern European neighbors, too. Poland, Hungary, and Czechoslovakia all wanted good relations with West Germany.[21] But the Poles, in particular, were unhappy about Kohl's treatment of the border issue. They found Kohl's unwillingness to make a binding statement on the final borders of a united Germany unsettling, despite the chancellor's protestations that he was prohibited from doing so until an all-German government and the Four Powers acted.

Poland's president, General Wojciech Jaruzelski, thought that Soviet troops might have to stay in Poland (thus securing the logistical support for their presence in eastern Germany) until Poland's borders won final recognition. Prime Minister Tadeusz Mazowiecki launched a major diplomatic initiative on February 21, sending letters to Bush, Gorbachev, Thatcher, and Mitterrand. He wanted definitive recognition of the existing border, the Oder-Neisse line (referred to as the Odra-Lusatian-Nysa line by the Poles). To make sure that he got it, he asked for the two German states to initial a treaty settling the border issue, which would then be signed by Poland and Germany after establishment of an all-German state. He formally asked that the Two Plus Four be changed to Two Plus Five, with Poland's participation formally recognized. Excluding Poland "from the relevant stage of the discussion" would, the prime minister argued, "be tantamount to a repetition of the Yalta formula of 1945." Handing the letter to the American ambassador in Warsaw, Foreign Minister Krzysztof Skubiszewski said that his government was making its "strongest possible" effort to influence the terms and process of German unification.[22]

The U.S. government was alone in expressing satisfaction with Kohl's position on the border issue. The Americans trusted Kohl's private promises and understood the delicacy of his domestic position as he tried to hold conservative support in an election year. Washington firmly believed that it was inconceivable that Kohl or any other German statesman would actually challenge the postwar borders. Lawrence Eagleburger, in Warsaw, assured Mazowiecki that there would not be "another Yalta" and that the United States would not "sell out" its friends.[23]

Bush Wins Kohl Over

Thus, in the middle of February the consensus on Germany was again threatening to unravel. There were many loose ends, the border issues and the exact nature of Germany's membership in NATO by far the most important of them. The Soviet Union was again bellicose, and the French, the British, and the East Europeans were sullen and anxious. As elections approached in the East, Kohl in the West was very far out on a limb in hoping to achieve unification through article 23.

The United States knew that the stakes were very high and that the Two Plus Four was a risky, if necessary, mechanism on which to depend. On February 14, the day after the Ottawa accord, Blackwill, Rice, and Zelikow met to talk through their concerns about how the new negotiating forum would actually operate. The NSC staff did not like the decision, but it had been made. Now it was time to make the Two Plus Four work. The outcome was a long memo for President Bush, drafted principally by Rice, "Preparing for the Six Power German Peace Conference."[24] It warned: "We should be under no illusions about the dangers that these talks pose. It is critical that we get the Administration's position formulated and then coordinated with the Allies so that we do not mismanage what will arguably be the most important set of talks for the West in the postwar period."

The NSC staff feared that the Soviets, previously so ineffective at influencing Germany's fate, had now been handed a powerful weapon that would both motivate and empower them to act. Using its place in the Two Plus Four, allied with a leftist East German government, Moscow might try to force the choice between unity and NATO before the West German electorate in a volatile election year. For Kohl, facing the opportunity to win reelection and go down in history as a modern-day Bismarck, "all else will become for him secondary and negotiable."

The key, then, was to design the Two Plus Four process so that Moscow could not use it effectively against American interests. Everything depended on "how carefully we structure the mandate of the Six Power discussions and whether we and our major Allies remain united on a common approach" to the profound security questions. Three tasks were then vital. First, commit the West Germans and other allies to a common position on the details of the security issues that would soon be so contentious. Second, delay. The Two Plus Four should start work very slowly while German unification was happening very quickly. This would also give the U.S. government time to collect its wits. Third, when the Two Plus Four started up, the subjects for discussion should be "as limited as possible—dealing only with the legal issues related to the end of Four Power rights, the consequences of the absorption of the GDR into the FRG, and the issue of what becomes of forces on the territory of Germany's eastern half."

At the State Department's European bureau, Seitz and Dobbins had come to similar conclusions. Both men had opposed the Two Plus Four idea. Now that it had been realized, they wanted to limit its scope for making mischief. Blackwill talked to Seitz; then Rice and Zelikow met with Seitz and Dobbins and cemented their agreement on a common attitude toward the new talks: delay, and seek a limited mandate. Seitz felt that Baker, Zoellick, and Ross had not yet decided what they wanted to do. The policy planning staff had prepared a paper that would give the Two Plus Four a broad writ to consider the future of German defense and European security. Then Seitz and Blackwill both promptly weighed in with their much more restricted design for the new forum.[25]

Seitz urged "a narrow approach to the Two-Plus-Four Conference." The only purpose of the negotiations should be "to turn over remaining four-power rights to a fully democratic, sovereign German state within the territory of the FRG and the GDR." In this scheme the Two Plus Four would *decide* only how to return full sovereignty to Germany. It would *discuss* but steer to other negotiations the contentious security issues, including a schedule for full withdrawal of Soviet troops from the former GDR. A sovereign Germany would decide on its own alliance commitments, and NATO issues would remain solely the business of NATO's members. Seitz knew that the Soviets would not like this, but Soviet interests could be considered in separate sets of negotiations. It would be vital to persuade the West Germans, Britain, and France to agree to this complex design.[26]

Zoellick, paying little attention to the policy planning staff advice, had already begun to think of the Two Plus Four as a "steering committee" with a narrow mandate. He readily worked his ideas, along with those of Seitz and Blackwill, into advice for Baker on how to describe the Two Plus Four plan to President Bush. Zoellick tended to see the Two Plus Four not as a process leading to a final settlement on Germany but as a "process of incremental consultations." It is apparent that Baker wanted to stress to Bush that he hoped to (1) reassure smaller allies that they would be consulted; (2) use the Two Plus Four narrowly as a forum more for consultation than for negotiation; (3) limit the Two Plus Four's mandate principally to surrendering Four Power rights and establishing the new Germany's borders; and (4) keep the Two Plus Four from even discussing a future Germany's sovereign choices about how it would defend itself. Baker did, however, want the Two Plus Four to discuss, but not to decide, some of the issues troubling Moscow. He thought he could bring the Soviets along, and he did not want to leave the field open for some Soviet-German deal.[27]

Zoellick knew that the NSC staff was worried about the potential for Soviet mischief in the Two Plus Four, but he believed that it could be managed in a way that gave the Soviets the appearance of influence without real power. He envisioned few substantive concessions. His position on the security questions was practically identical to the formulas coming from the White House. So Zoellick agreed with the need for delay in activating the Two Plus Four, especially at the ministerial level, and he also agreed on the need for a narrow forum rather than a broader negotiation that would encompass all of the Soviets' concerns. The European bureau, however, wanted to delay the start-up of the Two Plus Four until after Germany's internal unification was essentially complete. That was too much delay, Zoellick and Ross thought. It would place an intolerable strain on East-West relations and invite the Soviets to pressure the West Germans directly, excluding the United States.[28]

The West Germans were preoccupied with a major gamble on the terms of internal unification: a monetary takeover followed by a direct political takeover of the East German state by means of article 23. Teltschik, however, still unhappy about the outcome of the Genscher-Stoltenberg battle, appealed to the Americans to weigh in with the chancellor. There was a bit of scheming between Blackwill and Teltschik. Teltschik wanted to turn Kohl away from conceding any retreat of NATO "jurisdiction" from the GDR; Blackwill wanted to push Baker away from his public endorsement of the "jurisdiction" line, a position Baker had adopted at Genscher's urging and which he had already dropped. But on the eve of Kohl's departure, Teltschik warned the American ambassador about the need to "clarify" Baker's position, though he undoubtedly knew that Baker was actually repeating Genscher's Tutzing formula.[29]

Scowcroft and Blackwill were advising Bush to insist on a joint clarification of the NATO membership question along the lines of the formula Bush had sent to Kohl just before Kohl's meeting with Gorbachev two weeks earlier.[30] The time, they said, "has come for an honest and unadorned talk with Kohl about his bottom-line on security issues, despite the difficulty of pinning the Chancellor down." It must be clear that all of a united Germany would be covered by NATO; a united Germany would remain in NATO's integrated military command; the Western military presence in western Germany would be unaffected by unification; and the former GDR would have a "special military status," still to be defined. On the Two Plus Four, the briefing memo for Bush used material offered by Zoellick and stressed the need for delay and a narrow mandate. The memo to Bush noted that, by offering such unwavering support for unity, the president was in a strong position. Now was the time to use it "to cement a historic bargain: Kohl's pledge not to alter the form and substance of Germany's security commitments to NATO in exchange for a U.S. promise that the Two Plus Four process will not interfere with German unity."

The NSC and State Department staffs knew that this tough position would be hard for Moscow to accept. They were working to develop a package of incentives for Gorbachev punctuated by a planned Bush-Gorbachev summit that they hoped would be the most productive U.S.-Soviet summit of the postwar period. But the bottom line, come what may, was firm: "In the final analysis, Soviet leverage to influence the fate of Germany is marginal, however much Moscow complains. Stalin and his successors set as their principal goal for European security in the postwar era the fracturing of the FRG's ties to NATO. Adenauer said no. The West did not give in to Moscow's demands when the Soviets were strong; hopefully Kohl will agree at Camp David that we should certainly not do so now when the Soviet Union is weak."

Bush talked to Thatcher and Canadian prime minister Mulroney just before he met with Kohl. The conversations revealed that Bush had read, agreed with, and internalized all the key points covered in the briefing materials for the Kohl meeting. The conversations highlighted some of the possible dangers ahead. Thatcher, in addition to wanting Soviet troops to stay in Germany, also wanted the Two Plus Four to start work immediately. Mulroney was nettled by the signs that German unification was beginning to look more like a takeover. Bush said flatly that the United States would not stand in the way of unification and that Soviet troops should not remain in Germany.[31]

Camp David was a pleasant setting for Kohl and Bush to review plans for the months ahead. The Germans were flattered by the invitation; no chancellor had ever before been a guest at Camp David. The weather was cold, but a fire was burning in the hearth, and the lodgings were comfortable and unpretentious. Both Kohl and Bush were accompanied by their wives, and other members of Bush's family joined them at lunch. The Germans could tell that the atmosphere would be relaxed when Baker greeted the chancellor's party at Dulles International Airport wearing a red flannel shirt and cowboy boots.

The substantive talks began in the middle of the afternoon on Saturday, February 24, broke for a relaxing dinner, and then resumed the next morning.[32] Kohl had Teltschik and a couple of other staffers from the Chancellery along with him, but no one from the Foreign Ministry was present, not even the West German ambassador. Bush was joined only by Baker, Scowcroft, and Blackwill.

Kohl was in good form, thoughtful and well prepared. He explained how his plan for internal unification had changed. His own ten-point program of November 1989 had been swept away. He dated the decision to discard confederation and push for a quicker, more direct takeover to the beginning of February, "about three weeks ago," after it had become clear that Modrow's government had effectively collapsed. Now he wanted to achieve economic and monetary union as quickly as possible, on Western terms. That meant putting the currency system directly under the control of the Bundesbank and moving the GDR to a market economy immediately after the March 18 elections. The FRG would then soon take over financing old age pensions and unemployment benefits. He knew what he wanted, whereas the other political parties were all in disarray. In fact, Kohl said, "everyone is confused but me."

Kohl confided a vision of Germany's future in which the GDR might return to prosperity within three to five years. But he saw unification as an opportunity for West Germany, too. We are getting fat and lazy, he said. Now there is some adventure in our national lives. Kohl had known for weeks that Washington also favored unification at the fastest possible pace. He said that German-American friendship was stronger than it had ever been before in the entire postwar period. Bush did not question Kohl's internal plans for rapid unification; instead, most of the discussion was about how to achieve an equally quick resolution of the difficult international issues.

Chancellor Kohl was aware of public calls for him to settle the question of a future Germany's border with Poland, but he did not consider this a serious question. Of course, the vast majority of Germans favored the current Oder-Neisse line. But many Germans were still bitter about the loss of one third of prewar Germany, the expulsion of more than 12 million innocent people, and the deaths of 2 million German refugees who fled from the East in 1945. A way would be found to reassure the Poles that the border was safe. Legally, however, the FRG could not do this alone. Kohl thought that the Four Powers would ultimately play a crucial role in settling the matter for the world.

This brought Kohl to the process issues, to the question how the Two Plus Four would actually work. Both Kohl and Bush agreed that Poland should not be a formal participant. Kohl feared that the Poles might use such participation to hold a settlement hostage to demands for reparations—more compensation for Poland for wartime damage done by the Third Reich. Germany, Kohl explained, had already paid DM 150 billion to Poland, Israel, and individual claimants. Fifty years after the war the Germans would not pay more. Consultation would be a better way to ease Polish concerns. Bush suggested only that the more Kohl could do for the Poles, the better.

Bush and Baker then explained the U.S. idea of a narrow mandate for the Two Plus Four, and Kohl concurred. Bush said that he would hate to see the Soviets get involved in a German decision about the FRG's membership in NATO. Baker pointed out that the Two Plus Four could steer issues so that decisions could be made by the countries that had to be involved. No one would decide fundamental issues affecting other countries in their absence. This would not be another Yalta. And many issues would be left for the Germans themselves to resolve.

Bush and Kohl also agreed that the Two Plus Four should be slow to start work. Bush emphasized that the talks should not get in the way of West

Germany's dialogue about the terms of unification with East Germany. Starting the talks too soon might stimulate Soviet interference. Kohl wanted no Two Plus Four meeting before the March 18 East German elections. Baker was more anxious about the need to show the Soviets that their concerns were being addressed. But Kohl argued that, before March 18, the East Germans would only be spokesmen for the Soviets. Scowcroft agreed. Baker gave way. The British and the French, he said, cared more about an early start-up than he did. First Kohl, then Bush, settled the matter by agreeing to talk only to the British and the French.

The two leaders also agreed that allied consultations about the Two Plus Four should start soon, but the Two Plus Four itself would not meet until after March 18, with the first session, at the level of foreign ministers, occurring in May, before the Bush-Gorbachev summit meeting. They also agreed that the Two Plus Four should finish its work before November, prior to the CSCE summit in Paris.

The Two Plus Four forum would be central. Kohl was opposed to the Soviet idea of negotiating a German peace treaty. After all, he said, 110 countries were at war with Germany in May 1945. Both sides agreed to this point and on the need to keep the thirty-five–nation CSCE summit out of German issues as well. The Two Plus Four's work should be done by the fall so that the November CSCE summit in Paris could just bless what the Two Plus Four had accomplished.[33] Kohl also accepted Bush's iron linkage of the CSCE summit to the signing of a CFE treaty rearranging the balance of conventional military forces in Europe.

The substantive security issues were then discussed. Kohl heartily accepted Bush's argument for keeping U.S. troops in Germany. Kohl said that he wanted America in Europe, not just for its soldiers, but also to prevent construction of a Fortress Europe. Kohl thought, however, that the nuclear issue might be a difficult one for the German public. Both leaders also agreed that, after staying for some limited time, all Soviet troops should leave the territory of a united Germany. The status of American forces would not be equated with the position of the Soviets. You must stay, Kohl told the Americans, even if the Soviets leave Germany.

Bush repeatedly stressed the need to clarify a future Germany's status in NATO. It must have full membership in the alliance. Kohl wondered aloud if Germany should be handled the way France was handled, that is, outside NATO's military organization. Bush said that he hated to think of another France in NATO. Germany ought to be a full participant. Kohl then raised the specific question of NATO's presence in former East German territory.

He said that NATO units, including German forces dedicated to NATO, could not be stationed on East German soil.

As the conversations neared an end, Teltschik, having talked the matter over with Blackwill, urged everyone to agree that the limits would apply only to NATO "forces," but that NATO "jurisdiction" would indeed extend to all of the former GDR. The two had worked on a press statement that would publicly clarify the matter. Baker's response was crucial, since he was the one who had adopted the "jurisdiction" position at what he thought was Genscher's request. But Baker, who had already been consulted about the planned press statement, said Teltschik was right. He admitted that he had used the term only before he realized how it would affect the application of the North Atlantic treaty to the defense of all of Germany. Kohl then wanted to be sure that this clarification would be made public. Absolutely, Baker replied.

Having agreed on a joint German-American plan of action, Bush and Kohl mused about how to persuade the Soviets to go along. Bush said that, in his opinion, the Soviets were not in a position to dictate Germany's relationship with NATO. He was worried about the Soviet line that Germany should not stay in NATO but dismissed it: "To hell with that. We prevailed and they didn't. We can't let the Soviets clutch victory from the jaws of defeat."

Kohl saw the next months unfolding with the Americans pushing ahead on arms control while he pushed for EC integration with all his might, noting that the EC summit was planned for late April. Frank discussions would be needed with the Soviets, Kohl said, but he looked to the Americans to carry the burden of handling the issue of Germany's NATO membership outside the Two Plus Four framework. The Soviets should understand that the United States and the FRG were in total agreement. The time for games had passed. The Soviets might then name their real price for agreement.

Kohl wondered if their compliance might just be a matter of money. Bush wryly observed, "You've got deep pockets." But Kohl thought that Gorbachev would want to come to his decision directly with the American president— superpower to superpower. Baker had earlier compared the Soviet pronouncements to the opening move of a chess game that, at its end, would surely see the Soviets accepting Germany's membership in NATO. In the end, Kohl thought, Gorbachev would make the concession on Germany and NATO to the U.S. president. For that to happen, Baker thought, Gorbachev would need to see, on the one hand, that the Germans were unshakably behind full NATO membership but also, on the other, that the West was willing to take legitimate Soviet security concerns into account. That, Bush commented, was why the United States and Germany ought to have the closest possible consultation. We are going to win the game, he said, but we must be clever while we are doing it.

At the joint press conference following the talks, President Bush, as both sides had determined, announced the common agreement that

> a unified Germany should remain a full member of the North Atlantic Treaty Organization, including participation in its military structure. We agreed that U.S. military forces should remain stationed in the united Germany and elsewhere in Europe as a continuing guarantor of stability. The Chancellor and I are also in agreement that in a unified state, the former territory of the GDR should have a special military status, that it [referring only to the disposition of the GDR] would take into account the legitimate security interests of all interested countries, including those of the Soviet Union.

During the question and answer period Kohl again got in trouble over the border issue by repeating the formal legal position that the FRG lacked the capacity to settle the matter definitively on its own. Bush, for his part, had no difficulty saying—correctly—that the United States recognized the current East German–Polish border and considered it "inviolable" under the Helsinki Final Act of the CSCE.[34]

Kohl followed up on the Camp David meeting by arranging an extraordinary personal visit to NATO headquarters, where he personally reassured all the allies of his interest in their views and of Bonn's commitment to remaining a reliable and stable ally. The ambassadors were delighted with this gesture of support.[35]

Bush and Baker also followed up on the areas of agreement at Camp David. The secretary had on his desk a note telling him that French foreign minister Dumas attached "great personal importance" to starting the Two Plus Four talks soon, with meetings of officials to begin before the March 18 elections. Baker, in line with the discussions at Camp David, instructed his officials to tell the French, and the British, that the United States preferred to wait "until after 3/18."[36] Baker, conscious that Genscher had not been at Camp David, also wrote to his German counterpart to tell him of the agreement that "all of the territory of a united Germany would benefit from the security guarantee provided by the Alliance." Just to be clear, he added that references to limiting NATO jurisdiction were "creating some confusion" and should be avoided.[37]

Bush phoned both Mitterrand and Thatcher. Mitterrand was annoyed by Kohl's position on the border issue and thought that the Four Powers should take a stand, refusing to subordinate their strategic concerns to Kohl's domestic political interests. (Kohl, incidentally, waited more than a week before talking to Mitterrand about the Camp David meeting.) Bush offered soothing words about the respect Kohl bore the French president. Mitterrand closed by warning that the USSR was still a force to be reckoned with.

Thatcher was pleased about Kohl's stance on the NATO issue and did not renew her idea about leaving Soviet forces in Germany. She knew that Bush was opposed. Thatcher was more scornful than annoyed about Kohl's handling of the border issue, but Bush felt sure that happier news about Kohl's handling of the matter would be forthcoming.[38]

The Soviet Union had paid close attention to the outcome of the Bush-Kohl talks.[39] When Bush called Gorbachev on February 28, he began by recounting his public agreement on rapid German unification, full German membership in NATO, continued presence of American troops in Europe ("as long as the Europeans want them"), and the need for a "special status" for the former territory of the GDR.[40] Bush assured Gorbachev that the unification of Germany should not, however, abridge the legitimate security interests of any state in Europe.

Gorbachev reiterated his own government's faith in the "all-European process." The American president and Kohl might have a common view on security issues, but the Soviet Union did not have such a mutual understanding with the German chancellor. He was not sure that he saw a need to incorporate a united Germany into one alliance. "If we find that this would negatively affect the Soviet Union," he said, "we would have to think long and hard about it." Gorbachev appreciated Bush's effort to inform him personally and commented, referring also to the January 31 call, when Bush had consulted him about the U.S.-Soviet troop limit initiative, "That is twice, and I am in debt. I will have to draw some conclusions from this."

In Moscow the Bush-Kohl announcements spurred anxiety and the feeling that the Soviets were sitting, immobile, in their dug-in fortifications while the West was consolidating its strength. They, like the French and the British, were thinking constantly about how to use the Two Plus Four talks to play more of a role in the ongoing events.

Defusing the Polish Border Issue

All the governments that were worried about German unification seized on Kohl's reticence about the Polish border issue as a focal point for their anxieties and frustrations. Genscher announced that he could support Mazowiecki's proposal for negotiating a new Polish-German treaty that would settle the border question, to be signed after the unified German government came into being. Kohl was put on the spot at a cabinet session on February 28. That evening he and his advisers sat down and speculated about Genscher's political motives. Teltschik noted: "The Chancellor sees the international pressures and the domestic campaign against the background of the eight elections scheduled for this year. He knows that he must move himself further, but actually he doesn't want to." Kohl also had to decide how to present formally his emerging preference for a direct takeover of the GDR by means of article 23.[41]

Genscher put unremitting pressure on Kohl in private without openly attacking the chancellor in public. The two men were longtime political partners and were close personally, too, but tensions on this issue grew so severe that it looked to some as if the governing coalition might break apart. After prolonged debate among the coalition partners on March 5 and 6, Kohl gave in and the coalition agreed to offer the Poles a joint declaration confirming the current borders, to be issued by both the West German Bundestag and the East German Volkskammer. Kohl won agreement that such a declaration would be conditional on Poland's renouncing its claims for reparations (claims Poland had renounced vis-à-vis the GDR in 1953) and promising to respect the rights of the remaining ethnic German minority. Furthermore, the coalition formally agreed to support article 23 as the path to unification. The United States welcomed Bonn's decision publicly and privately.[42]

Chancellor Kohl presented the coalition agreement to the Bundestag on March 8. He then formally declared his support for article 23 as the instrument for unification. The FRG's Basic Law should not be revised, he maintained, even as the FRG worked out modalities for the transition to full application of West German law in the GDR. Kohl also strongly reaffirmed his agreement to keep the future Germany firmly integrated in the NATO alliance: "While some form of interim regulation has to be made for the present GDR territory . . . it is the objective of the Federal government headed by me to continue to completely close ranks with our Allies on this very decisive question." The Bundestag then adopted a declaration affirming that "the Polish people should know that its right to live in secure borders will not be called into question by us Germans through territorial claims, either now or in the future." The Bundestag further promised to settle the border issue definitively in a treaty to be signed between the all-German government and Poland. Poland's 1953 renunciation of reparations in its treaty with the GDR was duly noted.[43]

The West German policy declaration went some distance toward addressing the substance of Polish concerns. The American government was satisfied, and, privately, the British were satisfied too.[44] The Poles, however, had built up a good deal of momentum and continued to agitate for full participation in the Two Plus Four process.

Mazowiecki was encouraged by his visit to Paris on March 9. The French and the Poles had worked out a plan for partial Polish participation in the Two Plus Four, with a Two Plus Four session to be held in Warsaw. Mitterrand then held an extraordinary press conference with Mazowiecki, at which he had announced (without any prior discussion with Bonn) that the German-Polish treaty should be signed *before* German unification occurred, insisting that "a juridical act be negotiated as rapidly as possible, and in any case before the likely unification of the two German states." Mitterrand seemed to be seeking a confrontation with Kohl. The chancellor was furious. Here Kohl and Genscher had just agonizingly adopted a major new position, and within days the French president was publicly attacking it. Kohl expressed his unhappiness directly to Mitterrand in a telephone call. The French government soon muted its support for the Polish position.[45]

The American government gave no aid to this French-Polish initiative, telling Mazowiecki in a letter that the West Germans had made a "positive and important step toward settling the border question on a legal and permanent basis." Poland would be involved only in those Two Plus Four decisions that affected the vital interests of Poland; the terms of this involvement were left open. Genscher was soon able to secure direct agreement from the French that Poland would participate in Two Plus Four talks only "when the question of Poland's western border is considered." The West German foreign minister opposed any meeting in Warsaw. Faced with firm opposition from Bonn and Washington, France dropped its demand for concluding a new German-Polish treaty before unification.[46]

The Polish-German issue was defused in the second half of March, owing in large part to Bush's secret mediation between Kohl and Mazowiecki. Mazowiecki was on his way to Washington, where it was assumed he would press his case directly with the American president.[47] Bush called Kohl on March 15 to preview what he intended to say in his upcoming meeting with the Polish prime minister. He assured Kohl that he would stand by the Camp David understanding on the border issue and that the United States would not support Poland's claim to membership in the Two Plus Four.[48]

The leaders talked again on March 20. Kohl said Bush could tell Mazowiecki that he, Kohl, wanted to help Mazowiecki, but he also had to be sure that he could pull off his effort to accomplish Germany's unification. Kohl admitted that he did not usually admit this publicly, but obviously the election results had a bearing on these questions. Yet again, Kohl wanted Bush to have no doubt about his determination to accept the existing border. He was not hiding anything; there was no secrecy about his intentions. The borders were a bitter burden of history, but now was the time to settle the issue definitely for the future. Yet the all-German government, under international law, had to make the final settlement. Kohl could understand the Poles' wish for an earlier settlement, but there could be no doubt about the ultimate outcome: the West and East German parliaments would still represent the same attitudes.

Kohl then gave Bush more assurances for the American leader to offer Mazowiecki. Although he would not promise to negotiate a treaty for a united Germany before unification was achieved, Kohl would be willing to work out the relevant text privately with Mazowiecki in advance. Bush thought that these two pledges would be very reassuring. Kohl emphasized that these were promises he could keep. Bush asked Kohl if the chancellor wanted to communicate the idea of a private agreement on the text directly to Mazowiecki. Possibly, Kohl replied, but first he wanted to see what would happen after Bush tried out the idea on Mazowiecki, if Mazowiecki promised to keep the idea private.[49]

Mazowiecki arrived in Washington the next morning, March 21, and, after the welcoming ceremony on the South Lawn of the White House, the two leaders began a small meeting, each accompanied by only one adviser.[50] Germany was the first subject. Mazowiecki wanted a reconciliation with the past; he wanted to be forward-looking. But Mazowiecki did not want the western territories taken from Germany to be viewed as a gift from Stalin. Their status had to be guaranteed by all the powers, not just in a unilateral act by one of them. That was why Poland wanted to be included in the Two Plus Four and wanted a binding treaty recognizing the border. Declarations were just declarations. What the Poles needed was a treaty worked out before unification and signed afterward, for they feared that Germany would be less amenable to negotiations after unification.

Bush then worked hard to convince Mazowiecki that, at least on this matter, Kohl could be trusted. He explained Kohl's political problem and noted the strong language adopted by the Bundestag on March 8. Then he began to deploy the assurances he had discussed with Kohl the previous day. What if I could get Kohl to agree with you on the text of a treaty now? Bush asked. Would that help? He was convinced that Kohl had no secret desire to change the border. Mazowiecki was a bit skeptical about Kohl, but had to admit that the West Germans had acted to address Polish concerns. He wanted to study Bush's idea about a private, advance understanding of the text. Why couldn't the treaty be initialed before unification?

Bush then explained the problem: neither of the existing German states was the appropriate legal entity to negotiate such a treaty for the united Germany. Kohl had proposed common parliamentary resolutions, with a treaty to be concluded by the all-German government. Instead of asking to write and initial the treaty before unification and sign afterwards, Mazowiecki should think about persuading Kohl just to negotiate the text beforehand. Bush added his own weight to Kohl's assurances. The United States was not playing games. America trusted Kohl, but its policy did not rest on individuals. The United States could understand Poland's position on this issue.

Mazowiecki then suggested a proposal of his own. Poland did not believe in a neutral Germany. But something had to be done in a way to ensure Gorbachev's survival. The NATO solution was not acceptable to Gorbachev.[51] Perhaps forces of both the East and the West could remain in Germany. In other words, Mazowiecki was now presenting the proposal for the indefinite retention of Soviet troops in Germany which Thatcher had suggested to Bush nearly a month earlier.

Bush was also concerned about Gorbachev's fortunes. The political reforms were not yet irreversible. But that was a reason to try to remove all Soviet troops from Central and Eastern Europe while it was still possible. Soviet goodwill might not last. Bush also made it clear that the deployment of U.S. troops was a completely separate matter. American troops were a stabilizing force. If the Europeans did not agree, the U.S. soldiers would be out. Mazowiecki said that he understood. The meeting ended, and the ceremonial schedule resumed, including a state dinner that evening.

That same day Blackwill talked over the U.S.-Polish exchanges with Teltschik in Bonn, clarifying some confusion. The "text" that could be worked out in advance was not the entire text of a future Polish-German treaty but only the critical sentence or sentences addressing the border question. Once this language was worked out, it could be incorporated into the resolutions adopted later by the two German parliaments, then into the eventual treaty with a united Germany.[52]

Bush and Mazowiecki met again the next day. The Polish prime minister was still uneasy. Bush pointed out that Mazowiecki had already got Kohl to move a long way. But Bush was very direct: he would not publicly pressure Kohl to do more. He trusted the chancellor. A contented, unified Germany—under Kohl—would be easier to deal with on a number of issues. Resolutions followed by an early treaty would satisfy the United States.[53] Mazowiecki left

Washington knowing just what he could expect from the leading power of the West.

Having urged Mazowiecki to trust Kohl, Bush now called Kohl to urge him to trust Mazowiecki.[54] Bush reviewed the arguments he had made. He wanted to be sure there was no misunderstanding about Bush's offer to "persuade" Kohl to negotiate the key text of a treaty in advance. Kohl assured him that this was not a problem. The treaty, Kohl went on, would contain one key sentence that might read: "The Republic of Poland and the Republic of Germany do not make any border claims on each other, and they consider the existing border to be permanent." His idea was to find some area of agreement on the wording of that sentence. Then it would be written into the resolutions of the two German parliaments, which at the same time would call for completion of a treaty as soon as possible. The two German governments would then pass these resolutions to Warsaw, with assurances of their support for the parliamentary position. So the Poles would have assurances from the parliaments and the governments of both German states at the highest possible levels. Then no decent person could doubt German intentions.

Bush asked if Kohl would like to work out that sentence with Mazowiecki in advance. Bush had not committed Kohl to anything; in his talks with Mazowiecki the idea had been presented as Bush's own proposal. But, Kohl answered, we can further develop this idea. Exactly, Bush replied. Kohl thought that this would be a big concession but, after some open musing, agreed to pursue the language privately with Mazowiecki. Bush thought that the Poles were already feeling more reassured, and that this step could help settle the matter.

Kohl believed that the problem could now be managed in a reasonable way. He was right. The subsequent diplomacy to settle the Polish-German issue unfolded in line with these critical discussions between Bush, Kohl, and Mazowiecki. The language in the German parliamentary resolutions was the key text. It was discussed with the Poles in advance, and it accurately forecasted the later contents of the postunification Polish-German treaty.

One great irony was that the issue was propelled by the inability of the FRG to sign a treaty on behalf of the future united Germany. But the FRG's March decision (formally announced on March 8) to unify by means of article 23 made the point moot. If the FRG annexed the GDR, making it part of the existing Federal Republic, Bonn's past international legal obligations—including its 1970 treaty with Poland guaranteeing the borders—remained intact. That would have been enough to bind a united Germany to recognition of the Polish border.[55]

The West Confers on the Two Plus Four

On February 28, after the president's Camp David meeting with Chancellor Kohl, top subcabinet officials, "political directors," from the foreign ministries of the United States, West Germany, Britain, and France gathered in London for an exchange of views about how the Two Plus Four should work. Baker altered the traditional composition by asking Robert Zoellick to lead the delegation, accompanied by the State Department's usual political director, assistant secretary Raymond Seitz.[56] The delegation leaders at this meeting remained the same throughout the year: Zoellick, Dieter Kastrup from Bonn, John Weston for the British government, and Bertrand Dufourcq representing France.[57]

The first topic was one the Americans expected: How soon would the negotiations get under way? The British and the French wanted to move quickly. The Americans and the West Germans, following the understanding reached at Camp David, preferred delay. Kastrup began to give ground, but Zoellick would not. The group agreed with Zoellick's suggestion that any meeting of ministers would have to wait until after the East German elections. The Western diplomats also agreed to keep Germany out of the agenda for the CSCE summit. If, for some reason, unification was not concluded by the time the summit was held, the Two Plus Four would simply offer the other twenty-nine CSCE member states a progress report.

Turning to the substantive security issues, Kastrup presented the West German position on NATO membership. He still spoke of not extending NATO "jurisdiction" to East Germany (attributing the term to Baker!). Zoellick promptly clarified matters by reviewing the Camp David understandings. Zoellick further questioned the Genscher-Stoltenberg agreement by asking whether, if the German armed forces were kept out of eastern Germany, the FRG could avoid having a special "demilitarized" zone in its own country. He was against this, as were Weston and Dufourcq. Kastrup refused to engage, pleading a need for instructions. Zoellick urged him to tell Genscher that the other allies had raised a very large red flag on this issue.

A number of topics were touched on briefly, but all the diplomats soon realized that some important legal questions needed more careful study. If the FRG took over the GDR under article 23, which of East Germany's international obligations would be inherited by the Federal Republic? Kastrup assumed that Bonn would inherit those obligations that were consistent with existing FRG law, thus dropping the GDR's Warsaw Pact membership. But more study was needed. And just how would the external aspects of German unity be settled? Would there be a "peace settlement"? The British thought so, but Kastrup reported that his government was adamant about rejecting anything smacking of a "peace treaty" now, nearly fifty years after the end of World War II. Other questions arose about whether Berliners, still under Four Power rule, could vote in the upcoming federal elections. If so, preparations had to start soon. But moves to let Berliners vote as if they were part of West Germany rather than under Four Power rule might antagonize the Soviets at the beginning of the process.

The Soviet Union Prepares for the Two Plus Four

Not surprisingly, the West German and American goals for the talks clashed with those of the Soviet government. A working group on Germany had formed within the Foreign Ministry, and at this point its leading figures were deputy foreign minister Anatoly Adamishin and European department head Alexander Bondarenko. U.S. and Soviet interests were diametrically opposed. Just as the Americans wanted to delay the start of the Two Plus Four and circumscribe its jurisdiction, Moscow wanted to meet as soon as possible, and with the broadest possible mandate.

Moscow's immediate problem was to get the Two Plus Four into action. On March 2, two weeks after the meetings in Ottawa, Shevardnadze sent a terse letter to the other Two Plus Four foreign ministers proposing that, in the event of "unforeseen circumstances" connected to the upcoming GDR elections, any member of the Two Plus Four would have the right to call an urgent Two Plus Four meeting. If other ambassadors did not agree to the meeting within twelve hours, then the concerned country would "be free to act in response to the prevailing situation" while informing the others of its actions. Washington immediately sought further clarification of what "unforeseen circumstances" were contemplated and what sort of unilateral action the Soviets were thinking of taking. The Soviets were obviously worried about some sudden East German lunge toward unification after the March 18 elections. The French government saw this sign of Soviet anxiety as yet another reason to begin the talks as soon as possible.[58]

A few days later the Soviets tried again, formally proposing a Two Plus Four to be held at the "expert level" (i.e., political directors) on March 12 or 13 in Geneva.[59] The West German Foreign Ministry was ready to agree, and the United States joined in consenting to a first Two Plus Four meeting on March 14 in Bonn, not Geneva.

At the same time, the Soviet Union and East Germany were moving to counter the Kohl-Bush consensus on rapid unification. Moscow finally understood the point that Falin had made in January: Kohl was proposing a takeover of the GDR through article 23. Gorbachev met with Modrow in Moscow on March 5–6. Shevardnadze then announced that article 23 was an unacceptable and even "illegal" path to unification, since it would override East Germany's sovereign rights and its international obligations to its Warsaw Pact allies and to the Soviet Union. The Soviet ambassador to Washington, Yuri Dubinin, called on Zoellick and personally stressed the significance of Shevardnadze's stand.[60]

Gorbachev and Modrow emerged equally adamant on the issue of Germany's membership in NATO. Gorbachev told the press on March 6 that the Soviet Union could not agree to any form of participation of a unified Germany in NATO. "It is absolutely out of the question," he said. There must instead be a staged process, tied to the CSCE, leading to the transformation of both alliances into purely political organizations. In a vehement statement he attacked those who did not treat such questions seriously.

On returning to Berlin, Modrow also reported to the East German parliament that his coalition government had again agreed with the Soviets that NATO membership for a united Germany was unacceptable. The Soviet Union prompted precisely the response it had hoped for as the West Germans rushed to assure the USSR—and the German public—that no harm would come to Soviet interests. Genscher noted that "the alliances will increasingly become elements of cooperative security structures in which they can ultimately be absorbed." The last phrase was new and seemed not unlike the position of centrist SPD experts who believed that Germany's membership in NATO would be temporary since the alliance would dissolve within a year or two. SPD radicals were flatly opposed to German membership in NATO.[61]

The Soviet Union's preferences for the Two Plus Four began to emerge as well. The body would, in Shevardnadze's view, handle all security issues and borders, constrain any future German military threat, adopt guarantees against the rebirth of Nazism in German domestic politics, deal with Germany's alliance membership, address the status of all foreign forces on German soil, and consider financial and material claims against Germany left over from the war. The Soviet Foreign Ministry followed up with an official statement repeating these points and, in the harshest language yet, accused the FRG of massive interference in East Germany's internal affairs and of deliberately attempting to push the GDR into economic ruin.

These moves came too late from the point of view of Akhromeyev and retired veteran diplomat Georgi Kornienko. They later wrote angrily that "it was only in March, after the NATO train had left, or at least started to move, that we began making declarations about the impermissibility of incorporating the future Germany into NATO . . . and only at that time . . . a more or less detailed Soviet concept of the issues related to the reunification of Germany was announced in the form of a statement by the Foreign Ministry of the USSR. But it was too late."

Opening Skirmishes

The U.S. government believed that success in the Two Plus Four depended on a disciplined approach to the negotiations. The objectives and procedures of the upcoming talks had to be tightly coordinated. Thus, right after the Camp David meeting with Kohl, the government developed a detailed blueprint for the talks and circulated these plans to its allies. As these points were presented by American diplomats throughout Europe, the West German Foreign Office expressed some relief (at least to the Americans) that Washington was being so clear and so blunt as Moscow took a tougher line.[62]

The United States left no doubt about its view that the March 14 Two Plus Four meeting would be "preliminary and procedural, aimed at discussing modalities for later substantive sessions" that would take place only after there was a new GDR government, and after dialogue about internal unification had advanced.[63] But the NSC staff remained uneasy about the State Department's ability to limit the scope of the talks. Although Zoellick maintained that major security issues would be only discussed, not decided, in the Two Plus Four, White House aides feared that this precaution could "quickly lose all meaning" in the real setting of a negotiation. They even thought that President Bush might have to issue a formal National Security Directive confining the talks to the narrow agenda "before we are off to the races."[64]

The tension within the U.S. government finally disappeared after State Department officials joined their NSC staff colleagues in a long discussion, held at Zoellick's initiative, which hammered out an extraordinarily detailed common understanding of how the Two Plus Four would work. The Americans agreed on how they would handle a dozen issues. Kohl's choice to unify under article 23 was put off-limits for Two Plus Four discussion. The Americans argued that this was an internal German issue. Ross and Zoellick stressed the importance of bolstering Gorbachev by using the Two Plus Four to manage Soviet anxiety about Germany. But they agreed that there should be no meeting of Two Plus Four ministers until at least early April (after Baker met with Shevardnadze in Washington), and the NSC staff held out for postponing such a meeting until May.[65]

The NSC staff prepared a diagram to illustrate how the Two Plus Four would deal with various issues. For example:

- Four Power rights, including the fate of Berlin: decide in Two Plus Four.
- Borders: decide in Two Plus Four with sovereign German voice.
- NATO's obligations toward the former GDR: sovereign German decision; no discussion in Two Plus Four.
- German forces in GDR: sovereign German decision; could be discussed in Two Plus Four.
- Soviet troops in GDR: sovereign German decision and subject for bilateral German-Soviet agreement; could be discussed in Two Plus Four.
- Nuclear weapons in FRG: to be decided by Germany or in arms control negotiations; no discussion in Two Plus Four.
- German NATO membership: sovereign German decision; no discussion in Two Plus Four.
- Prohibition of German nuclear, biological, and chemical weapons: sovereign German decision; could be discussed in Two Plus Four.
- Size of the Bundeswehr: to be decided by Germany or in arms control negotiations; no discussion in Two Plus Four.[66]

Zoellick used this diagram in presenting the American stance at the Two Plus Four meeting and allied consultations.

On the eve of the Two Plus Four meeting, the four Western delegations met in Paris to coordinate their strategy. They had already agreed that the delegations would be small, only three members each. The American delegation at the political director level consisted of Zoellick, Seitz, and Rice. The West Germans were Kastrup, Elbe, and Peter Hartmann from the Chancellery staff.[67] The Americans pressed their narrow agenda and won agreement to exclude any discussion of the West German government's decision to unify by means of article 23.[68] Yet the French hedged, wanting the Two Plus Four to have a powerful writ to consider "political-military issues." Dufourcq had already had his own meetings with the Soviets and, like Moscow, had a substantial list of questions to be considered by the new forum, causing several clashes with Kastrup and with Zoellick. Both the British and the French also kept pressing for faster Two Plus Four action, rather than waiting for the West and East Germans to move closer to unification.[69] The atmosphere was tense at times, not always because of substantive differences, but perhaps exposing still lingering anxieties over what was about to happen.

The fractious allies met the next day in Bonn with the Soviets and the East Germans for the first Two Plus Four meeting. The Soviet team was headed by deputy foreign minister Adamishin along with Kvitsinsky, Moscow's ambassador in the West German capital.[70] Most Western positions on procedural issues were adopted without dissent. All agreed that the political directors' meetings would be held on German soil, in Bonn or Berlin. The Soviet Union presented the Shevardnadze proposal for emergency meetings within twelve hours should unforeseen circumstances arrive. Zoellick and Rice worked out a compromise requiring a longer period for notification and a detailed rationale for holding such a meeting.

The Americans were pleased that no future meetings were scheduled. Adamishin even agreed, after lengthy discussion, to the Western agenda, since its labels (borders, "political-military issues," Berlin, Four Power rights and responsibilities) were not clearly defined. The Americans and the West Germans opposed the notion that the Two Plus Four were negotiating a "peace settlement," though this language was favored by the Soviets (who wanted a formal peace treaty) and by the British.

Rice, writing back to the White House, reported that "the Soviets were not prepared to be very directive or clear about what they want. They held their fire today and seemed somewhat unprepared. That's the good news." The bad news, for Rice, were signs of weakening Western solidarity. The British wanted a peace treaty. The French did not care to coordinate Western views, claiming that they did not want to gang up on the Soviets. Both London and Paris wanted a broader Two Plus Four agenda, and the FRG was not resisting them as vigorously as the Americans would have liked. Zoellick, reporting to Baker, made similar points but was less concerned about the French. He thought that Paris would try to respect a common allied approach.[71]

The day after the Two Plus Four meeting broke up, Kohl called Bush to talk about what had happened. He suggested the following sequence of events: the GDR would form a new government; it would then decide in favor of monetary union and help slow the exodus of its people to the West; the FRG would next concentrate on getting a smooth settlement of external issues with its neighbors. Although Kohl did not say it, monetary union on Kohl's terms would pave the way to a quick takeover under article 23. So postponement of external issues until after a GDR decision for such a union would keep the Two Plus Four from being able to interfere with internal unification. Bush, of course, was not worried about such a scenario.

In Bonn, Kohl's mood had been shooting up and down. He had gone to the GDR and campaigned directly for the CDU alliance, encountering huge, cheering crowds. In six appearances he had spoken before about a million people, almost 10 percent of the electorate. Yet the stress was tremendous. He had undertaken an extraordinary gambit by publicly announcing the article 23 plan to take over the GDR. His coalition partner, Genscher, had forced him into a difficult confrontation with defense minister Stoltenberg, then to a much harder stand-down over the Polish border issue. He was furious with Mitterrand, then reconciled. The mood in the FRG was uncertain and anxious. So much hinged on the election in the GDR, and the polls were giving the SPD-East a clear plurality of 44 percent against only 20 percent for the conservative Alliance for Germany.[72]

The East German CDU had formed this tenuous alliance with two other conservative parties, the German Social Union (a counterpart to the Bavarian-based CSU) and Democratic Awakening. The CDU-East and its leader, Lothar de Maizière, had looked for some issue to highlight the difference between the Alliance for Germany and the SPD-East. That issue lay in the route to unity. A week before the March 18 vote the alliance had followed Kohl's lead and endorsed article 23. On March 13, at a rally in Cottbus, Kohl went further and promised East German voters that, after the West German takeover, their Ostmarks could be exchanged for the prized deutsche marks at a one-to-one rate. To his fellow West Germans Kohl could portray his choice of article 23 as a question of "whether we want this republic [the FRG] or another one."[73] To the East Germans he posed another question: After more than forty years of communist rule, do you want to try new social experiments or join a proven, prosperous democratic state?

The SPD-West had declared repeatedly for article 146, and the SPD-East had formally opted for this path at its February party convention. Some in the SPD-East and in the SPD-West (notably Herta Däubler-Gmelin) wanted to leave open the possibility of using article 23, and avoided speaking out against this option. This faction was effectively overruled in the SPD's formal party declaration, "Steps to German Unity," issued on March 9. The declaration envisaged transitional security arrangements in the process of unification which would replace both existing alliances with new structures based on the CSCE. Four Power rights would not end until the new security structures were in place. "Germany should not confront its partners and neighbors with faits accomplis," read the declaration. Unification would proceed only under article 146, with a new constitution that would change or augment the Basic Law as needed "by the creation of the federal state, or [by taking into account the] specific characteristics of the GDR."[74]

With the Christian Democratic and Social Democratic positions on unification now clearly distinguished for the East Germans, most analysts in early March, including the American embassy in East Berlin, thought that the Social Democrats, the SPD-East, were likely to win. According to a survey taken at the beginning of the month, about 34 percent of voters favored the SPD, about 30 percent backed the parties making up the Alliance for Germany, and the former Communist party—renamed the Party for Democratic

Socialism (PDS)—was in third place with a respectable 17 percent. The odds seemed long and bleak for Kohl and the CDU. He had defined the terms for unity when it seemed a distant possibility, and now the crucial vote to decide the question was about to take place in the East. It is no wonder that Horst Teltschik remembers Kohl as being so depressed that he wondered aloud whether he could just give up and go home. Kohl did not have long to wait for news that would restore his will to fight.[75]

A Stunning Victory in the East

In early March the Social Democratic leader in East Germany, Ibrahim Böhme, was already anticipating victory and deciding who would be in his government. Böhme did not have to worry about forming a government. In the first free election to be held in eastern Germany since 1932, the voters chose absorption into the more prosperous West. They voted decisively for Kohl's path to unity. The turnout was over 93 percent of the electorate, the margin of victory clear. The Alliance for Germany won over 48 percent of the electorate, the SPD about 22 percent. The former Communist party, the PDS, held some 16 percent of the voters, many in Berlin. The dissidents of 1989, New Forum and the like, running as Alliance '90, mustered less than 3 percent of the vote. Support for Kohl's plan was strongest among blue-collar workers and farmers, among practicing Protestants and Catholics, in rural communities, and in the southern provinces of Thuringia and Saxony. The Alliance for Germany, with 193 out of 400 seats in the East German parliament, easily formed a government dedicated to a rapid West German takeover under article 23. De Maizière and his colleagues ultimately formed a grand coalition in mid-April, including the SPD as a junior partner in order to have a comfortable two-thirds majority to effect constitutional changes and command a government with the appearance of consensus support. If there was a consensus, though, it was not for de Maizière. It was for Helmut Kohl's plan, his promises, and his Germany.[76]

The West Germans were exultant. "The sensation is perfect! . . . Who would have expected it?" Teltschik wrote in his diary. By March 20 Schäuble could report that the stream of refugees from East Germany was already diminishing. That same day Bush telephoned his congratulations to Chancellor Kohl: "You're a hell of a campaigner!" Kohl and his advisers quickly outlined their plans for internal unification. If the conservatives could sustain their momentum through the May 6 local East German elections, Kohl and his advisers thought that article 23 could be invoked in the summer or early fall of 1990, with economic and monetary union on Kohl's terms, that is, a Bundesbank takeover with effective West German management of the GDR economy, following shortly thereafter. Kohl hoped for agreement on the external aspects of unification by the fall of 1990, preferably before the CSCE summit. As for elections, Kohl remained more cautious. He wanted to go ahead with the December West German elections, then complete the formal unification of Germany in 1991—with new all-German elections held off until 1994. By the end of March Kohl was publicly revising this estimate. Now he expected all-German elections immediately after unification, in the second half of 1991.[77]

The March 18 GDR election results struck Moscow like a thunderbolt. The Soviet Union had counted on a more gradual process toward unification, based on an article 146 confederation route which a Social Democratic government could support. Expecting the SPD-East leader Böhme to be the next East German prime minister, Gorbachev and Shevardnadze had met with him in Moscow. Instead, the election results, which one Soviet official admitted to an American diplomat were "completely unexpected," seemed to be a mandate for a West German takeover under article 23, a path Moscow had publicly denounced. To make matters worse, Moscow had just finished a gloomy meeting of its erstwhile Warsaw Pact allies in Prague and was unable to rally a common approach on Germany, even on the issue of Germany's NATO membership.[78]

But the Soviet Union stood its ground. Shevardnadze, Baker, Genscher, and other dignitaries all gathered in Windhoek, Namibia, on March 20–22 to celebrate the independence of the new state.[79] They used the occasion for a series of lengthy bilateral meetings. Shevardnadze's position was essentially the same as it had been almost six weeks earlier, when Baker and Genscher had journeyed to Moscow. Shevardnadze was still worried about the power and intentions of a united Germany, still suggesting a neutral solution with the departure of both American and Soviet troops. He was not tempted by Genscher's Tutzing formula of not extending NATO jurisdiction eastward (and perhaps did not realize that Washington and Bonn had already dropped this formula and were now taking an even less compromising stance). Shevardnadze was convinced that the matter would ultimately have to be resolved, somehow, "at the highest levels." Baker also noticed that Soviet positions on arms control topics were hardening, with the Soviet military appearing to exert increasing influence.

Shevardnadze pressed Genscher to accept negotiation of a German peace treaty as the objective of the Two Plus Four. He wanted the negotiators to take a pencil and go through the Potsdam Declaration of 1945 line by line.

Genscher presented Bonn's arguments against a peace treaty. Baker and Genscher had a friendly discussion, though Baker did not go along with Genscher's ideas for handling the Poles or Genscher's plans for building up the CSCE, at least symbolically, by giving it responsibility for verifying arms control agreements in Europe (an idea with, from Baker's viewpoint, some serious substantive problems).

Perhaps the only glimmer of hope in the talks was in their tone. Baker reported back to Bush that Shevardnadze's mood, shadowed by developments in Germany and in Lithuania, "was more pensive than I have seen before." He and Gorbachev "seem to be genuinely wrestling with these problems, but have yet to fashion a coherent or confident response. They also have yet to shape their bottom lines." The Americans, Baker concluded, should therefore "not underestimate our ability to affect their choices and perhaps even the formulation of some of their options."[80]

The Western Policy Gathers Strength

A country's army prepares to fight a battle by refining a plan so soldiers know what to expect and what to do, and by gathering all the resources it can muster in order to carry out its plan. Diplomacy is not so different. Plans must be refined; political resources must be marshaled behind them. One symptom showing that an army is weak is if its plans are unclear or not thought through, so that soldiers from different units do not understand their mission well enough to adjust to the confusion of the battlefield. In diplomacy perhaps even more than in battle details matter. It is not enough to agree in principle. In the six weeks after the March 18 GDR elections, the Western diplomatic position had become much stronger in every respect and the Soviet position much weaker. The disparity became evident at the first major clash: the initial meeting of Two Plus Four ministers in early May.

President Bush and Chancellor Kohl were in complete agreement on their goals after Camp David.[81] Kohl had given repeated assurances to Bush on the matter of German membership in NATO. But Genscher had remained reluctant to come out and say that NATO's guarantees would apply to all of a united Germany. In a March 23 speech Genscher envisioned the alliances changing in two phases. First, they would cooperate more with each other. Second, the "cooperatively structured alliances will be converted into an association [*Verbund*] of common collective security." The alliances would create "new structures of security in Europe, in which they will increasingly be encompassed, and in which they can finally be completely absorbed."

Genscher never explained just what he meant by these ideas. Kohl chided Genscher about the mixed signals on NATO which seemed to be coming from the West German government and warned that such signals could encourage the Soviets.

After a subsequent meeting of Genscher's special working group on foreign and security policy on March 28, and a more definitive meeting of the Federal Security Council, chaired by Kohl, on April 2, top West German officials—from Kohl downward—began, like the Americans, to affirm publicly the extension of NATO defense obligations, continuing participation in NATO's military command, and unconditional support for the continued presence of American nuclear and conventional forces in Germany. Kohl now formally sided with Stoltenberg's argument that the eastern part of a united Germany ought *not* to be demilitarized. Kohl's Social Democratic opposition meanwhile clarified its rejection of each of these principles.

The sense of solidarity between the United States and the FRG was reinforced by Genscher's trip to Washington at the beginning of April. Genscher wanted to talk over what the Americans planned to say to Shevardnadze, who was about to arrive in Washington. Baker's meetings with Genscher went well, as did Bush's session with the West German foreign minister. There were no differences on the planned design for the Two Plus Four. Genscher was open and reassuring on the NATO issues, anticipating that the Soviets might offer to accept NATO membership in principle but attach unacceptable conditions to such an agreement. Not only did Genscher drop the language from his March 23 speech which had worried Kohl and the Americans, but he instead cast the job of developing new "cooperative security structures" as a task for the NATO alliance. He and Baker discussed ideas for strengthening the CSCE, with Genscher listing at least nine new ideas for CSCE institutions, but the ministers came to no firm conclusions.[82]

Genscher's Foreign Ministry officials continued to balk. At the next important Western consultation on Two Plus Four planning, on April 10, the British, represented by Weston, and Americans, by Zoellick and Seitz, asked for agreement on all the detailed elements of the NATO position. Kastrup still refused to agree that the North Atlantic treaty's defense commitments would apply to all of a united Germany. He conceded that Kohl had agreed to this stance but said that the matter was still being discussed by the coalition; in other words, Genscher was not yet ready to join in. Nor would Kastrup commit his ministry to retaining a mix of Western nuclear and conventional forces in Germany. Neither would he sign on to the U.S. and British position on the military status of the former GDR, which differed from February's Genscher-Stoltenberg declaration pledging the effective demilitarization of this region.[83] Publicly, however, Kohl was firm, and at least Genscher was quiet. He no longer openly contradicted the chancellor.

The pressure of impending German unification had driven the French government to seize on a more united Europe as its main hope for enmeshing a more powerful Germany in a net of European perspectives and obligations.[84] At the end of 1989 Mitterrand began to articulate his own vision for a new European confederation uniting all the countries of Europe. The West German government of Kohl and Genscher, sympathetic in principle to a more united Europe, felt obliged to respond. A turning point was reached in March 1990.

Kohl and Genscher were already sympathetic in principle to a more united Europe. Genscher, quoting Thomas Mann, reminded the Germans that "we do not want a German Europe, but a European Germany." A spring EC summit, scheduled to be held in Dublin during April (Ireland held the EC presidency), was set to consider new initiatives. Yet Kohl, uncertain about his own unification plans, had balked in January at accepting some of the more radical French proposals to proceed beyond the European exchange rate mechanism to further stages leading to a common European currency. The Bundesbank harbored serious reservations about this plan from 1989 on. Yet after the end of February, when Kohl chose the radical path to unity, gambling on a direct economic takeover followed by a direct political takeover under article 23, Kohl and his advisers felt an even stronger need to balance their bold moves with action to strengthen the European Community, as well as relations with France.

On March 13 Kohl spoke on the telephone with Jacques Delors, president of the European Commission. He declared his readiness to give more support to the process of European unity and asked to meet directly with the commissioners later in the month. Two days later Teltschik arrived in Paris for secret talks with Mitterrand's staff, led by Jacques Attali. They worked for a full day on a common French-German initiative for Europe. Not only would the FRG now sign on to rapid European economic and monetary union, but also the two governments were now ready to sponsor an initiative to negotiate the terms of a European *political* union. Teltschik talked to Attali again on March 20. Mitterrand was very pleased with the planned initiative. On March 23 Kohl, in a special meeting with EC commissioners in Brussels, and Genscher, in a speech to the Assembly of the Western European Union, both spoke out strongly in favor of increased European integration. Kohl unveiled the plan to negotiate political union, a plan he hoped would be adopted at the upcoming summit in Dublin. On April 2 Attali and Teltschik conferred again at length with their staffs in Bonn to hammer out the details of the Franco-German initiative, Genscher was working on the same day with Dumas and other ministerial colleagues. Both Mitterrand and Kohl approved the results, and a formal written proposal to begin negotiation of European political union was submitted by the two leaders to the EC on April 18.

The atmosphere at the special EC summit in Dublin on April 28–29 was completely different from the strained meetings of December 1989. To Teltschik it seemed that all of the EC countries had "made their peace" with the process of German unification. The Dublin summit also put the French-German proposal for negotiation of political union on the EC's agenda, thereby setting in motion a process that would lead, a year and a half later, to the Maastricht treaty which replaced the European Community with the present European Union.

Western solidarity was growing concerning the Two Plus Four Talks as well. The British Foreign Office had also become actively engaged in the effort to nail down the key details of Germany's continued membership in NATO. Careful planning for German unification revealed a number of crucial political and legal issues that had to be settled, from the form of a final settlement to securing allied rights to continue basing troops in the new Germany.[85] Not all of these legal issues needed to be settled right away, but they could raise some serious obstacles to the rapid unification deemed so essential by the Americans and the West Germans. Officials in both London and Paris doubted that all the legal tangles could be straightened out before the CSCE summit or even before internal unification. They held out the chance that the Four Powers might have to retain their ultimate authority over Germany until the new German government had followed through on some of the commitments (as on the Polish-German border) that the lawyers wrongly considered to be prerequisites for a final settlement.[86]

The political directors from the United States, West Germany, Britain, and France gathered in Brussels on April 10 to work on preparations for the Two Plus Four. The original plan to delay Two Plus Four talks was now an accomplished fact. All agreed that the Two Plus Four ministers should not meet for the first time until May 5, almost two months after the creation of the forum in Ottawa.

With Kohl's decisive victory in the East, the British and the French were noticeably friendlier toward the FRG. They retreated from their talk of a peace treaty between Germany and its former foes.[87] The French dropped their demand that the Two Plus Four consider the rights of Berliners to vote in the next West German election. The British and the French grudgingly went along with the West German and American views on how to handle the Polish border question. And all agreed to the American plan for limiting the mandate of the Two Plus Four.[88]

Resigned to the apparent inevitability of German unity, Prime Minister Thatcher began to play a more constructive role in a process she could not halt. On March 24 her staff arranged for her to meet a group of academics at her country home for a leisurely discussion of Germany. Her foreign policy adviser Charles Powell, who had served as a diplomat in Bonn, later said that he had arranged the meeting as a way of helping the prime minister come to terms with what was happening in Germany. Powell's confidential notes from the lengthy session, which were themselves another effort to sway Thatcher, noted in summary: "The weight of the evidence and the argument favoured those who were optimistic about life with a united Germany . . . Far from being agitated, we ought to be pleased . . . When it came to failings and unhelpful characteristics, the Germans had their share and perhaps more, but in contrast to the past, they were much readier to recognise and admit this themselves. The overall message was unmistakable: we should be nice to the Germans."[89]

Thatcher was indeed nice to Kohl when he visited England at the end of March. Their talks were cordial. She concentrated on the consequences of German unification for the NATO alliance. The atmosphere was not warm, but it had improved.[90] Bush then met with Thatcher in Bermuda. Sure of Britain's understanding for the American position on NATO, Bush hoped that this meeting would unite London with Washington on both the mandate and the outcome of the Two Plus Four.[91]

Bush laid out the American position in detail. Thatcher offered no objections.[92] Bush publicly announced their agreement that the Two Plus Four talks would "focus on bringing to an end the special Four Power rights and responsibilities for Berlin and Germany as a whole. A united Germany should have full control over all of its territory without any new discriminatory constraints on German sovereignty." In Bonn Teltschik noted with pleasure that this was the first public pronouncement from the British as well as the Americans on the goal of restoring full sovereignty to a united Germany.[93]

Bush then turned his attention to France. In less than a week he would meet with Mitterrand at Key Largo in Florida. For this meeting the Americans wanted to firm up a common position on both NATO and Two Plus Four plans. But the French sometimes seemed inclined more toward "post-Gaullist Gaullism" than to a readiness to put aside old biases and cope with a new situation. Yet from time to time Mitterrand expressed an interest in building closer ties between France and the United States.[94]

Bush sent Mitterrand a letter detailing American preferences in the diplomacy over Germany and Europe's future and recapitulating the points agreed on with Thatcher. "In no event should we allow Moscow to manipulate the Two Plus Four mechanism in ways that could fracture Western defense and Germany's irreplaceable part in it," Bush wrote. But also, "if NATO is allowed to wither because it has no meaningful political place in the new Europe, the basis for a long-term U.S. military commitment can die with it." This should be no threat to a stronger EC, Bush argued. He suggested that they agree that both organizations could talk about political and security issues and neither "should attempt to present the other with faits accomplis on matters where both have a proper interest."[95]

Mitterrand, when he met with Bush, suggested simply a common recognition that NATO would be the forum for organizing European security and "equilibrium." He pushed his European confederation idea into the background as a vision for the long term, building on the EC. But it would not exclude the United States. That would be idiotic, Mitterrand declared. He wanted continued close contacts between America and Europe, perhaps including a treaty between the United States and the European Community. NATO should stay, with France continuing to have its special role within the alliance. Furthermore, American troops must remain in Europe, and Germany had to stay in the alliance. Mitterrand was worried about German attitudes, fearing that a majority of Germans might give up on NATO or reject the continued presence of foreign troops. On the subject of the Two Plus Four talks, Mitterrand and his staff had no problem with Bush's public repetition of the same catechism announced after the meeting with Thatcher.[96]

After the meeting Bush reiterated the common line in a message to Kohl and to Thatcher, just to make doubly sure that the Western position on NATO and on the Two Plus Four was crystal clear. Kohl received the message after completing two days of meetings with the French president in Paris. Kohl had scrupulously stood by the agreed-upon position on both NATO and the Two Plus Four; there were no areas of disagreement. And Kohl was euphoric about the atmosphere of his one-on-one talks with Mitterrand. Teltschik could not remember a time when consultations among the allies had been "so active and so intensive."[97]

By the end of April, Bush and Kohl had every reason for optimism about the solidarity of the Western camp. The French-German initiative for political union of the European Community had improved relations with Paris and the atmosphere throughout Western Europe. The Americans had effectively locked up the debate over the goals of the Two Plus Four by the end of April.

At a special meeting of NATO foreign ministers, the United States won general assent to the detailed position that had already been worked out with the West Germans, the British, and the French.[98]

But the main focus of Kohl's attention was on the mechanics of internal unification, especially the plan for the economic and monetary takeover of East Germany. It was primarily the role of the U.S. government to tackle the other major task: to lead a visible, dramatic change in NATO's outlook and defense policy and to find a consensus stance on improving the CSCE, which together would help persuade the Soviets (and the German public) that Europe's political and security institutions were changing with the times and that a NATO strengthened by a united Germany would pose no real threat to the USSR.

Dealing with German unification meant dealing with every other major security issue vexing Europe. In December 1989 Baker had sketched a general picture of the new European architecture. By February 1990 officials in Washington realized that their plans needed to be, if anything, even more ambitious. They began preparing for a wholesale review of NATO's strategy. The White House decided that the stakes were so high and the issues so diverse that an entirely new interdepartmental group should be created to consider them: the European Strategy Steering Group. Blackwill and Rice approached Scowcroft with the idea, relying on Scowcroft's deputy Robert Gates to run the new body. Gates was skilled at interagency coordination— first sharpening differences between the agencies and then driving toward clear and decisive outcomes. Unlike the usual arms control working groups, this committee would include both Zoellick and Ross from the State Department. Membership of the group was kept very small, its papers very secret. The new group met for the first time on February 21.[99]

The most urgent question before the group was whether to proceed with plans for modernizing America's short-range nuclear missiles in Europe.[100] Congress was about to consider the administration's budget request for this modernization. After the May 1989 NATO summit the issue had been put on hold and fell out of the newspapers, but it had not disappeared. It was widely acknowledged in Washington that the current modernization plan, called FOTL (for "Follow-On to Lance," Lance being the aging missile then deployed in Europe) had no future. But how to kill it?

The Americans wanted to bury FOTL in a way that would not touch off a wider debate questioning the presence of U.S. nuclear forces in Europe or rule out some possible modernization of air-delivered systems later in the 1990s. They also remembered their promise to undertake a new set of arms control negotiations on short-range nuclear systems after the CFE treaty was completed. Kohl was understandably nervous about any action. At Camp David in February, Bush had told him, "FOTL is dead as a doornail," but the general position on keeping nuclear weapons in Europe had to be maintained. Kohl had agreed, but could not see how to avoid some sort of public debate after FOTL's cancellation became public. Kohl urged Bush not to give in to Soviet pressure, but to find some way to take the initiative rather than let Congress simply announce that the program was dead. Bush, Baker, Scowcroft, and Kohl weighed various solutions yet could come to no conclusion. The issue was unquestionably dangerous for the West; Scowcroft confided to a British visitor that a Soviet campaign against nuclear weapons was "tailor-made" for the current situation.

The other big question was how to adapt to German unification in the CFE talks on reducing and limiting the armies deployed in Europe. The Soviets would want some treaty, at some point, to impose fixed limits on the size of a united German army. The unhappy precedent for such limits was the 1919 Treaty of Versailles, which had imposed a ceiling of 100,000 soldiers on Germany. That limit had rankled as one of the treaty's humiliations, and no one in Germany had objected when their government evaded the limit and, under Hitler, threw it aside. Both the West Germans and the Americans were happy to limit a future German army, but only if and when all other national armies were limited as well in the next CFE negotiation, CFE II, scheduled to get under way after the current treaty was signed. In that way the Germans were not being singled out for discriminatory treatment. But even the current CFE talks were now stalled by growing Soviet opposition to the emerging treaty.[101]

The State Department had hoped to handle these and other issues with a NATO strategy review announced in 1990 and concluding with a NATO summit in 1991. But the White House wanted to move much faster. The outcome had to be visible in time to influence the diplomatic battle for Germany. At NATO Secretary General Manfred Wörner was also urging more rapid action.[102]

During March the NSC staff prepared an options paper for the short-range nuclear problem (the "how to kill FOTL" issue) which won agreement to a Bush initiative to deal with the subject. The initiative would cancel FOTL, as well as the planned modernization of the obsolete nuclear artillery shells deployed in Europe, and outline an approach to new arms control talks on short-range nuclear systems, to begin after the CFE treaty was concluded. With that plan settled, the FOTL initiative was pulled into the planned initiative for an early NATO summit. Baker, Cheney, Scowcroft, and Colin Powell all agreed, at the beginning of April, to link the nuclear announcement with an ambitious NATO summit plan. All of this would be announced in a presidential speech. Bush then previewed his plans at his April meetings with Thatcher and Mitterrand.[103]

Officials at the State and Defense departments still balked at the ambitious substantive agenda for this NATO summit and Bush's speech. But Blackwill won Zoellick's support for the plan, and the Pentagon's concerns were effectively overruled in another discussion of the matter, held at the White House, among Baker, Scowcroft, Cheney, and Powell.[104] The U.S. government also arrived at a position on the future of the CSCE.[105]

Bush delivered his speech on the future of NATO on May 4, in a commencement address at Oklahoma State University. He declared that, since America's fate had historically been inseparable from that of Europe, "the United States should remain a European power in the broadest sense—politically, militarily, and economically." Proposing an early NATO summit, he pledged that this meeting would "direct" the outcome of a review of strategy in four areas: (1) NATO's political role in the new Europe; (2) conventional defenses; (3) nuclear defenses; and (4) common Western objectives for the future of the CSCE.[106]

The conventional political wisdom on summit meetings is to downplay expectations. Since outcomes cannot be guaranteed, the press is less likely to be critical if it is not built up to expect great things. If the summit goes well, then the press and public are pleasantly surprised. That was the strategy that had worked so well for Bush at the May 1989 NATO summit. But Bush now bucked the conventional wisdom in his Oklahoma speech by promising results on a very ambitious agenda. He would be under a heavy burden to deliver the goods, and every NATO ally had the veto power to block him. Bush felt that he needed to get a bold promise on the table for his dealings with Moscow and gambled that he could devise initiatives great enough to satisfy Moscow, sound enough to strengthen the alliance, and appealing enough to command wide support from his European allies.

The Soviets Stay in Their Trenches

The U.S. strategy depended on Western coherence and unity and on Gorbachev's reluctance to take decisive action. Although Western policy made the dilemmas facing the Soviet Union sharper every day, the Americans believed that Gorbachev would avoid stating a "bottom line." That was fine for the United States because—with the East German election over—time was clearly the ally of the West.

The career officials in the Soviet Foreign Ministry, the Central Committee staff, and defense agencies had a conservative outlook. They found the notion of a united Germany in NATO unacceptable, a reversal of a position Soviet diplomats had maintained for forty years. To many of them incorporation of a united Germany into the West's military bloc would steal away the fruits of victory in the Second World War, a victory won at terrible cost to the Soviet people.[107] But their stance was essentially defensive and fixed. They knew what they did not want but organized no diplomatic campaign of their own, no coordinated counteroffensive undertaken with a careful eye to German domestic politics and bolstered by a readiness to court a tense international confrontation. There is no evidence that Gorbachev made a fundamental decision not to mount an effective defense. But ambivalence at the top translated into debilitation and inaction below.[108]

The Americans and the West Germans wanted more than bitter, frustrated acquiescence from the Soviet Union in a result Moscow felt powerless to affect. Bush, Baker, Kohl, and Genscher all hoped to find a way to reconcile the Soviet leadership to the outcome Washington and Bonn wanted. In Gorbachev's ambivalence they saw an opportunity to remold the way he and his advisers thought about their country's national interests, to see that, if other changes were made, a unified Germany fully involved in NATO might pose no threat and was even better than the available alternatives.

But top American officials believed from the beginning of 1990 onward that they were operating within a narrow window of opportunity. If the process of German unification could not be completed very soon, the United States and the FRG might find themselves dealing with a different kind of Soviet government and a more dangerous international environment. Margaret Thatcher visited Moscow in March and found Gorbachev unusually somber, even fatalistic. It was, she later told Bush, as if Gorbachev felt he had done his best and could no longer answer for the consequences.[109]

Shevardnadze visited Washington for lengthy substantive talks at the beginning of April.[110] The imminent danger of bloodshed in Lithuania overshadowed all other subjects. Shevardnadze saw in the Lithuanian crisis the potential collapse of perestroika. He confided to Baker that, even though he had often told reporters there was no alternative to perestroika, this was not true: "There is an alternative to perestroika. If perestroika doesn't succeed, then you are going to have the destabilization of the Soviet Union. And if that happens there will be a dictator." In this atmosphere there could be no progress on Germany. A working group, with Bondarenko on one side and Dobbins on the other, had little to report. Baker and Shevardnadze restated their countries' respective positions.

The Soviet posture had not changed materially since the end of January. Shevardnadze was encouraged in the briefing papers prepared for him to take a hard line on Germany, to leave no doubt that Moscow could and would defend its interests and those of the GDR.[111] Unification had to be a step-by-step process, with a transition period, and fully synchronized with the creation of new security structures arising from the CSCE process.[112] During the transition period both German states could retain their current alliance memberships. After the transition the Soviets could not accept membership of a unified Germany in NATO. Another solution must be found.

Furthermore, the troops of all Four Powers in Germany should remain where they were. Shevardnadze thought that the United States agreed (Baker corrected him). Germany must continue to renounce weapons of mass destruction and accept a ceiling on its armed forces, perhaps through the CFE framework. The external issues should be settled by a peace treaty, as envisioned at Potsdam in 1945, and—even if unification accelerated—the special status of West Berlin should remain unaffected until such a peace treaty was concluded. The two German states would also have to make treaty commitments to respect existing borders and economic obligations. The next Two Plus Four meeting should agree on the agenda and move on to substantive work. Shevardnadze openly deferred to his hard-line veteran adviser Bondarenko, saying that he dared not take a single step on Germany without him.

Shevardnadze grew impatient with the Americans' intransigence. Secretary Baker had not once even mentioned the Warsaw Pact. Did he think that the pact had already disintegrated? Both alliances should be transformed. There was a time when the Soviet Union had expressed interest in joining NATO. This was a painful issue, and both sides had to consider what options would be accepted by the Soviet people, not just by the Supreme Soviet. Baker did not budge. Shevardnadze's tone became even tougher. No one had yet removed any Four Power authority over Germany. Not one question would be resolved without the consent of the Soviet Union. The United States must give due consideration to solutions that would be acceptable to the USSR and the rest of the international community, including France, Britain, and all of Europe.

Shevardnadze met the next day with President Bush. Bush stressed American concerns about the danger a crackdown in Lithuania would pose for the cause of reform in the Soviet Union, but he made no threats of sanctions. The United States had made a conscious decision not to bluster over Lithuania. Bush was fearful of promising things he could not deliver and, as Rice later observed, "afraid to light a match in a gas-filled room."[113]

Bush carefully reviewed the American stance on Germany. He voiced his doubts about the value of any pan-European collective security system, which he said had been tried before and almost inevitably failed. But he said that he understood the Soviets' feelings about Germany, and he spoke of the enormous Soviet losses in World War II. We must convince you, he said, that German membership in NATO poses no threat to your country. Shevardnadze made little reply.[114]

Neither was Gorbachev displaying any signs of flexibility. When British foreign secretary Hurd saw the Soviet leader during an April 10 visit to Moscow, Gorbachev would not rule out using force in Lithuania. Nor did he give any ground on Germany. Indeed, he could not see how the CFE talks could progress to a conclusion without a suitable settlement of the German question. Yet Shevardnadze had indicated to Hurd that Moscow was going along with the American linkage of CFE completion to the convening of a CSCE summit.[115] The Soviet position was that there would have to be new cooperative security structures for all of Europe. These would presumably be ratified at the CSCE summit. Yet the Americans had insisted that this summit could not take place unless a CFE treaty was ready for signing.

Then, in an extraordinary speech in mid-April, Shevardnadze seemed to back away from his more confrontational stance.[116] It was as if another person—not the dogmatic foreign minister of the Washington meetings was now speaking. Facing a domestic audience, Shevardnadze scolded those who were trapped in the old thinking. The task here was not to convince Baker and Bush that the Soviet Union could defend its interest but to convince those at home that change was coming and that it might not be all bad.

Shevardnadze openly challenged the foundation of Soviet foreign policy (and the position on Germany) in responding to the criticisms voiced at the February party plenum. What, after all, were the critical security requirements of the Soviet Union? Emotionally, he too wanted the USSR to remain great. "But great in what? Territory? Population? Quantity of arms? Or the people's troubles? The individual's lack of rights? Life's disorderliness? In what do we, who have virtually the highest infant mortality rate on our planet, take pride?" Shevardnadze used the Soviet incursion in Afghanistan as an example of the "arrogance of statehood." He cited other examples of old thinking among those who, commenting on arms control talks, wanted to abandon the effort to renounce "a policy of strength." His central conclusion: "We live in a world of realities and a world of emotions. Realities dictate one line of conduct, feelings rise up against it."

On Germany Shevardnadze said only that "we need to find a solution which is accepted by the Soviet people and which gives them confidence that there will be no new military threat to us from German soil." Therefore, he declared, "there is no more important or crucial cause for Soviet foreign policy currently than the creation, together with other states, of a new system of security in Europe" by way of the CSCE.

Once again there were few proposals for bringing this new security system into being. Finally, in mid-April, the Soviets elaborated some CSCE proposals in a magazine article. In this article, which was leaked to the press, Shevardnadze called for CSCE summits every two years, CSCE ministerial sessions twice each year, creation of a CSCE secretariat, and—most important—establishment of a CSCE center for risk reduction and arms control verification, with consideration of a small pan-European peacekeeping force to assist in conflict resolution. NATO and the Warsaw Pact would continue to exist in the short term but evolve toward merger as the CSCE mechanism expanded. Germany could thus have "dual membership" in both NATO and the Warsaw Pact during this transitional period.[117] But neither Soviet leaders nor Soviet diplomats moved to press these proposals in foreign capitals.

The Soviets could feel their position on Germany slipping as the weeks went by without serious Two Plus Four talks and as Germany's internal unification gathered momentum. The Western policy of delay was having the desired effect. Finally, the Soviet Union was able to get the Two Plus Four ministers to meet, in Bonn, on May 4—nearly two months after the forum had been created at Ottawa. This would be the first real political discussion of the German question. The encounter was crucial, and the Soviet government—clearly now in a weakened position—mustered its strength for the battle.

The career bureaucrats in the Foreign Ministry, led by Bondarenko's German department, developed a formal and very conservative position, consistent with—even drawn from—the heritage of Soviet diplomacy on Germany dating back to the 1950s. Entirely separately Shevardnadze turned, as he had in December, to Tarasenko for an alternative approach. Shevardnadze was torn. Good relations with the West seemed essential for the progress of perestroika. But, as the Americans had seen in Washington, even Shevardnadze was not prepared to give in on the NATO issue.

The policy was too important to be determined by Shevardnadze alone, or even by Gorbachev. The matter had to be considered by the entire ruling Politburo. Shevardnadze's first position paper, based on Tarasenko's work outside the usual channels, adopted a cooperative, forthcoming stance, though it did not give in on NATO.[118] It met adamant opposition in the

Politburo, led by Yegor Ligachev, who had publicly warned of Soviet appeasement, of a "new Munich" over Germany, in February.

Shevardnadze's position paper was redrafted, following further advice from the German department. This more conservative paper did not give in to the West on NATO but implied that a concession was possible if the West met certain conditions, such as the creation of a pan-European security system. Moscow would be prepared to go along with an FRG takeover of the GDR by means of article 23—now a moot point, given the election results in the East. Shevardnadze managed to obtain as co-sponsors for his approach Yakovlev, KGB head Kryuchkov, and defense minister Yazov.

This approach was still not tough enough for the Politburo, or indeed for Gorbachev himself. Ligachev warned about "NATO approaching the borders of the [Soviet] Union." Gorbachev sided with Ligachev, calling for confrontation. Chernyayev, who was present, remembered a "stormy" speech in which Gorbachev had declared: We will not allow the GDR into NATO and that is the end of it, adding that he would even risk the collapse of the Vienna conventional arms control talks and the talks on strategic weapons, but would not allow this.

Shevardnadze and his co-sponsors remained silent. The most conservative possible position carried the day. It included a Foreign Ministry idea for separating internal unification and a settlement of Germany's external status. The two German states could rush to create a new Germany. But the new Germany's sovereignty and international alignment would remain unresolved until the international negotiations had reached a suitable outcome, however long that might take. In this way the Soviet Union would not have its hand forced by Kohl's internal plans.

Chernyayev, who had not been asked for his opinion, sent Gorbachev a note the next morning protesting that Ligachev's argument was "rubbish" and that many of the members of the Politburo lacked any expertise on Germany. This was 1945 thinking, he said, the "pseudo-patriotism of the crowd." Chernyayev feared that a negative, static defense, however stubborn, was doomed to fail: "Instead of putting forward the specific and rigid terms for our consent, we are heading toward a failure." But Chernyayev's complaints were too late. There is no evidence that Gorbachev heeded them at the time. Gorbachev may simply have been trying to cover his flanks, looking for room to maneuver toward a more conciliatory course in Lithuania. In any case, Shevardnadze now had his instructions to take to Bonn.

Other advisers, including Falin, thought that the Soviet Union could handle a confrontation. In May Falin would privately tell Soviet diplomats in Berlin that an extension of NATO had to be prevented at any cost, even if the price was moving in another million troops. Asked if this would lead to a mass exodus of East Germans westward, he reportedly replied, "Good riddance—we wouldn't have to feed them anymore." This attitude did not strike his listeners as unusual, and even Shevardnadze was just searching for other options while not ruling out a possible confrontation with the West.[119]

What would happen if Germany completed its internal unification and the external issues were stalemated, unresolved? This scenario had been considered, very discreetly, within the American and West German governments as early as February. Going ahead with German unification on Western terms, without Soviet support, would create an ugly contest of strength, played out in the last weeks of the West German election campaign. The Soviet Union could, at a minimum, simply refuse to relinquish its Four Power rights. After all, the Soviets still had more than 350,000 well-armed troops in the GDR and other means of backing up their diplomacy.[120] Would the West allow the process of unification to come to a halt?

The tentative answer, in both Washington and Bonn, was no. In March Zoellick had privately asked Genscher's staff how they were prepared to proceed if the USSR was determined to obstruct the achievement of unity. Their answer, and the American answer, was to approach Soviet concerns with sensitivity and reasonableness. But if, after doing so, the Soviets did not respond in kind, the Germans would have believed that they had discharged their responsibility.[121]

The West Germans and the Americans thought that Moscow had to be convinced, beyond any doubt, that the Soviet Union was isolated diplomatically. It must at least be clear that the costs of continued rigidity would be a deterioration in the smooth, stable relations so essential to the benign international environment in which the Soviet leaders could concentrate on domestic reform. To achieve this isolation, Western solidarity had to be complete. That was the purpose of the American and West German efforts during the time they had bought in March and April. Now, as ministers flew to Bonn, Western resolve would be tested.

The Two Plus Four Ministers Finally Meet

Kohl had used the six weeks after the East German elections to good effect. He had worked out the general approach to economic and monetary union. On May 2 the West German government joined with the new government of CDU-East leader Lothar de Maizière to proclaim agreement on the major principles.[122] The most radical path of West German takeover had been chosen, despite low-level Soviet protests.[123]

East German voters were going to the polls again on May 6, this time for communal (local) elections. The vote would be a barometer of continuing support for Kohl's program. Kohl had got an announcement together in time to make an impact on that vote, especially with the generous terms promised for Ostmark conversion into deutsche marks. But internally Kohl had made it clear that he would not raise West German taxes; nor would he let his historic bid for German unity be delayed by the macroeconomic doubts expressed by the Bundesbank.[124]

Nevertheless, the external issues remained entirely unsettled. The Western allies had coordinated their positions, capped by the meeting of NATO ministers on May 3. But many experts were pessimistic. Even in the U.S. government, State Department analysts thought that the prospects for continuing to keep American troops in Germany were "fairly bleak." Two Plus Four political directors had met on April 30 to prepare the way for ministers but made no progress, as the Soviets would not agree to the West's narrow proposed agenda for the talks.[125]

The American and West German policy continued to rest on a precise definition of success: German membership in NATO, paired with a still undefined package of changes in NATO and the CSCE that would help Moscow accept the Western objectives. Zoellick and Ross called this the "incentives package." Teltschik called it the "solution package."[126]

When Baker arrived in Bonn, he met with Kohl. The two men compared notes on the details of the policy positions and found that they were in complete accord. Afterward Kohl remarked to Teltschik that the American friends were "absolutely reliable. One could not wish for stronger support; he would not forget it."[127]

Both Chancellor Kohl and the arriving Western ministers also met with Shevardnadze. Kohl and Genscher explained the plans for economic and monetary union and introduced a new ingredient for Bonn's "solution package": a bilateral treaty of friendship and cooperation between Germany and the Soviet Union. This could be a vehicle for addressing Moscow's anxieties about its economic and political relations with the new Germany. Although little was said about the content of such a treaty, it was the symbolism of such an agreement that Bonn hoped would carry the most weight. Shevardnadze raised the possibility of getting hard currency credit from West Germany for the USSR. Kohl said that he would try to be helpful.[128]

Baker spent nearly four hours engrossed in his own talks with the Soviet foreign minister. He presented the American position in great detail, including the notion of the Two Plus Four as a "steering committee" with a narrow agenda for making decisions. Shevardnadze could not accept this and instead stressed the need to take time, not rush, to complete the work of the Two Plus Four. He objected to few of Baker's arguments but accepted none of the Western positions. Baker wrote to Bush that the Soviets "don't know how to square the circle. They're wrestling with it. I suspect that Gorbachev doesn't want to take on this kind of an emotionally charged political issue now, and almost certainly not before the [July 1990] Party Congress."[129]

The next day, May 5, the Two Plus Four ministers gathered and read their prepared presentations.[130] Knowing little about the internal debates in Moscow, having heard that Shevardnadze privately seemed eager to search for solutions, all the Western ministers were surprised by the grim, unyielding tone of the Soviet presentation. Everything associated with the Cold War, Shevardnadze said, was bound up in the fate of Germany. Nor could the feelings of the Soviet people be ignored. So nothing about Germany would be agreed to until a complete balance of interests was achieved.

What did Moscow want from the settlement? The treaty should deal with Germany's alliance membership and with the status of troops from all Four Powers. It had to confirm the legality of all occupation measures adopted by the Four Powers and place new restraints on German domestic politics to stop any rise of Nazism. NATO membership for a united Germany was out of the question; it would "create a dangerous military-strategic situation" for the USSR, and the Soviet people were "irreconcilable" on this point. Instead, Shevardnadze wanted to strengthen the CSCE to include a new European center "on the prevention of nuclear danger" that would be located in Germany, would build on existing Four Power military occupation regimes, and would have the goal—at least in part—of monitoring the "military-strategic situation in Germany."

It would take time to negotiate a treaty to deal with all these issues. So Shevardnadze deployed the idea of delinking the internal and external aspects of unification. Four Power rights would be maintained even after internal unification, to ensure that unification was "synchronized" with the creation of an entirely new European security system. Shevardnadze warned his colleagues that "we are neither playing nor bluffing here," and concluded his presentation with a blunt, emotional appeal:

Attempts to gain one-sided advantages, put our partner in a position of isolation, ignore his interests, be clever, or get the better of each other have always ended badly. They are all the more out of place in issues connected with Germany and with European stability and security.

Let us play this new, and last, game in German affairs in a businesslike way and with a full awareness of all the dangers that lie in wait for Europe on its path into the 21st century. I have in my time taken part in many negotiations and meetings. Yet I consider my participation in the work of the "Six" to be the most important and decisive task ever entrusted to me.

Although the Soviets had dropped any opposition to Germany's internal unification, Moscow's position on the external issues had actually hardened. The earlier notion of letting Germany belong simultaneously to both NATO and the Warsaw Pact had now been discarded. The notion of placing new international regulations on Germany's domestic politics in order to stop putative neo-Nazi movements was insulting to many Germans, and the new CSCE ideas seemed to amount to a CSCE police force, based on the old occupation regime, stationed in Germany in order to watch the Germans. With the Soviets asking that the connection between internal unification and external settlement be broken, Bonn faced the prospect of a unified Germany functioning under some sort of foreign supervision for years to come.

Even in retrospect Shevardnadze did not regret having taken such a strong stance in Bonn because he felt that NATO had not yet tried to transform itself into a different kind of alliance. In other words, the West had not yet delivered on the NATO design in its "incentives package," though Bush's NATO summit plans seemed promising.[131]

After the formal presentations the ministers began arguing about the agenda for the Two Plus Four. Western ministers were united and firm on keeping the agenda narrow. They finally agreed to include, under the general agenda of political-military issues, the creation of suitable security structures in Europe. Genscher had suggested "new" structures; Baker offered the word "suitable" in order to hold open the place of the structures that already existed (such as NATO). The Polish-German border question was discussed, with no one finding any point of dispute. Then the ministers turned to their press statement. Genscher presented a draft acknowledging that German unity would proceed "without delay." Shevardnadze balked, but East German foreign minister Markus Meckel said that "without delay" precisely described the situation. Finally, Shevardnadze went along with Baker's compromise: unity would occur "in an orderly way and without delay." With that the meeting came to an end.[132]

At the subsequent press conference reporters directed their questions only to the American and Soviet ministers. Shevardnadze projected an upbeat tone, talking about the "useful and constructive" discussion. Asked about substance, he referred reporters to his formal presentation, his government's "positions of principle."[133]

The first meeting to resolve the German question was over. The Soviet Union had been unyielding: a unified Germany must be neutral, outside the Western alliance system. The West was firmly united behind a position that Moscow could not accept. As the ministers returned to their capitals, they reflected on the looming stalemate—and on what they could do about it.

～ 7

Friendly Persuasion

AT THE BONN meeting of the Two Plus Four foreign ministers, Shevardnadze introduced a new proposal that would do away with the West's most important asset: the rapid pace of events. Since the end of January American and West German officials had decided to push for the fastest possible completion of internal unification. They hoped that the Soviet Union could be kept off balance, facing one unpalatable choice after another, ultimately accepting unity on Western terms as the least unfavorable solution. Now, under Shevardnadze's "decoupling" idea, the Germans would go ahead and unify quickly. But the Soviet Union would retain its Four Power occupation rights after unification until Moscow's concerns had been properly addressed. The Two Plus Four could take its time. Teltschik understood that "it would be extremely problematical if Germany was unified but neither internally nor externally was fully sovereign . . . The unity of Germany would be plagued by a large flaw."[1] With Four Power rights still in effect, the Germans would not be able to insist on the withdrawal of Soviet troops from their soil. Germany's alliance status would thus be clouded. The de facto unification of Germany while de jure occupation continued was not a very appetizing thought for the West.

American officials were unsettled to learn that Genscher was seriously considering the Soviet idea. The British were worried too. Douglas Hurd wrote to Baker, concerned that Genscher was "rather seduced" by Moscow's initiative. Hurd had learned from the Dutch that Genscher, in Brussels for an EC meeting on May 7, had given the Dutch foreign minister the impression that he was interested in the Soviet proposal. The British, now closely aligned with the American stance on Germany, vehemently opposed decoupling. In fact, if Moscow insisted on retaining its Four Power rights, the British were prepared to take a radical and somewhat dangerous step: deciding together with the Americans and the French to waive their own Four Power rights and leave Moscow standing alone as the sole claimant to occupation rights in Germany.[2]

The Americans believed at the time, and Frank Elbe has since confirmed, that Genscher was reluctant to reject Shevardnadze's idea out of hand because of Genscher's worries about Gorbachev's political future. Was a tough Western stand on German sovereignty worth the risk of destabilizing a friendly Soviet government? This, Elbe has written, is why Genscher reacted cautiously to Shevardnadze's proposal and did not rule it out.[3]

Genscher's argument had to be taken seriously. The maximal Western stance on Germany did indeed carry risks for the future of Gorbachev and perestroika. Genscher was not sure that these were the right priorities. Perhaps the West should be more flexible in order to keep a friendly Soviet government in power. Genscher may not have understood that the Americans had decided that the U.S. objectives for Germany were more important than protecting Gorbachev. The United States believed that a reaction to perestroika was already building, influenced strongly by domestic factors beyond American control.[4] For months this belief had driven the United States to act quickly, working to secure Soviet troop withdrawals from Eastern Europe, adamant that the Atlantic security system should stay intact. Some American officials also believed, if pressed, that if the West moved quickly and remained united, it could achieve its key objectives for Germany even if the USSR reversed course. These matters were so sensitive that they were seldom discussed candidly, even in private conversation, and rarely put down on paper. It was far easier to work from the assumption, which was also still plausible, that if managed correctly Gorbachev's government could be brought around.

Neither on this occasion nor on any other did Genscher have a chance to force all these hidden choices out into the open for full discussion.[5] On the morning of May 8, above a story that Elbe believes Teltschik helped plant, the *Frankfurter Allgemeine Zeitung* ran a front-page headline: "Genscher Welcomes Moscow's Readiness for the Separation of the Internal and External Aspects of Unification."

Kohl had already dismissed Shevardnadze's decoupling idea. Angry about Genscher's reported stand, Kohl and Seiters met with Genscher and heatedly criticized him for offering a new opening to the Soviets. Genscher is reported to have said that he had not accepted the idea but was just thinking about it. "With the Russians, that is all they need," Seiters is said to have replied. "For God's sake, let's not start something new now. We are in the middle of the stream and should move straight ahead." Kohl rebuked Genscher for undermining both government solidarity and the understandings with the United States. Kohl told Genscher that he had no time to be constantly straightening out problems caused by his foreign minister. The Americans were standing with the Germans, Kohl said, and there must be no under-the-table deals with Shevardnadze.

Later that day Kohl told CDU and CSU party leaders that any decoupling was out of the question, and Genscher, meeting with his FDP party colleagues, assured them that he hoped to wrap up both the internal and the external aspects of unification without delay, by the time of the November CSCE summit. According to Genscher and Elbe, the foreign minister never seriously entertained the decoupling proposal—he never even really understood it, they felt; and the whole affair was just a "storm in a glass of water." In any case, Genscher was not granted the leeway to consider Shevardnadze's proposal for long.

But Genscher was also saying things about NATO that troubled the U.S. government. In a radio interview Genscher pledged that "the part of Germany that is in NATO—will stay in NATO." Western officials thought that the question of extending NATO membership to all of Germany, not just the territory of the current Federal Republic, had been firmly settled for weeks. But this remark seemed even more worrying because, at the April 10 meeting of allied political directors, Dieter Kastrup had refused to endorse a clear position on the NATO issue. The Western understandings seemed in need of repair, lest an open rift should emerge that might confuse the allies and embolden the Soviet Union.[6]

Zoellick called Elbe to discuss Washington's unease with Genscher's statements.[7] Elbe said that Genscher was just trying to "pocket" the Soviets' willingness to let unification proceed without forcing them to admit that the result would be unification in NATO. Elbe assured Zoellick that there was no change of position; it was just a misunderstanding. To clarify matters, Zoellick and Blackwill prepared a letter from Baker to Genscher on May 9 detailing the arguments against decoupling and, referring to Genscher's radio interview, reiterating that the West should not accept, even temporarily, any qualification on Germany's NATO membership, "for then we may never be able to change it." Baker then sent parallel letters to Hurd in London and Dumas in Paris to make sure there were no other misunderstandings.

Genscher settled the decoupling issue definitively on May 10, when he reported to the Bundestag that "the German people are entitled to German unity and to the external aspects of unification being settled without delay. We do not want to encumber a united Germany with unsettled questions." Elbe told Zoellick that there were no disagreements, then Genscher assured

Baker in writing. But Genscher's message ducked the NATO issue which had been raised in Baker's letter. When Douglas Hurd came to Bonn a few days later, he was also reassured but found Genscher still elusive on the details of the allied position on NATO. Nonetheless, for the time being the Western governments appeared united. The mood in West Germany was ebullient, with economic and monetary union agreed to and the allies in accord on the external issues of German unity.

Reviewing the matter, Rice and Zelikow advised Blackwill, "We have essentially won the battle on the first phase [of the Two Plus Four]" by delaying the onset of the talks, winning Western agreement to the narrow mandate, and lining up allied agreement that the talks should restore full sovereignty to Germany. The Soviets, however, pressed for long, complicated negotiations on the external issues, first with their decoupling idea and then by pushing for a "peace treaty" at a conference that would include Italy, Belgium, Yugoslavia, Poland, and other neighbors of Germany. Gorbachev called for this elaborate conference on May 9, in his speech commemorating the anniversary of the 1945 Soviet victory over Germany.[8]

While the Soviets were desperately trying to buy time, Washington was convinced that the process of unification should go even faster. The current plan was for economic union to occur in July, the Two Plus Four to finish in October and "present their results" (Genscher's May 10 phrase) to the November CSCE summit, and the West Germans to hold federal elections in December, with complete unification in early 1991 and the first all-German elections later that year.

The NSC staff argued that Bonn should instead try to accomplish internal unification under article 23 at the same time as completion of the Two Plus Four, before the fall CSCE summit. They thought that "internal unification should not be an unsettled issue when the pan-European debating society is convened." Zoellick agreed, and the Americans quietly began to discuss contingency plans to prepare for the worst case. The United States, Britain, and France would indicate their readiness to give up their Four Power rights at the moment of German unification, even if the Soviets did not. As the White House staffers had argued, the Soviets "must know that, after a given date, the West will declare the game over, devolve their own Four Power rights, and deploy legal arguments to the effect that all Four Power rights—including the Soviets'—have now lapsed." Moscow would then have the unpopular task of insisting to the German people that they unilaterally retained occupation rights over the newly united and democratic German state. The West would prepare, in complete secrecy, an alternative arrangement to be used if a settlement including the Soviets could not be negotiated in time for unification in the autumn of 1990.[9]

Kohl had come to the same conclusion. He was encouraged by the essentially neutral outcome of the just concluded Two Plus Four ministerial meeting in Bonn. There was a spot of trouble domestically. On May 13 the CDU suffered losses to the SPD in the state elections held in Lower Saxony. Kohl feared that the SPD was scoring points with attacks on the cost of monetary union with the GDR. The German chancellor could not afford to give the West German electorate time to become disillusioned with the high costs of unity. Instead, Kohl gambled that he could turn the ebbing tide of voter sentiment in six months. On May 14 Kohl announced that he might advance the date of unification and consider a combined or concurrent election in the former GDR at the time of the scheduled federal election.[10]

The next day Kohl told Hurd, who was visiting Bonn, that the unification train was now arriving at the station. Either the Germans got on or they let it go, in which case there would not be another opportunity during his lifetime. Foreign policy, Kohl added, was like mowing grass for hay: you had to gather what you had cut in case of a thunderstorm.[11] Kohl too could see the ominous clouds gathering in Moscow.

A day after his meeting with the British foreign secretary, Kohl flew to Washington to talk matters over in person with George Bush.[12] This time Genscher and defense minister Stoltenberg came with him. The two leaders had no difficulty coming to a common understanding on achieving internal unification as quickly as possible. Kohl at one point stopped and offered Bush a warm tribute: I do not mean to embarrass you, he said. But for us Germans and Europeans George Bush is a stroke of good luck.

With little dividing them, the two leaders concentrated on the Soviet Union. Kohl saw the Bush-Gorbachev summit at the end of May as a turning point. Looking ahead, Kohl saw three events that would be crucial: the Bush-Gorbachev meeting, the July NATO summit in London, and the July G-7 economic summit in Houston. He urged Bush to set the direction for these events and give the West the leadership it needed. Kohl promised that Bush could count on his support.

The chancellor specifically pledged that in the months ahead he would be unshakable on the question of Germany's membership in NATO and the need to maintain the American military presence, including both nuclear and conventional forces, in Germany. In a small session Bush asked Kohl for his honest opinion about German public support for keeping the American soldiers on their territory. Kohl's answer was that U.S. troops were indispensable to NATO and NATO was indispensable to Germany. As he looked at the future of Europe even beyond the year 2000, he saw the Americans still present in Europe as a matter of course. If the Europeans allowed the Americans to leave, it would be a great defeat—a defeat on the scale of Wilson's failure to keep the United States engaged in Europe after World War I.

Both leaders agreed that Soviet troops should leave Germany soon after unification. Kohl and Genscher wanted to let them stay temporarily, for a period of no more than three years; the date must be fixed. Bush wanted Soviet troops to leave Germany as soon as possible; he thought that a withdrawal period of three years might be too generous. Genscher assured Bush that he wanted Soviet troops out, too, and that he rejected any attempt to equate the status of Soviet and American forces in Germany. Kohl became emotional. George, he said, don't worry about those who draw parallels between U.S. and Soviet forces. We will push this through. We'll put our political existence at stake for NATO and the political commitment of the United States in Europe.

The Soviets Ask for Money

The relationship with Bonn was now firmly set and would remain so until unification was complete. But the Soviet Union was another matter altogether. American officials would not compromise their objectives for Gorbachev's sake, but they still cared deeply about Gorbachev's future and the future of his "new thinking." Neither they nor the West Germans wanted to rely solely on their ability to isolate Moscow and turn back every Soviet diplomatic move. Thus, Washington and Bonn alike were working on an "incentives package" for the Soviets that might convince Gorbachev and at least some of his supporters that the USSR would remain an important player in the new European order.

The Americans began to move toward a design that rested on three assumptions. First, if the United States and West Germany took a measured approach on issues like the Baltic problem, and provided limited economic assistance to the USSR, the Soviet leader might be persuaded to close the deal on unification. Second, there had to be visible changes in NATO, so that the Soviet Union could accept the bitter pill of Germany's unification within the Western alliance. Third, the Germans would work out financial arrangements with the Soviet Union concerning the GDR's economic obligations and, perhaps, additional monetary assistance to the USSR. There was a kind of division of labor emerging between Bonn and Washington. It was now up to the United States to deliver reassurance and cover for the Soviet Union's acceptance of Germany unity—superpower to superpower.

But the Baltic problem was complicated for the United States. Washington could not simply countenance whatever the Soviets chose to do there. After the Lithuanians declared their independence in March, Gorbachev authorized military maneuvers in the republic, deployed additional KGB troops there, confiscated private weapons and disarmed the local national guard, seized printing presses and Communist party property, and imposed economic sanctions—including a cutoff of oil and natural gas. The American press was filled with calls for a forceful reaction from the United States. Bush resisted the pressure, with the State Department and White House carefully controlling the daily responses of press secretaries Margaret Tutwiller and Marlin Fitzwater to events in Lithuania.

Encouraged by Bush, Kohl and Mitterrand tried to defuse the crisis by sending a joint letter on April 26 to the Lithuanian leaders asking them to suspend their declaration of independence. The Americans debated hotly whether the United States should pressure the Lithuanians to accede to the German and French initiative. Gates, Blackwill, and Rice were opposed, arguing that Washington should not leave its fingerprints on an effort to dissuade the Baltic states from seeking independence. Scowcroft, Baker, and Ross, however, believed that the Americans could send an "indirect" message to the Lithuanians that they wanted to see a resolution. A delicately worded message was delivered to the Vilnius leadership by a third-party emissary. Primed by the Americans, the Lithuanians endorsed the Kohl-Mitterrand proposal in order to reduce tensions. Also primed by the Americans, Gorbachev's spokesman called the Lithuanian reaction encouraging. The Kremlin would consider reducing its natural gas embargo.

On May 1 the U.S. Senate voted to withhold trade benefits from the Soviet Union until Moscow lifted its embargo and began negotiating with the Lithuanians. On May 3 Bush met the Lithuanian prime minister, Kazimera Prunskiene, and she agreed that independence could be postponed until 1992 if there were constructive negotiations with Moscow.[13] When Bush saw Kohl, he conveyed his pleasure with the Kohl-Mitterrand letter, but reminded the chancellor that the United States was in no position to lean on the Lithuanians in the same way. Tensions eased for the moment. But, as the U.S.-Soviet summit approached, pressures grew on the administration to adopt the tougher line being urged on it by the Senate.

The Baltic crisis complicated the already difficult problem of when and how to provide economic assistance to the Soviet Union. The topic had surfaced at last when Shevardnadze spoke with Kohl in Bonn on May 4. Shevardnadze had finally asked for money. At the instruction of Gorbachev and Prime Minister Ryzhkov, Shevardnadze had requested financial credits, a line of hard currency credit that Moscow could use as foreign exchange in purchasing foreign goods. These would be loans, new debts for the Soviet government, but Gorbachev needed the money. The rapid January 1990 agreement to deliver emergency food aid had defused some of the anger Gorbachev had felt toward Kohl in December 1989. Now the West Germans, again in a diplomatic stalemate, realized that it would be hard for Moscow to sustain a full-fledged confrontation over unification at the very moment that Moscow was seeking financial assistance. Kohl was determined to help as much as he could.

Without informing his cabinet (but telling Genscher about Shevardnadze's request on May 7), Kohl contacted Hilmar Kopper of Deutsche Bank and Wolfgang Röller of Dresdner Bank. He decided to send Teltschik and the bankers to Moscow, in secret, to explore the Soviets' needs and possible responses.[14] On May 8 Kvitsinsky said that his government wanted DM 20 billion in credits (about $12 billion). Western governments should guarantee repayment of the loans, he said, to clear away any rumors that the Soviets were unreliable. This would open the way for the Soviets to get even more credits from the financial markets.

Teltschik soon learned from the bankers that the markets had lost confidence in Soviet creditworthiness because the USSR was not making timely payments on existing debts. It was obvious that the Soviets were experiencing an acute foreign exchange crisis, a smaller-scale version of the East Germans' problem. The West German government alone could not reverse this situation; at the very least a major multilateral Western effort would be needed. Teltschik and the bankers Kopper and Röller flew secretly on a West German military aircraft to Moscow, where they were met by Kvitsinsky, now assuming his new role as deputy foreign minister with responsibility for European affairs.

Teltschik met with Ryzhkov and Shevardnadze at the Kremlin on May 14. They were grateful for Kohl's quick response. They described a bleak economic picture. To maintain their reforms, they explained, they had to normalize the situation and keep living standards from sinking. Ryzhkov wanted an immediate extension of an unconditional credit of 1.5 to 2 billion rubles to meet current payments and quell whispering about Soviet creditworthiness. In the longer term they would require 10 to 15 billion more rubles, to be paid off over ten to fifteen years, with no payments due for five years. (At the time one ruble was equal to about one deutsche mark, or about 60 cents.)

Teltschik promised that Kohl would do what he could. He also made it clear that such support had to be part of a package that would include a solution to the whole German question. Shevardnadze agreed. The Soviets opened up their foreign exchange situation to the German visitors, disclosed more than DM 24 billion in outstanding foreign debts, a quarter owed to the Germans and most of the remainder owed, in order of importance, to Japan, Italy, France, Austria, and Britain.

Teltschik then met directly with Gorbachev, who again linked the credit issue to continuation of his overall program of economic reform and perestroika. Gorbachev liked the idea of a bilateral friendship treaty with Germany. It would be a pillar of his vision of the common European home. But on the security questions, Gorbachev said, he had to speak from the heart. These had to be handled in such a way that the people of the Soviet Union would not believe that the security of the USSR was endangered. He thought that the best solution was to go beyond both blocs, to get rid of both NATO and the Warsaw Pact. Teltschik gave no ground on the security issues, instead emphasizing the historic importance of a treaty between Germany and the Soviet Union as well as the Soviets' readiness to cooperate—in the context of a general solution to the German question. He reminded Gorbachev that the Soviet leader had once talked about bringing Kohl to the Caucasus to visit the region where he grew up. Would Gorbachev still be willing to do this? After the meeting Kvitsinsky remained behind and emerged to tell Teltschik that, yes, Gorbachev was interested in such a visit from Kohl. Teltschik returned to Bonn the same day, convinced that Kohl was finding the right ways to address some of the Soviet Union's central interests.

When Kohl met with Bush in Washington a few days later, the Soviet request for money was at the top of his agenda.[15] Privately, with only Bush, Scowcroft, and Teltschik present, Kohl disclosed the Soviet request to Bush and told him about Teltschik's trip to Moscow. Kohl expected the Soviets to make a similar request for credits directly to Washington, in part to buy wheat. Kohl said that his government would be willing to guarantee a loan of DM 5 billion (about $3 billion). Bush could not follow suit. Although he would not aggravate Gorbachev's problems with Lithuania, neither could he guarantee large loans to Moscow unless the Soviets changed their policy toward this Baltic republic. Bush also believed that handing the Soviets more debt, without real economic reforms in place, was not a good idea. He admitted, though, that Gorbachev sounded desperate.

Kohl urged Bush to change his mind. But Bush stood firm. Nor would he grant most favored nation trading status to the Soviets. Kohl predicted that Gorbachev would ask for money when he came to Washington for the summit meeting at the end of May. Bush still maintained that large loans would not be repaid under existing circumstances. Kohl disagreed. He urged Bush to help Gorbachev, not wait for him to be overthrown.

Did Kohl think that there would be a military takeover? Bush asked. Yes, said Kohl, by a civilian group backed by the military. He urged Bush again to think about the upcoming summit. Gorbachev needed to be able to stand beside the American president as an equal. Bush promised to treat Gorbachev as an equal, moving forward on political relations and arms control. But the United States would not give Gorbachev money, not unless the Soviets changed their policy toward Lithuania. Kohl promised to warn Gorbachev about the importance America attached to the Lithuanian problem and the need for further economic reform. Both Kohl and Bush agreed that their discussion must remain strictly confidential. Kohl's cabinet still did not know the details. The issue of economic assistance was left there for Bush to ponder as the U.S.-Soviet summit approached.

Moscow's "Surrealistic Jumble of Ideas"

In mid-May 1990 Kvitsinsky returned to Moscow to become Shevardnadze's deputy. His assignment was to get a firm grip on his country's German policy. He was depressed by what he found. Kvitsinsky looked at the Soviet positions and was disgusted. There were so many ideas on the table, none carefully put together or cogently presented. They amounted, he later wrote, to a "surrealistic jumble of ideas."[16]

The Politburo had handed Shevardnadze a tough line to take at the Two Plus Four ministerial meeting in Bonn. But Shevardnadze's reports of his meeting were clear: the West was firm and united. Soviet proposals had received no support whatsoever. He was impressed, however, by the friendliness he had encountered from the Western side. As he wrote in his memoirs: "They constantly assured me that they understood the special sensitivity of the Soviet Union to the events. I recall how Baker mentioned this factor, then said, 'We must find a solution where there won't be any winners and losers, but where everybody wins.'" Tarasenko recalled that Shevardnadze seemed happy after Bonn. He had done his best, and he could report that the hard-line position had failed. In the Kremlin Chernyayev also seized on the Bonn meeting as evidence that the current line of policy was bankrupt.[17] Naturally, both Shevardnadze and Chernyayev could only be helped in their internal struggle to win over Gorbachev by the discussions with Kohl on financial credits.

The conservatives, however, remained convinced that they were right. On May 9 Gorbachev had called for a peace treaty to be negotiated between Germany and all of its neighbors. His national security adviser, Marshal Akhromeyev, dismissed U.S. arguments about the value of anchoring Germany in NATO. He was attracted to the curious idea of establishing a new Four Power command in a united Germany, but warned that proceeding to unity without Soviet consent would create an "acute situation" and threaten all East-West relations. Defense minister Yazov linked any withdrawal of Soviet troops to the simultaneous removal of Western forces from German soil. Falin was even more intransigent. Presented with American arguments for German membership in NATO, he replied, "Don't treat us like kids." Falin too wanted permanent controls on Germany under Four Power auspices.[18]

These voices, particularly those of the professional military, were gaining influence in Moscow. During Baker's February trip to Moscow, Shevardnadze had offered a number of arms control concessions, but General Staff representatives had not been in the room. When Shevardnadze came to Washington in April, those agreements unraveled. This time a timid and cautious Shevardnadze was accompanied by the generals, who were clearly there to ensure that the General Staff's requirements were met. At one point Shevardnadze told Baker that the United States would simply have to deal with Akhromeyev on several key issues.

Throughout 1989 and the beginning of 1990, the Soviet military had been strangely silent about events in Germany. But as it became clear that developments in Germany and Eastern Europe were about to threaten the basic posture of the armed forces, the men in uniform started to find their bureaucratic footing. Chernyayev has said that it was the CFE negotiations that heightened the sensitivity of the armed forces to the Soviet Union's deteriorating position in Central Europe. The General Staff, headed by General Mikhail Moiseyev, moved decisively in the spring to circumvent the full effect of a CFE treaty's reductions and limits. Only later was the West able to appreciate the extent to which the CFE treaty and the battle over Germany served as turning points in the Soviet military's alienation from Gorbachev, a break with fateful consequences for the future stability of the Soviet Union.[19]

Secretary Baker viewed his May 16–19 trip to Moscow as "the last high-level opportunity to complete preparations for a productive, results-oriented summit." He intended to concentrate on the questions of Lithuania, Germany, and arms control.[20] But the talks in Moscow did not go well. Following his discussions with Shevardnadze on May 16–17, Baker reported to Bush that "after really slugging it out on the arms control issues," they had made only modest progress. The Soviet military was now playing a bigger bureaucratic role. Shevardnadze was obliged to read his whole arms control brief in front of his delegation, as if to show that he could be trusted to make the points. Other U.S. delegation members agreed that Shevardnadze was not in command of his material and seemed disorganized. To Baker Shevardnadze had seemed distracted "and a little overwhelmed by everything. The economic problems, the public mistrust, the sense of losing control, the fear of the nationality issue, and concerns about Germany all are weighing very heavily."[21]

On the final day of these Baker-Shevardnadze meetings, Shevardnadze suddenly canceled the morning session, an encounter Baker was depending on to break the logjam before the upcoming Washington summit. A frustrated Baker called Ross and Rice together and asked for their sense of what was going on. Rice and Ross decided to find out. They arrived at the Obsobnyak—the meetinghouse of the Foreign Ministry—to find the Soviets in the midst of an interagency meeting. Akhromeyev, Moiseyev, and Shevardnadze were all present. The Soviet leadership was clearly in no position to negotiate with the American secretary of state.

The Soviets were immobilized, and the CFE negotiations, so essential to progress on Germany and preparations for the fall CSCE summit, were stalled. As NSC staff arms control expert Arnold Kanter put it later, "We got nowhere." The Americans tried. Reginald Bartholomew and CFE ambassador James Woolsey introduced new proposals that went beyond what their NATO negotiating partners had agreed to offer, even beyond what other agencies had agreed to back in Washington. Shevardnadze conceded the American linkage between a CSCE summit at the end of 1990 and the signing of a CFE treaty, but he deferred on CFE substance to a working group where the Soviet delegates just asked questions about the new American ideas.[22]

The Americans and the Soviets did begin to explore ways to use CFE limits on military personnel to address the size of the German armed forces, the Bundeswehr, in a united Germany. The NATO allies had already agreed that a "follow-on" CFE negotiation, to begin after the current treaty was signed, could consider putting further limits on forces in a central zone of Europe, since such geographic limits were already part of the current CFE approach.[23] But the Soviets wanted to negotiate limits on German forces now, not later, and they wanted to do it in the Two Plus Four talks, not in CFE. Baker completely rejected this position. Shevardnadze asked if the matter could be discussed in Two Plus Four with special limits recorded in CFE. No, came Baker's answer.[24]

Discussions concerning the political questions pertaining to Germany's future were only slightly more fruitful. On the morning of May 18 Zoellick, Rice, and Seitz met with Kvitsinsky and Bondarenko to exchange working-level views on Germany. In an intense discussion Zoellick acknowledged how difficult the German issue was for the USSR. Washington was trying to be sensitive to this history. But long-term stability was the goal. That was why the United States did not want to single out Germany or discriminate against it. Zoellick presented the American concept of the Two Plus Four as a "steering group," a way of addressing the Soviet desire for "synchronization," with the Two Plus Four necessarily moving issues to the forums where they could legitimately be decided. For the first time Zoellick offered the Soviets a comprehensive picture of the "incentives" package meant to persuade Moscow to accept German membership in NATO. It was a nine-point package, bringing together in one presentation several sets of American and West German ideas, which Zoellick had assembled. The nine points were:

1. Follow-on CFE negotiations were needed to deal with the question of force size throughout Europe, including Central Europe. This was another reason to complete the current CFE treaty as quickly as possible, in order to move on to other issues.
2. The start of new arms control negotiations on short-range nuclear forces should be moved up.
3. The Germans had agreed to reaffirm that they would neither possess nor produce nuclear, biological, or chemical weapons.
4. No NATO forces would be stationed in the former territory of the GDR during a specified transition period.
5. The United States had proposed that Germany work out a respectable transition period for the withdrawal of all Soviet troops from German territory.
6. President Bush had called for a review of NATO strategy which would take into account the changes that had occurred in Europe. Put simply, NATO's posture would look very different in terms of both conventional and nuclear forces.
7. Germany's future borders must be settled.
8. The CSCE should be enhanced to ensure a significant role for the USSR in the new Europe. U.S. officials had called for a summer meeting to prepare new CSCE ideas, followed by a meeting of CSCE ministers in September, and capped by the CSCE summit in Paris (which,

Zoellick added, remained conditioned on conclusion of a CFE agreement).

9. Finally, the Americans believed that there must be a satisfactory treatment of the Soviet Union's economic ties with Germany, preferably in a way that benefited perestroika. This was, of course, an issue for the two German states to discuss with the USSR.[25]

Zoellick urged Kvitsinsky to accept German membership in NATO as the most stable solution, one that would eliminate any push by Germany to acquire an independent nuclear force of its own. The goal should be to achieve unification and terminate Four Power rights before the end of the year.

Kvitsinsky gave no ground, though he did not mention Gorbachev's peace treaty proposal of the previous week.[26] The Soviets, he said, were not afraid of a fait accompli, although there were those who talked as if they were. He added that some even thought that without Soviet consent the unification of Germany would not take place. The crux of the matter for Kvitsinsky was the relationship between what happened in the Two Plus Four and the development of the all-European process. Zoellick's nine points would have to be studied.

The Soviet Union still favored separating the question of achieving internal unification from that of relinquishing Four Power rights. Kvitsinsky said that his government would want to see how agreements were implemented by a new German government before giving up its Four Power rights. To illustrate what he had in mind for the Two Plus Four and German obligations, Kvitsinsky focused on the military strength of the future German armed forces. The Six, he said (the Soviets never liked the connotation of German primacy implied by the phrase "Two Plus Four"), could decide on a ceiling for the future Bundeswehr and could determine where forces would be deployed in Germany. A CFE II treaty could, as the Americans desired, include these German troop limits. But the decision of the Six would have to be respected and implemented regardless of what happened at the talks in Vienna. The United States should stop hiding behind references to CFE or other forums. Decisions to promote European stability had to be made now, in the Two Plus Four, for a second chance might not present itself.

The Americans, said Kvitsinsky, must have no doubt that, for Moscow, full German membership in NATO was out of the question. This was not a bargaining ploy. The prospect was unacceptable, and no Soviet parliament would approve a treaty allowing such a thing. If countries were worried about the behavior of a neutral Germany, they should solve that problem by setting down rules in the treaty being prepared by the Two Plus Four. Do not think, he added, that internal unification would solve the problem "automatically." Such an attempt would have negative consequences for many. Kvitsinsky concluded the discussion by saying that the Soviets could hardly imagine that Germany would adopt a position opposing the Soviet Union, the United States, or anyone else. That would be a tragedy for everyone.

Later the same day Baker tried out arguments similar to Zoellick's in a long meeting with Gorbachev.[27] Discussion of Germany dominated the private one-on-one discussion between the two men. Baker reassured Gorbachev that neither he nor President Bush had tried to exploit or gloat over the democratic revolutions in Central and Eastern Europe. The United States had initiated the Two Plus Four process, providing a mechanism Moscow needed to help manage its concerns. The United States had tried to address legitimate Soviet interests while showing that the issue could not and would not unfold without Gorbachev. He then detailed the nine-point incentives package.

Gorbachev moved the conversation to his agenda. He challenged the Americans' real intentions toward the Soviet Union, given the clashes over issues such as Lithuania and Germany. Then, just as Kohl had expected, Gorbachev made the same request for money that he had made to the West Germans. Gorbachev needed $20 billion in loans and credits to overcome a significant funding gap over the next few years. The United States had to be involved, at least symbolically, in the loan effort. The next few years would be critical in easing the transition to a market economy.

Baker could offer Gorbachev little encouragement. It was hard to justify spending U.S. taxpayers' money if the Soviets were subsidizing the Cubans and economically squeezing the Lithuanians. Baker was essentially making the same points Bush had made to Kohl, in Washington, the day before. On the German question, Gorbachev took detailed notes of Baker's presentation and his nine points. He approved much of it. But he said that it was impossible for the Soviet Union to accept a unified Germany in NATO. It would constitute a fundamental shift in the strategic balance of forces and jeopardize his program at home. "It will be the end of perestroika," he said.

The argument went back and forth. Gorbachev said, I know that Germany will be closer to you, but it should not be in the Western alliance. If that was unacceptable to the United States, then perhaps Gorbachev would seek Soviet admission to NATO. Gorbachev also put the German issue in a larger perspective. Resolving this matter, he declared, was a real test for the ability of the Americans and the Soviets to find a compatible approach, taking into account a balance of interests between the two countries. A solution had to be found. Both countries needed to think more about the issue. He would talk things over with President Bush when he came to Washington.

Reflecting on this meeting in a message back to Bush, Baker had three impressions. First, Gorbachev was clearly feeling squeezed and would probably react strongly to any action that compounded his political difficulties at home. Second, wrote Baker, "Germany definitely overloads his circuits right now. We ought to let the process go forward, continue to try to meet Soviet concerns, but not press them to accept our objective. It's best to let it happen." Third, given the preoccupation with Germany and Gorbachev's need to know how the German threat would be contained, "we probably will have to get more specific on how and when Bundeswehr limits are going to be achieved if we want a CFE agreement."

A few days after Baker left, Gorbachev, in an interview with *Time* magazine, said that the Soviet Union would "never agree to entrust to [NATO] the leading role in building a new Europe." He seemed to have hardened his position against including a unified Germany in the alliance, and claimed that Washington appeared ready to use any pretext to delay the departure of American troops from Europe. So both in private and in public, Gorbachev was apparently inflexible on the question of German membership in NATO. Gorbachev's adviser Vadim Zagladin told Rice in their second meeting within three months: "There used to be two Germanys—one was ours and one was yours. Now there will be one and you want it to be yours. That would be an unacceptable strategic shift in the balance of power." Later, Zagladin told another American that the NATO issue was a "deal-breaker" unless the alliance underwent some radical change.[28]

The Two Plus Four political directors met in Bonn on May 22. The Western allies easily achieved a common position in consultations prior to the start of the meeting. As planned, Bertrand Dufourcq, the chairman, proposed that the final settlement include (1) a preamble, giving a brief political declaration; (2) separate instruments on unity and borders, Berlin, and the termination of Four Power rights and responsibilities; and (3) acknowledgment by the Four Powers of other acts such as an expected Polish-German border treaty and amendments to the FRG's Basic Law which would repeal article 23 and other provisions allowing for the inclusion of additional territory into Germany. Annexation of East Germany would be the last use of article 23. But the meeting of the political directors was inconclusive. Bondarenko, representing the USSR, insisted that the Western outline was incomplete in its coverage of political and military issues. There was no real debate over these matters; the key issues were clearly being dealt with at a higher level.[29]

Within the allied camp a potentially serious disagreement had also emerged over the timing of a final settlement. British and French lawyers were convinced that the Two Plus Four could not resolve the issue of Germany's borders before Germany was unified. The FRG thought that both matters could be settled simultaneously. The dispute was significant because the British and French view led to the conclusion that the unification of Germany must precede conclusion of a settlement by the Two Plus Four. This threatened just the kind of decoupling of unification from the surrender of Four Power rights which America and Britain had considered so dangerous when it was first suggested by Shevardnadze at the beginning of May. The American lawyers sympathized with the British and French legal arguments, but they knew that those arguments led to a conclusion that the United States could not accept.

Interestingly, none of the lawyers appeared to grasp that the FRG's use of article 23 could make this worrisome legal debate irrelevant. If the GDR became part of the FRG under article 23, the unified Germany would not be a successor state to the FRG; it would be the *very same state* under international law, albeit larger. The FRG had already pledged, in 1970, that it would respect the existing borders of Poland. The Federal Republic had the legal authority to renew this pledge at any time. The pledge would bind a future enlarged FRG just as it had bound the Federal Republic in the past. All the Four Powers had to do was withdraw the qualification, the lien, they had claimed against the FRG's right to make this promise.[30] Fortunately, since U.S. and West German opposition to decoupling was so clear, the legal controversy subsided, and by the end of May only the French (and the Soviets) were still insisting that unification had to occur before Germany could reassure Poland in a binding fashion and Four Power rights could be relinquished.[31]

Limiting the Bundeswehr

Genscher recognized, as did Baker, the importance to Moscow of a guarantee concerning the size of Germany's future armed forces. The two foreign ministers were in agreement that this issue should be kept outside the competence of the Two Plus Four. But putting it off to the next CFE negotiation did not appear to satisfy the Soviets. So Genscher and his ministry developed a new CFE proposal to bring to Shevardnadze when the two ministers met in Geneva on May 23. They would propose adding a provision to the current CFE treaty specifying that no country could station more than

400,000 troops in the central zone, defined under the treaty draft as including Britain, France, Italy, East-Central Europe, and the western military districts of the USSR. This promise would not single out Germany alone, but it would effectively limit German forces while also limiting Soviet troop concentrations in the western Soviet Union (the "transitional" Soviet troops in eastern Germany would not be counted). Genscher was reported to be ready to add these new troop ceilings to the *current* CFE treaty, if that would close the deal.[32]

Scowcroft and the NSC staff believed that supporting Genscher's proposal would be a mistake. They identified several problems. First, Genscher's staff was miscalculating if they thought that Moscow could live with a ceiling of 400,000 Soviet troops in a zone that included the USSR's western military districts. U.S. officials believed that there were then about 1 million Soviet personnel in this zone. Exempting Soviet troops in the GDR was only a partial solution (and how would they be counted after they withdrew?). Second, the United States suspected that the West German government was not of one mind about this proposal. After all, FRG defense minister Stoltenberg had told American officials that he did not want Germany to be singled out for special troop limits.[33] Third, and perhaps most important, the proposal might open the door not to a deal but to a whole new set of debates that would bog down the ongoing CFE talks. The Soviets could offer a counterproposal (perhaps 200,000 troops in a smaller zone), and the West would find the negotiations stalled. Then that stalemate would in turn delay progress in the Two Plus Four. It is worth taking a moment to consider why these Americans feared that such a dry, technical arms control proposal could have momentous political implications.

The Western powers were trying to keep the nuclear and conventional arms control issues out of the Two Plus Four. The CFE talks were dealing with the problem of European forces. But if the talks were stalemated, then this failure might stop the Two Plus Four. The delay in CFE might also postpone the Paris CSCE summit, since it was now agreed that a CFE treaty had to be ready for signing before the leaders would come to Paris.

The American strategy for a narrow mandate in the Two Plus Four relied on delicate and precise timing, with all other European negotiations falling into place in time for Germany to be unifed before December; the next FRG elections would thus be all-German elections. Kohl apparently feared that he could lose the elections if they were held only in the Western half of Germany *and* unification was still unsettled. A victory for Oskar Lafontaine and the Social Democrats would then dramatically alter both U.S. and Soviet prospects for negotiating the future of Germany and all of Europe.

Scowcroft held a meeting with Baker, Cheney, and Powell. They agreed that

Genscher's idea was problematic, and that Washington had to do more than just criticize it. The United States had to find an alternative. The potential deadlock in CFE was now a real threat to the timetable for unification.[34]

While the Americans were tackling the CFE problem, Kohl wrote to Gorbachev on the issue of credits. His May 22 letter assured the Soviets that Bonn was willing to guarantee new, untied loans to Moscow of DM 5 billion (about $3 billion). Larger, long-term credits would require a multilateral Western effort. Kohl informed Gorbachev that he had already raised the matter with Bush and would soon raise it with his EC and G-7 partners as well. Kohl hoped that Gorbachev would approach Two Plus Four issues in this same spirit of cooperation and friendship.[35]

The next day Genscher met with Shevardnadze in Geneva. Genscher, like Kohl and the Americans, had always been encouraged by Shevardnadze's reasonable tone in discussing the NATO issue, even if he differed on substance. In Bonn, as in Washington, Shevardnadze was believed to be searching for a compromise. On May 14 a lengthy interview was published, in which Genscher confidently predicted that the Soviets would eventually agree to including a united Germany in NATO. Privately both the interviewer and Genscher's advisers wondered whether Genscher really felt as confident as he sounded.[36]

In Geneva Genscher and Shevardnadze had a friendly discussion, the atmosphere improved by Bonn's decision to offer Moscow the DM 5 billion in credit guarantees. Genscher outlined his own package of reassurances. On May 22 in Bonn Zoellick had debriefed Elbe so thoroughly on the nine-point proposal and on the Moscow talks that, as Elbe later put it, "Genscher could employ the same points in his conversation with Shevardnadze." But Genscher gave particular attention to certain points that he knew had special symbolic and psychological importance for the Soviets, such as caring for and respecting Soviet war monuments and military cemeteries in Germany. Shevardnadze had no problem with the proposed acceleration of internal unification. Moscow, he said, would not act like a "traffic policeman." Genscher urged Shevardnadze to deal with the issue of German troop limits in the CFE negotiations, not in the Two Plus Four. He persuaded Shevardnadze to agree that the matter could be handled in CFE as a "parallel process" to discussions of the problem among the Two Plus Four. Genscher apparently did not, however, present the details of his new CFE proposal to the Soviet foreign minister. He heard out a Soviet suggestion that future German armed forces be limited to no more than 250,000 to 300,000 soldiers, airmen, and sailors. Genscher explained why he could not accept any agreement that singled out Germans for unique limits on their forces.[37]

Genscher flew from Geneva to Paris, debriefed the French, and flew on to

Washington. He had been encouraged by the upbeat tone of his meeting with Shevardnadze. Bonn had also sent its economics minister, Helmut Hauss-mann, to Moscow to talk over how West Germany would deal with East German economic obligations to Moscow, as well as to start discussions on the economics of withdrawing Soviet troops from East Germany. On the crucial question how to handle German troop limits, Genscher told Baker that he had not yet given Shevardnadze the new proposal to amend the current draft of the CFE treaty with additional personnel limits applying to all armies in the broadly defined central zone of Europe. What, Genscher asked, did Baker think of this plan? Baker, aware of the misgivings that had surfaced in Washington, said that it was still being studied. He promised to finish his analysis soon.[38]

Genscher portrayed a Soviet leadership interested in compromise.[39] But Mitterrand had seen Gorbachev himself on May 25. Fully briefed by Bush about Baker's just-concluded talks, Mitterrand returned the favor by telling Bush all about his five hours of talks at the Kremlin, the majority of which was spent on the question of Germany. The report was bleak. Mitterrand found that Gorbachev's "hostility to the participation of a unified Germany in NATO does not appear to me as being either fake or tactical. On this subject, he is both firm and determined."

Gorbachev repeated to Mitterrand the warning he had made in the Polit-buro meeting at the beginning of May: if the West tried to confront the Soviet Union with a fait accompli on Germany, then the Soviet government would alter its behavior on many issues, including arms control in Europe. When Mitterrand argued for German membership in NATO, the Soviets hinted at the possibility of a French-style membership for Germany—outside the alli-ance's military command. Mitterrand received the impression that Gorbachev had little room for maneuvering either on Germany or on Lithuania. So Mitterrand thought that it would be very hard to try to achieve unification in the fall of 1990. As he put it, in his typically oblique way: "The usual course of diplomacy will not prevent a difficult climate in the summer and in the fall." Paris communicated the same pessimism to Kohl's office in Bonn. The Canadian foreign minister, Joe Clark, received a similarly bleak impression of Soviet attitudes when he met in Moscow on May 29 with Shevardnadze and Akhromeyev. Akhromeyev warned that ignoring Soviet views on Ger-many would bring about a changed Soviet foreign policy and a return to more offensive military doctrines. At the end of May the Soviet bureaucracy sent out a call for new CSCE structures that could replace NATO. All the signs indicated to Soviet experts in the State Department that Bush should "not expect to see much flexibility in the Soviet position" on Germany when Gorbachev came to Washington.

Yet only a few West Germans and a few Americans knew about Gorbachev's private requests for financial credits. Knowing this, they gave more credence to Genscher's optimism than to Mitterrand's and Clark's pessimism. The crucial insight into Soviet thinking would emerge in just a few days, when Gorbachev journeyed to Washington for his summit meeting with President Bush.

The Turning Point

By the end of May, as Gorbachev contemplated his trip to the United States, he faced a turning point in the course of East-West relations and perestroika. The stakes in continued cooperation with the West were enormous. Gorbachev and Shevardnadze had stated both publicly and privately that their first priority was domestic reform. That meant cutting military expenditures and avoiding the distraction of a major international crisis.

It also appears that both Gorbachev and Shevardnadze had vague but strong, perhaps exaggerated, hopes for Western economic assistance. They believed that a temporary infusion of capital, even if it increased Soviet indebtedness, could make the difference in effecting the all-important transition to a more viable economy. They obviously thought that a more prosperous future was linked somehow to increased trade and investment from the West. Their highest priority, domestic reform, was therefore tied inextricably to the notion of cooperation with the West.

The dilemmas they faced were acute. Up to 1989 the reforms may have encountered opposition at home, but they posed few costs to the Soviet Union's international position. The price was paid only in the devalued coin of Soviet influence in the third world and esoteric concessions in the START and INF talks. In return, Gorbachev had become the toast of world capitals, encouraging Marxist revisionists with the hope that socialism had finally acquired a human face. But 1989 had been a hard year, and the first half of 1990 had been even harder. The democratic revolutions in Eastern Europe had gone further and faster than Moscow would have liked. The Warsaw Pact was mortally wounded.

In the spring of 1990 the Soviet Union appeared to be resigned to the failure of its policy in Eastern Europe. A long document prepared by the Central Committee staff spoke matter-of-factly about the changed political and ideological face of Eastern Europe. The analysis warned Soviet leaders that they currently had no policy to respond to this situation. There was a vacuum, and the West was filling it. The USSR was withdrawing with "no rational explanation, with no regard for the immense material and spiritual investment that we made there." The policy guidance grasped at straws. There was still a chance to strengthen the Soviet cultural presence, interest in the Russian language, and so forth. Ties needed to be developed with youth, trade unions, feminists, and religious groups. The Central Committee staff even suggested to a leadership desperately short of hard currency that a new policy in Eastern Europe might require a certain financial investment. "We should not economize," the staff told their impoverished leaders, "because this is a matter of capital for the future."[40]

But the fact remained that Soviet policy in Eastern Europe—premised on the potential for reformed communism—was dead. Germany and Lithuania, however, were a different matter. The division of Germany and Soviet dominance of its eastern half could be considered the most important achievements of half a century of Soviet foreign policy. This Soviet emplacement in the heart of Europe was the highest and last remaining measure of meaning from the vast sacrifices endured during the Great Patriotic War. Now the West and NATO were threatening to overrun this bastion of Soviet power. It seemed inconceivable that the USSR could submit supinely to such a reverse. Gorbachev's own political survival could be jeopardized by such a concession, and Gorbachev would face a full congress of the Soviet Communist party in July.

Then there was Lithuania. Lithuania's declaration of independence in March 1990 was a blow aimed right at the authority that held together the Soviet Union itself. Gorbachev and Bush were both walking a tightrope. Gorbachev launched economic sanctions against Lithuania but held back from taking more violent measures. He rejected Lithuania's declaration of independence and opened talks in mid-May with Prime Minister Prunskiene on a possible "suspension" of the declaration. Bush meanwhile refused to sign a U.S.-Soviet agreement clearing the way for more normal trade between the two countries, and he refused to go along with the secret request for financial credits unless Gorbachev relaxed Soviet sanctions against Lithuania. Yet Bush would not order retaliation against Moscow, nor would he cancel the summit. Bush said privately at the time: "I don't want people to look back 20 or 40 years from now and say, 'That's where everything went off track. That's where progress stopped.'"[41]

The president had also refused to go along with extending large credits to Moscow unless the Soviet Union adopted major new economic reforms. Just as he was trying to defuse the Lithuanian crisis, Gorbachev was moving on the question of economic reform too. On May 24 Prime Minister Nikolai Ryzhkov announced a major new economic reform program, including increases in food prices. The cost of bread would triple. A wave of panic buying and public unrest followed. Gorbachev addressed the nation on television on May 27, pleading for calm. (The economic reform measures were eventually rejected by the Supreme Soviet before they could take effect.) So Gorbachev was trying to move forward but, as if to underscore his beleaguered political situation, on May 29 the Russian legislature chose Boris Yeltsin as its president despite Gorbachev's opposition.

On Germany Gorbachev was under pressure from much of the Politburo to maintain an unyielding policy. If he chose this option, he could move decisively and assert traditional Soviet national security requirements and prerogatives. He could state firmly that the Western approach was unacceptable and would lead to a major international crisis. He could present a detailed alternative plan, specifying the constraints to be placed on Germany. He could threaten to walk out on the Two Plus Four process unless the West let that mechanism address Soviet concerns.

This tough policy might have received a good deal of popular support and certainly would have been welcomed by key institutions within the government and the party. Even if the Soviet Union had not achieved all its objectives, Moscow might have recovered some of the bargaining leverage it had lost in the process. Kohl would have been on the defensive; his governing coalition might have fractured. The East German government would have been frantic as chances of an SPD victory in the federal elections rose. The shock might even have helped intimidate the Lithuanians and others who sought to exploit Soviet weakness.

Yet Gorbachev undoubtedly appreciated the dangers in this course of action. Soviet-German relations would have received a tremendous shock. The West German voters would quite possibly have blamed themselves and turned Kohl out. Or, if the Soviet diplomacy had struck the wrong note, it might have destroyed much of the goodwill Gorbachev had created among the German people. Soviet-American relations would also have been hurt. With political tensions running high, Germany's situation unstable, and arms control progress derailed, Europe could have descended into a renewal of the cold war. Some in the USSR were probably quite willing to accept such a development rather than be forced to sacrifice the fruits of victory in the Great Patriotic War. The questions for Gorbachev could not have been clearer: How high a price would the Soviet Union pay to stay on the path of cooperation with the West? Would the Soviet Union trade its power in Europe for Western help at home?

Bush, too, faced a difficult choice. Genscher feared that an uncompromising Western policy on Germany could threaten Gorbachev's political survival. Kohl, though not suggesting any compromises on Germany, had in effect warned Bush that a stingy policy denying financial credits to Gorbachev could push him out of power, to be replaced by a military-dominated ruler. As Bush prepared for the summit, he saw the need to offer Gorbachev at least the promise or appearance of tangible economic support. But neither Bush nor Kohl seems to have considered tempering his policies on Germany in order to protect Gorbachev.

As Bush approached the first of three critical summer meetings, he gathered his advisers in the Cabinet Room. He had been told that Gorbachev was "still groping for alternatives" on the fundamental German issue. The United States would demonstrate its understanding of Soviet concerns, but the bottom line, as Scowcroft advised Bush, was that "full German membership in NATO is not negotiable."[42]

Back in Bonn, Genscher was eager to add another persuasive offer to the U.S.-Soviet bargaining—the new proposal for limiting the future size of a German army. When meeting with Shevardnadze in Geneva, Genscher had held back his new plan for adding such limits to the current CFE treaty, waiting until he could gather more support both from the allies and at home. A skeptical Baker was withholding his blessing. Back in Bonn, Genscher pressed his plan on Kohl during a meeting on May 28. He urged quick action so that the plan could be given to the Americans to use a few days later with Gorbachev. Kohl wanted other agencies to have more time to consider the matter and put the issue off until the next evening, when he would bring Genscher together with the defense minister and Chancellery staff in his residence.

Teltschik used the time to call Washington. Speaking with Robert Gates, he asked if the Americans were interested in pushing the matter of limits on German armed forces at the summit with Gorbachev. Kohl wanted to be helpful. Would the White House like a troop limit proposal from Bonn? Gates said no; Washington thought that it would be premature to press such a new proposal. But he would talk with Scowcroft, and Bush and Kohl would discuss the matter over the telephone the next day. Blackwill told his contacts in Bonn's Defense Ministry that the Americans were skeptical of Genscher's suggestion. Whatever was done about German troop strength, it should not single out the Germans for unique limits. But this particular proposal had substantive problems, and it might actually stall both the ongoing CFE negotiation and, with it, the Two Plus Four. Finally, Washington felt that this matter could be saved for the diplomatic "endgame."

When Kohl convened his meeting on the night of May 29, Genscher reviewed his idea about troop limits and said that he thought Baker was positively inclined. (Perhaps Genscher had misunderstood Baker's reserve.)

Then Stoltenberg spoke in favor of maintaining the current position: German troop strength would be limited only in a future CFE treaty. In those future talks Stoltenberg would support a limit of 430,000. Kohl decided to hold off on any decision. Genscher pleaded for immediate approval of his proposal for current CFE treaty limits. He wanted to get the Americans to use the idea in Bush's meetings with Gorbachev over the next few days. That would show Gorbachev how hard the West was trying to address Soviet concerns. This, he said, was the way to get over the current impasse in the talks. Stoltenberg was unconvinced, and Kohl promised only to discuss the matter with Bush.

The next day Kohl talked to Bush. The Chancellery and the Defense Ministry had already passed the word that the "Hartmann initiative" (named for West Germany's ambassador to the CFE talks) was off. Ten minutes after Scowcroft talked to Teltschik, Bush repeated the message directly to Kohl: it was good of Kohl to offer help on the German troop limits issue, but it was premature to propose a new idea for handling the problem. Kohl replied: "The wind blew some rumors my way." But no proposals would be made to the Soviets until both he and President Bush had agreed first. Bush could rely on that, Kohl promised.[43]

Kohl also wanted to review the bidding on two other issues, NATO and financial credits. On NATO membership, Kohl wanted Bush to know that he could rely on full West German support, that the West German position was in complete accord with the American view. Whatever happened, Kohl would stand side by side with Bush. On the sensitive issue of credits, Kohl again urged Bush to try to find a way to help Gorbachev. Bush doubted that there would be any breakthrough on Germany at the summit, but he returned to his earlier conversation with Kohl about credits for Moscow. He noted Gorbachev's interest in this question when Baker had visited Moscow. Bush said that he was still constrained by Soviet behavior toward Lithuania, but he would instead try to move forward on arms control issues.[44]

Later that day, May 30, Gorbachev arrived in Washington. He had just come from Canada. Prime Minister Mulroney had talked privately with Gorbachev in Ottawa, almost entirely about Germany, then warned Bush that Gorbachev had described the German question as a litmus test for U.S.-Soviet relations and had shown no flexibility. Gorbachev seemed to think that the Germans were being manipulated by Washington into an unreasonable position on NATO membership. Mulroney thought that Gorbachev needed more time; he needed to see how NATO could change to become less threatening to the Soviet Union.[45]

On the morning of May 31 Gorbachev was formally welcomed in a ceremony on the South Lawn of the White House. Guns boomed; a fife and drum corps dressed in the eighteenth-century uniforms of the Continental Army paraded for the leaders. After the opening ceremony Bush and Gorbachev walked from the South Lawn into the Oval Office for a private meeting, joined only by Scowcroft, Chernyayev, and their interpreters. Gorbachev promptly turned to the issue of American economic help for perestroika. A U.S.-Soviet trade agreement was essential. It was the one matter under discussion that might make a favorable impact at home. Gorbachev knew that Lithuania was still a problem for the Americans. He pledged to avoid a violent solution by pursuing a peaceful dialogue with the Lithuanian leaders. Bush was noncommittal. In another room Baker and Shevardnadze were replaying the same discussion. Shevardnadze was particularly emotional, admitting that he had rarely spoken like this before, but a U.S.-Soviet trade agreement was "extremely important" for Gorbachev's standing at home, to defend the Soviet leader's policy of cooperation with the West.[46]

Gorbachev returned to the Soviet embassy for a luncheon with American intellectuals and celebrities and then came back to the White House for an additional meeting.[47] The main subject was Germany and the future of Europe. Bush wanted to tackle this difficult subject right from the start. Naturally he knew that the open question of the trade agreement still lurked in the background. Bush began the Cabinet Room discussion by delivering a carefully prepared presentation on Germany that reviewed the nine-point plan for addressing legitimate Soviet concerns about unification and Germany's membership in the NATO alliance. Bush then reiterated and defended the U.S. position on the NATO issue and the workings of the Two Plus Four. He stressed to his Soviet audience that NATO would be a stabilizing force for Germany, giving the Germans confidence about their security and making it less likely that they would trouble their neighbors or want their own nuclear weapons.[48]

Gorbachev presented his alternative. A united Germany could be a member of both military alliances, or it could be a member of neither. Moscow could live with either possibility. In a rambling presentation Gorbachev said that letting a united Germany join only NATO would "unbalance" Europe. He repeatedly referred to the need for a long transition period. Perhaps by the end of this period Germany could be anchored in both NATO and the Warsaw Pact. As part of the transition both alliances would be transformed into political organizations. "You are a sailor," he told Bush. "You will understand that if one anchor is good, two anchors are better." Gorbachev felt that if the United States and the USSR could decide on how to proceed, the Germans would surely agree.

Bush thought that the fundamental difference between the two governments was that the Soviet Union was deeply suspicious of Germany and America was not. But Bush thought that Germany could potentially be a strong friend to the Soviet Union, just as it was a friend of the United States. Germany had built a true democracy. Bush reiterated that he had tried to avoid embarrassing the Soviet Union. He had not gloated when the Berlin Wall opened up. But he believed that a unified Germany in NATO was the most stable solution for Europe's security.

Gorbachev agreed that the U.S. presence was stabilizing. This presence was linked to NATO. Fine; new structures could come later. But first NATO must change. Gorbachev said that he understood the feelings of the Germans, but he could not overlook the attitudes of his own people. He repeated his suggestion of membership for a united Germany in both alliances. The Two Plus Four could conclude a settlement renouncing Four Power rights. Then there would be a transition period, lasting for years, during which the alliances would be transformed. Gorbachev seemed to imply that agreement on this transition process and its outcome could clear the way to completion of the CFE treaty.

The foreign ministers then weighed in. Baker talked about plans for the NATO summit in July, and he reviewed the nine-point plan. Shevardnadze returned to the idea of German membership in both alliances. Gorbachev added that perhaps any country could join either alliance. After all, Stalin, Roosevelt, and Churchill had all been part of a coalition. Gorbachev casually wondered if the Soviets should apply to join the North Atlantic Alliance. Bush, with a smile, wondered how Marshal Akhromeyev—sitting across the table—would like serving under an American NATO commander.

Baker talked about the possibility of some sort of agreement between NATO and the Warsaw Pact to show that friendly relations had replaced hostile confrontation. Gorbachev described how the alliances might turn into more political bodies, exchanging views, as NATO doctrine changed. But Germany could not be in just one structure; that would upset the European balance.

President Bush then introduced an argument that other U.S. and West German officials had begun to employ at lower levels. Under the CSCE principles in the Helsinki Final Act, all nations had the right to choose their own alliances. So Germany should have the right to decide for itself which alliance it would join.[49] Was this not so? Gorbachev nodded and agreed matter-of-factly that this was true.

The Americans were startled. They could see Akhromeyev and Falin, on the Soviet side, shifting in their seats. Blackwill whispered to Zoellick, sitting next to him, that he would pass a note to the president. Zoellick agreed.

Blackwill jotted down a quick note pointing out to President Bush that, surprisingly, Gorbachev had just supported the U.S. position that nations have the right to choose their own alliances. Could the president get Gorbachev to say it again?

Bush could. "I'm gratified that you and I seem to agree that nations can choose their own alliances," he said. Gorbachev answered: "So we will put it this way. The United States and the Soviet Union are in favor of Germany deciding herself in which alliance she would like to participate" after the conclusion of the Two Plus Four settlement. Bush then suggested an alternative formula: "The United States is unequivocally advocating Germany's membership in NATO. However, should Germany prefer to make a different choice, we will respect it."

Gorbachev agreed with this formula. Meanwhile many of his aides could not conceal their distress. Zoellick recalled the scene as "one of the most extraordinary" he'd ever witnessed. There was a palpable feeling—conveyed through expression and body language—among Gorbachev's advisers of almost physically distancing themselves from their leader's words. Then Gorbachev appeared to return to the familiar Soviet stance, describing the notion of a prolonged transition period during which Europe would change in order to accommodate a unified Germany. Gorbachev slipped Falin a note asking him to explain why the Soviets considered a pro-NATO solution unacceptable. Falin scribbled "I am ready," and sent it back. Gorbachev nodded, and as Falin launched into his presentation, Gorbachev conferred with Shevardnadze. When Gorbachev reentered the discussion, he proposed that Shevardnadze work with Baker on the German issue. Oddly, Shevardnadze at first openly refused, right in front of the Americans, saying that the matter had to be decided by heads of government. Gorbachev asked him again. Shevardnadze relented and agreed to explore the matter with Baker.

As the meeting ended, Bush and his advisers were in accord. There had been no misunderstanding: Gorbachev had indeed agreed that a united Germany could choose to be a full member of NATO. Back at the Soviet residence in Washington, Falin later recalled, Gorbachev complained about Shevardnadze's passivity, and expressed unhappiness that the foreign minister had done nothing to explore what kinds of variations the Americans might be prepared to accept on the NATO issue. Perhaps Shevardnadze, having been rebuffed by Gorbachev and others in the Politburo earlier in the month, was reluctant to stick his neck out. If Gorbachev, who had overruled Shevardnadze then, wanted to make concessions now, let him take the responsibility.

But now Gorbachev had made a concession, and the entire Soviet delegation knew it. Immediately after the meeting, on the lawn of the White House, Akhromeyev practically assaulted Chernyayev, interrogating him about Gorbachev's comments. Had they been written down as part of his briefing papers? Why had Gorbachev said what he'd said? Chernyayev replied that the comments were spontaneous; he did not know why the Soviet leader had chosen to make them on the spot.[50]

Gorbachev's and Shevardnadze's behavior at the meeting seemed, and still seems, quite unusual. It is actually very rare in diplomacy to change one's mind right at the table. The best interpretation consistent with the available evidence is that Gorbachev's resolve had been weakening, little by little, even before he arrived in Washington. Nothing that the Soviet Union suggested about Germany seemed to be working. The Politburo discussions in May had led directly to Shevardnadze's failure in Bonn. The Soviet leader had made all the old arguments to Baker, then to Mitterrand, then to Mulroney. Finally, as he faced Bush in Washington, something snapped. Bush's invocation of the right to choose one's alliance system may have caught Gorbachev off guard. Chernyayev recalled later that it would not have been logical to reject this idea since Gorbachev had already granted that a united Germany would be fully sovereign. Indeed, Gorbachev had often adopted the rhetoric of free choice and national self-determination. So when Bush struck the wall of resistance from this new angle, it suddenly cracked.

Gorbachev went on with his schedule: a formal dinner at the White House in the evening, breakfast with congressional leaders the next morning, June 1. Gorbachev kept pressing for the trade agreement. On Germany Gorbachev outwardly seemed as tough as ever. He complained to the American congressmen, "We are being squeezed out" of Europe, and "pressure is being applied for a unilateral advantage of the other side." Should an imbalance develop in Europe, Moscow would have to "reconsider" and "reassess" its arms control positions. Gorbachev explained his economic difficulties and asked the congressmen to back a trade agreement. The agreement would not bring quick results, said Gorbachev, since "the trade relationship between us now is so primitive," but "I think it is very important that you make this gesture mostly from a political standpoint."[51]

Gorbachev returned to the White House later that morning, and he and Bush talked further about the trade agreement. Bush had checked views around his administration and on Capitol Hill. Opinions were divided, but Baker recommended going ahead with the deal. The administration should try to negotiate some links to Soviet behavior in Lithuania, but the United States had to deliver this visible support to reform. Shevardnadze had been persuasive on this issue. Bush agreed. It is probable that Gorbachev's apparent move on Germany contributed to the president's decision to help the beleaguered Soviet leader.

Bush took time out to call Kohl and tell him about the previous day's discussion of Germany.[52] Bush mentioned Gorbachev's "screwy" idea of simultaneous membership in two alliances, but he thought that Gorbachev was as concerned with the nature of NATO as with whether Germany should be a part of it. In other words, Gorbachev could clearly be influenced by a genuine effort to change the nature of the alliance, to ease its anti-Soviet orientation. Bush had read Gorbachev article 2 of the North Atlantic Treaty, which described NATO's broad political mission. Bush believed that Gorbachev's views were not fixed, and that the upcoming NATO summit could be vitally important. Offhandedly Bush mentioned that Gorbachev had "kind of agreed" that Germany should have the right to decide whether to be a full member of NATO.

Kohl wanted to know where matters stood on providing economic aid to the USSR. Bush replied that, though the trade agreement was being discussed, the proposal for credits had not come up. Bush thought that Gorbachev might wait for a more private setting the next day at Camp David. Kohl reaffirmed his stance on the NATO issue, explaining at length why he thought the FRG should not even discuss the possibility of leaving the alliance.

Realizing that Kohl had not caught the point about Gorbachev's conceding Germany's right to choose to be in NATO, Bush asked Kohl directly if he had any problem saying that, under the Helsinki Final Act, Germany had the right to make that choice. Kohl assented but was still preoccupied with the economic issue. Bush interrupted again, emphasizing what Gorbachev had said about Germany's right to choose. Kohl, however, remained caught up in the discussion of the Soviet economy throughout the rest of the conversation. It was as if the information was so startling that, even if Bush put a headline on it, it simply did not register.

Bush returned to his talks with Gorbachev. Arms control discussions dominated the meetings during the day on June 1, with some hard-won progress on START and a little movement on CFE. But in the press and among Bush's advisers, suspense was growing about the fate of the U.S.-Soviet trade agreement. The White House had scheduled a ceremony at the end of the day on June 1 to announce the agreements that had been concluded. Gorbachev arrived. A few top officials on both sides huddled privately outside the East Room, where the ceremony was to take place. "Are we going to sign the trade agreement?" Gorbachev asked.

Yes, Bush replied. Furthermore, he would meet Soviet demands and drop

U.S. insistence on explicit conditions tying the agreement to events in Lithuania. He would condition it only on passage of the new Soviet law liberalizing emigration (a long-standing American demand). The White House staff frantically scurried to find a copy of the trade agreement to sign. With Bush and Gorbachev impatiently looking over their shoulders, James Cicconi, the president's staff secretary, and Rice worked feverishly to include comments about the agreement in Bush's remarks. After delaying the scheduled start of the ceremony, the two leaders entered the East Room and made their announcements. Bush did not stress the linkage of the trade agreement to a new Soviet emigration law in his public remarks, merely mentioning that we "are looking forward to the passage of a Soviet emigration law." This was, Michael Beschloss and Strobe Talbott later commented,

> a classic example of Bush's preferred way of dealing with Gorbachev—and a good illustration of why that way was often so effective. Bush had granted the Soviets something they desperately wanted, and he had made the favor conditional on a major concession on their part. Yet by treating the whole issue in such a low-key, almost offhand manner—and by not rubbing Gorbachev's nose in the Soviet concession—he had managed to impose exactly the sort of linkage between U.S.-Soviet trade and the Kremlin's policies toward its own citizens that previous Soviet leaders had always found not only objectionable but unacceptable.[53]

There was nothing to announce on Germany.

Later that night Bush's aides thought of a way to capitalize on Gorbachev's concession on Germany. The NSC staff drafted a statement for the president to deliver at the joint press conference that would close the summit on Sunday morning, June 3. The statement would help nail down Gorbachev's assent to the principle that any state was free to choose its alliance status, even if the United States and the USSR had different ideas about what that choice should be. Bush would say: "On the matter of Germany's external alliances, I believe, as do Chancellor Kohl and members of the Alliance, that the united Germany should be a full member of NATO. President Gorbachev, frankly, does not hold that view. But we are in full agreement that the matter of alliance membership is, in accordance with the Helsinki Final Act, a matter for the Germans to decide." To make sure that Gorbachev was "in full agreement" with this statement, Rice passed the draft to Soviet ambassador Bessmertnykh for his review. Bessmertnykh, a seasoned diplomat, naturally discussed Bush's planned statement with Gorbachev and his staff.

Meanwhile, Bush and Gorbachev flew off to Camp David for relaxed and private discussions, mostly about regional issues around the world.[54] Gorbachev, as Bush had expected, raised the question of U.S. extension of financial credits to Moscow. Bush said that he wanted to help but needed to see more economic reforms, movement on Lithuania, and a reduction of subsidies to Cuba. Progress on Germany would also create the right political climate for Bush to seek money from the Congress. Bush did pledge that the G-7 would consider a broad multilateral assistance program, including substantial credits, at the Houston summit in July, to be held right after the NATO summit in London.

Reviewing developments in the third world, Gorbachev and Bush seemed to their aides to be genuinely conversing and exchanging ideas without inhibitions or pretense. At dinner Gorbachev looked untroubled, serene. With the trade agreement signed, the atmosphere was warm and friendly. Yet Blackwill and Rice waited tensely throughout the night for the Soviet reaction to the draft presidential announcement. Finally, early Sunday morning, Bessmertnykh passed the word to Blackwill: Gorbachev had no objection to the president's planned remarks. Bush proceeded to make his statement as prepared.

None of the reporters at the press conference appeared to notice the significance of Bush's statement. Nor did American officials call attention to it. They sensed that Gorbachev had finally turned a corner in his approach to the German question, but the situation was tentative and shaky. If the Americans whooped and gloated, Gorbachev—embarrassed politically— might quickly retrench, and positions would harden, as had happened after the February meeting with Kohl. The concession was in the record, and the Americans would work behind the scenes to consolidate progress until the Soviets themselves were ready to acknowledge the fundamental shift in their position. In the same low-key spirit Bush carefully reported on this passage in his statement in phone calls to Kohl, Thatcher, and Mitterrand but did not dramatize the concession. He instead emphasized the need to follow up with a successful NATO summit in July. None of the other leaders appeared, at least at first, to grasp the significance of the Soviet move; none even inquired about it. (Teltschik, however, noted that this was "a sensation.") Mitterrand did remark shrewdly that Gorbachev would be counting on achieving his security objectives through West Germany's domestic politics. Bush then followed up with written messages. Again Bush's tone was cautious: "We, of course, will have to see whether this reflects real flexibility in the Soviet position."[55]

But, as Chernyayev recalled, the Americans were correct to take the exchange on Germany's right to choose very seriously.[56] When asked later by the American scholar Hannes Adomeit just when the Soviet Union agreed to membership of a united Germany in NATO, Chernyayev "unhesitatingly" answered, "On May 30, at the Soviet-American summit in Washington."[57]

It was a turning point. From this time on, Gorbachev never again voiced adamant opposition to Germany's presence in NATO. Both he and Shevardnadze instead began to press for the West to deliver on the nine-point plan, especially the changes in NATO, at the alliance's upcoming summit in London. Those deeds and the domestic calendar, dominated by the July party congress, would determine when the time was ripe to acknowledge publicly a new Soviet approach to the German question. In the meantime there would be no discussion of Germany in the Politburo, no debates among the collective leadership that might tie the hands of either Gorbachev or Shevardnadze. The German issue was thus contributing to a broader decision to discard the old apparatus used for governing the Soviet state.

After the Washington summit both Baker and Shevardnadze traveled from Washington directly to Copenhagen for the conclusion of a conference that was the major CSCE human rights event of the year. They returned to the topic of Germany after a day of speechmaking in Denmark. Shevardnadze had already taken time out during the day for a brief discussion with Genscher, but he settled in that evening for another long talk with the American secretary of state.[58]

Baker raised the topic of Germany by asking whether Shevardnadze was interested in the idea of some agreement between NATO and the Warsaw Pact. This was something the Soviets had suggested. What did Moscow want? Shevardnadze said that no specific proposal was ready, but perhaps it might include ideas such as a commitment to "no first use" of nuclear weapons. Baker warned that this idea might be difficult to sell, but one had to see a proposal. Shevardnadze promised to provide a proposal within ten days.

Shevardnadze added that the United States should come out and say what Baker was saying privately, that the Soviet Union was no longer perceived as an enemy. Baker took the point. Shevardnadze then returned to the idea of the transition period which he and Gorbachev had developed in Washington. Decisions had to be made on how long the period would last and what role it would play.

Perhaps knowing that the Americans believed that events in Germany were now moving on a fast timetable toward unity and all-German elections by the end of the year, Shevardnadze then made a startling assertion. He said that the Soviets had intelligence confirming their suspicion (which Shevardnadze had briefly voiced to Baker in Washington) that the Germans would not be proceeding toward unification as quickly as expected. There has been "some very hot stuff that's been cooking," Shevardnadze said. He knew about Kohl's plans to complete internal unification by the fall of 1990, but he was not sure that it would happen. Moscow had it on good authority that many members of the East German government would not accept Kohl's plans, for they thought that Kohl was artificially stepping up the pace of unification. So it appeared likely that the pan-German elections would not be held until 1991. Shevardnadze was not positive that this would happen, but he wanted to brief the secretary on what he knew. Under the circumstances the idea of a longer transition period might make sense.

Baker was reserved. He certainly hoped that the Soviets would not want to hold up German sovereignty if political and economic union was going forward. That would cause deep resentment in Germany. If internal unification took longer, then the need for an external settlement might not be as pressing. But Baker hoped that Shevardnadze would not create an artificial transition period simply to drag out the conclusion of the external aspects of unification. Progress on that matter should be related to progress on political and economic union. If it weren't, the Soviet Union would end up isolating itself, especially if it tried to prevent sovereignty after unity.

That would not happen, Shevardnadze assured him. Soviet relations with Germany would be based on equality and respect. Then he said, even if Germany remains in NATO, or for that matter wants to become a member of ASEAN (Association of Southeast Asian Nations), we are going to develop our relations with them, and we are not going to create artificial difficulties. If the Soviets were really trying to impair the process, Shevardnadze added, they would not have consented to the Two Plus Four mechanism. They would have kept the Germans out of the process and treated this as purely a Four Power matter under the 1945 Potsdam declaration. But the Soviets did not want to try to struggle against the current by "going upstream."

Baker then turned to a key Soviet concern: limits on German armed forces. Shevardnadze was willing to work from the American idea of promising to set limits in a future CFE negotiation. As Shevardnadze had told Genscher, he would be satisfied with a West German declaration of the level that would be acceptable in such a future treaty. The Soviets would not let this matter delay conclusion of the CFE treaty currently being negotiated in Vienna. An appropriate promise, from the Soviet perspective, would be to limit German armed forces to between 200,000 and 250,000 (about half the size of the existing West German armed forces). The West Germans, he said, were talking about 280,000 to 300,000.

Shevardnadze was clearly moving toward a compromise. He was prepared to accept the basic Western approach for handling the problem of German troop limits, with the Germans pledging a figure now that would be codified only after all the other nations of Europe had accepted limits on their own armed forces. Shevardnadze actually thought that the Germans were being more forthcoming than was really the case. Neither Chancellor Kohl nor the Defense Ministry had agreed (or ever would agree) to a number this low. Either Shevardnadze had misunderstood the West German position or one of Genscher's diplomats had conveyed promises he could not keep.[59]

Baker believed that the stalemate had been broken. The muddled views of the new East German foreign minister, Markus Meckel, could safely be ignored.[60] If Gorbachev had agreed with traditional definitions of Soviet security, he would have made a stand in Washington. He did not. There was still work to do, particularly on the NATO summit. But Baker now believed that if Washington delivered a "transformed NATO" and a reasonable out-come at the Houston economic summit, the Soviet Union would be prepared to seal the German deal. Tarasenko recalled later that Gorbachev and Shevardnadze had a long talk in June. They worried about their slipping influence, knowing that the GDR had become little more than a curiosity in the politics of German unification. Perhaps the Soviets hoped against hope that their intelligence about moves to slow German unification would prove to be right. But, failing that, there was little of real import that the Soviet Union could do now. Given the fact that, in Shevardnadze's terms, the current had become very strong, neither he nor Gorbachev wanted any longer to swim against the tide.

～ 8

The Final Offer

THE U.S.-SOVIET meetings in Washington and Copenhagen signaled a turning point, the end of real Soviet opposition to a united Germany's full membership in the NATO alliance. The Americans wondered about Shevardnadze's surprising prediction that unification was about to be disrupted by the new East German government. But top U.S. officials felt sure that Shevardnadze was wrong. They knew that Chancellor Kohl had met privately with East German prime minister Lothar de Maizière on May 28 and secured his agreement to the fast timetable. The economic union treaty would be ratified by the Bundestag in June and go into effect on July 2. Accession under article 23 would take place before the end of the year, in time for all-German federal elections to select the next chancellor.[1]

Chancellor Kohl himself flew to Washington in early June, his third such trip in about three months, for a low-key meeting with President Bush. Arriving without Genscher or the large entourage he had brought with him in May, the chancellor wanted a direct discussion of the strategy to be used in pursuing unification to a successful conclusion. The Americans were especially curious about how Kohl planned to handle the issue of limits on German troop strength.

NATO foreign ministers had just met at Turnberry in Scotland. There the West German arms control commissioner, Josef Holik, had circulated with Genscher's approval yet another proposal for future German troop limits. Holik's plan would put a binding cap on the armed forces of all countries in Central Europe. The Soviets and other NATO and Warsaw Pact countries outside Central Europe would simply promise not to increase their military manpower in Europe, and all parties would agree to join the Central European states, including Germany, in accepting negotiated manpower ceilings during the next phase of conventional arms control talks. Bush's staff did not treat this Foreign Ministry proposal as a definitive view of the West German government. Instead they wanted Bush to find out Kohl preferences so the Americans and West Germans could get together to hammer out a common line.[2]

On this trip to Washington Kohl had an interesting request. He wanted to tour Arlington National Cemetery, the ceremonial resting place for many veterans and soldiers who had fallen in America's wars. Brent Scowcroft walked among the white tombstones with the German chancellor, who mused about past conflicts. Scowcroft was struck by Kohl's detailed grasp of military as well as political history.[3] On the evening of June 8 Kohl came to the White House for a small dinner with Bush, Baker, and Scowcroft.[4] Kohl's main message was very clear: NATO membership for Germany was essential and nonnegotiable. But NATO must show that it was ready to adapt. He wanted to help work on the plan for the NATO summit, and offered to send Teltschik to Washington for private talks. Secrecy was vital. Kohl was also intrigued by the idea of offering to conclude a NATO–Warsaw Pact nonaggression treaty.

Bush was not interested in a nonaggression pact. Making some agreement with the Warsaw Pact, he thought, might actually prop up this disintegrating Soviet-dominated alliance. The pact nations had just concluded a summit meeting in Moscow, where both Hungarian and Czech leaders had spoken bluntly of their desire to distance themselves from any further military alignment with the Eastern bloc. The Warsaw Pact was becoming at best a political organization, if it could hold together even on that basis. But Gorbachev did seem to want some NATO–Warsaw Pact treaty that he could then present as a way of keeping the door open to a new all-European security structure to take the place of both old alliances.[5]

Bush and Baker differed on this question. Baker had been toying with the idea of a NATO–Warsaw Pact agreement for weeks. He had discussed it with his NATO counterparts and was reluctant to let the notion go. Baker conceded that the West should not lend legitimacy to the dying Warsaw Pact. Yet if some sort of innocuous agreement between the two alliances might persuade the Soviets to accept full German membership in NATO, Baker wanted to consider it.

On the problem of German troop limits, Bush and Kohl took for granted that the Germans should not be singled out for special constraints and that the issue should be kept out of the Two Plus Four. Kohl seemed unaware, or uninterested, in the proposal his arms control commissioner, Josef Holik, had floated at the Turnberry NATO meeting. But Kohl understood that the Soviets would require some sort of commitment from Germany to limit its armed forces. He accepted this, commenting on the Russians' searing memory of the 20 million people they had lost during the Second World War. Kohl's problem was to fix on the right figure for the future Bundeswehr. He had not done this yet, in part because he was still puzzling over what to do with the current East German army. But Kohl promised that he would arrive at a number, and would consult with the Americans, sometime during the next few weeks.

Kohl and Bush also reviewed the status of economic aid to Gorbachev. Kohl was proceeding with his unilateral guarantee of DM 5 billion (about $3 billion) in new private loans. But the larger Soviet request was for credits of about $20–25 billion. That was the number Gorbachev had used in May with Teltschik and Baker. This was a matter for the autumn that would have to be discussed at the July G-7 summit in Houston. Bush told Kohl that he had already warned Gorbachev that his administration would have a great deal of trouble supporting major loans to the USSR without changes in Soviet policy toward Cuba and Lithuania.

With a fairly clear understanding between Bush and Kohl about what needed to be done in the coming weeks, Kohl returned to Germany. The agreed-on acceleration of the internal timetable for unification became evident to the German public. As Kohl and de Maizière had decided, the CDU-East announced on June 12 its support for federal elections in December, to be held as an all-German vote. The FDP, led by Lambsdorff and Genscher, fully agreed with Kohl's plan.[6]

Kohl continued to wonder if the voters would be willing to pay the high cost of unification. After all, polls in late May showed that only about 28 percent of West Germans were prepared to make financial sacrifices to achieve unification, and a majority feared a rise in unemployment and damage to the currency. The opposition, led by SPD candidate Lafontaine, was steadily pressing the political logic expressed by these numbers.[7] Kohl did not believe that he could let up. The timetable depended, of course, on concluding the Two Plus Four process in 1990. The chancellor remained publicly adamant that internal and external aspects of unification were inseparable. The entangled set of planned agreements meant that in only a few months a final settlement on Germany would have to be concluded, any outstanding difficulties with Poland would have to be resolved, a CFE treaty would have to be completed, and the CSCE summit would need to bless these results.[8]

Designing a Settlement Document

Preparations for a Two Plus Four settlement were continuing. The West Germans were pursuing their own efforts to ease any Polish concerns, including revisions of the German Basic Law and citizenship laws to allay any fears of German revanchism.[9]

Two Plus Four political directors conferred again on June 9 at the Schloss Niederschönhausen in East Berlin. The delegates avoided the "sequencing" problem and concentrated more usefully on determining the borders of a united Germany. All parties agreed that the final settlement had to deal with borders. The political directors were further able to agree that a united Germany would "comprise the territory of the Federal Republic of Germany, the German Democratic Republic, and the whole of Berlin." Both German governments duly promised to renew this pledge in a binding treaty with the Poles, renounce territorial claims against any country, and amend any part of the West German constitution that might seem inconsistent with this pledge. (Articles of the Basic Law dealing with possible paths to unifying Germany, such as articles 23 and 146, would therefore be deleted after unification was accomplished.) The Four Powers would take note of these commitments and "state that the provisional character of Germany's borders has ended." Although there were no disagreements about where the borders should be, much time was taken up in crafting language to avoid prejudicing the lawyers' argument about sequencing. Seitz drily reported to Zoellick that "this minuet consumed at least three hours."[10]

Gorbachev and Shevardnadze had made concessions in Washington and Copenhagen, but the momentum created by the Soviet and East German bureaucracies continued as they pressed the same hard-line proposals that Shevardnadze had been obliged to make at the May ministerial.[11] The Western representatives told the Soviets bluntly that they were not interested in these ideas, and the two sides simply agreed to disagree. They scheduled another meeting of political directors to try to iron out some of these differences on June 20, just before the next scheduled meeting of ministers on June 22.[12] The Soviets remained immovable, perhaps waiting to see what NATO would do at its upcoming summit meeting.

The new East German prime minister, CDU-East leader Lothar de Maizière, visited Washington in June.[13] It was the first and last time an East German head of government would meet with an American president. Bush and de Maizière had a friendly conversation, and the East German leader clearly relished the historic occasion. But Bush wanted de Maizière to know that the Americans did not think that the East Germans were playing a constructive part in the Two Plus Four talks. De Maizière had also met with Gorbachev in Moscow and had come away with the impression that Gorbachev would have trouble accepting German membership in NATO unless certain undefined elements were added to the package. Whatever the Soviet

Union's economic problems might be, economic assistance would not be enough to quell the anxiety of the Soviet people.

Bush made clear that, whatever was done to reassure the Soviets, there could be no parallel treatment of allied and Soviet troops. The allied presence was wanted; the Soviets were not. De Maizière had little quarrel with this. Indeed, when Baker remonstrated with him about East Germany's position in the Two Plus Four, de Maizière just shrugged and said that there was no need to convince *him*. (He was alluding to the fact that his foreign minister, Markus Meckel, was from another party, the SPD-East, part of his ruling coalition.) De Maizière said that he knew nothing about Meckel's proposal to Baker in Copenhagen for creating a special neutralized security zone in Central Europe. He had never supported such ideas and had first heard about them in the press.

Another glimpse of Gorbachev's thinking came from Margaret Thatcher. She journeyed to Moscow to see the Soviet leader on June 8. Just before leaving, she spoke with Baker, who was in Great Britain for the NATO meeting in Scotland. Thatcher, like Bush, was suspicious of any NATO–Warsaw Pact agreement, which she called a "curious" idea. Baker said that Shevardnadze had promised him a detailed proposal. Thatcher commented scornfully that the Soviets would not soon provide details. They were not that kind of government. They work, she said, from one day to the next, armed only with slogans. Baker thought that the Soviets were just throwing balls into the air to see if any would be caught. He promised, however, to try to give them "political cover" for the hard decisions they had to make on Germany and NATO. Baker warned Thatcher to expect a Soviet request for financial credits. Here Thatcher was at least as skeptical as the Americans. She thought that with the Soviet economy in its current condition, any new loans would be wasted. She preferred to offer technical assistance to help advance Soviet reform—what the British called a "know-how fund."[14]

Returning from Moscow, Thatcher was able to give Bush fresh firsthand impressions of the situation.[15] Gorbachev had talked of creating a market economy and a new constitutional relationship with the republics. He had clearly been impressed by his visit to the United States, and was full of anecdotes about his experiences in America. He seemed to feel that he had established a very good personal relationship with the president.

Thatcher and Gorbachev had spent most of their time discussing the security of Europe and the problem of Germany and NATO. She had stood by Kohl's schedule for rapid unification, synchronized with a settlement of external issues. Gorbachev's thinking still seemed to be evolving, with evident inconsistencies and contradictions. But, somewhat to her surprise, he never ruled out German membership in NATO, though he had wondered aloud about different types of membership—from the French model to that of Denmark or Norway. He kept talking about establishing a pan-European security organization to transcend the present alliances. Yet he seemed to realize that this was not practicable.

Thatcher was now, like Baker, ready to see merit in the idea of a NATO–Warsaw Pact joint declaration. And, like Baker, she saw the potential for something less than the nonaggression pact Kohl had spoken of, something that would help Gorbachev without "giving away anything significant." Gorbachev had also mentioned the idea of a CSCE center for preventing conflict. Thatcher urged President Bush to press forward quickly on possible diplomatic opportunities before Soviet thinking congealed around a firm negative position. She felt sure that the USSR would ultimately accept a united Germany in NATO "and that we need not, in practice, pay a high price for that."

Gorbachev had also pronounced himself heartily sick of the Lithuanian problem. Thatcher did not think that it ranked high on his list of priorities. She had visited the Ukraine and Armenia and was struck by the strength of nationalist sentiment. All in all, she felt that Gorbachev had no early respite in sight, although, she said, "it is hard to see that anyone else could have a better chance of surmounting the problems and getting through in reasonable order."

Waiting for NATO to Act

With the moment of truth drawing closer, Genscher accelerated his efforts with the Soviet Union. Shevardnadze had asked him to make a symbolic pilgrimage of respect for the Soviet Union's tragic history with Germany by meeting him in Brest. The city's past was richly symbolic for many reasons. It was the place where Lenin had been forced to sign a humiliating peace treaty with Germany in 1918. The memories were bitter for the Poles, too, since Brest-Litovsk had been part of an independent Poland. But Shevardnadze probably intended to invoke a personal memory, for it was in Brest that his brother Akaky had died—fighting to defend the city in 1941. Now, at this moment of judgment over Germany's future, Genscher would journey with Shevardnadze to Akaky's grave.[16]

The emotion of the moment—as Genscher solemnly laid a wreath on Akaky Shevardnadze's grave—probably advanced the cause of German unity far more than the talks. The discussions were comprehensive but merely went over old ground. For the first time Shevardnadze did explore the various ways Germany might affiliate itself with NATO; but the Western position was now well settled, and Genscher offered him no encouragement. They talked principally about crafting an agreement between NATO and the Warsaw Pact. Genscher was skeptical about arrangements between the two alliances, but he agreed on the need to reshape relations for the new era. All parties hoped that the upcoming NATO summit would provide an important opportunity to begin this process.

Shevardnadze still held out for a transition period, with Four Power rights remaining in force long after internal unification had occurred, though he could not specify how long this transition period might last. Genscher rejected such decoupling. Why, he asked, was a transition period necessary? Shevardnadze replied that during the transition period agreement would be completed on a changed relationship between the Warsaw Pact and NATO and there would be some resolution of the problem of Four Power military presence in Germany. Shevardnadze wanted Soviet troops to remain in Germany as long as American and even British and French forces stayed in the FRG. The transition period would also have to include an agreement on the size of German armed forces and a clear disposition of the international agreements of the German states (especially the GDR's obligations toward the USSR). Finally, the transition period would last until the question of a new European security structure had been resolved. The Soviet Union needed answers to these questions before giving up its right to keep forces in Germany.

Genscher argued that Germany, once unified, should be fully sovereign. Genscher also stressed this point at the postmeeting press conference, and his staff noted that Shevardnadze chose not to challenge him publicly on this position. Genscher's staff also told American officials that their minister had strongly rejected any effort to equate the presence of U.S. and Soviet forces in Germany.

The size of Germany's future armed forces was the subject of a one-on-one discussion between the two ministers. This issue was clearly critical. Genscher wanted an arrangement negotiated in Vienna to limit the forces of a united Germany, but without discrimination or special treatment. Once a deal was struck at the CFE talks in Vienna, it could be noted in the Two Plus Four talks. Genscher was flexible on the form; the agreement could declare an intent to limit forces in future talks or even be made part of the current CFE treaty. There was no talk of specific numbers. As in Copenhagen Shevardnadze appeared to accept this approach. So the three key issues seemed to be the question of NATO, the timing of an end to Four Power rights (the "transition period"), and setting limits on Germany's future armed forces.

Meanwhile, Gorbachev wrote to Kohl thanking him for arranging financial credits, but also stating that the external aspects of German unification would have to be settled at the CSCE summit. He gave no hint of any important movement on the substantive issues when he spoke to the Supreme Soviet. But in the give-and-take afterward Gorbachev emphasized his hope that NATO might be changed significantly at its upcoming London summit.[17]

Kohl wrote back to Gorbachev telling him that the Western side wanted to conclude the external aspects of unification *before* the CSCE summit. Kohl requested further negotiations on the arrangements for the DM 5 billion credit agreed to in May, and Gorbachev in reply set dates for those talks and for Kohl's visit to Moscow in the middle of July—after the results of the NATO and G-7 summits were known, and after what promised to be a difficult Communist party congress for the Soviet leader.[18]

Genscher and Shevardnadze met again on June 18, this time in the West German city of Münster.[19] Genscher's FDP colleague in the cabinet, Jürgen Möllemann, who hailed from Münster, helped arrange a tumultuous welcome for the Soviet visitor. Again the theme was that of a new relationship between NATO and the Warsaw Pact. Again Shevardnadze emphasized how much depended on the results of the London NATO summit.

Shevardnadze had set down his ideas for a NATO–Warsaw Pact agreement in writing and had sent his more formal proposal to all CSCE foreign ministers. The two ministers discussed this proposal and many of the related ideas for new political structures. Genscher liked the emerging plan for a joint NATO–Warsaw Pact declaration on European security and hoped to persuade the alliance to include this point in the communiqué issued from the NATO summit.

Shevardnadze also had surprisingly modest suggestions for enhancing the CSCE. He did not advocate a great leap forward into a new European security system. Using ideas the Americans, West Germans, and British had all mentioned, Shevardnadze suggested creating a secretariat, which would give permanent institutional support for high-level meetings, a conflict prevention center (duties unclear), and a center to monitor military activities (duties also unclear). The proposal at the Bonn Two Plus Four meeting six weeks earlier for a Four Power–based center in Germany to watch over German military activities had apparently been dropped. There was little new discussion of how to limit future German armed forces.

The meaning of Shevardnadze's "transition period" had become confused. Now, meeting with Genscher, Shevardnadze dropped the idea completely. Privately, Tarasenko gave Frank Elbe a paper that he and Teymuraz Stepanov of the planning staff had put together. The paper abandoned the demand to keep Four Power rights in force until after the transition period. In other words, it reflected the position Shevardnadze had taken privately with Baker at Copenhagen. Tarasenko told Elbe not to worry; the Soviet position would follow this paper. Elbe trusted Tarasenko, knowing of his close relationship to Shevardnadze, and understanding how Soviet bureaucratic conflicts had divided the Foreign Ministry. Tarasenko's prediction proved to be accurate.

The Western allies hoped that the Two Plus Four ministerial meeting would offer clearer insight into where the Soviets stood. The ministers were scheduled to gather in Berlin on June 22. Political directors from the six participating states convened in Bonn on June 20. The agreement on borders was quickly polished off, ready for the approval of the ministers. Then they turned to other issues. Zoellick, chairing the meeting, had worked on a draft outline for the entire settlement. The other Western allies concurred with this outline. The Soviets, however, balked at provisions returning Berlin to the Germans and giving up other Four Power rights. Nor did agreement seem any closer on the contentious political-military questions.[20]

As soon as Baker arrived in Berlin, he sought out Prime Minister de Maizière to follow up on the session with Bush and again urge the GDR leader to moderate his country's support for Soviet positions in the Two Plus Four. He had little success. Obviously nervous about Soviet resistance on the NATO issue, de Maizière claimed that he had just returned from Paris, and Mitterrand had been only "casual" about the question of Germany's alliance status. Mitterrand had seemed more interested in the development of new all-European security structures at the CSCE summit. But, Baker pressed, did Mitterrand really say that these new structures would replace the existing ones? De Maizière conceded that Mitterrand had not gone so far. De Maizière, however, thought that the West should plan to replace the current NATO system.

Baker disagreed. De Maizière equivocated. Finally de Maizière came to the heart of the matter. The Soviet Union was beginning to play hardball in the GDR. Other aspects of unification were moving quickly, and the East German people now counted on unification's happening soon. But the Soviets had said that unification would be "problematic" without a settlement of the external aspects. Dmitri Yazov, in Berlin for a Warsaw Pact defense ministers' meeting, had reiterated this position personally to de Maizière. If the external issues were not resolved, de Maizière feared that the situation could become quite difficult. Unity amid such discord might be bad for Germany. The Soviets were starting to suspend their previously scheduled troop withdrawals from the GDR. De Maizière could not rule out the possibility that fighting might break out between Soviet troops and East German civilians.

Baker reviewed the U.S. stance. Although there might be a transition period for Soviet forces, the stationing of foreign troops would be a question for the sovereign German state to decide. That, De Maizière replied, was the crux of the matter. For the Soviets such German authority was unacceptable. The Soviets could not imply that they had lost the gains of World War II. The Four Powers should strike a deal.[21]

This encounter turned out to be a preview of the entire ministerial.[22] Despite the ceremonial joint viewing of the dismantlement of Berlin's Checkpoint Charlie, the famed entry point to the American sector, East and West remained quite separate at the negotiating table. The ministers easily blessed the language of the agreement on borders, and agreed to invite the Polish foreign minister to the next Two Plus Four meeting in Paris to endorse it. But when the ministers turned to other settlement issues, the familiar debates were renewed. The flexibility and reasonableness that had been evident in Washington and Copenhagen evaporated. Meckel, the East German foreign minister, led off the Eastern attack, noting the need to deal with the military status of Germany and to put ceilings on and secure the withdrawal of all Four Power forces. Shevardnadze promptly agreed.

Shevardnadze's own lengthy prepared intervention set the tone by reminding the delegates that the date marked the forty-ninth anniversary of the "fascist" attack on the USSR. His presentation seemed to be built on the guidance that had been prepared for him in April — guidance he had not followed. At that time the foreign minister had been advised to make absolutely clear that German participation in the Western alliance was unthinkable. Now he took that advice. First, he said, the alliances must be transformed. Next, he turned to the Soviet draft for a settlement document. Although he was flexible on form, agreeing that no peace treaty was needed, he showed no flexibility on substance. The Soviet draft contained a number of provisions that were utterly unacceptable to the Western countries. It was, Elbe remembered, like stepping into a "cold shower."

The Soviets were not going to be merely passive objects of Western diplomacy. Deputy foreign minster Kvitsinsky, sitting at Shevardnadze's side during the Berlin meeting, had thought that the Soviets were being taken for granted by the West. He felt that Shevardnadze was carrying "unimaginable" burdens at an "insane" pace, flying here and receiving people there. Kvitsinsky had become Shevardnadze's deputy in May and was now making his mark, sorting out the mess that had passed for Soviet policy. Kvitsinsky feared what a few Western officials had secretly contemplated: that the Western powers might negotiate their own settlement with Germany, excluding the Soviets, as they had done in concluding the postwar peace treaty with Japan. The West had now built up terrific momentum. Shevardnadze, on the defensive, was meeting constantly with Western ministers. Kvitsinsky later wrote: "All that happened because we had to try, under the worst time pressure, to achieve an optimal result in a game in which we, from day to day, had lost one trump card after another." Playing the one remaining trump, the Soviet military presence in Germany, would have caused such a crisis that this option was ruled out by the Soviet leadership.[23]

Now Kvitsinsky was determined to slow the tide of events by firmly asserting this stance again in a draft treaty. An expert working group headed by Bondarenko had prepared the draft. Kvitsinsky wanted to deliver a shock, to force the Western ministers to take account of the Soviet position on a transition period and the need for changes in Europe's security structures. It was this tough attitude which had already intimidated de Maizière and inspired Meckel to enter the fray.

The Soviet draft stipulated that the settlement document would be an interim one only. Four Power rights and responsibilities would remain in force after unification. In 1992, nearly two years after internal unification, a conference of Two Plus Four foreign ministers would examine Germany's behavior under the interim settlement and then decide how and when to terminate Four Power rights over Berlin and Germany as a whole. The following provisions would be included in the interim settlement:

- All East German international agreements would remain in force for a transition period of at least five years after unification. During this time a united Germany could seek bilateral modifications. The division of Germany between the Warsaw Pact and NATO, however, "shall not be changed, and the competence of the Warsaw Treaty and NATO respectively shall not extend to territories that did not fall within their scope." The settlement would also promise various improvements of the CSCE process.
- Troops of all Four Powers would remain in Germany through at least the five-year transition period after unification. While they stayed, their status would be governed by previous agreements concluded by the GDR or FRG.
- Ceilings on German armed forces would be imposed both in quantity (no more than 200,000 to 250,000 for all branches combined) and in quality, so that German forces would be "structurally modified to render them incapable of offensive action." These ceilings would be implemented within three years after unification.
- After these ceilings were implemented, the troop contingents of all Four Powers would be reduced to no more than half their former

strength. Subsequently they would be either withdrawn or retained only "within token levels." All U.S., British, and French forces would be forbidden from entering the territory of the former GDR.

- The current West German Bundeswehr and East German National People's Army would be confined to the former territories of their respective states. After three years new restrictions would confine only the permanent bases used by these forces to the western and eastern portions of a united Germany (the draft spelled out the lines of demarcation), effectively creating a demilitarized zone through the middle of Germany. This settlement would remain in effect until both NATO and the Warsaw Pact were dissolved or Germany withdrew from both alliances.

- After unification Four Power rule of Berlin would end, and the troops of all Four Powers would leave Berlin within six months. All allied institutions in Berlin would be closed. (This meant, of course, that Berlin would be left for years in a region of Germany where Soviet troops remained and from which all Western forces were still excluded.)

- There would be a prohibition on German military action that would extend to any military activities of third states conducted on German territory, directed against "anybody."

- There would be a ban not only on German possession of nuclear, biological, and chemical weapons but also on German participation in decision making concerning the use of such weapons. (This provision would actually reduce the existing West German participation in NATO organizations.)

- There would be categorical German acceptance of all prior Four Power decisions on de-Nazification, demilitarization, and democratization within the respective zones of occupation. These decisions could not be reexamined by German legislatures or courts. (This would exempt Soviet occupation confiscations or other acts from any German review.)

- The settlement would restrict German domestic political activity to prevent any resurgence of Nazism or national socialist political movements.

Shevardnadze was eager to conclude this interim settlement document in time for the November CSCE summit. Therefore, he also proposed that the periodic Two Plus Four meetings be replaced by a standing negotiation process, to meet continuously until the work was done.

While Shevardnadze was speaking, Baker passed Genscher a note asking, "What does this mean?" Genscher wrote back: "Window dressing." Baker nodded in agreement. But the presentation was so formidable and so detailed that it had to be taken seriously even as it clashed jarringly with their private impressions of Shevardnadze's stance. Douglas Hurd opened the Western critique of Shevardnadze's proposal. Baker was especially blunt. He said that, after reading the plan, all he could say was, "So much for German sovereignty." He also rejected the procedural idea of trying to keep the Two Plus Four process running continuously. Genscher believed that the final settlement should terminate Four Power rights and not leave issues unsettled. Germany must be fully sovereign at the time of unification. Singling out Germany for all these special limits would violate this principle. Mutual confidence, not mutual mistrust, must be the basis for the agreement.

The session then broke for lunch. Baker tried to divert attention from the specifics of the Soviet paper. He suggested that the group concentrate on listing all the issues that needed to be addressed and specifying the forum in which they should be handled.

After lunch Meckel, as chairman, put forward Baker's idea. But he then made a ludicrous if dangerous suggestion: the ministers should not leave the Two Plus Four table until they had agreed on a future security architecture for Europe and the timetable for its construction. He also circulated a paper calling for a ceiling on German armed forces of 300,000 and a transitional period to last until "final agreement is reached on a European security system." Shevardnadze urged the ministers to look at the proposed Soviet draft again and adopt the idea of a standing negotiation. Otherwise the next Paris ministerial would find much yet to be done and could take an unpleasant turn.

Baker and Genscher pushed the group at least to prepare a list of the areas of disagreement and decide where each matter should be handled. Genscher noted that the CFE should resolve force issues, the NATO summit should deal with the alliance's future, and the CSCE summit should address the future of that institution. Baker also asked for agreement that the goal of the exercise was to achieve full German sovereignty at the moment of unification in such a way that Germany was not singled out for special limits. Hurd backed him. But how, Shevardnadze asked, could we speak of a unified Germany without singling it out? With that inconclusive coda, the meeting ended.

Speaking to the press at a joint news conference, the ministers downplayed the points of controversy at the meeting. Shevardnadze did stress publicly the importance he placed on the upcoming NATO summit meeting in London. Portraying the Soviet approach as constructive, Shevardnadze went so far as to say, "We intend to have final agreement that will resolve all aspects of German unity before the end of the year." This statement was plainly contradictory to the position he had just put on the table, and entirely incompatible with the spirit of the Soviet draft settlement. Either Shevardnadze did not understand this position or he sought to conceal it from public scrutiny, which would be odd, since the Soviet proposal had been made available to the press. Elbe could tell himself that this was why Tarasenko had given him the "non-paper" in Münster: it was to let the West Germans know that they should not take the forthcoming Soviet position at face value.[24]

Because of Kvitsinsky's efforts the Soviet Union had finally found its footing on the solid ground of traditional Soviet security interests. Kvitsinsky's strategy was elegant, but it had come too late. The West had consolidated its position. The fatal flaw, though, was that other Soviet officials had effectively undermined any credible threat of confrontation. In Washington Gorbachev had shown the crack in the Soviets' resistance. Then Shevardnadze's private discussions, especially with Baker in Copenhagen, had further revealed his underlying readiness to find a compromise solution. Just as Central Committee staffer Portugalov had (inadvertently) undercut Soviet diplomacy at key points in late 1989, Tarasenko's "non-paper" given to Elbe in Münster had (this time quite deliberately) undercut the effect of Kvitsinsky and Bondarenko's move in Berlin. Tarasenko had been annoyed in December 1989 when Shevardnadze had accepted Kvitsinsky's tougher approach to the German question. This time it was Tarasenko who sabotaged the deputy foreign minister's plan, with Shevardnadze's approval.

Still, U.S. officials were surprised by and concerned about Shevardnadze's performance. Baker confronted Shevardnadze with questions at a private two-and-a-half-hour meeting that night at the Soviet residence in Berlin.[25] As in Copenhagen, only Ross, Tarasenko, and the interpreters were with them. This was probably the most intense of all the U.S.-Soviet exchanges on the subject of Germany during the year of turmoil which had begun in the fall of 1989.

Baker was direct. He told Shevardnadze that he was surprised by the Soviet paper. He had been hopeful after Copenhagen and had briefed President Bush accordingly. Now the paper moved in the opposite direction, very clearly singling out Germany for special treatment. It separated the issues of unification and German sovereignty and equated the U.S. and Soviet military presence, even though Gorbachev had recognized the need for American troops to stay in Europe and Germany. "What's happened between Copenhagen and here?" Baker asked. The Americans had tried to be responsive to

Soviet concerns. Shevardnadze also knew that it had been a stretch to conclude the commercial trade agreement in Washington. Now this paper represented a dramatic departure from what Baker had understood in Copenhagen to be the Soviet position. He hoped that Shevardnadze could tell him
what was happening. President Bush had to know. The United States was
reviewing the issue of economic support for the Soviet Union. The decision
would be a hard one. At a minimum, said Baker, "you really need to level
with me now about what's going on with regard to Germany. I can deal with
the true picture, but I need to know what it is."

Shevardnadze briefly defended the document. Then he conceded that in
working on this proposal, the Soviets "were guided by our domestic situation." The mood in the country was not good, and it would be irresponsible
not to take this into account. True, the Soviet government now wanted the
American military to stay in Germany. But it was hard to explain all this to
the Soviet people. The European process had to be more dynamic, Shevardnadze continued. A lot would depend on the kind of statement that came
from the NATO summit in London. Progress on the CFE and CSCE issues
was important, too. So, the Soviets' proposals did not represent their ultimate
position. A solution had to be found. But, said Shevardnadze, "we are facing
a crisis situation, a political crisis as well as an economic crisis, and it's not
easy to convince our people today of what we're doing." There was "tremendous" opposition. Maybe later there could be an adjustment, Shevardnadze
conceded. But it was very important to see a statement from London demonstrating change. The Soviet leaders needed to be able to show their people
that they faced no threat—not from Germany, not from the United States,
and not from NATO. He mentioned an article published by one of his critics,
titled "Free Cheese Can Only Be Found in a Mouse Trap."[26]

Baker understood. He could not go into detail on all the U.S. plans for the
NATO summit, but he felt sure that Shevardnadze would be pleased with the
outcome if Washington could persuade its allies to accept the U.S. proposal.
Baker's only worry was that, with this position now public, it would be hard
for Shevardnadze to compromise and walk away from it. Shevardnadze
understood but emphasized again the importance of the London NATO
summit.

Baker, feeling that he needed to show a flash of steel, then said: "In the
final analysis Germany will unify, and we are prepared, with others, to grant
Germany the sovereignty it deserves and it is due. We are going to make every
effort to accommodate your security concerns as we move forward, and I
hope you will not be isolated in opposition to German sovereignty." After
offering some arguments to use in defending a suitable outcome to the Soviet

people, Baker repeated, "At the end of the day we take the position that Germany is going to be fully sovereign and they are not going to be singled out." In friendship Baker told Shevardnadze that, to answer the question why the United States would stay in Europe, it was because the American presence had always been based on the consent of the countries concerned. Maybe it was too much for the Soviet public to accept, but the reality was that there was an important difference between the U.S. presence in Europe and the historical Soviet presence.

Baker had hinted that the Western allies might terminate their Four Power rights unilaterally, leaving the Soviets isolated. The Americans and the British had toyed with the idea in April. There had been no formal deliberation in the U.S. government to lead to this policy decision. It is not clear whether Baker had discussed this particular contingency with President Bush. Yet no one at the top levels of the government doubted for a moment Bush's resolve on the goal of restoring full German sovereignty, nor was there was any reason to doubt that Bush would follow the U.S. position to the logical conclusion Baker had just spelled out. But Baker did take a chance. It is not clear that the Western allies would have made good on this gamble had they been forced to the wall.

Shevardnadze raised the stakes even higher, but on a different front. The domestic situation was very difficult, and the easiest thing for both him and Gorbachev would be to leave the stage altogether. But they knew who would replace them and what kind of order that would produce, and they knew what would happen in Europe, and not only in Europe, and so they knew that they would have to pass this test. Shevardnadze admitted that the Soviet proposal was an unpleasant surprise. But some decisions in Moscow had to be made collectively. Alluding to the May Politburo decision, he said that this was not just a document from the president and the foreign minister.

Baker now backed off. He could see how embattled the foreign minister was. The United States would endeavor to take care of Soviet concerns in the proper forum, Baker assured him. All the issues need not be handled in the final settlement. That was reflected in the nine points. But, Shevardnadze answered, the nine points were known only to a few people in the USSR. That was why the NATO message from London was so important. It would be seen by everybody. If the statement that came out of London opened up the possibility of building relations between states that had been parties to different alliances, that would be very positive. Baker, without elaborating, said that he felt sure Shevardnadze would be happy with the London NATO summit. Shevardnadze, in return, said that he valued this assurance very highly.

The ministers then turned to the question of limits on future German armed forces. Shevardnadze said that Genscher wanted a limit in the current CFE treaty that would apply to all countries in Central Europe. This approach seemed feasible. Baker, however, was cautious, perhaps remembering the negative White House reaction to this idea when it was first floated in May. He renewed the idea, discussed at Copenhagen, of a promise to embed a particular ceiling in a future treaty that would put similar ceilings on the troops of other nations. As at Copenhagen, Shevardnadze was willing to consider this option.

Shevardnadze also returned to the question of economic aid for the USSR, looking ahead to the G-7 summit in Houston. America wanted to help, but there were some serious legal problems. Above all, the Soviet Union had to proceed with fundamental economic reform. No one in the administration wanted to repeat the mistake made with Poland in the 1970s, when a great deal of money was transferred but there had been no reform. There would also be questions about Soviet defense spending.

Shevardnadze was so focused on the outcome of the London summit that Baker decided to preview the U.S. proposals to be presented there for strengthening the CSCE. The list included regular ministerial meetings, a regular schedule of review conferences, a new CSCE secretariat to coordinate these activities, a CSCE elections commission, a conflict reduction center, and a new CSCE parliament based on the parliamentary assembly of the Council of Europe and including representatives from all CSCE states. He did not know if America's allies would agree to the list, but it went a long way toward addressing Soviet concerns. (In fact, only a few NATO allies had heard about these and other American proposals for the summit.)

Shevardnadze promised to keep the information strictly confidential. These were very serious steps. If they were accepted and adopted, the Soviets would be able to concede that the CSCE process was based on a firm foundation. It would lay the basis for substantive guarantees of security and stability. He valued this information very much and regarded it as quite important. Baker added that the United States still did not see the CSCE as a replacement for NATO. Shevardnadze understood.

The two men then parted. Baker thanked Shevardnadze for staying up so late. Shevardnadze suggested that the meeting with Baker had been no less important than the Two Plus Four meeting itself. On the plane trip back to Moscow Shevardnadze had a lot to think about. Kvitsinsky thought that he seemed pensive and troubled. As the officials took stock of what had happened, Shevardnadze passed the draft treaty he had presented in Berlin, which had caused so much controversy, back to Kvitsinsky (who had not attended

Kohl and Gorbachev at the Kremlin, February 1990. Seated from left to right: Teltschik, Kohl, Anatoly Chernyayev, and Gorbachev. (Private collection)

Kohl, Bush, and Baker relax at Camp David, February 1990. (Bush Presidential Materials Project)

Kohl greets new GDR prime minister, Lothar de Maizière. (German Information Center)

The first meeting of Two Plus Four ministers at the "round table with sharp corners," Bonn, May 1990. Genscher, in the left foreground, is conferring with Peter Hartmann on his left and Dieter Kastrup on his right. The bearded gentleman in the right foreground is the new GDR foreign minister, Markus Meckel. On the other side of the table is Baker, flanked by Zoellick to the left and Seitz to the right, with Margaret Tutwiler, Vernon Walters, and Blackwill sitting behind them. At the table to the right of the Americans are (from left to right) Kvitsinsky, Shevardnadze, and Alexander Bondarenko. (Bundesbildstelle Bonn)

Bush's menu for Gorbachev. (KAL, Cartoonists and Writers Syndicate)

Gorbachev and Bush in the Oval Office, May 31, 1990. (Bush Presidential Materials
Project)

The dismantling of Checkpoint Charlie, Berlin, June 1990. (Private collection)

Genscher, Gorbachev, and Kohl in the Caucasus, July 1990. (Private collection)

The final settlement for Germany is prepared by the political directors, Berlin, September 1990. From left to right: Zoellick, John Weston, Bondarenko, Kastrup, Bertrand Dufourcq, and Helmut Domke. (Private collection)

The Day of German Unity, October 3, 1990. From left to right: Genscher, Hannelore Kohl, Helmut Kohl, Richard von Weizsäcker, and de Maizière. (German Information Center)

the meeting with Baker) and asked him the rhetorical question: "What, out of this paper, will probably be left?"[27]

On another plane, this one headed for Washington, the American secretary of state walked back to the reporters' cabin. Speaking on background, to be quoted only as "a senior administration official," Baker urged the journalists to consider the Soviet proposal "a document that has been thoroughly reviewed on an overall interagency basis in Moscow. Someone made the point, I think, that it was at least in part for domestic Soviet consumption and I think that's very valid . . . I think that the [July] Party Congress plays an important role in this and I don't think it should be seen as unusual that [Shevardnadze] might have more flexibility after the Party Congress than he would before."[28] After the party congress, of course, Shevardnadze would also know the outcome of the NATO summit.

Preparing for the NATO Summit

President Bush had raised expectations for the summit when he described an ambitious agenda in his May 4 speech at Oklahoma State University. He had promised that the summit would show the alliance adopting a more political, less military, role, that it would change the posture and strategy of both conventional and nuclear forces, and that it would chart a new course for the CSCE. Both the Defense Department and the State Department bureaucracy had hoped for a more modest agenda, one that would simply launch a review of NATO strategy so the alliance could take the time to deliberate over such important changes. But the White House, and Baker's circle, favored a more decisive event. In this judgment they had the valuable support of NATO's secretary general, Manfred Wörner, who could appreciate the difficulty of the task but also, as a West German politician, could sense the need for dramatic action. The summit declaration, he told Bush, should not just pose questions about NATO's future purpose. It should provide answers.[29]

But bureaucratic preparations for the NATO summit were disjointed. Every bureaucracy in Washington seemed to be reflecting on some aspect of NATO's future—but there was no overall strategy to hook the pieces together.[30] Ideas for the CSCE were being considered in many quarters.[31] The West Germans, with Italian support, set out the broadest range of ideas, with language suggesting that the CSCE would become *the* central structure in the new Europe, including "an all-embracing European security architecture." Bonn was pushing for almost any CSCE move that could be reduced to writing, while the Americans tried "to keep their CSCE aspirations earth-bound."[32] Soviet proposals for further extension of CSCE continued to dwell on the creation of all-European security structures to replace both alliance systems.[33] In Washington at the end of May, Raymond Seitz led an interagency review of options for strengthening the CSCE. He was surprised and pleased to find that the NSC staff's usual disdain for CSCE had been replaced by strong support for new institutions.[34]

But at NATO Wörner was a very worried man. NATO's most important meeting in its history was fast approaching. The Soviet foreign minister had virtually put the fate of German unification within the alliance in the alliance's own hands. And yet the bureaucracy was grinding on as it had done for forty years, during the deep freeze of the Cold War. Wörner wrote to Baker at the end of May warning him that the summit "has already been widely and publicly billed as the most significant reappraisal of the Alliance's role since the mid-1960s and as responding to the biggest political changes since NATO's foundation." Wörner did not have any particular policies to recommend. Nor did U.S. diplomats at NATO. Ambassador William Taft was primarily concerned that more urgent activity might "increase the chances of early and significant differences with the Allies."[35]

Bush was publicly committed to an ambitious summit. In mid-May Blackwill and Zelikow prepared both a list of summit initiatives and a draft summit declaration. Upon reading them, Scowcroft declared them "really forward-looking." But Scowcroft expected bureaucratic wrangling at NATO to kill or water down the most ambitious ideas. The ideas for enhancing NATO's political role were:

- To involve, for the first time, the former enemies of the Warsaw Pact directly in NATO's activities and deliberations. The alliance would invite the USSR and East European governments to come to NATO and establish diplomatic liaison missions with ambassadors accredited to the alliance. Their representatives could then work directly with Western representatives and staff at alliance headquarters on issues of common concern.[36]
- To invite Gorbachev to address NATO and propose that the SACEUR (Supreme Allied Commander for Europe), General John Galvin, visit Moscow for talks with senior Soviet military authorities.

After Soviet forces left Eastern Europe and a CFE treaty was implemented, NATO could:

- End the current "layer cake" system of national corps sectors in Germany and replace it with truly multinational corps, including U.S. forces, deployed in locations that might be different from their wartime areas of operations. The units in these corps would be assigned in peacetime to NATO's integrated military command rather than just earmarked for the command in wartime, thereby giving a German general (commanding Allied Forces Central Europe, AFCENT, under SACEUR) much more authority over the peacetime deployment of allied troops in Germany.[37]
- Move away from the old strategic doctrine of forward defense toward a new doctrine emphasizing mobility, building on concepts being developed in the Pentagon and in NATO's military command structure.
- Ensure that future conventional arms control negotiations would seek national limits applied throughout Europe. NATO could also promise to seek deep cuts by each participant in CFE II talks of up to one half of their conventional armed forces in Europe.[38]

In considering NATO's nuclear strategy, Blackwill and Zelikow suggested that:

- NATO replace its strategic doctrine of "flexible response" with a new doctrine of "minimum deterrence for permanent peace." In substance, the nuclear weapons employment guidelines would abandon reliance on the *early* first use of nuclear weapons in a conflict (while not endorsing the doctrine of no first use itself).
- NATO radically and unilaterally reduce its stockpile of U.S. theater nuclear weapons to no more than one thousand warheads, eliminating three fourths of U.S. nuclear weapons then located in Europe. All U.S. nuclear artillery shells would also be withdrawn unilaterally, with the Soviets asked to reciprocate.
- The West announce its position for the upcoming SNF (short-range nuclear forces) arms control negotiations. The goal of the talks would be the phased global elimination of all American and Soviet SNF missile forces (not including air-delivered systems).

The laundry list of institutional ideas for CSCE should be trimmed to just a few:

- New schedules for regular meetings of leaders and ministers—an idea included on almost every country's list of initiatives.
- Creation of a small CSCE secretariat to be located in Prague.
- Creation of a CSCE center for crisis management to base both the in-

formation clearinghouse functions envisioned by the State Department (and the West Germans) and any new mechanism for the conciliation of international disputes.

- Establishment of a CSCE parliament, the Assembly of Europe, to be based on the existing parliamentary assembly of the Council of Europe in Strasbourg (also the location of the EC's European Parliament), to include representatives from all CSCE member states. This suggestion corresponded to Soviet interest in such an institution, and used the Council of Europe structures in which Shevardnadze had earlier displayed some interest.[39]

Zelikow drafted a possible NATO summit declaration to show how the initiatives could be embodied in a short, nonbureaucratic document, vividly phrased and easy to understand. Blackwill told him, "Picture Gorbachev as the person who will be reading this."[40]

At the end of May the departments of State and Defense were formally asked to present ideas for the NATO summit.[41] Gates reconvened his European Strategy Steering Group to begin polling the State and Defense departments for their ideas on June 4 (the day after Gorbachev's departure from Washington). The discussion was general and unfocused. Reginald Bartholomew, representing the State Department, warned against gimmicks ("newfangled ideas") to boost NATO's political role. Seitz said that NATO had to be something more than "just a club of jolly good chaps." But Lieutenant General Howard Graves, representing the Joint Chiefs of Staff, came ready to outline possible moves away from the conventional NATO strategy of forward defense to a strategy of "forward presence." The uniformed military was also ready to talk about the use of multinational corps.

Gates summarized the emerging consensus. No one questioned the need for the NATO summit in London to close the book on one phase of history and open another. Officials needed to keep their eye on the primary strategic issue: how to end up with a unified Germany in NATO. Gates asked Blackwill and Kanter to organize working groups to develop additional ideas for both political and defense topics at the summit.

Gates turned to another topic: limits on the Bundeswehr and CFE. A State Department paper suggested that the United States "act as the catalyst in forging an Allied consensus [on Bundeswehr limits] that addresses Soviet concerns."[42] Blackwill and Zelikow were opposed to the State Department's ideas, and Scowcroft thought that efforts to crank up such proposals were premature. On May 29 the German government had reportedly decided against making any new proposals for personnel limits in the current CFE talks.[43] Gates said flatly that not a single idea could be raised with the allies until the German chancellor and the American president had approved it.

On June 7 Warsaw Pact leaders met in Moscow and issued a communiqué promising to "review the character, functions and activities of the Warsaw Treaty" and start the pact's "transformation into a treaty of sovereign states with equal rights, formed on a democratic basis." The results of the review would be announced before the end of November. Privately, as East German premier de Maizière mentioned to Bush in Washington four days later, several East European ministers already knew that this review would lead to a dead end. Among the more outspoken was the newly elected (in May) noncommunist Hungarian prime minister, Jozsef Antall, who told newspaper reporters, "Our country won't remain as a member of this organization under any circumstances . . . The organization can neither be modernized, nor be made democratic."[44] The day after the Warsaw Pact meeting, NATO foreign ministers issued a communiqué of their own after meeting in Turnberry. The document was unremarkable but conciliatory, reading: "We extend to the Soviet Union and to all other European countries the hand of friendship and cooperation." New initiatives were clearly being left for the NATO summit in London the next month.[45]

Deliberations in Washington on a NATO summit package were picking up speed. Blackwill and Kanter had run their working group sessions. On June 11 Gates again convened subcabinet officials to review progress.[46] There was a debate over whether to propose a NATO–Warsaw Pact joint declaration. James Dobbins from the State Department supported the idea, which he knew Baker favored. Wolfowitz from Defense, backed by NSC staff, was more skeptical.

As an alternative Gates suggested an invitation to the Eastern European states and the Soviet Union to establish liaison missions at NATO. "Wow!" was Bartholomew's first reaction. Would we bring the East Europeans into the alliance structure? Create some form of associate relationship? The word "liaison" was too clever. Blackwill portrayed the idea as a bold response to Gorbachev's fear of isolation from the new Europe. Just as the United States had an ambassador accredited to the European Community, so there could also be Polish or Soviet ambassadors accredited to NATO. There were obvious risks, but the Europeans were looking for innovative initiatives from the U.S. president.

Zoellick intervened to keep the idea of the NATO–Warsaw Pact declaration alive. Shevardnadze had promised to suggest some specific language. This issue was important to the Soviets. Baker's view, Zoellick said, was that Washington should not be paralyzed by the old notion of the Warsaw Pact, which was now moribund. There was no need to throw the declaration idea out the window.

The group then returned to the issue of limits on future German armed forces. On June 8, at the Turnberry ministerial meeting, the West German arms control commissioner had circulated a new Foreign Ministry proposal: Germany could commit itself to a national ceiling on troop strength if other nations would promise that they too would eventually accept similar national ceilings. German national limits would become binding only when all other states accepted binding national limits as well. American officials liked the idea.

But the American officials needed to understand the status of the Holik proposal within the Bonn government. The West German position remained murky on a key point: When would ceilings on German and other individual national manpower actually be set down on paper and codified in a treaty? The FRG initially indicated that such ceilings would be part of CFE I, the ongoing CFE talks. This approach threatened to put too great a burden on current negotiations, which had to be finished in time for the November 1990 CSCE summit. But putting off agreement to future talks was not likely to satisfy Moscow.[47]

The final offer that emerged from these June deliberations was a variant on the Holik proposal. This variant, which won the agreement of both Kohl and Stoltenberg and was well received in Washington, put off all agreements on national manpower ceilings to a limited follow-on negotiation (CFE I-a). But, to satisfy the Soviets, the Germans would offer a nonbinding promise stating the troop limit they intended to accept in this future negotiation. Furthermore, the Germans would offer this assurance in the ongoing CFE talks, though their promise would not be codified in the CFE treaty itself. In this way the Soviets would have some assurance about future German troop strength, but the Germans would not be legally bound by this assurance until all the other countries had accepted national troop ceilings too. Thus, Germany would not be the only country singled out for limits on its armed forces.[48]

The NSC staff was assigned the task of drafting the NATO summit declaration. (Gates knew that such a draft had been readied weeks earlier.) Zoellick stressed that the draft declaration had to *look* different, nonbureaucratic, like a message direct from Bush to other heads of government, not from one diplomat to another. The next day Blackwill privately gave Zoellick a copy of the draft, making him the first person to see it outside the White House.

Gates reconvened his group the next day to work harder on defense and arms control ideas. Zoellick urged a stronger commitment to multinational corps. Gates joined him. Although Wolfowitz was hesitant, Graves from the Joint Chiefs was supportive. For Gates the issue was *how* to develop multinational corps structures, not *whether* to do it. President Bush was concerned that people would equate the American and Soviet presence. The multinational approach would plainly distinguish the U.S. presence in Germany from the Soviet one.

Zoellick pressed the idea of subordinating American and other forces to NATO command structures in peacetime, not just in the contingency of a war. Was that possible? Graves was receptive, but more analysis was needed on the precise command arrangements. Gates again emphasized the president's openness to new ideas. The United States was prepared to contemplate this kind of command structure. Wolfowitz and Graves agreed. The goal would be multinational corps under the operational control of NATO in peacetime (and hence with a German general in the chain of command above all foreign forces in Germany, commanding Allied Forces Central Europe under the American Supreme Allied Commander for all of Europe). The declaration could promise to examine how to reach this objective.

On the matter of U.S. nuclear forces in Europe, no one questioned the need to revise the strategy of flexible response, though the participants speculated about a label for describing the new strategy. Zoellick noted that the East Germans wanted NATO to adopt the doctrine of no first use. Wolfowitz and Blackwill were opposed. Why not consider it? Kanter asked.

Wolfowitz reiterated arguments Kanter already knew well. NATO's goal was not to make Europe safe for conventional war. A greatly reduced level of conventional forces would make conventional defenses more fragile, less certain. The alliance should not rely on a purely conventional deterrent. Ronald Lehman, the director of the Arms Control and Disarmament Agency, agreed. Blackwill added that a U.S. no first use proposal would cause a political crisis with the British and the French, who would then be under pressure to reconsider their own nuclear doctrines. Gates pressed for something the president could say to show that NATO was adapting to the new military circumstances. There was clearly general support for moving toward a strategy that ended reliance on the early first use of nuclear weapons.

Before the meeting Blackwill had devised new language, a sentence for the draft summit declaration that would read: "Indeed, in this new Europe, Alliance nuclear weapons will truly become weapons of last resort." Blackwill had asked Zoellick to introduce the "last resort" language as it would carry more weight coming from the State Department. Zoellick agreed. At the meeting he suggested using the phrase "last resort" to describe the new strategy of no early first use. Gates, following the script, said that he liked the idea. Wolfowitz murmured his assent. Everyone agreed that Washington could announce unilateral plans for deep cuts in its nuclear stockpile and for the withdrawal of all nuclear artillery shells from Europe.

Gates then set the schedule for further work. Baker, Cheney, Powell, and Scowcroft would consider the draft summit declaration within a week. This subcabinet group would meet one more time to prepare the way. Gates promised an NSC staff draft of the declaration for the next meeting. To ensure secrecy the draft declaration would not be handed out until the meeting itself.[49] This critical meeting of Gates's group was scheduled for June 18.

In the meantime, Shevardnadze had finally sent along the details of his proposed NATO–Warsaw Pact joint declaration. It was neither empty nor innocuous. The Soviet bureaucracy had made use of every dusty idea from its Cold War attic. The draft declaration proposed that the alliance agree to:

- create a joint NATO–Warsaw Pact pan-European collective military alliance open to all CSCE states
- establish new "multilateral forces," including forces of neutral states, to maintain peace between East and West
- eliminate the automatic requirement of NATO allies to come to one another's aid in the event of attack
- limit NATO defense obligations if an ally used force in Europe and promise adoption of sanctions against the ally
- exclude the former GDR from NATO treaty protection
- engage in no first use of nuclear weapons
- withdraw all U.S. nuclear forces in Europe
- withdraw all U.S. conventional forces from Germany as Soviet troops left the GDR
- create demilitarized zones in Central Europe (not to affect the USSR)
- withdraw naval and air forces that could be used for "surprise offensive actions and large-scale operations" from Europe

This draft was a blow to the State Department, which had hoped to support a NATO–Warsaw Pact declaration because the idea plainly mattered to Shevardnadze, the West Germans liked it, and State thought it could do little harm. But practically all the proposals in this declaration were anathema to the Americans, portending long and complicated negotiations. The NSC staff had been suspicious of the idea all along. They advised Scowcroft that "the problems with the Soviet proposal are so pervasive, and so tied to the basic approach of the document, that we believe it is not a useful basis for further discussion . . . There are at least a dozen major ideas in the Soviet proposal which we consider so unacceptable as to be nonnegotiable." Most of the

NATO allies also reacted negatively. But the West Germans and British still hoped to salvage the idea if the joint declaration could be made sufficiently dull and unobjectionable.[50]

Before officials gathered in the White House Situation Room on June 18, Blackwill told Gates that he thought there were seven really important initiatives in their draft declaration. If all seven were approved, the document would clear the threshold. But all of them had to be adopted in order to build up enough cumulative weight for the declaration to have the desired impact on Moscow. For Blackwill the "big seven" were:

- inviting former enemies to open permanent liaison missions with their ambassadors at NATO
- promising to seek cuts of up to half the conventional forces of states participating in a CFE II negotiation
- reshaping NATO conventional forces with a dramatic new emphasis on multinational corps under multinational control
- eliminating U.S. nuclear artillery, making deep stockpile reductions, and announcing a new nuclear doctrine of "last resort" use
- announcing ambitious new goals for the upcoming SNF arms control negotiations (along with massive unilateral reductions and the doctrine of last resort)
- pledging that NATO would devise a new military strategy that would replace both "flexible response" and "forward defense"
- pointing to the new CSCE institutions the alliance would work to create, including a new CSCE center for the prevention of conflict

Gates agreed that the draft could not afford to lose any of these ideas as it was watered down in interagency discussion.

Gates opened his meeting on June 18 with a Pentagon briefing on future U.S. military commitment to Europe.[51] The U.S. presence required a corps of two divisions, but its exact size would be based less on war-fighting needs than on judgments about the appropriate proportion of U.S. participation in NATO's forces and the need to have an evident readiness to receive and utilize reinforcements.

The group then turned to the latest draft for the proposed NATO summit declaration. Gates warned that there could be no leaks. The United States had to "show the beef" and give Gorbachev the ammunition he needed to defend a decision to accept the unification of Germany in NATO. The officials agreed to propose permanent liaison missions to NATO. They could not agree to the idea of a NATO–Warsaw Pact joint declaration. The issue was left for cabinet officials to decide. So too was the future of conventional arms control.[52] The NSC staff proposed that the United States seek cuts in national forces "by as much as one half in some instances" to prevent any country from maintaining disproportionate military power in Europe.[53]

The Joint Chiefs of Staff were now prepared to go along with peacetime organization of multinational corps in NATO, even the unprecedented integration of these corps into NATO's peacetime command structure. The military balked, however, at the final step of committing U.S. units to the peacetime command of a non-U.S. general. This issue was also left for principals to decide.

The State Department refused to agree to the proposals to eliminate nuclear artillery unilaterally and withdraw three fourths of American nuclear weapons based in Europe. Significantly, the Pentagon posed no objection to these decisions. State Department officials feared that these steps might trigger a new nuclear debate in Germany. It was agreed, therefore, to avoid detailed proposals for new SNF arms control talks.[54]

Officials also wrangled about how to guide NATO's new military strategy. Zoellick defended the language which declared that "nuclear weapons in this new Europe will truly become weapons of last resort." The phrase was designed to express the sense of reduced reliance on nuclear defenses and the move away from plans for early first use. Zoellick lost his patience. Did the group realize how many of the initiatives were still bracketed, how close they were to losing the declaration's big ideas? Assistant Secretary of Defense Stephen Hadley then settled the issue by offering a compromise formulation that preserved the new approach and muted the critics.

But Arms Control and Disarmament Agency director Lehman also objected to the language that called flatly for replacing "flexible response" and "forward defense" with new allied strategies. Again there were worries about London's reaction. Hadley and Gates offered a way to soften the language with a promise to "move away from" the old strategies. This was agreed to. Finally, the group quickly agreed on the list of new CSCE institutions in the NSC staff's draft. With this agreement the meeting ended.

The next day the principals—Baker, Cheney, Powell, and Scowcroft—gathered informally in Scowcroft's office to decide the fate of the declaration.[55] The declaration was not new to any of them, of course. Their decision-making style was to let lower-level officials do what they could, then concentrate only on the issues that were left. President Bush was also aware of what was under way. He had communicated his wish for an ambitious declaration. But Bush did not intervene directly in these deliberations. He had delegated a task and the necessary authority to his subordinates; his philosophy was then to step back and let them do their work.

The principals moved briskly through the draft text. They approved the invitation to Warsaw Pact countries to "come to NATO, not just to visit, but to stay," with permanent liaison missions to the alliance. Baker and Ross renewed the push toward a NATO–Warsaw Pact declaration. Baker knew that both the Germans and the British were willing to go along with this idea. Ross drafted a new paragraph in which NATO made a solemn commitment to nonaggression and invited the Warsaw Pact to reciprocate. This idea captured some of the spirit of the joint declaration idea and Kohl's notion of a "nonaggression pact" without actually trying to negotiate such a treaty. All agreed to Baker's proposal. It was not a joint declaration but a reciprocal exchange of declarations, so the process would not become bogged down in negotiating an unacceptable Soviet draft.

Turning to the issue of future conventional arms control, the group pledged to seek "further far-reaching reductions of the offensive capabilities" of forces in Europe, but the principals decided to drop the provocative promise of reductions "by as much as one half in some instances." Baker's approach reflected Seitz's and the European Bureau's preference for focusing on a more limited follow-on negotiation that would resolve the German troop limits problem without being encumbered by more ambitious goals.

The critical factor dooming more ambitious conventional arms controls was Scowcroft's caution. Although the radical plan had been developed by Scowcroft's own staff, upon reflection Scowcroft, like Seitz earlier, judged that the more ambitious strategy was premature and could turn out to be unnecessary. The passage of time has shown that Scowcroft and Seitz were probably right (and Zelikow was probably wrong).[56]

The principals endorsed all the other major initiatives. Powell went along with the strong language moving NATO toward multinational corps in peacetime, led by corps commanders reporting through NATO's multinational structure (which included the German commander for forces in Central Europe). The alliance would further commit itself to the complete elimination of nuclear artillery shells.[57] A specific promise to reduce the Europe-based stockpile of nuclear weapons by three fourths was dropped for fear it would spotlight for the German public the number of warheads (more than a thousand) that would remain.[58] The Bush administration later decided to go ahead and unilaterally withdraw most nuclear warheads in Europe back to the United States anyway.

Baker, Scowcroft, Cheney, and Powell firmly supported "a new NATO strategy making its nuclear forces truly weapons of last resort." They further approved the agreed-on language announcing that alliance military strategy would be "moving away from 'forward defense' toward a reduced forward presence and modifying 'flexible response' to reflect a reduced reliance on nuclear weapons." With those decisions the text of the proposed declaration was settled. President Bush readily approved the outcome. The NSC staff had developed a short declaration, stripped of bureaucratic language, that would change NATO's relationship with its Warsaw Pact adversaries, revise the nature of its military deployments, overturn its past military doctrines, and suggest ways of turning the CSCE into a permanent feature of Europe's political landscape. In less than a month an extraordinary interagency effort had produced a thoroughly analyzed American proposal which preserved the same style, length, and menu of initiatives.

Forty-eight hours after the cabinet-level review in Washington, the draft summit declaration was delivered to Helmut Kohl, Margaret Thatcher, François Mitterrand, and Manfred Wörner. It remained to be seen whether Bush could win the agreement of the fifteen other NATO countries to his plan for transforming the North Atlantic Alliance.

Bringing the Allies Along

For weeks Washington had been convinced that the kind of extraordinary summit declaration that was needed would not be produced through the usual NATO bureaucratic process. Ordinarily states would make their proposals for language at NATO headquarters. These proposals would then be combined by NATO's international staff (under a NATO assistant secretary general) into a draft, with bracketed alternate positions and national footnotes. This draft would then be reviewed painstakingly, line by line and word by word, in NATO's Senior Political Committee by career diplomats from the sixteen national delegations. Then the draft would be considered by the nations' ambassadors to the alliance, meeting as permanent representatives to the North Atlantic Council.

The United States maintained that a political declaration from the heads of government at such a historic moment should be free of the jargon, nuanced expression, and lowest common denominator content that usually emerged from the traditional process. Such a process rarely strengthened ideas; it diluted them. This was not because the diplomats were invariably stolid and unimaginative. Even the brightest and most creative diplomats lack the authority to take risks, deviate from established routines, or abandon traditional national postures when new approaches are suggested. Early reports from NATO only confirmed White House fears.

At the May 1989 NATO summit the problem had been solved by crafting a discrete initiative on one subject, conventional arms control, and grafting this onto the remainder of the declaration. Language on the other key subject, short-range nuclear forces, was haggled over by ministers at the summit. But this solution would not work for a declaration that had to act comprehensively on a range of subjects. Nor could secrecy be maintained if most of the major U.S. initiatives were presented at NATO weeks in advance.

So the White House perceived a difficult political problem in getting the "design" it felt was needed out of the London summit. The NSC staff conjured up a strategy for achieving approval of the declaration.[59] The internal work was accomplished in Washington by the group Gates chaired. The White House intended to circumvent the entire NATO process with a direct proposal from President Bush to his counterparts, to include the full text of the declaration. Baker and his circle agreed. As the president's own proposal, the U.S. draft declaration would thus escape revision by career officials. It would be negotiated only at the NATO summit itself, and only at the political level, by foreign ministers or heads of government themselves.

The plan rested conceptually on three theories of persuasion: (1) if the United States pushed hard for its desired outcome at this moment in history, one or two leaders might dislike a passage here or there, but it would not be possible for them to rally a countervailing coalition behind a comprehensive alternative; (2) if Bush proposed the plan directly to his counterparts and confined any discussion to the level of ministers at the summit meeting itself, the allies would likely raise only those concerns that genuinely troubled the political leadership; and (3) if Bush trusted Baker to handle the negotiation of the document in London, Baker could be relied on to preserve its essential content.

It was a risky plan. The NATO bureaucratic process existed for a reason: to assure heads of government that, by the time they arrived, most of the work would already have been done and most disagreements ironed out. The leaders could concentrate on a few key issues, confident that a final document was practically ready for publication. If Bush bypassed this process, he had to gamble that he could swing other governments behind him. If several representatives arrived at the summit unhappy with the document and prepared to renegotiate numerous provisions, there was no guarantee that an adequate product could be worked out in time, and no guarantee that the public would not witness the spectacle of open disagreement among leaders. Given the expectations that had been attached to the London summit, such a fractious outcome would be disastrous. Even under the best of circumstances some governments, and practically all of their NATO representatives, were likely to resent such a highhanded American approach and contemplate possible outlets for this resentment.

Still, this was the course Bush, Scowcroft, and Baker adopted. Baker's role was critical. He would bear the major burden of defending the American draft. The president had a good deal of faith in Baker's ability to conduct such a negotiation, for he knew that Baker understood what the document had to accomplish.

Bush would begin by sharing his draft with a few key leaders. Meanwhile, the NATO process would be allowed to rumble along while the American initiative was secretly being discussed by a few heads of government. On June 21 Bush sent letters explaining his plan, and enclosing his draft declaration, to Kohl, Thatcher, Mitterrand, Andreotti, and Wörner. To maintain secrecy, each letter was sent through special channels rather than using embassies to deliver the messages. Bush's letter declared, "We are at a pivotal moment." The Soviet Union would soon decide whether to acquiesce amicably in the unification of Germany as a full member of NATO. The American people were forming judgments about the relevance of NATO to the new Europe. The new democratic leaders of Eastern Europe were still unsure what to think about NATO and its part in European security. "In sum," Bush wrote, "this NATO summit is likely to fix the image of what our Alliance stands for during this period of historic change."[60]

Teltschik was jubilant as the letter arrived at the Chancellery in Bonn. Bush, he noted in his diary that night, "has gone on the offensive. With [this proposal] he has surprised all the other NATO partners, ourselves included. There exists no corresponding plan in the federal government. But the proposal makes clear the extent of German-American agreement and Bush has once more proved himself to be extraordinarily helpful. We are now sure that the NATO summit will be a success and will formulate the right message for Gorbachev."[61] Wörner was equally ecstatic. The NATO secretary general quickly wrote back that when he received the message, he was tempted to break out the champagne. The package was "excellent," he said, just the "clear message that we need at London. In short, I am enthusiastic about the draft." Wörner went on, "You are correct in noting that the declaration is ambitious, but as we agreed before, ambition is called for."[62]

Margaret Thatcher, however, was not so happy with this "lively draft." She was concerned that the U.S. proposal did not strike the right balance between NATO's fundamental purpose and a solid military strategy. "We should not adopt a declaration which contains some eye-catching propositions before we have really worked out the underlying strategy," Thatcher said. She opposed the change in NATO nuclear strategy as well as the promises for future conventional arms control. She feared that the tone of the declaration would make people think there was no longer any danger of conflict, so she also opposed the invitation to the East to set up missions at NATO. "Won't people ask," she wrote to Bush, "what is the point of defence and security if we are letting those who were so recently our bitter foes—and at worst could become so again—so close to the innermost councils of our defense and preparedness?" She preferred to concentrate on CSCE and negotiation of a NATO–Warsaw Pact joint declaration. Thatcher therefore suggested that officials from the United States, Britain, France, the FRG, and Italy get together and come up with an entirely new draft: "That will be the best way to ensure that there is Allied unity at the summit itself."[63]

Blackwill reflected on how to proceed procedurally and discussed the problem with Zoellick. Wörner had suggested making the U.S. proposal at NATO on June 29. "Too early," Blackwill decided. (The summit would be held July 5–6.) He feared that the American draft "would leak, and worse, be pawed over" by the many diplomats assigned to NATO. With Zoellick's concurrence, Blackwill instead suggested to Scowcroft that President Bush send his message directly to the remaining allied heads of government on July 2 in order to enlist their support and further isolate Prime Minister Thatcher. Then the text would finally be proposed at NATO on July 3. At that time Ambassador Taft would reveal that the president's text would be discussed only in London, by heads of government and foreign ministers. Taft would propose a special session of foreign ministers in London, on July 5, to go over the draft. Bush, Baker, and Scowcroft approved.[64]

Wörner was willing to go along with the U.S. preference for managing NATO discussion of the summit declaration. He had just talked to Thatcher, though, and knew of her reaction. So he cautioned the Americans that Washington had now embarked on "a very high risk strategy for the summit." Allied concerns about both substance and procedure would be aroused, and getting the needed agreement would not be easy. If the plan misfired, there would be a failure no one could afford. So it was essential that, having launched this high-level effort in this extraordinary way, the U.S. government display "considerable toughness and determination" to see the declaration through.[65]

Bush made another attempt to persuade Thatcher to accept his ideas. He sent a message on July 1 responding point by point to each of her concerns.[66] On the question of nuclear strategy, he argued, "I worry that if we say nothing about the future of flexible response and our strategy for deterrence at this summit, we will just allow the advocates of no first use and denuclearization to set the terms for the debate, including in Germany." Flexible response had, as a matter of necessity, relied on early use of nuclear weapons. That necessity would clearly vanish with the massive reductions of Soviet military power in Europe required by the CFE treaty nearing conclusion in Vienna.

Bush went on: "If I am asked in London at a press conference after our summit whether NATO will adapt its nuclear strategy in response to these changes, I could say we are studying it. But then we have failed to offer leadership. If I say flexible response would continue, unaffected by these new circumstances, then it will be much harder to maintain a consensus behind NATO's nuclear deterrent. And if I say NATO's strategy will be different, don't we have to say something to define this new direction?"

The bottom line was this: "If we do not make bold moves at the London summit . . . we will fail to meet the public test we both agree the declaration must pass . . . In their private meeting in Berlin, Shevardnadze told Jim Baker no less than four times how important the NATO summit would be in shaping Soviet attitudes on the vital questions that Moscow must answer during the next few months. I am also aware that Helmut Kohl will be in Moscow on July 15–16. He should take with him a clear Alliance position on just how we will (and will not) adapt to the new realities in Europe." Thatcher's desire to convene a group to prepare a fresh draft was rejected. "We will be able to work on the specific language of the document in London," said Bush. Prime Minister Thatcher was now left to decide whether she was willing to risk an Anglo-American clash at this vital meeting of NATO leaders.

Kohl and Mitterrand had talked about Bush's proposal over breakfast while they were in Dublin for an EC summit meeting. Mitterrand agreed with most of it, though he was worried that the multinational corps idea might strengthen NATO's military structures, and he thought that the changes in nuclear strategy went too far. Teltschik called Blackwill to convey Kohl's pleased reaction to the proposal. Blackwill in turn urged Teltschik to help line up French and German support in London so that Thatcher would be isolated. Briefed by Teltschik, Kohl talked to Genscher. They decided to send Kastrup, Teltschik, and Klaus Naumann from the Defense Ministry to Washington to work with the Americans on the summit declaration. Scowcroft warned Teltschik, however, that such U.S.-German consultations would only inflame British hostility and suspicion about the preparation of the document. Wörner had called Scowcroft with more concerns about reactions among other NATO allies. Scowcroft and Teltschik agreed that Bonn should just offer some written suggestions.[67]

Teltschik sent on a West German draft declaration that used many of the American ideas but pressed for a more formal NATO–Warsaw Pact nonaggression agreement, soft-pedaling the idea of a NATO multinational corps (to avoid antagonizing the French) and changes in NATO military strategy (to avoid starting a public debate over nuclear weapons).[68] The Chancellery draft included the current German troop limits proposal (the so-called Holik proposal), but in the original form, which called for all parties to negotiate national troop limits during the current CFE negotiations. The Americans still preferred not to burden the ongoing CFE talks or hand the Soviets a golden opportunity to tie up a Two Plus Four settlement they did not like and a CFE treaty they did not care for either.

Scowcroft wrote back to Teltschik that the Holik proposal in this form meant that all twenty-three countries participating in the CFE negotiations "would have to agree on the size of the Greek armed forces, the Turkish armed forces, and so on for every country in Europe. We are especially worried that trying to accomplish this formidable task in the current CFE negotiations could indefinitely delay the conclusion of a CFE treaty (a development the Soviet military might actually welcome). It is also possible that Gorbachev could use this notion and its inherent complexity to delay resolution of the Two Plus Four process."

Teltschik took these arguments seriously. The West German Defense Ministry also preferred to negotiate all national limits in future talks, after the current CFE treaty was signed and the fate of Soviet troops in Europe became clear. Defense minister Stoltenberg told Kohl for the first time, on July 2, that he could accept a limit of fewer than 400,000 troops for Germany's future armed forces.

The top West German leadership then met to finalize a position on limiting their armed forces. They agreed to accept the American and Defense Ministry preference for negotiating their own and all other national limits in a follow-on CFE discussion, not in the current treaty negotiations. The Germans could introduce their future stance as a unilateral commitment during the current talks. They disagreed only about the number. Genscher favored 350,000; Kohl and Stoltenberg preferred 400,000. Kohl feared that an offer of 350,000 would eventually mean a compromise outcome of 280,000, which was too low. Genscher then sought out Teltschik and explained that there was no danger of watering down the position because the German number would not be negotiated—it would just be a unilateral statement. Kohl and Teltschik conferred again, and Kohl settled on an ideal of 370,000, but decided he would be willing to go as low as 350,000 if all other questions could also be settled.[69]

The Americans meanwhile were discussing their NATO summit plan with the French president.[70] Mitterrand, aware of Kohl's positive reaction, wrote to Bush to say that he liked the tone of the declaration and the way the Americans had replaced the idea of a NATO–Warsaw Pact joint declaration with an offer of reciprocal declarations of their "will for non-aggression." Mitterrand objected, however, to including new initiatives on NATO multinational corps. He also wanted to keep from making "overly precise proposals" on permanent CSCE institutions until the Paris summit. His staff later developed a lengthy substitute draft on CSCE to replace the U.S.-proposed language, though they had no quarrel with the American list of institutional initiatives.

Mitterrand joined with Thatcher in questioning the Americans' proposed changes in NATO nuclear strategy. He thought that a "last resort" concept was inconsistent with effective deterrence, that to be effective, the threat of using nuclear weapons had to involve early use. Since France was not part of NATO's integrated military command, said Mitterrand, he would not try to tell other members of NATO what military strategy they ought to adopt. But French doctrine, "which complements, I think usefully, the strategy of NATO," relied on the threat of early first use of nuclear weapons.

French officials also conveyed their dissatisfaction with the offer to bring Warsaw Pact ambassadors to NATO. They did not want NATO to take on such a political role. Mitterrand's interpretation of his understanding with Bush at their April Key Largo meeting was that NATO should be limited to "the examination among Allies of the security problems related to the [military] balance in Europe."

Bush quickly responded to Mitterrand's concerns in a message sent on July 1. He offered no changes in his proposed declaration, promising only that "we can work on specific adjustments to the declaration when we get to London." But he pledged that nothing in the draft "is meant either to challenge France's traditional relationship to the Alliance or reduce France's flexibility as it considers its future defense arrangements in Europe."[71]

On the whole, the reaction from key allied leaders was mixed. Every major idea in the draft text was opposed by at least one of Bush's counterparts and supported by at least one of the leaders. As Blackwill reported to Scowcroft and Gates, "It is perhaps not surprising that the net effect if we took all the changes would be to drain the Declaration of its substance." The Americans agreed that the only course was to press ahead without making any changes in the U.S. proposal and simply try to carry the day when the foreign ministers attacked the text in London.[72]

As planned, Bush's proposal was put forward at NATO headquarters on July 2. NATO diplomats grumbled about the American insistence on deferring any drafting to the summit itself. Spanish president Felipe Gonzalez had urged Bush directly to let NATO ambassadors redraft the declaration. But at NATO headquarters Wörner stoutly resisted pressure to start drafting and quashed an international staff "annotation" of Bush's proposal. Ambassador Taft concluded that "we are in pretty good shape." As Washington had hoped,

Taft thought, many of the diplomats' objections would "not appeal to foreign ministers as much as their bureaucracies hope." Yet there would still be "plenty of tough negotiation in London." Taft added, "There will be some hard feelings, but we have what we wanted."[73]

Meanwhile Bush was preparing himself for the London summit. His senior advisers traveled to the Bush summer home in Kennebunkport, Maine, on July 2 for a series of briefings on policy toward Germany and Europe and on the status of the various initiatives. Zoellick set the tone in an opening briefing, "The NATO Summit: German Unification and the Soviet Audience." Zoellick's paper declared, "This NATO summit is NATO's major opportunity within this sequence [of events in 1990] to define its positions on the key political and security issues in play during the sprint to the CSCE Summit and All-German elections."[74]

To rally backing in London from some smaller allies and friends, on July 3 Bush telephoned the Belgian, Dutch, and Danish prime ministers. In each telephone conversation he found firm agreement on the critical importance of the summit and received the assurances of support that he had hoped for.[75]

Heads of government assembled in London on July 5 amid the palatial surroundings of Lancaster House, which had been the site of the successful 1979 negotiations for the settlement that turned Rhodesia into Zimbabwe.[76] Wörner opened the session by declaring that President Bush's draft would be the basis for further work, with foreign ministers personally taking charge of negotiating the text. Bush addressed the gathering, explaining each of the initiatives in the draft, warning that the summit "may be our last chance to indicate the changing nature of our Alliance before the Soviets and Eastern Europeans and others make their decisions on German unity and CFE and for the CSCE summit."

Prime Minister Thatcher promptly replied by voicing her concern about the declaration's promise of new conventional arms control to seek "further far-reaching reductions" of offensive capability and criticizing the change to a nuclear strategy of "last resort." As she put it:

> Although a great deal of what President Bush says about nuclear weapons is very welcome, I am concerned that we don't misinterpret the same words. To me the expression "weapons of last resort" is very clear. Last resort: last means last and nothing else and yet I am told that it is not so, that the expression is ambiguous. But I have often read confusing words in communiqués and found them very confusing; but to be told that clear words are confusing is, to me, a new dimension of diplomacy. Of course, as colleagues

round this table will know, I never had much use for diplomacy anyway, and I've got on very well without it.

She understood the need for the alliance to "match the moment," but "not at the expense of our future defence and security."

Chancellor Kohl spoke next, helping to offset the effect of Thatcher's address by lining up directly behind the United States: "I would like to support President Bush in what he has said here. The message to go out from the NATO Summit meeting here is of enormous importance for Central and Eastern Europe." More leaders spoke. Then the assembly adjourned for lunch. When they reconvened, the speeches continued, but the real work had moved to another room in Lancaster House, where the foreign ministers were haggling over the text of the declaration itself.

The foreign ministers worked over the four and a half pages of text until after midnight. The White House reliance on Baker's negotiating skills paid off. With Hans van den Broek chairing the session with agility and forcefulness, the text of the declaration emerged relatively unscathed from the hours of debate. British foreign secretary Hurd did what he could to adjust language on the defense and arms control points, but he had been instructed not to force an open breach in allied councils. He did pare down the declaration's promise of further far-reaching reductions in conventional forces in Europe to the more anodyne promise that future measures might further limit such forces.[77] Yet the brevity and nonbureaucratic tone of the declaration was preserved, as were almost all the principal initiatives. Van den Broek, presenting the new text to heads of government the following day, could triumphantly claim, "We have been able to accommodate [Allied] viewpoints without losing the imagination and punch of the message which this Declaration conveys."

The proposal for a NATO–Warsaw Pact joint declaration that "we are no longer adversaries" was endorsed and strengthened—as the West Germans and British had hoped, but it was still short of a "nonaggression pact." France fought the idea of inviting Eastern European countries to send their ambassadors to NATO, but it was a losing battle. When the issue was referred to the heads of government, French foreign minister Dumas accepted a compromise that dropped the specific reference to ambassadors but retained the declaration's landmark plea to the states of the East "to come to NATO, not just to visit, but to establish regular diplomatic liaison with NATO." These seeds quickly sprouted. By the end of the following year they had grown into a new organization linked to the alliance and designed to include the East in NATO's deliberations—the North Atlantic Cooperation Council (NACC).

This institution was, in turn, to lead by 1994 to creation of the Partnership for Peace, to bring former Warsaw Pact adversaries even closer to NATO's security deliberations.[78]

Taking advantage of the West German decision to adopt the American-preferred variant on the Holik proposal for handling future German troop limits, the summit declaration included a statement of the new position. The declaration promised that "a commitment will be given at the time of signature of the CFE Treaty concerning the manpower levels of a united Germany."[79] The declaration's promise of fundamental changes in the posture of NATO's conventional forces was retained. Led by the French, the allies excised the language committing to the peacetime integration of national forces into multinational corps under NATO's integrated military command. But the pledge to "rely increasingly on multinational corps made up of national units" was retained, and has since become a singular characteristic of the alliance's military reorganization. Also left intact were the assurance that much smaller restructured units would replace the force structure of the past.

The proposal to eliminate all nuclear artillery shells from Europe, if the Soviets would reciprocate, was adopted by the allies, as was the language, which Thatcher and Mitterrand had so disliked, promising a change in NATO nuclear strategy to make "nuclear forces truly weapons of last resort." Both "forward defense" and "flexible response" were explicitly consigned to the past. A review to elaborate these new strategic principles was put in motion (with conclusions that were ultimately adopted in November 1991 at a NATO summit in Rome). All of the institutional innovations for the CSCE proposed in the U.S. draft were adopted as well.

The only jarring note as heads of government finished their endorsement of the declaration's text was struck by Mitterrand. Near the end of the meeting he delivered a curious presentation in which he essentially distanced himself, and France, from the entire result. Mitterrand had long hoped that a comprehensive review of NATO military strategy would be a drawn-out process in which France might find a way to participate constructively. He was irritated by the abrupt American effort to force the direction of this review and bulldoze Bush's proposed text through the alliance. His pique at the U.S. success in this effort (and President Bush's refusal to accept his warning against changing NATO's nuclear strategy) was evident for months after the summit ended.[80]

An annoyed Mitterrand promptly announced, shortly after the summit, that France would pull all of its nearly fifty thousand troops out of Germany by 1994, would not join any multinational units, and would not allow any multinational units to be stationed in France. Mitterrand did not bother to inform the Franco-German Defense Council, which existed to consider common security concerns, of his decision before he announced it. This extraordinary move did not affect NATO implementation of the summit initiatives, although it did perhaps undermine Germany's faith in the credibility of French commitments. The hasty call to withdraw French troops from Germany was quietly superseded in 1991, when France developed the idea of a Franco-German corps in order to press its conception of a European defense identity in the closing phase of negotiations over the Maastricht treaty on European political union. The whole affair now appears to have reflected little more than erratic statesmanship born out of France's sense of frustration.[81]

The Americans, the West Germans, and most of the other allies were very pleased, however, with the summit's outcome. The full text of the declaration was published in the *New York Times* on July 6. European press reaction was overwhelmingly, even extravagantly, positive. But the most important reaction would be that coming from Moscow.

The Houston Summit

As *Air Force One* flew from London to Houston, Bush, Scowcroft, and Blackwill drafted a letter to Gorbachev, telling him what they thought they had just accomplished at the NATO summit.[82] The letter was transmitted to Moscow by radio from the airplane. When the letter arrived in Moscow, the American diplomat running the embassy that day, Michael Joyce, rushed it to the Congress of People's Deputies, where Gorbachev was defending his policies. Chernyayev came out of the meeting to take the letter from Joyce. He read it quickly and then looked up. "This is indeed an important letter," he said, then brought it in to his chief.

The letter explained clearly what the allies had done in London, and how each of the NATO initiatives responded to Soviet concerns. In other words, the letter said: We promised you that we would move on our nine points; now we have delivered on our promise. As Bush put it:

> I listened carefully to what you said during those most helpful discussions [in Washington].
> Working solely from a draft text I circulated to my NATO counterparts, we a few hours ago issued a declaration that promises the Alliance's transformation in every aspect of its work and especially of its relationship with the Soviet Union. As you read the NATO declaration, I want you to know

that it was written with you importantly in mind, and I made that point strongly to my colleagues in London.

Mr. President, we have important decisions before us as we work toward Europe's reconciliation . . . I hope today's NATO declaration will persuade you that NATO can and will serve the security interests of Europe as a whole.

I have been watching the developments at your Party Congress these past days with the greatest interest and have admired the way you have handled the burgeoning democratic process in your country. As you know, I have stressed repeatedly to the American people how much I support your efforts in this regard.

Mr. President, we have witnessed remarkable changes in the world and in our relationship. I hope that what has perhaps been the most important NATO summit meeting in its history will push U.S.-Soviet relations to an even higher plane in the period ahead.

With this letter and the NATO declaration from London, the United States, West Germany, and their allies had delivered what amounted to their final offer for settlement of the German question. Their position on German membership in NATO was clear. They had established just how far NATO was willing to go in adapting to meet Soviet concerns. They had described how they were willing to handle the issue of German troop strength.

The only other element in this final bid was the economic one. Gorbachev had asked both the West Germans and the Americans for large-scale aid. Bonn was taking care of the Soviet request for an immediate credit line of DM 5 billion (about $3 billion), and on June 27 the credits were finally extended, to run over a twelve-year period. The West Germans also knew that they would be assuming the short-term costs of maintaining Soviet forces in eastern Germany which had been borne by the GDR. In 1990 these costs were expected to amount to another DM 1.4 billion, or about $850 million. But Gorbachev wanted a broader Western program of assistance on a large scale, amounting to at least $15–20 billion. This would require a Western consensus, since the aid would come mainly from international financial institutions such as the International Monetary Fund. But such consensus for large-scale aid did not exist.

Bush had already indicated, both to Kohl and to Gorbachev, that he could not easily endorse this larger program of assistance. It would be economically unsound until Moscow was prepared to adopt a genuine reform program, and it would be unsustainable politically unless the Soviets dropped their blockade of Lithuania and curtailed their massive subsidies to Cuba. Kohl had worked hard to help Gorbachev. He had won Mitterrand's backing for more ambitious aid, though the backing was almost entirely rhetorical, and at a June 25–26 EC summit Kohl, with Mitterrand, urged his European counterparts to join in endorsing a major aid program for Moscow.[83]

Thatcher was a strong supporter of Gorbachev. But she could not back any aid program until the Soviets undertook the economic reforms that would make such assistance worthwhile. As she recalled later, "I took most satisfaction . . . at this Council from stopping the Franco-German juggernaut in its tracks on the question of financial credits to the Soviet Union." She did not think that giving former communist countries or the communist USSR even more debt "would do them any favours." Above all, she did not want Western money to become "an oxygen tent for the survival of much of the old system." Kohl and Mitterrand pressed their case over dinner on the night of June 25. Thatcher opposed them. She found the utter lack of any serious economic analysis appalling, and argued that "no board of directors of a company would ever behave in such an unbusiness-like way. We should not do so either." She insisted on a proper study of the situation before any decision was made to dispense large sums of money. The argument continued into the EC session on the morning of June 26, but Thatcher's approach prevailed.[84]

Kohl did not respond to the economic arguments. There is no evidence that the Germans had made any serious analysis of how the $15–20 billion in credit would help perestroika. That, for Kohl, was not the point—any more than he had made a serious analysis of the form or effect of a European political union before he had become a cosponsor of that enterprise. After all, his primary motive in both cases was political—the need to make powerful symbolic gestures. Kohl supported a move to political union because he believed in the European ideal and believed that the Germans now had to show themselves to be placing Europe ahead of German nationalism. Gorbachev wanted help. An aid program would help keep Gorbachev in power. And a friendly Gorbachev seemed vital for pulling off Kohl's bid for rapid, untroubled unification. If the EC could not be persuaded to support large-scale credits, Kohl would get the next best thing: at least Gorbachev would see that Kohl had done his best to get the money. As Teltschik noted after the Dublin summit: "For Kohl it was important to keep his word that he would push for support to the Soviet Union in multilateral fora. With Mitterrand's help this became a main issue at the European summit. That is surely helpful for the whole atmosphere between us and the Soviet Union."[85]

In Houston, Kohl and Mitterrand urged their colleagues to be forthcoming in responding to the Soviet request for large-scale credits. Bush had already communicated a willingness to help, but, like Thatcher, he thought that the first constructive step should be to study the situation and determine what assistance was needed and what Moscow would have to do in return. The reluctance of the Americans and the British was shared by the Japanese and the Canadians. So the G-7 leaders in Houston, picking up the suggestion that emerged from the Dublin EC summit, asked the IMF to begin a crash study of Soviet economic needs, to be completed by the end of the year. This landmark study laid the foundation for a future program of assistance; but that was all Moscow would get for now.[86]

The West had made its best and final offer to secure Soviet acquiescence to the rapid unification of Germany on Western terms. Kohl would return to Moscow in mid-July, just before the next Two Plus Four ministerial meeting in Paris. But there was now broad consensus: the terms of the Western offer were no longer negotiable. The key decision rested with the Soviets. The allies awaited Moscow's reply. They did not have to wait long.

~ 9

Germany Regains Its Sovereignty

IN MID-JULY Gorbachev decided to settle the German issue and put it behind him. For about a month the Soviet government's behavior had been very difficult to read. There were two personas—one public and the other very private. Formal public policy on Germany had been fixed, in its essentials, for about two months. That was when the Politburo forced Shevardnadze to carry his hard-line message to the first meeting of Two Plus Four ministers in Bonn. The Politburo's stance in May was not all that different from the policy the Soviet government had adopted, together with East German leader Hans Modrow, at the end of January. The only concession to the dramatic internal developments in Germany had been the decision to decouple internal unification from the satisfactory settlement of all external issues. Shevardnadze proceeded in June to propose a draft NATO–Warsaw Pact declaration that would dismantle both alliances, effectively neutralize Germany, and obtain the withdrawal of all foreign forces from German soil. Then, at the Two Plus Four ministers' meeting in Berlin, Shevardnadze presented a draft settlement for Germany that was consistent with the established policy line.

But Gorbachev's own resolve on the NATO issue had begun to weaken at the Washington summit with Bush at the end of May. From that time forward he had been passive in public and uncertain in private. One of the conservatives on the Central Committee staff, Nikolai Portugalov, later said that what had happened in Washington "was so unprofessional, so unexpected, that all of us were startled. Of course, now it looks like 'tout est pour le mieux.' But then it looked awful, scandalous. We could and should have asked Kohl to accept a French-style military status for Germany. That was not done because Shevardnadze was pressing Gorbachev with his 'concessions to the

Americans' line.'" Valentin Falin was even more bitter, calling Shevardnadze "the Americans' most powerful agent of influence."[1]

There is no evidence that Shevardnadze knew in advance of the Washington summit about any Gorbachev plan—if there was one—to concede Germany's right to remain in NATO. But one thing is clear: Shevardnadze and Gorbachev made a decision shortly thereafter to try to put in place the most crucial moves of the "endgame" on German unification. They knew that their influence was slipping. The GDR was being rapidly absorbed into the FRG. Two Plus Four meetings had become virtually Four Plus One, with the Soviet Union on the short end.

Soviet positions became pro forma in the Two Plus Four. On July 4, at another meeting of political directors, the Soviet representative, Alexander Bondarenko, offered nothing new but did confide that Shevardnadze had not even been seen around the ministry for several days.[2] While carrying out the Politburo's script in public, Shevardnadze had begun to stall, waiting until the West could deliver its promised transformation of the NATO alliance. At the same time, diplomatic activity swirled around Gorbachev's requests for substantial credits from America, the FRG, and other Western countries. And Gorbachev and Shevardnadze made sure that their hands were not tied by any further discussion of Germany or other European security issues in the Politburo. "All decisions after Bonn [the early May Two Plus Four ministerial] were taken out of the Politburo's hands," Sergei Tarasenko recalled. The moves in July were never discussed there. The opposition would have been too great. Once he moved, Tarasenko adds, "Shevardnadze played such a quick game—others could never catch up."[3]

Shevardnadze and Gorbachev faced a timing problem. They knew that the twenty-eighth congress of the CPSU would be the conservatives' "best and perhaps last chance to reassert control before the country sped off in a new, democratic direction." The conservatives had just dominated a Russian party conference. There had been an all-out assault on the Soviet Union's "ruinous" foreign policy. A leading critic, the general commanding the Volga-Urals military district, had declared: "Germany is being reunited and will probably be a member of NATO . . . Only our own scientist-chaps twitter on about the fact that no one intends to attack us . . . That formula is calculated to appeal to the feeble-minded."[4]

Gorbachev had little capital left with conservative forces. He had already moved to resolve the Lithuanian crisis which had shadowed his reform efforts at home and his relationships abroad. On June 29 Lithuania accepted a variant of the Kohl-Mitterrand proposal and suspended its declaration of independence. The next day Gorbachev lifted the Soviet blockade.

The party congress began on July 2. Gorbachev defended his program against conservative attacks. Responding to the criticism that he had "lost" Eastern Europe, Gorbachev answered that he had decided not to use "the methods we used in the past." He said as little as possible about Germany, instead emphasizing his fundamental choice for cooperation and "the inclusion of our national economy in the world economy." Shevardnadze defended his foreign policy record to the assembled delegates, amid shouted boos. Kvitsinsky, who was present, recalled later that Shevardnadze only barely averted "an explosion in the assembly hall." Shevardnadze reportedly felt angry and dejected that Gorbachev had done little to defend him at the meeting. Gorbachev's main concern was to secure a mandate for his domestic reform program, and his hopes for dramatic change were at their height.[5]

Gorbachev again proved to be a master of Kremlin politics. He had lined up his supporters for the congress and clearly knew that he had the strength to withstand a vote of no confidence. The Soviet leader, who had threatened to resign, emerged victorious—winning reelection to the post of general secretary by a three-to-one margin. His candidate for deputy party leader, the Ukrainian Vladimir Ivashko, soundly defeated Yegor Ligachev in an even more lopsided tally. When Gorbachev met Helmut Kohl in the second week of July in Moscow, he was flushed with his recent victory over Ligachev and his "ultras."[6] Gorbachev told Kohl that his party congress had paralleled the fiery and epochal gatherings of the October revolution; the eleven-day congress kept reminding him of John Reed's book *Ten Days that Shook the World.*

Maneuvering brilliantly between right and left, Gorbachev also prepared to cut a deal with Boris Yeltsin. He agreed to launch a new market reform plan that would compete against the bureaucratic proposals developed by his own prime minister, Nikolai Ryzhkov. The working group charged with the development of the plan was stacked with Gorbachev supporters, such as Sergei Shatalin, and Yeltsin advisers, including Grigory Yavlinsky. This group drafted a truly ambitious "500-day plan" for dramatic reform. An all-Union treaty would be prepared to attend to the nationalities question. Gorbachev was bubbling over with plans to remake his country.[7]

Yet colder weather would soon follow. The national security establishment was increasingly hostile and unreconciled to the new agenda. Even as party conservatives were being routed at the congress, reactionaries in the police, the army, and the KGB were gaining strength. The shift was obvious to those who encountered these hard-liners in arms control negotiations or noticed the estrangement of Shevardnadze from the security institutions he claimed to represent. Yet the most destructive effects of the Thermidorian reaction were yet to come. Months later a panicked Gorbachev would lunge toward the conservatives, making an alliance with those who would ultimately betray him. Yakovlev would resign in November and Shevardnadze in December, warning darkly of an impending coup. And Yeltsin would deal the Soviet Union a mortal blow by ripping out its Russian core. All that lay in the not too distant future.

But July 1990 was the Indian summer of perestroika. With the party congress over and Kohl already scheduled for a visit to Moscow, Gorbachev decided that it was time to resolve the problem of German membership in NATO, and with it the German question. The NATO summit announcement was a catalyst. Shevardnadze had referred to it over and over in his private talks with Baker and Genscher. He recalled in his memoirs how "in the extremely inflamed atmosphere of the [party] Congress it was difficult to breathe. My personal fate was on the line . . . The Congress gave vivid testimony to the growth of opposition to our policy. In my circumstances, it was especially important to see some encouraging response from 'the other side' (the West). Otherwise, we would be in an untenable position. When the news came out about the NATO session in London, I knew there had been a response."[8]

Shevardnadze was waiting in his office for the first word of the London communiqué. Tarasenko, who was with him, later recalled that when they received the text from the wire service, they "immediately, within an hour," analyzed it and wrote an official response for the Foreign Ministry. "If we hadn't done that," Tarasenko recalled, "Marshal Akhromeyev would have had time to put his own spin on the document." Gorbachev and Shevardnadze wanted to place the Soviet reaction in a larger context, one that could relate the NATO move to the controversial public debate over policy toward Germany. For the same reasons Gorbachev's interpreter and aide, writing under a pseudonym, also quickly published a positive appraisal of the NATO initiatives in the Soviet press.[9]

Shevardnadze shaped the initial Soviet government reaction to the London declaration, applauding it as "realistic and constructive." Although it was still too early to judge whether the declaration marked "a turning point and a day of renewal," Shevardnadze considered it "certain, however, that the decisions adopted move in the right direction and pave the way to a safe future for the entire European continent." Now, with the NATO states actually opening the door to new contacts for Eastern nations with the alliance, he thought, "one can say that things began to move." The promised change in NATO military strategy "signals a sober evaluation" of the new environment in Europe, said Shevardnadze, especially the moves away from the concepts of forward defense and flexible response. "This signifies potentially important decisions."[10]

Despite the Soviet Union's positive response to London, the United States and the FRG thought that Gorbachev would probably wait before making a major move to settle the German question. It had been characteristic of him to avoid painful decisions until the last possible moment. Perhaps he would wait to see how the Two Plus Four talks progressed. The allies did know, however, that they had narrowed Soviet options dramatically. The Soviets could no longer hope to obstruct the next stage of internal unification. Because of the extraordinarily able and energetic efforts by Bonn, economic and monetary union took effect as scheduled on July 1. East Germans began exchanging Ostmarks for deutsche marks. West German goods flooded East German shops. East–West German border checks disappeared. The stunning metamorphosis of East Germany into a new society had begun.

Negotiations of the second state treaty on political union started on July 6 and moved quickly. Bonn predicted that the treaty would be completed in August and ratified in September.[11] The Soviet Union was almost out of time and out of weapons with which to stop unification from occurring essentially on Western terms.

Gorbachev and Shevardnadze decided to settle the issue of Germany's membership in NATO once and for all when Kohl came to the Soviet Union. According to Chernyayev, Gorbachev himself had decided that he no longer feared NATO, and no longer really believed that German membership in NATO posed a real threat to the USSR. His greatest worries were about the reaction of his domestic enemies. Chernyayev underscored the gravity of the decision, noting: "If there had been a coup against Gorbachev in August 1990, this [German] question would have been in the forefront . . . Look at the Central Committee, two-thirds of them were against Gorbachev and Shevardnadze. There was a genuine danger of a coup. So domestically the London summit was extremely important. It was the kind of thing used to stabilize Gorbachev's ship." Gorbachev himself reflected to Bush in September 1990 that "enormous efforts were required, tremendous work and political will," to deal with the German issue, "to overcome the old approaches which seemed unquestionable, to act according to the changing reality."[12]

With the party congress at an end, Gorbachev was at his point of maximum strength. He must have known that he would need every ounce of that strength for the coming battle for economic reform that lay just ahead. On the last day of the congress Gorbachev sent a message to Kohl: How would the German leader like to start his visit in Moscow but then go on with Gorbachev to visit Gorbachev's home region, the Caucasus? Of course Kohl would be happy to accept this offer. Teltschik saw this as a signal. If Gorbachev intended a confrontational visit, surely he would not be inviting the chancellor to his hometown. Teltschik was right.[13]

A Pleasant Surprise for Kohl

The West Germans were "dead-tired" (Teltschik's phrase) after three summits in two weeks (EC summit in Dublin June 25–26, NATO summit in London July 5–6, G-7 summit in Houston July 9–11).[14] But they did not need to work hard on the policy positions they would bring to Moscow. All the essential elements of the West's final offer were already fixed: the scope of the Two Plus Four talks, the position on termination of Four Power rights and immediate restoration of full German sovereignty, the details of full German membership in NATO, the ways in which NATO would adapt to the new environment, and the manner in which German troop strength would be dealt with. Teltschik and Scowcroft had again gone over the details of the troop strength issue in Houston. The Americans and the West Germans were in full accord. The West Germans had also told Moscow of their willingness to conclude a Soviet-German nonaggression treaty. But the substance of this treaty would not affect Bonn's alliance commitments in any way, and negotiation of its text had not yet begun. The Western positions on all these issues were set.

On economic incentives, the West had delivered all it was prepared to deliver at that time: the West German credit of DM 5 billion had been arranged. Positive signals had been given about a broader program of assistance, but nothing would be forthcoming until after the IMF study was completed, in 1991 at the earliest.

The only loose end was the exact number for a ceiling on German troop strength. The formula was understood: there would be a political declaration in the current CFE talks setting the figure Germany would accept in the follow-on talks, at which time all the other participants would accept similar limits on their own forces. Kohl had narrowed the number down to 350,000–370,000, a range with which the Americans were comfortable. In May the White House and the Chancellery had agreed that commitment to a specific number should wait for the endgame. Teltschik had told Scowcroft in Houston that Kohl was now prepared to give Gorbachev a figure if the Soviets accepted the principle of full German membership in NATO. Was this a problem for Washington? Scowcroft agreed that this approach was fine.

On the day Kohl and Genscher returned to Bonn from Houston, the chancellor chaired a last cabinet meeting to review the bidding. Genscher reported on the status of the Two Plus Four negotiations. He also mentioned that he had had little luck in trying to bring the East German foreign minister, Markus Meckel, around to a more supportive stance. The Americans had met with Meckel in Washington on July 13 but had not had much success with him either. Genscher described the current Soviet proposals on political and security questions as unacceptable, though Shevardnadze had indicated that these positions were not the last word.[15]

The Chancellery played down public expectations for Kohl's trip. No breakthrough was expected, they said. Privately the Germans were more hopeful, especially in light of the invitation to visit Stavropol and the Caucasus, but were still uncertain about what to expect.[16]

Two days after returning to Bonn from Houston, Kohl took off for Moscow. On Saturday evening, July 14, the Germans again reviewed their negotiating position.[17] It seemed clear to Teltschik that this was probably the most important foreign trip ever taken by the chancellor. They focused on what seemed to be the two biggest obstacles on the road to unity: completely terminating Four Power rights and responsibilities and securing agreement to full NATO membership for a united Germany. But they felt that their positions on both issues were clear.

Kohl still had not set the final number for the future size of the Bundeswehr. On the plane to Moscow he and Genscher clashed. Swinging back toward the Defense Ministry's preferences, Kohl suggested 400,000. Genscher insisted on 350,000. Kohl accused the Free Democratic party of seeking to establish a professional army, since he believed 350,000 was too low a figure to sustain a continuation of conscription. Genscher considered the accusation insulting. Kohl asked that the FDP hold a presidium in order to decide a party position on the issue. Genscher refused to call a presidium for an issue he thought was so obvious, and threw the suggestion back at Kohl. Why didn't he call a CDU party gathering to decide the matter? But as quickly as Kohl had started the argument, he put it aside. Teltschik wrote in his diary that Kohl frequently saw such arguments as a means to an end. Once he had aired the dispute, it was easier to settle it. After all, the men were coalition partners, not friends. The two essentially split the difference and arrived at a figure of 370,000.

As Gorbachev prepared for the German chancellor's visit, Falin made one last desperate effort to persuade the Soviet leader to take a harder line.[18] He sent Gorbachev an "energetic" memo warning him that this meeting was the last decisive opportunity to protect Soviet interests. Receiving no reply, Falin finally called Gorbachev and asked for ten or fifteen minutes of his time. Gorbachev promised to call him later in the evening. Finally, fifteen minutes before midnight, Gorbachev called back. "What do you want to tell me?" he asked.

Falin outlined three points. First, he wanted Gorbachev to oppose FRG annexation of the GDR by means of article 23. He could not bear the "moral and political costs" of obliterating the GDR's economic structures, and he feared that the takeover would criminalize what the GDR had done over the course of forty years. A "hundred thousand people" might be hauled into court. Second, Falin wanted Gorbachev to stand against participation of a united Germany in NATO. At the least Gorbachev should insist on a French-style membership, which would take Germany out of the alliance's integrated military command, and expulsion of all nuclear weapons. Third, all questions concerning Soviet property rights should be handled as political decisions to keep the Soviets from being entangled in endless debates about environmental damage or other claims, as was already the case in Czechoslovakia and Hungary.

Gorbachev asked a few questions, then concluded the conversation by saying, "I will do what I can. Only I fear that the train has already left." Gorbachev and Shevardnadze did not bring their planned position with Kohl before the Politburo. They could not risk another debate before the collective leadership. They would go it alone.[19]

Kohl arrived on July 14. As the German party dined that night in Moscow, they received the report on Manfred Wörner's meetings with the Soviets earlier that day. Wörner had come to Moscow right after the NATO summit in order to convey personally NATO's direct offer of friendship to the Soviet government. He had been warmly welcomed and had received almost unqualified praise for the alliance's London declaration. Kohl was encouraged.[20]

Kohl and Gorbachev met the next day, July 15, in Moscow at a guest house of the Soviet Foreign Ministry.[21] A palatial neo-Gothic building on Alexei Tolstoy street, the house had belonged to a wealthy mercantile family until after the October revolution, when Georgi Chicherin—commissar for foreign affairs in the 1920s—had diverted it to its new function.

Kohl, Teltschik, Gorbachev, and Chernyayev met alone with their interpreters. Kohl said that although he had been too young to fight in the Second World War, both he and Gorbachev were old enough to have memories of those years. Perhaps they could now do something about addressing that history. Gorbachev agreed. He had been ten years old when the war began and could remember it well. It was no longer important who had won and who had lost. They were now all living together in one world. When Gorbachev spoke of the two countries, he spoke of Germany and Russia, not the Soviet Union.

Kohl then reviewed the outcome of the recent summits and the situation in the GDR, which was getting worse from day to day. Kohl wanted to settle three sets of issues in order to allow for timely conclusion of the Two Plus Four talks and the CSCE summit. These were the withdrawal of Soviet troops from the GDR, the membership of a united Germany in NATO, and the future limits on Germany's armed forces. When the Two Plus Four process ended, Germany's full sovereignty must be restored.

Gorbachev replied that now was the time to clear up these questions and make decisions about further work. Interestingly, Gorbachev then emphasized the progress in Soviet-American relations. It was especially important, he said, that President Bush had decided to strengthen U.S.-Soviet ties. The closeness of the chancellor to the American administration was very important. He was disturbed, he said, that the Americans had thought at first that the USSR "may be thinking about dislodging the U.S. from Europe. In a meeting with Bush I stated firmly that the presence of U.S. forces in Europe is stabilizing." Kohl then praised Bush's part in orchestrating the NATO and G-7 summits. Washington had no misgivings about progress in German-Soviet relations. It must be very clear that good German-Soviet connections were linked to good ties with America.

Gorbachev agreed that NATO had moved toward becoming a more political alliance. "Now the political context is better than two to three months ago," Gorbachev said. "The present transformative movement of NATO, the strengthening accent on the political sphere of activities. In London a large step was taken on the road to throwing off the chains of the past." The same was true for the declarations of the West German government and the chancellor. Kohl had led the German people step by step toward solving their problems. What had happened in the past could not be forgotten, but now it was possible to change things for the better.

Gorbachev then gave Kohl a paper titled "Reflections on the Content of a Treaty of Partnership and Cooperation between the USSR and Germany," which addressed the planned bilateral treaty. Then Gorbachev turned to the question of Two Plus Four issues and, without further ado, delivered the decisive concessions that would move the talks forward.

First, he said, a united Germany should be made up only of the FRG, GDR, and Berlin within their current borders. Second, Germany would have to renew its renunciation of nuclear, biological, and chemical weapons. Gorbachev knew that Kohl already accepted this. Third, the military structures of NATO should not be extended to the territory of the GDR. Transitional arrangements would have to be made for a temporary Soviet troop presence. Last, Four Power rights would end.

Kohl quickly asked whether Germany, at the time of unity, would be fully sovereign. That was obvious, Gorbachev replied. But an agreement needed to be reached to allow Soviet forces to stay in Germany for a "three to four year period." Kohl agreed.

On the key question of NATO membership for a united Germany, Gorbachev made it clear that, de jure, the question was simple. De facto it was more complicated because NATO authority ("Geltungsbereich") should not be extended to the territory of the GDR. Gorbachev said: "A unified Germany will be a member of NATO. De facto the former territory of the GDR will not be a sphere of NATO activity as long as Soviet forces are located there. The sovereignty of a unified Germany in any case will not be in doubt." The leaders agreed again that a transitional stationing of Soviet forces for three or four years would not be a problem. Kohl offered West German assistance in helping the soldiers return to the Soviet Union and adjust to civilian life.

In this way—matter-of-factly and without fanfare—the Soviet leader agreed to German membership in NATO. Kohl showed no visible reaction. But Teltschik wrote later that his pen was flying over the paper and he had to tell himself to try to concentrate, to get every word the translator was saying. But he knew that there was no misunderstanding.

Then came what Teltschik called Gorbachev's "second surprise": the Soviets were ready to terminate Four Power rights immediately on concluding a final settlement in the Two Plus Four talks. Soviet troop stationing rights for a further three or four years would be addressed in a separate agreement.

To ensure that there was no misunderstanding Kohl summarized what he had heard, and Gorbachev recapitulated his position point by point. The meeting ended after nearly two hours of talks. As Teltschik wrote in his diary: "The breakthrough is accomplished! What a sensation! We had not expected such clear promises from Gorbachev. All the signals were certainly positive, but who had predicted such a result? For the Chancellor this conversation is an unbelievable triumph." Kohl gave few overt clues to his feelings, letting the mask slip only in a long look at Teltschik that revealed his satisfaction.

The two leaders then were joined by their ministers, who had been holding their own parallel discussions. Gorbachev announced that the day's meeting was extraordinary and would have an important place in the history of the bilateral relations between the two countries. He now relaxed and talked about the situation in the Soviet Union for the first time that day. The party congress had, he declared, been extraordinarily important, not just for the Soviet Union but for Europe and the entire world. The coming weeks would see decisions leading the USSR toward a market economy. The prime minister would present a plan to the Supreme Soviet in September. The summer months would be full of activity, including preparation of an all-Union treaty.

Gorbachev also made his first mention of economic matters. The DM 5 billion credit had come at the right time. Kohl commented that the whole morning's conversation had gone extremely well. It was a historic moment in world politics.

Gorbachev had not pressed Kohl for more money as part of the deal. But in separate discussions his deputy prime minister, Stepan Sitaryan, had raised the issue of aid with Kohl's finance minister, Theo Waigel, and got nowhere. Waigel made it "unmistakably clear" that the FRG would pay nothing beyond the DM 5 billion credit agreed to in May. More aid would have to come from concerted international action, screened through the IMF process set in motion at the G-7 summit in Houston. Sitaryan complained that the IMF would be too slow; the USSR had a "mountain" of foreign debts and an immediate need for billions of dollars. Waigel did not budge, though Sitaryan continued to press the issue throughout Kohl's visit.[22]

Gorbachev invited his guests to lunch. The atmosphere was convivial, with due recognition paid to the estimable qualities of Russian vodka and German beer. Tribute was also offered to German footballers. Gorbachev and Ryzhkov expressed gratitude that the FRG had started to pick up the GDR's old financial obligations in hosting the hundreds of thousands of Soviet troops stationed there. Lunch was followed by a brief press conference, where the statements were upbeat but vague. Then the Germans left for the airport.[23]

After a two-hour flight the Germans arrived in Stavropol in the Caucasus. They were taken to the seat of the republic's government, where Gorbachev had worked for nine and a half years. Gorbachev gave a guided tour, showing his old office. Reminders of the Great Patriotic War were everywhere—in a monument in the square outside, in the group of veterans Gorbachev and Kohl met with as they strolled outside.[24] Gorbachev recounted how he had first met Shevardnadze in Stavropol in 1979, and how they had agreed on the need to work together to rescue their country. This was especially clear to them after the invasion of Afghanistan. Out of this time, he said, perestroika was born.

Then the leaders were convoyed back to the airport to board helicopters for their next destination, in the Caucasian countryside. Farmers and their wives came to meet the men in suits as they descended from their helicopters, bringing the traditional greeting of bread and salt. Gorbachev showed Kohl the proper way to tear off a piece of bread, salt it, and eat it. Both leaders chatted with the farmers for half an hour and then took off again. At sunset they arrived at a hunting lodge in the mountains. There Raisa Gorbachev was waiting for them, picking flowers. Everyone changed into casual clothes and surveyed the beautiful countryside.

Dinner conversation touched on light politics and anecdotes. Gorbachev recalled that when the Germans had occupied his village, a friendly soldier named Hans had stayed in his parents' house. After the Germans left, Stalin's police arrested and deported the village elders as collaborators. Gorbachev also told a joke: There was a long line in front of a grocery store in Moscow.

A man waiting in line became furious and rushed up to the proprietor, saying that he wanted to kill the man responsible. The proprietor said, "The line for that is on the other side of the store, but it's a lot longer than the one here."[25]

During their travels Gorbachev had asked Kohl privately how much he was willing to reduce the Bundeswehr in a united Germany. As planned, Kohl gave him the figure of 370,000. Gorbachev said that he had expected a greater reduction. Kohl argued that he needed an army of at least this size in order to sustain conscription and avoid relying on a purely professional soldiery. Kohl later thought that this argument had clinched the issue.[26]

Late that night, after the drinks and dinner, the Germans gathered in a billiard room at the lodge to talk about the day's events. Kohl joined them and finally told them all what had happened in Moscow earlier in the day. The basis for agreement was at hand. The group moved to another room. The chancellor told them that Gorbachev had made it clear that Germany could remain in NATO. The precedents of the 1950s were in his thoughts. This would not be the tradeoff of reunification for neutrality that Stalin had proposed in 1952, he said. "This was a price I was not ready to pay!" Much still remained to be done. But Kohl no longer bothered to conceal his delight. "Never in my life have I had to work so hard," he said. "But never in my life have I also been so happy."[27]

On Monday morning, July 16, Kohl reviewed Teltschik's draft statement. Then the group gathered at a long table.[28] The leaders moved quickly to substance.[29] The agreements from the previous day's private conversation were reviewed. Then Genscher intervened. The final settlement of the Two Plus Four had to be completed before the CSCE summit, a choice of alliance had to be made, and it had to be clear that the Germans wanted full membership in NATO. Gorbachev expressed himself plainly. If a united Germany had full sovereignty, it obviously could choose its alliance membership. That meant it could choose NATO, but there was no need to emphasize this point. Soviet troops were to stay in eastern Germany during a transition period, but this would be regulated by a treaty with the Germans, and the Soviet military presence would not call into question the full sovereignty of a united Germany. Genscher recapitulated what he had heard. Gorbachev agreed, repeating it point by point—as he had with Kohl in their smaller meeting the day before.

Gorbachev repeated that he would expect NATO "structures" not to be extended to the former territory of the GDR for as long as Soviet troops were stationed there. This would make it easier for the Soviet people to understand that the Germans had the right to choose their alliance, and that NATO was their choice. Kohl and Genscher were insistent that these restrictions would last only so long as Soviet troops remained in Germany. After the Soviet troops left, Germany could make its own sovereign decisions. Everyone agreed. Genscher also made it clear that there could not be different security zones for the two parts of a united Germany. NATO's security guarantees under articles 5 and 6 of the Washington treaty would apply to the entire territory of a united Germany. This point was independent from the issue of extending the stationing of NATO troops to all of Germany. But he and Kohl agreed that while Soviet troops were still stationed in the former GDR, Bundeswehr units there would not be integrated into NATO.

As for the length of the transition period during which Soviet forces could remain in Germany, Gorbachev spoke of five to seven years. Kohl reminded Gorbachev that the previous day he had suggested three to four years, a period Kohl considered more realistic. Gorbachev appeared to be satisfied.

The two sides then turned to the FRG assumption of East German economic commitments, especially for the support of Soviet troops in the former GDR. There was a general discussion of economic opportunities and Kohl's hopes for further support of reform. Gorbachev agreed that Prime Minister Ryzhkov would write to the Germans about the GDR's financial obligations. A settlement seemed possible. Kohl said that he would be ready for such discussions. Both sides agreed that there should be two treaties, one to govern the temporary presence of Soviet troops and the other to settle the financial arrangements for their departure.

Moving on to the issue of future troop limits for a united Germany, Shevardnadze immediately proposed the 350,000 figure, which he may have got earlier from Genscher. Then Genscher explained his government's position: the Germans would declare during the CFE talks in Vienna the limit they would accept in the follow-on negotiations once the other participating states accepted similar limits. He repeated the number Kohl had stipulated: 370,000. Kohl added that he expected that reductions to this level would be complete by the time the Soviets withdrew their forces from Germany, that is, in three or four years. Gorbachev had been persuaded by Kohl the day before to accept the figure of 370,000, and the Soviet leader declared his agreement.

After a placid discussion of the border question, the group turned to the issue of their statement to the press. Kohl summarized the main results using the press conference statement Teltschik had drafted the night before. Gorbachev agreed. Kohl then invited Gorbachev to make a return visit to Germany, and the Soviet president accepted. The two leaders, Gorbachev commented, had come a long way in the past two or three months.

The talks had gone on for four hours. Teltschik was surprised that Gorbachev had been so easily persuaded to allow units of the Bundeswehr to be stationed in the former territory of the GDR immediately after unification and to let these troops be integrated into NATO as soon as the Soviet troops had departed. NATO's security guarantees would cover all of Germany from the day of unification. This, he thought, finally brought the German position back to the original American and FRG Defense Ministry preferences of early February. After the previous day's breakthrough in Moscow, all the outstanding questions about Germany's military status were now clarified. There was no longer any doubt that, on the day of unification, Germany would regain its full sovereignty.

Teltschik thought that it was Gorbachev personally, assisted by Shevardnadze, who had made all the most important decisions. Gorbachev had completely dominated the two days of discussions from the Soviet side, impressing the Germans with his mastery of the issues.[30] But the tenor of the discussions could leave little doubt that Gorbachev had made up his mind how to settle these issues before Kohl's plane landed in Moscow. There were no serious disagreements, and the Soviets had made no significant new requests. The Soviet leadership, recognizing that the final offer of the Western alliance was already on the table, had decided that they had no choice but to accept it—graciously and without acrimony. When Teltschik broke away from the party to put the finishing touches on the press statement, his draft, prepared the previous evening, needed few changes.

The group moved a few hundred yards away to the Zheleznovodsk sanatorium, where the press had gathered. Gorbachev briefly opened the news conference. Then Kohl delivered his statement.[31] He noted that the two countries had agreed to a treaty governing their future political relations and observed that all parties understood that the Two Plus Four talks must be finished in time to present the results to the November CSCE summit in Paris. He then itemized eight points of agreement:

1. A unified Germany would comprise the Federal Republic of Germany, the German Democratic Republic, and Berlin.
2. Once unification was accomplished, the rights and responsibilities of the Four Powers would be completely terminated; a unified Germany would enjoy full and unrestricted sovereignty.
3. A unified Germany, exercising its unrestricted sovereignty freely and by itself, could decide which alliances to belong to, if any, in accord with the CSCE Final Act. It was the view of the government of the Federal Republic of Germany that the unified Germany should be a member of the NATO alliance. Kohl was sure that this was in accordance with the view of the German Democratic Republic.
4. The unified Germany and the Soviet Union would conclude a bilateral

treaty for carrying out the withdrawal of Soviet troops from the German Democratic Republic within three to four years. At the same time, a transitional treaty would cover the consequences of the introduction of the deutsche mark in the German Democratic Republic.

5. For as long as Soviet troops remained stationed in the former territory of the German Democratic Republic, NATO structures would not be extended to this part of Germany. The immediate application of articles 5 and 6 of the NATO treaty would remain in effect. Unintegrated units of the Bundeswehr—that is, units of the Territorial Defense—could be stationed immediately after unification in the territory of the German Democratic Republic and Berlin.

6. For as long as Soviet troops remained in the former territory of the German Democratic Republic, troops from the three Western powers would remain in Berlin. The FRG government would seek to conclude agreements with the three Western governments to regulate the stationing of their troops in Berlin.

7. The Federal Republic of Germany, at the time of the Vienna negotiations, would declare its commitment to reduce the level of armed forces of a united Germany to 370,000 over a period of three to four years, the reduction to come into force the day the first Vienna agreement took effect.

8. A unified Germany would renounce the production, storage, and use of nuclear, biological, and chemical weapons and remain a member of the Non-Proliferation treaty.

Gorbachev then delivered a more extensive statement, describing the warm atmosphere of the Soviet-German talks, and paying particular attention to the "stimulus from London," where NATO had taken a "historic turn." He said, "I should say it straight, that were it not for this second element it would have been difficult for Herr Chancellor and I both yesterday and today to work effectively in a spirit of mutual understanding and arrive at what he has already said." The press conference over, the Germans flew home.

"Really, It's Like Heaven and Earth"

The news from the Caucasus was met around the world with surprise and relief. Allied leaders issued welcoming statements. On his first day back in Bonn, Kohl briefed his cabinet, phoned Bush to brief him personally, and sent letters reporting on the meetings to Thatcher, Mitterrand, and Andreotti.

The Americans were as surprised by Kohl's announcement as Teltschik had been when Gorbachev made the concessions in Moscow. Until the press beamed his words across the world, Kohl and his party had been unable to communicate what had happened in Moscow and the Caucasus to anyone in the West, even their own government. The Soviet-German itinerary had taken the Germans to remote locations during their first day of talks, so that as a practical matter Kohl and Genscher were not able to communicate securely.

Not understanding this, American officials were annoyed that they had not been informed. But the agreement was a good one. The Germans had done precisely what they had told the president they would do. Yet American reporters traveling with Baker to Paris could observe firsthand the surprise of U.S. officials and quickly but erroneously concluded that the Germans had left Washington behind in striking a deal with the Russians.[32]

The next ministerial meeting of the Two Plus Four in Paris, which began little more than a day after the Kohl-Gorbachev talks ended, was anticlimactic. Shevardnadze and Genscher reported on the agreements reached during their just concluded talks in the Soviet Union. Shevardnadze said that the problem now was to turn the agreement on principles into a Two Plus Four document ready for approval at the next meeting of ministers—to be held in Moscow less than two months later, on September 12.

The only unhappy minister was the East German, Markus Meckel. Meckel complained that several questions still needed to be settled between the two Germanys. The East Germans were furious because they had little information about the Soviet-German talks. They had received only a hasty debriefing from Kvitsinsky and practically no information from the West Germans. Meckel had worked out ambitious plans for East German initiatives and activity in the Two Plus Four, based on the SPD-East's ideas for resolving German unity, such as expelling all nuclear weapons from Germany. That balloon was now punctured. As one participant in the East German team bitterly recalled, "The objective of running an independent East German foreign policy ended with the agreement in the Caucasus."[33]

When ministers reconvened in the afternoon, they welcomed a special guest, Polish foreign minister Skubiszewski. Skubiszewski had already met with Genscher, so there were no real substantive disputes between the FRG and Poland. The paragraphs of the Two Plus Four agreement concerning the border issue had been agreed upon in June. Poland no longer insisted on concluding a Polish-German treaty before unification. Genscher promised that the FRG would sign a bilateral treaty with Poland as soon as possible after unification. The Poles were content.[34] The ministers then held their press conference, with Skubiszewski invited to speak first in order to declare his satisfaction with the session's results.[35]

Baker and Shevardnadze met the next morning for more than two hours.[36]

They relaxed a bit, and Shevardnadze offered the most detailed explanation he would ever give Baker of how he and Gorbachev had decided to move when they did to settle the German question. Shevardnadze stressed his appreciation of U.S. efforts to obtain the London declaration. Without that "one declaration it would have been a very difficult thing for us to take our decisions on Germany," he said. Those statements had allowed the USSR to adopt a new policy. "If you compare what we're saying to you and to Kohl now, with our Berlin document [of June 22]," said Shevardnadze, "it's like day and night. Really, it's like heaven and earth . . . The London session and our Party Congress is what made this possible." Before the Congress it would have been impossible to speak of terminating Four Power rights, or to make new decisions on Germany's alliance status, or even to make the decision to withdraw Soviet troops from Germany. Shevardnadze admitted that the Soviets knew before the congress that they would have to withdraw their forces from Germany, but "the balance of forces and the balance of senior political figures was very different before the Party Congress." But even after the congress it would not have been easy to move if it had not been for "the London statements." He told Baker: "You've really made an effort to take into account all our problems and our concerns, and that's what made so much possible."[37]

Baker then explained how the United States had managed the preparation of the London declaration in order to keep it from being watered down. He described the unprecedented procedures and recounted how he had used Shevardnadze's own statements on the importance of the summit document in order to move his allied colleagues. "We wanted it to be a hard-hitting document that you could use, and use in a sense during the Party Congress," he said. Naturally the United States had watched the outcome of the congress with interest and appreciation. Baker and President Bush had especially noted Shevardnadze's significant speech. "The bottom line, the President and I have felt for over a year, [is] that you and President Gorbachev have a vision and a sense of history that corresponds to ours," Baker told him. "This is an historic opportunity to bring about the reconciliation of the East and West— an opportunity never presented before." They had already seized this opportunity and Baker hoped they would continue to make use of it. Shevardnadze agreed, harking back to the vision of the future both men had shared at their meetings in Wyoming in the fall of 1989. He gave credit to the Germans, too, for understanding Soviet concerns. The handling of the Bundeswehr issue had been especially important.

Baker expressed satisfaction that the U.S. approach to the recent meetings had helped make it possible for the two sides to move forward. "Frankly," he confided, "I was quite worried, notwithstanding what you told me, when you tabled that paper that you gave . . . in Berlin." It had seemed then that the political constraints might prove too great. It was important to keep moving quickly. To be sure, President Bush was enjoying a very long period of public approval. But, "in the nature of things, that's not likely to continue forever," said Baker. Domestic concerns would rise to the fore. So he urged continued rapid movement "between now and the end of the year." Of course, Baker could not know how prescient his prediction would be. He did not know that two weeks later Iraq would invade Kuwait, or that by the end of the year Shevardnadze would no longer be foreign minister.

Shevardnadze, for the moment, was equally inclined to think about the longer term. He saw no problem with the current German leadership. It was the future leaders, five or ten years hence, that concerned him. "In principle, we have decided we will build a new relationship with a unified Germany," he said. But in his view the quality of U.S.-Soviet relations would remain the key security assurance for his country. The two men then reviewed specific issues, from ideas for technical assistance for the Soviet economy to plans for completing the work in the CFE talks.

Preparation of a Two Plus Four settlement document accelerated. The Two Plus Four political directors gathered in Bonn on July 19 and agreed on where and how all disputed issues were to be addressed. Although the East Germans still lacked instructions on many issues and were delaying work, the officials were nonetheless able to decide which issues should be handled by sovereign German decision, which in the final settlement document, and which in some other forum. The scope of the final settlement was thereby narrowed, as the West had hoped. Final negotiation of the text of the agreement was planned for the first week of September. All parties expected the document to be ready for approval at the next meeting of Two Plus Four ministers, to be held in Moscow the following week. Genscher and Shevardnadze spoke to each other by telephone in late July. Shevardnadze had made clear his desire to wrap up quickly all remaining issues related to German unity.[38]

The Western countries soon had reason to be doubly grateful that the most difficult decisions were behind them. On August 1 Iraq invaded Kuwait and the Persian Gulf crisis began, dominating the policy agenda of leaders around the world. As Teltschik later noted:

The immediate USA reaction and its energetic engagement make it clear how happy we can be that the most important foreign policy questions linked to German unity have been clarified. In the first half of the year the energies of the world powers were concentrated practically exclusively on

Germany. It was our luck that no other decisive event diverted the attention of our American partner. I ask myself if we would have been so fortunate as to so smoothly get through the necessary decisions at the American-Soviet summit, the special summit of NATO and the world economic summit, if the Gulf conflict had begun about two months earlier.[39]

On August 10 the NATO foreign ministers gathered in Brussels for a special meeting. This time their topic was the war in the Gulf, not Germany or the future of the alliance. Near the end of the ministerial Genscher reported to his colleagues that the date for German unification would have to be advanced to October owing to the rapidly deteriorating economic conditions in the GDR. No one even commented on his remarks; the other ministers were too preoccupied with the new crisis. Bush telephoned Kohl twice in August; both times the only topic was the Gulf crisis. "How much things have changed," Teltschik wrote after one of these talks, "not one more word in the discussion on German questions!"[40]

The Germans were drawn to problems closer to home. Although individual East German consumers were now better off, the economy of the GDR had been crippled by monetary union. East German consumers were buying Western goods, so GDR manufacturers had lost their domestic market. The GDR's most important trading partner was the Soviet Union. But the USSR could not pay for East German imports once they were priced in hard currency. Complete collapse would follow quickly unless the GDR could be absorbed rapidly into the West German network of social and economic assistance.

Pressure mounted for quicker unification. The SPD-East began pressing for the GDR to unite with the FRG in mid-September, if not sooner. Soberer heads, including Genscher, made it clear that accession had to wait at least for conclusion and ratification of the second state treaty on the terms of political unification, allow time for re-creation of the five former Länder, and await signature of a Two Plus Four accord. The Germans hoped that all these events could occur in September, with unification taking place the following month. All-German elections were still scheduled for December.[41]

The second state treaty, or the unification treaty, had proven to be a more complex undertaking than the Germans had realized when negotiations began in early July. Bonn's leaders at the talks were interior minister Wolfgang Schäuble and Rudolf Seiters from the Chancellery. The East German side was led by Günter Krause from Lothar de Maizière's office.[42]

The takeover of a country is no simple matter. The major issues in the inter-German talks on the second state treaty included:

- the timing and manner of article 23 accession (which would affect the timing of all-German elections)
- financial rights and distribution of tax revenue among and to the new East German Länder (an especially thorny issue since money given to poor West German Länder might now be diverted to the even poorer eastern German ones);
- transitional legislation on social issues such as abortion rights (East German law had been much more permissive)
- cataloguing East Germany's thousands of international obligations and establishing which of these would be assumed by the FRG[43]
- deciding whether to locate the capital of a united Germany in Berlin or in Bonn
- setting guidelines for adjudicating thousands of decades-old claims of West German citizens to property in the GDR
- arranging trusteeship for East German state enterprises destined for privatization
- application of European Community law to the GDR
- a host of other questions ranging from the administration of East German universities to language protecting the rights of the GDR's small Sorbian minority.[44]

But despite the number of issues to be settled, the unification treaty was completed on schedule at the end of August after four rounds of East-West German talks. What remained was to complete the documents that would establish the international status of a united Germany. The Two Plus Four document, of course, still needed to be concluded. But first the Germans had to tie up some loose ends, in particular the bilateral agreements with the Soviets and with their Western allies to end the legacy of postwar occupation.

Money for the Soviet Union

Bonn had promised to negotiate a new treaty of friendship between a united Germany and the Soviet Union, a document that would symbolize a new era of cooperation between the two historic adversaries. The idea had originated in the Chancellery, and Kohl had followed through on that promise when he visited the USSR. He had thought of this treaty almost as a personal agreement between the two leaders, and suggested that it be negotiated by Teltschik and Chernyayev. Chernyayev, wondering if Kohl might have some sort of "Genscher complex," promptly passed the matter along to Shevardnadze and

Kvitsinsky. The details of the treaty quickly engaged Bonn's Foreign Ministry too, with Kastrup taking the lead.[45]

There were actually treaties on three different subjects to be negotiated between the Germans and the Soviets, with the FRG acting as the agent for a united Germany. First there was the general treaty on future political relations with the USSR, the treaty Kohl and Teltschik had emphasized. But there was also a need to agree on the disposition of the GDR's economic obligations to the Soviet Union, and for a treaty governing the status of Soviet forces and their withdrawal from Germany, as well as the "transitional" financial arrangements for these forces. The West Germans and Soviets had about six weeks to complete all of this work, since they wanted these accords to be ready by the time the Two Plus Four settlement was approved at the September ministerial meeting in Moscow.

The general treaty proved to be the easiest. Its terms set a program for annual German-Soviet summits and biennial meetings of foreign and defense ministers. Other articles covered everything from cultural cooperation to the maintenance of Soviet war monuments. Far and away the most significant article was the "nonaggression commitment," article 3, in which both countries promised never to use their armed forces against each other or any other state "except for the purpose of individual or collective self-defense." And they pledged never, under any circumstances, to be the first to use armed force against another state. Both countries also promised not to aid any state that had committed aggression against the other. Nothing in the treaty undermined Germany's established commitments to NATO strategy or force deployments. Indeed, article 21 specified that "the present Treaty will not affect the rights and obligations arising from existing bilateral and multilateral agreements which the two sides have concluded with other States."[46]

The general treaty therefore served its purpose of providing a symbolic break with the past, though it broke no important new ground. The United States was never anxious about the content of this treaty. While in Berlin in early September to conclude the preparation of the Two Plus Four settlement, Zoellick and his delegation had actually declined a West German briefing on these bilateral negotiations because they were short of time, trusted German intentions, and foresaw no worrisome issues. The general treaty was finally signed by Germany and the USSR on November 9, as a capstone for Gorbachev's visit to the newly united German nation.[47]

It was more difficult to dispose of East Germany's many economic obligations toward Moscow. The USSR and the GDR were bound by numerous published and unpublished treaties, protocols, and constitutional documents. As with most trade in COMECON, the Eastern bloc trade organization, the two governments had been obliged to negotiate terms for all major commercial exchanges since the value of their money and the prices of their goods bore no necessary relation to any underlying market reality. These were, in essence, elaborate barter arrangements.

Quite early in the unification process, in order to reassure Moscow, the FRG had pledged to honor the GDR's long-term economic obligations toward Moscow. Only later in 1990, as it explored GDR files with the new government, would Bonn be able to evaluate fully just what these obligations entailed. In June, after initial negotiations in connection with the FRG-GDR monetary union, the West Germans had hoped to maintain deliveries of East German goods, but now priced them in deutsche marks in an attempt to fix some exchange rate between the Western currency and the "transferrable rubles" Moscow used as a medium for some of its foreign exchange. The West Germans hoped that after a couple of years conditions would have evolved enough to allow trade based entirely on market terms. West Germany's costs in maintaining a transitional Soviet troop presence in Germany would, it was hoped, be offset by deliveries of Soviet commodities.[48]

As for the treaty governing the interim stationing and status of Soviet forces in Germany, the most difficult problem here was to fix the financial terms for the transitional support and eventual withdrawal of these troops. In both this agreement and the economic one, the key issues were the amount of money the FRG was prepared to spend in assuming the old East German obligations and resettling the Soviet troops back home.

Kastrup and Kvitsinsky met on August 14–15, Genscher and Shevardnadze on August 16–17, and Waigel and Sitaryan on August 23–24. They had exchanged draft treaties and begun work on the structure of the documents. There would be four treaties in all: the general treaty on political relations, the transition treaty on financial arrangements for withdrawing Soviet forces, a treaty on the trade obligations of the GDR, and a treaty governing the interim status of Soviet forces in the former GDR.

Time pressure became intense. The final scheduling decisions were being made for unification and the all-German elections. But the FRG-Soviet bilateral negotiations began to stall.[49] On August 27 Genscher received a startling letter from Shevardnadze. The Soviet military had apparently declared that it was technically impossible to withdraw their forces from the GDR within three or four years, as Gorbachev had promised. Instead it would take at least five to seven years (the period the Soviets had initially proposed in Stavropol before Kohl reminded Gorbachev of his promise). Shevardnadze acknowledged that a period of three to four years had been agreed to in July, but Gorbachev had linked his promise to getting enough material and financial support for the Soviet forces from the German side. There the German proposals were, according to Shevardnadze, completely insufficient. If a solution could not be found on the issue of support, then the date for withdrawing Soviet troops would have to be changed.

Shevardnadze's letter also listed a series of objections to the security provisions in the general treaty and the economic and financial treaties, and pressed for a number of additional German commitments on security questions in the Two Plus Four settlement document. The Soviet foreign policy and security bureaucracies had clearly caught their breath and decided to weigh in with their demands.

The next day Kvitsinsky met with Teltschik in Bonn. He said that both the union treaty's handling of the nationalities issue and the quarrels over economic reform had placed the Soviet leadership in another critical domestic situation. This was the background for the Soviet stance on the transition treaty. The attitude of the Soviet military was especially critical. There had to be money for transport costs, new housing, and the support of Soviet troops in the GDR. Kvitsinsky also spoke of the need to extend the period of withdrawal to six years.

Feeling the pressure, Kohl met on August 29 with Genscher, Waigel, and economics minister Helmut Haussmann. They believed that the general treaty could be concluded on schedule. But they wondered where in the Federal budget they could find the money for these new demands. Genscher kept up the pressure, reminding the group that the major bilateral issues had to be settled in less than two weeks, by the time of the Moscow Two Plus Four ministerial on September 12. Kohl decided to be generous on the issue of housing construction for returning troops but remain tough on the question of costs so long as they were stationed in Germany. President Bush, meanwhile, was also pressing Kohl for money to help those countries affected by the economic sanctions against Iraq.

As if all this were not enough, the Soviets suddenly delivered a new request for the transfer of subsidized food, like the one Bonn had provided at the beginning of the year. Since the subsidies would be used to purchase produce from East German farmers, and since this produce could not easily be sold in Western markets anyway, the FRG quickly agreed to the new assistance, worth about DM 1 billion (about $600 million), in effect an agricultural subsidy for East German farmers.

Waigel and Sitaryan talked again on September 3–4. The sides were still far apart. Kohl confided his worries to Teltschik on September 5. They both now felt overwhelmed by the scale and complexity of the ongoing negotiations and by the constant time pressure. The general treaty seemed to be under control, with Genscher handling the issues. The economic treaty was initialed by Haussmann and Sitaryan on September 6.

The transition treaty clearly presented the most difficult problem just because of the amounts of money being demanded by the Soviets. On September 5 the new Soviet ambassador to Bonn had spelled out the Soviet requests: DM 3.5 billion for stationing costs; DM 3 billion for transport costs; DM 11.5 billion for building 72,000 houses as well as necessary schools and stores; DM 500 million for retraining; and up to DM 17.5 billion for Soviet-owned real estate in the GDR, a total of DM 36 billion (over $20 billion). These numbers far exceeded the West German planning assumptions in July, when experts from the Finance Ministry, Foreign Ministry, and Chancellery had expected the package to cost DM 1.25 billion in the first year and a total of DM 4.25 billion over the four-year withdrawal period. Now the Soviets were demanding a sum eight times this size, and the Moscow Two Plus Four ministerial was only a week away.[50]

Kohl phoned Gorbachev on September 7, their first direct conversation in the nearly two months since their meetings in the Soviet Union.[51] Both were satisfied with progress on the general treaty and looked forward to signing it after unification. But the treaties governing the financial arrangements for Soviet forces and their withdrawal still presented problems. Kohl made an offer: a total of DM 8 billion, concentrated on housing construction (Bonn officials expected these contracts to go to East German firms, so at least this money would come back to Germany).

Gorbachev, who had been so friendly in Moscow and the Caucasus, was now stern and unyielding. Kohl's figures, he said, would lead to a dead end. His accounting showed that the housing and necessary infrastructure for returning soldiers alone would cost DM 11 billion, and the transport and maintenance costs had to be added in as well. All these matters were linked inextricably to one another. Then Gorbachev delivered a hard punch. He made it clear to Kohl that the final settlement in the Two Plus Four talks could not be concluded without results in the bilateral negotiations and without a solution to the financial questions. The Soviet Union, which had seemed to be out of options in July, had suddenly found a new approach. Moscow would hold the German settlement hostage, count on the time pressures on Kohl, and make a final pitch for financial assistance of all kinds.

Kohl hoped that, with goodwill, the two sides could find a way out. Gorbachev replied that he found the situation very alarming. Kohl pointed out that he was making good on the new agreement to deliver food supplies and consumer goods.[52] He urged Gorbachev to join him in trying to solve these problems and speak again about them on Monday, September 10.

Teltschik describes this conversation as "really dramatic." He was surprised at how hard Gorbachev pushed Kohl for further financial assistance. The Soviet leader was "visibly disappointed" with Kohl's DM 8 billion offer, and the Germans understood perfectly that he had linked this issue to the completion of the critical diplomacy during the coming week. Teltschik, shaken, was now sure that "our offer could not be the last word."

Intensive negotiations followed over the weekend in Moscow between Waigel and Sitaryan. Sitaryan had named a total figure of DM 16–18 billion. The Soviet numbers still seemed extremely high, and Waigel proposed a total figure no greater than DM 11–12 billion. When Gorbachev and Kohl spoke again on Monday, September 10, the haggling resumed. Kohl referred to the possibility of future economic assistance to the USSR. Gorbachev replied candidly that the matter had less to do with help for the Soviet Union than with the process of German unification. He was fighting many battles with his government, his military, and his financial officials. He called for agreement on a sum of DM 15 billion.[53]

Kohl saw that he had to make a decision. He offered to supplement the standing German offer of DM 12 billion with an interest-free credit of DM 3 billion. (The West German Finance Ministry had already prepared for this fallback position.) Gorbachev was happy. Horst Köhler of the Finance Ministry flew to Moscow to work out the details. Kohl called Bush the next day to brief him on the outcome of these discussions. He had not asked the American president to intervene with Gorbachev or to prepare options for a response if the Soviets carried out their threat of suspending progress in the Two Plus Four talks. Overwhelmed by events and eager to achieve a quick settlement with Moscow, the West Germans did not mount effective resistance when, finally, Moscow named a price.[54]

With the basic agreement on financial issues in place, the last remaining bilateral problem between the FRG and USSR was to complete the treaty on the terms for interim stationing and withdrawal of Soviet troops in Germany. This treaty, initialed on September 27, was not particularly controversial and achieved the principal German objectives. Withdrawal was to be complete in four years, by the end of 1994. Soviet military activities were circumscribed, and German sovereignty over all of eastern Germany was firmly established. The Germans resigned themselves to the need for significant environmental cleanup efforts at vacated Soviet installations, with the treaty urging only that Moscow "avoid further damage." A German-Soviet commission was established to resolve disputes over the treaty's implementation.[55]

Future Relations with the Americans

As the Germans hastily forged the basis for postunification relations with the Soviet Union, they confronted questions of future dealings with their allies, too.

In the aftermath of the NATO summit in London and Kohl's successful visit to the Soviet Union, West German leaders felt a sense of deep gratitude to the United States and warmly appreciated Washington's role in the achievement of German unity. Genscher prepared an article, published in August, which he circulated in late July to all German media and foreign newspaper offices in Germany. The article, titled "The Americans and Us," praised the American nation and its current leaders in extravagant terms. "Never has America's influence on developments in Europe been as great as it is today," the article concluded, "not in the sense of domination but of partnership . . . The attitude of the United States during this historic period is the crowning of the German-American friendship, which will endure. Thank you America."[56]

The United States had an early chance to test these good feelings. There were over two dozen significant bilateral issues for American-German relations presented by the coming unification of Germany. For example:

- Allied rights to station troops in Germany under the Presence Convention of 1954 expired, under the convention's terms, with a German "peace settlement." Germany would have to determine a new basis for permitting a continued allied military presence, and decide whether to amend the agreement regulating the status of these forces on German soil. Other changes would be needed in NATO's Air Defense Identification Zone for Germany and the Four Power military liaison missions that operated throughout the country.
- The basis for the allied troop presence in Berlin had an independent source: sovereign allied control over the city. When this expired, a new basis for the continuing presence of such forces would have to be agreed to with Germany. Allied troops' access to Berlin, their status, their training rights, and their command structure would all need to be redesigned, while the costs of the presence would have to be handled on an entirely new basis.
- U.S., British, and French airlines had enjoyed special aviation rights in Berlin under the occupation regime. These rights, along with special inter-German service rights, would also have to be renegotiated,

along with new mechanisms for handling air traffic control in the city.

- Various property claims from U.S. citizens and the international Jewish community were pending against the GDR. These needed to be settled, along with various property issues relating to Berlin and the future of entities such as the RIAS (Radio in the American Sector) broadcasting station and the Berlin Document Center archives of Nazi-era material.

The United States formally requested bilateral negotiation of these issues at the beginning of August, and the British and French made similar requests.[57]

The most important issue for the United States was to ensure a smooth transition in the stationing rights and status of allied forces in western Germany and Berlin. The German public's views about the continued presence of U.S. and other allied forces on their soil were mixed. There was solid support for a continued presence, but this support could be undermined by noisy disagreements during a negotiation about continued rights or status. U.S. officials agreed that extension or renewal of past agreements would be the best and easiest course.[58]

American (and British) officials were therefore dismayed when West German lawyers, at a late July meeting of Western legal experts, offered a different approach to the stationing and status issues. These officials proposed a draft document that would curtail the existing NATO Status of Forces Agreement (SOFA) and supplemental agreement covering the status of allied forces. The West German lawyers wanted to negotiate an entirely new stationing treaty. The U.S. chargé in Bonn, George Ward, promptly conveyed Washington's concerns about opening this "Pandora's box" to Genscher's top aide, Frank Elbe.[59]

Elbe explained that he, Kastrup, and their legal adviser preferred to make as few changes as possible in the documents governing the allied military presence. But the SPD and the Greens party might press for a different policy. In 1989 the SPD had announced with some fanfare the positing of a "Great Questionnaire" about allied basing rights. Elbe promised to look into the matter further. The United States also determined that the FRG Defense Ministry preferred the simple approach, at least to get through the period surrounding unification. Nevertheless, the lawyers in the Foreign Ministry continued to pursue an entirely new agreement, "free of any elements of old thinking." Separate agreements would be worked out with each of the six allied countries with troops stationed in Germany, and then each of these interim agreements would have to be ratified by the West German parliament—all in little more than a month. Working-level officials at the Chancellery were aware of the Foreign Ministry contretemps but seemed to have no particular opinion about it. As details of the FRG legal position became clearer, the American embassy in Bonn grew alarmed.

On August 16 Baker wrote to Genscher, asking him to extend the existing agreements with a clean multilateral solution rather than negotiate a new series of bilateral accords. He also hoped for rapid movement on a stationing agreement for allied forces in Berlin.[60] Once Genscher became involved, his positive feelings toward the United States seemed to carry more than enough weight. The obstacles began to melt away. Bonn agreed to all of Baker's requests. The United States sent a negotiating team, headed by Ambassador Nelson Ledsky, to work out the details. As new problems arose at the working level, Baker intervened to straighten the problems out directly with Genscher. Kastrup was already uncomfortable with the approach his Foreign Ministry lawyers had been taking, and Genscher delivered on his promises to settle the issues along the lines he had agreed to with Baker.[61]

The United States then successfully negotiated three agreements with the FRG during the next two weeks: a renewal of the 1954 Presence Convention providing a legal basis for stationing of all allied troops in the FRG; a new stationing agreement for British, French, and American troops in Berlin after Four Power rights ended; and an agreement covering the de facto extension of the NATO SOFA to the former GDR.[62]

Other bilateral issues were settled more easily and less formally. The Americans needed assurances that a united Germany would address the outstanding claims of Jewish victims from the Nazi era and of American property owners against the former GDR. A private agreement between Lufthansa and Pan American Airways helped ease resolution of the civil aviation issues. Appropriate letters and assurances were attached to the final settlement when it was later presented for ratification to the U.S. Senate.[63]

A Final Settlement

During August the Western allies worked from an American outline to draft a final document. The Soviets first began to exchange views about the text of a settlement with the West Germans, in Moscow on August 16–17, in addition to the talks on the four bilateral treaties then being concluded. Kastrup and Kvitsinsky followed up with in-depth talks in Bonn on August

27–28.[64] Negotiation of the settlement document took place in four days of intense discussions among Two Plus Four political directors in East Berlin at the beginning of September. Two issues emerged as especially difficult.[65]

1. *How and when could NATO "structures" enter the former GDR?* All the Two Plus Four countries had now agreed that Germany would be a full member of NATO but that, at least while Soviet troops remained, NATO "structures" would not extend to the former GDR. What exactly did this mean? The West Germans, apparently after discussing the issue with the Soviets during the Genscher-Shevardnadze meetings on August 16–17 in Moscow, first proposed a blanket prohibition on any movement of American, British, or French forces into the former GDR. The other allies considered this language too confining, given possible contingencies for NATO defense in a crisis, or in maneuvers and exercises or troop transits. The West interpreted the Caucasus press statement as a limit only on the stationing of foreign forces, not on all temporary movements. NATO aircraft, for example, would certainly be flying over eastern German airspace and helping to defend it.[66]

The allied countries agreed that they would not move their nuclear weapons east into the former GDR. This was a symbolic concession, since only German forces would be permanently deployed in eastern Germany, and the Germans had already forsworn any possession of nuclear weapons. The Soviets, in the East Berlin settlement talks, pressed to exclude all dual-use weapon systems, effectively excluding anything that could fire or launch a nuclear weapon. This position was plainly unacceptable to the West, since it would keep aircraft or artillery from being deployed in the former GDR. The Americans suggested that the dual-use systems be handled as they were in the CFE treaty, but the Soviets balked. Bondarenko complained that this would violate the understanding reached in the Caucasus. Kastrup said that he had been at those meetings (Bondarenko had not) and that the dual-capable issue had not even come up. Kastrup checked with the Chancellery, which confirmed that there had been no discussion of the matter. Bondarenko insisted that the question had been settled in the Caucasus. The political directors were stalemated.

2. *Handling future limits on German armed forces.* Gorbachev and Shevardnadze had agreed that future German armed forces would be limited to 370,000, but this limit would be codified only after other European countries had accepted similarly binding limits on their armed forces. The Germans would promise unilaterally to reduce their forces to this level. The question that remained was where and how the Germans would make this promise.

The Soviets still wanted the commitment to be sealed somehow in the current CFE treaty. Shevardnadze had raised this point with Baker when the two ministers met in Siberia at the beginning of August. Baker again wanted to keep this German undertaking from impeding the completion of the CFE treaty. The Germans would make their pledge separate from the treaty itself but connected to it—just as the Americans and Soviets had exchanged a reciprocal pledge in February about limits on their forces stationed in Europe.

Shevardnadze wanted the matter to be raised in the CFE setting in some way. Baker was satisfied with any solution that did not put the issue in the treaty. The NATO allies worked out a common approach for Genscher to present to Shevardnadze in Moscow. Genscher and the East German foreign minister would go to Vienna and, at a CFE negotiating session, make unilateral statements about their future plans. This took place on August 30. The East German governing coalition had broken up and de Maizière had personally taken over the Foreign Ministry, so Genscher, accompanied by de Maizière, stated in Vienna that the FRG undertook within three or four years to reduce the personnel strength of its armed forces to 370,000. Genscher stated that Bonn "assumed" that in future conventional arms control negotiations other countries in Europe would make similar commitments to limit their personnel strength. That pledge was repeated in the final settlement as a quotation of the Germans' promise, with the provision that the other signatories only "take note" of Genscher's statement. Under international law this pledge was politically but not legally binding.[67]

In the Berlin negotiations Bondarenko introduced a new idea by proposing to link the completion of Soviet troop withdrawals from Germany to Germany's fulfillment of its promise to reduce its armed forces to 370,000 as part of parallel limits on other European armed forces. In other words, Soviet soldiers would stay until the Germans had completed their reductions, regardless of when or whether a future arms control treaty was concluded. The French, British, and American delegates totally opposed this provision. But, after lengthy argument, the delegates drafted language that was deliberately ambiguous.

The Soviets and the Germans agreed in the settlement that the withdrawal of all Soviet troops "will be completed by the end of 1994" but stipulated that this was "in connection with" the FRG's pledge to reduce its forces. So the Soviets had established some vague linkage which, in a small way, did single out the Germans for a uniquely binding constraint on their armed forces— though only until the end of 1994. Kastrup welcomed this Soviet compromise language. The West could claim that the Soviet withdrawal pledge was specific and unequivocal, that it was doubly guaranteed by the Soviet-German bilateral agreement on troop withdrawal, and that "in connection with" did not qualify the Soviet promise. But this was a weak argument. The Americans found themselves by the end of the discussion in the awkward position of being more worried about this "singularization" than Kastrup was, so they let the matter go. But they advised Baker of their concern.

Bondarenko also tried to create provisions in the settlement for verifying Germany's renunciation of nuclear and biological weapons and the size of its armed forces. None of the Western countries would support this. Bondarenko, after three days of talks, then complained bitterly that all the others seemed to oppose Soviet draft language on every issue. There appeared to be a "law," he said, against supporting Soviet proposals.[68]

Zoellick and Seitz left Berlin and traveled on to Helsinki, where they met the party that had arrived for President Bush's meeting with Gorbachev, their third face-to-face encounter since Bush had taken office.[69] Shevardnadze wanted to talk about CFE issues and Germany. He felt reassured in the (mistaken) belief that Genscher had promised to keep nuclear-capable aircraft out of the former GDR after unification. This was incorrect, since practically all modern military attack aircraft are capable of carrying nuclear weapons. Baker said that he would not try to limit German sovereignty, but the United States would only sign up to the agreement announced in the Caucasus— which referred to nuclear weapons, not to dual-capable delivery systems. Baker also stressed that, although NATO had agreed not to station foreign forces in the former GDR, this did not prohibit other kinds of movements. Shevardnadze said that he was concerned about military exercises, not other kinds of temporary transits of foreign forces.

Shevardnadze felt sure that Genscher had been ready to compromise on this point. He told Baker that surely Genscher would not have suggested something without discussing it with the Americans. Shevardnadze said that he had called Genscher two days before, and Genscher had told him he was in touch with the Americans. Well, Baker replied, Genscher called and asked me to help him solve the matter here in Helsinki. That is what he said to me, Shevardnadze exclaimed. He said to raise it with Baker. I told him that we are dealing with the sovereign rights of Germany, so why should I raise it with Baker?

Baker repeated his understanding from the West Germans: that there had been no discussion of or agreement on dual-use systems, only nuclear weapons. Baker explained that the Soviet position would keep practically all artillery out of the former GDR. Shevardnadze appeared not to understand that most artillery is dual-capable, since it can fire nuclear-armed shells. (Such shells had been widely deployed in the Soviet as well as the American military.)

Baker reiterated the American's lingering concern over the theoretical linkage between German troop reductions and the withdrawal of Soviet forces from Germany. He warned that this could become a real problem unless the other issues were settled. The ministers then turned to a discussion of the Persian Gulf crisis.

The Two Plus Four political directors met again on the eve of the arrival of their ministers to try to wrap up remaining differences the day before the final settlement on Germany was to be signed. Genscher and Baker had talked through the key issues in advance, arriving at common positions. The issue of dual-capable weapon systems was solved by qualifying the Soviet-proposed language with the American formula offered in Berlin, which had been hammered out in advance by Kastrup and Elbe with Kvitsinsky and Bondarenko. Genscher and Baker had agreed on this approach, and after lengthy debate the Soviets accepted it. Other issues remained unresolved as the ministers began to arrive.[70]

On the day the final settlement was to be signed, September 12, the Soviets were satisfied with the state of their bilateral negotiations with the Germans and were ready to join in a declaration suspending Four Power rights. Gorbachev and Kohl had settled the money issue two days earlier. Baker also decided to go along with the final settlement's treatment of Soviet withdrawals and promised German force reductions.

But it was a last-minute quarrel among the Western allies that most threatened the successful conclusion of the Two Plus Four. There was still—at this late moment—no agreement on the extent of allowed NATO activities in the territory of the former GDR. Although Elbe later singled out the British for their rigid tone on this issue, commenting derisively about Weston wearing his Royal Marines tie, the Americans were equally adamant—if not as outspoken. Zoellick privately advised Baker on his arrival that the Soviet draft, with its blanket exclusion of allied forces from eastern Germany, "represents a Soviet effort to disassociate Germany's NATO allies from part of its territory and people . . . It is incompatible with the supposed Soviet willingness to permit Germany to choose its Alliance . . . It is also yet another permanent infringement on German sovereignty."[71]

It had been agreed since July that the German armed forces, even if integrated into NATO's military command, could be stationed or deployed anywhere in Germany after Soviet forces left the former GDR in 1994. It was also agreed that foreign forces would not be stationed in the former GDR or carry out "any military activities there" until after Soviet troops were withdrawn at the end of 1994. Thereafter the West was willing to concede that foreign troops would not be "stationed" in the former GDR.

On September 11 the political directors agreed to Kvitsinsky's proposal that foreign forces would be "neither stationed nor deployed" in eastern Germany, provided it was understood that the term "deployed" ruled out only large-scale NATO maneuvers and did not affect smaller-scale transits or training exercises. Kastrup, responding to a Kvitsinsky suggestion, further suggested that the FRG was prepared to state that, in interpreting this provision, it would take everyone's interests into account. Weston said that Britain would interpret such a statement to mean that smaller maneuvers could be permitted, with the decision in each case resting with the sovereign German state. The French and the Americans offered similar interpretations. Weston still preferred a U.S. proposal stipulating that "deployed" referred only to large-scale maneuvers. Zoellick thought that the issue should be passed to the ministers to solve, but Kastrup wanted to keep working on the problem. The positions of the two sides were very close. It was Kvitsinsky, chairing the meeting, who suggested to the exhausted officials that it was fruitless to continue debating the topic and proposed that they adjourn for the night.[72]

The West Germans saw the British as impeding a settlement on this issue by talking of the need for NATO "maneuvers" with non-German forces in eastern Germany. Genscher leaned hard on Hurd to relax his opposition in a meeting at the German ambassador's residence on the eve of the ministerial. Genscher claimed that the British were threatening a collapse of the ministerial and a failure to conclude a final settlement. According to Elbe, Hurd gave way and instructed his aide to call off Weston. Weston, however, continued to argue that NATO needed to preserve its ability to fulfill its defense commitments to eastern Germany.

Shevardnadze, in his memoirs, recalled being informed late that night, presumably by Kvitsinsky, that one country "was demanding the addition of a clause extending the zone of possible NATO maneuvers to the territory of the former GDR." He passed back a message saying that, if his colleagues adopted such an article, "the meeting the next day would not be held. In other words, there would be no treaty, and it would be their fault."[73]

Genscher, returning to his hotel to discover that the issue had not been settled, was furious.[74] He could not understand what Hurd was doing. He and his advisers thought then, as Elbe states in his memoirs, that Hurd had probably received further instructions directly from Prime Minister Thatcher in London. Elbe recalled a Bonn diplomat speculating that the British were trying to spoil the German settlement out of pique over their loss of Great Power status.

Genscher angrily declared that he would go to the signing ceremony the next day: "We will see who does not come." The world press, he thought, would reveal who was responsible for any failures. Elbe, in his memoir, even quotes, without comment, Kvitsinsky's suspicion that some of Germany's allies wanted to sabotage the whole process of German-Russian reconciliation and arms control. Elbe's use of Kvitsinsky to level this charge is ironic, since it was actually Kvitsinsky who had terminated the discussion of the problem during the meeting of political directors, and it was also Kvitsinsky who presumably then advised Shevardnadze that the Soviet government should threaten to cancel the signing of the treaty.

Oddly, Elbe's account says nothing about the American role to this point. Yet no country had more influence on the NATO issue than the United States, and no government had more influence with the British government. The omission is telling. It suggests that the Americans agreed with the British—which was the case—and that the West Germans knew it. Rather than explain to Genscher that the political directors' discussion had finally sputtered out in a combination of British and American stubbornness and the Soviet chair's impatience, Kastrup—who had tried to keep the discussion going—apparently found it easier to blame the British. Or so he was understood to do. It is possible, however, that the West Germans knew that Zoellick was immovable but were waiting for Baker to arrive.

We do know that in the middle of the night Genscher, frustrated and angry about the "British problem," went to get Baker out of bed, though Baker's aides preferred not to wake the weary secretary of state. Genscher threatened to "wake him myself." American staff members were startled to see the West German foreign minister, Elbe and Kastrup in tow, sweep into Baker's corridor at the Hotel International well after midnight. Dressed in his pajamas, Baker was roused for a meeting in his suite with the anxious West German foreign minister. According to Elbe, Baker promised to help ensure that nothing would keep a Two Plus Four agreement from being signed as planned.

What Elbe does not mention is that Baker, not wavering from the American position, worked out with Genscher the possibility of leaving the term "deployed" in the text, perhaps with an oral explanation that this would not apply to "large-scale" maneuvers. No one could write a satisfactory legal definition that excluded such "large-scale" movements without prohibiting transits, training activities, or other contingencies important to NATO's defense of Germany. Genscher came back to his hotel at 2:30 in the morning and briefed the just-arrived East German prime minister/foreign minister de Maizière on the situation.

"Toward morning," Shevardnadze later recalled, "I was informed that the proposal [to extend NATO maneuvers] had been withdrawn." Since there had been no such proposal to begin with, it is hard to tell how Kvitsinsky's reports to him had changed during the night, or whether Kvitsinsky felt he had already dared enough in using Shevardnadze's clout to intimidate the Western delegates. In any case, when the Western ministers gathered for breakfast at the French ambassador's residence, Genscher pulled the French foreign minister aside, pleading with him, "Roland, I have never asked you for a favor. But now you must help me. Make the situation clear to Hurd." Kastrup had already drafted a statement along the lines of his suggestion the night before: the Germans would define "deployed" to take account of everyone's interests. No one had opposed the idea, and it preserved the concept of the sovereign Germany's right to make decisions.[75] Baker and Hurd readily agreed to incorporate this language.

Weston had first addressed the issue of permissible military activities in Berlin on September 6. He had explained that NATO was obliged to defend eastern Germany, and unless expressly excluded, such activities were within the jurisdiction of the allies involved and the host country. Bondarenko accused Weston of wanting maneuvers to take place in eastern Germany. Weston immediately replied that he had said only that this would be a question for Germany and its allies to decide. Zoellick joined in, asserting that a newly sovereign Germany had to be permitted to make these choices. So the "new" proposal in Moscow mirrored the stance the British and Americans had taken literally from the moment the issue had first arisen.[76]

The Two Plus Four ministers then gathered, with only a few aides present, and quickly agreed to the Western proposal. The meaning of the term "deployed" was to be described in an "agreed minute" stating that any questions about the term "will be decided by the government of the united Germany in a reasonable and responsible way taking into account the security interests of each contracting party."[77]

Then in the late morning the formal meeting began with a flurry of emotional remarks. Several ministers referred to a "long road" that had arrived at a destination. But the longest speech was given by the man whose country was about to be signed out of existence, East German prime minister de Maizière, whose government was in such disarray that he had to act as his own foreign minister. Shortly thereafter, the document was signed in a brief and simple ceremony.

Gorbachev met with Genscher that afternoon. Referring to his rough handling of the West German foreign minister in December 1989, Gorbachev recalled their "hard conversations."[78] Now Gorbachev wanted to turn the page and talk of a new Europe.

Indeed it was a new Europe, with a unified Germany at its heart. In the Berlin declaration of June 5, 1945, and the Potsdam declaration of August 2,

1945, the victorious powers had assumed supreme authority over Germany and defined their responsibility for the future fate of a defeated and ruined nation. Now, on September 12, 1990, in Moscow, the World War II victors gave up that responsibility and blessed the re-creation of a united German state. As Shevardnadze said, there were no winners and no losers. The "German question" would never again threaten European peace. Perhaps as a reminder of the Soviet Union's historic role in shaping the issue, the hosts gave all delegations—except the Germans—a history of the Great Patriotic War.

The division of Europe had been healed with an end to the partition of Germany. The Cold War was over, and Europe was whole and free. The terms of the final settlement were complete. At a CSCE ministerial meeting in New York two weeks later, the governments signed the declaration suspending Four Power rights at the moment of German unification. The declaration took effect on October 3, 1990. Germany was sovereign again.

Epilogue: Germany Unified and Europe Transformed

ON OCTOBER 3, 1990, the Federal Republic of Germany absorbed the German Democratic Republic. The German people turned to the hard work of integrating the new Länder, and two different societies, into one democratic state.

Germany signed bilateral treaties with the Soviet Union in Bonn on November 9, 1990, the anniversary of the opening of the Berlin Wall. A bilateral treaty, as promised, was signed on November 14 reaffirming the border with Poland, and in June 1991 Poland and the new Germany concluded a treaty of friendship.

All signatories to the final settlement ratified the treaty, the Senate of the United States voting unanimously in favor. Although the task was more difficult in the Soviet Union, Gorbachev and Shevardnadze won approval in the Supreme Soviet, despite Falin's last-minute effort to rally the diehard conservative opposition. The settlement entered into force in March 1991.

The unification of Germany left no western outpost for Soviet forces. Postwar European politics had been conducted in the shadow of a massive presence of Soviet conventional forces for almost fifty years. At the end of 1990 this fundamental feature of a divided Europe and a divided world was quickly unraveling. The Treaty on Conventional Armed Forces in Europe was signed in Paris on November 19 at the CSCE summit. The withdrawal of Soviet forces from Central and Eastern Europe was already well under way, but the CFE treaty ensured that all Soviet forces in Europe, including European Russia, would be reduced to half their former size and remain under those limits for the foreseeable future. In the spring of 1991 all European states issued political declarations concerning the maximum size of their armed forces. Germany was thus not singled out when it made the same commitment.

The Germans reduced their armed forces, which budget pressures drove below the 370,000-man ceiling, so that by the middle of 1994 the Bundeswehr numbered just 357,000 personnel. The Soviet Union completed the withdrawal of its forces from eastern Germany ahead of schedule in 1994. More than half a million soldiers, dependents, and civilians departed with 2.7 million tons of materiel and more than 12,000 armored fighting vehicles. The majority of American forces have left Germany since 1990; more than 100,000 will remain for the foreseeable future.

In the final act of the end of Germany's occupation, American, British, and French forces left Berlin on September 8, 1994, to proclamations of gratitude and friendship. Russian forces had left one week earlier, unhappy that they were not permitted to participate in the gala Western ceremony. As of September 1994 the Bundeswehr, integrated in NATO's military command, was free to deploy to any part of Germany.[1]

Western institutions emerged from the unification of Germany and the end of the Cold War transformed but fundamentally intact. NATO remains to this day Europe's premier security institution. The alliance's political and military infrastructure played a notable role in supporting the U.S.-led coalition's military effort against Iraq in 1990–91. Ironically, the alliance fired shots of military engagement for the first time in its existence after the Cold War was over, as it was called on to punish Serbian aggression in Bosnia.

NATO has become a magnet for its former adversaries in search of credible security assurances in a less settled Europe. The alliance formed the North Atlantic Cooperation Council in 1991, building on the liaison concept which had first surfaced in NATO's London declaration of 1990. In 1994 NATO responded even more formally to the East European clamor to join the alliance, creating the Partnership for Peace, a halfway house for the new democracies.

The European Community emerged from the process of German unification transformed as well. France and Germany accelerated European integration in order to give a more powerful unified Germany a home in a unified Europe. During the spring and summer of 1990 key decisions were made that led to the negotiation of the Maastricht treaty. The present European Union was created when that treaty was signed in December 1991.

The hasty quality of those decisions in 1990 was in part a product of French dismay and frustration over developments in Germany. The Germans just wanted to establish irrefutable credentials as good Europeans. But the rush to European political and monetary union was costly, sparking a financial backlash in 1992, and at the end of 1994 raising fundamental questions about the future shape and direction of the European Union.

Counterfactual propositions are, of course, difficult to defend. We do not know how the world would have looked had Germany unified on different terms or at a different time. But the centrality of Germany to Europe means that the character of the new German state that emerged—fully sovereign and unequivocally anchored in Western institutions—will determine in large part the shape of the new Europe. The decisions that were taken by the leaders who suddenly found themselves face to face with the German question determined not only Germany's path to unity but the outlines of Europe's future as well.

One thing is certain: German unification took place with uncommon speed and as amicably as any major negotiation in recent memory. There were those at the time who questioned if it might have gone too fast. But one wonders how different the course of German unification might have been had the difficult decisions been left to November or December 1990, when Shevardnadze resigned in protest against Gorbachev's Faustian bargain with the reactionaries. Less than a year after the final settlement the Soviet Union collapsed. Would it have been easier to negotiate Germany's future with fifteen newly independent states?

No one understood the issues of timing better than Helmut Kohl. He has reaped both the praise and the blame appropriate to the momentous role that he played in his country's headlong rush toward unity. Kohl was reelected with a comfortable margin of victory in December 1990. Although the difficult period of adjustment to the unification of East and West continued to prompt questions about his leadership, Kohl was narrowly reelected yet again in October 1994, a victory that made him the longest-serving and most influential chancellor since Konrad Adenauer.

Yet the story of Helmut Kohl and German unity is not about the chancellor's vision but about his extraordinary feel for the pulse of the German people. It is fitting that it was Kohl who sensed the latent urge for unity in the East German people and, drawn to unity himself, found a way to shape that longing into a force that could not be denied. Always conscious of history, throughout his career Kohl has had an unfailing instinct for the politics of the street. If the recalcitrant Honecker had reacted sooner, had Krenz been more skillful, or had Modrow not arrived on the scene too late, Kohl might not have had the chance to channel the hopes of the East German people.

Like the storming of the Bastille at the outset of the French Revolution, the story of Germany's unification will always begin with common people—

with the exodus of men and women fed up with deprivation and tired of the assault on human dignity proffered by the East German regime. But it was Helmut Kohl who gave expression to that desperation and set the course toward a united Germany. Kohl took a tremendous chance in placing unification on an international agenda that was not quite ready for it. He found his European allies to be wary of a unified Germany despite forty-five years of extraordinary friendship. The British and the French emerge from this story as somewhat secondary players. Those who were present at the press conference of the first Two Plus Four ministerial will never forget that there was not a single question for the British, the French, or the representative of the dying East German regime. The solution to the German question was seen to rest with the United States, the Federal Republic, and the Soviet Union.

It is tempting to read this as evidence of the decline of French and particularly British power in Europe. But influence and power are not synonymous. The British and the French were weaker—economically, politically, and certainly militarily—at the end of World War II than in 1989. Yet they wielded great influence in the decisions concerning postwar Germany. At the end of the Cold War London and Paris reacted and followed; they did not lead.

The United States did offer leadership, deciding early that it was committed to German unity and communicating that clearly and often to Kohl. This permitted the German chancellor to follow his instincts, assured of the backing of Germany's most powerful ally. Whenever Kohl wanted to push harder or faster, he turned to George Bush for support. He found that the American president believed in the promise the West had made to Adenauer: the Federal Republic of Germany was an incubator for German democracy until the day the German people could be joined together in one state. In 1989 Bush told Kohl unambiguously that he was ready to deliver on that bargain.[2]

Timing was of the essence for Bush, too. In October 1990, when the instruments of ratification for German unification were sent to the American Congress, he took note in a brief and simple Rose Garden ceremony, hastily arranged and jammed into a presidential schedule otherwise devoted to building the coalition against Saddam Hussein. The Americans had moved on to the first crisis of the post–Cold War world and talk of a new world order that had less to do with Europe than with the pressures of civil wars and small conflicts across the globe.

The end of the Cold War left the Americans with new dilemmas. With the retreat of the Soviet armed forces back to the territory of Russia, the United States stood as the only military power with global reach and global responsibility. In trying to discharge those responsibilities, George Bush collided with America's festering ambivalence about its role in the world. The country found little joy in the West's Cold War victory, only questions about what the forty-five-year commitment had done to America at home. For some, President Bush became an object of ridicule, a man seen as out of touch with the aspirations and concerns of his own country. Confronted with the results of that judgment, he said with resignation on the night of his electoral defeat: "The democratic process has taken its course. And I believe in democracy."

For George Bush the Cold War in Europe had been the defining characteristic of the international system. Even more than his predecessor, Ronald Reagan, he could not imagine an end to the Cold War that did not leave Europe whole and free. It fell to him to deliver on that promise. And he did. It is perhaps characteristic of Bush that he did so quietly and sometimes inarticulately, leaving little public record of his impact. That problem is symptomatic of a larger one, however. In the White House the tension between the need for quiet diplomacy and the pressure for publicity is very great. The press wants to know what the president has done for world peace *today*—in time for the evening news or the morning's headlines. But that runs counter to the demands of those times when one must permit an adversary to save face or work behind the scenes so that others can rightfully take the lead. In the case of German unification, Bush did not want to overshadow Kohl or publicly dominate Gorbachev. But in choosing to play his role offstage, he made an inviting target for those who wanted to believe that he was just a bystander.

The Bush administration was riveted on the institutions—principally NATO—that had sustained the Western alliance and American power in Europe for forty-five years. History will judge whether that preoccupation turns out to have been warranted. In this sense Europe had been transformed by a general acceptance of the Western status quo. NATO remained; American troops and nuclear weapons stayed in Europe; and German power continued to be tightly integrated into the postwar structures. The Americans repeatedly defended the stabilizing virtues of this arrangement to the Soviets, and the arguments had a real impact on them. So one security system collapsed, but the other remained intact, ready to become a foundation for reconstruction of the whole.

The Clinton administration found NATO a vital institution for pursuing its goals, as new conflicts and challenges arose in and around Europe. It also inherited a German friendship that was secure and sound. Most important, in 1993 the new president found a democratizing Russia that was a willing partner for the United States, not a bitter and humiliated power bent on recapturing a lost role in Europe. The Cold War did not have to end this way, but the legacy of friendship was immediately clear when in August 1990 the United States sought and unexpectedly received Moscow's support against Iraq, the USSR's most valued client in the Middle East.

The Soviet Union's quiet death is still one of the most stunning events in modern history. When the hammer and sickle came down from above the Kremlin for the last time, on December 25, 1991, the state that Lenin built was finished. Ironically, those had been Josef Stalin's words to his foreign minister V. M. Molotov as German tanks roared across the Soviet border in June 1941.

We will never know precisely how to weigh the role of the unification of Germany in the collapse of the Soviet Union. Gorbachev's German policy undermined his political base at home and emboldened rebel nationalists throughout the USSR. The terms of unification ended the Soviet Union's reign as a dominant European power. With no East German anchor, the Warsaw Pact collapsed a few months later as Eastern European regimes rushed to negotiate the withdrawal of Soviet forces from their territory. Pushed back to the Ukraine, the socialist empire did not stop unraveling until it had receded to the approximate frontiers of Peter the Great's Russia.

The irony is that the Cold War could not have ended and Germany could not have been unified without the Soviet Union's renunciation of conflict and class struggle in Europe. Scholars will long study and try to understand why Gorbachev made the choices he did. He never intended to destroy Soviet power in Europe. He only wanted to place it on a different and more legitimate foundation.

Instead, the last great European empire—built in part on coercion and in part on the myth of the "new Soviet man"—simply crashed down around him. Gorbachev's return from captivity at the Black Sea, where he had been held by coup plotters in August 1991, marked the last sad chapter for a man who is one of modern history's great figures. He did not understand what was happening to him or to his country, as he tried in vain to resurrect a Communist party that could govern a multiethnic state. At that moment Boris Yeltsin treated the soon-to-be-deposed leader like a confused child, demanding that he sign documents leading to the Soviet Union's dissolution. It was a poignant scene for those who remembered Gorbachev as the triumphant catalyst for change.

But as sad as that day was for Gorbachev the man, the world could not mourn the Soviet state. The Soviet Union had been a militarized and threatening power, bent on repressing its own people and stifling the human spirit. When it collapsed, Ronald Reagan's memorable words rang true. It was indeed a "sad experiment" practiced on a huge and helpless population.

Martin Malia has captured brilliantly the "Soviet tragedy." The Bolshevik Revolution ripped Russia out of Europe and set it in opposition to everything Western at a time when tsarism—for all its excesses—was beginning to modernize the vast empire. Lenin fully intended and believed that Bolshevik Russia would regain its roots in a communist Europe. Stalin was not willing to take that chance, and instead built a secretive, suspicious, and Byzantine state, fittingly housed within the walls of the fifteenth-century fortress that is the Kremlin. Seventy years of separation from Europe's development was interrupted only by an uneasy marriage between Stalin and the Western allies to defeat an even more dangerous tyrant in Germany. But after the war the Soviet Union returned to isolation, wrapping itself again in secrecy and hostility toward the West.

For Gorbachev and those around him this was wrong. These men believed in a Europe of common values, where reformed and humane communist states would find their place. The Soviet Union would be the heir to Russia's European legacy and a respected member of a common European home. But there was no place for the Soviet Union in a Europe of common values. The former East German prime minister Lothar de Maizière remembered an exchange with Gorbachev at the Moscow signing ceremony for the final settlement on Germany. De Maizière reminded Gorbachev about his reputed warning to Erich Honecker that "those who come too late are punished by life." Gorbachev "laughed somewhat bitterly and said with resignation, 'Yes, but do you know whether we have all come much too late?'"[3]

That place in Europe has been filled by Russia, not by the Soviet Union. Boris Yeltsin, Gorbachev's rival, was invited into the councils of the West—the G-7, NATO, the Council of Europe. Worries may persist that Russia is bent again on reconstructing its empire, but there is little concern that it will be a menacing military power on the continent any time soon.

The chance to unify Germany on Western terms was given to Kohl, Bush, Mitterrand, and Thatcher because the East German people's thirst for freedom survived the years of Europe's ideological division. An exhausted Soviet Union could no longer mount effective resistance in Eastern Europe to the pull of liberty and prosperity. But history is littered with missed opportunities. The leaders who saw their chance acted with skill, speed, and regard for the dignity of the Soviet Union. As a result, Europe bears scars but no open wounds from German unification. That is a testimony to statecraft.

Notes

To help distinguish government documents from published materials, we have cited such unpublished documents with abbreviated dates (e.g., 30 Nov 89 for November 30, 1989). Telegrams to or from American embassies are cited by what the State Department calls message reference numbers, usually accompanied by the subject line of the message and always accompanied by the date of transmission. So, for example, State 306045, "Meeting in Moscow," 27 Jun 90, would be a telegram sent overseas from the State Department, with the given subject line, on June 27, 1990. Brussels 4567 gives the number of a telegram sent to Washington by the American embassy in Brussels, just as EmbBerlin 4567 would be the number of a telegram sent to Washington by the American embassy in East Berlin (the embassy in West Germany was in Bonn). "Secto" means a telegram sent to Washington by the secretary of state's traveling party. "USBerlin" is the American mission in West Berlin, "USNATO" the American mission to the North Atlantic Treaty Organization headquarters in Brussels. All U.S. government memoranda are cited in this form: [name, not title, of official author] to [name of addressee], "[subject line, if any]," date memo was sent.

Bureaus of the State Department also have standardized abbreviations. EUR is the Bureau for European and Canadian Affairs. EUR/CE is that bureau's office for Central European affairs. EUR/RPM is the bureau's office for regional political-military (NATO) affairs. L is the Office of the Legal Adviser and L/EUR that bureau's office for European matters. PA is the Bureau for Public Affairs, S/P the policy planning staff. In the intelligence community there are also abbreviations. NIC is the National Intelligence Council (coordinating the views of all U.S. intelligence agencies, including the CIA). SOV M is a memo from the CIA office for Soviet affairs, and EUR M a memo from the CIA office for European affairs, both in the CIA Directorate for Intelligence (which does intelligence analysis, as distinct from directorates that carry out clandestine operations or scientific research).

Other commonly used abbreviations in the notes are FBIS-SOV (Foreign Broadcast Information Service, Soviet Union), *Vestnik* (*Vestnik Ministertsva Inostrannykh del SSR*, a journal that recorded the official activities of the Soviet Foreign Ministry), and FRUS (Foreign Relations of the United States), the principal published archives of U.S. foreign policy.

Preface

1. Genscher quoted in Richard Kiessler and Frank Elbe, *Ein runder Tisch mit scharfen Ecken: Der diplomatische Weg zur deutschen Einheit* (Baden-Baden: Nomos, 1993), pp. 14–

15; Timothy Garton Ash, *In Europe's Name: Germany and the Divided Continent* (New York: Random House, 1993), p. 343.

2. For "greatest triumph," see Karl Kaiser, *Deutschlands Vereinigung: Die internationalen Aspekte* (Bergisch Gladbach: Bastei Lübbe, 1991), p. 16; for "most hated developments," see Alexander Bessmertnykh quoted in a 1991 interview in Michael Beschloss and Strobe Talbott, *At the Highest Levels: The Inside Story of the End of the Cold War* (Boston: Little, Brown, 1993), p. 240.

3. See, e.g., the interview excerpts with Helmut Kohl, Hans-Dietrich Genscher, Horst Teltschik, Eduard Shevardnadze, Vyacheslav Dashichev, Nikolai Portugalov, and Rainer Eppelmann in Ekkehard Kuhn, *Gorbatschow und die deutsche Einheit: Aussagen der wichtigsten russischen und deutschen Beteiligten* (Bonn: Bouvier, 1993), pp. 8–11.

Introduction

1. "Declaration Regarding the Defeat of Germany and the Assumption of Supreme Authority by the Allied Powers," signed at Berlin, June 5, 1945 at 6:00 P.M. Berlin time, reprinted in U.S. Department of State, *Documents on Germany, 1944–1985* (Washington, D.C.: Department of State, 1986), pp. 33–38.

2. This account is based on Rice's recollection of the ceremony.

1. When Did the Cold War End?

1. Herbert Butterfield, *The Whig Interpretation of History,* 1st American ed. (New York: Scribner, 1951), p. 12.

2. Raymond L. Garthoff, *The Great Transition: American-Soviet Relations and the End of the Cold War* (Washington, D.C.: Brookings Institution, 1994), pp. 770–772.

3. Butterfield, *The Whig Interpretation of History,* pp. 39–40.

4. See Alexander Dallin and Gail W. Lapidus, eds., *The Soviet System in Crisis: A Reader of Western and Soviet Views* (Boulder, Colo.: Westview Press, 1991).

5. This was, in fact, Shevardnadze's phrase in discussions with Gorbachev about the state of the Soviet Union in 1985. He describes the evolution of his thinking and that of other "new thinkers" in Eduard Shevardnadze, *Moi vybor: v zashchitu demokratii i svobody* (Moscow: Novostii, 1991), pp. 193–220.

6. Judith Goldstein and Robert Keohane, in their volume *Ideas and Foreign Policy: Beliefs, Institutions, and Political Change* (Ithaca, N.Y.: Cornell University Press, 1993), put it this way: "Ideas help to order the world . . . Insofar as ideas put blinders on people, reducing the number of conceivable alternatives, they serve as invisible switchmen, not only by turning action onto certain tracks rather than others . . . but also by obscuring the other tracks from the agent's view" (p. 12).

7. The debate between Stalin and his competitors for Lenin's throne has been largely obscured by the ruthless means that he used to weed out the opposition. But in this debate Stalin emphasized his theory for achieving "socialism in one country": that is, progress toward socialism in the USSR did not have to wait upon the achievement of worldwide revolution. This debate about "socialism in one country" is perhaps the crucial ideological turning point for the Soviet Union's course in the post-Lenin era. The question was whether the Soviet Union could survive without a global proletarian revolution. This was more than a matter of academic debate; it would determine whether the Soviet Union made building socialism at home its highest priority or tried to foment revolution abroad. The proponent of "permanent revolution," Lev Trotsky, while far more articulate and

urbane, lacked a realistic plan for dealing with the Soviet Union's immediate circumstances of weakness and vulnerability in 1926–27. Depending as it did, even rhetorically, on revolutionary uprisings in the capitalist world, Trotsky's prescription simply did not accord with the world in which the Soviet Union found itself. Stalin resolved any dilemma between the international movement and the Soviet Union's existence: "An internationalist is one who is ready to defend the USSR without reservation, without wavering, unconditionally; for the USSR is the base of the world revolutionary movement and this revolutionary movement cannot be defended unless the USSR is defended." J. V. Stalin, *Ob oppozitsii* (Moscow: Gosudarstvennoe Izdatel'stvo, 1928), pp. 220–293. The Soviet Union would prepare to go it alone, but as a temporary condition until the revolution triumphed in the capitalist world and provided a more hospitable international environment. Martin Malia has resurrected this debate in *The Soviet Tragedy: A History of Socialism in Russia, 1917–1991* (New York: Free Press, 1994). The implications of "socialism in one country" for Soviet foreign and military policy are discussed in Condoleezza Rice, "The Making of Soviet Strategy," in *Makers of Modern Strategy: From Machiavelli to the Nuclear Age,* ed. Peter Paret, with the collaboration of Gordon A. Craig and Felix Gilbert (Princeton: Princeton University Press, 1986), pp. 648–676.

8. Ed Hewett discusses the marginalization of the Soviet economy in Ed A. Hewett with Clifford G. Gaddy, *Open for Business: Russia's Return to the Global Economy* (Washington, D.C.: Brookings Institution, 1992), pp. 1–32.

9. The best work on the Soviet Union's earliest conceptions of CMEA remains Michael Kaser, *COMECON: Integration Problems of the Planned Economies,* 2d ed. (London: Oxford University Press, 1967).

10. A simple example is illustrative. The technology that permits multiple telephone lines on one instrument and that makes it possible to switch easily from one line to another was denied to the Soviet Union because it would have made it possible for the military quickly to establish alternative nodes of communication if the primary link was destroyed. Thus, visitors to the offices of high-ranking Moscow officials often noticed that there were several telephones rather than several lines on one instrument, as is common in the West. It was often said that one could tell how important a Soviet official was by the number of phones on his desk.

11. The correlation of forces was a model that tried to assess the relative economic, military, and political strengths of an alliance or countries. It tried, as Coit Blacker has noted, to put the analysis of international relations on a more "scientific" basis, since the Soviets, as good Marxists, were unimpressed with "bourgeois" analyses, which seemed to them subjective and inconclusive. See Coit D. Blacker, *Hostage to Revolution: Gorbachev and Soviet Security Policy, 1985–1991* (New York: Council on Foreign Relations Press, 1993), p. 13.

12. See Coit D. Blacker, "The Kremlin and Detente: Soviet Conceptions, Hopes, and Expectations," in *Managing U.S.-Soviet Rivalry: Problems of Crisis Prevention,* ed. Alexander L. George (Boulder, Colo.: Westview Press, 1983), pp. 119–137.

13. This presented a paradox for the Soviet leadership. As a clear stakeholder in international stability and thus a status quo power, the Soviet Union often faced difficult choices between moving its own "socialist alternative" forward and reaping the benefits of recognition as a superpower in the international order. The historian Alexander Dallin often quipped that this led to a simultaneous "need to enjoy and need to destroy."

14. See Brezhnev's speech to the plenary session of the Soviet Communist party (CPSU) Central Committee on October 25, 1976, reprinted in *Pravda,* October 26, 1976, pp. 1–3.

15. Kiron Skinner has demonstrated that U.S. frustration and inability to respond to Moscow led Presidents Nixon and, later, Carter to begin, with little success, to link Soviet behavior to what Moscow was thought to want most—major arms control agreements that codified the status quo. See Kiron Skinner, "The Politics of Weakness and the Politics of Strength: American Use of Security Linkage during the Carter Era" (Ph.D. diss., Harvard University, 1994).

16. On the debate over the Soviet military buildup, see Franklyn D. Holzman, "Soviet Military Spending: Assessing the Numbers Game," *International Security*, 6 (Spring 1982): 78–101; John Prados, *The Soviet Estimate: U.S. Intelligence Analysis and Russian Military Strength* (New York: Dial Press, 1982); William Zimmerman and Glenn Palmer, "Words and Deeds in Soviet Foreign Policy: The Case of Soviet Military Expenditures," *American Political Science Review*, 77 (June 1983): 358–367; Abraham S. Becker, *Sitting on Bayonets: The Soviet Defense Burden and the Slowdown of Soviet Defense Spending* (Santa Monica, Calif.: RAND/UCLA Center for the Study of Soviet International Behavior, December 1985); and Franklyn D. Holzman, "Politics and Guesswork: CIA and DIA Estimates of Soviet Military Spending," *International Security*, 14 (Fall 1989): 101–131.

17. William Perry, at the time a Carter administration defense official who was one of the fathers of the "off-set" strategy, discusses the plan in *The Role of Technology in Meeting the Challenges of the 1980s* (Stanford: Arms Control and Disarmament Program, Stanford University, 1982).

18. See Barry R. Posen and Stephen W. Van Evera, "Reagan Administration Defense Policy: Departure from Containment," and Alexander Dallin and Gail W. Lapidus, "Reagan and the Russians: United States Policy toward the Soviet Union and Eastern Europe," in *Eagle Defiant: United States Foreign Policy in the 1980s*, ed. Kenneth A. Oye, Robert J. Lieber, and Donald Rothchild (Boston: Little, Brown, 1983), pp. 67–104, 191–236; and Robert Jervis, *The Illogic of American Nuclear Strategy* (Ithaca, N.Y.: Cornell University Press, 1984).

19. See the revealing transcript of the May 1983 Soviet Politburo meeting published in "More Documents from the Russian Archives," *Cold War International History Project Bulletin*, 4 (Fall 1994): 77–80; see also Jonathan Haslam, *The Soviet Union and the Politics of Nuclear Weapons in Europe, 1969–87: The Problem of the SS-20* (London: Macmillan, 1989).

20. The Soviets seemed scornful, at least at first, about the viability of the program as a nuclear shield. Scientists in the Soviet Union did not believe that it could work. The earliest comment from military leaders on SDI was rather dismissive of its effect on Soviet nuclear forces, noting that countermeasures were readily available. Later, though, Soviet military officers began to wonder aloud if SDI was really a means by which to protect the United States from Soviet retaliation once Soviet nuclear forces had been partially destroyed in a nuclear first strike. They pointed out that the Soviet Union had signed the 1972 Anti-Ballistic Missile treaty in part to prevent the Americans from acquiring just such a strategic option. See Sidney D. Drell, Philip J. Farley, and David Holloway, *The Reagan Strategic Defense Initiative: A Technical, Political, and Arms Control Assessment* (Cambridge, Mass.: Ballinger, 1985); and David Holloway, "The Strategic Defense Initiative and the Soviet Union," *Daedalus*, 114 (Summer 1985): 257–278.

21. The best-known article is Nikolai Ogarkov, "In Defense of Socialism: History's Experience and the Present Day," *Krasnaya zvezda*, May 9, 1984, p. 2. The Ogarkov episode is examined in Brian A. Davenport, "The Ogarkov Ouster: The Development of Soviet Military Doctrine and Civil-Military Relations in the 1980s," *Journal of Strategic Studies*, 14 (June 1991): 129–147. Although the more politically sensitive Sergei F. Akhromeyev

succeeded Ogarkov, his analysis of the general military balance was not very different. At the time of the Persian Gulf war in 1990, he told Rice that he suspected the United States of planning the war against Saddam Hussein which it had always intended to fight against Soviet military forces—one heavily dependent on the rapid transmission of information to independent weapons-carrying platforms at the front. He was right, of course.

22. The resource-intensive, centrally directed method for achieving technological breakthroughs is discussed in several works by David Holloway; see "Innovation in the Defence Sector" and "Innovation in the Defence Sector: Battle Tanks and ICBDs," in *Industrial Innovation in the Soviet Union,* ed. Ronald Amann and Julian Cooper (New Haven: Yale University Press, 1982), pp. 276–367, 368–414.

23. N. Kapchenko, "Imperialist Foreign Policy at the Present Stage of the General Crisis of Capitalism: The General Crisis of Capitalism and the Growing Aggressiveness of Imperialism," *International Affairs* (Moscow), 3 (March 1982): 66–69.

24. Fine short portraits of Gorbachev are offered by his aide Anatoly Chernyayev in "The Phenomenon of Gorbachev in the Context of Leadership," *International Affairs* (Moscow) (June 1993): 37–48, and by a Western journalist acquainted with Gorbachev, Robert Kaiser, in *Why Gorbachev Happened: His Triumphs, His Failure, and His Fall,* rev. ed. (New York: Simon and Schuster, 1991), pp. 21–92. See also Anatoly Chernyayev, *Shest' let s Gorbachevym: Po dnevnikovym zapisyam* (Moscow: Progress Publishers, 1993). On the German occupation and the deportations of the Karatchay, Kalmyks, and other peoples in the wake of the German retreat, see Michel Tatu, *Mikhail Gorbachev: The Origins of Perestroika,* trans. A. P. M. Bradley (Boulder, Colo.: East European Monographs, 1991), pp. 6–10.

25. George Shultz, *Turmoil and Triumph: My Years as Secretary of State* (New York: Charles Scribner's Sons, 1993), p. 1108, recounting a December 1988 meeting at Governor's Island, New York.

26. Anatoly Chernyayev remarked that he was always amazed at how much Moscow's specialists on America liked America while some of the experts on Germany (such as Bondarenko) seemed to dislike the Germans. "Whatever their views," he said, "they respected the Germans but they did not like them." Rice interview with Chernyayev, Moscow, June 1994; letter from Chernyayev, February 1995.

27. Eduard Shevardnadze, *The Future Belongs to Freedom,* trans. Catherine Fitzpatrick (New York: Free Press, 1991), p. 13.

28. Quoted in Don Oberdorfer, *The Turn: From the Cold War to a New Era, The United States and the Soviet Union, 1983–1990* (New York: Poseidon Press, 1991), p. 119.

29. See J. L. Scherer, *Soviet Biographical Service,* 1 (April 1985): 31; 2 (June 1986): 56.

30. Rice interview with Tarasenko, Moscow, October 1991; Zelikow interview with Tarasenko, Providence, June 1993; *The Tauris Soviet Dictionary: The Elite of the USSR Today* (London: I. B. Tauris and Co., 1989), p. 421.

31. For background, see Sergei Grigoriev, "The International Department of the CPSU," unpublished ms.; Mark Kramer, "The Role of the CPSU International Department in Soviet Foreign Relations and National Security Policy," in *Soviet Foreign Policy: Classic and Contemporary Issues,* ed. Frederick Fleron, Jr., Erik Hoffmann, and Robbin Laird (New York: Aldine de Gruyter, 1991), pp. 444–463.

32. See Jeffrey Gedmin, *The Hidden Hand: Gorbachev and the Collapse of East Germany* (Washington, D.C.: AEI Press, 1992), pp. 13–14, 46–47.

33. The early caution as well as the subsequent, more radical steps are detailed in Blacker, *Hostage to Revolution.*

34. The professional military opposed unilateral and asymmetrical arms control reductions. See Condoleezza Rice, "Is Gorbachev Changing the Rules of Defense Decision-Making?," *Journal of International Affairs,* 42 (Spring 1989): 377–397.

35. Chernyayev, *Shest' let s Gorbachevym,* pp. 255–260; Rice interview with Chernyayev, Moscow, June 1994.

36. Quoted in Seweryn Bialer and Joan Afferica, "The Genesis of Gorbachev's World," *Foreign Affairs,* 64 (1985): 612. See also Ronald D. Asmus, J. F. Brown, and Keith Crane, *Soviet Foreign Policy and the Revolutions of 1989 in Eastern Europe* (Santa Monica, Calif.: RAND Corporation, 1991), p. 11.

37. For the full text, see *Pravda,* November 8, 1987, p. 1. For detailed accounts of Gorbachev's dealings with East European leaders in 1987 and 1988, see Georgi Shakhnazarov, *Tsena Svobodyi: Reforma Gorbacheva glazami ego pomoshnika* (Moscow: Zevs, 1993), pp. 95–120.

38. In 1987 Gorbachev had read the writings of Nikolai Bukharin, a leading party figure of the 1920s and 1930s who had been executed by Stalin, prompted by Stephen Cohen's gift of his book on the debates of the Stalin era. Rice interview with Chernyayev, Moscow, June 1994. This is not the only instance in which Western scholarship helped reintroduce Russians to their own past.

39. Chernyayev, *Shest' let s Gorbachevym,* pp. 184–186, 213–218. Gorbachev would later put his ideas into a series of speeches and articles. See, e.g., "Sosialisticheskaya ideya i revolutsionnaya perestroika," *Kommunist,* 18 (December 1989): 3–20.

40. On the scholarly debates and the key scholars who contributed to the "new thinking," see the very good account in Jeff Checkel, "Ideas, Institutions, and the Gorbachev Foreign Policy Revolution," *World Politics,* 45 (January 1993): 271–300.

41. Both Yakovlev and Shevardnadze discuss these themes in detail in their written recollections. See Alexander Yakovlev, *Muki prochteniya byitiya: Perestroika: nadezhdyi i real'nost* (Moscow: Novosti, 1991), esp. pp. 73, 91; and Shevardnadze, *Moi vybor,* esp. pp. 85–93. Yakovlev, in particular, links the confrontational division of the world along class lines to Stalinism.

42. Shevardnadze speech to the scientific-practical conference of the USSR Foreign Ministry reprinted in *Pravda,* July 26, 1988, p. 4.

43. Yegor Ligachev speech reprinted in "Za delo—bez raskachki," *Pravda,* August 6, 1988, p. 2.

44. Mikhail Gorbachev, "Speech to Council of Europe," reprinted in *Pravda,* July 7, 1989, pp. 1–2.

45. Rice discussions with Gorbachev, Moscow, June 1994, and other informal discussions with Gorbachev while Rice was in the government.

46. The conversation took place in the second expanded session held aboard the Soviet passenger liner *Maxim Gorkii,* December 3, 1989. Rice was the note taker for the American side at this meeting. The Soviet notes from this session are published in Mikhail S. Gorbachev, *Gody trudnykh reshenii, 1985–1992: izbrannoye* (Moscow: Al'fa-Print, 1993), pp. 176–179.

47. Some of the more interesting groundwork for this shift had been laid by Soviet academics almost a decade earlier. Among the more important participants in the debate are Oleg Bogomolov, Karen Brutents, and Yuriy Novopashin. For a thorough examination of the scholarly debates that laid the basis for the revocation of the Brezhnev doctrine and rejection of a segregated "socialist community of states," see Jonathan Valdez, *Internationalism and the Ideology of Soviet Influence in Eastern Europe* (Cambridge: Cambridge University Press, 1993).

48. Don Oberdorfer, "Thatcher: Gorbachev Has Ended Cold War," *Boston Globe*, November 18, 1988, p. 7; Shultz, *Turmoil and Triumph*, pp. 1131, 1138.

49. Ronald Reagan, "Address to Members of the British Parliament," 8 Jun 82, in *Public Papers of the Presidents: Ronald Reagan* (Washington, D.C.: Government Printing Office, 1982), bk. 1, pp. 742–748.

50. Address of Vice President George Bush at the Hofburg, Vienna, 21 Sep 83, in *Department of State Bulletin*, 83 (November 1983): 19–23.

51. The recollection of Whitehead's intervention comes from Rice's discussion of the Bush trip with a State Department official in 1989.

52. Address by Ronald Reagan, Berlin, 12 Jun 87, in *Public Papers* (1987), bk. 1, pp. 634–637; Willy Brandt, *Erinnerungen* (Zurich: Propyläen, 1989), p. 55. The language in Reagan's speech reportedly originated with a White House speech writer, Peter Robinson. Lou Cannon, *President Reagan: The Role of a Lifetime* (New York: Simon and Schuster, 1991), p. 774. Reagan wrote that he mentioned Berlin at the 1988 Moscow summit, see Ronald Reagan, *An American Life* (New York: Simon and Schuster, 1990), pp. 705–707. Chernyayev found no mention of the subject in Soviet records of these talks. Letter from Chernyayev, February 1995. Reagan's "Berlin initiative" became a working-level proposal to regularize Four Power controls. A proposal for talks was passed to the Soviets six months after Reagan's speech. While Moscow debated its response, the East Germans weighed in with what a Soviet diplomat called their "100 percent negative attitude." Another ten months passed before the Soviet government replied to the Americans. The West did not return to the matter until the summer of 1989, after the Bush administration revived the issue during the president's visit to West Germany. See Igor Maximychev, "What 'German Policy' We Need," *International Affairs* (Moscow) (September 1991): 53, 58–60.

53. Shultz, *Turmoil and Triumph*, p. 1138.

54. Zelikow interview with Scowcroft, Washington, D.C., June 1994.

55. The "wrong mistakes" quote is from Zelikow's recollection of Bush's response to compliments at a lunch with Irish prime minister Charles Haughey in February 1990.

56. The Bush quote is from Ross to Baker, "Thoughts on the 'Grand Design,'" 16 Dec 88 (transition team memo); Zelikow interview with Scowcroft, Washington, D.C., June 1991.

57. Bush used the "doing nothing stupid" phrase with a group of Soviet specialists during one of his first briefings on events in Eastern Europe. Rice was present at this Kennebunkport briefing in February 1989. The incident is also reported in Michael R. Beschloss and Strobe Talbott, *At the Highest Levels: The Inside Story of the End of the Cold War* (Boston: Little, Brown, 1993); account of Baker's team is from Ross to Baker, "Thoughts on the 'Grand Design'"; Zelikow interviews with Baker, Houston, January 1995, and Zoellick, Washington, D.C., January 1995.

58. Impressions of the period between January and mid-May 1989 are reflected in Beschloss and Talbott, *At the Highest Levels*, pp. 17–68.

59. Rice's recollection of Kennebunkport briefing for Bush on Eastern Europe, February 1989.

60. Bush address to the citizens of Hamtramck, Michigan, 17 Apr 89, in *Public Papers of the Presidents: George Bush*, bk. 1, p. 432. Raymond Garthoff, in *The Great Transition*, p. 606, asserts that the timing of Bush's speech on the day Solidarity was legalized was a coincidence. It was not. The speech was timed to follow the Warsaw announcement. The Polish government agreed to hold free parliamentary elections in June. The "roundtable" developed the procedures for these elections. The Hungarians followed this example after the shakeup of their government in June 1989, effectively creating a multiparty political

system before fully free elections were held in March 1990. See Timothy Garton Ash, *The Magic Lantern: The Revolution of '89 Witnessed in Warsaw, Budapest, Berlin, and Prague* (New York: Random House, 1990), pp. 25–60; Bernard Gwertzman and Michael T. Kaufman, eds., *The Collapse of Communism,* rev. ed. (New York: Times Books, 1991), pp. 3–40, 110–137, 161–163, 253–254.

61. Zelikow interview with Zoellick, Washington, D.C., 1991.

62. Final version of State Department paper responding to NSR-5, as conveyed in transmittal memo from Levitsky to Scowcroft, 11 Mar 89.

63. "Summary of Conclusions for Deputies Committee Meeting on NSR-5, U.S. Relations with Western Europe (Political and Security Aspects)," 20 Mar 89.

64. Beschloss and Talbott, *At the Highest Levels,* pp. 38–39.

65. Account based on Henry A. Kissinger, "A Memo to the Next President," *Newsweek,* September 19, 1988, pp. 34, 37; Ross to Baker, "Thoughts on the 'Grand Design'"; Ross to Baker, "Shaping Soviet Power," 21 Feb 89; Zelikow interview with Baker, Houston, January 1995; Beschloss and Talbott, *At the Highest Levels,* pp. 14–17, 19–21, 45–46; and Thomas L. Friedman, "Baker, Outlining World View, Assesses Plan for Soviet Bloc," *New York Times,* March 28, 1989, p. A1.

66. Scowcroft to Bush, "The NATO Summit," 20 Mar 89. On March 26 the president noted to Scowcroft that he had "read this with interest!" The President marked up the memo, underscoring and checking the paragraph on the priority to be attached to policy toward Germany.

67. The "commonwealth of free nations" phrase was introduced in President Bush's Mainz address, 31 May 89, *Public Papers* (1989), bk. 1, p. 652, and subsequently elaborated on by Bush in a speech in Leiden on American relations with Europe, July 17, 1989; ibid., bk. 2, pp. 977–978, 979. The concept, simplified as the "commonwealth of freedom," was also discussed in another Bush speech, delivered to the Czech Federal Assembly in Prague on 17 Nov 90; see *Public Papers* (1990), bk. 2, p. 1625.

68. Scowcroft to Bush, "The NATO Summit," p. 2.

69. Arnaud de Borchgrave, "Bush 'Would Love' Reunited Germany," *Washington Times,* May 16, 1989, p. A-1; Zelikow interview with Bush, Houston, January 1995.

70. Blackwill to Scowcroft attaching a draft "Memorandum for the President on Dealing with the Germans," May 11, 1989. The quoted passage is from the enclosed memo to the president. Months later, on August 7, Scowcroft actually forwarded the memo to the president with minor changes to reflect the passage of time. Bush read and initialed the memo on September 9, 1989, nine days before making another significant comment to reporters on German unification in Helena, Montana. The Zoellick quote is from Zoellick to Baker, "NATO Summit—Possible Initiatives," 15 May 89.

71. Good pictures of conventional arms control issues as they stood in the spring of 1989 can be found in Barry M. Blechman, William J. Durch, and Kevin P. O'Prey, *Regaining the High Ground: NATO's Stake in the New Talks on Conventional Armed Forces in Europe* (New York: St. Martin's Press, 1990); and Richard A. Falkenrath, *Shaping Europe's Military Order: The Origins and Consequences of the CFE Treaty,* CSIA Studies in International Security, no. 6 (Cambridge, Mass.: MIT Press, 1995), pp. 29–48. Blackwill and Zelikow were both inclined to favor a push on conventional arms control, having contributed in 1986 and 1987 to developing the West's conceptual approach for the new Negotiations on Conventional Armed Forces in Europe (CFE) in Vienna. Blackwill had headed the U.S. delegation to the earlier generation of conventional arms control talks in 1985–86; Zelikow had worked for Blackwill and for Blackwill's successor, Stephen Ledogar.

72. Zelikow interview with Baker, Houston, January 1995; Soviet notes of Baker's

meeting with Gorbachev on May 11 are published in Gorbachev, *Gody trudnykh reshenii*, pp. 136–148. For the atmosphere surrounding Baker's trip to Moscow, see Beschloss and Talbott, *At the Highest Levels*, pp. 61–68. On the Soviet CFE move, see Falkenrath, *Shaping Europe's Military Order*, pp. 49–50 and note 13.

73. See May 19 Baker notes on his May 17 meeting on his copy of Zoellick to Baker, "NATO Summit—Possible Initiatives," 15 May 89. For the Bush quote and a good account of the May frenzy, see Oberdorfer, *The Turn*, pp. 347–351.

74. On the Bush CFE initiative, see Blechman, Durch, and O'Prey, *Regaining the High Ground*, pp. 65, 69. As a result, "by May 1989 the essential structural elements of the CFE treaty had been defined." Falkenrath, *Shaping Europe's Military Order*, p. 54. On the "enthusiastic welcome" for Bush's initiatives from both the Bonn government and the opposition Social Democratic party (SPD), see Dennis Bark and David Gress, *A History of West Germany: Democracy and Its Discontents*, 2d ed. (Oxford: Blackwell, 1993), pp. 575–577. Bush's reflections on the significance of the 1989 NATO summit for his presidency were related to Rice in 1993 discussions. For the Bush quote, see Oberdorfer, *The Turn*, p. 351.

75. *Public Papers* (1989), bk. 1, p. 638. Paragraph 26 of the NATO summit declaration, adopted on May 30, 1989, states: "We seek a state of peace in Europe in which the German people regains its unity through free self-determination" (ibid., p. 625).

76. Address by Bush, Mainz, 31 May 89, in *Public Papers* (1989), bk. 1, pp. 650–654. The "Europe whole and free" phrase was in the original State Department draft written by Harvey Sicherman.

77. Zelikow interviews with Scowcroft, Washington, D.C., 1991. The Mainz speech, as redrafted by Zelikow and the White House speech writing staff before the trip and en route to Europe, referred more directly to German unification.

78. This initiative, the seed that ultimately produced the CSCE's Office of Free Elections, had been suggested to Rice by Stephen Sestanovich; Rice then passed it on to Zelikow for use in the speech. On the West German philosophical debate over whether CSCE norms should extend from individual liberties to matters of democratic governance, see Timothy Garton Ash, *In Europe's Name: Germany and the Divided Continent* (New York: Random House, 1993), pp. 263–264.

79. Bark and Gress, *History of West Germany*, p. 581.

80. Oberdorfer, *The Turn*, pp. 351–352. Bush had told his staff during the transition that he thought Eastern Europe was the most exciting place in the world. Zelikow interview with Zoellick, Washington, D.C., January 1995.

81. On West German perceptions of America's "new orientation," see Richard Kiessler and Frank Elbe, *Ein runder Tisch mit scharfen Ecken* (Baden-Baden: Nomos, 1993), pp. 16–21.

82. On the evolving Soviet attitude toward Germany and Kohl's 1988 visit, see Michael Sodaro, *Moscow, Germany, and the West: From Krushchev to Gorbachev* (Ithaca, N.Y.: Cornell University Press, 1990), pp. 322–357. See also Ash, *In Europe's Name*, pp. 105–112; Gedmin, *The Hidden Hand*, pp. 46–47; F. Stephen Larrabee, "Moscow and the German Question," in *The Germans and Their Neighbors*, ed. Dirk Verheyen and Christian Soe (Boulder, Colo.: Westview Press, 1993), pp. 212–215. On West German political pressures to help Gorbachev in 1987 and 1988, see Bark and Gress, *History of West Germany*, pp. 475–476, 481–484.

83. Rice interviews with Shevardnadze and Tarasenko, Moscow, October 1991; see interviews by Ash with Shevardnadze, Yakovlev, and Chernyaev quoted in Ash, *In Europe's Name*, pp. 108–109; Chernyaev, *Shest' let s Gorbachevym*, p. 302–304. On the views of

Dashichev as well as Falin and Portugalov, see also Gedmin, *The Hidden Hand*, pp. 46–51. For even earlier evidence of Gorbachev's belief that Germany would someday be reunified, see Hannes Adomeit's excellent article "'Midwife of History' or 'Sorcerer's Apprentice'? Gorbachev, German Unification, and the Collapse of Empire," *Post-Soviet Affairs*, 10 (August–September 1994): 197, 202–203 (on Gorbachev's 1975 visit to the FRG).

84. Letter from Chernyaev, February 1995; Ash, *In Europe's Name*, p. 108; Chernyaev, *Shest' let s Gorbachevym*, pp. 153–155. In the official account of the meeting, Gorbachev is reported to have added that the matter must be left to history, and "if anyone were to take a different path, the consequences would be very serious. There should be the utmost clarity about this." "M. S. Gorbachev's Meeting with R. von Weizsäcker," *Pravda*, July 8, 1987, pp. 1–2. See also Hans-Peter Riese, "Die Geschichte hat sich ans Werk gemacht," *Europa-Archiv*, 4 (1990): 117, 118. Much of the effect of Gorbachev's generous tone was further undermined during von Weizsäcker's visit when former foreign minister Andrei Gromyko, then chairman of the Supreme Soviet, instructed the ambassador to the FRG, Yuli Kvitsinsky, to comment scornfully about von Weizsäcker's references to the all-German consciousness. A summary of the private exchange was then deliberately published in the Soviet press. Chernyaev, annoyed, asked Gorbachev to intervene to deal with this "stupidity." Gorbachev expressed indifference. The next day Chernyaev complained about the publication of the exchange. Shevardnadze supported him. Gorbachev, changing the subject, replied that he liked von Weizsäcker and found him interesting, but he had not come to a clear official position that would allow him to react to Gromyko's stance. Yakovlev and Chernyaev later arranged to have a fuller and fairer version of von Weizsäcker's remarks published in the Soviet press. Chernyaev, *Shest' let s Gorbachevym*, pp. 155–156.

85. Mikhail Gorbachev, *Perestroika: New Thinking for Our Country and the World* (Cambridge: Harper and Row, 1987), pp. 199–200.

86. Sodaro, *Moscow, Germany, and the West*, p. 353. Kvitsinsky, the Soviet ambassador to West Germany, strongly agrees: "Moscow did not want to lose the GDR" and reacted in 1989 under the "pressure of events." Julij A. Kwizinskij, *Vor dem Sturm: Erinnerungen eines Diplomaten* (Berlin: Siedler, 1993), p. 421. When the GDR leaders asked Moscow what Gorbachev had told von Weizsäcker, East German records note that top Soviet officials recounted the exchange with the assurance that "the USSR would allow no speculation about the 'German nation.' The defence of the interests of the GDR was a cornerstone of Soviet policy." For this quotation and another discussion of Dashichev's views, see Ash, *In Europe's Name*, pp. 109–110, 495, based on an interview with Dashichev and East German archives of the July 1987 discussions between Hermann Axen and Anatoly Dobrynin.

87. For Kohl's remarks, which in another gesture of friendliness were carried by the Soviet press, see *Pravda*, October 25, 1988, p. 2. A brief extract captures the tone: "The truth remains, however: This division is unnatural. The community of the Germans is a historical and human reality which politics cannot ignore. We respect the existing boundaries, yet we want all Germans—like all Europeans—to be able to choose their fate freely and to come together in mutual freedom" (ibid., p. 22).

88. Chernyaev, *Shest' let s Gorbachevym*, p. 262; letter from Chernyaev, February 1995.

89. See *Izvestiya*, October 16, 1988, quoted in Larrabee, "Moscow and the German Question," p. 214.

90. Ash, *In Europe's Name*, pp. 118, 498 (from an October 1991 interview with Kohl).

91. Chernyaev recalled instead Kohl's complaint about continuing disagreements

over German unity. See Chernyayev, *Shest' let s Gorbachevym*, pp. 290–91. Gorbachev, asked about Kohl's recollection, said that the conversation was philosophical, not political, with no such discussion of economics. Letter from Chernyayev, February 1995.

92. Gedmin, *The Hidden Hand*, pp. 51–52; Sodaro, *Moscow, Germany, and the West*, pp. 355–362.

93. The text of the declaration was negotiated principally between Dieter Kastrup and Alexander Bondarenko, representing their respective foreign ministries. Zelikow and Rice interview with Horst Teltschik, Gütersloh, June 1992. For the text of the Bonn Declaration of Mikhail Gorbachev and Helmut Kohl, June 13, 1989 (in German), see *Texte zur Deutschlandpolitik*, ser. 3, vol. 7, 1989 (Bonn: Deutscher Bundes-Verlag, 1990), pp. 148–153.

94. According to Teltschik the original draft of the Bonn Declaration, as received from the Foreign Ministry, contained no language at all on self-determination for the Germans. The phrase mentioning "self-determination" was added by Kohl, in part to test the Soviet reaction. Teltschik and his colleagues were surprised that the Soviets raised no objection. Zelikow and Rice interview with Teltschik, Gütersloh, June 1992. The full sentence reads: "Die uneingeschränkte Achtung der Grundsätze und Normen des Völkerrechts, insbesondere Achtung des Selbstbestimmungsrechts der Völker." *Texte*, pp. 150, 151. See also Ash, *In Europe's Name*, pp. 113–117. For official Soviet accounts of the Gorbachev trip to the FRG, see "Ofitsial'ny vizit M. S. Gorbachev v FRG," *Vestnik*, July 1, 1989, pp. 12–13. The explicit recognition offered to differing social systems was, for Moscow, a key aspect of the "Basic Principles" of U.S.-Soviet relations agreed between Richard Nixon and Leonid Brezhnev in May 1972. Of course, the context for this language was quite different for Gorbachev in 1989. On 1972, see Raymond Garthoff, *Detente and Confrontation: American-Soviet Relations from Nixon to Reagan* (Washington, D.C.: Brookings Institution, 1985), pp. 290–296.

95. Unnamed "key author" of draft CDU policy statement quoted from 1988 interview with A. James McAdams in *Germany Divided: From the Wall to Reunification* (Princeton: Princeton University Press, 1993), p. 191 n. 36. The original discussion paper produced by the CDU party commission would have downplayed the goal of political reunification, but the document finally adopted at the June 1988 Wiesbaden CDU party conference was wrested back to language mirroring the time-honored usage of the FRG's Basic Law. See Ash, *In Europe's Name*, pp. 446–447; and Karl-Rudolf Korte, *Die Chance genutzt* (Frankfurt: Campus, 1994), p. 20 n.11.

96. Schäuble address to the Evangelical Academy, Bad Boll, February 25, 1989, quote in *Texte*, p. 47; see also the statement of the government's position by FRG inner-German minister Dorothee Wilms (CDU), address to the Friedrich-Ebert Stiftung, Bonn, January 24, 1989, quoted ibid., p. 28. For Teltschik, see *General Anzeiger*, July 6, 1989, quoted in McAdams, *Germany Divided*, pp. 191–192.

97. Zelikow and Rice interview with Teltschik, Gütersloh, June 1992.

98. Vernon A. Walters, *Die Vereinigung war voraussehbar: Hinter den Kulissen eines entscheidenen Jahres—Die Aufzeichnungen des amerikanischen Botschafters*, trans. Helmut Ettinger (Berlin: Siedler, 1994), p. 27 (meeting with Foreign Office state secretary Hans Lautenschläger).

99. Zelikow and Rice interview with Teltschik, Gütersloh, June 1992.

100. Charles Gati, *The Bloc That Failed: Soviet–East European Relations in Transition* (London: I. B. Taulris, 1990), pp. 65–135; and J. F. Brown, *Surge to Freedom: The End of Communist Rule in Eastern Europe* (Durham, N.C.: Duke University Press, 1991), pp. 48–70.

101. For the "kindergarten" remark, see Zelikow interview with Chernyayev, Moscow, January 1994. For the rest, see Adomeit, "'Midwife of History' or 'Sorcerer's Apprentice'?," p. 209; see also Wjatscheslaw Kotschemassow, *Meine letzte Mission* (Berlin: Dietz, 1994), pp. 49–60; Günter Schabowski, *Das Politbüro: Ende eines Mythos,* ed. Frank Sieren and Ludwig Söhne (Reinbek bei Hamburg: Rowohlt, 1990), pp. 34–36.

102. Kotschemassow, *Meine letzte Mission,* pp. 121–129, 143–144, 148–155; Reinhold Andert and Wolfgang Herzberg, eds., *Der Sturz: Erich Honecker in Kreuzverhör* (Berlin: Aufbau, 1990), p. 62; Zelikow interview with Chernyayev, Moscow, January 1994.

103. David Childs, *The GDR: Moscow's German Ally,* 2nd ed. (London: Unwin Hyman, 1988), p. xii.

104. Ash, *The Magic Lantern,* p. 64. On the East German government's use of forced "exit" as a tool of control, see Albert O. Hirschman, "Exit, Voice, and the Fate of the German Democratic Republic: An Essay in Conceptual History," *World Politics,* 45 (January 1993): 183–185. On the loosening of general travel restrictions, "It is conceivable that between one-fifth and one-quarter of the total East German population found itself in the Federal Republic at one time or another [just] in 1987"; McAdams, *Germany Divided,* p. 167. The discussion that follows also draws on these additional sources for the internal political environment of the GDR in the 1980s: the account of Bonn's representative in East Berlin during much of the decade, Hans-Otto Bräutigam, in "Die deutsche Geschichte ist voller Spaltung," *Die Zeit,* January 13, 1989; Childs, *The GDR;* Daniel Hamilton, "Dateline East Germany: The Wall behind the Wall," *Foreign Policy,* 76 (Fall 1989): 176–197; Manfred Lötsch (a sociologist in the GDR), "From Stagnation to Transformation: The Sociology of the 'GDR Revolution,'" in *The German Revolution of 1989: Causes and Consequences,* ed. Gert-Joachim Glaessner and Ian Wallace (Oxford: Berg, 1992), esp. pp. 43–50; McAdams, *Germany Divided,* pp. 175–193; and A. James McAdams, *East Germany and Detente: Building Authority after the Wall* (Cambridge: Cambridge University Press, 1985).

105. See Armin Mitter and Stefan Wolle, eds., *Ich liebe euch doch alle!: Befehle und Lageberichte des MfS Januar-November 1989,* 3d ed. (Berlin: BasisDruck, 1990), p. 28. The eighty-two-year-old Mielke had helped purge noncommunist republicans in the international brigades in Spain in the 1930s. He had worked for the East German security apparatus from its inception, before the GDR became a state, and had headed the security ministry for thirty-two years; Childs, *The GDR,* pp. 355–356.

106. For the "taboo" quote, see Schabowski, *Das Politbüro,* p. 36; for the "wallpaper" quote, see interview with Kurt Hager, the GDR's chief ideologue and minister for culture and science, in "Jedes Land wählt seine Lösung," *Stern,* April 9, 1987.

107. On the "touch of shame" one member of the East German Politbüro felt about the "manipulated and falsified" election results, see Günter Schabowski, *Der Absturz* (Berlin: Rowohlt, 1991), pp. 172–177.

108. Estimate from now public Stasi report in Gert-Joachim Glaessner, "Political Structures in Transition," in Glaessner and Wallace, *The German Revolution of 1989,* p. 13.

109. Reinhold quoted in Asmus, Brown, and Crane, *Soviet Foreign Policy and the Revolutions of 1989 in Eastern Europe,* p. 85.

2. Revisiting the German Question

1. Alexis de Tocqueville, *Recollections,* ed. J. P. Mayer, trans. Alexander Teixiera de Mattos (London: Harvill Press, 1948), pp. 67–68.

2. Fritz Stern, *Dreams and Delusions: The Drama of German History* (New York: Random House, 1987), p. 119.

3. Gerhard L. Weinberg, *A World at Arms: A Global History of World War II* (New York: Cambridge University Press, 1994), pp. 898–899.

4. Elie Wiesel, *From the Kingdom of Memory: Reminiscences* (New York: Schocken, 1990), p. 195.

5. See Adam Ulam, *Expansion and Coexistence: Soviet Foreign Policy, 1917–1973*, 2d ed. (New York: Praeger, 1974), pp. 156–169.

6. A useful summary of the development of the German question in the postwar period is Frank Ninkovich, *Germany and the United States: The Transformation of the German Question since 1945*, updated ed. (New York: Twayne, 1995).

7. British memorandum of conversation from Bevin's March 24, 1947, meeting with Stalin, reprinted in Department of State, Office of the Historian, *Foreign Relations of the United States, 1947:3* (Washington, D.C.: Department of State, 1972), p. 279; hereinafter *FRUS*.

8. Communiqué of the Tripartite Conference of Berlin (Potsdam), 1 Aug 45, art. VIII(B); reprinted in Department of State, *Documents on Germany, 1944–1985* (Washington, D.C.: Department of State, 1986), p. 63.

9. Declaration Regarding the Defeat of Germany and the Assumption of Supreme Authority with Respect to Germany, 5 Jun 45, in Department of State, *Documents on Germany*, p. 33.

10. Harold Zink, *The United States in Germany, 1944–1955* (Princeton, N.J.: Van Nostrand, 1957), p. 89.

11. Address by Secretary Byrnes, Stuttgart, 6 Sep 46, in *Documents on Germany*, pp. 94–96.

12. On Marshall in Moscow, see Philip Zelikow, "George C. Marshall and the 1947 CFM Meeting in Moscow," ms. pending publication. Quotations are from Marshall to President Truman and Lovett, 17 Mar 47, in *FRUS*, 1947:2, pp. 256–257; and Forrest Pogue, "George C. Marshall and the Marshall Plan," in *The Marshall Plan and Germany: West German Development within the Framework of the European Recovery Program*, ed. Charles Maier with Günter Bischof (New York: Berg, 1991), p. 49.

13. Michael Howard, introduction to Olav Riste, ed., *Western Security: The Formative Years* (Oslo: Norwegian University Press, 1985), p. 14.

14. See, e.g., Vojtech Mastny, *Russia's Road to the Cold War: Diplomacy, Warfare, and the Politics of Communism* (New York: Columbia University Press, 1979), pp. 310–311; William Taubman, *Stalin's American Policy: From Entente to Détente to Cold War* (New York: Norton, 1982), pp. 99–165.

15. Ulam, *Expansion and Coexistence*, pp. 402–403.

16. Viktor L. Mal'kov, "Commentary," in *Origins of the Cold War: The Novikov, Kennan, and Roberts "Long Telegrams" of 1946*, ed. Kenneth M. Jensen, 2d ed. (Washington, D.C.: U.S. Institute of Peace, 1993), pp. 76–77.

17. Stalin quotation is from East German archival records of his December 1948 meeting with the East German communist leader Wilhelm Pieck; see Dietrich Staritz, "The SED, Stalin, and the German Question: Interests and Decision-Making in the Light of New Sources," *German History*, 10 (October 1992): 274, 281. See generally Norman M. Naimark, *The Russians in Germany* (Cambridge: Harvard University Press, 1995).

18. Wolfram P. Hanrieder, *Germany, America, Europe: Forty Years of German Foreign Policy* (New Haven: Yale University Press, 1989), p. 6.

19. See Kennan to Marshall and Lovett, "Policy Questions Concerning a Possible German Settlement," 12 Aug 48, in *FRUS*, 1948:2, pp. 1287–97. On the development of this proposal, see the excellent study by Wilson D. Miscamble, *George F. Kennan and the Making of American Foreign Policy, 1947–1950* (Princeton: Princeton University Press, 1992),

pp. 145–147; and Anders Stephanson, *Kennan and the Art of Foreign Policy* (Cambridge, Mass.: Harvard University Press, 1989), pp. 130–145.

20. George F. Kennan, *Memoirs, 1925–1950* (New York: Random House, 1967), p. 258.

21. George F. Kennan, untitled paper, 8 Mar 49, in *FRUS*, 1949:3, pp. 96–98.

22. On the reaction to Kennan's proposal, see *FRUS*, 1948:2, pp. 1287–88 n. 1.

23. See Policy Planning Staff, "Position to Be Taken by the U.S. at a CFM Meeting," 15 Nov 48, in *FRUS*, 1948:2, p. 1324; Kennan, *Memoirs, 1925–1950*, pp. 418–446.

24. Dean Acheson, *Present at the Creation: My Years in the State Department* (New York: W. W. Norton, 1969), p. 288.

25. Bevin to Acheson (recounting a trip Bevin had just made to Berlin and the British zone), delivered 10 May 49, in *FRUS*, 1949:3, pp. 870–871; see also the message from the Foreign Office in London to the British embassy in Washington which was passed by the embassy to American officials on 10 May 49, ibid., pp. 867–869.

26. Acheson to President Truman (summarizing his explanation to a meeting of the National Security Council on May 18, 1949), quoted in Miscamble, *Kennan and the Making of American Foreign Policy*, p. 171 n. 126.

27. Paul H. Nitze with Ann M. Smith and Steven L. Rearden, *From Hiroshima to Glasnost: At the Center of Decision, A Memoir* (New York: Grove Weidenfeld, 1989), pp. 71–72. As late as February 1951 Acheson mused to Secretary of Defense George Marshall about "the possibility of withdrawal of troops in Germany." He "recalled that the Military had been against this sometime back and he wondered if there was any change in their attitude at this time." Marshall and others convinced Acheson that the old idea had now been overtaken by events. Hermann-Josef Rupieper, "American Policy toward German Unification, 1949–1955," in *American Policy and the Reconstruction of West Germany*, ed. Jeffrey Diefendorf, Axel Frohn, and Hermann-Josef Rupieper (New York: Cambridge University Press, 1993), pp. 55–56.

28. Convention on Relations between the Three Powers and the Federal Republic of Germany, May 26, 1952, as modified by the Paris Accords of October 1954; reprinted in Department of State, *Documents on Germany*, pp. 425–430. The term "European community" was meant as a general idea. The European Community as an institution had not yet been created.

29. See HICOG 1644, 24 Feb 50, and Office of German Political Affairs, "German Unity and East-West Political Relations within Germany," 13 Mar 50, both in *FRUS*, 1950:4, pp. 602–605, 608–611, and n. 4, 605.

30. Rupieper, "American Policy toward German Unification," p. 50.

31. Soviet note, 10 Mar 52, in *FRUS*, 1952–1954:7, pp. 169–172. See Gerhard Wettig, "Stalin and German Reunification: Archival Evidence on Soviet Foreign Policy in Spring 1952," *Historical Journal* 37 (1994): 411–419. On West German reaction to this note, see Rolf Steininger, *Eine vertane Chance: Die Stalin-Note vom 10. März 1952 und die Wiedervereinigung* (Bonn: Dietz, 1985), pp. 30–42. This book was controversial within Germany for its assertion that Adenauer had "lost" a chance to reunify his country by being so wedded to the Western political-military system. As the debate over German unification reignited in 1989, this thesis seemed quite relevant. Steininger's book was translated into English and published as *The German Question: The Stalin Note of 1952 and the Problem of Reunification*, ed. Mark Cioc, trans. Jane T. Hedges (New York: Columbia University Press, 1990).

32. McCloy to Robert Bowie, 13 Mar 52, quoted in Thomas A. Schwartz, *America's Germany: John J. McCloy and the Federal Republic of Germany* (Cambridge, Mass.: Harvard University Press, 1991), p. 380 n. 54. On the views of East German leaders, see Staritz, "The SED, Stalin, and the German Question," pp. 284–289.

33. State 2209, 22 Mar 52, in *FRUS*, 1952–1954:7, pp. 189–190.

34. Steininger, *The German Question*, p. 121.

35. Pollak to Jessup, "Departmental Views on Germany," 2 Apr 52, in *FRUS*, 1952–1954:7, pp. 194–196. Steininger examined these deliberations but erroneously concluded that the State Department was opposed to reunification. Steininger, *Eine vertane Chance*, pp. 72–75. In fact, Bohlen reluctantly summarized a consensus reaching the conclusion quoted in the text.

36. Moscow telegram to State, 25 May 52, in *FRUS*, 1952–1954:7, p. 253. See also Schwartz, *America's Germany*, pp. 267–269.

37. See Christian F. Ostermann, "The United States, the East German Uprising of 1953, and the Limits of Rollback," paper for the Cold War International History Project, Woodrow Wilson International Center for Scholars, Washington, D.C., December 1994. Eisenhower letter to Adenauer, 23 Jul 53, in *FRUS*, 1952–1954:7, pp. 493–494. For a sense of the underlying private ambivalence, see NSC 160/1, "United States Position with Respect to Germany," August 1953, ibid., pp. 514–515.

38. See James Richter, "Reexamining Soviet Policy towards Germany during the Beria Interregnum," paper for the Cold War International History Project, Woodrow Wilson International Center for Scholars, Washington, D.C., June 1992. For evidence of the shadow this episode cast on the later behavior of Soviet officials, see Valentin Falin, *Politische Erinnerungen*, trans. Heddy Pross-Weerth (Munich: Droemer Knaur, 1993), pp. 315–316, 497; Julij A. Kwizinskij, *Vor dem Sturm: Erinnerungen eines Diplomaten*, trans. Hilde and Helmut Ettinger (Berlin: Siedler, 1993), p. 13.

39. See the record of the NSC meeting on July 28, 1955, in *FRUS*, 1955–1957:5, p. 531.

40. Note from the USSR to the United States, 27 Nov 58, in Department of State, *Documents on Germany*, p. 555; see Hope M. Harrison, "Ulbricht and the Concrete 'Rose': New Archival Evidence on the Dynamics of Soviet–East German Relations and the Berlin Crisis, 1958–1961," Working Paper no. 5, Cold War International History Project, Woodrow Wilson International Center for Scholars, May 1993.

41. Interview of President Kennedy by Alexei Adzhubei, editor of *Izvestiya*, Hyannis Port, 25 Nov 61, in Department of State, *Documents on Germany*, p. 802; Nikita S. Khrushchev, *Khrushchev Remembers: The Last Testament*, trans. and ed. Strobe Talbott (Boston: Little, Brown, 1974), pp. 501–509. The Soviets had been especially worried about the combined prospects of a Germany reunified under West German domination coupled with the fear that such a Germany might acquire nuclear weapons. See Marc Trachtenberg, *History and Strategy* (Princeton: Princeton University Press, 1991), pp. 169–234. But Kennedy's escalation of the military confrontation in 1961 may have cowed Khrushchev into taking a more defensive stance, reflected in Khrushchev's authorizing construction of the Berlin Wall. See Trachtenberg, *History and Strategy*, pp. 218–222.

42. Adenauer quoted in diary of Heinrich Krone; see Daniel Körfer, *Kampf ums Kanzleramt: Erhard und Adenauer* (Stuttgart: Deutsche Verlags Anstalt, 1987), p. 636. On Kennedy's view of Adenauer, see the well-documented but unflattering picture of Kennedy's thinking offered in Frank Mayer, "Adenauer and Kennedy: Distrust in German-American Relations," *German Studies Review*, 17 (February 1994): 83–104.

43. On the transition in West German thinking, see Arnulf Baring with Manfred Görtemaker, *Machtwechsel: Die Ära Brandt-Scheel* (Stuttgart: Deutsche Verlags-Anstalt, 1982), esp. pp. 197–236; and Peter Bender, *Neue Ostpolitik: Vom Mauerbau bis zum Moskauer Vertrag* (Munich: Deutscher Taschenbuch, 1986). The actual phrase "change through rapprochement" ("Wandel durch Annäherung") was first used by Egon Bahr, then SPD leader Willy Brandt's press spokesman, in remarks that accompanied a formal address delivered by Brandt at the Protestant Academy in Tutzing in June 1963. See Timothy Garton Ash, *In Europe's Name: Germany and the Divided Continent* (New York: Random

House, 1993), pp. 65–67. It was therefore no coincidence that more than twenty-six years later, in January 1990, Foreign Minister Genscher chose this same venue in Tutzing to explain his views about the path to German unity.

44. Brandt interview in *U.S. News and World Report,* December 29, 1969, quoted in Ash, *In Europe's Name,* p. 134. See treaty between the Federal Republic of Germany and the Soviet Union, signed in Moscow, 12 Aug 70, in Department of State, *Documents on Germany,* pp. 1103–5. This treaty included an exchange of notes from the FRG to the United States, Britain, and France and from the United States, Britain, and France to the FRG reiterating the "immutability" of quadripartite rights. Department of State, *Documents on Germany,* pp. 1100–1101. Similar sets of notes were exchanged in connection with the treaty between the Federal Republic of Germany and Poland concerning the basis for normalizing their mutual relations, signed in Warsaw, 7 Dec 70, and the Treaty on the Basis of Relations between the Federal Republic of Germany and the German Democratic Republic, signed in Berlin, 21 Dec 72. Department of State, *Documents on Germany,* pp. 1125–27, 1215–31.

45. As early as 1961 Kissinger had privately advised President Kennedy to view Willy Brandt, then a leading opposition figure in the SPD, as an attractive alternative to Adenauer and suggested that the SPD's greater interest in accommodating Soviet anxiety about Germany meant that "a gain in Socialist strength would be favorable for us in the long run." Quoted in Mayer, "Adenauer and Kennedy," p. 85.

46. See sec. 1(A), principles I and X, of the Final Act of the Conference on Security and Cooperation in Europe, Helsinki, 1 Aug 75, in Department of State, *Documents on Germany,* pp. 1287–88, 1291. For background on the negotiation of this key language, with Kissinger carrying the water for the West Germans, see the account of an American diplomat, John J. Maresca, *To Helsinki: The Conference on Security and Cooperation in Europe, 1973–1975* (Durham, N.C.: Duke University Press, 1983), pp. 110–116.

47. Helsinki Final Act, in Department of State, *Documents on Germany,* p. 1288; also Seitz to Zoellick, "Helsinki Final Act and German Unification," 12 May 90.

48. Address by President von Weizsäcker, Düsseldorf, 8 Jun 85, in Department of State, *Documents on Germany,* p. 1415. On the "European peace order" see, e.g., address by Hans-Dietrich Genscher, Potsdam, 11 Jun 88, in Hans-Dietrich Genscher, *Unterwegs zur Einheit: Reden und Dokumente aus bewegter Zeit* (Berlin: Siedler, 1991), pp. 151–169.

49. Hanrieder, *Germany, America, and Europe,* pp. 179–180. Egon Bahr was arguing by the 1980s that even paying lip service to the goal of reunification had become "hypocritical." Quoted in David Marsh, *The Germans: A People at the Crossroads* (New York: St. Martin's Press, 1990), p. 58.

50. Ash, *In Europe's Name,* p. 178.

51. Ibid., pp. 152–176, 188–189; A. James McAdams, *Germany Divided: From the Wall to Reunification* (Princeton: Princeton University Press, 1993), p. 176. On current political debates in Germany over the assignment or avoidance of blame for this result, see A. James McAdams, "Revisiting the *Ostpolitik* in the 1990s," *German Politics and Society,* 30 (Fall 1993): 49–60.

52. Brandt quoted in McAdams, *Germany Divided,* p. 134. By 1984 only 17 percent of West Germans reported in a poll that they considered reunification "possible" within the next thirty years. Gebhard Schweigler, "German Questions or the Shrinking of Germany," in *The Two German States and European Security,* ed. F. Stephen Larrabee (New York: St. Martin's Press, 1989), p. 94. In 1985 Timothy Garton Ash wrote a fine essay capturing such German attitudes on their national question; see *The Uses of Adversity: Essays on the Fate of Central Europe* (New York: Random House, 1989), pp. 71–104.

53. Rommel quote and subsequent quotations by Schmidt and Kohl are taken from interviews conducted by, and Kohl press conference quoted in, Marsh, *The Germans*, pp. 55, 115–118.

3. The Fall of Ostpolitik and the Berlin Wall

1. The April 1989 poll, conducted by Emnid, was reported in *Der Spiegel*, April 10, 1989, p. 156. The poll showed that only 56 percent of West Germans thought that unification should remain a goal of FRG policy. In 1987, 80 percent of West Germans had backed the goal, but at that time only 3 percent thought that it would ever happen. Silke Jansen, *Meinungsbilder zur deutschen Frage* (Frankfurt: Peter Lang, 1990), p. 98.

2. Dieter Grosser, "Triebkräfte der Wiedervereinigung," and Friedrich Kurz, "Ungarn 89," in *Die sieben Mythen der Wiedervereinigung: Fakten und Analysen zu einem Prozeß ohne Alternative*, ed. Dieter Grosser, Stephan Bierling, and Friedrich Kurz (Munich: Ehrenwirth, 1991), pp. 37–38, 123–124, and 130 (for the quote from Nemeth, interviewed by Kurz). The American embassy in East Berlin also received this explanation of how East Germans would be handled after checking with Hungarian diplomats. G. Jonathan Greenwald, *Berlin Witness: An American Diplomat's Chronicle of East Germany's Revolution* (University Park: Pennsylvania State University Press, 1993), pp. 6, 22–23.

3. Schabowski in an interview with Elizabeth Pond, quoted in Pond, *Beyond the Wall: Germany's Road to Unification* (Washington, D.C.: Brookings Institution, 1993), p. 90.

4. By mid-1989 there were approximately five hundred opposition groups operating under the aegis of the Protestant church (which included both Lutherans and Calvinists in a decentralized structure of lay synods). These groups were publishing small newsletters, officially intended for internal church use only but actually reaching a broader readership. After the rigged May elections the groups came out of the churches and started demonstrating in Dresden and Leipzig. Six main groups emerged during the summer months, the most visible being New Forum. See *Politische Zielvorstellungen wichtiger Oppositionsgruppen in der DDR* (Bonn: Gesamtdeutsches Institut, 1990), pp. 2–3. Demonstrators became bolder too. For example, after police broke up a July 7 demonstration by detaining 97 people, 140 more met at an alternative site and demonstrated for reform. Armin Mitter and Stefan Wolle, eds., *Ich liebe euch doch alle!: Befehle und Lageberichte des MfS Januar-November 1989* (Berlin: Basis Druck, 1990), pp. 108–109.

5. EmbBerlin 6311, "The GDR's Silent Crisis: A Commentary," 4 Aug 89.

6. See, e.g., Eagleburger (Acting) to the President, 24 Aug 89 (for his evening reading); Eagleburger (Acting) to the President, 29 Aug 89 (for his evening reading). A good reflection of ambivalence among the department's German experts can be found in Marc Fisher, "The Unanswered 'German Question,'" *Washington Post*, July 27, 1989, p. A25. Bush's rhetoric was duly noted by diplomats and commentators in West Germany, but Fisher quotes the prominent West German professor Karl Kaiser's comment, "You Americans have taken our reunification debate far more seriously than we have." The Soviets, Kaiser said, simply would not allow a political reunification of Germany.

7. Ross to Baker, 9 Aug 89. There is no evidence that Baker read or acted on this paper. The formal dialogue the policy planning staff recommended was not initiated.

8. *Pravda*, August 12, 1989, p. 5, quoting a letter-writing campaign of "ordinary citizens" in the East German official newspaper, *Neues Deutschland*.

9. Greenwald, *Berlin Witness*, pp. 99, 105.

10. See Kurz, "Ungarn 89," pp. 135–140 (drawing heavily from discussions with Nemeth).

11. Dennis Bark and David Gress, *A History of West Germany: Democracy and Its Discontents, 1963–1991*, 2d ed. (Cambridge: Basil Blackwell, 1993), pp. 597–598.

12. See A. James McAdams, *Germany Divided: From the Wall to Reunification* (Princeton: Princeton University Press, 1993), p. 188.

13. Seiters made his appeal on August 9. See Deutschland Archiv, *Chronik der Ereignisse in der DDR* (Cologne: Verlag Wissenschaft und Politik, 1990), pp. 1–2; Antonius John, *Rudolf Seiters: Einsichten In Amt, Person und Ereignisse* (Bonn: Bouvier, 1991), p. 73.

14. Quoted in Greenwald, *Berlin Witness*, p. 105.

15. See Friedrich Karl Fromme, "Die Bundesrepublik hat Deutschen aus der DDR Schutz zu gewähren als deutschen Staatsangehörigen," *Frankfurter Allgemeine Zeitung*, August 21, 1989, p. 3.

16. Konrad H. Jarausch, *The Rush to German Unity* (New York: Oxford University Press, 1994), p. 28; Bark and Gress, *Democracy and Its Discontents*, pp. 589–594, 608–613; "Das droht die DDR zu vernichten," *Der Spiegel*, August 14, 1989, p. 18.

17. "Surprise" quote is from Zelikow interview with Kastrup, Bonn, December 1994; Zelikow and Rice interview with Teltschik, Gütersloh, June 1992; letter to Honecker, mid-August (probably August 19 or 20), 1989, in Peter Przybylski, *Tatort Politbüro: Honecker, Mittag und Schalck-Golodkowski*, vol. 2 (Berlin: Rowohlt, 1992), p. 110; see also Ralf Georg Reuth and Andreas Bönte, *Das Komplott: Wie es wirklich zur deutschen Einheit kam* (Munich: Piper, 1993), pp. 56–58.

18. Kurz, "Ungarn 89," pp. 131–134.

19. Ibid., pp. 145–156.

20. Account based on Zelikow interviews with Genscher, Wachtberg-Pech, December 1994; Teltschik, Munich, December 1994; and Kastrup, Bonn, December 1994. See also Richard Kiessler and Frank Elbe, *Ein runder Tisch mit scharfen Ecken: Der diplomatische Weg zur deutschen Einheit* (Baden-Baden: Nomos, 1993), p. 30; Kurz, "Ungarn 89," pp. 156–157; John, *Seiters*, p. 82.

21. Gyula Horn, *Freiheit, die ich meine: Erinnerungen des ungarischen Aussenministers, der den Eisernen Vorhang öffnete*, trans. Angelika and Peter Mate (Hamburg: Hoffmann und Campe, 1991), pp. 312–326; Kurz, "Ungarn 89," pp. 158–160.

22. See Wjatscheslaw Kotschemassow, *Meine letzte Mission* (Berlin: Dietz, 1994), p. 163; Memorandum of conversation (hereinafter Memcon) for Honecker meeting with Gorbachev, Moscow, 28 Jun 89, published in Daniel Küchenmeister with Gerd-Rüdiger Stephan, eds., *Honecker Gorbatschow: Vieraugengespräche* (Berlin: Dietz, 1993), p. 209.

23. Ibid., pp. 219–220. Egon Krenz, then a member of the East German Politbüro, said later that he had no doubt about Gorbachev's support for the East German state. Ekkehard Kuhn, *Gorbatschow und die deutsche Einheit: Aussagen der wichtigsten russischen und deutschen Beteiligten* (Bonn: Bouvier, 1993), pp. 25–26 (transcripts of interviews conducted in preparation for a German television documentary). For Gorbachev's vague recollections of his three "vier augen" conversations with Kohl in Bonn, see Kuhn, *Gorbatschow und die deutsche Einheit*, pp. 35–36.

24. The U.S. account of the meeting was reported in Bonn 28695, 7 Sep 89.

25. Kurz, "Ungarn 89," p. 161.

26. Rice interview with Tarasenko, Moscow, October 1991.

27. See M. Podklyuchnikov, *Pravda*, August 12, 1989, p. 3; M. Podklyuchnikov, *Pravda*, August 13, 1989, p. 5; Czech article from *Trybuna Ludu*, August 18, 1989, reprinted in *Sovietskaya Rossiya*, August 20, 1989.

28. See reportage in *Izvestiya* and *Trud* daily from September 13–16, 1989, and TV program *Novosti*, September 11, 1989, in *FBIS-SOV* 89–175, September 12, 1989, p. 32.

29. *Pravda*, August 19, 1989, p. 3.

30. *Pravda*, August 21, 1989, p. 1. Rakowski's comment is reported in the same article, and there is extensive coverage of the strikes in Poland on pp. 5–6.

31. Carried on Warsaw Television Service, August 17, 1989; in *FBIS-SOV* 89–158, August 18, 1989.

32. *Izvestiya*, August 24, 1989, p. 2.

33. On this point, see, e.g., Herbert Kremp, "A Gorbachev Doctrine for Eastern Europe," *Die Welt am Sonntag* (Hamburg), August 20, 1989, p. 2, in *FBIS-SOV* 89–161, August 22, 1989, pp. 20–21.

34. Shevardnadze, Yakovlev, Yazov, and Kryuchkov to members of the Politburo, "Ob obstanovkiye v ol'she, vozmozhnykh variantakh ego razvitiya, perspektivakh sovetskopol'skikh otnoshenii," Notes from Protocol no. 166 for the Meeting of the Politburo of the Central Committee, 28 Sep 89, in the Center for the Storage of Contemporary Documentation (TsKhSD), Moscow, no. P166/23. See also cable from Soviet Embassy, Warsaw, "O kontaktakh Solidarnosti s Nezivisimymi politicheskimi dvizheniyami vostochno-evropeiskikh stran," 8 Feb 90, in TsKhSD, Moscow.

35. Rice interview with Tarasenko, Moscow, October 1991.

36. Ibid.

37. Gorbachev's surprise at Ligachev's invocation of his name is from Rice communication with Chernyayev, September 1994. For the Foreign Ministry reaction, see *Pravda*, September 14, 1989, p. 5.

38. The account of Gorbachev's reluctance is based on Zelikow interview with Chernyayev, Moscow, January 1994. The cautious statement was made by Foreign Ministry spokesman Gennady Gerasimov in a press briefing on September 15, reported in *Izvestiya*, September 16, 1989, p. 2.

39. *Krasnaya zvezda*, September 28, 1989, p. 2.

40. Michael Beschloss and Strobe Talbott, *At the Highest Levels: The Inside Story of the End of the Cold War* (Boston: Little, Brown, 1993), pp. 107–108.

41. See TASS International Service (Moscow), "TASS Statement Supports GDR in FRG Campaign," 11 Sep 89, in *FBIS-SOV* 89–175, September 12, 1989, p. 32; Central Committee Secretariat, "O zayavlenii TASS v podderzhku Germanskoi Demokraticheskoi Respubliki," Note to Protocol no. 165 for the Meeting of the Politburo, 11 Sep 89, in TsKhSD, Moscow, no. P165/6. See also Yevgeniy Grigoryev, "Reading the Script, or Something about Bonn's Predictability," *Pravda*, September 23, 1989; A. Pavlov, "On the Wrong Track," *Pravda*, September 23, 1989, p. 5; and Moscow Television Service, the *World Today* program, 27 Sep 89, all in *FBIS-SOV* 89–188, September 29, 1989, pp. 31–33.

42. Julij A. Kwizinskij, *Vor dem Sturm: Erinnerungen eines Diplomaten* (Berlin: Siedler, 1993), p. 14. Although Kvitsinsky thought that Moscow was too complacent about the CDU party conference, others confirm that his reports on the Bremen meeting prompted the addition of a sharp warning to Shevardnadze's speech to the UN General Assembly at the end of September. Zelikow interview with Pavel Palazschenko, Moscow, January 1994. On Kohl's remarks and the Bremen conference, see "Kohl: Freiheit und Einheit fuer alle Deutschen," *Frankfurter Allgemeine Zeitung*, September 12, 1989, p. 6. Kohl's conservative CSU coalition partner Theo Waigel, in Munich, quickly made clear that all this talk was about human conditions, not about changing borders. See "Wiedervereinigung und Aussenpolitik," *Frankfurter Allgemeine Zeitung*, September 13, 1989, p. 4.

43. Memcon for meeting between Baker and Shevardnadze, September 21, 1989, 6:30–8:30 P.M., en route to Jackson Hole, Wyoming. The only listed participants in the discussion are Baker and Shevardnadze. Dennis Ross was the U.S. note taker. Tarasenko joined

Shevardnadze. Shevardnadze did not discuss the GDR crisis during his meeting in Washington with Bush or in larger meetings between the two delegations.

44. For Shevardnadze's speech, see "The Fate of the World Is Inseparable from the Fate of Our Perestroika," *Pravda*, September 27, 1989, pp. 4–5. The Soviet criticism of West German behavior was certainly being noticed in Washington. See, e.g., item in National Intelligence Daily, 30 Sep 89, titled "USSR: Critical of Renewed German Reunification Debate."

45. Horn, *Freiheit, die ich meine*, p. 327.

46. Kiessler and Elbe, *Ein runder Tisch mit scharfen Ecken*, pp. 30–31, 35–36.

47. See ibid., pp. 36–44; John, *Seiters*, pp. 82–104; Pond, *Beyond the Wall*, pp. 97–98. The Baker-Genscher exchange is from Zelikow interview with Genscher, Wachtberg-Pech, December 1994.

48. TASS, Moscow World News Service, "GDR Decision Guided by Justice," October 2, 1989, in *FBIS-SOV* 89–90, October 3, 1989, pp. 23–24.

49. TASS, "GDR Protests West Germany's Breach of Trust," October 2, 1989, in *FBIS-SOV* 89–190, October 3, 1989, pp 24–25.

50. This description is drawn from Werner Maser, *Helmut Kohl: Der Deutsche Kanzler* (Frankfurt: Ullstein, 1990); Guenter Muechler and Klaus Hofmann, *Helmut Kohl: Chancellor of German Unity* (Bonn: Federal Press and Information Office, 1992); Oskar Fehrenbach, "Helmut Kohl," in *Die Bundeskanzler*, ed. Hans Klein (Berlin: Edition Q, 1993), pp. 345–414; Werner Filmer and Heribert Schwan, *Helmut Kohl* (Duesseldorf: Econ, 1985); and Reinhard Appel, ed., *Kohl: Im Spiegel seiner Macht* (Bonn: Bouvier, 1990).

51. Peter Merkl, *German Unification in the European Context* (University Park: Pennsylvania State University Press, 1993), pp. 42–43.

52. On the conservative Tendenzwende, see Jeffrey Herf, *War by Other Means: Soviet Power, West German Resistance, and the Battle of the Euromissiles* (New York: Free Press, 1991).

53. On Schäuble, see Werner Filmer and Heribert Schwan, *Wolfgang Schäuble: Politik als Lebensaufgabe* (Munich: Bertelsmann, 1992).

54. Filmer and Schwan, *Helmut Kohl*, pp. 204–208.

55. Kiessler and Elbe, *Ein runder Tisch mit scharfen Ecken*, p. 121. On Kastrup, see also Udo Bergoff, "Im Profil," *Süddeutsche Zeitung*, March 15, 1990, p. 4.

56. For an illustration of this prevailing view from a relatively conservative commentator, see Friedrich Karl Fromme, "Flüchtlinge und deutsche Frage," *Frankfurter Allgemeine Zeitung*, September 26, 1989, p. 1.

57. "Kohl in Bremen als CDU-Vorsitzender wiedergewählt," *Frankfurter Allgemeine Zeitung*, September 12, 1989, p. 1.

58. *Pravda*, September 23, 1989, p. 5.

59. From Gorbachev's speech in East Berlin for the fortieth anniversary celebration of the GDR, published in *Izvestiya* and *Pravda*, October 8, 1989.

60. Baker's formal meeting with Genscher in New York at the time of the UN General Assembly session featured little discussion of East German developments. Genscher discussed the refugee problem and the need to engage East German opposition groups. He asked if Baker was planning to go to the GDR. Baker said he was not considering such a visit. The unification issue was not mentioned. Secto 14013, 28 Sep 89.

61. See Bonn 28695, September 7, 1989. For the Genscher interview, see *Der Spiegel*, September 25, 1989.

62. Bonn 29066, 11 Sep 89. Seiters replied cautiously, urging that America only help knock down intellectual and spiritual walls between the two Germanys in support of

reform. Eagleburger's message on unification was apparently his own idea, based on his understanding of where Bush stood. The briefing papers prepared for Eagleburger did not cover this point. But the U.S. ambassador to Germany, former Army general and intelligence official Vernon Walters, was outspoken in predicting that unification could be coming soon. Walters has built his memoirs around this very point. Vernon A. Walters, *Die Vereinigung war voraussehbar: Hinter den Kulissen eines entscheidenen Jahres—Die Aufzeichnungen des amerikanischen Botschafters,* trans. Helmut Ettinger (Berlin: Siedler, 1994), esp. pp. 25–41. Walters's intuitive and prescient prediction was not accompanied at the time by any notable analysis of the political situation or advice about what the United States should do. Even in his memoirs Walters seems more interested in railing against Baker and Baker's aides for having ignored or mistreated him than in analyzing the policy issues that were streaming past him.

63. Bush received another memo from his staff sympathetically discussing German aspirations for unity. Scowcroft to President Bush, "Dealing with the Germans," 7 Aug 89. Blackwill had drafted this memo on May 11; Bush did not read and initial it until September 9.

64. When Hungary annulled its agreement with the GDR and opened its border with Austria to departures by GDR citizens, Baker perceptively analyzed this development to President Bush. The next morning, in its briefings for top officials, the CIA underscored how serious this step would be for the GDR, and also noted the harsher Soviet criticisms of the West German government. See Baker to the President (for his evening reading), 11 Sep 89. Neither Baker's memo nor the CIA piece discussed the choices being made in West German policy. The U.S. embassy in East Berlin and the Department of State's European Bureau, now headed by Raymond Seitz, predicted that the GDR was headed toward "short-term stagnation," with the party facing a choice betwen hard-liners and reformists. See EmbBerlin 7534, 13 Sep 89; Seitz to Eagleburger, "GDR Adrift," 18 Sep 89.

65. *Public Papers of the Presidents: George Bush, 1989,* bk. 2 (Washington, D.C.: Government Printing Office, 1990), p. 1221. Jim Hoagland, "Honecker's Goetterdaemmerung," *Washington Post,* September 18, 1989, p. A19; Enno von Loewenstern, "German Unification Bobs Up in Refugee Flood," *Wall Street Journal,* September 18, 1989. The week before Flora Lewis had advised the administration "Go Slow on Germany," *New York Times,* September 12, 1989, p. A25.

66. Memcon from meeting with Waigel in the Oval Office on September 26.

67. Laurence H. McFalls, *Communism's Collapse, Democracy's Demise?: The Cultural Context and Consequences of the East German Revolution* (London: Macmillan, 1995), pp. 48, 49–53.

68. Robert Darnton, *Berlin Journal, 1989–1990* (New York: W. W. Norton, 1991), p. 11; see also pp. 96–98. The best single summary of the day's events in Leipzig, based on primary sources, is Elizabeth Pond, "The Day Leipzig's Residents Defied Their Masters," *Wall Street Journal* (Europe), October 7, 1994.

69. "From 1967 on, the Stasi even maintained a series of internment camps to herd dissidents into on some future day of reckoning, along with lists of up to 200,000 intended victims. Periodically, it conducted exercises to prepare for this final defeat of 'counterrevolution,' and district administrators of the operation continued to meet and plan for it up through early October 1989. Heinz Eggert—Protestant pastor and then, after unification, Saxony's interior minister—discovered just how up-to-date these plans were kept when he found out that one of the detention centers was to have been located 150 yards from his own house. Eggert joked later to a former Stasi officer that he could have walked to the camp. The officer replied, 'You, Herr Eggert, would not have reached it alive.'" Pond,

Beyond the Wall, pp. 80–81. On Mielke's orders see also Pond, "The Day Leipzig's Residents Defied Their Masters."

70. See, e.g., Reuth and Bönte, *Das Komplott;* Lally Weymouth, "Germany's Urge to Merge," *Washington Post,* March 4, 1990, p. C1. Wolf had created a sensation by publishing a book, *Die Troika,* which had contained an unmistakable attack on the current East German leadership and a plea for reformed socialism. See Markus Wolf, *Die Troika* (West Berlin: Claassen, 1989); Franz Löser, "Die Dreharbeiten sind in vollem Gange!: Gedanken zu Markus Wolfs Troika," *Deutschland Archiv,* no. 6 (1989): 639–642; and, on both Wolf and his book, Jeffrey Gedmin, *The Hidden Hand* (Washington, D.C.: AEI Press, 1992), pp. 82–84.

71. For the "sterility" phrase, see Igor Maximychev, "End of the Berlin Wall," *International Affairs* (Moscow) (March 1991): 100, 103. On contacts in the summer of 1989 between East German SED officials (and Markus Wolf) with disgruntled Soviet Germanists, including Falin, see Reuth and Bönte, *Das Komplott,* pp. 91–92; Gerhard Wettig, "Die sowjetische Rolle beim Umsturz in der DDR und bei der Einleitung des deutschen Einigungprozesses," in *Der Umbruch in Osteuropa,* ed. Jürgen Elvert and Michael Salewski (Stuttgart: Franz Steiner, 1993), pp. 44–45, 51.

72. Account based on Zelikow and Rice interview with Sergei Grigoriev, Cambridge, Mass., February 1995; see Erich Honecker, "GDR vhod ego piyat'letnii," *Pravda,* October 4, 1989.

73. See *Pravda* coverage of the trip, October 7–9, 1989.

74. Ibid.

75. For the quoted passage from the stenographic record of Gorbachev's meeting with the SED Politbüro, Berlin-Niederschönhausen, 7 Oct 89, see Günter Mittag, *Um Jeden Preis: Im Spannungfeld zweier Systeme* (Berlin: Aufbau, 1991), pp. 367, 370. For the Honecker meeting with Gorbachev, see Memcon for Honecker's meeting with Gorbachev, Berlin-Niederschönhausen, 7 Oct 89, in Küchenmeister and Stephan, *Honecker Gorbatschow,* pp. 240–251; Kotschemassow, *Meine letzte Mission,* pp. 109–110. For Gorbachev's own recollection of the messages he thought he was conveying, see interview excerpts in Kuhn, *Gorbatschow und die deutsche Einheit,* pp. 48–49, 50–51. For Krenz's recollections, see Egon Krenz with Hartmut König and Gunter Rettner, *Wenn Mauern Fallen: Die friedliche Revolution—Vorgeschichte, Ablauf, Auswirkungen* (Vienna: Paul Neff, 1990), pp. 86–87; Günter Schabowski, *Das Politbüro: Ende eines Mythos,* ed. Frank Sieren and Ludwig Söhne (Reinbek bei Hamburg: Rowohlt, 1990), pp. 73–75; Michael Sodaro, *Moscow, Germany, and the West: From Khrushchev to Gorbachev* (Ithaca, N.Y.: Cornell University Press, 1990), pp. 377–378; and Wettig, "Die sowjetische Rolle," pp. 49–50.

The phrase about life punishing those who fall behind actually reads, in the East German notes: "Ich halte es für sehr wichtig, den Zeitpunkt nicht zu verpassen und keine Chance zu vertun. Die Partei muss ihre eigene Auffassung haben, ihr eigenes Herantreten vorschlagen. Wenn wir zurückbleiben, bestraft uns das Leben sofort." For a perceptive comment on this language, see a letter to the editor from Heinz Geyr, "Originalton Gorbatschow," *Frankfurter Allgemeine Zeitung,* December 5, 1991, p. 8. For Gorbachev's comment to Krenz that he was actually talking about himself, see Memcon for meeting between Egon Krenz and Mikhail Gorbachev, Moscow, 1 Nov 89, in Bundesarchiv, Abt. Potsdam, E1–56320. On the translation error of the "life punishes" comment from its Russian original, see Portugalov interview excerpt in Kuhn, *Gorbatschow und die deutsche Einheit,* p. 48.

76. See Kotschemassow, *Meine letzte Mission,* pp. 168–169. Kochemasov's description of the episode was first reported in Stanislav Kondrashov, "Our Place in the World, or

Home Thoughts from Abroad," *Izvestiya*, April 30, 1990, p. 5, in *FBIS-SOV* 90–086, May 3, 1990, pp. 20, 23.

77. Zelikow interviews with Chernyayev and Igor Maximychev, Moscow, January 1994; Krenz interview excerpt in Kuhn, *Gorbatschow und die deutsche Einheit*, p. 54; Schabowski, *Der Absturz*, pp. 262–263; Schabowski, *Das Politbüro*, pp. 140–141; Gedmin, *The Hidden Hand*, pp. 104–105, 115; Pond, *Beyond the Wall*, pp. 106, 122–124 (based on firsthand evidence from Soviet, East German, and West German sources). Maximychev concluded that "Moscow was neither the initiator of Honecker's resignation nor the force behind it . . . [Gorbachev] merely acknowledged the change of leadership in the GDR and signified his readiness to cooperate with Egon Krenz." Igor Maximychev, "Possible 'Impossibilities,'" *International Affairs* (Moscow) June 1993: 109.

78. Maximychev, "Possible 'Impossibilities,'" p. 109.

79. Anatoly Chernyayev, "Obidiyeniye Germanii: Kak eto byilo?," unpublished ms. given to Rice in Moscow, June 1994; see also the discussion of Soviet and Stasi conspiracy theories in Pond, *Beyond the Wall*, pp. 122–127.

80. Maximychev, "End of the Berlin Wall," p. 104; see also Pond, *Beyond the Wall*, pp. 120–121; Krenz, *Wenn Mauern Fallen*, pp. 88–89, 144–145; Schabowski, *Das Politbüro*, pp. 110–111.

81. Pond, *Beyond the Wall*, pp. 121–122. Among the many accounts of the October protests and the downfall of Honecker, see also Kotschemassow, *Meine letzte Mission*, pp. 173–177; Bark and Gress, *Democracy and Its Discontents*, pp. 603–645; and Jarausch, *The Rush to German Unity*, pp. 33–48.

In Washington, Secretary of State Baker was attentive to developments in the GDR. While reading his briefing papers for an October 10 meeting with West German defense minister Gerhard Stoltenberg, Baker passed over the top four defense-related items on the agenda to underscore all the talking points prepared for him under the fifth and last item—inter-German affairs. Baker then turned his report to the president on the Stoltenberg meeting into an opportunity to comment accurately that the East German regime seemed to be at a turning point, about to choose between reform and repression. See Seitz to Baker, for his October 10 meeting with Stoltenberg, 6 Oct 89 (as marked up by Baker); Baker to President Bush (for his evening reading), 11 Oct 89.

82. On the offer to refugees, see interview with Wolfgang Meyer, *Neues Deutschland*, October 21/22, 1989, p. 1; on the dissatisfaction of the demonstrators with Krenz's first moves, see Maximychev, "End of the Berlin Wall," pp. 104–105; Jarausch, *The Rush to German Unity*, pp. 46–49, 51–52, 59–61.

83. On the Kohl-Krenz call, see the transcript published in *Der Spiegel*, December 3, 1990.

84. For the Krenz government's explanation to Washington of its plans, see Eagleburger to President Bush (for his evening reading) on Eagleburger's meeting with GDR deputy foreign minister Kurt Nier, 23 Oct 89. The American embassy in East Berlin estimated that "it is too early to say with confidence that he [Krenz] is sincere much less that he is likely to be successful, but a few more days like this most recent one will at least convince all observers that he has correctly identified his immediate challenge and that he is working at it"; EmbBerlin 8568, 26 Oct 89. Krenz "has done a lot in a short time, but he has not yet much affected the tough odds against him"; EmbBerlin 8683, 2 Nov 89. "The slogans on the banners and the mood of the marchers remain well in advance of where the new man yet says he is willing to lead the GDR, but he is showing far too much skill and adaptability to be written off prematurely"; EmbBerlin 8734, 6 Nov 89. Both the West Germans and the Americans had heard, however, that the Soviets themselves considered

Krenz a transitional figure. For the West Germans, see Kiessler and Elbe, *Ein runder Tisch mit scharfen Ecken*, p. 45 (on what Falin told Willy Brandt during Brandt's October 1989 visit); for the Americans, see CIA reports at the time and Dobbins (Acting) to Eagleburger, "Critical GDR Central Committee Plenum," 6 Nov 89.

85. The account that follows is based on Memcon for meeting between Egon Krenz and Mikhail Gorbachev, Moscow, 1 Nov 89, in Bundesarchiv, Abt. Potsdam, E1–56320. We are indebted to Charles Maier for helping us locate this document. On the circumstances of the meeting and some additional reflections, see the Krenz interview excerpts in Kuhn, *Gorbatschow und die deutsche Einheit*, pp. 56–60. Georgi Shakhnazarov was the note taker for Gorbachev; we do not know who accompanied Krenz. The discussion reveals that Gorbachev had a perception of Kohl similar to opinions often found in the West German SPD, probably a reflection of Falin's role with Shakhnazarov in preparing Gorbachev for this meeting.

86. Rice interview with Chernyayev, Moscow, June 1994.

87. Baker to President Bush (for his evening reading), 10 Oct 89. This note provided the State Department's first formal comment for the president on developments in the GDR: "All the [West German political] parties agree that the GDR must remain stable if it is to reform. Kohl and the SPD opposition thus appear to have buried the hatchet for now on what was becoming a divisive domestic issue." A week later the State Department (like most West Germans) still believed that after an initial flurry of debate, the FRG had "elected to continue its current policy of pursuing 'small steps' toward the GDR and calling on the GDR leadership to pursue a course of reform." Seitz to Kimmitt, for his October 24 meeting with Ambassador Barkley, 17 Oct 89; see also EmbBerlin 8466, "GDR Crisis: The Honecker Era Fades Quickly," 20 Oct 89; Seitz to Eagleburger, for his October 20 meeting with Ambassador Barkley, 19 Oct 89: "It is not yet clear what course Krenz will follow . . . It is not yet clear how the FRG will respond to the succession of Krenz to the leadership position." For an indication of even more uncertainty, see Mulholland (Assistant Secretary for Intelligence and Research) to Kimmitt, "The German Question Revidius," 19 Oct 89 (drafted by Phil Kaplan): "There is no way of divining just how the German debate will evolve in the medium term. There are too many possibilities . . . We cannot foresee exactly how all this will evolve, whether towards unification, confederation or some other form. Nor, in the present political environment, can we foreclose repression in the East or a sudden collapse of the GDR regime leading to its consolidation with the FRG. In a five year perspective these prospects may appear still more possible."

88. Bonn 34271, "The German Question and Reunification," 25 Oct 89.

89. Ibid.

90. In Washington, the National Intelligence Council (guided by the national intelligence officer for Western Europe, Martin van Heuven) believed that Bonn regarded the debate on German reunification mainly "as a factor complicating its more immediate commitment to a CSCE process and a European framework of detente." NIC, "Executive Brief: Outlook for East Germany," October 27, 1989. A member of the State Department's policy planning staff, Roger George, traveled to the FRG and GDR in October. His report, read by Ross and Zoellick, provides a good summary of the spectrum of West German opinion on the national question at the time. He noted that Chancellery and Foreign Ministry officials in Bonn were discouraging speculation about changing the 'political map' of Europe. But, George thought, "We have only begun to see the renewed ferment on the 'German Question.'" He noted that Ambassador Barkley in East Berlin seemed to differ with State's European bureau (EUR) and the embassy in Bonn. EUR and the Bonn embassy were inclined to follow the West German lead and take on the national question

if the West Germans wished. George, through his representation of Barkley's views, was of the opinion that the United States should not be guided by the FRG (presumably since it might go too far) but had a broader interest in assuaging British and French fears about German motives. George suggested that Washington stop endorsing the term "reunification" and instead substitute the milder term "reconciliation" to describe the way in which Germans might achieve their national aspirations. George to Ross, 26 Oct 89.

91. Zelikow and Rice interview with Teltschik, Gütersloh, June 1992.

92. See, e.g., interview with Secretary Baker on NBC-TV, *Meet the Press,* October 8, 1989 (pp. 7–8 of PA transcript, PR no. 186).

93. On October 16 Baker was to address the Foreign Policy Association in New York. The main focus was how to find "points of mutual advantage" in U.S.-Soviet relations. Scowcroft felt that, since Kohl was still offering carefully nuanced statements on unification, the United States should do the same. Bush had in fact endorsed unification in his May *Washington Times* interview and again during his Montana press conference in September. But Scowcroft drew a distinction between press interviews and deliberate, formal policy statements by top administration officials. So, in the portion of his speech dealing with Germany, Secretary Baker said: "Of course the United States and our NATO partners have long supported the *reconciliation* of the German people. Their legitimate rights must some day be met. But let me be clear—*reconciliation* through self-determination can *only* be achieved in peace and freedom. Normalization must occur on the basis of Western values with the end result being a people integrated into the community of democratic European nations [emphasis added]." Ross and Zoellick, briefing reporters on the speech, were forced into the kind of argument Genscher and most other West German officials made, placing the issue in the context of a broader evolutionary process of European integration and the general acceptance of Western values. Department of State Background Briefing on U.S.-Soviet Relations, October 16, 1989, pp. 3–5. This account is based on Zelikow interviews with both Scowcroft and Zoellick in 1991.

Throughout October working-level officials within the State Department had been involved in a separate, parallel debate about what Baker should say about unification. State's policy planning staff was both more worried about German movement toward reunification and more interested in developing an active U.S. policy to steer West German policy. So Ross privately urged Baker early in October to think about how to engage the Germans in a "sensible discussion of reunification without misleading them or alarming the other allies," and to consider the need for U.S. initiatives. Ross attached a paper prepared by a member of his staff, Roger George, reviewing U.S. policy. See Ross to Baker, "Reunification Revisited," 5 Oct 89. The memo was passed directly to Baker without any attempt to seek agreement on the text from State's European bureau.

Again, George argued that FRG leaders were not being "up-front" about their real plans. He thought, with some accuracy, that West German leaders were privately moving more toward reunification than they would reveal in their public comments. The United States therefore had the choice of either putting "its money where its mouth is" with a more activist policy on reunification or staying with "the current policy of benign neglect." He then detailed the "obvious" drawbacks to pushing reunification. George recommended that the United States dampen speculation about reunification and support political reform in the GDR. George to Ross, "Reunification Revisited," 27 Sep 89, attaching a copy of Bonn 29785, "The German Question: Back on the FRG Agenda," 14 Sep 89. George's paper did not mention Bush's public remarks on the issue of unification.

The European bureau did not agree with the policy planning staff. In a separate memo sent to Baker at about the same time, Raymond Seitz and James Dobbins were advising the secretary that "the foundations of postwar Europe are shifting." Although they concluded that "for most Germans, the vision of a united Germany has not yet become an operational policy objective to be actively pursued," EUR thought that the push for change would come not from the more cautious and self-satisfied West Germans but from the East German people: "Popular forces in the East could push events more rapidly than now foreseen toward new arrangements for Germany." EUR cared little for the new government in the GDR, concluding that there was "little useful business we can do with the current GDR leadership." On unification itself, Seitz and Dobbins viewed support for eventual unification as good both for public purposes and on the merits. They argued that the U.S. position should follow the mainstream West German lead, supporting the goal of unity without prejudging or trying to prescribe exactly how or when unification might be achieved. EUR shared its memo with the policy planning staff, which attached a dissent. Seitz through Kimmitt to Baker, "The Future of Germany in a Fast-Changing Europe," 10 Oct 89 (drafted by Dobbins).

These serious policy differences were presented in an information memo, not an action document. Baker was not obliged to make a choice between them. Had he chosen the policy planning staff view, he would have encountered some resistance from the White House. Though interesting, this internal State Department debate is only a footnote in this history because it got no notice from Baker, Zoellick, or even Ross. Zelikow interview with Baker, Houston, January 1995. For example, the policy planning staff's October 5 memo had urged Baker to stop using "reunification" in favor of "self-determination." Yet Ross personally cleared the NSC staff's draft national security directive language on Germany, with its explicit endorsement of possible "unification." Ross also joined with Zoellick in drafting language for Baker that explicitly endorsed the possibility of unification, both in Baker's October 8 press appearance and in the draft "points of mutual advantage" speech.

94. Memcon of the president's telephone call from Chancellor Kohl, Oval Office, 23 Oct 89 (note taker was NSC staffer Robert Hutchings). On the morning of this call President Bush and other top officials had been briefed by intelligence analysts on "German Reunification: What Would Have to Happen?" They explained that, for Germany to be reunited, East Germany would have to allow democratic choice, Soviet attitudes would need to change, Western allies would need to cooperate (and the FRG underestimated the opposition they would face from London and Paris), West German domestic support would have to be strong, and Bonn would need to tackle the problem of external alignment. They feared that Bonn might agree to attenuate or even drop its NATO ties. Having heard such a briefing, Bush would have been especially sensitive to the impact of Kohl's request on West European and German opinion.

95. R. W. Apple, Jr., "Possibility of a Reunited Germany Is No Cause for Alarm, Bush Says," *New York Times*, October 25, 1989, p. 1; see also p. A12.

96. The story is told, significantly, in Kiessler and Elbe, *Ein runder Tisch mit scharfen Ecken*, p. 57, remarking on the importance of Bush's position for Bonn's diplomacy.

97. Conor Cruise O'Brien, "Beware, the Reich is Reviving," *Times* (London), October 31, 1989; reprinted in Harold James and Marla Stone, eds., *When the Wall Came Down: Reactions to German Unification* (London: Routledge, 1992), p. 221. O'Brien notes that, according to press reports, even some advisers to Kohl were dismayed by Bush's comments, fearing they "might fuel expectations of the unification on the far right in West Germany" (ibid.).

98. There were other signs of Bush's thinking. When Bush met with NATO secretary general Manfred Wörner on October 11, he (as with Waigel on September 26) ignored the

GDR and asked directly how Wörner handled the reunification question, both for NATO and as a German. Wörner, a longtime CDU politician and pro-American conservative, answered that, first, he told people the situation was untenable, that there must be self-determination for all, including East Germans. NATO had accepted the goal of overcoming the division of Europe. Second, he told people that unification was not a policy problem "for tomorrow." The main thing was to persuade the Soviets to allow continued change in Eastern Europe and the GDR. Gorbachev, Wörner warned, would not let the GDR leave the Warsaw Pact. "If it leaves, that is the end. He needs the GDR in order to keep the others in." Bush wondered if he could persuade Gorbachev to let the Warsaw Pact go, to decide its military value was no longer essential. "That may seem naive," Bush said, "but who predicted the changes we are seeing today?" Wörner thought this scenario was unrealistic. The pact was the Soviet Union's great legacy from World War II, the emblem of its status as a great power. The president acknowledged that he might not be able to persuade Gorbachev. "I was just thinking," he said. Memcon for meeting in Oval Office with Manfred Wörner, 11 Oct 89.

99. Between mid-September and mid-October 1989, media opinion on the prospect of German reunification was split, with the majority favoring caution. In one survey of editorial opinion, "the question of German reunification was raised by 10 papers. Nine saw reunification creating problems Western Europe may be unready to face." Kennedy (acting assistant secretary of state for public affairs) to Eagleburger, "Editorial Comment on the East German Exodus," September 29, 1989. For examples of such caution, see "How to Slow the East German Exodus," *New York Times,* October 6, 1989, p. A30; and John Hughes, "Deutschland uber Alles?," *Christian Science Monitor,* October 13, 1989, p. 18. But for more positive views of German reunification, see Richard C. Hottelet, "Once Again, the 'German Question,'" *Christian Science Monitor,* October 6, 1989, p. 19; Enno von Loewenstern (of *Die Welt*), "France's Germanophobia Cannot Block Reunification," *Wall Street Journal,* October 9, 1989.

100. See Address on Arms Control and Q-and-A Session by Secretary Baker before the Commonwealth Club in San Francisco, October 23, 1989. While Baker was trying to emphasize the process by which unification should be accomplished rather than the goal itself, the United States was engaging in quiet contingency planning to consider extreme scenarios of chaos in East Germany. In October Scowcroft and Gates had asked the NSC staff to prepare crisis contingency plans in a restricted group for several possible developments, including events in the GDR and Berlin. The contingencies included widespread violence in the GDR, a major challenge to allied status in Berlin, regime collapse or near-collapse in the GDR, and Soviet military intervention. James Dobbins at the State Department convened meetings to discuss the group's work, and a planning paper drafted for the NSC staff by Robert Hutchings was ready by early November. These plans framed U.S. objectives for managing such contingencies but did not detail exactly what would be done. The work became moot, and none of the papers was ever utilized. The contingency planning was part of a broader effort which also included plans for possible developments in Poland and Hungary. See Zelikow through Blackwill to Scowcroft, 16 Oct 89.

101. "Erklärung der Bundesregierung . . .," *Bulletin* (Bonn, Presse und Informationsamt der Bundesregierung), no. 123 (1989), p. 1053. For grudging acceptance of Kohl's line, even from SPD leader Vogel, see "Kohl: Die SED muss auf ihr Machtmonopol verzichten," *Frankfurter Allgemeine Zeitung,* November 9, 1989, p. 1. Elizabeth Pond, citing an anonymous West German Chancellery source, asserts that Kohl's linkage of aid to comprehensive political reform was suggested by an unnamed "East German middleman" (*Beyond the Wall,* p. 131 and n. 2). The editorial board of the *Washington Post* promptly criticized Kohl

for his comments, warning of the dangers posed for European stability by the accelerating movement toward reunification. See "Toward German Reunification," *Washington Post*, November 9, 1989, p. A22.

102. Quoted in "Wir müssen Kurs halten," *Der Spiegel*, September 25, 1989, pp. 16–17.

103. Margaret Thatcher, *The Downing Street Years* (New York: HarperCollins, 1993), p. 792. Soviets present at the meeting accept these accounts, with Chernyayev recalling that Thatcher was voicing concerns about Germany as early as April 1987. Zelikow interviews with Chernyayev and Pavel Palazschenko, Moscow, January 1994. Chernyayev's published account of the September meeting with Thatcher does not mention Germany, instead focusing on what Gorbachev considered most important—his internal situation within the Soviet Union. See Anatoly Chernyayev, *Shest' let s Gorbachevym: po dnevikovym zapisyam* (Moscow: Progress Publishers, 1993), pp. 298–299.

104. Zelikow interviews with the head of the Foreign Office's West European department at the time, Hillary Synnott, and Britain's then–deputy chief of mission in Bonn, Pauline Neville-Jones, London, June 1992. A copy of the Foreign Office paper, "The German Question," was shared in 1989 with U.S. officials.

105. Stanley Hoffmann, "French Dilemmas and Strategies in the New Europe," in *After the Cold War*, ed. Robert Keohane, Joseph Nye, and Stanley Hoffmann (Cambridge, Mass.: Harvard University Press, 1993), p. 134.

106. Unofficial translation of President Mitterrand's remarks, provided to the U.S. government by the Press and Information Service of the French embassy in Washington, D.C. The French ambassador to Washington, Lothar de Margerie, told Undersecretary of State Robert Kimmitt that he thought Mitterrand's comments displayed great courage. Eagleburger (Acting) to President Bush (for his evening reading), 7 Nov 89. Bush clearly took note of Mitterrand's position and chose, as Ambassador de Margerie and Eagleburger had suggested, to characterize the French position as positive. See, e.g., "Q and A Session with Reporters," 9 Nov 89, in *Public Papers*, 2:1490.

107. EmbBerlin 8783, 8 Nov 89; see also the more detailed analysis in EmbBerlin 8764, "GDR Crisis: As the Plenum Meets, Can the SED Seize Its Slender Chance?," 8 Nov 89. West German ambassador to the United States Jürgen Ruhfus told Kimmitt that Krenz was increasing his freedom to maneuver but confided that Bonn was pessimistic about a new SED government's chances for survival. The British ambassador to Washington, Antony Acland, said he was "nervous about something going very wrong." The State Department reported these remarks to President Bush. Eagleburger to President Bush (for his evening reading), 7 Nov 89.

108. Students of the politics of the former GDR will find it interesting that when Krenz and Gorbachev discussed East German party figures, it was clear that Gorbachev had a good opinion of Modrow. But Gorbachev reserved his strongest praise for longtime party veteran Willi Stoph, who he had thought had done the best he could while working with Honecker. Both Gorbachev and Krenz had blamed Günter Mittag for the GDR's deplorable economic problems. See Memcon for Krenz-Gorbachev meeting, 1 Nov 89.

109. The quotation appears in Maximychev, "Possible 'Impossibilities,'" pp. 112–113, without an explanation of its origin. Maximychev elaborated on the background of the quotation in an interview with Zelikow, Moscow, January 1994. See also Kotschemassow, *Meine letzte Mission*, p. 110 (placing "We will not forgive" on October 7). On the Soviet support for Krenz, see also Ivan Kusmin (KGB resident in East Berlin), "Da wussten auch die fähigsten Tschekisten nicht weiter," *Frankfurter Allgemeine Zeitung*, September 30, 1994, p. 14. Gorbachev frequently called Kochemasov, an unusual step for a head of state. See Kotchemassow, *Meine letzte Mission*, p. 177.

110. See Memcon for Krenz-Gorbachev meeting; Krenz interview excerpt in Kuhn, *Gorbatschow und die deutsche Einheit*, p. 59.

111. Zelikow interviews with Tarasenko, Providence, June 1993; and Maximychev, Moscow, January 1994; Valentin Falin, *Politische Erinnerungen,* trans. Heddy Pross-Weerth (Munich: Droemer Knaur, 1993), pp. 488–489. For variations on this account, see the excellent reconstruction in Igor Maximytschew and Hans-Hermann Hertle, "Die Maueröffnung: Eine russisch-deutsche Trilogie," *Deutschland Archiv* 27 (November 1994): 1137–1158; and Kotschemassow, *Meine letzte Mission,* pp. 185–186; Igor Maximytschew, "Was ist bei euch los?," *Der Spiegel,* October 31, 1994, p. 43.

112. Maximychev, "End of the Berlin Wall," pp. 106–107 (based on numerous discussions with East German officials); and Maximytschew and Hertle, "Die Maueröffnung," pp. 1146–1148.

113. In Bonn, for example, "there were no preparations or contingency plans for this situation, which had always been talked about, but in truth was considered most improbable. There was also no warning from the intelligence services." Kiessler and Elbe, *Ein runder Tisch mit scharfen Ecken,* p. 45. Kiessler and Elbe go on to criticize the West German intelligence service, the Bundesnachrichtendienst (BND), for having written reports that ignored the people of the GDR and focused only on the governing communist elite.

114. See Krenz, *Wenn Mauern Fallen;* Hans Modrow, *Aufbruch und Ende* (Hamburg: Konkret Literatur, 1991), p. 25; Heinrich Bortfeldt interview with Modrow, March 1993, in GDR Oral History Project, Hoover Institution, box 2, pp. 15–16; Reuth and Bönte, *Das Komplott,* p. 160. Early accounts of the opening of the wall sometimes inaccurately assert that Gorbachev had approved the decision. The Soviet government had blessed a liberalization of travel laws but was taken aback—like everyone else—by what happened on the night of November 9–10. See Pond, *Beyond the Wall,* p. 309 n. 7.

115. Darnton, *Berlin Journal,* p. 85.

116. Schabowski, *Das Politbüro,* pp. 138–139. Unless otherwise cited, this account of the opening of the Berlin Wall is drawn from Krenz, *Wenn Mauern Fallen,* pp. 161–195; Schabowski, *Das Politbüro;* Gedmin, *The Hidden Hand,* pp. 109–110; Pond, *Beyond the Wall,* pp. 132–134; Maximychev, "End of the Berlin Wall," pp. 106–108; Maximytschew, "Was ist bei euch los?"; Kusmin, "Da wussten"; and Greenwald, *Berlin Witness,* pp. 258–265. For the U.S. embassy's reporting of the events, see EmbBerlin 8820, "GDR Plenum: Virtually Free Travel and Emigration in Force Immediately," 9 Nov 89; EmbBerlin 8823, ". . . And the Wall Came (Figuratively) Tumbling Down," 10 Nov 89.

4. The Goal Becomes Unification

1. Horst Teltschik, *329 Tage: Innenansichten der Einigung* (Berlin: Siedler, 1991), pp. 11–12.

2. Ibid., p. 13.

3. Richard Kiessler and Frank Elbe, *Ein runder Tisch mit scharfen Ecken: Der diplomatische Weg zur deutschen Einheit* (Baden-Baden: Nomos, 1993), p. 46; Teltschik, *329 Tage,* pp. 15–18; Vernon A. Walters, *Die Vereinigung war voraussehbar: Hinter den Kulissen eines entscheidenden Jahres—Die Aufzeichnungen des amerikanischen Botschafters,* trans. Helmut Ettinger (Berlin: Siedler, 1994), pp. 82–87.

4. For the November 10 speeches by Brandt, Genscher, and Kohl, see Bundesministerium für innerdeutsche Beziehungen, *Texte zur Deutschlandpolitik,* scr. 3, vol. 7-1989 (Bonn: Deutscher Bundes-Verlag, 1990), pp. 399–407. On the Kvitsinsky call, see Teltschik, *329 Tage,* pp. 19–20. A text for Gorbachev's message to Kohl is in East German archives. "Mündliche Botschaft Michail Gorbatschows an Helmut Kohl," Stiftung Archiv der Parteien und Massenorganisationen der DDR in Bundesarchiv (SAPMO), JIV 2/2A/3258K, 13 Nov 89.

5. A poll conducted by the GDR Academy of Sciences for West German Media found, in early December, that 71 percent of respondents were against unification and 27 percent in favor. "Ein Staat, Zwei Staaten?," *Der Spiegel,* December 18, 1989, p. 89. This survey may have been moderately skewed toward SED respondents. Another survey, also flawed, estimated that, at the end of November, 48 percent of East German women favored unification. Elizabeth Pond, *Beyond the Wall: Germany's Road to Unification* (Washington, D.C.: Brookings Institution, 1993), pp. 135, 310 n. 13. See also G. Jonathan Greenwald, *Berlin Witness: An American Diplomat's Chronicle of East Germany's Revolution* (University Park: Pennsylvania State University Press, 1993), p. 274.

6. Greenwald, *Berlin Witness,* p. 269.

7. See Pond, *Beyond the Wall,* p. 134.

8. Greenwald, *Berlin Witness,* pp. 272–275. Greenwald's views did not reflect U.S. government policy. Nevertheless, at the State Department's European bureau, Dobbins agreed to let Greenwald submit his piece to the *Los Angeles Times* "out of generosity and the belief that events would soon overtake it, not because he agreed." Ibid., p. 278. In fact the piece was indeed overtaken by events and was not published.

9. On the Kohl-Thatcher call, see Margaret Thatcher, *The Downing Street Years* (New York: HarperCollins, 1993), pp. 792–793; Teltschik, *329 Tage,* p. 21. The November 8 intelligence briefing for President Bush was part of a series Blackwill and Rice had arranged in order to prepare Bush for his Malta summit meeting with Gorbachev. In addition to Bush, participants in the November 8 meeting were Baker, John Sununu (White House chief of staff), Scowcroft, Gates, Blackwill, Rice, Ross, Dobbins, Curt Kamman (deputy assistant secretary of state for Eastern Europe and the Soviet Union), and four analysts from the CIA. The description of the briefing is based on interviews with Dobbins, Blackwill, and one of the CIA analysts.

10. *Public Papers of the Presidents: George Bush* (1989), bk. 2 (Washington, D.C.: Government Printing Office, 1990), pp. 1488–89. The discussion took place at 3:34 P.M. on November 9, or about 9:30 P.M. in Berlin.

11. On the Kohl-Bush call, see Teltschik, *329 Tage,* p. 22; Memcon of telephone call from Chancellor Kohl, 10 Nov 89 (the note taker was Gates). Bush later referred to Kohl's words of gratitude in his televised Thanksgiving address to the nation, delivered from Camp David on November 22, 1989. The president called this "fitting praise from a good friend."

12. Teltschik, *329 Tage,* pp. 22, 24. The list of participants in this late-night session is a roster of Kohl's inner circle: Schäuble, Chancellery minister Rudolf Seiters, finance minister Theo Waigel, inner-German minister Dorothee Wilms, Hans ("Johnny") Klein (Kohl's press spokesman), and Teltschik.

13. Teltschik, *329 Tage,* p. 23; for text of the Gorbachev messages, see State 363047, 11 Nov 89; "Mündliche Botschaft an Mitterrand, Thatcher und Bush," in SAPMO, JIV 2/2A/ 3258K.

14. State 363047, 11 Nov 89; Teltschik, *329 Tage,* p. 23; see also Baker to President Bush (for his evening reading), 13 Nov 89. Teltschik believes that Gorbachev's message was also delivered to Willy Brandt, a leading figure in the opposition SPD. Zelikow and Rice interview with Teltschik, Gütersloh, June 1992. If this assertion is true, it is notable that the Soviet government would convey confidential diplomatic messages to opposition politicians in order to intervene in West German politics.

15. Memcon for telephone call from FM Genscher to Secretary Baker, 10 Nov 89 (note taker was an S/S-O watch officer). Genscher repeated the assurances about Germany's ties to the West in a November 11 briefing in Bonn for NATO ambassadors. See Bonn 35783,

"Genscher Briefs Allies on Developments in GDR and Chancellor's Poland Trip," 11 Nov 89.

16. Memcon of telephone call from Secretary Baker to Foreign Secretary Hurd, 11 Nov 89 (note taker was an S/S-O watch officer). For Baker's own handling of public reaction, see PA transcripts of his appearances on CBS-TV's *This Morning* (November 10), ABC-TV's *Good Morning America* (November 10), and ABC-TV's *This Week with David Brinkley* (November 12).

17. See State 364359, 14 Nov 89; and Bush's reply to Gorbachev in State 369390, 17 Nov 89. For the Thatcher message, see letter from UK ambassador Acland to Scowcroft, 15 Nov 89.

18. For Gerasimov's comments, see Michael Beschloss and Strobe Talbott, *At the Highest Levels: The Inside Story of the End of the Cold War* (Boston: Little, Brown, 1992), pp. 136–137. An East German copy of the Soviet record of the Genscher-Shevardnadze call is "Inhalt des Telefongesprächs zwischen Schewardnadse und Genscher," in SAPMO, JIV 2/2A/3258K.

19. An East German copy of the Soviet record of the call is "Information über den Inhalt des Telefongesprächs zwischen Gorbatschow und Kohl," in SAPMO, JIV 2/2A/3258K. Excerpts from the Soviet memcon of the call are in Anatoly Chernyaev, *Shest' let s Gorbachevym: po dnevikovym zapisyam* (Moscow: Progress Publishers, 1993), p. 305; and Alexander Galkin and Anatoly Chernyayev, "To Truth, and Only Truth: Memoirs in Connection with Remembrances," *Svobodnaya Mysl'* (January–February 1994): 19, 24; these can be supplemented by Teltschik's recollections in *329 Tage*, p. 28.

20. Teltschik, *329 Tage*, p. 28.

21. See Igor Maximychev, *Poslednii god GDR* (Moscow: Mezhdunarodniye Otnosheniya, 1993), pp. 85, 92–93. For the Dumas visit, see *Pravda*, November 15, 1989, p. 6; on the West German reaction, see Teltschik, *329 Tage*, p. 31. On the drumbeat of public statements coming from the Soviet government in opposition to German unification, see Fred Oldenburg, "Sowjetische Deutschland-Politik nach der Oktober-Revolution in der DDR," *Deutschland Archiv*, 23 (January 1990): 68–76.

22. Chernyayev, *Shest' let s Gorbachevym*, pp. 304–305.

23. After Kohl talked to Krenz on November 11, Rudolf Seiters traveled to East Berlin and received a more detailed picture of what the East Germans wanted. Teltschik, *329 Tage*, pp. 27, 30–31.

24. Ibid., pp. 32–34.

25. Kohl's statement to the Bundestag, "Erklärung der Bundesregierung zur Lage in der DDR," in *Texte zur Deutschlandpolitik*, pp. 412–421. McAdams is mistaken in asserting that Kohl was trying to slow down the pace of change in the GDR. A. James McAdams, *Germany Divided: From the Wall to Reunification* (Princeton: Princeton University Press, 1993), p. 204.

On terminology, *reunification* and *unification* were used almost indistinguishably in 1989 to refer to the re-creation of a unified German state (in German, *Wiedervereinigung* and *Vereinigung*). *Reunification* was (and still is) the most common usage. It implied, however, that the German state that existed before 1945 and was divided after the war was being brought back together; indeed, the FRG itself defined reunification in its Basic Law by reference to the borders of Germany in 1937. Yet the old Germany was not being put back together, particularly since the "Eastern territories" would remain part of Poland and the Soviet Union. Therefore, U.S. officials tried to use only the term *unification* to describe the process of re-creating a single German state. That will be the usage herein as well, unless the source material uses a different term. For a prescient discussion of this point, see Karl Kaiser, "Unity for Germany, Not Reunification," *New York Times,* October 6, 1989, p. A31.

26. Konrad H. Jarausch, *The Rush to German Unity* (New York: Oxford University Press, 1994), p. 63; on the Soviet view of Modrow, see M. Podklyuchnikov, *Pravda,* November 20, 1989, p. 6, in *FBIS-SOV* 89–224, November 21, 1989, p. 35; Novosti interview with Nikolai Portugalov, in *Frankfurter Rundschau,* November 17, 1989, p. 2, in *FBIS-SOV* 89–222, November 20, 1989, p. 33; Jeffrey Gedmin, *The Hidden Hand* (Washington, D.C.: AEI Press, 1992), p. 112. For sober accounts of the limited Soviet role in the rise of Modrow, see Elizabeth Pond, "A Wall Destroyed: The Dynamics of German Unification in the GDR," *International Security,* 15 (Fall 1990): 35, 44 n. 18; Gerhard Wettig, "Die sowjetische Rolle beim Umsturz in der DDR und bei der Einleitung des deutschen Einigungprozesses," in *Der Umbruch in Osteuropa,* ed. Jürgen Elvert and Michael Salewski (Stuttgart: Franz Steiner, 1993), pp. 56–57; Hans Modrow, *Aufbruch und Ende* (Hamburg: Konkret Literatur, 1991), p. 92; see also Valentin Falin, *Politische Erinnerungen,* trans. Heddy Pross-Weerth (Munich: Droemer Knaur, 1993), p. 488.

27. *Texte zur Deutschlandpolitik,* pp. 422–429.

28. The UN General Assembly had agreed, for example, that the UN Charter protected the right of "establishment of a sovereign and independent State, the free association or integration with an independent State or the emergence into any other political status freely determined by a people." UNGA Res. 2625 (25), October 24, 1970.

29. On the theoretical question whether Kohl was actually obliged by international law and FRG constitutional law to adopt this narrower stance, see Joachim Frowein, "Deutschlands aktuelle Verfassungslage," *Veröffentlichungen der Vereinigung der deutschen Staatsrechtslehrer,* 49 (1990): 12. These arguments turn, in part, on whether "Germany" continued to exist as an entity under international law, an entity whose existence as a unified state was suspended in 1945 but not terminated. The majority of experts accept that this was the case. See I. D. Hendry and M. C. Wood, *The Legal Status of Berlin* (The Hague: Grotius, 1987), p. 19; Gilbert Gornig, "The Contractual Settlement of the External Problems of German Unification," *Aussenpolitik,* III/1991: 4. For the minority view that "Germany" had ceased to exist during the 1940s, a view sometimes but not always espoused by the Soviet government, see Hans Kelsen, "The Legal Status of Germany According to the Declaration of Berlin," *American Journal of International Law,* 39 (1945): 518.

30. Pond, *Beyond the Wall,* p. 135. An excellent running chronology of daily events in the GDR during 1989 and 1990 is provided in Deutschland Archiv, *Chronik der Ereignisse in der DDR* (Cologne: Verlagwissenschaft und Politik, 1990).

31. On November 26 a group of thirty-one writers, respected reform Marxists, church figures, and opposition leaders all joined in a published appeal to their East German countrymen to "insist on GDR independence" and not to accept "a sell-out of our material and moral values and have the GDR eventually taken over by the Federal Republic." Within two weeks 200,000 people had signed this manifesto of "antifascist and humanist ideals." A prominent group of West German intellectuals responded with a parallel manifesto rejecting unification and dangerous nationalism. Jarausch, *The Rush to German Unity,* p. 67.

32. The day after the wall was overrun, Scowcroft had commissioned another interagency examination of options for U.S. policy on the question of German unification. The small group of working-level officials, led by Dobbins, quickly agreed that the main issue was to choose between emphasizing German self-determination, letting Kohl set the pace for progress toward unity, or supporting early Four Power intervention to regulate the process. Hutchings through Blackwill to Scowcroft, "Paper on German Reunification,"

11 Nov 89. Bush was also urged by Henry Kissinger, who visited the White House for dinner on November 13, to keep open his rhetorical acceptance of possible unification. Beschloss and Talbott, *At the Highest Levels,* p. 138.

Baker was also receiving advice on the issue of German unification within his department. The Office of the Legal Adviser had already prepared a background summary of allied rights in Germany. Sofaer through Kimmitt to Baker, "Allied Rights in Germany," 30 Oct 89 (forwarded by Kimmitt on November 10). Dobbins quickly drafted and sent Baker the European bureau's recommendations. Baker was advised to avoid any suggestion of a U.S.-Soviet "superpower condominium" to dictate events in Germany. Any U.S. economic aid to the GDR should be tied to free elections—the same condition Kohl had imposed on West German aid. On reunification Dobbins argued that the United States should resist calls to take the lead in setting out a blueprint for change in Europe or assert Four Power rights. Instead, Dobbins urged that Washington keep the emphasis on German self-determination. Staying away from Four Power intervention would avoid a Soviet veto as well as the appearance of trying to block German national aspirations. Baker highlighted this analysis and noted his agreement with its conclusion. Dobbins, however, urged that the United States work with its allies on guidelines for channeling movement toward unification. "We now need to begin considering how Germany's Western ties can in practice be assured in a transformed European context," he wrote. Again, Baker agreed. Dobbins (Acting) through Kimmitt to Baker, "The Wall Breached: Implications for Malta, Your Trip to Europe, Relations with the GDR, and the Reunification Debate," 11 Nov 89.

Baker's policy planning staff also forwarded separate analyses to Baker. The key memo, drafted this time by Ross and staffer Francis Fukuyama (instead of Roger George), argued, with Dobbins's concurrence, that any process leading to unity had to start with internal reform in the GDR to allow free elections. Although a subsequent move to unification seemed more distant, Ross and Fukuyama recommended that the United States confront the unity question soon—at least to help manage disparate views within the alliance. They noted that unification could evolve in several ways and that the Americans should not insist on a particular outcome. But Washington could enunciate some key principles: true self-determination, with an outcome acceptable to Germany's neighbors; unification, with Germany remaining in NATO and the EC; and movement toward unity in a gradual step-by-step process, with respect for postwar borders. The United States could also embed its views on Germany in a broader vision of Europe's future "architecture," including change in NATO and U.S.-EC relations. The United States could also start talking more to the British, French, Germans, and Soviets. Ross to Baker, "How to Approach the German Unity Issue," 13 Nov 89; see also Ross to Baker, "GDR," 9 Nov 89. And see Ambassador Walters's belated complaint about endorsing "reconciliation" instead of "reunification," in Bonn 35777, "Discussion of German Unity by USG Spokesman," 10 Nov 89.

33. Teltschik, *329 Tage,* p. 36; Memcon of telephone call from Kohl to President Bush, 17 Nov 89 (note taker was Rice).

34. Thatcher, *The Downing Street Years,* pp. 793–794; Teltschik, *329 Tage,* pp. 37–38.

35. Interdepartmental paper, "Handling the German Question at Malta and Beyond," p. 7, attached to Hutchings through Blackwill to Scowcroft, "The German Question," 20 Nov 89. The paper was drafted by Dobbins, Jack Seymour from the State Department's German desk, and Jim Holmes from the policy planning staff. On the term "German self-determination," see also the interesting memo from Mulholland (INR) to Kimmitt, "German Self-Determination: Three Components," 21 Nov 89 (drafted by Bowman Miller). The National Intelligence Officer for Europe, Martin van Heuven, believed that "the Kohl government will continue to be cautious in pressing the reunification theme

for fear of adding to the current political turbulence in East Germany and out of concern not to trouble relationships with its West European partners . . . For now, Bonn's policy will be continued incremental steps." National Intelligence Council Memo for the Record, "A German Peace Treaty," 15 Nov 89. He also thought that the intelligence community agreed "unfolding events are making it clear that political reunification is not in the offing for now" because the East German people did not want it, dissident leaders hoped to keep a distinctive East German identity, democratic elections would *reinforce* rather than weaken East German separateness, and "Bonn also does not want to destabilize the European situation by active pursuit of reunification." National Intelligence Council Memo for the Record, "German Reunification," 14 Nov 89.

36. Ross to Baker, "How to Approach the German Unity Issue," 13 Nov 89.

37. Memcon for President Bush's meeting with FRG Foreign Minister Genscher, 21 Nov 89. On Genscher's meetings at the State Department, see Baker to President Bush (for his evening reading), 21 Nov 89; see also Seitz to Baker, "Meeting and Luncheon with Hans-Dietrich Genscher," 18 Nov 89. Seitz's briefing memo followed the agreed-upon line endorsing German self-determination which could lead to unification, while adding cautiously, "Like the FRG and other European governments, we believe it is premature to put German unification on the international agenda."

38. Memcon for General Scowcroft's meeting with Foreign Minister Genscher, 21 Nov 89 (note taker was Robert Hutchings); Zelikow interview with Genscher, Wachtberg-Pech, December 1994. In Bonn Genscher's report to the Chancellery about his Washington visit emphasized the positive American stance toward the possibility of German unification. Teltschik, *329 Tage,* pp. 47–48.

39. See Address by Prime Minister Thatcher at the Guildhall, November 13, 1989; Thatcher, *The Downing Street Years,* p. 793; message from Prime Minister Thatcher to President Bush (sent through special channels), 16 Nov 89. For more on British attitudes toward Germany in 1989, see Karl-Günther von Hase, "Britische Zurückhaltung: zu den Schwierigkeiten Englands mit der deutschen Einheit," *Die Politische Meinung* (November–December 1990): 13–18; Richard Davy, "Grossbritannien und die Deutsche Frage," *Europa Archiv,* February 25, 1990, pp. 139–145; Günther Heydemann, "Britische Europa-Politik am Scheideweg: Über Deutschland nach Europa?," *Deutschland Archiv* (December 1989): 1377–82.

40. Memcon of phone call from Thatcher to the President, 17 Nov 89 (note taker was Zelikow).

41. Scowcroft to President Bush, "Meeting with Prime Minister Margaret Thatcher," 22 Nov 89, forwarded from Zelikow through Blackwill to Scowcroft, "Briefing Materials for the President's Meeting with Prime Minister Thatcher at Camp David," 21 Nov 89. Bush also underscored the recommendation that he tell the prime minister he would "respond negatively to any Soviet request for special US-USSR arrangements on Germany, or Four Power talks, or other devices that shift the focus at this time from the pressing need for reform and democracy in the GDR."

42. The discussion that follows is based on Thatcher, *The Downing Street Years,* p. 794; Memcon for meeting with Prime Minister Margaret Thatcher, Camp David, 24 Nov 89 (based on notes taken by Scowcroft).

43. Memcon of phone call to President Mitterrand, 17 Nov 89 (note taker was Adrian Basora).

44. Message from President Mitterrand to President Bush, 27 Nov 89 (U.S. translation), attached to Hutchings through Blackwill to General Scowcroft, "The President's Telephone Call to President Mitterrand," 29 Nov 89. Speaking to Bush again on November

30 (after Kohl had announced his program for unification to the Bundestag), Mitterrand again avoided any direct comments on Germany. But, describing his plans for the Malta summit, Bush repeated twice that despite Gorbachev's concern about premature reunification, he would "go in a forward-leaning position" on Germany. Mitterrand said that he was not worried and had full confidence in President Bush. Memcon of phone call to President Mitterrand, 30 Nov 89 (note taker was Hutchings); account of Genscher talks is from Zelikow interview with Genscher, Wachtberg-Pech, December 1994; on West German unhappiness with Mitterrand's travel announcements, see Teltschik, *329 Tage*, p. 47. For more background on French views of Germany in 1989 and 1990, see Walter Schütze, "Frankreich angesichts der deutschen Einheit," *Europa Archiv*, February 25, 1990, pp. 133–139; Ingo Kolboom, "Vom 'Gemeinsamen Haus Europa' zur 'Europäischen Konföderation'—François Mitterrand und die europäische Neuordnung, 1986–1990," in *SOWI-Sozialwissenschaftliche Informationen*, no. 4 (October–December 1990): 237–246. French mass opinion was apparently less troubled by the prospect of German unification. Renate Fritsch-Bournazel, *Europe and German Unification* (Providence: Berg, 1992), pp. 174–175.

45. For the chorus of caution on the editorial pages of American newspapers, see, e.g., "German Reunification," *Washington Post*, November 12, 1989, p. D6 (advising the West to be satisfied with movement short of political unification); Anne-Marie Burley, "High-Stakes Poker at the Berlin Wall," *New York Times*, November 13, 1989, p. A21 (calling for preservation of a stable GDR); Stephan-Gotz Richter, "Overloading Noah's Ark," *Washington Post*, November 14, 1989, p. A25 (arguing that East Germans would not want unification); Tom Wicker, "Decline of the East," *New York Times*, November 14, 1989, p. A31 (advising the West to be satisfied with a more democratic GDR); Christopher Layne, "Do Something Bold in Central Europe," *Wall Street Journal*, November 14, 1989 (suggesting an initiative trading unification for German neutralization, with Germany remaining in the EC but not in NATO); William Echikson, "Two (Safe) Germanys," *Christian Science Monitor*, November 16, 1989, p. 19 (urging the United States to pressure Kohl to abandon the goal of reunification); Elie Wiesel, "I Fear What Lies beyond the Wall," *New York Times*, November 17, 1989, p. A39; Stephen Rosenfeld, "Striking a Balance on Germany," *Washington Post*, November 17, 1989, p. A23 (calling for more "awareness of where the undisciplined sentiment for self-determination can lead"); editorial, "One Germany: Not Likely Now," *New York Times*, November 19, 1989, p. 22 ("For many different and sound reasons, hardly anybody wants reunification to happen"); and Theo Sommer, "A Dog That Doesn't Bark," *Newsweek*, November 20, 1989, p. 39 (the title was a metaphor for the reunification issue). George Kennan was also quoted as cautioning that now was "not the time to raise the subject" of German reunification. Jim Hershberg, "German Reunification: A Tale of Two Plans," *Christian Science Monitor*, November 29, 1989, p. 19.

For examples of the minority who took a more welcoming view of the prospect of German unification, see Jim Hoagland, "Reunification: What's the West's Plan," *Washington Post*, November 13, 1989, p. A13 (urging the United States to begin seriously negotiating terms of an all-German settlement); David Broder, "Our Great Mission in Europe," *Washington Post*, November 15, 1989, p. A21; editorial, "East Germany's Future," *Washington Post*, November 22, 1989, p. A22; and Joseph Nye, Jr., "Designs for Europe: An Occasional Series," *New York Times*, November 26, 1989.

46. Interview with foreign journalists, November 21, 1989, in *Public Papers*, pp. 1588–89.

47. Gorbachev's words on November 17 were repeated to the press by one of the visitors, Bundestag president Rita Süssmuth (the other was French National Assembly

president Laurent Fabius); see Deutsche Press Agentur report, November 17, 1989, in *FBIS-SOV* 89–222, November 20, 1989, p. 34.

48. Descriptions of this meeting are drawn from Teltschik, *329 Tage*, pp. 43–44; Novosti interview, "Two Systems, One Nation," in *Frankfurter Rundschau*, November 17, 1989, p. 2, in *FBIS-SOV* 89–222, November 20, 1989, pp. 33–34.

49. On Kohl's motives, see Teltschik, *329 Tage*, pp. 41–58.

50. See Pond, *Beyond the Wall*, p. 136.

51. Description of speech preparation is from Zelikow interview with Teltschik, Munich, December 1994; for the rest, see *Der Spiegel*, November 20, 1989, pp. 16–17 (Emnid survey); Teltschik, *329 Tage*, p. 41 (ZDF Politbarometer survey); Lafontaine in *Süddeutsche Zeitung*, November 25–26, 1989, quoted in McAdams, *Germany Divided*, p. 206 n. 74.

52. *Die Tageszeitung*, November 23, 1989, quoted in Daniel Hamilton, *After the Revolution: The New Political Landscape in East Germany* (Washington, D.C.: American Institute for Contemporary German Studies, 1990), p. 13. On developments in the GDR, see Pond, "A Wall Destroyed"; and Hamilton, *After the Revolution*. The number of East German emigrants in November 1989 is from Karl Kaiser, "Germany's Unification," *Foreign Affairs*, 70 (1990/91): 179, 184.

53. Helmut Kohl, "Zehn-Punkte Programm zur überwindung der Teilung Deutschlands und Europas," in *Texte zur Deutschlandpolitik*, pp. 426–433.

54. Teltschik, *329 Tage*, p. 58. For further evidence that Kohl and his advisers were trying to shape East German opinion, not just respond to it, note that on the day the speech was given, Teltschik told Ambassador Walters that "there was not much open talk of reunification in the GDR at present," though "as millions of East Germans visited the FRG, that could change." Bonn 37206, "Teltschik Briefing on Kohl Speech on German Unity," 28 Nov 89. Elizabeth Pond originally argued that Kohl saw the oncoming public clamor for unification within East Germany and was trying to slow it down to a manageable pace. She subsequently and correctly abandoned this argument, but her original position was cited approvingly by James McAdams, who also mistakenly saw Kohl's move as an effort to slow the pace of change. Compare Pond, "A Wall Destroyed," p. 57 and nn. 45 and 46, with Pond, *Beyond the Wall*, p. 137; and see McAdams, *Germany Divided*, p. 205.

55. Teltschik, *329 Tage*, p. 58; Jarausch, *The Rush to German Unity*, pp. 68–69.

56. Teltschik, *329 Tage*, pp. 50–58; Bonn 37206, "Teltschik Briefing on Kohl Speech on German Unity," 28 Nov 89. Teltschik briefed the U.S. ambassador, Walters, along with the British and French ambassadors. He told Walters that Kohl had already sent the details of his speech to Bush. Unfortunately, probably because of difficulties in communicating the eleven-page message either in Bonn or in Washington, the message arrived at the end of the day, hours after the story had been broadcast all over the world. U.S. officials were irritated at first by the lack of consultation, since Bush had always been so scrupulous in consulting with Kohl. The annoyance was eased once the message arrived and when Kohl called Bush the next day. The Soviets were thrilled to have been briefed by Teltschik and told *Izvestiya* that this was evidence of the warming relationship with the FRG. See *Izvestiya*, November 29, 1989, p. 3.

57. This account is based on the recollections of Dobbins and John McLaughlin, the analyst who joined Dobbins in making the presentation.

58. From undated paper in Zoellick's office files, probably prepared to brief Baker for a press conference on November 29. Zoellick may have drawn on a short factual summary, George to Ross and Zoellick, "Kohl's Ten-Point Plan," 28 Nov 89.

59. Message via special channels from Chancellor Kohl to President Bush, 28 Nov 89 (sent from Bonn in English); the contents are also quoted in Teltschik, *329 Tage*, p. 54.

60. Letter from Krenz to President Bush, 28 Nov 89. See also Baker to President Bush (for his evening reading), 28 Nov 89.

61. The account that follows is drawn from Memcon for President Bush's phone call with Chancellor Kohl, 29 Nov 89; for the staff advice before the call, see Hutchings through Blackwill to General Scowcroft, "The President's Telephone Call to Chancellor Kohl," 28 Nov 89.

62. *Public Papers*, 1989, bk. II, p. 1603. Bush was referring to his speeches at Boston University (May 21), in Mainz (May 31), and in Leiden (July 17).

63. Kiessler and Elbe, *Ein runder Tisch mit scharfen Ecken*, pp. 51–53.

64. As he prepared for the Malta summit, Bush invited Mulroney and his foreign minister, Joe Clark, to Washington to brief him on their trip to the Soviet Union. For their comments on Soviet views of Germany, see Memcon of dinner with Prime Minister Mulroney, 29 Nov 89. It can be assumed, especially since Bush and Mulroney were known to be friends, that the Soviet leaders anticipated that what they told the Canadians would be passed on to the American president.

65. For Gorbachev's remarks, see *Pravda*, November 17, 1989, pp. 1–2. One German observer asserts that Gorbachev's comments were strengthened when they were reported in print. Hans-Peter Riese, "Die Geschichte hat sich ans Werk gemacht," *Europa Archiv* (April 1990): 117, 121.

66. Julij A. Kwizinskij, *Vor dem Sturm: Erinnerungen eines Diplomaten,* trans. Hilde and Helmut Ettinger (Berlin: Siedler, 1993), pp. 16–17. For the explanation for Soviet inaction after the opening of the wall as a result of Gorbachev's hope that Krenz and Modrow would stabilize the situation, see Vyacheslav Dashichev, "On the Road to German Reunification: The View from Moscow," in *Soviet Foreign Policy, 1917–1991: A Retrospective,* ed. Gabriel Gorodetsky (London: Frank Cass, 1993), pp. 170, 173.

67. Kwizinskij, *Vor dem Sturm,* p. 17.

68. Scowcroft to President Bush, "The Soviets and the German Question," 29 Nov 89. Markings on the memo indicate that Bush read it.

69. CIA, "The German Question and Soviet Policy," SOV M 89–20089X, 27 Nov 89. It is doubtful that the president or his cabinet-level advisers actually read this twenty-page analysis, but it was reviewed by key subcabinet officials before the Malta meeting. The CIA analysts did not know about the Soviet statements to the Canadians recounted by Mulroney to Bush. There was no evidence that Shevardnadze sympathized with the pragmatists, though—as with Gorbachev—there were conflicting indications about Yakovlev's views. Veteran advisers on Germany, such as Valentin Falin, were considered to be strongly opposed to reunification, and military opinion was thought to be divided. No Soviet officials at any level had indicated any willingness to accept a unified Germany entirely inside NATO. The debate was over whether, as a historical or policy matter, Germany should be unified at all.

70. In his speech in Rome, Gorbachev emphasized the philosophy of perestroika: "We have abandoned the claim to have a monopoly on truth; we no longer think we are the best . . . We have now decided, firmly and irrevocably, to base our policy on the principle of freedom of choice . . . We are getting to know ourselves, revealing ourselves to the world, and discovering the world." *Pravda*, December 2, 1989, p. 2; see also "Press-konferentsiya v Milane," *Pravda*, December 3, 1989, p. 2.

71. The account that follows is based on the Soviet memcon of this meeting, published in Mikhail S. Gorbachev, *Gody trudnykh reshenii, 1985–1992: izbrannoye* (Moscow: Al'fa-Print, 1993), pp. 173–176. For other published accounts of the meeting based on interviews with participants, see Beschloss and Talbott, *At the Highest Levels,* pp. 154–156, 157–158;

Don Oberdorfer, *The Turn: From the Cold War to a New Era: The United States and the Soviet Union, 1983–1990* (New York: Simon and Schuster, 1991), pp. 378–379. For the American notes, see Memcon of First Expanded Bilateral Session with Chairman Gorbachev, December 2, 1989. Bush was accompanied at this session by Baker, Sununu, Scowcroft, Undersecretary of Defense Paul Wolfowitz, Zoellick, Blackwill, and an interpreter. Gorbachev was joined by Shevardnadze, Yakovlev, Bessmertnykh (then first deputy foreign minister), Chernyayev, Anatoly Dobrynin (then foreign policy adviser to Gorbachev), Akhromeyev, and their interpreter. For some background on the decision to meet in Malta and Bush's preparations for the meeting, see Beschloss and Talbott, *At the Highest Levels,* pp. 139–152; Oberdorfer, *The Turn,* pp. 375–376. For Bush's key briefing materials on Germany at Malta, see Presidential Briefing Book, "Presidential Presentations," 29 Nov 89. This book was prepared by Scowcroft, Rice, Ross, Blackwill, Zoellick, and Zelikow. It was distinct from the regular briefing materials normally compiled for such trips, and its contents were very closely held. See papers titled "Key Points to Be Made in Subsequent Presentations" and, for a longer presentation, "The Future of Germany," and notional Gorbachev presentation and suggested presidential response to possible surprises in a paper titled "German Peace Treaty."

72. This account is based on verbatim excerpts from the Soviet notes taken at the meeting, quoted at length in Chernyayev, *Shest' let s Gorbachevym,* pp. 309–310, which appear to be from this one-on-one session. Similar records from the American side are unavailable. But Bush and Scowcroft later debriefed aides about the meeting, and the Soviet account dovetails with the recollections of Blackwill and Rice, as well as the more general accounts offered to journalists. See Beschloss and Talbott, *At the Highest Levels,* pp. 156–157. While Bush and Gorbachev were having their one-on-one meeting, Shevardnadze was in another room telling Baker of the deep unease his government felt about German unification and revanchist statements coming out of West Germany.

73. For the Soviet memcon of this session, described in the account that follows, see Gorbachev, *Gody trudnykh reshenii,* pp. 176–179; for the American notes, see Memcon for Second Expanded Bilateral Session (on the *Maxim Gorkii*), 3 Dec 89. In this session Bush was accompanied by Baker, Sununu, Scowcroft, Lieutenant General Howard Graves (assistant to the chairman of the Joint Chiefs of Staff), Ross, Rice, and the interpreter. Gorbachev was joined by Shevardnadze, Yakovlev, Bessmertnykh, Chernyayev, Dobrynin, Akhromeyev, and their interpreter. The language quoted in the discussion that follows is from the primary sources. For similar accounts based on interviews with participants, see Beschloss and Talbott, *At the Highest Levels,* p. 162; Oberdorfer, *The Turn,* pp. 381–382.

74. Scowcroft took notes for the American side in this conversation. For the content, see Beschloss and Talbott, *At the Highest Levels,* p. 164.

75. Remarks of President Bush and Chairman Gorbachev and a question-and-answer session with reporters at Malta, December 3, 1989, in *Public Papers* (1989), bk. 2, pp. 1877–78.

76. Anatoly Chernyayev, "The Phenomenon of Gorbachev in the Context of Leadership," *International Affairs* (Moscow), (June 1993): 48.

77. S. F. Akhromeyev and G. M. Kornienko [a former deputy foreign minister who retired in 1988], *Glazami Marshala i Diplomata* (Moscow: Mezhdunarodniye Otnosheniya, 1992), pp. 253–254, 259.

78. For the German account of this meeting, see Teltschik, *329 Tage,* pp. 62–64; for the American notes, see Memcon of meeting with Chancellor Kohl at Château Stuyvenberg, Brussels, 3 Dec 89; the account that follows also draws on Zelikow interview with Scowcroft, Washington, D.C., June 1991. See also Scowcroft to President Bush, "Scope Paper—Your Bilateral with Chancellor Kohl" (in-trip briefing materials).

79. See PA transcript, Press Conference by Secretary Baker on Bush-Gorbachev Malta Meeting, the White House, 29 Nov 89, pp. 7–8.

80. The earlier Ross-Fukuyama formula had included a qualifier, "if there is unification." That phrase was dropped. The language referring to Four Power rights was new, added because the embassy in Bonn had complained of Kohl's persistent failure to refer to these rights and because of the Americans' care to mention their legal obligation for Berlin and "Germany as a whole." See Bonn 37736, "Kohl's Ten-Point Program—Silence on the Role of the Four Powers," 1 Dec 89.

81. The text of the intervention was subsequently released to the public. "Outline of Remarks at the North Atlantic Treaty Organization Headquarters in Brussels," December 4, 1989, in *Public Papers* (1989), bk. 2, pp. 1644–47. Bush passed along his four principles on Germany directly to Gorbachev. See President Bush to President Gorbachev, 8 Dec 89. For a sense of the positive press reactions to Bush's handling of the Malta-Brussels trip, see News Conference in Brussels, 4 Dec 89, in *Public Papers*, 1989, bk. 2, pp. 1647–49; Scowcroft to President Bush, "European Press Reaction to the NATO Summit and Your Speech on the Future of Europe," 6 Dec 89.

82. Teltschik, *329 Tage*, pp. 64–67; Zelikow interview with Blackwill, Cambridge, Mass., 1991. Despite growing calls for U.S. troop cuts in Europe, American public support for the military commitment remained solid in late 1989. In 1982 about 66 percent of Americans had wanted to maintain or increase U.S. troop strength in Europe; in November 1989, despite the political changes on the Continent, this figure had shrunk by only 8 points, to 58 percent. The success of the May 1989 NATO summit may have played a part, as did wariness about future Soviet intentions and the uncertain political situation— themes repeatedly emphasized by President Bush. On the polling data, see Tutwiler to Baker, "Support for NATO and U.S. Troops in Europe," 8 Dec 89.

83. Thatcher, *The Downing Street Years*, pp. 795–796.

84. Teltschik, *329 Tage*, p. 67.

85. For the official Soviet report on the Warsaw Pact summit meeting, an account of which follows, see "Vstrecha rukovoditelye godsudarstvuchastnikov Varshavskogo Dogovora [Meeting of the leaders of the Warsaw Pact member states]," *Vestnik*, December 31, 1989, pp. 42–45. For the account of a participant as told to a journalist, see Oberdorfer, *The Turn*, pp. 384–386. Although Krenz insisted on going to Moscow with Modrow, the Soviets pointedly publicized Gorbachev's meeting with Modrow, treating the now discredited Krenz as a nonperson. Ralf Georg Reuth and Andreas Bönte, *Das Komplott: Wie es wirklich zur deutschen Einheit kam* (Munich: Piper, 1993), pp. 185–186. Modrow later recounted the message from Gorbachev to Rudolf Seiters. Teltschik, *329 Tage*, p. 68.

86. See Deutschland Archiv, *Chronik der Ereignisse*, pp. 33–34; Pond, *Beyond the Wall*, pp. 140–145; Jarausch, *The Rush to German Unity*, pp. 70–76. In Washington, Blackwill convened a meeting of CIA and DIA analysts to review the situation in the GDR on December 7, and the U.S. government closely monitored developments for signs of a breakdown of public order. Soviet forces remained quiet. See Benko (analyst attached to Blackwill's office) through Blackwill to Scowcroft, "Intelligence Community Assessment of Current Tensions in the GDR," 7 Dec 89.

87. See *Krasnaiya zvezda* and *Izvestiya*, December 5 and 6, 1989. For the reports on emergency measures taken by Soviet troops, see the same newspapers for December 8 and 9, 1989.

88. Kwizinskij, *Vor dem Sturm*, p. 17. Wjatscheslaw Kotschemassow, *Meine letzte Mission* (Berlin: Dietz, 1994), pp. 195–196.

89. According to both Tarasenko and Chernyayev, the Soviet leadership was becoming worried that the real problem for them if Germany unified would be a witch-hunt carried

out against those who had "lost East Europe and Germany." Tarasenko claims that by the end of 1989, he and others knew that the unification of Germany was inevitable and were trying to figure out a strategy to keep this development from bringing down Gorbachev's government. Rice interviews with Tarasenko, Moscow, October 1991, and Chernyayev, Moscow, June 1994. This evidence is not reliable for characterizing the whole Soviet diplomatic effort, but it does offer insight into the way domestic concerns were already shadowing Soviet policy.

90. This discussion is based on Soviet memcon, "Zapis besedy M. S. Gorbacheva s Ministrom inostrannykh del' FRG G. D. Gensherom," 5 Dec 89, made available to authors by Alexandra Bezymenskaya. See also Chernyayev, *Shest' let s Gorbachevym*, pp. 306–309. The "left no doubt" quotation is from Kiessler and Elbe, *Ein runder Tisch mit scharfen Ecken*, p. 70. Shevardnadze's reference to Hitler was in the context of an alleged German "diktat" in forcing the annexation of a neighbor. For Genscher's own account to his counterparts of his meeting in Moscow, see State 3834. "12/13/89 Quadripartite Ministers' Meeting," 5 Jan 90. See also *Pravda,* December 6, 1989, p. 1, and *Izvestiya,* December 6, 1989, p. 4. Shevardnadze's public criticism of Genscher was especially sharp. Teltschik was surprised by the Soviet hard line after Bush's report of his more temperate talk with Gorbachev in Malta (*329 Tage,* p. 68). Echoing Gorbachev's line (which he may have helped write), Valentin Falin told the British ambassador in Moscow on December 7 that the USSR thought Kohl, demonstrating "national egoism," had broken a promise to Gorbachev not to undertake any pan-German initiatives. On the hardening Soviet line, see the analysis sent urgently to Washington in Moscow 35285, "Soviet Concerns about Germany," 9 Dec 89. The Falin comment was passed along by the British to their American colleagues in Moscow. Soviet deputy foreign minister Anatoly Adamishin also went out of his way on December 11 to convey a message in Paris to the assistant secretary of state for human rights, Richard Schifter, that, in part because of domestic criticism, Moscow was "deeply concerned" over the possibility of early German reunification. (Schifter heard concerns from senior officials in the French Foreign Ministry as well.) See Schifter to Baker, "Soviet Concern over German Reunification and French Thoughts Thereon," 15 Dec 89.

91. See TASS reports, December 5, 1989, in *FBIS-SOV* 89–233, December 6, 1989, p. 51. The *Pravda* reports for the next day, December 6, are similar.

92. See reports of the Gorbachev speech in *Pravda,* December 10, 1989, pp. 1–3.

93. Soviet memcon, "Zapis besedy M.S. Gorbacheva s prezidentom frantsii F. Mitteranom," 6 Dec 89, made available to authors by Alexandra Bezymenskaya. For French foreign minister Dumas's account of the meetings in Kiev, see State 3834, "12/13/89 Quadripartite Ministers' Meeting," 5 Jan 90. Mitterrand told Kohl, over breakfast during the EC summit on December 9, that Gorbachev had displayed "astonishing" inner peace about Germany but might react differently if developments moved too quickly toward unification. The Germans noticed that Mitterrand said nothing about the French side of this conversation. As usual, Kohl tried to downplay any concern about unification taking place anytime soon. Teltschik, *329 Tage,* p. 71.

94. Thatcher, *The Downing Street Years,* p. 796.

95. Ibid., pp. 796–797.

96. Zelikow interview with Genscher, Wachtberg-Pech, December 1994; Conclusions of the Presidency, European Council, Strasbourg, December 8 and 9, 1989. See also Scowcroft to President Bush, "Mitterrand and the Strasbourg Summit," 13 Dec 89 (drafted by Blackwill). The CIA pointed up the similarities between the president's four principles on Germany and the EC's Strasbourg statement in an informal chart, "Conditions for German Reunification," which Blackwill passed to General Scowcroft on December 13.

97. Teltschik, *329 Tage*, p. 70.

98. See untitled note from Seitz to Baker, 4 Dec 89 (with Zoellick's annotated recommendation and Baker's marginal note), in Zoellick's office files. The concerns about preconditions for a CSCE summit influenced Baker's advice to Bush, just before his December 16 meeting with Mitterrand on the island of St. Martin, that Gorbachev's CSCE summit proposal "puts the cart before the horse" by not letting the allies decide first "what such a meeting might accomplish." Baker to President Bush, "Thoughts for the Mitterrand Meeting," Secto 19021, 16 Dec 89 (cabled from Brussels).

99. Scowcroft to President Bush, "Mitterrand, the Germans, U.S.-EC Cooperation, and the CSCE," 15 Dec 89 (drafted by Blackwill). See also Mitterrand's and the president's public comments at their St. Martin news conference. *Public Papers* (1989), bk. 2, p. 1713.

100. For the proposal and the quote from the French official, see Jim Hoagland, "Germans and French," *Washington Post*, December 14, 1989, p. A31.

101. See Baker to President Bush (for his evening reading), 8 Dec 89; this account also draws from Zelikow's notes on Blackwill's conversations with Kimmitt and others at State and with officials at the British embassy. On the background of the "Berlin initiative," see Maximychev, "What 'German Policy' We Need," pp. 58–60.

102. The account that follows is from Zelikow interviews with Genscher, Wachtberg-Pech, December 1994, and Kastrup, Bonn, December 1994; see Kiessler and Elbe, *Ein runder Tisch mit scharfen Ecken*, pp. 73–74; Teltschik, *329 Tage*, pp. 75, 79; USBerlin 3510, "Four-Power Talks on Berlin Initiative: December 11, 1989," 11 Dec 89; see also Bonn 39821, "Follow-Up on Four Power Talks in Berlin," 21 Dec 89. On the furious reaction in the West German press, see Pond, *Beyond the Wall*, p. 168. For the Soviet official's comment, see Maximychev, "What 'German Policy' We Need," p. 62.

103. Kiessler and Elbe, *Ein runder Tisch mit scharfen Ecken*, p. 55.

104. The account that follows is drawn from Zelikow interview with Baker, Houston, January 1995, and Memcon of meeting with President Mitterrand, St. Martin, 16 Dec 89. See also Scowcroft to President Bush, "Scope Paper—Your Meeting with President Mitterrand," 15 Dec 89 (drafted by Basora and Blackwill); and Scowcroft to President Bush, "Mitterrand, the Germans, U.S.-EC Cooperation, and the CSCE," December 15, 1989 (drafted by Blackwill).

105. See CIA, "East Germany: Movement toward Democracy and Reunification," 11 Dec 89; Munich 4955, "Bavarians and the Reunification Question," 15 Dec 89; Bonn 38006, "Kohl's Ten-Point Program: A Burst of Criticism and then More Embracing," 5 Dec 89; Claus Gennrich, "Genscher Pledges Respect for Soviet Security Interests," *Frankfurter Allgemeine Zeitung*, December 13, 1989, p. 4; Bonn 38015, "The SPD and the German Question," 5 Dec 89; and other U.S. intelligence reports.

106. See address of Secretary Baker, Berlin Press Club, 11 Dec 89, State Department transcript released to press.

107. This was the judgment in Bonn at both the Chancellery and the Foreign Ministry. See Teltschik, *329 Tage*, p. 78; Kiessler and Elbe, *Ein runder Tisch mit scharfen Ecken*, pp. 58–59. See also the appraisal (and *Die Welt* quote) in Pond, *Beyond the Wall*, pp. 153–154. For Bush's Brussels remarks, see note 81. On the speech, see also the background briefing in PA transcript, Briefing by Senior State Department Officials (Ross and Zoellick) in Berlin, 12 Dec 89. For Shevardnadze's comment, see USNATO 7044, "IS Notes of Soviet Foreign Minister Shevardnadze's Meeting with NATO SYG Wörner at NATO Headquarters—December 19, 1989," 19 Dec 89. Baker apparently discussed the main elements of his speech with President Bush before his departure, on December 9 or 10. See Dobbins to Baker, "Talkers for Use with the President," n.d. (probably 8 Dec 89). The handwritten annotations on the State Department file copy of this memo are Zoellick's, but the memo

was also marked up by Baker in a manner indicating that he probably used it to brief Bush.

108. The account of this meeting is drawn from Teltschik, *329 Tage,* p. 77; State 408228, "Secretary's December 12 Meeting with Chancellor Kohl," 26 Dec 89. Before Baker's trip, officials in Washington were so worried about West Germany's antagonizing other governments that they had considered whether Baker should give Kohl a letter from Bush highlighting the need for improved U.S.-FRG consultations during the period ahead. A draft was prepared, but the president decided that such a letter was unnecessary. On the border issue, Kohl had offered private assurances at the EC summit in Strasbourg similar to those he extended to Secretary Baker. The Dutch were reportedly satisfied with these assurances. The Hague 10159, "German-Polish Border: Dutch Claim Germans Gave Assurances at EC Summit," 20 Dec 89.

109. CIA, "The Changing Relationship between the Two Germanys: Prospects and Implications," EUR M 89–20218, November 29, 1989 (Baker's marked-up copy in Zoellick's office files).

110. For the account of the adviser whose advice was rejected, see Walters, *Die Vereinigung war voraussehbar,* pp. 65–66.

111. The following account of the Potsdam meetings is based on Brussels 16024, "Fast-press: Background Briefing by Senior Administration Official (Baker) Tegel Airport en route Brussels, Dec 12," 13 Dec 89; PA transcript, "Background Briefing by Senior State Department Officials" (given by Ross and Zoellick in the press bus in Potsdam en route to Tegel Airport), 12 Dec 89; Modrow, *Aufbruch und Ende,* p. 94; and Zelikow's own recollections of the trip.

112. For accounts of this dinner and the next morning's breakfast, see Kiessler and Elbe, *Ein runder Tisch mit scharfen Ecken,* pp. 74–75 (quoting Genscher and Baker; Elbe was present); State 3834, "12/13/89 Quadripartite Ministers' Meeting," 5 Jan 90.

113. On the comment from Mitterrand's adviser Jean-Louis Bianco, see Teltschik, *329 Tage,* p. 96.

114. Kohl's message was sent to Moscow on December 14. Gorbachev's message was waiting when Kohl returned on December 18 from a visit to Hungary. Teltschik, *329 Tage,* pp. 80–81, 85.

115. Rice interview with Tarasenko, Moscow, October 1991. Teltschik was told this by the Soviets as well. Zelikow and Rice interview with Teltschik, Gütersloh, June 1992.

116. Baker to President Bush (for his evening reading), December 20, 1989. On Kohl's trip to the GDR, see Teltschik, *329 Tage,* pp. 87–96.

117. Kiessler and Elbe, *Ein runder Tisch mit scharfen Ecken,* p. 47; emphasis added. Elbe remembers that Zoellick replied to the December warning by agreeing, "We also see it that way."

5. The Process Becomes the Two Plus Four

1. The following account of the preparation of the speech was relayed to the authors in two interviews with Tarasenko, Moscow, October 1991, and Providence, June 1993. Tarasenko was assisted by Teymuraz Stepanov from Shevardnadze's policy planning unit.

2. Quotations from this speech are drawn from "Europe: A Time of Change—E. A. Shevardnadze's Speech at the European Parliament Political Commission," *Pravda,* December 20, 1989, p. 4.

3. Ibid.

4. See Eduard Shevardnadze, *Moi vybor: v zashchitu demokratii i svobody* (Moscow:

Novostii, 1991), pp. 229–230. For a contemporary analysis of the speech, see CIA, "An Analysis of Shevardnadze's Seven Questions on German Unification," SOV M 89–20099, 29 Dec 89. To place the speech in the context of political developments within the Soviet Union, see Moscow 37130, "Gorbachev's Foreign Policy Facing Critical Tests," 23 Dec 89.

5. The account of Genscher's reference to the *Bild* article was given to Zelikow by an official who was present. The article must have been Karl-Ludwig Günsche, "Schewardnadse: Sieben Bedingungen für die Einheit," *Bild-Zeitung*, December 20, 1989. It is conceivable that Genscher or his staff had some hand in this article, but there is no evidence for this. See also Richard Kiessler and Frank Elbe, *Ein runder Tisch mit scharfen Ecken: Der diplomatische Weg zur deutschen Einheit* (Baden-Baden: Nomos, 1993), pp. 68–72; Horst Teltschik, *329 Tage: Innenansichten der Einigung* (Berlin: Siedler, 1991), pp. 92–93. American analysts thought that West German moderates, who believed that Kohl was risking an international crisis, might even be hoping that the stern Soviet warnings would somehow slow Kohl down. See CIA, "German Reaction to Shevardnadze's Speech," EUR M 89–20254, 29 Dec 89.

6. For the Süssmuth and Kohl statements, see *Frankfurter Allgemeine Zeitung*, December 30, 1989, p. 5; *General Anzeiger*, January 2, 1990, p. 2; see also Bonn 40202, "CDU Leaders React to Criticism of President von Weiszaecker's Call for Recognition of Poland's Western Border," 29 Dec 89; Bonn 79, "Poland's Western Border: Kohl Calls 'Unacceptable' Proposal for Joint FRG-GDR Declaration," 2 Jan 90.

The legal issue was whether the FRG had the capacity to settle the border with Poland. As we saw in Chapter 2, the Four Powers had reserved ultimate authority over the border of Germany in the Berlin declaration and Potsdam agreement of 1945, with the Western allies recognizing the continued reservation of their rights in all subsequent agreements, such as the Relations Convention of 1955 and the Quadripartite Agreement of 1971. Furthermore, the West Germans had argued, with support from the United States and Great Britain, that "Germany" still existed as a passive subject of international law, awaiting its eventual reestablishment as a unified state. Only such a reestablished Germany could conclude a final agreement on its borders. The Polish and East German position, occasionally shared by the Soviets, was that "Germany" had been extinguished in 1945. The FRG and the GDR were its successors. These two states had declared their assent to the existing GDR-Polish border in the 1950 Treaty of Görlitz (GDR-Poland) and the 1970 Treaty of Warsaw (FRG-Poland). See, e.g., Władysław Czaplinski, "The New Polish-German Treaties and the Changing Political Structure of Europe," *American Journal of International Law*, 86 (1992): 163, 164; Jochen Frowein, "Legal Problems of the German Ostpolitik," *International and Comparative Law Quarterly*, 23 (1974): 105.

7. See Konrad Jarausch, *The Rush to German Unity* (New York: Oxford University Press, 1994), pp. 76–89, 91–92; Elizabeth Pond, *Beyond the Wall: Germany's Road to Unification* (Washington, D.C.: Brookings Institution, 1993), pp. 145–152; Teltschik, *329 Tage*, p. 95.

8. On the January 4, 1990, meeting with Mitterrand, see Teltschik, *329 Tage*, pp. 97–100. Neither the West German nor French foreign ministries appear to have been represented at these talks.

9. For the account that follows, see Hutchings through Blackwill to Scowcroft, "Responding to a Soviet Call for a German Peace Conference," n.d. (written in late December 1989). The memo contained a draft memo embodying these views which Scowcroft could forward to President Bush. Scowcroft noted his disagreement, however, and declined to forward the memo to the president. This account is based on the documents and Zelikow interview with Scowcroft, Washington, D.C., 1991.

10. State 11920, "Shevardnadze Message on Germany—Corrected Text," 12 Jan 90. The

move was anticipated in national intelligence daily item, "Four-Power Talks and Reunification," 5 Jan 90.

11. State 13681, "Response to Shevardnadze's Proposal for Four-Power Exchange on Germany," 13 Jan 90; Bonn 1390, "Response to Shevardnadze's Proposal for Four-Power Exchange on Germany," 16 Jan 90; State 13666, "Followup on Four-Power Talks in Berlin," 13 Jan 90; Bonn 1510, "Meeting with UK and French Ambassadors on Shevardnadze Message and Berlin Initiative," 17 Jan 90. The final Western reply included the notion that Four Power diplomats resident in Berlin could coordinate with the FRG and GDR as needed on traditional Four Power issues such as the status of Berlin and public safety in the city. This was a British suggestion made in the hope of softening the allied refusal to agree to the main points of the Soviet note.

12. See Bonn 1899, "Ambassador's Discussion with Foreign Minister Genscher, January 19," 19 Jan 90; EUR/CE (Skinner) to Embassy Bonn, "QUAD Political Directors' Meeting in Washington, January 23," 23 Jan 90.

13. See State 29161, "Soviet Demarche on Direct Elections in Berlin, Activities by Neo-Fascist Forces," 27 Jan 90; Bonn 3160, "Soviet Demarche on Direct Elections in Berlin, Activities by Neo-Fascists," 31 Jan 90; and Seitz to Baker, "Soviet Demarches on Germany," 27 Jan 90 (drafted by Alexander Vershbow and Pierre Shostal). On initial Western consideration of the elections issue, see also State 14289, "Direct Election and Voting Rights of Berlin Bundestag Deputies," 14 Jan 90. From Moscow, U.S. ambassador Jack Matlock urged Washington to offer the Soviets some framework for discussing the changes in Germany and Eastern Europe. He suggested a group to explore the issues a CSCE summit might consider. Moscow 2333, "Dealing with Soviet Concerns about Germany," 19 Jan 90.

14. Sources for this account of conditions in the GDR in January 1990 are Jarausch, *The Rush to German Unity*, pp. 95–107; Pond, *Beyond the Wall*, pp. 170–171; Discussion Paper for Europe PCC on GDR, "GDR Policy Review," 9 Jan 90; USBerlin 213, "The Momper-Modrow Discussions on the Internal GDR Situation," 22 Jan 90; Bonn 1973, "FRG Economics Ministry on Inner-German Economic Developments," 22 Jan 90; CIA, "Appraisal of Situation—Increasing Uncertainty and Growing Prospects for Confrontation in East Germany," 24 Jan 90.

15. This account of the evolution of Kohl's thinking in January relies on Teltschik's day-by-day diaries, *329 Tage*, pp. 104–127; Zelikow and Rice interview with Teltschik, Gütersloh, June 1992; Bonn 2631, "Chancellery Readout on Inner-German Relations," 26 Jan 90; Bonn 2422, "Ambassador's Conversation with Chancellor Kohl, January 24, 1990," 25 Jan 90; authors' information about the conversation between Chancellor Kohl and British ambassador Christopher Malaby in Bonn on January 25; Deutschland Archiv, *Chronik der Ereignisse in der DDR* (Cologne: Verlagwissenschaft und Politik, 1990), pp. 46–50; and Pond, *Beyond the Wall*, pp. 170–171. A good sense of the contemporary mood can be captured by reading the proceedings of a January 24–25, 1990, conference in Bonn, well attended by East and West German luminaries. Both Teltschik and Egon Bahr presented papers on the international issues, previewing debates still to come. See Hans Süssmuth, ed., *Wie geht es weiter mit Deutschland?* (Baden-Baden: Nomos, 1990); for the Teltschik paper, see pp. 119–127.

16. See Hutchings to Gantt (for Scowcroft and Gates), "PCC on U.S.-GDR Relations," 11 Jan 90 (sent via electronic mail), reporting on the PCC recommendations with which Hutchings, in attendance, had concurred. Scowcroft sent back the report with the note: "See me." Scowcroft made it clear that the GDR would not be treated in a manner comparable to the aid efforts being devised for the new democracies in Poland and Hungary.

17. Blackwill to Scowcroft, "1990," 19 Jan 90.

18. Hutchings through Blackwill to Scowcroft, "Your Breakfast with Kissinger: Managing the German Question," 26 Jan 90; Zelikow interviews with Baker, Houston, January 1995, and Zoellick, Washington, D.C., January 1995.

19. Rice to Blackwill, "Thinking about Germany," 23 Jan 90.

20. Wjatscheslaw Kotschemassow, *Meine letzte Mission* (Berlin: Dietz, 1994), pp. 204–209; Eduard Shevardnadze, *Izvestiya*, January 19, 1990, p. 5; see also the public statements surrounding the visit of East German foreign minister Oskar Fischer to Moscow at the same time, "Rabochii vizit O. Fishera v SSSR," *Vestnik*, February 15, 1990, pp. 19–20. Teltschik characteristically glossed over the negative aspects of Shevardnadze's *Izvestiya* article, preferring to comment on its relaxed tone, which he interpreted as showing a readiness to compromise. Teltschik, *329 Tage*, pp. 112–113. Teltschik again could find statements in press interviews with Central Committee staffers, including Portugalov, that seemed to indicate a more tolerant Soviet attitude (though the Central Committee staff was actually anything but tolerant within the internal deliberations of the Soviet government). Ibid., pp. 113–114.

21. The following account of the January "crisis staff" meeting is based on Georgi Shakhnazarov, *Tsena svobody: reformatsiya Gorbacheva glazami ego pomoshchnika* (Moscow: Zevs, 1993), pp. 125–127; Anatoly Chernyaev, *Shest' let s Gorbachevym: po dnevikovym zapisyam* (Moscow: Progress Publishers, 1993), pp. 346–347; Valentin Falin, *Politische Erinnerungen*, trans. Heddy Pross-Weerth (Munich: Droemer Knaur, 1993), pp. 489–490; interview with Falin quoted in Ekkehard Kuhn, *Gorbatschow und die deutsche Einheit: Aussagen der wichtigsten russischen und deutschen Beteiligten* (Bonn: Bouvier, 1993), p. 94; Zelikow interview with Chernyaev, Moscow, January 1994; and Alexander Galkin and Anatoly Chernyaev, "K pravdy i tol'ko odinaya pravda: Memoiri v svazi Vospominaniyem," *Svobodnaya Mysl'*, nos. 2–3 (January–February 1994): 19–29. The Falin account, though vaguer and confused about timing, is generally consistent with Chernyaev's and Shakhnazarov's version except for two details. Falin names defense minister Dimitri Yazov, who just listened, as a participant in the meeting; and Falin names Shakhnazarov as a supporter of Chernyaev's position, whereas Chernyaev (and Shakhnazarov's own account) indicates that Shakhnazarov supported Falin. The consideration of Soviet troop withdrawal from the GDR should be placed against the nuanced Soviet reaction to Gregor Gysi's proposal for withdrawals of all foreign troops in Shevardnadze's January 22 *Izvestiya* article.

The Soviet request to the FRG for foodstuffs was delivered directly from Kvitsinsky to Kohl on January 8, with Kvitsinsky stressing Soviet disappointment with the record so far of assistance resulting from the agreements at the June 1989 Kohl-Gorbachev summit in Bonn. Kohl seized on this opportunity to assuage Soviet hostility, instructed his agriculture minister Ignaz Kiechle to move on the request, and had finalized his government's plans by January 24. See Teltschik, *329 Tage*, pp. 100–102, 109, 114. At the same time, the Soviet government finally agreed to Kohl's proposal for a visit to Moscow, a request that had been pending for more than a month.

22. For the following account of Modrow's talks with Gorbachev, see Hans Modrow, *Aufbruch und Ende* (Hamburg: Konkret Literatur, 1991), pp. 120–123; Kotschemassow, *Meine letzte Mission*, pp. 211–217; and interviews with Gorbachev, Modrow, and Manfred Gerlach excerpted in Kuhn, *Gorbatschow und die deutsche Einheit*, pp. 100–103. For the public commentary, see TASS, "Talks Begin with Gorbachev," January 30, 1990, in *FBIS-SOV* 90–020, January 30, 1990, p. 22; TASS, "Shevardnadze Outlines Policy on German Unity," February 2, 1990, in *FBIS-SOV* 90–024, February 5, 1990, pp. 33–35; Bericht des

Bundesministerium für innerdeutsche Beziehungen, in *Materialen zur Deutschlandfragen* (Bonn: Kulturstiftung der deutschen Vertriebenen, 1989–1991), pp. 243–244; "Rabochii vizit G. Gysi v SSSR," *Vestnik*, February 28, 1990, pp. 4–5. For the notice taken of these comments in Bonn and Washington, see Teltschik, *329 Tage*, pp. 120–121; Baker to President Bush (for his evening reading), 30 Jan 90. For the full text of Modrow's plan, see Ingo von Münch, ed., *Dokumente der Wiedervereinigung Deutschlands* (Stuttgart: Alfred Kroner, 1991), pp. 79–81.

23. Letter from President Gorbachev to President Bush, 2 Feb 90 (quoting unofficial translation provided by Soviet embassy). Although Chernyayev contends that Gorbachev had decided on a six-power forum at the January meeting of his crisis staff, it is noteworthy that the Soviet government was still proposing only a Four Power approach in this letter to Bush. On the disconnection between this crisis staff and the traditional Foreign Ministry and Central Committee bureaucracies, see Hannes Adomeit, "Gorbachev, German Unification, and the Collapse of Empire," *Post-Soviet Affairs*, 10 (1994): 197, 215–217.

24. For the account that follows, see Margaret Thatcher, *The Downing Street Years* (New York: HarperCollins, 1993), pp. 797–798.

25. See Blackwill to Scowcroft, "Germany," 30 Jan 90. This memo attached a draft memo for Scowcroft to forward to President Bush, "A Strategy for German Unification," laying out the proposed policy. The blueprint (outlined in eight points) was in the draft memo to the president. A copy of this package was also passed informally to Secretary Baker and Zoellick at the State Department. To ensure secrecy, this memo and others were forwarded outside the normal paperwork system. We have been unable to determine when the "strategy" memo was actually forwarded by Scowcroft to Bush. We do know that Scowcroft agreed at the time with Blackwill's argument.

26. On the policy planning staff (S/P) Roger George, with Peter Hauslohner, first drafted a memo to Ross, "German Confederation in a New NATO," apparently around mid-January. The head of the European bureau's German desk, Pierre Shostal, then prepared a counterdraft. George told Shostal that S/P's recommendations reflected a consensus among the staff but admitted that Ross himself had some doubts about the memo's recommendations. On January 23 George gave Shostal a redraft of the S/P memo, now framed as a memo to Zoellick, reiterating the original arguments. Shostal renewed his effort to substitute a counterdraft, framed as a memo through Kimmitt to Baker (January 29). See also, for similar views, draft memo from Shostal and McKinley through Dobbins to Seitz, "U.S. Goals for a Future Germany," 30 Jan 90, drafted by EUR desk officer Andrew Goodman. After more debate about how to combine the competing S/P and EUR memos into a memo for Zoellick, the effort was abandoned at the beginning of February. This debate had little effect on U.S. policy. It is doubtful that Zoellick, or even Ross, read any version of the S/P memo beyond George's first draft. Zoellick was influenced instead by the NSC staff analysis he had received informally. It was the NSC staff's more inflexible stand on NATO that Zoellick—with a significant modification— later passed on to Baker.

27. See Bonn 1904, "Chancellor Kohl's Press Remarks on German Unification and NATO," 19 Jan 90; authors' information on discussion between British ambassador Christopher Malaby and Von Weiszäcker. See also Mulholland to Eagleburger, "German Unity: Kohl Escalates His Demands," 22 Jan 90 (arguing, entirely mistakenly, that Kohl thought the Bush-Baker four principles of December were meant as roadblocks to unity, so Kohl was now defying the United States).

28. The discussion that follows is based on Ross and Zoellick to Baker, "Germany:

Game Plan for Two Plus Four Powers Talks," 30 Jan 90. This memo drew on and revised an earlier set of ideas for the Two Plus Four written by Roger George as a draft note for Ross to send to Baker. George's draft had captured the idea of wanting to do "more than say no to Four Power Talks, which leaves the Soviets outside the process, capable of creating trouble," and the need to condition creation of a Two Plus Four forum on explicit acknowledgment that the self-determination process "could" lead to unification. But the draft was murky on other key points. It implied that Four Power talks might still be appropriate, prompting Zoellick to note in the margin, "Too much." George's original draft also envisioned, as Genscher did, the CSCE summit "as the place to present an allied-endorsed German unity plan, developed by the two Germanies." In addition, as we mentioned earlier, George and his S/P colleagues were writing other papers in late January that referred consistently to Four Power talks as the vehicle for negotiating the possible withdrawal from Germany of both U.S. and Soviet troops. See "Action Plan: Two Plus Four Talks," undated S/P note to Zoellick (apparently written around the third week of January). The best published account of the development of Two Plus Four, though it underestimates how fully elaborated the plan was before it was discussed with the West Germans, is Pond, *Beyond the Wall,* pp. 176–178.

29. For the discussion that follows, see Seitz to Baker, 1 Feb 90 (with attached McKinley comments annotated by Zoellick), and Zoellick's cover note forwarding the package to Baker.

30. See Scowcroft to President Bush, "CFE Reductions," 16 Jan 90, attaching separate memos from Cheney, Scowcroft, and Baker. The NSC staff approach that was ultimately adopted was crafted by Blackwill and Zelikow with Arnold Kanter and Heather Wilson from Kanter's defense and arms control directorate in the NSC staff, then refined by Scowcroft.

31. Scowcroft considered a compromise between the NSC staff and State Department positions that would proceed to a conclusion of a CFE treaty with the 275,000 figure and then, just before signing, add a protocol changing the number to 200,000. This idea was weighed and then discarded, for reasons described in Blackwill and Kanter to Scowcroft, "CFE Move on Manpower: The Protocol Idea," 25 Jan 90.

32. Teltschik, *329 Tage,* p. 117; Memcon for phone call from the president to Chancellor Kohl, 26 Jan 90 (Zelikow was note taker).

33. For the account that follows, see Memcon for the president's call to President Mitterrand, 27 Jan 90 (Heather Wilson was note taker).

34. Memcon of president's call to Prime Minister Thatcher, 27 Jan 90 (Zelikow was note taker).

35. Teltschik, *329 Tage,* p. 123. The account of the Eagleburger-Gates discussions is drawn from ibid., p. 119; and Zelikow's notes of Gates's debriefing after he returned to Washington. On their meeting with Thatcher, see also Paris 2912, "Meeting with Mrs. T.," 29 Jan 90.

36. Letter from President Bush to President Gorbachev, 31 Jan 90; Michael Beschloss and Strobe Talbott, *At the Highest Levels: The Inside Story of the End of the Cold War* (Boston: Little, Brown, 1992), pp. 177–178; Memcon of the president's call to President Gorbachev, 31 Jan 90 (Rice was note taker). The NATO allies formally welcomed the president's troop cut initiative first as an arms control measure and second because they understood that Bush was placing a floor under the U.S. troop commitment. The Soviet press spokesman pronounced Bush's move "a step in the right direction." See memos from Baker to President Bush (for his evening reading), 1 and 2 Feb 90.

37. From point 4 of outline for Baker's meeting with President Bush, 31 Jan 90 (these

outlines were usually prepared by Zoellick for Baker). The preparatory notes for the meeting allude to the Two Plus Four process, though, and it is unclear whether Baker raised this idea with President Bush. The outline erroneously treats the concept of a "demilitarized" eastern Germany as identical to Genscher's suggestion that the former GDR remain outside NATO.

38. For the account that follows, see Memcon of the president's meeting with Foreign Secretary Hurd, 29 Jan 90. See also State 54508, "British Foreign Secretary Hurd's Meeting with Secretary Baker, January 29, 1990," 20 Feb 90; and Baker to President Bush (for his evening reading), 29 Jan 90. The account of the discussions with Scowcroft are from Zelikow's notes of the meeting. According to Beschloss and Talbott, Hurd opposed the Two Plus Four idea, saying that he preferred "Four-plus-Zero," meaning "leaving the Germans out" (*At the Highest Levels,* p. 185), a statement repeated in Kiessler and Elbe, *Ein runder Tisch mit scharfen Ecken,* p. 88. We have not found any evidence to support this assertion. The American position on the CSCE summit was developed in January by the State Department's European Bureau and the NSC staff. See Seitz through Kimmitt, McCormack, and Bartholomew to Baker, "Framing the Basis for a 1990 CSCE Summit," 11 Jan 90. On January 22 Zoellick told Seitz that Baker agreed with the EUR recommendations and would review the issue with the White House.

39. The account that follows is drawn from Zelikow interviews with Genscher, Wachtberg-Pech, December 1994, and with Kastrup, Bonn, December 1994; also Hans-Dietrich Genscher, "German Unity in the European Framework," Tutzing Protestant Academy, 31 Jan 90. Quotations are from the English-language translation prepared for Genscher and passed by him to Baker when the two men met in Washington on February 2. See also Bonn 3400, "Genscher Outlines His Vision of a New European Architecture," 1 Feb 90. For a rather general discussion of the thinking behind the Tutzing formula, see Kiessler and Elbe, *Ein runder Tisch mit scharfen Ecken,* pp. 77–80.

40. See Bonn 2169, "Genscher's Views on the German Question," 23 Jan 90 (the Genscher-Mathias conversation took place on January 23); Teltschik, *329 Tage,* p. 117; FBIS translation of "Austrian Press interview with Genscher in Bonn on January 21," Vienna Television Service in German, 21 Jan 90; CIA report, "Foreign Minister Genscher's Views on German Unification, Four-Power Meetings, Future European Security Structures, and SNF," 29 Jan 90; Bonn 1899, "Ambassador's Discussion with Foreign Minister Genscher, January 19," 19 Jan 90.

41. Kiessler and Elbe, *Ein runder Tisch mit scharfen Ecken,* p. 80.

42. See the untitled briefing paper on the Genscher meeting Zoellick prepared for Baker, 2 Feb 90. In setting down these points, Zoellick drew to some extent on George through Holmes to Ross and Zoellick, "The Genscher Visit: Working the Unification Issue," 1 Feb 90.

43. Kiessler and Elbe, *Ein runder Tisch mit scharfen Ecken,* pp. 86–87; Pond, *Beyond the Wall,* p. 178. Kiessler and Elbe mistakenly assert that Blackwill was also involved in devising the Two Plus Four plan which Elbe accepted, although they appear to know that Blackwill was against the idea. Compare Kiessler and Elbe, *Ein runder Tisch mit scharfen Ecken,* pp. 87, 88–89. Although there is evidence that the idea of a six-power forum had occurred to officials in Bonn, none of them had developed the idea to include, for example, the express commitment to unification.

44. The following account of Genscher's visit is drawn from Kiessler and Elbe, *Ein runder Tisch mit scharfen Ecken,* p. 89; draft report on the meeting prepared on February 2 by Seitz for Baker to send to Scowcroft in Germany; from PA transcript, "Departure Remarks by Secretary Baker and Foreign Minister Genscher," 2 Feb 90; and from Zelikow

interviews with Zoellick, Washington, D.C., 1991. Genscher says this account of the meeting is inaccurate; letter from Genscher, April 1995. Don Oberdorfer's brief description of the Baker-Genscher meeting, though apparently based on an interview with Zoellick, is inaccurate; see Don Oberdorfer, *The Turn: From the Cold War to a New Era, The United States and the Soviet Union, 1983–1990* (New York: Simon and Schuster, 1991), pp. 393–394.

45. See USBerlin 406, "Momper's Nine-Point Paper for German Unity," 6 Feb 90.

46. The account that follows is drawn from Teltschik, *329 Tage*, pp. 126–127; Scowcroft to President Bush, "Trip Report: Wehrkunde Conference in Munich, FRG February 3–4, 1990," 5 Feb 90; also Zelikow interviews with Blackwill, Cambridge, Mass., 1991. For the policy-making environment in Washington at this time, see Peter Riddell and Lionel Barber, "Americans Turn Attention to German Reunification," *Financial Times*, February 5, 1990.

47. See Scowcroft to President Bush, "Trip Report"; Bonn 3968, "Unification: Increasingly, It's Seen as Coming Soon," 6 Feb 90; Bonn 4193, "German Unification: Further Developments Coming Thick and Fast," 7 Feb 90; EmbBerlin 844, "German Unification on March 19?," 9 Feb 90.

48. Blackwill to Scowcroft, "The Beginning of the Big Game," 7 Feb 90. See also Moscow 2679, "U.S.-Soviet Relations on the Eve of the Ministerial: The View from Moscow," 23 Jan 90.

49. The account of this meeting is drawn from Oberdorfer, *The Turn*, p. 394; Secto 01005, "Secretary's Meeting with Foreign Minister Dumas, February 6, 1990," 7 Feb 90.

50. Baker to President Bush, "My Visit to Czechoslovakia," Secto 01009, 8 Feb 90 (cabled from Moscow).

51. See "Debate Speech by Ye. K. Ligachev," *Pravda*, February 7, 1990, p. 6; "Speeches in the Discussion of the Report [to the Central Committee]," *Pravda*, February 7, 1990, pp. 5–6. The latter is reprinted in Ligachev's memoir, Yegor K. Ligachev, *Zagadka Gorbacheva* (Novosibirsk: Interbook, 1992), pp. 98–99. See also the summary of the Soviet debate in Oberdorfer, *The Turn*, pp. 389–391. Beschloss and Talbott report that Yakovlev clashed at this time with Falin and other hard-liners (*At the Highest Levels*, p. 186), but there is no evidence to confirm a break at this time between Yakovlev and others on the Central Committee staff. Although Yakovlev did defend Gorbachev against the attacks from Ligachev, his public position was otherwise close to the prevailing line.

52. The account that follows is based on Memcon of Second One-on-One Meeting with Foreign Minister Shevardnadze, Osobn Guest House, Moscow, 8 Feb 90. The note takers were Ross and Tarasenko. The burden of historical feeling about Germany and Shevardnadze's desire for a much more gradual process of unification are also evident in Shevardnadze's memoirs. See Shevardnadze, *Moi vybor*, pp. 235–237.

53. The account that follows is based on Memcon of meeting with President Gorbachev at the Kremlin, February 9, 1990. Baker was accompanied by Dennis Ross, who took notes, and an interpreter. Gorbachev was joined by Foreign Minister Shevardnadze, a note taker, and an interpreter.

The account of Baker's discussion of Germany in his Moscow meetings in Beschloss and Talbott, *At the Highest Levels*, pp. 183–184, 185–186, is inaccurate. It quotes Gorbachev describing worries about Germany, though the quotes are actually paraphrases of what Shevardnadze, not Gorbachev, said in the foreign minister's earlier, separate meeting with the American secretary of state. Beschloss and Talbott quote Gorbachev's comments on the NATO issue accurately in some respects but inaccurately in others. They also have Gorbachev grudgingly conceding only that the Two Plus Four "might be suitable" but refusing to commit himself to support Baker's design. In fact, as we mention in the text, Gorbachev responded quite positively to the idea, in part because the January "crisis staff" meeting had already considered a possible "six-power" forum. Don Oberdorfer's more reliable account of the Baker meetings in Moscow has some similar problems that seem to stem in part from the way Baker and his aides summarized these meetings to reporters; see Oberdorfer, *The Turn*, pp. 394–396.

Baker's caution in describing the Soviet reaction to the Two Plus Four idea deserves notice. Although Baker summarized the reaction in the same way ("might be suitable") in his subsequent letter to Kohl, and may have also described it to reporters in these terms, the summary was actually Baker's careful, lawyerly understatement of a much more positive reaction. Readers will have noted that, in the same way, Baker repeatedly told the Russians that the Germans had not "committed" themselves either, though Baker already had Genscher's agreement in his pocket, because Baker knew that he had not yet secured agreement from Kohl. For Baker "commitment" was a term that meant a formal, binding promise. Baker could not get such a commitment from Gorbachev because he could not formally propose an agreement to Moscow that was not yet blessed by America's allies (or indeed by parts of his own government).

54. On the discussions about Germany with subcabinet officials, see Memcon of meeting between Seitz and deputy foreign minister Anatoly Adamishin, 9 Feb 90. For Soviet reports of Baker's visit, see "Ofitsial'ny vizit J. Baker v SSSR," *Vestnik*, February 28, 1990, pp. 5–6; and Shevardnadze's press conference, TASS, "Shevardnadze Answers Questions," February 10, 1990, in *FBIS-SOV* 90–029, February 12, 1990, pp. 24–29.

55. See PA transcript, Secretary Baker's Press Conference, Novosti Press Center, Moscow, 9 Feb 90, pp. 5, 10–11. The press missed Baker's deliberate vagueness on the key point about NATO "jurisdiction," an issue hardly anyone understood at that point. Instead, the press jumped on Baker's accidental reference to German "association" with NATO. There were then numerous press stories about a supposed U.S. concession to accepting only "association." These stories were entirely baseless, since Baker in fact took pains to correct his slip of the tongue during his press conference. The next day either Zoellick or Ross, speaking to the press on background, had to put an end to the "association" issue: "It's membership, it's membership, it's membership, okay?" PA transcript, Background Briefing by Senior Administration Official, Sofia, Bulgaria, 10 Feb 90.

56. Kiessler and Elbe, *Ein runder Tisch mit scharfen Ecken*, p. 91.

57. Scowcroft to President Bush, "Message to Kohl," 8 Feb 90 (drafted by Blackwill and Zelikow).

58. For the following account, see Scowcroft to President Bush, "Message to Kohl"; Blackwill to Scowcroft, "State Department Draft Message to Kohl," 8 Feb 90. The previous day Blackwill and Zelikow had drafted for Scowcroft a catalogue of the complete spectrum of possible German affiliations to NATO and outcomes for the U.S. security presence. See "German Unity: Variations on the Theme," 8 Feb 90 (a copy was passed to Zoellick after his return to Washington).

59. This reference to NATO's "original political role" alludes to an interpretation Zelikow was offering at the time, arguing that the NATO treaty had originally served as a statement of U.S. commitment to Europe's future before the later decisions were made, after the outbreak of the Korean War, to commit large numbers of U.S. combat troops to Europe as part of far more elaborate efforts to deter and repel a potential Soviet attack.

60. See message from President Bush to Chancellor Kohl, 9 Feb 90 (sent via special channels); the contents are also summarized in Teltschik, *329 Tage*, pp. 134–135; Beschloss and Talbott, *At the Highest Levels*, p. 187.

61. *Public Papers of the Presidents: George Bush, 1990*, bk. 1 (Washington, D.C.: Government Printing Office, 1990), p. 266.

62. For the account that follows, see Secretary Baker to Chancellor Kohl, 10 Feb 90 (delivered by U.S. diplomats to Kohl on his arrival in Moscow). The contents of the letter are quoted at length in Oberdorfer, *The Turn,* p. 396; and also described in Kiessler and Elbe, *Ein runder Tisch mit scharfen Ecken,* p. 95; Teltschik, *329 Tage,* pp. 137–138; and Beschloss and Talbott, *At the Highest Levels,* p. 187. A copy of this letter was reviewed by the White House before it was sent. (Bush's own letter had already gone out.) By getting White House clearance for this letter, Baker was also—in effect—getting the first written White House clearance for a written proposal of his Two Plus Four idea. When the NSC staff attempted to block agreement to this approach a few days later, they were forced to confront the fact that Baker had already won a good deal of support for his idea from the West German chancellor and foreign minister, as well as from Gorbachev, and the approach to Kohl had been sent with a formal White House clearance.

63. See Teltschik, *329 Tage,* pp. 137–138; Kiessler and Elbe, *Ein runder Tisch mit scharfen Ecken,* pp. 95–96; Bonn 5456, "Meeting with FRG Political Director Kastrup," 16 Feb 90; Bonn 4761, "Teltschik Readout on Kohl's Visit to Moscow," 12 Feb 90.

64. On Kohl's discussions in Moscow, see Teltschik, *329 Tage,* pp. 138–141; interviews with Teltschik and Gorbachev excerpted in Kuhn, *Gorbatschow und die deutsche Einheit,* pp. 108–109; Anatoly Cherniaev, "Gorbachev and the Reunification of Germany," in *Soviet Foreign Policy, 1917–1991: A Retrospective,* ed. Gabriel Gorodetsky (London: Frank Cass, 1993), p. 167 (though mistakenly calling this a telephone conversation and dating it February 11 instead of February 10); Bonn 4761, "Teltschik Readout on Kohl's Visit to Moscow," 12 Feb 90; and CIA reports circulated to U.S. officials at the time.

65. See Teltschik, *329 Tage,* pp. 142–143; the venomous comments about Teltschik are in Kiessler and Elbe, *Ein runder Tisch mit scharfen Ecken,* p. 98; for Portugalov's comments downplaying the Moscow meeting, see the interview excerpted in Kuhn, *Gorbatschow und die deutsche Einheit,* pp. 111–112; and Pond, *Beyond the Wall,* pp. 179–180. For the public commentary, see *Europa-Archiv,* April 25, 1990, pp. 192–193.

66. See State 49194, "Eagleburger-Dubinin Meeting on Germany," 14 Feb 90; Eagleburger (Acting) to President Bush (for his evening reading), 13 Feb 90. Falin blasted both the Bush and Genscher formulas for suggesting NATO membership for a united Germany; see interview with Rudolf Augstein, *Der Spiegel,* February 19, 1990, pp. 168–172. For Bondarenko's public effort to set the record straight from the Foreign Ministry, see A. P. Bondarenko, "The Truth Is This," *Trud,* February 18, 1990, p. 3, in *FBIS-SOV* 90–040, February 28, 1990, pp. 23–24. In their notes to Washington, London, and Paris, the Soviets did admit that they had agreed to a six-power forum. Only in the message to the Americans, the Soviets added a proposal for trilateral discussions involving the United States, the USSR, and the FRG, cutting out the British and the French. The United States did not pursue this suggestion, and it was dropped.

67. Soviet Memcon, "Zapis osnovnogo soderzhaniya telefonnoso razgovora M. S. Gorbacheva s predsedatelem Soveta Ministrov GDR H. Modrovem," 12 Feb 90, made available to authors by Alexandra Bezymenskaya; communication from Chernyayev, February 1995.

68. Zelikow helped pass this message to Baker. See also Beschloss and Talbott, *At the Highest Levels,* p. 189.

69. At this NATO caucus Baker and Genscher also briefed their NATO colleagues on their respective meetings in Moscow. Neither alluded specifically to the Two Plus Four mechanism then being negotiated (account based on Zelikow's notes from the caucus).

70. This account is based on Zelikow's recollection of events, including the drafting of the Ottawa compromise on U.S.-Soviet troop limits. See also Beschloss and Talbott, *At the Highest Levels,* p. 190. Documentary records from Baker's various meetings are frag-

mentary. See also Zelikow through Blackwill to Scowcroft, "Impressions from the Ottawa Conference," 14 Feb 90. The Pentagon was later annoyed that Baker's arrangement confined them to only 30,000 troops outside of Central Europe. Civilian and military defense officials wanted more room to mix and match according to force planning needs and availability of bases and felt that Baker had hurried the process to conclusion without letting their representatives participate in the negotiations or allowing them adequate time to consult about the deal with the secretary of defense or Joint Chiefs of Staff. But Baker had negotiated the accord based on force levels the Defense Department had earlier recommended to President Bush as adequate.

71. Memcon of breakfast with Prime Minister Mulroney and Foreign Minister Shevardnadze, Prime Minister's Residence, 12 Feb 90.

72. See Kiessler and Elbe, *Ein runder Tisch mit scharfen Ecken,* pp. 99–100; Shevardnadze, *Moi vybor,* pp. 225–227, 231–233. The background of the Two Plus Four was well described in the detailed background press briefings conducted by Zoellick and Ross at the time. See PA transcript, "Background Briefing by Senior Administration Officials," 12 Feb 90, pp. 5–8 (Zoellick is the briefer in the cited portion); PA transcript, "Department of State Background Briefing on Results of Ottawa Ministerial," 14 Feb 90 ("First Official" is Ross; "Second Official" is Zoellick).

73. See Kiessler and Elbe, *Ein runder Tisch mit scharfen Ecken,* pp. 103–104; Zelikow's recollections and draft State Department cable, "Ottawa: Allied Ministers' Meeting on CFE and German Unity Statement," 15 Feb 90. See also The Hague 1387, "Dutch Reactions to Ottawa Agreement on Handling German Reunification," 15 Feb 90. The Canadian ambassador to the United States, Derek Burney, later told Blackwill that his government, hosting the meeting but unaware of the Two Plus Four discussions, felt like the piano player in a whorehouse, watching the customers going up and down the stairs, hearing the bedsprings creak, and just playing along. Interview with Blackwill, Cambridge, Mass., August 1994.

74. Account based on Zelikow interviews with Baker, Houston, January 1995, and Genscher, Wachtberg-Pech, December 1994; Kiessler and Elbe, *Ein runder Tisch mit scharfen Ecken,* p. 101. On the calls themselves, see Teltschik, *329 Tage,* p. 146; Memcons of calls between the president and Chancellor Kohl, February 13, 1990 (note taker for both calls was Hutchings). Kiessler and Elbe repeat a story that the Americans called Kohl because Teltschik had called the White House in order to use the Americans to delay agreement to a Two Plus Four process that would move bureaucratic control over the German question to Bonn's Foreign Office. Kiessler and Elbe, *Ein runder Tisch mit scharfen Ecken,* p. 101. This remarkable assertion speaks volumes about the poisoned relationship in Bonn at the time between the Foreign Office and the Chancellery. Teltschik did call Blackwill, but only to express concern about how little information either of them had about what was happening in Ottawa. Interview with Blackwill, Cambridge, Mass., 1994. It is highly doubtful that Teltschik would have opposed the Two Plus Four idea since he knew Kohl liked it and, even more important, knew that Kohl had already agreed with Gorbachev to support Baker's plan. Bush and Scowcroft, not knowing about the understanding between Kohl and Gorbachev, had their own reasons for wanting to confer with Kohl.

75. Account based on Zelikow interviews with Scowcroft and Zoellick, Washington, D.C., 1991; authors' recollections; and Blackwill to Scowcroft and Gates (via Gantt and Edwards), "Six Power Conference," 13 Feb 90 (electronic mail messages sent at 1559 and 1900 EDT).

76. Pond, *Beyond the Wall,* p. 181; Kohl and Falin quoted in Beschloss and Talbott, *At the Highest Levels,* p. 190.

77. For the account that follows, see Memcon for president's meeting with Manfred

Wörner, Camp David, 10 Feb 90 (the Memcon in the official records is incorrectly dated). Bush was joined for this meeting by Vice President Quayle, Scowcroft, U.S. ambassador to NATO William Taft IV, Eagleburger, deputy secretary of defense Donald Atwood, and Blackwill. Wörner was accompanied only by James Cunningham, an American diplomat detailed to the secretary general's private office.

78. See, e.g., the interview with Shevardnadze on board the aircraft returning from Ottawa to Moscow, M. Yusin, "Eduard Shevardnadze . . .," *Izvestiya,* February 20, 1990, p. 5 (an interview later referred to in his memoirs, *Moi vybor,* p. 232); and for the military perspective, see Yuri Teplyakov, "My otvykli razoruzhat'sya," *Moskovskiye Novosti,* February 25, 1990, p. 7 (interview with deputy commander of the Strategic Rocket Forces Lieutenant General Igor Sergeyev: "All the theoretical discussions about changing [NATO] from a military to a political pact are cold comfort. It's playing with words.")

79. Interview in *Der Spiegel,* February 19, 1990, pp. 168–172. Shevardnadze later told Teltschik that, during the January policy review, Falin had spoken in support of directly threatening military intervention in Germany. Falin denied it, but Teltschik did not believe him. Zelikow and Rice interview with Teltschik, Gütersloh, June 1992.

6. The Design for a New Germany

1. "Remarks on Signing the Urgent Assistance for Democracy in Panama Act of 1990 and a Question-and-Answer Session with Reporters," in *Public Papers of the Presidents: George Bush, 1990,* bk. 1 (Washington, D.C.: Government Printing Office, 1990), pp. 244–246. The Ottawa accord was well received in the United States. Tom Wicker spoke for many in commenting that the agreement appeared to place the administration "on top, if not literally in control, of the swiftly evolving situation in Europe." Richard Cohen remarked: "President-bashing may be as warmly satisfying as hot soup on a cold day, but sometimes the facts make it difficult . . . As a West German official put it, the non-vision President had vision after all." The majority of editorial comment followed suit, though some journalists continued to voice their fears of a united Germany. See Tom Wicker, "The Score at Ottawa," *New York Times,* February 15, 1990, p. A31; Richard Cohen, ". . . And Diplomats," *Washington Post,* February 21, 1990, p. A21. On the general positive reaction, see also Tutwiler to Baker, "Editorial Comment on Ottawa Ministerial," 7 Mar 90. For another example of such comment, see "Steering the German Steamroller," *New York Times,* February 15, 1990, p. A30, which, curiously, gave most of the credit for the accomplishment to Genscher rather than Baker. In fact, some commentators thought that Bush had adopted a "laissez-faire approach" to developments in Germany; see Robert Hunter, "The Transition to One Germany," *Christian Science Monitor,* February 21, 1990, p. 18. Others even thought that Bush was opposed to rapid German unification; see, e.g., "The Germanys: Marching to Unity," *Time,* February 12, 1990, p. 30. Owing, however, to the skillful background briefing of Zoellick and Ross, many journalists grasped the significance of the sequencing concept of the Two Plus Four, which put internal German moves toward unity before negotiation of the external aspects of unification. See "Germans and Their Neighbors," *Washington Post,* February 19, 1990, p. A18; and "Reunifying Germany," *Washington Post,* February 15, 1990, p. A24, which nonetheless notes anxiously, "One is entitled to be a bit nervous about the speed of it all and to expect that the unifiers will proceed with the utmost care."

More overt fears of Germany were evident in "An Agreeable Unity," *Christian Science Monitor,* February 15, 1990, p. 20, as well as frank hostility from A. M. Rosenthal, "Until Shadows Vanish," *New York Times,* February 15, 1990, p. A31, and William Safire, "Kohl at

Camp David," *New York Times,* February 23, 1990, p. A31. For counterarguments to allay such fears, see, e.g., Henry Ashby Turner, "Baseless Fears of a Unified Germany," *New York Times,* February 11, 1990, p. 25; George Will, "Europe's Furled Banners," *Newsweek,* February 26, 1990, p. 72. Some also recognized the formidable challenges involved in the first step, economic merger; see, e.g., "German Digestion," *Wall Street Journal,* February 16, 1990, p. A12.

2. See Henry Kissinger, "Delay Is the Most Dangerous Course," *Washington Post,* February 9, 1990, p. A27. Also raising some of the same questions is Flora Lewis, "Peace before Power," *New York Times,* February 17, 1990, p. 27. A contemporary sample of a more "liberal," though far vaguer, approach to some of these questions can be found in Hunter, "The Transition to One Germany," p. 18.

3. Horst Teltschik, *329 Tage: Innenansichten der Einigung* (Berlin: Siedler, 1991), p. 122.

4. Teltschik was paraphrasing Kohl's remark to CDU and CSU parliamentarians on February 6, 1990. See Teltschik, *329 Tage,* pp. 125, 129; Bonn 5708, "East German Resettlers Force Up-Front FRG/GDR Economic and Monetary Union; Result Will Be De Facto Unification," 21 Feb 90; the 340,000 figure is from Kohl's February 15 statement to the Bundestag in *Materialen zu Deutschlandfragen* (Bonn: Kulturstiftung der deutschen Vertriebenen, 1989–1991), pp. 52–56.

5. Teltschik, *329 Tage,* pp. 130–133; see also Theo Waigel with Manfred Schell, *Tage, die Deutschland und die Welt veränderten: Vom Mauerfall zum Kaukaus, die deutschen Währungsunion* (Munich: Bruckman, 1994), pp. 17–20; Jürgen Gros, *Entscheidung ohne Alternativen?* (Mainz: Forschungsgruppe Deutschland, 1994); Bonn 4612, "Teltschik Flap Notwithstanding, Bonn Does Not See Imminent GDR Economic Collapse, but GDR Acceptance of Monetary Union Is Likely February 13," 12 Feb 90; Stuttgart 301, "Spaeth Asks GDR to Surrender Unconditionally," 13 Feb 90. Konrad Jarausch, *The Rush to German Unity* (New York: Oxford University Press, 1994), p. 109, shows Pöhl bowing to "political pressure" at the February 7 cabinet meeting and Kohl ignoring warnings about economic and social disruption, arguing against approaching the problem with a "mercenary mind." But the only primary source cited is Teltschik, who offers the detailed and entirely different portrait of the meeting summarized in the text. The quote about the "mercenary mind" used by Jarausch actually comes from Kohl's ruminations the next day, when he was expressing his great satisfaction with the way Pöhl had handled the monetary union question on television the night before. Teltschik, *329 Tage,* pp. 132–133.

6. See Hans Modrow, *Aufbruch und Ende* (Hamburg: Konkret Literatur, 1991), pp. 127–136; Kohl and Modrow press conferences reprinted in *Europa Archiv,* April 25, 1990, pp. 194–199; Teltschik, *329 Tage,* pp. 144–145; Jarausch, *The Rush to German Unity,* p. 110 (citing the transcript of the Kohl-Modrow talks as well as published sources); Bonn 4951, "GDR Prime Minister Modrow Accepts Chancellor Kohl's Offer of Economic/Monetary Union; Implementation ASAP after GDR Elections," 13 Feb 90; Bonn 5102, "Chancellery Debriefing of Modrow Visit," 14 Feb 90; EmbBerlin 1571, "Modrow Reports on Moscow Trip, Cites U.S. Senators on Polish Border," 9 Mar 90.

7. Kohl statement in *Materialen zu Deutschlandfragen,* pp. 52–56.

8. See Teltschik, *329 Tage,* pp. 147–148 (describing Genscher's February 14 presentation to the cabinet committee on German unity); Baker to President Bush (for his evening reading), 22 Feb 90 (describing Baker's February 21 meeting with FRG interior minister Wolfgang Schäuble).

9. An excellent summary of the arguments on article 23 versus article 146 can be found in "Grundgesetz oder 'neue Verfassung'?: Die Kontroverse über die Artikel 23 und

146 des Grundgesetzes," in *Die Wende in der DDR,* ed. Gerhart Maier (Bonn: Moeller-Druck, 1991), pp. 73–83. Article 146 of the Basic Law did not itself require the convocation of a national assembly. It said only: "This Basic Law loses its validity on the day on which a constitution enters into force which has been adopted by the German people in a free decision." The name Basic Law itself originally had an interim quality, the implication being that the Basic Law would eventually be superseded by a constitution. Since the West German government had maintained since 1950 that such a constitution would be prepared by an all-German, freely elected national assembly, Article 146 was interpreted as referring to this sequence of events. See also Bonn 6138, "Constitutional Aspects of German Unification," 23 Feb 90. On the working group's early attraction to article 23, see Teltschik, *329 Tage,* pp. 128, 152–153.

10. See Bonn 5102, "Chancellery Debriefing of Modrow Visit," 14 Feb 90; Bonn 6138, "Constitutional Aspects of German Unification," 23 Feb 90; Bonn 8004, "German Unification: The Politics of Article 23 v. Article 146," 9 Mar 90.

11. See CIA, "The Germanys: Increasing Party Ties and the March GDR Elections," EUR M 90–20043, 15 Feb 90; Bonn 5143, "Visit of PDAS Dobbins to Bonn," 15 Feb 90 (especially comments of CDU Secretary General Volker Rühe); Dobbins to Seitz, "Current German Attitudes on Reunification," 15 Feb 90 (reporting on his just concluded visit to Munich, Bonn, and Berlin); FBIS, "East, West SPD Joint Statement on Security," East Berlin ADN International Service in German, 12 Feb 90; and the joint "Erklärung zum Weg zur deutschen Einheit" issued by both SPD parties February 19, 1990, in *Materialen zu Deutschlandfragen,* pp. 192–193. The SPD joint statement also called for much earlier external intervention by the Four Powers in the unification process, envisioning a conference in the second half of April which would also include all of Germany's neighbors, whose views would "be dealt with as a matter of the highest priority."

12. The following account is based on Zelikow interview with Klaus Naumann, Bonn, December 1994; Jörg Schönbohm, *Zwei Armeen und ein Vaterland* (Berlin: Siedler, 1992), pp. 22–23. See Genscher-Stoltenberg statement in *Bulletin: Presse- und informationsamt der Bundesregierung,* no. 28 (1990): 218; Richard Kiessler and Frank Elbe, *Ein runder Tisch mit scharfen Ecken: Der diplomatische Weg zur deutschen Einheit* (Baden-Baden: Nomos, 1993), pp. 81–85; Teltschik, *329 Tage,* pp. 147–152; Zelikow and Rice interview with Teltschik, Gütersloh, June 1992; Bonn 5672, "Genscher Calls for Demilitarized GDR; Stoltenberg Forced to Accede," 20 Feb 90.

In his memoir Elbe argues defensively that Genscher never wanted to keep German armed forces out of the former GDR, creating a permanently disarmed eastern zone in a united Germany. Instead, he seems to argue both that Genscher was obliged to adopt a position excluding the Bundeswehr as an expedient to manage the Soviet danger and that Genscher's position actually kept all options open. The latter argument becomes even more strained as Elbe asserts that the American "special military status" formulation equally kept all options open. Kiessler and Elbe, *Ein runder Tisch mit scharfen Ecken,* pp. 81–82. The American position specified explicitly that all German territory, including the former GDR, would be part of NATO. By promising only a "special military status," the United States kept open the option of deploying NATO-assigned troops, including the Bundeswehr, in the GDR—an option Genscher had expressly ruled out. Genscher (and Elbe) understood the distinction quite well, especially since, as we shall see, Baker called the matter to Genscher's attention in a pointed message sent after Kohl and Bush agreed to the American formulation at their Camp David meeting later in February. Having firmly stated that Genscher never wanted to keep the Bundeswehr out of the GDR, Elbe must wrestle with the categorical exclusion of German armed forces used at Genscher's insistence in the February 19 joint statement. The best he can do is to say that this position meant "nothing" since the matter would later be clarified in the Two Plus Four negotiations. Elbe is on firmer ground in noting that Kohl himself was trying to dodge the issue in, for example, his February 15 Bundestag speech, holding obliquely that no "units and institutions" ("Einheiten und Einrichtungen") of NATO would move eastward into the former GDR.

13. Moscow 5553, "As Germany Goes . . . So Go the Soviet Germanists?," 15 Feb 90; CIA, "Gorbachev's Germanists," SOV M 90–20026X, 26 Feb 90. The Soviet Foreign Ministry's German working group was headed by first deputy foreign minister Anatoly Kovalyov and included deputy foreign minister Anatoly Adamishin, Alexander Bondarenko, Sergei Tarasenko, and deputy foreign minister for arms control Viktor Karpov. See also Moscow 7200, "Soviet-FRG Bilaterals on German Question," 1 Mar 90; USBerlin 553, "Soviet Minister's View of Situation in Berlin and the GDR and Concerns about German Reunification," 17 Feb 90.

14. Moscow Domestic Service, "Gorbachev Discusses German Reunification," February 21, 1990, in *FBIS-SOV* 90–035, February 21, 1990, pp. 50–53.

15. For American and West German reactions to Gorbachev's remarks, see Baker to President Bush (for his evening reading), 21 Feb 90; Teltschik, *329 Tage*, p. 155; Bonn 5836, "Genscher Comments on Gorbachev's *Pravda* Interview," 21 Feb 90 (Genscher highlighting need for both alliances to be redefined in the context of a new overarching European security structure). For the collegium statement, see TASS International Service (Moscow), "Foreign Ministry Collegium Statement on Germany," February 24, 1990, in *FBIS-SOV* 90–038, February 26, 1990, p. 1. Tarasenko confirms that the collegium statement was intended as a "slap at Kohl." Zelikow interview, Providence, June 1993. For the Shevardnadze statement in Ottawa, see *Pravda*, February 16, 1990, p. 5. See also Moscow 5968, "Gorbachev on German Unification," 21 Feb 90; Moscow 6456, "Collegium Statement on Politico-Military Status of United Germany," 25 Feb 90; CIA, "Moscow's Game Plan for Six-Power Meetings on German Unification," SOV M 90–20025, 20 Feb 90; Moscow 6450, "Shevardnadze on 'The German Question and Soviet-Polish Relations,'" 24 Feb 90. See generally Mulholland to Kimmitt and Zoellick, "Soviet Attitudes on German Reunification," 27 Feb 90.

16. Mitterrand made his public comments in an interview released on February 14. "German Reunification: Interview with President Mitterrand," February 14, 1990; English translation provided to U.S. government by the French embassy. Interestingly, the embassy chose to delete some of the more disturbing parts of the interview in the translation they gave to the Americans. The complete text of the press interview was reported and commented on in Paris 5018, "President Mitterrand on Architecture: Is the French President Afraid of History After All?," 14 Feb 90. The next day Mitterrand met with Kohl and told him that a unifying Germany seemed to be a historic reality whether one liked it or not—though Mitterrand assured his guest that he was one of the ones who liked it. Both men agreed that the West should keep some fixed number of troops in Germany even if the Soviets left. Teltschik thought that the meeting had gone wonderfully well; but one French participant told American diplomats that their side had been disappointed. Teltschik recalls Kohl applauding the principle of faster movement toward European union. The French noted that he rejected the specific proposal for moving up the intergovernmental conference to negotiate economic and monetary union. Teltschik recalls that Kohl offered private assurances that he would respect the Oder-Neisse border; the French found Kohl cagy on the border issue. Teltschik remembers Mitterrand strongly opposing a

German peace conference; the French reported that they grudgingly were going along with a settlement based only on the Two Plus Four. Compare Teltschik, *329 Tage*, pp. 150–151, with Paris 5447, "Elysée Readout on Kohl/Mitterrand Dinner: You Don't Bring Me Flowers Anymore," 17 Feb 90. For more background on French policy toward Germany at this time, see Karl Kaiser, *Deutschlands Vereinigung: Die Internationalen Aspekte* (Bergisch Gladbach: Bastei Lübbe, 1991), pp. 64–68; and the negative commentary on Germany among the French political class described in Ingo Kolboom, *Vom geteilten zum vereinten Deutschland: Deutschland-Bilder in Frankreich* (Bonn: Europa Union Verlag, 1991), pp. 47–48.

17. Message sent through special channels from the U.S. embassy in Budapest, "What Happened to the Spirit of Kennebunkport?," 20 Feb 90, written by NSC staffer Adrian Basora and distributed only at the White House. The reference is to the harmonious meeting between Bush and Mitterrand at Kennebunkport in May 1989.

18. See Paris 4475, "French Views on the New European Architecture: Following History," 9 Feb 90; Paris 6853, "French Views on the Soviet Union and Germany: Seitz-Blot Consultations, Paris, February 27," 2 Mar 90.

19. On the press interview, see "Thatcher Sees East European Progress as More Urgent than Germans," *Wall Street Journal*, January 26, 1990, p. A12; and the German reaction in Teltschik, *329 Tage*, pp. 115–116. The account of the Chequers meeting is based on Zelikow interview with Charles Powell, London, June 1993; and Alan Clark, *Diaries* (London: Weidenfeld and Nicolson, 1993), p. 276. The meeting should not be confused with another Chequers discussion on Germany, this time with academic experts, in March.

Thatcher's worries about the Germans were also reinforced by the equally worried Italian prime minister, Giulio Andreotti, when the two leaders met in London on February 23. Genscher traveled to Italy on February 21 to assuage concerns and patch over the anger caused by his harsh words in Ottawa. The Italians found him "Janus-like," combining conciliation and arrogance. Baker tried to ease European worries by at least promising all the NATO ministers, in writing, that he would consult with them at every stage of the Two Plus Four process. On Italian attitudes, see Rome 3881, "Genscher, Italy, and Europe," 24 Feb 90; Rome 4306, "MFA Weighs in on Two Plus Four; Andreotti and CSCE," 1 Mar 90; Rome 4447, "Readout on 2/23 Andreotti/Thatcher Meeting: German Unification and NATO," 2 Mar 90. For other European and Canadian concerns, see, e.g., The Hague 1639, "Further GON Reactions to 2 Plus 4 Approach to German Reunification," 26 Feb 90; Brussels 3021, "FM Eyskens Rejects SNF Modernization, Complains about German Unification Procedure," 26 Feb 90; Ottawa 1661, "Canadian Concerns about 'Two Plus Four' and NATO's Future," 28 Feb 90. On Baker's assurances and assurances from Bush conveyed by Wörner, see State 54339, "Letter from Secretary to NATO Foreign Ministers," 19 Feb 90; Dobbins (Acting) through Kimmitt to Baker, "Proposed Message from the Secretary to NATO Foreign Ministers," 17 Feb 90; USNATO 877, "Wörner Briefing of Permreps on Discussions at Camp David and Ottawa," 13 Feb 90; Brussels 2951, "Letter from the Secretary to NATO Foreign Ministers," 23 Feb 90.

20. The account that follows is based on Margaret Thatcher, *The Downing Street Years* (New York: HarperCollins, 1993), pp. 798–799; Memcon for telephone conversation with Prime Minister Thatcher, 22 Feb 90 (Zelikow was note taker). Thatcher says she learned afterward that Bush objected to her argument that Soviet military power could help preserve the balance of power in Europe, thinking that she was proposing an alternative alliance to NATO. So, she concludes, "it was the last time that I relied on a telephone conversation to explain such matters." There is, however, no reason to believe that Bush misunderstood what Thatcher was proposing. Her suggestion was clear enough, and

Bush's views on keeping Soviet troops in Germany were, as we shall see, consistent and unshakable. It is possible that someone was too polite in later explaining to Thatcher's staff why Bush found her argument objectionable. Bush's closing suggestion of U.S.-British-French consultations, the "triumvirate," eventually emerged in the form of separate bilateral talks in April with both Thatcher and Mitterrand, not a threesome, which would have aroused German fears and suspicion.

21. The views of the new democratic Czech government, headed by President Vaclav Havel and Foreign Minister Jiri Dienstbier, were pro-Western and lined up with centrist West German opinion, exemplified by Genscher. They supported German membership in NATO, but hoped that both military alliances would soon be transformed into something new. Bush welcomed Havel to Washington for a state visit in February 1990, and the two men found a common stance on Germany. See Memcon for meeting with President Havel, Cabinet Room, 20 Feb 90; Kimmitt (Acting) to President Bush (for his evening reading), 20 Feb 90.

22. Letter to President Bush from Prime Minister Tadeusz Mazowiecki, 21 Feb 90; and the comments in Warsaw 2677, "Prime Minister's Letter to President," 21 Feb 90. See also Krzysztof Skubiszewski, "Die völkerrechtliche und staatliche Einheit des deutschen Volkes und die Entwicklung in Europa," *Europa Archiv*, March 23, 1990; Hans-Adolf Jacobsen and Mieczyslaw Tomala, eds., *Bonn-Warschau 1945–1991: Die deutsch-polnische Beziehungen: Analysen und Dokumentation* (Cologne: Verlag Wissenschaft und Politik, 1992).

23. For the public U.S. position on the border issue, see statement by deputy press spokesman Richard Boucher, Department of State daily press briefing, 15 Feb 90. Baker met with FRG interior minister Wolfgang Schäuble on February 20 and immediately said that he could not understand why the Germans would not offer the Poles a binding legal declaration to put aside the border dispute. Schäuble then explained the international legal obstacle keeping the FRG from making a statement binding upon a subsequent united German state. Wolfgang Schäuble, *Der Vertrag: Wie ich über die deutsche Einheit Verhandelte,* ed. Dirk Koch and Klaus Wirtgen (Stuttgart: Deutsche Verlags-Anstalt, 1991), pp. 59–60. For initial U.S.-FRG consultations on assurances that could be offered to the Poles, see State 54183; Bonn 5459, "Polish Concerns on German-Polish Border," 17 Feb 90. These assurances were presented as proposals from Seitz to Kastrup. On Eagleburger's talks, see Warsaw 2785, "The Deputy Secretary's Meeting with Prime Minister Mazowiecki," 23 Feb 90.

24. For the following account, see Scowcroft to President Bush, "Preparing for the Six Power German Peace Conference," 15 Feb 90, and Robert D. Blackwill, "German Unification and American Diplomacy," *Aussenpolitik*, III/1994 211, 214–215.

25. Seitz chaired the first meeting of a newly formed Germany Task Force on February 15. He and Dobbins, aided by deputy legal adviser Michael Young, rebuffed the suggestion from another of the State Department's German experts, Nelson Ledsky, that a peace treaty was needed to settle Germany's fate and future borders. Dobbins and Rice both argued against letting the Two Plus Four consider the status of Western forces based in the FRG, although the head of the department's Soviet desk believed that the Soviets would insist on it. After the meeting Seitz and Dobbins met privately with Rice and Zelikow and confirmed their agreement on what they thought was the proper approach. Authors' recollection; Zelikow to Scowcroft and Gates, "Initial Interagency Discussion of a Six Power Conference on Germany," 15 Feb 90. The "Bonn Group" of diplomats who regularly considered Four Power (Quadripartite) issues tried to take on the job of designing the Two Plus Four forum, with the American representative proposing the idea on a personal basis to his British, French, and West German colleagues. The Bonn embassy was promptly told (informally) that the matter would be handled at the political level and

decided in Washington. All American embassies were then cautioned to "avoid specula-tion" about what the Two Plus Four would do. See Bonn 5284, "Bonn Group Discussion on a Two-Plus-Four Conference on German Unity: Berlin and Germany-as-a-Whole Issues," 15 Feb 90; State 64344, "German Unification, Two Plus Four, and NATO," 28 Feb 90.

For the policy planning staff views given to Zoellick, see Holmes and George to Ross and Zoellick, "Next Steps on Two Plus Four," 15 Feb 90. Their plan would assign to the Two Plus Four consideration of the "long-term status of German and foreign forces" as well as a future Germany's treaty commitments to NATO and the European Community

26. Seitz to Zoellick, "Agenda and Strategy for the Two-Plus-Four Conference," 16 Feb 90.

27. Account based on Zelikow interviews with Baker, Houston, January 1995, and Zoellick, Washington, D.C., January 1995; annotated copy of Zoellick to Baker, "Proposed Agenda for Meeting with the President," 16 Feb 90, 1:30 P.M. Annotations on the document are in Baker's handwriting, and Baker's characteristic checkmarks beside points may indicate which ones he covered with Bush. The "incremental consultations" quote is from Zoellick to Baker, "Two Plus Four: Advantages, Possible Concerns, and Rebuttal Points," 21 Feb 90.

28. See Zoellick to Baker, "Two Plus Four: Advantages, Possible Concerns, and Rebut-tal Points," 21 Feb 90; Zoellick's handwritten notes, "2 + 4 Timing," from his office files; informal EUR paper, "Managing 'Two-Plus-Four' Consultations on German Unification," n.d. (20–21 Feb 90); and Zoellick's marked-up copy of this paper in his office files.

29. See Bonn 5833, "Teltschik's Preview of Camp David," 21 Feb 90.

30. The discussion that follows is based on Scowcroft to President Bush, "Meeting with German Chancellor Helmut Kohl," February 22, 1990 (drafted by Zelikow with Blackwill and forwarded by Blackwill to Scowcroft). Zoellick had passed his suggestions for the briefing paper to Blackwill, outlining the Two Plus Four approach he had worked out, blending in Seitz and Dobbins's "discuss/decide" analysis of the narrow mandate: "In general, Two-Plus-Four can exchange views on many topics, but it can decide very few." Blackwill could find little to criticize in Zoellick's papers, but he was still worried that the State Department would not stick to the narrow mandate; he feared that Baker would "find the prospect of negotiating the future security structure of Europe in the Two Plus Four ministerial context irresistible." See Zoellick papers (passed to NSC staff on 22 Feb 90) "Our Objectives for Chancellor Kohl's Visit" and "Key Themes for Camp David." For the Blackwill comments forwarding these papers to Scowcroft, see Blackwill to Scowcroft, "State Department Papers on Two Plus Four Talks," 23 Feb 90 (which also forwarded the even more cautious EUR paper, "Managing 'Two Plus Four' Consultations," which Zoellick had subsumed into his own work, but which EUR had passed separately to the NSC).

31. Memcon of telephone conversation with Prime Minister Mulroney, 24 Feb 90 (Zelikow was note taker). Canadian diplomats were worried that Germany might opt for neutrality and thought that strong U.S. leadership was needed to help keep Germany in the alliance. See Eagleburger (Acting) to the President (for his evening reading), 2 Mar 90 (on Marchand meeting with Kimmitt). In addition to calling Thatcher and Mulroney, Bush also tried to speak with Mitterrand before Kohl arrived, but the White House was unable to agree with the Elysée Palace on a mutually convenient time for the call. A convenient time to talk was finally found on February 26.

32. The account of these talks is drawn from Teltschik, *329 Tage*, pp. 158–162; memo-randum of conversations with Chancellor Kohl, February 24–25, 1990 (Blackwill was note taker for the meetings).

33. Immediately upon Kohl's return to Bonn, his staff received a note from the East

German Foreign Ministry on how to "embed unification in the all-European process." The East Germans wanted to be sure unification was not complete until the CSCE summit could consider the external issues. The Americans and the West Germans had already ruled out this approach at Camp David. Anyway, Teltschik noted in his diary, "this GDR-government will only be in office a few more days." Teltschik, *329 Tage*, p. 163.

34. "Joint News Conference Following Discussions with Chancellor Helmut Kohl of the Federal Republic of Germany," *Public Papers* (1990), pp. 305–313.

35. Teltschik, *329 Tage*, pp. 170–171; USNATO 1496, "March 8 NAC on German Unification: Kohl Seeks to Reassure the NATO Permreps; Allies Stress the Need for Extensive NATO Consultations 'Synchronous' with Two Plus Four," 9 Mar 90. British foreign secretary Hurd also made progress in talking through the specific NATO issues in his March 12 visit to Bonn. See, e.g., London 5013, "March 12 Hurd Meeting with Kohl and Genscher," 13 Mar 90.

36. See note from Kimmitt to Baker, "German Unification," 23 Feb 90, and Baker's handwritten reply, dated February 25.

37. State 63344, "Message to Genscher," 28 Feb 90; see also Dobbins through Kimmitt and Bartholomew to Baker, "NATO and German Unification: Message to Genscher," 27 Feb 90.

38. Memcon of telephone conversation with President Mitterrand, 26 Feb 90 (note taker was the director of the White House Situation Room, Cornelius O'Leary); Zelikow notes from Bush telephone conversation with Prime Minister Thatcher, 26 Feb 90. The French anger about Kohl's handling of the Polish border question spilled over into Dumas's public remarks during a March 1 speech in Berlin. Dumas also wanted the Two Plus Four to start work immediately, the proposal he had made to Baker a week earlier, which Baker had turned down. On this episode and Kohl's March 5 call to Mitterrand, see Teltschik, *329 Tage*, pp. 164–165, 167; USBerlin 717, "French FM Visits Berlin," 2 Mar 90; USBerlin 838, "Addendum on French FM Visit to Berlin," 13 Mar 90. For more on Bush's views of Germany after his meeting with Kohl, see Memcon of Bush's meeting with Berlin's governing mayor Walter Momper, 27 Feb 90. Momper wanted American troops to stay in Berlin as long as Soviet soldiers were there, and unlike some of his SPD colleagues, he was against the withdrawal of all Western forces from a united Germany. Momper's administration in West Berlin was already planning the future of the entire city. See USBerlin 471, "Quick Unity of East and West Berlin?," 9 Feb 90.

39. For a sampling of public commentary, see TASS, "TASS notes Kohl-Bush News Conference," February 25, 1990, and TASS, "Kornilov Comments," February 26, 1990, in *FBIS-SOV* 90–038, February 26, 1990, pp. 1–2; Moscow Domestic Service, "Bush-Kohl Talks Create 'Fresh Misgivings,'" February 26, 1990, in *FBIS-SOV* 90–039, February 27, 1990, p. 9; A. Blinov, *Izvestiya*, February 27, 1990, p. 4.

40. For the discussion that follows, see Memcon for telephone conversation with Gorbachev, 28 Feb 90 (Rice was note taker); Igor Maximychev, *Krusheniye: Rekviyem po GDR* (Moscow: Mezhdunarodniye otnosheniya, 1993), pp. 132–133, and, for Maximychev's similar views at the time, EmbBerlin 1323, "Soviet Ambassador Worries about Rapid German Reunification," 28 Feb 90. Zelikow passed this cable on to Scowcroft on March 1, noting that Maximychev's distress about Soviet inertia and his hopes that early Two Plus Four action would get Moscow's attention were both good reasons to oppose early activation of the Two Plus Four process. Having seen this cable and another paper making the same point, Scowcroft asked, "Can't we get this notion to Baker, or at least Zoellick?" Notation on Blackwill to Scowcroft, "The Impact of the Two Plus Four Talks on Soviet Policy toward Germany," 27 Feb 90. Soviet inaction is blamed for the Bush-Kohl an-

nouncement in Sergei Akhromeyev and Georgi Kornienko, *Glazami marshala i diplomata* (Moscow: Mezhdunarodniye otnosheniya, 1992), pp. 259–260.

41. Teltschik, *329 Tage*, p. 164. On the evening of March 5 Kohl again discussed the issue of article 23 versus article 146 with Seiters, Schäuble, Teltschik, and other advisers. They were all united in support of using article 23. Ibid., p. 167.

42. On the internal debate and the March 6 coalition decisions, see Teltschik, *329 Tage*, pp. 165–168; Kiessler and Elbe, *Ein runder Tisch mit scharfen Ecken*, pp. 116–117; Schäuble, *Der Vertrag*, pp. 60–65; Baker to President Bush (for his evening reading), 5 Mar 90; Baker to President Bush (for his evening reading), 6 Mar 90; Bonn 7347, "Coalition Agrees on Joint Statement on Polish Border," 6 Mar 90. There are indications that Genscher was concerned about international reaction to the "takeover" inherent in article 23, but there is no evidence that Genscher actually opposed this crucial choice.

Kohl promptly informed Bush about the coalition decision, and Bush cabled back his assurance of support. Message from Chancellor Kohl to President Bush (sent via special channels), 6 Mar 90; message from President Bush (sent via special channels), 8 Mar 90 (actually sent March 7, Washington time). The messages are discussed in Teltschik, *329 Tage*, p. 170. Genscher also passed word of the coalition agreement to Baker, through a call from Elbe to Zoellick on March 6. See Zoellick to Baker, "German Coalition Agreement on a Polish Border Treaty," 6 Mar 90. Elbe told Zoellick that Genscher had no particular dispute with Kohl over choosing the article 23 path to unification but that Genscher, worried about the foreign reaction, preferred not to publicize the choice.

43. See *Bulletin*, no. 34 (1990): pp. 265–268; Jacobsen and Tomala, *Bonn-Warschau*, pp. 523–524; Teltschik, *329 Tage*, p. 169. Kohl's fears about Polish reparation demands and other desiderata were not entirely baseless. Eighty-three percent of Poles surveyed in the spring of 1990 thought that German unification presented a threat to Poland. The same percentage supported German reparation payments for Polish slave labor in World War II. Fifty percent wanted further limits on the civil rights of ethnic Germans still living in Poland. See Friedrich Ebert Stiftung, "Der deutsche Einigungsprozess aus polnischer Sicht," *Forum Deutsche Einheit: Aktuelle Kurzinformationen*, no. 5/90 (Hof: Mintzel-Druck, 1990).

44. Teltschik, *329 Tage*, p. 171. Hurd conveyed the British approval to Genscher when they met in Bonn on March 12.

45. See Teltschik, *329 Tage*, pp. 171–172; Paris 7991, "MFA Readout on Jaruzelski/Mazowiecki Visit," 12 Mar 90.

46. See State 79390, "Dumas Letter on Two Plus Four and the Polish-German Border," 13 Mar 90; Warsaw 3768, "Polish Foreign Minister Suggests 2 Plus 4 Meeting in Warsaw," 12 Mar 90; Paris 8101, "Dumas Letter on 'Two-Plus-Four' and the Polish/German Border," 13 Mar 90; Dobbins (Acting) through Eagleburger to Baker, "Expected Call from French Foreign Minister re Poland and Two plus Four," 12 Mar 90, and cover note attached to this memo from Eagleburger, dated March 13. On the Genscher-Dumas statement, see Bonn 8488, "FRG-French Declaration on Polish Participation in Two-Plus-Four Talks," 14 Mar 90. Baker took the unusual step of calling Teltschik on March 13, just before his subordinates began the first Two Plus Four meeting, to find out if Kohl had any opinion about the idea of holding a Two Plus Four meeting in Warsaw. Teltschik called Baker on March 14 to inform him that both Kohl and Genscher were opposed to such a meeting. He conveyed the same view to Blackwill at the White House. Teltschik, *329 Tage*, p. 175. For Bush's letter to Mazowiecki, see State 81152, "Presidential Letter to Prime Minister Mazowiecki on Polish Borders and Two Plus Four Talks," 14 Mar 90 (drafted by NSC staff); see also Gates to President Bush, "Your Meeting Today with Leaders of the Polish

American Congress at 2:00 P.M.: New Developments on the Issue of Polish Participation in the Two Plus Four Process," 14 Mar 90.

47. In early March members of the State Department's policy planning staff proposed a U.S. move toward Poland, writing to Ross and Zoellick. The staff knew that State's European bureau would have a "strongly negative reaction" to their idea. They were right, and there would have been equally adamant opposition from the White House, but the proposal was not seriously considered either by Ross or by Zoellick. See Fox and George to Ross and Zoellick, "Polish-German Border Resolution," 9 Mar 90, and attached cable to be sent from Zoellick to Dieter Kastrup (drafted by George). The "strongly negative reaction" quote is from the March 9 cover note endorsing the proposal from the policy planning staff's deputy director James Holmes, passing the paper to Zoellick's special assistant, Nick Burns.

48. See Teltschik, *329 Tage*, p. 176; Memcon of telephone conversation with Chancellor Kohl, 15 Mar 90 (Hutchings was note taker); Scowcroft to President Bush, "Your Telephone Conversation with Chancellor Kohl, March 15, 1990," 16 Mar 90. Representatives of the Polish-American Congress had met with the president on March 14 and had urged him to join Mazowiecki in issuing just the kind of joint statement Kohl feared. The White House view of the border issue is summarized in Blackwill, "German Unification and American Diplomacy," pp. 216–217.

49. The account that follows is based on Teltschik, *329 Tage*, p. 179; Memcon of telephone conversation with Chancellor Kohl, 20 Mar 90 (note taker was Hutchings).

50. Memcon for meeting with Prime Minister Mazowiecki, 21 Mar 90 (Scowcroft was note taker). Bush was joined only by Scowcroft and an interpreter. Mazowiecki was accompanied by Ryszard Wojtkowski, director of his private office, and an interpreter.

51. While rejecting the neutrality solution, Polish officials were still avoiding open endorsement of the NATO alternative. Mazowiecki's plea for the United States to find some other way of addressing Soviet concerns was entirely consistent with Foreign Minister Skubiszewski's longer explanation of Poland's position more than a week earlier. See Warsaw 3768, "Polish Foreign Minister Suggests 2 Plus 4 Meeting in Warsaw," 12 Mar 90.

52. See Teltschik, *329 Tage*, p. 181; Hutchings through Blackwill to Scowcroft, "Telephone Call to Chancellor Helmut Kohl of the Federal Republic of Germany, March 23, 1990," 22 Mar 90.

53. Memcon for follow-up meeting with Prime Minister Mazowiecki, 22 Mar 90. The participants were the same as in the small meeting the previous day (see note 50). See also "The President's News Conference," 22 Mar 90, in *Public Papers* (1990), pp. 460–463. Mitterrand's support for Mazowiecki in their Paris talks has already been mentioned. Thatcher, though her government had approved of the March 6–8 coalition decisions, blasted Kohl's stance on the border issue in an interview published in *Der Spiegel*, March 26, 1990, pp. 182–187.

54. The following account is drawn from Memcon of telephone conversation with Chancellor Kohl, 23 Mar 90 (Hutchings was note taker). Zoellick urged Secretary Baker to be sure to read this Memcon, and Baker later noted that he did (on or about March 31; see his notations).

55. Warsaw kept pressing for advance negotiation of a German-Polish treaty, though tensions had eased. Genscher was prepared to meet these demands and negotiate a treaty that would be initialed before unification. Kohl overruled Genscher, knowing that Bush would back him up. The FRG continued to refuse a formal prenegotiation of a treaty between Poland and a united Germany. But Kohl, as promised, used the Polish–West German dialogue as a way to negotiate the crucial border-related sentences of such a

treaty, which were then embedded in the parliamentary resolutions passed, as he had pledged, in the early summer of 1990. On Genscher's March plans, see Teltschik, *329 Tage*, p. 179 (on March 19 meeting between Kohl, Genscher, and Stoltenberg); Secto 2045, "Secretary's Meeting with FRG Foreign Minister Genscher, March 21, 1990," 24 Mar 90 (on meeting in Windhoek, Namibia). See also Michael Ludwig, *Polen und die Deutsche Frage* (Bonn: Europa Union, 1990), pp. 73–74; Warsaw 6452, "Polish/FRG/GDR Draft Treaty on Border Issue," 30 Apr 90; Warsaw 9216, "Polish Approach to Two-Plus-Four Talks," 13 Jun 90. For the parliamentary resolutions, see *Materialen zu Deutschlandfragen*, pp. 75–76, 80–83.

The State Department's lawyers did not grasp the significance of article 23 and the FRG's signing of past treaties and a current Two Plus Four settlement document. In late April they still anticipated a "catch-22" in that the FRG and GDR "cannot fix (or make treaty commitments regarding) a united Germany's borders until they are united and, as a political matter, the Four Powers probably cannot bless German unification until the border question is addressed." Young (deputy legal adviser) to Zoellick and Seitz, "Legal Constraints on Timing of Settlement," 27 Apr 90.

56. Zoellick had to leave early, before the conclusion of the London meeting, so Seitz represented the United States in discussions of some topics. The U.S. foreign policy structure does not have a political director, in the same sense as in other European capitals, so Washington designates different officials to play this role, depending on the negotiation. On European issues, however, the assistant secretary of state for European and Soviet affairs was usually considered the political director.

57. For an account of the London meeting, see Zoellick to Baker, "Quad Meeting Discussion of German Unification and Two-plus-Four," 1 Mar 90. The following detailed account of the meeting is drawn from final draft of State Department reporting cable, "German Unification: Initial Three-Plus-One Allied Consultations (Part One of Two) and (Part Two of Two)," 4 Mar 90. On the Germans' initial concerns about their status in the talks and the pronounced opposition to a peace treaty, see Kiessler and Elbe, *Ein runder Tisch mit scharfen Ecken*, pp. 106–113; Teltschik, *329 Tage*, pp. 172–173.

58. See Teltschik, *329 Tage*, p. 167; Dobbins (Acting) through Kimmitt to Baker, "Letter from Shevardnadze Proposing Two-plus-Four Contingency Consultations Mechanism," 2 Mar 90; State 68751, "Shevardnadze Letter to Secretary on 'Two-Plus-Four' Mechanism," 3 Mar 90; Moscow 7472, "Shevardnadze Letter to Secretary on 'Two Plus Four' Mechanism," 3 Mar 90; Moscow 7532, "Shevardnadze Letter to Secretary on 'Two Plus Four' Mechanism,'" 5 Mar 90; EmbBerlin 1407, "Shevardnadze Letter to Secretary on 'Two-Plus-Four' Mechanism," 5 Mar 90; Bonn 7216, "Kastrup on Two Plus Four Mechanism," 5 Mar 90; Paris 7024, "Shevardnadze Letter to Secretary on 'Two-Plus-Four' Mechanism: French Thoughts," 5 Mar 90.

59. Untitled and unsigned text of note, 5 Mar 90 (S/S Log #9005019).

60. In the discussion that follows, for the Gorbachev interview, see *Pravda*, March 5, 1990; for the Shevardnadze interview (published in an East German magazine and thus clearly aimed at the East German audience), see TASS, "Shevardnadze Discusses German Unity in Interview," March 7, 1990, in *FBIS-SOV* 90–046, March 8, 1990, pp. 37–40. For the Foreign Ministry statement, see TASS, "Foreign Ministry Make Official Statement," March 13, 1990, in *FBIS-SOV* 90–050, March 14, 1990, pp. 2–3. For the quote from Akhromeyev and Kornienko (Kornienko had been the top deputy to Shevardnadze's long-serving predecessor, Andrei Gromyko), see S. F. Akhromeyev and G. M. Kornienko, *Glazami Marshala i Diplomata* (Moscow: Mezdonarodniye Otnosheniya, 1992), p. 26. On Gorbachev's meeting with Modrow, see Hans Modrow, *Aufbruch und Ende* (Hamburg:

Konkret Literatur, 1991), pp. 137–141; Moscow Television Service, "Gorbachev Comments before Meeting," March 6, 1990, and TASS, "Gorbachev-Modrow Meeting Detailed," March 6, 1990, both in *FBIS-SOV* 90–045, March 7, 1990, pp. 24, 26–27; Moscow 7912, "GDR Premier Modrow's Visit: German Unity, NATO Membership, Two Plus Four," 7 Mar 90; EmbBerlin 1571, "Modrow Reports on Moscow Trip, Cites U.S. Senators on Polish Border," 9 Mar 90. On Dubinin and Zoellick, see Baker to President Bush (for his evening reading), 8 Mar 90; State 87582, "Zoellick-Dubinin March 7 Discussion of Germany," 19 Mar 90. For additional background, see S/P—Hauslohner to Zoellick, "Recent Soviet Statements on Germany," 8 Mar 90. For acknowledgment of the Soviet pronouncments in Bonn, see Teltschik, *329 Tage,* pp. 168–169, 170. For analysis of the Soviet stance by the American embassy, see Moscow 8211, "Soviet Views on the Future Status of Germany: NATO, Neutral or Neither?," 10 Mar 90; Moscow 8648, "Soviets Move Publicly to 'Put the Brakes' on German Rush for Unification," 14 Mar 90: "To Moscow, the rush toward German unification is not unlike a large Mercedes barreling down the autobahn showing little regard for public safety . . . Moscow is sending the message that unless Kohl (and others) are prepared to meet the Soviets part-way, Germany's journey to reunification could be far lengthier and slower than expected."

61. See Hans-Dietrich Genscher, "German Unity as a Contribution to European Stability," *Nordsee-Zeitung,* March 3, 1990 (translation provided by FRG government); and the anodyne reference in Kiessler and Elbe, *Ein runder Tisch mit scharfen Ecken,* p. 107. The pro-NATO SPD opinion mentioned refers to the views conveyed by Horst Ehmke and Dietrich Stobbe to Eagleburger in a Washington meeting on March 7. Willy Brandt was also part of this relatively pro-NATO faction of the SPD. Opposed to NATO membership were the party's chancellor candidate Oskar Lafontaine and Egon Bahr, and the SPD had prepared a party platform calling for the dissolution of both alliances. See Scowcroft to President Bush, "SPD Thinking on a United Germany" (date unknown but probably the last week of March); Baker to President Bush (for his evening reading), 7 Mar 90 (on Eagleburger meeting). Ehmke also thought that unification was proceeding too quickly, but he got no support from Eagleburger. On the interplay between outside attitudes and domestic politics in shaping West German positions on security, see the useful analysis in CIA, "Initial Security Options for a United Germany," EUR 90–10005, Mar 90. On the uncertainties in German opinion on NATO, see Seitz to Baker, "West German Public Opinion Fluid on NATO, U.S. Forces, and the Eastern Threat," 19 Mar 90; Bonn 6979, "FRG Public Opinion on the Threat from the East, the Image of NATO, and the Presence of U.S. Forces," 2 Mar 90; Bonn 7256, "The German Question and Alliance Security," 6 Mar 90. For the pro-NATO views of West German defense officials, see, e.g., Bonn 7009, "General Naumann on Security Policy Issues," 2 Mar 90.

62. State 76007, "German Unification, Two-Plus-Four, and Germany in NATO," 9 Mar 90 (drafted by Brunson McKinley in EUR and Zelikow). See Bonn 7849, "German Unification," 9 Mar 90, for the FRG reaction.

63. State 74775, "'Two-Plus-Four' Consultations," 8 Mar 90; State 78499, "Explaining March 14 Two Plus Four Meeting," 10 Mar 90.

64. Rice through Blackwill to Scowcroft, "Mounting Problems with 2 + 4," 28 Feb 90.

65. For more detail on the conclusions, see Zelikow through Blackwill to Scowcroft, "Discussions with State on Plans for Two Plus Four Meeting on March 14," 9 Mar 90. These internal understandings are also reflected in EUR/RPM (Caldwell) and EUR/CE (Shostal) to Zoellick and Seitz, "Preparing for Your Paris One-Plus-Three, March 13, 1990," n.d.

66. Zelikow through Blackwill to Scowcroft and Gates, "The Two Plus Four Agenda,"

12 Mar 90. See also the summaries of how other countries viewed the Two Plus Four talks, in George to Zoellick and Ross, "The Two-Plus-Four Tightrope," 12 Mar 90; EUR (Dobbins), "National Agendas for the Two-Plus-Four Meeting," n.d.

67. The U.S. State Department had made an important judgment to include Rice from the NSC staff, thereby giving more White House cover for their activities and including an official nominally responsible for representing the views of other interested agencies. The West German Foreign Ministry needed a chancellery representative for similar reasons, compounded by the needs of the different political parties represented by Genscher and Kohl. Kastrup and Elbe had known Hartmann, a career diplomat, for years, and they felt confident that he understood "how to combine loyalty to the Chancellor with loyalty to his old house." Kiessler and Elbe, *Ein runder Tisch mit scharfen Ecken,* p. 119.

68. According to Dufourcq, the Quai's legal experts thought that the Soviets had a legal right as one of the Four Powers to veto a German choice of article 23 over article 14. There was a precedent. France had given its permission when Bonn used article 23 for the accession of the Saarland to the FRG. Weston said that the British lawyers had a different opinion. But Zoellick and Kastrup insisted that, regardless of the law, the West should argue that the matter was outside the purview of the Two Plus Four. State Department lawyers in Washington and Bonn could find legal grounds both for and against a claimed Soviet veto power. See State 81208, "Soviet Legal Argument Barring German Use of Article 23 for Reunification," 14 Mar 90; Sofaer to Zoellick, "GDR Accession under Article 23 of the FRG Basic Law," 5 Apr 90.

69. See "One Plus Three Meeting," detailed memcon of March 13 discussion prepared by Rice; Zoellick's notes from meeting in his files; and Zelikow through Blackwill for Scowcroft and Gates, "Readout on March 13 Meeting Between US, UK, French, and FRG Representatives for March 14 Two Plus Four Discussion," 13 Mar 90 (based on call from Rice). A response to Shevardnadze's March 2 letter was also discussed, and the bland American reply was sent on March 18. On some of the particular French suggestions annoying the West Germans, see Bonn 7849, "German Unification," 9 Mar 90; Bonn 7220, "Berlin Voting Issue: Paris Wants to Put Issue in the Two-Plus-Four Mechanism," 5 Mar 90; State 75918, "Berlin Aviation: French Proposal to Raise the Issue in March 14 Two-Plus-Four Meeting," 9 Mar 90.

70. The Modrow government in the GDR was represented by Ernst Krabatsch, Herbert Suess, and Karl Seidel. Adamishin was accompanied by Kvitsinsky, Mikhail Timoshkin, and the head of the German desk, Valeri Rogoshin. Dufourcq was backed by Denis Gauer and Thierry Dana. Weston was assisted by department head Hillary Synnott and policy planner Jonathan Powell.

71. See "Two Plus Four Talks," 14 Mar 90 (memcon prepared by Rice); Zoellick's notes from the meeting and notes passed during the meeting between Zoellick, Seitz, and Rice, in Zoellick's office files; message sent through special channels from Rice to Scowcroft, Gates, and Blackwill, "2 + 4 Meeting 14 March 1990," 14 Mar 90; Zoellick to Baker, "Background on Two-Plus-Four for Namibia Meetings," 16 Mar 90.

72. The first set of surveys, conducted by the Leipziger Zentralinstitut für Jugendforschung, was published in *Der Spiegel,* March 12, 1990, p. 40. The 44/20 survey, by Infratest, is cited in Teltschik, *329 Tage,* p. 173.

73. Many in the West German SPD wanted a different republic. See, e.g., the interview with SPD Presidium member Gerhard Schröder in *Süddeutsche Zeitung,* March 14, 1990, p. 12; excerpts of interviews in Maier, *Die Wende in der DDR,* p. 79. The FRG Basic Law could be amended only by a two-thirds majority in both the Bundestag and the Bundesrat, which the SPD obviously lacked. West German constitutional lawyers believed that a

constituent assembly under article 146 would probably operate by majority vote. Given the delicate electoral balance in the West, an SPD victory in the East—even a plurality—would almost certainly mean an all-German constituent assembly in which the SPD would have the necessary majority to shape the constitution of a united Germany. See Bonn 8004, "German Unification: The Politics of Article 23 v. Article 146," 9 Mar 90. A representative contrast of views can be found in the exchange between Schäuble and SPD-East leader Markus Meckel in "Anschluss ist ein falscher Begriff," *Der Spiegel*, March 19, 1990, pp. 48–57.

74. On the politics of the path to unification, see Elizabeth Pond, *Beyond the Wall: Germany's Road to Unification* (Washington, D.C.: Brookings Institution, 1993), pp. 198–199; Bonn 8004; Bonn 7780, "SPD Declaration on 'Steps to German Unity,'" 8 Mar 90; and intelligence analyses of the domestic debate.

75. The poll numbers, somewhat more optimistic than the Infratest survey cited by Teltschik, were reported from the Leipziger Zentralinstitut für Jugendforschung and the Institut für Marktforschung, in "Umfrage sieht Verluste der Ost-SPD," *Frankfurter Allgemeine Zeitung*, March 9, 1990, p. 4. The West German political parties reportedly spent about DM 20 million in the Eastern election campaign. Deutsche Press Agentur, "20 Millionen Mark 'Demokratiehilfe,'" *Süddeutsche Zeitung*, March 17/18, 1990, p. 1.; Teltschik, *329 Tage*, p. 173. For the American embassy's preelection assessments, see EmbBerlin 1554, "GDR Election Overview: More Unclear with Each Passing Day," 9 Mar 90; EmbBerlin 1553, "Peanuts, Popcorn, Cracker-Jack: The GDR Party Landscape," 9 Mar 90. In Washington, Dobbins at State and Zelikow at the NSC staff both refused to endorse or prepare papers with predictions of an SPD victory because they thought that public opinion in the GDR was too volatile and they considered the polling utterly unreliable.

76. EmbBerlin 1569, "SPD Chairman Boehme Discusses Democratization and Unification with Ambassador," 9 Mar 90. The election day's cover of *Der Spiegel* read simply: "Kohl's Triumph." Among the best accounts of the campaign and election are "Es gibt keine mehr," *Der Spiegel*, March 19, 1990, pp. 20–33; Timothy Garton Ash, "The East German Surprise," *New York Review of Books*, April 26, 1990, p. 14; Jarausch, *The Rush to German Unity*, pp. 115–128; Pond, *Beyond the Wall*, pp. 199–201; Martin Mantzke, "Eine Republik auf Abruf: Die DDR nach den Wahlen vom 18. März 1990," *Europa Archiv*, April 25, 1990, p. 287; Maier, *Die Wende in der DDR*, pp. 83–88; and Daniel Hamilton, *After the Revolution: The New Political Landscape in East Germany* (Washington, D.C.: American Institute for Contemporary German Studies, 1990), pp. 14–18, 42–43. Plans to convert Ostmarks to deutsche marks at a one-to-one rate were agreed on within the governing coalition by the end of February, and Otto Lambsdorff, FDP party chairman, assured Secretary Baker on March 1 that the FRG could manage monetary union on these terms. Baker to President Bush (for his evening reading), 1 Mar 90.

77. See Teltschik, *329 Tage*, pp. 173–176; Bonn 10349, "German Unification: Kohl Says All-German Elections in the Second Half of Next Year," 29 Mar 90; Bonn 9413, "Teltschik's Comments on German Unification and Future European Security Arrangements," 22 Mar 90; and intelligence reports circulated at the time.

78. See Moscow 9214, "Warsaw Pact Meeting and GDR Elections Spell Trouble for Soviet German Policy," 19 Mar 90; and, for the public line, TASS, "Termed Useful, Necessary," March 17, 1990, in *FBIS-SOV* 90–053, March 19, 1990, pp. 4–5. For Soviet commentary on the GDR elections, blaming the past Stalinist leadership for bringing socialism into disrepute and steadfastly maintaining Moscow's positions on the external issues, see Igor Maximychev and Pyotr Menshikov [both then serving at the Soviet embassy in East Berlin], "One German Fatherland?," *International Affairs* (Moscow), July

1990, pp. 31–38; "Yedinaya Germaniya i eyo sosedi," and Ye. Tsedilina, "Ob'yedineniye: pervyi etap," *Mirovaya Ekonomika i Mezhdunarodniye Otnosheniya*, no. 8 (1990): 68–79. On March 19 the Soviets also received the unhelpful American reply to Shevardnadze's March 2 proposal for setting up a mechanism for urgent Two Plus Four consultations on Germany. State 87148, "Secretary's Response to Shevardnadze's Proposed Procedure for Urgent Consultations on Germany," 18 Mar 90.

79. In the account that follows, for the Shevardnadze-Baker, Baker-Genscher, and Genscher-Shevardnadze talks in Namibia, see Memcon for meeting with Minister Shevardnadze, Windhoek, 20 Mar 90 (Shevardnadze-Baker) (Ross was note taker); Secto 2045, "Secretary's Meeting with FRG Foreign Minister Genscher, March 21, 1990," 24 Mar 90; Kiessler and Elbe, *Ein runder Tisch mit scharfen Ecken*, pp. 109–110; Bonn 10177, "FRG Foreign Minister Genscher's Meeting with Soviet Foreign Minister Shevardnadze, March 22, 1990," 28 Mar 90 (based on Kastrup debriefing to ambassadors in Bonn); Teltschik, *329 Tage*, p. 181 (summarizing Genscher's report back to Kohl). In Bonn Kvitsinsky reiterated Soviet concerns about the NATO issue directly to Kohl on March 22. Teltschik, *329 Tage*, pp. 179–181.

80. Secto 2017, "Memorandum for the President: Namibia, March 20," 20 Mar 90 (sent from Windhoek).

81. For the following account, see Hans-Dietrich Genscher, *Unterwegs zur Einheit: Reden und Dokumente aus bewegter Zeit* (Berlin: Siedler, 1991), pp. 257–268 (for March 23 speech in Luxembourg to the Assembly of the Western European Union); Teltschik, *329 Tage*, pp. 182–184, 190; Bonn 11684, "Teltschik's Views on European Security Issues," 11 Apr 90. For reflections of these FRG positions in Kohl's statements at the time, see David Marsh, "Kohl Sees Unified Germany in EC Union," *Financial Times*, April 2, 1990, p. 4 (based on March 30 interview with Kohl); FBIS translation of Kohl interview on French television, Antenne-2, March 29, 1990 (recorded on March 27). For an indication of CSU support for Kohl's policies on security (and Poland), see also Baker to President Bush (for his evening reading), 5 Apr 90 (reporting on Washington visit of CSU Bundestag faction leader Wolfgang Bötsch). The April 2 Federal Security Council meeting was chaired by Kohl and attended by Genscher, Stoltenberg, Seiters, Teltschik, Kastrup, and Klaus Naumann (then head of Stoltenberg's planning staff).

The SPD position on security policy was first redefined after the March 18 GDR election by a working group (Fortschritt 90) headed by Lafontaine, which called on March 20 for the dissolution of military blocs, a linkage of German unification to the development of a new all-European security system, the abolition of nuclear deterrence, and withdrawal of all nuclear weapons from German soil. At no point did the document endorse continued German NATO membership, however qualified. These and other steps announced in the document would have eliminated the basis for a continued U.S. military presence in Germany, and the SPD drafters of the document were undoubtedly cognizant of this fact. Somewhat more moderate voices in the SPD—such as Willy Brandt, Hans-Jochen Vogel, Walter Momper, Karsten Voigt, Horst Ehmke, and Andreas von Bülow, who were prepared to endorse some transitional and qualified NATO membership for a united Germany— were unable to rally a party consensus that could overshadow the even more leftist views of Lafontaine, Egon Bahr, and others. See Bonn 9527, "Lafontaine Working Group Announces 12-Point Disarmament Program—Calls for Ultimate Dissolution of Military Blocs, Interim Changes in NATO Strategy," 22 Mar 90; Bonn 10020, "SPD Leadership Positions on German Membership in NATO," 27 Mar 90.

82. See Genscher's April 6 speech to the American Society of Newspaper Editors, published in Auswärtiges Amt, *Deutsche Aussenpolitik 1990/91: Auf dem Weg zu einer*

europaeischen Friedensordnung (Munich: Bonn Aktuell, 1991), pp. 103–105; the well-informed reflection of views held among Genscher's staff evidenced in "We Need a Treaty," *Der Spiegel,* April 23, 1990; intelligence reports circulated at the time on Genscher, "Changing Assessment of the CSCE Process and German Unification"; Memcon of President Bush's meeting with Foreign Minister Genscher, 4 Apr 90; Scowcroft to President Bush, "Meeting with Foreign Minister Genscher," 3 Apr 90. Bush and Baker followed up their mediation efforts at the time of Mazowiecki's visit by going over draft text on the key border issue which Genscher had brought with him. The West Germans planned to discuss this privately with the Poles before inserting it into the parliamentary resolutions.

83. When Seitz complained about Kastrup's stance, Kastrup answered testily that neither Baker nor Hurd nor Dumas had tried to pin Genscher down yet on all of these points. First, Kastrup said, we should see what the Soviets say. After all, the principle of full German membership in NATO is the important point. Neither the Americans nor the British were satisfied with this reply. See State 154104, "German Unification: Highlights of April 10 Meeting of One-Plus-Three States," 14 May 90; Dobbins to Baker, 10 Apr 90 (passing along a report phoned in by Seitz); and Zoellick's handwritten notes from the April 10 meeting (in his office files).

84. For the account that follows, see Teltschik, *329 Tage,* pp. 172–173, 175–176, 179, 181–182, 195, 200, 207; Pond, *Beyond the Wall,* pp. 210–213; Thatcher, *The Downing Street Years,* p. 760. On the German attitudes toward monetary union and the opposition of the Bundesbank, see W. R. Smyser, *The Economy of United Germany: Colossus at the Crossroads* (New York: St. Martin's Press, 1992), pp. 233–248. Genscher's quote from Thomas Mann is from his March 23 address, in Genscher, *Unterwegs zur Einheit,* pp. 257–268. For a Genscher pledge of pro-European sentiment to Mitterrand in November 1989, see Kiessler and Elbe, *Ein runder Tisch mit scharfen Ecken,* p. 60. For American reactions to the Franco-German initiative, see, e.g., Baker to President Bush (for his evening reading), 27 Mar 90 (reporting on Kohl's visit to the European Commission, based on an account of the meeting from Delors's staff).

The EC's fundamental legal problem with incorporating the GDR was solved when Kohl chose article 23 because there was no change in EC membership. Other legal issues, from voting rights in the European Parliament to the application of EC trade and agricultural policies, were adequately resolved within the community by the time of the Dublin summit in April. On the EC and German unification, see Barbara Lippert, Rosalind Stevens-Ströhmann, Dirk Günther, Grit Viertel, and Stephen Woolcock, *German Unification and EC Integration: German and British Perspectives* (New York: Council on Foreign Relations, 1993); David Spence, *Enlargement without Accession: The EC's Response to German Unification,* RIIA Discussion Paper no. 36 (London: Royal Institute for International Affairs, 1991); and Bertelsmann Stiftung, *Die doppelte Integration: Europa und das grossere Deutschland* (Gütersloh: Bertelsmann Stiftung, 1991).

85. See Zelikow to Blackwill, "German Unification: Identifying Issues for Early US Decision," 21 Mar 90; Zelikow to Dobbins (listing NSC suggestions for decision issues), 27 Mar 90. The British offered an excellent list of questions about NATO to the U.S. government on March 27. See George and Holmes to Zoellick, "British Paper on Germany and NATO," 30 Mar 90. Seitz and Dobbins convened the interagency Germany Task Force on March 30 to organize the preparation of the necessary analytical papers.

86. For discussions about the legal issues at the time, see Sofaer to Zoellick, "GDR Accession under Article 23 of the FRG Basic Law," 6 Apr 90; Bonn 8005, "Maksimychev's Views on German Unification and the Soviet Legal Position," 9 Mar 90; Bonn 10722, "Views of FRG Foreign Office Deputy Legal Adviser Eitel on Unification-Related Legal

Issues," 2 Apr 90; Seitz through Kimmitt and Zoellick to Baker, "Draft Preparatory Paper on 'Options for a Settlement on Germany' to be Distributed to UK, FRG, and France," 4 Apr 90; Young (Sofaer's deputy legal adviser) to Zoellick and Seitz, "Summary of Impressions from German Unification Legal Consultations with British, French, and West Germans," 9 Apr 90 (elaborated in Paris 11635; London 7341); Seitz to Zoellick, "Soviet Approach to German Unification, including Current Applicability of the Potsdam Agreement," 6 Apr 90. The Germany Task Force, under the direction of Seitz and Dobbins, was also commissioning analytical papers on the various legal issues.

87. On April 10 Weston simply urged that the matter be referred to the lawyers. London then formally dropped its peace treaty position for, the Americans were told, "both legal and political reasons." But the British lawyers still thought that Four Power rights over Germany would need to remain in force for some time after the unification of the two German states. See Weston to Seitz, 23 Apr 90, and attached paper, "German Unification and a Settlement: Legal Aspects—UK Comments."

88. See State 154104, "German Unification: Highlights of April 10 Meeting of Officials of One-Plus-Three States," 14 May 90; note from Dobbins to the Secretary, April 10, 1990 (passing along phoned-in report from Seitz); Zoellick's handwritten notes from the April 10 meeting (in his office files); Scowcroft to President Bush, "Officials-Level Meeting of the 'One Plus Three' on German Unification," 19 or 20 Apr 90 (drafted by Rice with Blackwill); informal Zoellick paper, "Thatcher Meeting—Key Points," 11 Apr 90 (annotated by Baker).

89. Zelikow interview with Powell, London, June 1993; Powell's complete notes were later published (after being leaked to news magazines) as "What the PM Learnt about the Germans," in *When the Wall Came Down*, ed. Harold James and Marla Stone (London: Routledge, 1992), pp. 233–239. The academics invited to Chequers on March 24 were Timothy Garton Ash, Gordon Craig, Lord Dacre (Hugh Trevor-Roper), Fritz Stern, Norman Stone, and George Urban. Powell's notes were originally meant to be seen by Thatcher herself and only a few others. Only seven copies were distributed, with instructions that they were not to be reproduced. After the notes were leaked a few months later, the subsequent investigation found that at least 193 copies of the notes were floating around the British government.

When the notes were leaked, most of the commentary focused on the fact that Powell's notes mentioned agreement on some pejorative German national traits. So some of the academics present wrote that they had said nothing of the kind. See, e.g., Timothy Garton Ash, "The Chequers Affair," *New York Review of Books*, September 27, 1990. Ash does not comment, however, on why Powell might have written such things in a paper intended almost exclusively for the eyes of Margaret Thatcher. Powell may have been echoing Thatcher's prejudices in order to persuade her to accept an ultimate conclusion he knew she disliked—in effect dressing up an unappealing meat with some well-liked sauce.

90. See Teltschik, *329 Tage*, pp. 188–189; Thatcher's address to the Königswinter Conference, Cambridge, 29 Mar 90 (with Kohl sharing the dais); Bonn 11183, "The Anglo-German Summit Viewed from Bonn: Progress on Bilateral Relations, but Still No Warm Feelings for Mrs. Thatcher," 5 Apr 90. For NSC staff speculation about the increasing convergence of policy views between Britain and France, see Scowcroft to the president, "Meetings with Prime Minister Thatcher," 10 Apr 90 (drafted by Zelikow through Blackwill).

91. See Scowcroft to President Bush, "Meetings with Prime Minister Thatcher," 10 Apr 90 (drafted by Zelikow and Blackwill). For general background, see also London 7247, "Your Meeting with Thatcher in Bermuda," 11 Apr 90.

92. Memcon for meetings with Prime Minister Thatcher, 13 Apr 90.

93. *Public Papers* (1990), p. 570; Teltschik, *329 Tage*, p. 196.

94. The "post-Gaullist Gaullism" phrase is Stanley Hoffmann's. Illustrations of the American perspective can be found in Scowcroft to President Bush, "Reviving the Spirit of Kennebunkport," 2 Apr 90 (drafted by Basora and Zelikow through Blackwill); Seitz through Kimmitt to Baker, "France and European Institutional Architecture," 8 Mar 90; see also Basora to the File, "General Scowcroft's March 8 Lunch with Jacques Attali," 10 Mar 90. Attali then saw the Two Plus Four as a way to manage a "runaway Germany." See also intelligence reports circulated at the time on Mitterrand's desire to reorient French strategic policy.

95. Message from President Bush to President Mitterrand, 17 Apr 90; see also Scowcroft to President Bush, "Letter to President Mitterrand," 16 Apr 90.

96. See Memcons for meetings with President Mitterrand, 19 Apr 90, and *Public Papers* (1990), p. 597. Mitterrand's tone was noticeably more positive about NATO and the American role in Europe than the tone heard by Baker in his separate conversation with Dumas.

97. Teltschik, *329 Tage*, p. 210; message from President Bush to Chancellor Kohl at the Chancellery, 25 Apr 90; message from President Bush to Prime Minister Thatcher, 25 Apr 90. On the Mitterrand-Kohl summit in Paris, see Teltschik, *329 Tage*, pp. 207–210; Paris 13158, "Fifty-Fifth Kohl-Mitterrand Summit," 27 Apr 90.

98. Bush conveyed the proposed policies for Germany and the Two Plus Four in a message sent to all NATO heads of government and NATO Secretary General Wörner on May 1 and 2. NATO ambassadors had already acknowledged FRG acceptance that the defense obligations under articles 5 and 6 of the North Atlantic Treaty would extend to all the territory of a united Germany. USNATO 2381, "Further NATO Discussion of German Unification," 18 Apr 90. On the May 3 ministerial session, see USNATO 2843, "Secretary Baker's May 3 NAC Intervention," 10 May 90; USNATO 2844, "May 3 NATO Ministerial—Part I," 10 May 90; USNATO 2845, "May 3 NATO Ministerial—Part II," 10 May 90; USNATO 2726, "Press Conference by Secretary of State James A. Baker, III," 3 May 90.

99. See Bartholomew to Baker, "NATO Review," 15 Feb 90; Rice through Blackwill and Kanter to Gates, "First Meeting of the European Strategy Steering Group," 21 Feb 90. The members of the European Strategy Steering Group were Gates (chair); NSC staff members Blackwill, Kanter, and Zelikow; State Department officials Zoellick, Bartholomew, Ross, and Seitz; officials from the Office of the Secretary of Defense Paul Wolfowitz and Stephen Hadley; representatives from the Joint Chiefs of Staff (Admiral David Jeremiah and Lieutenant General Howard Graves); CIA representatives Richard Kerr and John McLaughlin; and Arms Control and Disarmament Agency director Ron Lehman.

Scowcroft, Gates, and Blackwill planned the group, in part, as a way of adapting to their analysis of the bureaucratic politics at work. Undersecretary of state for international security policy Reginald Bartholomew and undersecretary of defense for policy Paul Wolfowitz were starting to organize such deliberations under their leadership. Blackwill wanted these reflections to be run by the White House, where he could exert more influence over them, and where the group could be chaired by the powerful and very capable Gates. Blackwill also thought that the group ought to extend beyond the usual circle of arms control officials to include Zoellick and Ross. Since State Department's protocol might make it difficult for Zoellick to chair a State-led group rather than the (nominally) more senior Bartholomew, running the group from the White House also made it easier to transcend the department's own bureaucratic rivalries.

100. For the discussion that follows, see Teltschik, *329 Tage,* pp. 160–161; Memcon for meeting with Helmut Kohl, 24–25 Feb 90. Scowcroft made his remark to Sir Percy Cradock on April 24, according to the author's notes from the meeting.

101. See Bonn 9413, "Teltschik's Comments on German Unification and Future European Security Arrangements," 22 Mar 90; Bonn 11684, "Teltschik's Views on European Security Issues," 11 Apr 90; USVienna 585, "CFE: Disintegration of the Warsaw Pact and German Unification," 23 Feb 90.

102. See Zelikow through Blackwill and Kanter to Gates, "Your Meeting of the European Strategy Steering Group on March 16," 15 Mar 90 (and attached departmental papers); Zelikow to Blackwill, "NATO Strategy Review Subgroup Meeting," 29 Mar 90. Blackwill presented the NSC staff's preferred approach to other officials on March 29, urging a major NATO summit in July. Ross agreed with him. Dobbins and Wolfowitz wanted more time to deliberate on NATO's future strategy and doubted that there was enough time to get agreement on a substantive summit declaration. See Zelikow's notes of the meeting. Wörner conveyed his views during an early April visit to Washington.

103. The cabinet officials made this decision on April 4. The decision won support from NATO supreme military commander U.S. General John Galvin when he met with Scowcroft on April 12. Wörner led a supportive but general discussion of the plan among NATO ambassadors on April 17. See USNATO 2357, "April 17 Permrep Lunch: Discussion of a NATO Summit," 17 Apr 90. The U.S. mission to NATO was not well informed about the details of the secret plans being hatched in Washington. On the development of the new NATO nuclear policy, see Zelikow through Blackwill and Kanter to Scowcroft, "Moving Toward a USG Decision on the Future of US Nuclear Forces in Europe," 31 Mar 90 (and attached options paper). On the State Department's different vision for NATO summit plans, see Seitz through Zoellick and Bartholomew to Baker, "Where We Stand on FOTL, INF Arms Control, NATO Strategy, NATO Summit, and CSCE," 12 Apr 90.

104. The cabinet-level decision took place on April 16. On the plans for Bush's speech and the dispute with the Pentagon, see Zelikow through Blackwill and Kanter to Scowcroft, "NATO Strategy and the Future of US Nuclear Forces in Europe: Issues for Decision," 4 Apr 90; Zelikow through Blackwill and Kanter to Gates, "Your Meeting of the European Strategy Steering Group on April 6," 5 Apr 90 (and attached outlines); Zelikow through Blackwill and Kanter to Scowcroft, "Your Meeting to Discuss a Possible Presidential Speech on European Security and NATO on April 16," 13 Apr 90.

105. A State Department policy planning staff paper, "CSCE: Looking Ahead," was reviewed at the March 16 meeting of the European Strategy Steering Group. It was drafted by James Holmes, Lynne Davidson, and Roger George. Ross suggested to Baker on April 19 that the United States should "*explore* the role that CSCE might play in a future all-European security arrangement and how NATO can be a component of such a system. Despite current skepticism at the NSC, the U.S. cannot afford to be seen as retarding the formation of structures which so many Europeans view as the wave of the future." Ross to Baker, "How to Think about NATO This Spring," 19 Apr 90 (drafted by John Reichart and Bob Einhorn). This memo contained no specific proposals and was not shared with the State Department's European bureau. Blackwill and his staff had a wide-ranging discussion with Scowcroft on ideas for NATO on April 16. They then suggested that a CSCE security institution be set up as a "conflict prevention center" largely concerned with confidence building. Blackwill suggested creating an all-European parliament under the auspices of the CSCE.

106. Address by President Bush at Oklahoma State University, Stillwater, Oklahoma, 4 May 90 (drafted mainly by Zelikow and Blackwill). Bush previewed his plans to all NATO

leaders in individually tailored messages sent on May 1–2. See Zelikow through Blackwill and Kanter to Scowcroft, "Message to NATO Leaders," 1 May 90. The West Germans had been thinking about a slower schedule for action in NATO and had not focused on the substance of needed changes. But Teltschik comments that Bush's proposals were received positively as ideas that seemed sure to improve the prospects for a successful outcome in the Two Plus Four talks, "the right step at the right time." Teltschik, *329 Tage,* pp. 205, 214–216. On May 2 Baker previewed the upcoming speech in a letter to Shevardnadze that also dealt with outstanding issues in the CFE talks.

107. See, e.g., from top diplomats and military advisers, TASS, "Adamishin Interviewed on German Unification," March 21, 1990, in *FBIS-SOV* 90–056, March 22, 1990, p. 4; interview with Marshal Akhromeyev in Vladimir Ostrovsky, "We Cannot Agree to an Imbalance of Forces," *Zolnierz Wolnosci* (Warsaw), March 20, 1990, p. 7, in *FBIS-SOV* 90–057, March 23, 1990, pp. 17–18; TASS, "Soviet Government Statement," March 27, 1990 in *FBIS-SOV* 90–060, March 28, 1990, pp. 24–25.

108. It also created an atmosphere in which some subordinates lacked adequate guidance. Thus, Portugalov, working for Falin on the Central Committee staff, who had inadvertently done so much to embolden Kohl and Teltschik in November 1989, had another long talk with Teltschik on March 28 in which he opposed NATO membership for a united Germany but, by alluding to a host of ideas being considered in the Soviet government, conveyed a message of irresolution. Portugalov seemed to think that he could trade West Germany's flexibility on its alliance status for Soviet flexibility on whether the diplomatic settlement should take the form of a peace treaty. Teltschik wrote: "The Chancellor, whom I spoke with immediately after [my meeting with Portugalov], expressed his satisfaction that the positions of the Soviet leadership continued to appear so open and flexible." Teltschik, *329 Tage,* p. 188. Portugalov said that he was acting with Chernyayev's approval.

109. Informal notes on president's telephone conversation with Prime Minister Thatcher, March 28, 1990 (Zelikow was note taker).

110. This account is based on Memcon of conversation with Shevardnadze, 4 Apr 90, in Baker's office.

111. The tough Soviet stance on Germany is strongly reflected in the briefing papers prepared for Shevarnadze before his trip. See Politburo position paper sponsored by Lev Zaikov, Kryuchkov, Shevardnadze, Yakovlev, Yazov, Oleg Baklanov, and Igor Belousov, "O direktivax dlya peregovorov Ministra inostrannyikh del SSSR c Prezidentom SShA Dz. Bushem i Goscydarstvennyim sekretaryem Dzh Bekerom," 31 Mar 90, in Center for the Storage of Contemporary Documentation (TsKhSD), Moscow, no. 184. A second document prepared specifically for the meeting with Bush makes essentially the same points. See Politburo directive "Dlya besedi ministra inostrannyikh del SSSR s Prezidentom SShA Dzh. Byushem," n.d., in TsKhSD, Moscow, no. 184.

112. This point and the account that follows are based on Memcon for meeting with Foreign Minister Shevardnadze (Second Small Group: Regional Issues), 5 Apr 90.

113. The Rice quote is in Don Oberdorfer, *The Turn: From the Cold War to a New Era* (New York: Simon and Schuster, 1991), p. 404; and Michael Beschloss and Strobe Talbott, *At the Highest Levels: The Inside Story of the End of the Cold War* (Boston: Little, Brown, 1992), p. 205, where it is accompanied by descriptions of Bush's effort to walk a tightrope in stating American policy on Lithuania.

114. Memcon for the president's meeting with Foreign Minister Shevardnadze, April 6, 1990.

115. See London 7298, "Gorbachev-Hurd Discussion on Lithuania and Germany," 12 Apr 90; *Pravda,* April 11, 1990, pp. 1–2.

116. For the account that follows, see TASS, "Shevardnadze Gives Speech on 'Sensitive Problems,'" April 18, 1990, in *FBIS-SOV* 90–076, April 19, 1990, p. 1. For a pro-NATO position from Soviet intellectuals, see, e.g., Vyacheslav Dashichev interviewed by Manfred Schell, "A United Germany Must Be Bound within the Framework of NATO," *Die Welt*, March 20, 1990, p. 9, in *FBIS-SOV* 90–056, March 22, 1990, pp. 28–30; Major General Geli Batenin, "Preferred Variety: All of Germany in NATO," *Berliner Zeitung*, May 4, 1990, p. 3.

117. See Eduard Shevardnadze, "Towards a Greater Europe—The Warsaw Treaty Organization and NATO in a Renewing Europe," *NATO's Sixteen Nations* (May 1990); Seitz to Baker, "Shevardnadze Article to be Published in May 90 Issue of 'NATO's Sixteen Nations,'" 19 Apr 90.

118. In the discussion that follows, the description of the May policy debate is based on authors' interviews with Tarasenko and Chernyayev, along with Chernyayev's published account, based on his original notes; see Anatoly Chernyayev, *Shest' let s Gorbachevym: po dnevikovym zapisyam* (Moscow: Progress Publishers, 1993), pp. 347–348. The accounts are consistent, except that Tarasenko alludes to two Politburo meetings and Chernyayev offers a detailed account of only one, clearly the decisive session. It is hard to find Politburo documents for these sessions, so it is possible that these were informal leadership gatherings rather than formal Politburo meetings. For a sense of Shevardnadze's ambivalence at the time, see Eduard Shevardnadze, *Moi vybor: v zashchitu demokratii i svobody* (Moscow: Novostii, 1991), pp. 232–233. The Americans did not know about the Politburo debates, and had more of a sense of the fluid discussions swirling around the nongovernmental institutes. Marshal Akhromeyev did, however, tell Ambassador Jack Matlock that Germany's political-military status was a "grassroots issue" in the USSR, one that concerned the entire military, millions of common people, and the top echelons of both the Soviet government and the Communist party. See Moscow 14624, "Can a United Germany Remain in NATO? Many Soviets Think So, but Seek 'Unconventional Recipes' and More Ideas from the West," 1 May 90; Moscow 14438, "Two Plus Four—Soviets Look to Ministerial and Summit; Bondarenko Takes Lead in Berlin," 27 Apr 90.

119. Igor Maximychev, "Possible 'Impossibilities,'" *International Affairs* (Moscow) (June 1993): 112. Maximychev does not attribute the "million troops" to Falin in his published article, but later clarified the origin and circumstances of the remarks in an interview with Zelikow, Moscow, January 1994. Understandably Falin does not mention such talk in the memoir he wrote for German book buyers, but he makes no effort to conceal his vitriolic hostility to the notion of letting a united Germany become a full member of NATO. At the very least, he writes, Moscow should have insisted on Germany's leaving the NATO military command (like France) and the "minimum Minimorum" should have been the withdrawal of all nuclear weapons out of all Germany. He believes that 84 percent of the Germans would have backed such a Soviet stand. See Valentin Falin, *Politische Erinnerungen*, trans. Heddy Pross-Weerth (Munich: Droemer Knaur, 1993), p. 494.

120. For some disturbing postunification revelations about the high level of offensive planning and readiness among the Soviet and East German forces stationed in the GDR, see Lothar Rühl, "Offensive Defence in the Warsaw Pact," *Survival*, 33 (September–October 1991): 442–450.

121. See, e.g., Zoellick to Baker, "Background on Two-Plus-Four for Namibia Meetings," 16 Mar 90, p. 10.

122. On the formation of de Maizière's coalition government, see Jarausch, *The Rush to German Unity*, pp. 128–134.

123. A Soviet note on April 19 protesting the impending agreement on economic and monetary union was dismissed by Teltschik because it was delivered by low-level diplomats and in the form of a "non-paper" rather than, for example, a letter from Shevardnadze

or even Gorbachev. On April 23 Kvitsinsky apparently disavowed his government's own demarche as premature, since the text of a planned economic and monetary union treaty was not yet available for review. Teltschik, *329 Tage*, pp. 202–203, 205.

124. See Teltschik, *329 Tage*, pp. 203–204; Dobbins (Acting) through McCormack to Baker, "Two Germanys Announce Agreement on Principles for Economic and Monetary Union," 3 May 90.

125. For the "bleak" assessment, see Burleigh (Acting) to Kimmitt, "Maintaining US Forces in a United Germany—An Uphill Battle," 11 Apr 90. For a survey of West German opinion read by U.S. officials revealing areas of vulnerability, see USIA Office of Research, "West Germans Want Unified Germany in NATO, Majority Finds Pace of Unification Too Fast," 9 May 90 (survey conducted on April 25–28). On the April 30 meeting of Two Plus Four political directors, see Teltschik, *329 Tage*, pp. 212–213; State 139175, "April 30 Two-Plus-Four Officials Meeting," 1 May 90; and Zoellick's notes from the meeting in his office files. The meeting was held in East Berlin and chaired by the East German Foreign Ministry's parliamentary state secretary Hans Misselwitz.

126. Ross and Zoellick to Baker, "Scene-Setter: Two-Plus-Four Ministerial," n.d. (but appears to be 1 or 2 May 90); see also the briefing papers prepared for Baker's trip to NATO and Bonn, including Seitz letter to Baker, 20 Apr 90, attaching "Strategy for Dealing with the Soviets," 19 Apr 90 (drafted by desk officer Andrew Goodman and cleared throughout the department); Seitz through Kimmitt to Baker, "Managing German Unification: Planning for the Two-plus-Four Ministerial and the US-Soviet Summit," 25 Apr 90 (passed with a note from Kimmitt emphasizing the need to take "an active lead *now*" in shaping NATO's approach to all the European defense and arms control issues). A number of other briefing papers were prepared, going well beyond what Baker needed at the time, but forcing a major consolidation of U.S. analysis on many details and bringing a massive quantity of information before Zoellick, Blackwill, Ross, and other key sub-cabinet officials. For Teltschik's use of "solution package," see *329 Tage*, p. 195 (entry for April 16).

127. For more details, see Teltschik, *329 Tage*, pp. 217–218, 221 (for the Kohl quote); State 154634, "Secretary's Bilateral with Chancellor Kohl," 14 May 90.

128. Shevardnadze was scheduled to see Genscher but not Kohl. At the last minute Teltschik asked the Soviets whether Shevardnadze wanted to see the chancellor. Of course, Kvitsinsky said, but Genscher's people had said it was not possible. Furious, Teltschik quickly arranged the meeting himself after checking with Kohl. On the meeting itself, see Teltschik, *329 Tage*, pp. 218–221. The idea for the German-Soviet treaty was evidently conceived in the Chancellery after being suggested in an April 4 meeting with nongov-ernmental experts from academia and the media, including Boris Meissner. On April 23, having discussed the idea with Kohl, Teltschik tried it out on Kvitsinsky and received what he thought was a "euphoric" reaction. Shevardnadze referred to Kvitsinsky's report of this meeting when he met with Kohl. Ibid. pp. 192–193, 204–207. Teltschik elaborated on the thinking behind the idea in an interview with Zelikow and Rice, Gütersloh, June 1992.

129. Secto 6013 (from Bonn), "Memorandum for the President, Bonn, May 4, 1990: My Meeting with Shevardnadze," 5 May 90.

130. The text of Shevardnadze's presentation was published in *Izvestiya*, May 7, 1990, p. 3. For the other ministerial presentations, all of which were later released to the press, see State 159968, "Two-Plus-Four Bonn Ministerial Interventions," 18 May 90; see also Kiessler and Elbe, *Ein runder Tisch mit scharfen Ecken*, pp. 122–126.

131. For Shevardnadze's reflections, see *Moi vybor*, pp. 232–233. The same point is emphasized in Kiessler and Elbe's analysis of Shevardnadze's position in *Ein runder Tisch*

mit scharfen Ecken, pp. 124–125. CIA analysts took a less anxious view of Shevardnadze's speech, emphasizing that Moscow would let Germany unify, and noting signs of flexibility in Shevardnadze's attitude toward the problem. They thought of the speech as an opening bid for future bargaining. CIA, "An Analysis of Shevardnadze's Speech at the Two-Plus-Four Talks," SOV M 90–20062, 17 May 90. For a similarly nuanced reaction from Teltschik, ever determined to see the bright side or signs of flexibility in any Soviet statements, see *329 Tage,* pp. 221–224.

132. Account based on the original notes taken during the meeting both by Zoellick and by Blackwill, in their respective office files.

133. For the press conference, see *Bulletin,* no. 54 (1990): 421–424; and, for a fairly typical but astute press reaction, see Claus Gennrich, "Moskau will die deutsche Einheit bald," *Frankfurter Allgemeine Zeitung,* May 7, 1990, p. 1.

7. Friendly Persuasion

1. Horst Teltschik, *329 Tage: Innenansichten der Einigung* (Berlin: Siedler, 1991), p. 225.

2. Zelikow interview with Pauline Neville-Jones, London, June 1992; the Hurd quote is from a message about his trip sent by Hurd to British diplomats in Washington for discussion with the Americans. Hurd repeated to Kohl, on May 15, the British readiness to give up Four Power rights at the moment of unification. Teltschik, *329 Tage,* p. 235. This contradicts Elizabeth Pond's assertion that the British, like the French, supported continuing Four Power supervision. Elizabeth Pond, *Beyond the Wall: Germany's Road to Unification* (Washington, D.C.: Brookings Institution, 1993), p. 214.

3. See Richard Kiessler and Frank Elbe, *Ein runder Tisch mit scharfen Ecken: Der diplomatische Weg zur deutschen Einheit* (Baden-Baden: Nomos, 1993), pp. 126–129; Pond, *Beyond the Wall,* pp. 213–214.

4. On American intelligence estimates of the Soviet Union between 1989 and 1991, see Harvard University Kennedy School of Government Case, "The CIA and the Fall of the Soviet Empire: The Politics of 'Getting It Right,'" C16–94–1251.0. In fact, the Bush administration had formed a highly secret contingency planning group to examine potential American responses to the catastrophic failure of Gorbachev's policies and attendant instability in the Soviet Union.

5. The account that follows is drawn from Kiessler and Elbe, *Ein runder Tisch mit scharfen Ecken,* pp. 126–129; Pond, *Beyond the Wall,* pp. 213–214; Claus Gennrich, "Genscher begrüsst Moskaus Bereitschaft zur Trennung der inneren und äusseren Aspekte der Vereinigung," *Frankfurter Allgemeine Zeitung,* May 8, 1990, p. 1; Zelikow and Rice interview with Teltschik, Gütersloh, June 1992; Zelikow interview with Genscher, Wachtberg-Pech, December 1994; and Teltschik's somewhat reticent published account in *329 Tage,* pp. 224–226. Teltschik denies planting the Gennrich article. Interview with Zelikow, Munich, December 1994. The quotations from the meeting between Kohl, Seiters, and Genscher are from an account conveyed informally to American officials at the time from a Foreign Ministry source who heard an account of the meeting from Genscher. The account is consistent with other evidence. A Chancellery official later told Pond how relieved he was that Teltschik left the full details of this episode out of his published diary. Pond, *Beyond the Wall,* p. 323 n. 4. Blackwill called Teltschik to confirm that the United States strongly agreed with the position being taken by the Chancellery, and Elbe alludes to Blackwill's concerns as well.

6. Kiessler and Elbe refer to the May 7 interview with *Deutschlandfunk* without mentioning this language; see *Ein runder Tisch mit scharfen Ecken,* p. 126. American

officials spotted Genscher's formulation of the NATO position in a report on the interview carried on the UPI wire in a May 7 story filed by Joseph Fleming.

7. The account that follows is based on State 148610, "Message to Foreign Minister Genscher," 9 May 90; State 154828, "Message to Foreign Ministers Hurd and Dumas," 15 May 90; Baker to President Bush (for his evening reading), 10 May 90 (Elbe had faxed to Zoellick a copy of Genscher's May 10 statement to the Bundestag); Genscher to Baker, 16 May 90 (delivered in Washington and transmitted to Baker in Moscow). For Genscher's Bundestag statement, see Hans Viktor Böttcher, ed., *Materialen zu Deutschlandfragen: Politiker und Wissenschaftler nehmen Stellung, 1989–91* (Bonn: Kulturstiftung der deutschen Vertriebenen, 1991), pp. 62–65. Genscher gave press interviews denying that he had ever supported decoupling. See, e.g., *Der Spiegel*, May 14, 1990, pp. 28–30. On May 10 Kohl also addressed the Bundestag, but limited his remarks to a report on the special EC summit in Dublin and the progress of negotiations with the GDR on economic and monetary union. British officials debriefed American diplomats on Hurd's May 15 talks with Genscher in Bonn. For a sense of West German confidence and warm feelings toward the United States and President Bush's "fantastic" support for Germany, see Memcon of President Bush's meeting with CSU Chairman and Finance Minister Theo Waigel, 8 May 90.

8. See Rice and Zelikow to Blackwill, "Two Plus Four: The Next Phase," 10 May 90; M. S. Gorbachev, "Lessons of War and Victory," *Pravda*, May 9, 1990, pp. 1–5.

9. Rice and Zelikow to Blackwill, "Two Plus Four: The Next Phase"; see also Zoellick's notes to himself, dated May 9, in his office files. This proposal turned in part on a question of international law. Could three of the Four Powers give up their Quadripartite rights without the consent of the fourth? Zoellick, advised by State Department lawyers, was doubtful. The United States had insisted for decades, beginning with the second Berlin crisis (1958–1961), that one of the Four Powers (in this case the USSR) could not unilaterally abandon its rights over Berlin to the Germans (in this case the GDR). The State Department lawyers, led by Michael Young and Dan Koblitz, had not written a formal opinion stating that Four Power rights could be extinguished only if all Four Powers agreed. After all, once such an opinion was drafted, it could prove quite inconvenient should the United States government later decide that a different view was politically essential. But the lawyers, steeped in years of efforts to protect allied rights in Berlin, clearly disapproved of any policy that endorsed the principle of unilateral abrogation of Four Power rights. When Baker traveled to Bonn, his briefing papers on this point said only: "If the Soviets try to hold up termination of rights pending a substantive arrangement more to their liking, we may find ourselves in a bargaining situation." Secretary's Briefing Papers, "Two-plus-Four Talking Points: Termination of Four-Power Rights," 24 Apr 90.

Rice and Zelikow understood this legal argument but thought that the West, in the final analysis, had to be able to counter a Soviet attempt to insist on retention of Four Power rights. So Rice and Zelikow believed that a legal defense, if a thin one, would have to be constructed by adopting the old Soviet arguments of the 1950s, strengthened by the genuine self-determination of the German people.

10. See "Die CDU will jetzt gesamtdeutsche Wahlen um die Jahreswende," *Frankfurter Allgemeine Zeitung*, May 15, 1990, p. 1; Eagleburger (Acting) to President Bush (for his evening reading), 15 May 90; Mulholland to Zoellick, "FRG: Kohl's Call for Early All-German Elections," 21 May 90.

11. On the Hurd-Kohl meeting, see Teltschik, *329 Tage*, p. 235; Bonn 15540, "Hurd's May 15 Visit to Bonn," 16 May 90 (based on firsthand British reports of the meeting).

12. On the Bush-Kohl conversations, see Teltschik, *329 Tage*, pp. 236–239; Memcons for president's meetings with Chancellor Kohl, 17 May 90. For Eagleburger's separate meetings with Genscher, see Eagleburger to President Bush (for his evening reading), 17 May 90; Dobbins (Acting) to Zoellick, "The Kohl-Genscher Visit," 18 May 90. The same concerns about the future of American troops in Germany and forthright West German support for a continued U.S. presence dominated the president's meeting a week later with the chairman of the FDP, Otto Lambsdorff. See Memcon for president's meeting with Otto Graf Lambsdorff, 24 May 90. During this discussion Bush suggested that, both to help get rid of Soviet troops and to give economic incentives to Moscow, Bonn should offer to build housing for withdrawn troops. U.S. officials noticed that Chancellor Kohl began referring to this idea in conversations around the end of May, but this may just have been a coincidence.

13. Account based on Rice's recollections; see Michael Beschloss and Strobe Talbott, *At the Highest Levels: The Inside Story of the End of the Cold War* (Boston: Little, Brown, 1992), pp. 202–207 for the remainder of the account.

14. The account that follows is drawn from Teltschik, *329 Tage*, pp. 221, 226–228, 230–235. Beschloss and Talbott assert that, during his trip to Moscow, Teltschik pledged to Gorbachev that Bonn would finance and provision the Soviet troops in Germany for several years, and would build housing for them when they returned to the USSR; see *At the Highest Levels*, p. 209. But this account is contradicted by the only published primary source, Teltschik's recollections, and appears to confuse the May 1990 discussion of credits with issues discussed months later.

15. The discussion that follows is drawn from Teltschik, *329 Tage*, pp. 237–238; Memcon for Oval Office meeting with Chancellor Kohl, 17 May 90.

16. Julij Kwizinskij, *Vor dem Sturm: Erinnerungen eines Diplomaten,* trans. Hilde and Helmut Ettinger (Berlin: Siedler, 1993), p. 16 (the German phrase is "surrealistischen Wust von Ideen").

17. Eduard Shevardnadze, *Moi vybor: v zashchitu demokratii i svobody* (Moscow: Novostii, 1991), p. 247; Anatoly Chernyayev, *Shest' let s Gorbachevym: po dnevikovym zapisyam* (Moscow: Progress Publishers, 1993), p. 348; Zelikow interviews with Tarasenko, Providence, June 1992, and Chernyayev, Moscow, January 1994.

18. These opinions were conveyed to a RAND Corporation group, led by James Thomson, that visited Moscow in mid-May. See the report on the trip drafted by Thomson and John Van Oudenaren and sent by Thomson to various U.S. officials, "Soviet Views on Germany," 24 May 90 (Blackwill forwarded his copy of the report to Scowcroft and Gates).

19. Chernyayev quoted from remarks at a February 1993 conference at Princeton, published in Fred I. Greenstein and William C. Wohlforth, eds., *Retrospective on the End of the Cold War* (Princeton: Center of International Studies, 1994), p. 22. Chernyayev also discussed Mikhail Moiseyev's stance on CFE, an attitude well known to U.S. officials. The Americans did not know about the plans for CFE circumvention, however, and could only reconstruct the circumstances later. The draft CFE treaty would effectively have halved Soviet armored equipment west of the Urals. One measure for avoiding enormous reductions was to begin massive movements of armored equipment from Europe to Asia before the treaty came into effect. These movements were probably approved in 1989 and were well under way on a vast scale by the fall of 1990. Other more flagrant measures for circumventing CFE became a subject of acrimonious East-West negotiations in the fall and winter of 1990–91. On these turning points in political-military decision making and the effects on the Soviet political system as a whole, see Harry Gelman, *The Rise and Fall*

of National Security Decisionmaking in the Former USSR (Santa Monica, Calif.: RAND Corporation, 1992), esp. pp. 37–40. For military anger over Germany, see also the early but perceptive analysis in John Van Oudenaren, *The Role of Shevardnadze and the Ministry of Foreign Affairs in the Making of Soviet Defense and Arms Control Policy* (Santa Monica, Calif.: RAND Corporation, 1990), pp. 55–61; for helpful background, see also Benjamin S. Lambeth, *Is Soviet Defense Policy Becoming Civilianized?* (Santa Monica, Calif.: RAND Corporation, 1990), pp. 35–53.

20. Baker to President Bush, "May Moscow Ministerial," 15 May 90.

21. Secto 7013 (from Moscow), "Memorandum for the President: Moscow, May 17," 18 May 90; Zelikow's notes of debriefing from Rice and Kanter after their return from Moscow.

22. Zelikow's notes of debriefing from Kanter. American CFE negotiators were usually scrupulous about never going beyond what their NATO partners had agreed to offer. That they broke NATO discipline on this occasion is an indication of the exceptional urgency attached to progress in CFE. Baker did warn his NATO colleagues on May 14 that in Moscow he would be "probing Soviet bottom lines" in CFE by discussing U.S. ideas. "Some of these ideas have been discussed within the Alliance in general terms, but I will present these solely as U.S. views that still require Allied agreement." The U.S. suggested revised limits for combat aircraft, a higher allowance for Soviet equipment in Europe under the CFE treaty's "sufficiency rule," a new approach on numbers of inspections, a new position on how to define armored equipment covered by the agreement, and other measures. See State 154365, "CFE: Letter to Allied Foreign Ministers," 14 May 90.

23. Woolsey suggested a new approach to handling follow-on CFE talks that would have affected the Bundeswehr issue, but the idea was not approved. For the details, see privacy channel message from Gates and Kanter to Scowcroft and Blackwill, 15 May 90 (May 16 in Moscow); Wilson through Gordon (Acting) and Blackwill to Scowcroft, "Moscow Ministerial: CFE Personnel Limits," 16 May 90; privacy channel message from Scowcroft to Gates and Kanter, 16 May 1990.

24. Account based on Zelikow's notes of debriefing from Kanter.

25. On May 11 the State Department's European bureau had been asked to draft a checklist of ideas for the "package." Unable to wait for completion of this work, Zoellick went ahead and worked up the nine points offered in Moscow. The European bureau eventually produced a checklist that refined and added to the nine points, but Zoellick decided to stay with the list he had already introduced.

26. For the discussion that follows, see Moscow 17086, "May Ministerial: Counselor Zoellick's Meeting with Soviet MFA Officials Kvitsinskiy and Bondarenko on Germany, Cyprus, and Other Subjects," 23 May 90.

27. In the account that follows, for the Zoellick-Ross drafted presentation on Germany which Baker took into his meeting with Gorbachev, see briefing paper, "One-on-One Points: Gorbachev Meeting," n.d. On the Baker-Gorbachev meeting itself, see Secto 7015 (from Moscow), "Memorandum for the President: Moscow, May 18," 19 May 90. Ross, Shevardnadze, Tarasenko, and interpreters were also present for the one-on-one session. On the Baker discussions in Moscow generally, including details on Lithuania and START, see Beschloss and Talbott, *At the Highest Levels,* pp. 210–213. Beschloss and Talbott erroneously report the exchange over the $20 billion credit request as occurring in the May 15 meeting with Shevardnadze, not in the May 18 meeting with Gorbachev. For Teltschik's reaction to Baker's presentation of the nine-point package, see *329 Tage,* pp. 241–243. Scowcroft phoned Teltschik on May 22 to let him know that there had been no breakthrough on German issues.

28. See Baker to President Bush (for his evening reading), 23 May 90; Seitz through Kimmitt to Baker, "Assuring Gorbachev on NATO and Eastern Europe," 26 May 90 (drafted by EUR/SOV office director Alexander Vershbow). The *Time* interviewers, editor in chief Jason McManus and Strobe Talbott, gave an advance copy of excerpts from the Gorbachev interview to American diplomats on condition that the excerpts not be disclosed to *Time*'s commercial competitors. See Moscow 17109, "Gorbachev *Time* Interview—German Question," 23 May 90. For the Zagladin comment (to Larry Horowitz, an aide to Senator Edward Kennedy), see Foley to Eagleburger, "Kennedy Advisor in Moscow," 29 May 90 (Eagleburger passed this memo on to Baker as "worth a glance").

29. On the meeting, see note from Dobbins (Acting) to Baker, 22 May 90 (passing along a telephone debriefing from Seitz); and Baker to President Bush (for his evening reading), 24 May 90. Meanwhile, a number of issues concerning Berlin were being discussed in the "Bonn Group," which had long served as a vehicle for consultations on Berlin among the three allied powers and the FRG. See Seitz to Zoellick, "The Bonn Group and Its Current Agenda," 12 May 90. Near the end of May a special Berlin working group was created, based in Berlin, to review allied legislation affecting Berlin and to prepare for the smooth termination of Four Power rights. See Bonn 16565, "Berlin Working Group—Agreement on Mandate," 25 May 90.

30. At issue were diverging views of the capacity of the FRG, before unification, to make binding commitments about the nature of its borders after unification. But "from the way German reunification took place, the identity of the subject of international law called the Federal Republic of Germany was clearly not affected in any way . . . All treaties concluded by the Federal Republic of Germany, as well as its membership in international organizations, remain unaffected by the accession of the GDR." Jochen Abr. Frowein, "The Reunification of Germany," *American Journal of International Law,* 86 (1992): 157; and see idem, "Völkerrechtliche Probleme der Einigung Deutschlands," *Europa Archiv,* 45 (1990): 234. Even if the law of state succession applied to the controversy (which it did not, since such rules applied only to disposition of legal obligations incurred by the former GDR), this body of international law has traditionally viewed border treaties as commitments that "run with the land" and thereby bind the successor state. To be sure, the Ostpolitik treaties had qualified the FRG's legal capacity, reserving the final disposition of borders until a "peace treaty" settled the ultimate nature of Germany in the manner envisioned in Potsdam and other postwar conventions. But since the Two Plus Four settlement would include Four Power blessing of a final border arrangement, thereby removing any qualification on the FRG's capacity to affirm such commitments, the old qualifications would become moot. The West German government at first mangled this straightforward legal analysis by using claims of incapacity in order to avoid having to negotiate and initial, or sign, a treaty with Poland before unification was complete. But Bonn could have climbed out of the box by claiming that, if unification occurred under article 23, the border with Poland was already settled by the 1970 Treaty of Warsaw and would be doubly settled by signing the Two Plus Four agreement. In Bonn as in Washington, deferring to flawed legal analysis made an already difficult policy problem even harder. For more on the legal arguments in Western capitals, see, e.g., Young to Zoellick and Seitz, "Legal Constraints on Timing of Settlement," 27 Apr 90; London 9466, "Consultations on Legal Issues Pertaining to German Unification," 16 May 90; Young to Zoellick and Seitz, "Legal Analysis of British and French Comments on U.S. Settlement Options Paper," 14 May 90.

31. For details on the internal U.S. debate of this misconceived "sequencing" issue, which could have had such serious consequences if the European bureau had not persuaded Zoellick to adopt a sensible position, see Young to Zoellick, "Position Paper on

Sequencing of German Unification and Settlement," 25 May 90 (sent without EUR clearance); and attached draft paper (May 29), "U.S. One Plus Three Paper on Sequencing/Simultaneity of German Unification and Settlement"; May 17 L draft of "A Settlement on Germany" (circulated by L/EUR, Koblitz to other State offices on May 17); Seitz (actually signed out by Dobbins) to Zoellick, "L's Draft for 'A Settlement on Germany,'" 29 May 90 (sent without L's clearance). Zoellick's concurrence with the EUR objections is noted on the copy of the memo in his files.

Allied lawyers met again in Paris on May 31. At this meeting Young listed options for a solution without declaring a preference. Apparently unaware of the known preferences of the president and his secretary of state on the question when Four Power rights should be abandoned, Young presented his office's proposal, which would condition a final Two Plus Four settlement on later ratification of the German-Polish treaty. The FRG lawyers immediately rejected this approach since, among other problems, it would make termination of Four Power rights dependent on the actions of Poland. The French representative, deputy legal adviser Edwige Belliard, continued to insist that a Two Plus Four settlement could take place only after unification so that it could incorporate commitments made by the unified German state. See Paris 16828, "Legal Experts Meeting on German Unification, Paris, May 31, 1990," 6 Jun 90.

32. Bonn's CFE ambassador Rüdiger Hartmann informed his American counterpart, Woolsey, of Genscher's plan on May 23. Woolsey liked the idea, seeing it as another opportunity to reopen the Ottawa manpower limits, which he knew were so objectionable to the Pentagon. See USVienna 1494, "CFE: Genscher Initiative on Personnel," 24 May 90.

33. Stoltenberg and Klaus Naumann, then the Defense Ministry's head of policy planning, discussed their concerns with U.S. officials, including Scowcroft, during a visit to Washington on May 1. Naumann told Blackwill that the Federal Security Council had decided that the FRG would say nothing to Moscow committing Germany to manpower ceilings in the central region, especially without solid comparable ceilings on Soviet manpower. See Zelikow through Blackwill and Kanter to General Scowcroft, "Your Meeting with FRG Minister of Defense Gerhard Stoltenberg on May 1," 30 Apr 90.

34. The arguments against the Genscher plan were laid out in a paper by Zelikow, "Four Options to Unblock the CFE I Personnel Issue," 24 May 90; and Kanter and Blackwill to Scowcroft, "Your May 25 Meeting on Arms Control," 24 May 90. The account of Scowcroft's May 25 meeting is based on Zelikow's notes of the debriefing he received at the time.

35. Teltschik, *329 Tage,* pp. 243–244.

36. See the informative interview "Nicht den Buchhaltern überlassen," *Der Spiegel,* May 14, 1990, pp. 28–30 (the quote about the Soviets ultimately going along is on p. 30); for the opinions of the interviewer (Kiessler) and Elbe, see *Ein runder Tisch mit scharfen Ecken,* pp. 135–136.

37. For the coordination with Zoellick, see Kiessler and Elbe, *Ein runder Tisch mit scharfen Ecken,* p. 150; on the Geneva talks, see ibid., pp. 145–147; Claus Gennrich, "Auch die Sowjetunion hält Eile bei der Vereinigung der beide deutsche Staaten für geboren," *Frankfurter Allgemeine Zeitung,* May 25, 1990, p. 2; and the debriefings given to Kohl, reported in Teltschik, *329 Tage,* p. 249, and to Baker, reported in Baker to President Bush (for his evening reading), 25 May 90.

38. Baker to President Bush (for his evening reading), 25 May 90. On May 30 Kastrup went to Moscow for follow-up discussions with Kvitsinsky, but at that time the main action had shifted to the U.S.-Soviet summit in Washington.

39. In the account that follows, for Mitterrand's report to Bush, see the message sent from the Elysée Palace to the White House through special channels, 22 May 90; letter from Mitterrand to Bush, delivered on 30 May 90; and Paris 15967, "Mitterrand's Moscow Meetings with Gorbachev on May 25," 28 May 90. On reports of the Canadian visit to Moscow, see Seitz to Baker, "Shevardnadze's Talk with Foreign Minister Clark," May 30, 1990. Shevardnadze referred to Gorbachev's *Time* interview in calling once again for rapid creation of totally new all-European structures to help solve the problems associated with the "building of German unity." He stressed the need for a consensus solution; see Eduard Shevardnadze, "Europe: A Generation's Mission," *Izvestiya,* May 30, 1990, p. 5. On the Foreign Ministry proposal, which Teltschik found encouraging, see *329 Tage,* p. 247. As to the prediction of the State Department's Soviet experts, Attali, on Mitterrand's behalf, conveyed an identically bleak assessment of the Moscow meetings to Teltschik in Bonn; see Teltschik, *329 Tage,* pp. 247–248, 250.

40. Central Committee staff to members of the Politburo, "O svazi otnosheniyakh c vostochnym-evropa," May 1990, in Center for the Storage of Contemporary Documentation (TsKhSD), Moscow.

41. See Don Oberdorfer, *The Turn: From the Cold War to a New Era, The United States and the Soviet Union, 1983–1990* (New York: Simon and Schuster, 1991), p. 404 (Bush quote is from Oberdorfer interview with Rice).

42. We have not located any formal memcon for the meeting with Gorbachev in the Cabinet Room on May 29. Rice was present at the meeting. The quotations are from the briefing paper for the meeting drafted by Zoellick and read carefully by Bush (he checked off or underscored each point as he went through the paper). The account is also based on Zoellick's annotations of his paper showing his planned presentation, and on Rice's recollection of the meeting. For the briefing paper, see Scowcroft to President Bush, "Briefing on Germany—The Future of Europe," 27 May 90; copy of "German Unification—Two Plus Four Process," 25 May 90 in Zoellick's files. Bush was given an analytical paper prepared by the CIA, "Soviet Policy on German Unification," which he also marked up. The Scowcroft quotation is from a separate briefing paper, part of the "real" briefing book for the summit meeting; see Scowcroft to President Bush, "Your Meeting with Gorbachev," n.d. (drafted by Rice). This and other memos fully described the serious political situation confronting Gorbachev at home in Moscow.

43. The Bonn-Washington exchanges over German troop limits are detailed in Teltschik, *329 Tage,* pp. 249–253; the account dovetails with Zelikow's notes at the time of debriefings about the call to Gates and Blackwill's discussion with the West German Defense Ministry; also with Bonn 17082, "German Policy on Bundeswehr Limits in CFE Context," 31 May 90; and Memcon for President Bush's telephone conversation with Chancellor Kohl, 30 May 90 (Hutchings was note taker). In Washington later on May 30 Arnold Kanter chaired an interagency meeting reviewing more formal U.S. analyses of options for limiting German troops. The group agreed that Washington should wait for a proposal from the Germans and not raise the topic with Gorbachev unless the Soviets presented a proposal of their own. The only substantive ideas that commanded agreement were so lackluster that the NSC staff told Scowcroft they were not worth any further discussion. See Wilson through Kanter and Blackwill to Scowcroft, "CFE—Bundeswehr Personnel Limits," 31 May 90.

44. Memcon for telephone conversation with Chancellor Kohl, 30 May 90 (Hutchings was note taker).

45. Memcon for telephone conversation with Prime Minister Mulroney, 30 May 90

(Basora was note taker). Bush had also spoken on the phone with Mulroney for a partial debriefing on the Canadian-Soviet talks on May 29, and the president had already described his attitudes to Mulroney in an earlier conversation on May 24.

46. See Oberdorfer, *The Turn*, pp. 414–415; Beschloss and Talbott, *At the Highest Levels*, pp. 217–218 (both sources are accurate, based on interviews with participants).

47. We have been unable to locate a memcon for this meeting in the American archives, but part of the Soviet memcon is quoted in Chernyayev, *Shest' let s Gorbachevym*, p. 348. Other details in the discussion that follows are drawn from Zelikow's interviews with participants at the meeting (Chernyayev, Blackwill, and Zoellick); Zoellick's and Blackwill's handwritten notes; Valentin Falin, *Politische Erinnerungen*, trans. Heddy Pross-Weerth (Munich: Droemer Knaur, 1993), pp. 492–493; Beschloss and Talbott, *At the Highest Levels*, pp. 219–220 (the Open Skies discussion they mention actually took place in a different meeting); and Oberdorfer, *The Turn*, pp. 417–418. Participants on the American side in this May 31 meeting were Bush, Baker, Sununu, Scowcroft, Gates, Zoellick, Blackwill, and an interpreter. (It is possible that Seitz or Ambassador Matlock may also have been present.) Gorbachev was accompanied by Shevardnadze, Ambassador Bessmertnykh (who had recently replaced Dubinin), Chernyayev, Akhromeyev, Falin, Dobrynin, and possibly one or two other officials, as well as an interpreter.

48. Bush stayed close to a prepared presentation titled "The Future of Europe: Germany, NATO, CFE, and CSCE." His talking points were drafted by Ross and Rice, then edited and refined by Blackwill, Zoellick, and Zelikow.

49. The language appears in "Principle I" of the "Principles Guiding Relations between Participating States" in "Basket I" of the Helsinki Final Act of 1975, dealing with security questions: "They [the participating states] also have the right to belong or not to belong to international organizations, to be or not to be a party to bilateral or multilateral treaties including the right to be or not to be a party to treaties of alliance; they also have the right to neutrality." Within the American government Zoellick had seized on this principle months earlier as a way to strengthen the West's position, since the CSCE document, though not legally binding on signatories, was one of the few bodies of principles clearly agreed to by both sides.

50. Rice interview with Chernyayev, Moscow, June 1994.

51. The conversation was recorded by CNN, with Gorbachev and the congressmen apparently unaware that the TV cameras were broadcasting their conversation live to the world—and to Bush, who was watching in the Oval Office. Oberdorfer, *The Turn*, pp. 418–419; Beschloss and Talbott, *At the Highest Levels*, pp. 221–222.

52. The following account is drawn from Memcon for telephone conversation with Chancellor Kohl, 1 Jun 90 (Hutchings was note taker).

53. Beschloss and Talbott, *At the Highest Levels*, p. 224; the account in the text is also based on Oberdorfer, *The Turn*, pp. 418–423; and, of course, on Rice's recollection of the events.

54. The account that follows is based on authors' recollections; Oberdorfer, *The Turn*, pp. 423–429; Beschloss and Talbott, *At the Highest Levels*, pp. 224–227; "News Conference of President Bush and President Mikhail Gorbachev of the Soviet Union," June 3, 1990, in *Public Papers of the Presidents: George Bush, 1990*, bk. 1 (Washington, D.C.: Government Printing Office, 1990), p. 874.

55. See Teltschik, *329 Tage*, pp. 255–258; Memcon of telephone conversations with Chancellor Kohl and Prime Minister Thatcher, 3 Jun 90 (Hutchings was note taker); Memcon for telephone conversation with President Mitterrand, 5 Jun 90 (Basora was note taker); message from President Bush to Chancellor Kohl, sent through special channels,

4 Jun 90; message from President Bush to Prime Minister Thatcher, sent through special channels, 4 Jun 90. Bush told both Kohl and Thatcher about the private discussions of credits and economic aid. A further indication of the significance West German officials attached to the Washington summit is the extensive treatment given to this meeting in Kiessler and Elbe, *Ein runder Tisch mit scharfen Ecken,* pp. 147–152.

56. Zelikow interview with Chernyayev, Moscow, January 1994.

57. Hannes Adomeit, "Gorbachev, German Unification, and the Collapse of Empire," *Post-Soviet Affairs,* 10 (August–September 1994): 197, 229 n. 28.

58. The account that follows is based on Zelikow interview with Tarasenko, Providence, June 1993; Memcon for meeting between Baker and Shevardnadze, Soviet Residence in Copenhagen, 5 Jun 90. The only others present were Ross, Tarasenko, and the two interpreters.

59. It is hard to trace where Shevardnadze might have gained the impression that Genscher was willing to accept such a low troop limit. Genscher and Shevardnadze had discussed German troop limits in Geneva on May 23. According to Elbe, Shevardnadze then proposed a number between 250,000 and 300,000 (Kiessler and Elbe, *Ein runder Tisch mit scharfen Ecken,* p. 146), but Shevardnadze two weeks later proposed to Baker the lower figure of 200,000 to 250,000. Elbe does not mention whether his side had offered any number. Teltschik has Genscher urging a ceiling of 350,000 as he debriefed Kohl on May 28. On May 29 Stoltenberg stood by the figure of 400,000 (including 30,000 naval personnel), and Kohl refused to resolve the dispute at that time. As late as June 5 Stoltenberg was still maintaining a figure between 380,000 and 420,000, while Kohl had not yet revealed his hand; see Teltschik, *329 Tage,* pp. 249–251, 258. Two other possible sources of Soviet misinformation were Kastrup, who had visited Moscow at the end of May, and West German CFE ambassador Rüdiger Hartmann. We have no evidence on what these diplomats were saying to the Soviets about the troop limits issue at the end of May.

60. See State 190169, "Secretary's Meeting with GDR Foreign Minister, June 5, 1990," 12 Jun 90.

8. The Final Offer

1. See Zelikow to Scowcroft, "The President's Meeting and Dinner with Chancellor Kohl on June 8," 7 Jun 90.

2. Ibid. See also USVienna 1566, "CFE: GDR Rep on Germany, NATO, and Bundeswehr Personnel Limits," 2 Jun 90. For more insights into the internal tensions within the West German government over the German troop limits question and the problem of the Soviet Union, see USVienna 1627, "CFE: Visiting FRG Official on the Germans, the Soviets, and CFE," 9 Jun 90.

3. Zelikow interview with Scowcroft, Washington, D.C., January 1994.

4. For the account that follows, see Teltschik, *329 Tage,* p. 262; Memcon for President Bush's meeting and dinner with Chancellor Kohl, 8 Jun 90.

5. On this Warsaw Pact summit, see Julij A. Kwizinskij, *Vor dem Sturm: Erinnerungen eines Diplomaten,* trans. Hilde and Helmut Ettinger (Berlin: Siedler, 1993), pp. 33–36. East German prime minister de Maizière, who was present at the June 6 meeting in Moscow, debriefed Seiters, Schäuble, and Teltschik on June 8; see Horst Teltschik, *329 Tage: Innenansichten der Einigung* (Berlin: Siedler, 1991), p. 261.

6. See, e.g., "Alle werden sehen: Es geht," *Der Spiegel,* June 11, 1990, pp. 18–22.

7. See, e.g., Emnid poll results published in *Der Spiegel,* May 28, 1990, pp. 39, 42, and interview with Lafontaine in the same issue, pp. 26–29.

8. For good analyses of these developments, along with insight into the important choices involved in how the ruling coalition sought to structure the election procedures, see Bonn 18417, "German Unification: Momentum Building Fast for All-German Elections This Year," 13 Jun 90; and Bonn 19136, "East and West CDU Want Unification in December Immediately after FRG/GDR Parallel Elections," 20 Jun 90.

9. Since May the Kohl government had expected first to issue joint declarations from the West and East German parliaments, following the declarations with confirmation of intentions by each government. Then—immmediately *after* unification—Germany would definitively settle the border question with a binding treaty. The joint parliamentary declaration was passed, as promised, on June 21. Hans Viktor Böttcher, ed., *Materialen zu Deutschlandfragen: Politiker und Wissenschaftler nehmen Stellung, 1989–91* (Bonn: Kultur-stiftung der deutschen Vertriebenen, 1991), pp. 75–76. Although the substance of a Polish-German agreement was still being debated, by early June FRG officials believed that the Poles would be satisfied just to see the contents of the treaty agreed to before unification and were no longer demanding that the treaty itself be concluded or initialed before unification occurred. See Bonn 17862, "Two-Plus-Four Talks: Polish Border Issue," 8 Jun 90; Seitz to Zoellick, "Nonborder Polish Issues at Two-plus-Four Talks," 16 Jun 90; and Bonn 19525, "June 21 Joint Bundestag/Volkskammer Declaration on the Polish Border," 22 Jun 90. But see also Warsaw 9216, "Polish Approach to Two-Plus-Four Talks," 13 Jun 90. On the dilemmas facing Bonn in deciding whether and how to amend the citizenship provisions of the Basic Law (article 116), see CIA, "German Unification and the Politics of Article 116," EUR M 90–20153, 15 Jun 90; draft memo from L (Young) to Zoellick and Seitz, "FRG Nationalities Law and the Polish-German Treaty," 15 Jun 90. For more on the continuing and somewhat surreal legal arguments about the issue of "sequencing," see L-prepared Two Plus Four paper, "Sequencing of Unification and Settlement," 13 Jun 90; Young to Zoellick and Seitz, "Review of UK Compromise Sequencing Outline," 14 Jun 90. But see George to Zoellick, "Sequencing" (n.d., apparently June 14 or 15, urging that "termination of Four Power rights regarding borders will not be effective until a Polish-German treaty is ratified").

10. Seitz to Zoellick, untitled report with attached papers, 11 Jun 90. Seitz led the U.S. delegation at this meeting.

11. The Americans understood that, if they agreed to such limits on German political behavior, the Four Powers would in effect become legal guarantors of Germany's behavior, giving the Four Powers incalculable leverage over future German security decisions and opportunities for mischief in German domestic politics.

12. The U.S. delegation included Seitz and Rice from the NSC staff. The Soviet team was led by Alexander Bondarenko and the East Germans by Hans-Jürgen Misselwitz. The other allied faces were familiar: Weston from London, Dufourcq from Paris, and Kastrup from Bonn. See draft State Department cable, "June 9 Two-Plus-Four Officials' Meeting: Detailed Report of Discussions," 12 Jun 90; Seitz to Zoellick, 11 Jun 90; EmbBerlin 3684, "June 9 Two-Plus-Four Officials Meeting: Points for Use in Briefing NAC," 11 Jun 90.

13. The account that follows is based on Memcons from Cabinet Room meeting and luncheon meeting with Prime Minister de Maizière, 11 Jun 90. De Maizière was not accompanied by Meckel or by any of Meckel's key advisers. Bush sent messages to Kohl, Mitterrand, and Thatcher reporting on this meeting, as a vehicle for reiterating U.S. preferences for a narrow mandate for the Two Plus Four, no singularization of Germany, and no parallel treatment of foreign troops stationed in Germany. Bush wanted the others

to lean on the East Germans, too. Messages sent through special channels, 12 Jun 90. The message to Kohl is accurately described in Teltschik, *329 Tage,* p. 274. For more on De Maizière's notion of his GDR government as a bridge to the USSR, see "De Maizière schlägt gemeinsame Tagungen von NATO und Warschauer Pakt vor," *Frankfurter Allgemeine Zeitung,* May 30, 1990, p. 2. A good review of GDR foreign policy during the spring and summer of 1990 is Hans Misselwitz, "Diplomacy of German Unity: GDR Views," unpublished paper presented to the American Institute for Contemporary German Studies, June 1991. On Meckel's stance at Copenhagen, and the allied reaction, see also Ulrich Albrecht, *Die Abwicklung der DDR: die 2 | 4 Verhandlungen, ein Insider bericht* (Opladen: Westdeutscher Verlag, 1992), p. 80; and on the West Germans' dismay with Meckel's stance in the Two Plus Four, see Teltschik, *329 Tage,* p. 285. For Soviet coverage of de Maizière's meeting with Gorbachev, see "Vstrechi M. S. Gorbacheva," *Vestnik,* July 15, 1990, p. 18.

14. State 200531, "Secretary Baker's Meeting with Prime Minister Thatcher, June 8 at Turnberry, Scotland," 21 Jun 90.

15. The account that follows is based on Margaret Thatcher, *The Downing Street Years* (New York: HarperCollins, 1993), pp. 804–807; also from the Soviet memcon, "Zapis besedy M. S. Gorbacheva s premer-ministrom Velikobritaniya M. Tetcher," 8 Jun 1990, made available by Alexandra Bezymenskaya; message from Prime Minister Thatcher to President Bush (sent through special channels), 11 Jun 90; detailed debriefing from the original British reporting cable given, on instructions, to Zelikow on June 12; and debriefing given to Teltschik, described in *329 Tage,* p. 266. See also the message from Prime Minister Thatcher to President Bush (sent through special channels), 17 Jun 90 (replying to Bush's message on the de Maizière meeting). For more on U.S. consultations with the French government during this period, see Basora to File, "Attali/Scowcroft Meeting Today," 15 Jun 90. Attali wanted more pressure put on Bonn to meet Polish demands. Scowcroft was unsympathetic.

16. Brest had been Polish for several centuries before it was absorbed into the Russian Empire during the 1795 partition of Poland between Russia, Prussia, and Austria. It became Polish again between 1919 and 1939, when it went back to the Russians in another German-Russian deal. Teltschik at the Chancellery was worried about the effect on the Poles of a German-Russian meeting at this site, and Genscher personally assured the Polish foreign minister that no offense was intended by the choice of a city that meant so much to Shevardnadze. On this issue and the talks themselves, see Richard Kiessler and Frank Elbe, *Ein runder Tisch mit scharfen Ecken: Der diplomatische Weg zur deutschen Einheit* (Baden-Baden: Nomos, 1993), pp. 154–157; Teltschik, *329 Tage,* pp. 267–268, 272–274; Bonn 18254, "Genscher-Shevardnadze Discussions in Brest," 12 Jun 90; USNATO 3465, "FRG's Kastrup Briefs the NAC June 13 on Genscher-Shevardnadze Meeting in Brest," 14 Jun 90.

17. See Teltschik, *329 Tage,* p. 265; question and answer session with Gorbachev at the Supreme Soviet, broadcast live on Moscow Television Service, June 12, 1990, and Gorbachev's prepared address to the Supreme Soviet, both in *FBIS-SOV* 90–114, June 13, 1990, pp. 45, 46–47, 53. Beschloss and Talbott characterize Gorbachev's June 12 remarks as a "cave-in" made to look "principled and tough." They then interpret a routine Bush comment on these remarks as his reaction to Gorbachev's "playing the good loser." Michael Beschloss and Strobe Talbott, *At the Highest Levels: The Inside Story of the End of the Cold War* (Boston: Little, Brown, 1992), p. 231. But a closer study of what Gorbachev said reveals no significant departures from the past Soviet stance, except in the tone of his exchange during the question and answer session. The notion that East Germany might remain an "associate member" of the Warsaw Pact is not notably different from the earlier idea of a united Germany's keeping membership in both alliances. At this time, as we

know from Thatcher's account, Gorbachev was also still toying with ways to dilute Germany's membership in NATO.

18. Teltschik, *329 Tage,* pp. 275–276.

19. The account that follows is based on Kiessler and Elbe, *Ein runder Tisch mit scharfen Ecken,* pp. 157–159; Zelikow interview with Tarasenko, Providence, June 1993; Kastrup's debriefing to Teltschik, in *329 Tage,* pp. 276–278; Kastrup's debriefing to NATO, in USNATO 3565, "FRG Political Director Briefs the NAC June 19 on Genscher-Shevardnadze Meeting in Muenster," 19 Jun 90; and the official Soviet debriefing provided to the Americans and reported in State 209211, "Soviet Nonpaper on Shevardnadze-Genscher Meeting in Münster," 27 Jun 90. Kastrup did not mention the Elbe-Tarasenko conversation to anyone. Curiously, Elizabeth Pond, citing anonymous West German Foreign Ministry sources, has written that Tarasenko's "non-paper" in Münster "foreshadowed the final deal. United Germany could stay in the NATO alliance; NATO structures could not extend to the former GDR so long as Soviet troops remained there, but that territory would nonetheless fall under the guarantee of the Western alliance." Elizabeth Pond, *Beyond the Wall: Germany's Road to Unification* (Washington, D.C.: Brookings Institution, 1993), p. 217. Her sources exaggerated. Elbe does not say that the Soviets went so far, Tarasenko denies it, and abundant evidence about Genscher's and Shevardnadze's subsequent behavior contradicts the story.

20. See EUR/CE (Goodman) to various working-level officials in the State Department, "Negotiating History of Two-plus-Four," 21 Sept 90, pp. 6–7. On the U.S. draft outline, see Zoellick's markup of "A Basic Outline for Elements of a Final Settlement," passed to Zelikow on June 18; Foulon (Zoellick's staffer) to Zoellick, "Draft Settlement Outlines," 13 Jun 90.

21. State 222614, "The Secretary's June 22 Meeting with GDR Premier de Maizière," 10 Jul 90.

22. The account that follows is based on Kwizinskij, *Vor dem Sturm,* pp. 40–46 (including the text of the Soviet draft treaty); Kiessler and Elbe, *Ein runder Tisch mit scharfen Ecken,* pp. 160–163; State 248717, "June 22 Two-Plus-Four Ministerial in Berlin: Account," 28 Jul 90; Blackwill's handwritten notes from the ministerial meeting; text of Shevardnadze's intervention distributed by Soviet delegation; and Secto 10012 (from Baker's aircraft), "Briefing Points on June 22 Two-Plus-Four Ministerial for Use at NATO Permrep Meeting on Jun 25," 23 Jun 90. For Teltschik's reactions to the ministerial, see *329 Tage,* pp. 284–286.

23. Kwizinskij, *Vor dem Sturm,* pp. 39–40.

24. On the press conference, see Department of State, "Press Conference Following Berlin Two-Plus-Four Ministerial," East Berlin, 22 Jun 90. For Elbe's thoughts, see Kiessler and Elbe, *Ein runder Tisch mit scharfen Ecken,* p. 162. Zoellick, in subsequent background briefings, informed American reporters quite fully about the positions presented by all sides at the meeting. Zoellick told them: "The train to German unification is leaving the station—it's well on the track and fundamentally the Soviets are going to have to face the choice of whether they want to get on the train or isolate themselves." He further implied, refusing to elaborate, that Shevardnadze's proposal could have been aimed at a Soviet domestic audience. See Department of State, "Background Briefing by Senior State Department Officials," 22 Jun 90. For typical West German press reactions, see Christoph Bertram, "Stagnieren unter Zeitdruck," *Die Zeit,* June 29, 1990, p. 6; "Schewardnadse plädiert für 'Übergangsfristen' nach der Einheit," *Frankfurter Allgemeine Zeitung,* June 23, 1990, p. 1.

25. The following account is based on Memcon for meeting with Foreign Minister

Shevardnadze, 22 Jun 90, Soviet Residence, Berlin (prepared by Ross). As he did on the margins of Shevardnadze's meeting with Genscher in Münster, Tarasenko assured Ross, like Elbe, not to take Shevardnadze's public statements at face value. Some quotation marks in the text are applied to passages that appear in the memcon to have been taken down practically verbatim. The material presented as direct quotations from Baker and Shevardnadze is from Beschloss and Talbott, *At the Highest Levels*, p. 233; these are not actual quotations taken down at the time, but are quotations from another source—apparently Ross—who later told reporters what had been said, with some simplification and amplification.

During this meeting there was a brief but interesting discussion of Boris Yeltsin. Baker left the room briefly, and Ross used the lull to suggest that Shevardnadze and Gorbachev should try to work closely with Yeltsin and secure his cooperation in their policy initiatives. Baker returned during this exchange and added his support for this suggestion. Shevardnadze's reaction was positive but noncommittal.

26. The article must be the one by Vladimir Ostrovskiy, "The Only Free Cheese Is in a Mousetrap," *Rabochaya tribuna*, June 12, 1990, pp. 1, 3, in *FBIS-SOV* 90–115, June 14, 1990, pp. 5–7. It presented the views of Oleg Baklanov, a party secretary on the CPSU Central Committee who had held responsibility for defense industry matters, was an adviser to Gorbachev, and was named by Gorbachev in 1991 to head a revived Defense Council, the top national security decision-making body of the state. Gorbachev came to regret the elevation of this conservative, since Baklanov became a primary plotter of the attempted August 1991 coup against the Soviet president. See Harry Gelman, *The Rise and Fall of National Security Decisionmaking in the Former USSR* (Santa Monica, Calif.: RAND Corporation, 1992), pp. viii–ix.

27. Kwizinskij, *Vor dem Sturm*, p. 47.

28. Department of State, "Background Briefing by Senior Administration Official," Berlin Tegel Airport en route to Shannon, Ireland, 23 Jun 90.

29. Wörner and Scowcroft, joined by Zelikow and Wörner's staffer James Cunningham, had discussed summit plans over dinner on May 6. The next morning Wörner met with Bush at the White House. See Memcon for meeting with Manfred Wörner, Oval Office, 7 May 90. In this meeting Bush even wondered whether NATO, as a symbolic gesture, should change its name.

30. On the state of NATO nuclear discussions in early May, see "Agreed Minute" from meeting of NATO Nuclear Planning Group, Kananaskis, Canada, 9–10 May 90; Seitz through Kimmitt and Bartholomew to Baker, "TASM, SNF Negotiations, Germany, and Unification," 14 May 90. The capable U.S. chairman of the high-level group for nuclear defense planning was assistant secretary of defense Stephen Hadley. On the relatively modest State Department agenda for the NATO summit, hoping to shield the alliance from any new controversy, see Dobbins (Acting) and Clarke (assistant secretary of state for political-military affairs) through Kimmitt and Bartholomew to Baker, "Gameplan for Spring NATO Meetings and NATO Summit," 22 May 90.

31. On discussion of ideas for the CSCE, see speech by Genscher, "The Future of a European Germany," to the American Society of Newspaper Editors, Washington, D.C., 6 Apr 90; State 158722, "CSCE: Message from the Secretary," 17 May 90 (sent to all CSCE posts; updated an April 24 version for NATO allies with a review of developments and U.S. policy on Germany); message from Foreign Secretary Hurd to Secretary Baker, 1 May 90; Dobbins to Zoellick, "CSCE: Update on Preparations for Copenhagen Meeting," 4 May 90.

32. See Dobbins to Zoellick, "U.S./FRG Perspectives on CSCE at NATO," 19 May 90;

and attached paper circulated by the German NATO delegation, "CSCE-Summit Working Group," 16 May 90. The stimulus to expand the CSCE's elaboration of common political principles to include market economics and election guidelines had come from the United States in 1989. As a result, two CSCE meetings were ultimately scheduled to develop such principles. The Bonn CSCE meeting on economic cooperation in Europe, held in March 1990, had been quite successful in articulating a surprisingly broad area of agreement on market principles for the economic organization of society. The Copenhagen meeting on election guidelines was scheduled for June. See Vojtech Mastny, ed., *The Helsinki Process and the Reintegration of Europe, 1986–1991: Analysis and Documentation* (New York: New York University Press, 1992), pp. 187–257; John Fry, *The Helsinki Process: Negotiating Security and Cooperation in Europe* (Washington, D.C.: National Defense University Press, 1993), pp. 143–156.

33. For a definitive portrait of how Soviet thinking on CSCE had evolved, see Eduard Shevardnadze, "Europe: A Generation's Mission," *Izvestiya,* May 30, 1990, p. 5.

34. See Dobbins (Acting) through Kimmitt and Bartholomew to Baker, "CSCE: 'Institutionalization' and the U.S.-Soviet and NATO Summits," 22 May 90; Seitz to Zoellick, "Results of May 25 PCC on CSCE," 2 Jun 90. For development of CSCE political norms on respect for fundamental freedoms and the rule of law, see Baker speech, "CSCE: The Conscience of the Continent," Copenhagen, 6 Jun 90; Seitz through Kimmitt to Baker, "Results of the CSCE Copenhagen Meeting," 2 Jul 90. The American delegation to Copenhagen was headed by Ambassador Max Kampelman.

35. See USNATO 3203, "Letter to Secretary Baker from SYG Wörner Concerning the Turnberry Ministerial and the London Summit," 30 May 90; USNATO 3188, "London Summit Declaration: Wörner's Outline," 30 May 90; USNATO 3211, "The London NATO Summit and Next Steps in Conducting the Alliance's Review of Military Strategy," 31 May 90.

36. Zelikow had first suggested inviting Warsaw Pact countries to establish diplomatic liaison missions to Rice, who encouraged it, and to Blackwill, who was skeptical. Zelikow then raised the idea in an April 16 discussion with Scowcroft. Rice again supported it. By mid-May Blackwill was persuaded that the liaison missions idea could become the foundation for establishing a new set of relationships between NATO allies and the individual states of the Warsaw Pact (though not between NATO and the doomed pact itself), while also addressing the desires of East European states to begin developing closer ties to NATO.

The initial Blackwill-Zelikow list of initiatives had also included a proposal that formal ties be established between NATO and the European Community, linking the North Atlantic Council and European Political Committee processes as well as NATO's secretary general and the European Commission's president in a network of regular contacts. But this idea, with its focus on relations within Western Europe, detracted from the West-East emphasis of the summit declaration, and so it was not pursued. The idea has some small historical interest, however, because it reflected a judgment that NATO should seek to build some sort of bridge to the European Community. After Blackwill's departure from the NSC staff in July 1990, Zelikow (later with Blackwill's successor, David Gompert) continued to support new NATO-EC linkages during the debate over European security architecture and the role of the Western European Union in late 1990 and 1991.

37. NATO defense authorities were already moving to consider more use of multinational units, in part because the Belgians and the Dutch would no longer be fielding enough troops to make up a national corps. Zelikow thought that multinational corps would depart from the "occupation" look and make an American military presence in Germany sustainable for the long haul as the Germans were given more authority over the forces deployed on their soil. Blackwill and Zelikow were encouraged by reports of

praise for a multinational corps from the West German Chancellery. See Bonn 14094, "More on the Future of the Bundeswehr and NVA," 4 May 90. Other NSC staffers were more cautious, as was the Defense Department. On June 7 Scowcroft asked NATO Supreme Allied Commander for Europe (SACEUR) General John Galvin what he thought of the multinational corps concept. Galvin voiced his strong support. He had done the homework and supported an ambitious approach to the multinational corps concept. Account based on Zelikow's notes from the meeting and subsequent discussion with General Galvin.

38. The approach was based on a model that would set a common cap on the forces any country could maintain within a particular subregion of Europe (using the CFE demarcation of subzones). In early May Zelikow prepared a paper analyzing CFE II arms control options, which included an option for deep cuts using such national ceilings. The outcome was that net Soviet advantages allowed under CFE I would be substantially reduced. U.S., British, French, and German forces alone would be adequate to outnumber all Soviet forces in the European portion of the USSR. The Soviet military advantage against its Eastern European neighbors would also be greatly reduced. See, e.g., Annex A, "Options" (especially options 4 and 5), to the longer paper at Tab 2 attached to Blackwill and Kanter to Gates, "Your Meeting of the European Strategy Steering Group on June 18," 15 Jun 90.

39. On the CSCE parliament idea, Shevardnadze's interest in the Council of Europe was reported in Strasbourg 61, "Shevardnadze on the Council of Europe (COE)," 14 Mar 90. The idea of greater use of the Council of Europe in bridging East-West differences was being actively promoted by the Council's Secretary General, Catherine Lalumière. See also London 4473, "WEU SYG Van Eekelen on German Unification, NATO, and the CSCE," 6 Mar 90. Blackwill suggested the idea of a CSCE parliament to Scowcroft on April 16. Zelikow recommended attaching Blackwill's idea to the existing COE parliamentary assembly. Later, in his May 30 *Izvestiya* article, Shevardnadze suggested a parliamentary assembly of Europe in terms almost identical to the NSC staff's budding proposal.

40. See "Possible Presidential Initiatives to Announce Publicly at the NATO Summit," 23 May 90, and "London Declaration on a Transformed North Atlantic Alliance," passed informally to Scowcroft and Gates, also attached to Blackwill and Kanter to Gates, "Your Meeting of the European Strategy Steering Group on Monday, June 4," 2 Jun 90. The description of this submission in Beschloss and Talbott, *At the Highest Levels*, pp. 234–235, is inaccurate.

41. The account that follows is based on Zelikow's notes from European Strategy Steering Group meeting, 4 Jun 90. See also Blackwill and Kanter to Gates, "Your Meeting of the European Strategy Steering Group on Monday, June 4," 2 Jun 90.

42. See Wilson through Kanter and Blackwill to Scowcroft, "CFE—Bundeswehr Personnel Limits," 31 May 90. The State Department paper was titled "Dealing with Soviet Desires for German Limits," and attached as Tab 6 in Blackwill and Kanter's June 2 memo to Gates, cited earlier. Kanter agreed that any proposal must be "made in Germany" but backed the kind of proposed limits officials in his working group were prepared to support. Blackwill and Zelikow objected to those ideas on substance, origin (American rather than German), and timing (too soon).

43. Bonn 17082, "German Policy on Bundeswehr Limits in CFE Context," 31 May 1990.

44. See "Warsaw Pact States' Declaration," *Pravda*, June 8, 1990, p. 1A, in *FBIS-SOV* 90–111, June 8, 1990, pp. 10–11; Reuters dispatch from Bonn, "Hungarian Premier Says Warsaw Pact Should Be Dissolved," June 16, 1990 (reporting on an interview for the West German newspaper *Welt am Sonntag*).

45. The Turnberry communiqué did seal the agreement of all alliance members that

a unified Germany had to "be a full member of this Alliance, including its integrated military structure . . . The security guarantee provided by Articles 5 and 6 of the North Atlantic Treaty will extend to all the territory of a united Germany." As the diplomatic impasse over German unification reached its peak, Kohl's government would be able to point to the unanimous wish of his allies as he fended off pressures for compromise at home or abroad. See "Message from Turnberry," communiqué issued by the ministerial meeting of the North Atlantic Council at Turnberry, United Kingdom, 7–8 Jun 90; Kiessler and Elbe, *Ein runder Tisch mit scharfen Ecken,* pp. 153–154. Elbe considered the Turnberry meeting "a decisive chess move of West German diplomacy." He attached more weight to the importance of the conciliatory expressions of goodwill, recounting how Baker "in a formulation that until then would have been 'Genscher-typischen,'" called for a revolution in NATO's thinking about the East. Elbe gives Kastrup credit for telling Genscher that the NATO bureaucracy-produced communiqué was not good enough, thus prodding Genscher to insist on a communiqué that "extends the hand of friendship."

46. The following account is based on Zelikow's notes of the meeting. For background, see Zelikow through Blackwill and Kanter to Gates, "Meeting of the European Strategy Steering Group on June 11," 9 Jun 90.

47. See Kimmitt (Acting) to President Bush (for his evening reading), 18 Jun 90.

48. On the original Holik proposal and the ultimate variant discussed between Bonn and Washington early in July, see Rice (actually Zelikow) through Blackwill and Kanter for Gates, "Your European Steering Group Meeting on Follow-On Conventional Forces Negotiations and the NATO Summit," 28 Jun 90; EUR briefing paper for Paris Two Plus Four Ministerial, "Limiting German Manpower Levels: The U.S. Perspective," n.d.

49. An extraordinary concern about secrecy had dominated all the deliberations of the European Strategy Steering Group. Even the existence of the group was not publicly known at that time. The account of the June 12 meeting is based on Zelikow's notes. For background and copies of the working group papers discussed herein, see Zelikow through Blackwill and Kanter to Gates, "Meeting of the European Strategy Steering Group on June 11," 9 Jun 90.

50. Shevardnadze to Baker, 13 Jun 90; transmitted to certain diplomatic posts in State 193792, "Soviet Proposed NATO-WTO Declaration," 15 Jun 90. For an analysis of the Soviet proposal, see Zelikow through Blackwill and Kanter to Scowcroft, "Soviet Proposal for Joint NATO–Warsaw Pact Declaration: A Preliminary Analysis," 18 Jun 90. On NATO discussion of the proposal, see USNATO 3579, "Soviet Proposal for a NATO-WTO Joint Declaration," 20 Jun 90; USNATO 3591, "June 20 NAC Discussion of Soviet Proposal for a NATO-WTO Joint Declaration," 21 Jun 90. For British views of a NATO–Warsaw Pact declaration, see Seitz to Zoellick, "June 20 One-plus-Three Meeting: British Ideas on a NATO-Warsaw Pact Declaration," 18 Jun 90 (with British paper attached).

51. The account that follows is based on Zelikow's notes of meeting with Gates and meeting of group on June 18. For background on the meeting, see Blackwill and Kanter to Gates, "Your Meeting of the European Strategy Steering Group on June 18," 15 Jun 90; Zoellick to Blackwill, "Attached Draft," 14 Jun 90.

52. See Seitz and Clarke through Kimmitt and Bartholomew to Baker, "Arms Control in Europe: CSCE Mandate Talks?," 15 Jun 90. Ambassador Woolsey and the CFE delegation in Vienna were cautious; they also wanted to avoid any early talks on a new CFE mandate, but they shared the NSC staff's skepticism about trying to go for a quick CFE I-a accord. See, e.g., USVienna 1724, "CFE and the London-NATO Summit," 19 Jun 90.

53. The NSC staff analysis to support the "up to one half" deep cuts approach was the Zelikow-drafted Annex A (option 5) to the revised NSC staff (Kanter-Wilson) paper,

"CFE II Objectives." For the version of this paper being considered on June 18, see Tab 2 attached to Blackwill and Kanter to Gates, "Your Meeting of the European Strategy Steering Group on June 18," 15 Jun 90.

54. Wolfowitz visited U.S. military commanders in Europe during mid-June. NATO and U.S. supreme commander General John Galvin was opposed to unilateral withdrawal of Lance missiles or nuclear artillery, preferring to hold these moves back as bargaining chips for an SNF arms control negotiation. But neither the Office of the Secretary of Defense (OSD) nor the Joint Chiefs chose to press this case in Washington.

55. Participants in the June 19 principals' meeting were Baker, Cheney, Powell, Scowcroft, Ross, Hadley, Graves, and Blackwill (and possibly Gates). We have not located any written notes for this meeting. But Ross, Hadley, Graves, and Blackwill all came to Zelikow's office immediately after the meeting to dictate the revisions to the draft declaration. This account is based on that debriefing, on Zelikow's notes of the meeting with Scowcroft just prior to the principals' discussion, and on Zelikow through Blackwill and Kanter to General Scowcroft, "Your Meeting with Your Counterparts on the NATO Summit, Tuesday, June 19," 19 Jun 90.

56. The nature and scope of CFE follow-on negotiations continued to be debated within the government. The NSC staff, joined by OSD and Arms Control and Disarmament Agency, preferred to hold open all options for an ambitious and more open-ended follow-on negotiation. See Rice (actually Zelikow) through Blackwill and Kanter for Gates, "Your European Steering Group Meeting on Follow-On Conventional Forces Negotiations and the NATO Summit," 28 Jun 90; State 214255, "NATO Summit and Future Conventional Arms Control," 30 Jun 90 (instructing embassies to hold open the option for ambitious follow-on talks); see also USVienna 1866, "CFE: Summit Discussions over Follow-On Negotiations," 2 Jul 90; USNATO 3790, "HLTF: Draft Language for London Summit Declaration," 2 Jul 90.

57. Thatcher had just informed President Bush of her government's plan for SNF arms control. Unlike the U.S. approach, which concentrated on land-based missiles, the British approach included other systems and agreed on aggregate requirements for cuts (to a number well above zero) that could be satisfied by some combination of artillery and missile systems. The British thought that their strategy would deflect public attention from the decision that air-delivered systems ought to be omitted from the categories being negotiated while allowing a formula to be developed that would protect these systems just as effectively. Promising the unilateral withdrawal of artillery would therefore have immediately ruled out adoption of the preferred British approach to future negotiations, and the American leaders were unwilling to dismiss London's thoughtful views out of hand. For the British views, see, e.g., message from Prime Minister Thatcher to President Bush (sent through special channels), 17 Jun 90.

58. Hadley told other officials that his NATO high-level group and the nuclear planning group were ready to accept the unilateral elimination of nuclear artillery shells and radical reductions in the theater stockpile. All understood that NATO was moving toward complete reliance on offshore and air-delivered systems. This account is based on Zelikow's notes of the meeting of Kanter's working group on June 7.

59. On the development of the NATO consultation plan, see the "Next Steps with Allies" section of Zelikow through Blackwill and Kanter to Scowcroft, "Your Meeting with Your Counterparts on the NATO Summit, June 19," 19 Jun 90; "Future Work" portion of Zelikow through Blackwill and Kanter to Gates, "Meeting of the European Strategy Steering Group on June 11," 9 Jun 90; and the notes from Zelikow to Blackwill minuted on USNATO 3188 and USNATO 3211, 31 May 90, in Zelikow's files. For a sense of the state

of preparations in NATO's international staff (with a draft declaration accompanied by three separate annexed declarations on arms control, CSCE, and defense), see Roberts (secretary of NATO's Special Political Committee) to NATO SPC Members, "Summit Declaration (DSD/1 Revised)," 21 Jun 90.

60. Messages from President Bush to Chancellor Kohl, Prime Minister Thatcher, President Mitterrand, Prime Minister Andreotti, and Secretary General Wörner, 21 Jun 90.

61. Teltschik, *329 Tage*, pp. 281–282.

62. Message from Wörner to President Bush (sent through special channels), 25 Jun 90. Wörner suggested the addition of language to the declaration restating the Western position on German unification, and this was done. The quotation of Wörner's note in Beschloss and Talbott, *At the Highest Levels*, p. 235, is not a direct quotation of Wörner but a quote of someone else's recollection of Wörner's reaction.

63. Thatcher had been uneasy about Bush's April decision, announced in May, to push for an early and decisive NATO summit. She explains her reaction to Bush's proposed summit declaration, especially the disagreement over NATO nuclear strategy, in *The Downing Street Years*, pp. 810–811; see also message from Prime Minister Thatcher to President Bush (sent through special channels), 25 Jun 90. The U.S. proposal had not caught London by surprise. The British embassy in Washington was extraordinarily, even uniquely, knowledgeable about the development of the U.S. ideas and had provided useful advice about some of them.

64. Bush did send a copy of the draft declaration to Canadian prime minister Mulroney on June 27. On the choreography at NATO, see Blackwill to Scowcroft and Gates, untitled, 25 Jun 90; USNATO 3675, "Further Comments on Summit Declaration," 25 Jun 90; State 211592, "Managing NATO Discussion of Summit Declaration," 29 Jun 90.

65. See USNATO 3771, "Discussion with Secretary General Wörner on Managing NATO Discussion of Summit Declaration," 29 Jun 90. Wörner had to cancel NATO meetings and suspend a process that had already produced a revised draft declaration with more lengthy annexes. See USNATO 3750, "London Summit Declaration: June 28 I.S. Draft," 28 Jun 90. On the Wörner-Thatcher discussion, see USNATO 3784, "SYG Wörner's June 29 Discussion with Prime Minister Thatcher on the NATO Summit Declaration," 29 Jun 90.

66. The account that follows is drawn from message from President Bush to Prime Minister Thatcher (sent via special channels), 1 Jul 90. Thatcher discusses this exchange of messages in her memoirs and asserts that, because of her messages, "some of the more eye-catching and less considered proposals were dropped." Thatcher, *The Downing Street Years*, p. 811. This assertion is incorrect. The only proposal significantly diluted under British pressure was the promise of "further, far-reaching reductions" in a future conventional arms control treaty to be negotiated after CFE was signed. That dilution was negotiated in London at the drafting session of foreign ministers.

67. Teltschik, *329 Tage*, pp. 287–289.

68. For the discussion that follows, see ibid., pp. 289–293; message from Teltschik to Scowcroft (sent via special channels), 27 Jun 90; message from Scowcroft to Teltschik (via special channels), 30 Jun 90. See also Bonn 20259, "Kohl and Genscher on Force Levels of a United Germany in Vienna CFE Talks," 28 Jun 90. Scowcroft also called Teltschik on June 29. They agreed that there were no basic differences in their approach, but Scowcroft reiterated the White House's determination to avoid any drafting work on Bush's proposal until the leaders arrived in London. Teltschik, *329 Tage*, p. 291.

69. Teltschik, *329 Tage*, pp. 293–296. On the morning of July 3 Kohl discussed the troop limits issue with Genscher, Stoltenberg, Seiters, Kastrup, Naumann, and Teltschik.

Then, after a full cabinet meeting to discuss the 1991 budget, Genscher met privately with Teltschik, followed by further discussion between Teltschik and Kohl. Although the West Germans had agreed that the treaty codifying national limits on all the armed forces in Europe, including the German Bundeswehr, would be concluded after the current CFE treaty was signed, there was continuing uncertainty on the extent to which they would be bound to accept these limits later.

70. For the discussion that follows, see message from President Mitterrand to President Bush (sent via special channels), 29 Jun 90. Mitterrand's security adviser, Admiral Jacques Lanxade, met with Scowcroft on June 29. Lanxade also met privately with Blackwill. For background, see Hutchings through Blackwill for Scowcroft, "Your Meeting with Admiral Lanxade, June 29," 28 Jun 90. NSC staffer Basora was traveling to Paris and, with U.S. embassy officer Kim Pendleton, met with Mitterrand's counselor Hubert Vedrine on July 2. Basora then conveyed a detailed description of the Elysée Palace's attitude toward the declaration, including the text of France's lengthy proposed counterdraft to replace the U.S. language on CSCE. Paris 19892, "Elysée Comments on NATO Draft Declaration," 3 Jul 90.

71. Message from President Bush to President Mitterrand (sent via special channels), 1 Jul 90.

72. See Blackwill to Scowcroft and Gates (via electronic mail to their assistants Florence Gantt and Diane Edwards), "Allied Responses to Our Draft Declaration," 30 Jun 90.

73. See message from President Gonzalez to President Bush (sent via special channels), 3 Jul 90; USNATO 3804, "London Summit Declaration: July 2 NAC," 2 Jul 90; USNATO 3805, "Strategy for the London NATO Summit—The President's Intervention and Managing the Declaration Drafting Process," 2 Jul 90; USNATO 3831, "The London NATO Summit Declaration—July 3 Discussions among NATO Permreps on Drafting Procedure," 3 Jul 90. Taft recommended that in London the political directors go over the draft before the ministers worked on it themselves. This advice was not heeded. He also underscored the need for a strong chairman in the ministerial negotiation, recommending Dutch foreign minister Hans van den Broek—a welcome suggestion in Washington, where officials recalled Van den Broek's skill in managing the ministerial negotiations at the May 1989 NATO summit. The Norwegian foreign minister would ordinarily have served as the chairman, but Wörner helped to put Van den Broek in the chair.

74. See Zelikow through Blackwill and Kanter to Scowcroft, "Briefings on the NATO Summit at Kennebunkport on July 2," 28 Jun 90; and Scowcroft to President Bush, "Preparing for the NATO Summit: Briefings in Kennebunkport on July 2" (probably forwarded to Bush on June 29 or 30). The Zoellick briefing paper was an attachment to Scowcroft's memo. The president's package also included a paper from EUR, "NATO and Its Future Political Role"; an NSC staff paper, "Conventional and Nuclear Arms Control"; a copy of a memo from JCS chairman Powell to Zelikow, "Pre-Summit Briefing at Kennebunkport—Defending Europe," 27 Jun 90; and another EUR paper, "NATO Summit: CSCE Proposals," 28 Jun 90. James Cicconi's handwritten notes of the meeting in Kennebunkport on the morning of July 2 have been preserved, and the briefing materials also capture both the tone and the substance of the discussions. Joining Bush at this briefing were Quayle, Baker, Cheney, Powell, Brady, Scowcroft, Bartholomew, Wolfowitz, Zoellick, Seitz, Ross, Blackwill, Zelikow, and the White House staff secretary, James Cicconi.

75. On the phone calls, see Memcons of telephone conversations between the President and Prime Minister Martens, Prime Minister Schlueter, and Prime Minister Lubbers. All the calls were made from Kennebunkport.

76. The account that follows is drawn from Teltschik, *329 Tage*, pp. 298–301; Zelikow's notes of the meeting; and verbatim NATO transcripts of the summit meeting, document C-VR(90)36. The account of this session and of Thatcher's remarks in Beschloss and Talbott, *At the Highest Levels*, pp. 235–236, is inaccurate and misleading. They report an exchange between Baker and Thatcher which did not take place, at least not during one of the London summit sessions, and misconstrue her reference to Alan Clark's book *Barbarossa* as anti-German. She actually referred to both Clark's and Casper Weinberger's recent books as parables on the theme of preparedness. Teltschik, who was present, also noticed no particular animus against Germany in Thatcher's remarks. Neither should readers rely on Beschloss and Talbott's summary of the summit declaration. They are incorrect in asserting that Kohl had dropped his opposition to singling Germany out for special troop limits.

77. When this language was referred to heads of government for their final approval, Genscher intervened to say that this correction must have been a typing error: surely it should have read "reduce," not "limit." Hurd, who had forced this compromise, drily assured the group, "I don't think there is a mistake in the drafting."

78. By 1991 several of the East European states were already openly expressing interest in joining the NATO alliance itself. The original concept for the diplomatic liaison missions anticipated this development. The idea was founded on the belief that any credible security guarantees for these countries could not be manufactured by a treaty but had to evolve from years of deepening political and military cooperation in alliance councils. The diplomatic liaison missions, and later the North Atlantic Cooperation Council, were designed to be the vehicles for this evolution.

79. For this and other language, see "London Declaration on a Transformed North Atlantic Alliance" (full text), 6 July 1990, reprinted in *Survival*, 32 (September–October 1990): 469–472; Teltschik, *329 Tage*, pp. 301–304; record of NATO summit heads of government session on July 6, NATO document C-VR(90)36, pt. 2; and fact sheets on NATO summit initiatives issued in London by the White House Press Office, 6 Jul 90.

80. In a discussion of French attitudes in a July 16 meeting of the Gates group, Bartholomew and Hadley said that some French officials had hoped the NATO leaders would announce a major restructuring of NATO responsibilities between U.S. and European defense components, although Paris had not actually proposed this idea. Everyone wanted to find a way to bring France into the review process put in motion by the London declaration, though not, as Wolfowitz commented, at the expense of kicking the United States out of Europe. He thought, quite rightly, that some of the French security ideas tended to prophesy an American departure and then offer solutions that would help realize such predictions. Bartholomew described French attitudes at this time as "a form of existential pessimism." See Zelikow's notes from European Strategy Steering Group meeting, 16 Jul 90.

81. See, e.g., Joachim Fritz-Vannahme, "Die Geschichte machen die anderen," *Die Zeit*, July 20, 1990, p. 4. In mid-July Blackwill met with Mitterrand's chief security adviser, Admiral Jacques Lanxade, and they agreed on the need for a confidential bilateral dialogue on strategic issues. The dialogue would be between officials from the Elysée Palace and the White House, in part because Lanxade disliked Reginald Bartholomew of the State Department and in part because of the notoriously poor relations between Baker and Dumas. Although Blackwill left the government in July, the U.S.-French plan went ahead. Discussions began in the fall of 1990, boosted by the cooperative spirit that prevailed between Bush and Mitterrand and between their chief security advisers, Scowcroft and Lanxade, during the Persian Gulf crisis. With relations between Baker and Dumas con-

tinuing to go downhill and Scowcroft and Lanxade working well together, the effort was orchestrated entirely between the NSC staff (in particular Basora, Zelikow, and later David Gompert) and Mitterrand's advisers at the Elysée Palace (especially Lanxade, Pierre Morel, and Caroline de Margerie). There were several productive meetings in both Washington and Paris. Tensions eased, and the two countries began to recognize their opportunity to end the old transatlantic feud over allied nuclear strategy.

82. For the letter and the account of its delivery, see message from Moscow to White House, sent via privacy channels, 7 Jul 90.

83. The West Germans had continued financial negotiations with Moscow during June over the DM 5 billion credit and the arrangements for picking up existing East German obligations to the Soviet Union. On these talks and on the Kohl-Mitterrand discussions of aid to Gorbachev, see Teltschik, *329 Tage*, pp. 274–275, 279–280, 283–284.

84. Thatcher, *The Downing Street Years*, pp. 762–763.

85. Teltschik, *329 Tage*, p. 288. The Dublin summit also went beyond the general commitment to political union agreed to in April to schedule an intergovernmental conference (IGC) that would negotiate a treaty establishing a European union. Whatever one's view of this enterprise, it is hard to dispute the factual accuracy of one aspect of Thatcher's account of this decision: the leaders made this decision although they "were either unable—or perhaps at this stage unwilling—to spell out precisely what political union meant for them. Top marks for calculated ambiguity, however, must have gone to Sig. Andreotti, who suggested that although we must set up an IGC on political union, it would be dangerous to try to reach a clear-cut definition of what political union was." The chairman, Irish prime minister Charles Haughey, concluded the discussion by assuring the gathering that the worrisome or objectionable dangers Thatcher had warned about, whatever they were, would "be excluded from political union." Thatcher, *The Downing Street Years*, p. 762.

86. This account is based on Zelikow's recollections, and Teltschik, *329 Tage*, pp. 289, 305–310. Gorbachev had written to Bush on July 4 about the upcoming G-7 summit in Houston. He thanked Bush for having agreed to grant GATT observer status to the USSR, noted that the December 1989 USSR-EC trade agreement had begun to operate, and praised the just-concluded Washington agreement as a "genuine 'breakthrough'" in U.S.-Soviet economic relations. He therefore asked Bush, as chairman of the G-7 meeting, to direct the summit toward "working long-term agreements on large-scale credit and investment cooperation which in effect would be a serious factor of stabilization and a transition to the market economy in the USSR." Bush's July 6 letter on the NATO summit promised a more detailed reply later on G-7 matters, and Bush later conveyed the G-7 decision to initiate an IMF study of the Soviet economy, while observing that Western aid prospects "would be enhanced by your decisions to take more radical steps toward the construction of a market economy, by shifting substantial resources from the military sector, and by reducing your support to nations that promote regional conflicts." Japan's concerns about "the Northern Territories" were also noted. See Burns through Rice and Deal to Scowcroft, "Letter from the President to President Gorbachev on the Houston Summit," 13 Jul 90.

Beschloss and Talbott portray Kohl as having argued for aid to Gorbachev at the NATO summit in London, and they say that Bush, eager to avoid alienating Kohl, did not object; see *At the Highest Levels*, p. 236. In fact, Kohl did not push the credit issue in London, and he was well aware of Bush's objections, since they had discussed the matter both in person and over the telephone in May and June. This book also has Gorbachev pleading for aid in a letter to the G-7 leaders and threatening that "without this radical step, a further renewal of our society will not be possible." They then interpret this blunt threat as Gorbachev's effort "to extract a bribe for consenting to a united Germany in NATO." But the words "radical step" in the quote from Gorbachev's July 4 letter was not a reference to Western aid. The phrase referred to Gorbachev's internal reforms. Western aid is mentioned only obliquely in this message. If Gorbachev was attempting to "extract a bribe," he was not relying on this letter to convey such a demand (and he did not get the bribe).

9. Germany Regains Its Sovereignty

1. Michael Beschloss and Strobe Talbott, *At the Highest Levels: The Inside Story of the End of the Cold War* (Boston: Little, Brown, 1992), pp. 238–239.

2. Seitz to Baker, untitled, 4 Jul 90.

3. Zelikow interview with Tarasenko, Providence, June 1993. Falin also discusses the circumvention of all the usual organs of collective leadership. Valentin Falin, *Politische Erinnerungen,* trans. Heddy Pross-Weerth (Munich: Droemer Knaur, 1993), p. 495.

4. On the conservatives' "last chance," see Robert Kaiser, *Why Gorbachev Happened: His Triumphs, His Failure, and His Fall,* rev. ed. (New York: Simon and Schuster, 1991), p. 337. The quotation from the conservative attack is from Moscow Television Service, "Makashov Addresses 19 June Russian Conference," June 19, 1990, in *FBIS-SOV* 90–120, June 21, 1990, p. 92.

5. For Kvitsinsky's account of the debates, see Julij A. Kwizinskij, *Vor dem Sturm: Erinnerungen eines Diplomaten,* trans. Hilde and Helmut Ettinger (Berlin: Siedler, 1993), pp. 37–38; for a good general summary of the congress's first week, see Kaiser, *Why Gorbachev Happened,* pp. 336–348. Gorbachev's lengthy opening speech to the congress is excerpted in Mikhail S. Gorbachev, *Gody trudnykh reshenii, 1985–1992: izbrannoye* (Moscow: Al'fa Print, 1993), pp. 218–222. For Shevardnadze's embattled appearance, see Moscow Television Service, "Shevardnadze Speech," July 3, 1990, in *FBIS-SOV* 90–129-S, July 5, 1990, pp. 7–10; and "Foreign Minister Shevardnadze," July 7, 1990, in *FBIS-SOV* 90–131-S, July 9, 1990, pp. 47–50. Gorbachev's allies thought that Falin was stirring up some of the attacks against Shevardnadze. It is noteworthy that Falin describes his position as: "Unification— yes, annexation [*Anschluss*]—no." Falin, *Politische Erinnerungen,* p. 490. Ligachev used the exact same formulation in one of the attacks on Shevardnadze during the party congress. See TASS, "Ligachev, Shevardnadze Cited," July 7, 1990, in *FBIS-SOV* 90–131-S, July 9, 1990, p. 57. For more illustrations of the attacks on Shevardnadze and more of the debate on Germany, see *Pravda,* July 11, 1990, pp. 5–6, quoted in *Current Digest of the Soviet Press,* 42, no. 33 (1990): 18–19; Moscow Television Service, "Mikulin on Foreign Policy," July 5, 1990, in *FBIS-SOV* 90–130-S, July 6, 1990, p. 10 (Major General Ivan Mikulin was an active-duty officer serving with Soviet forces in Hungary); *FBIS-SOV* 90-130-S, "Baklanov on Peace Initiatives," pp. 13–14 (Central Committee party secretary Oleg Baklanov); TASS, *FBIS-SOV* 90-130-S, p. 16 (for reports of public defense offered by Kvitsinsky and Falin). Shevardnadze's disappointment with Gorbachev is reported in Beschloss and Talbott, *At the Highest Levels,* p. 234.

6. Horst Teltschik, *329 Tage: Innenansichten der Einigung* (Berlin: Siedler, 1991), p. 325.

7. For the Gorbachev quote to Kohl, see Teltschik, *329 Tage,* p. 325. For the second week of the congress, see Kaiser, *Why Gorbachev Happened,* pp. 348–356. On the Shatalin plan and the differences between it and the Ryzhkov plan, see Ed Hewett, "The New Soviet Plan," *Foreign Affairs,* 69 (Winter 1990–91): 146.

8. Eduard Shevardnadze, *Moi vybor: V zashchitu demokratii i svobody* (Moscow: Novostii, 1991), p. 239.

9. Zelikow interviews with Tarasenko, Providence, June 1993, and Pavel Palazschenko, Moscow, January 1994. Palazschenko's praise for NATO's good "first step" was published as P. Vorob'yev, "Zhit' Bez Vraga: NATO peresmatrivaet vboyu rol'," *Trud*, July 25, 1990. Beschloss and Talbott are incorrect in saying that Baker forwarded an advance copy of the London declaration to Shevardnadze; see *At the Highest Levels*, p. 237. Baker, in the June 22 Berlin meeting with Shevardnadze, only revealed the planned American CSCE initiatives. Shevardnadze's and Tarasenko's problems become clearer when they saw how conservatives on the Central Committee staff, such as Falin and Portugalov, were framing the NATO summit for the Soviet public. See press reports in *FBIS-SOV* 90–128, July 3, 1990, p. 4, and *FBIS-SOV* 90–129, July 5, 1990, pp. 4–6. For Akhromeyev's later appraisal of the London NATO announcements, see S. F. Akhromeyev and G. M. Kornienko, *Glazami Marshala i Diplomata* (Moscow: Mezhdunarodniye Otnosheniya, 1992), pp. 260–261, though Akhromeyev credits the London NATO decisions as the first of three reasons why the Soviets withdrew their objections to full German membership in NATO.

10. "Comments by Soviets on NATO," *New York Times*, July 7, 1990, p. 5; TASS, "Shevardnadze on NATO Communiqué," July 6, 1990, in *FBIS-SOV* 90–131, July 9, 1990, pp. 2–4. See Baker to President Bush (for his evening reading), 13 Jul 90.

The most negative reaction to the London NATO declaration came from East Germany, though from Foreign Minister Meckel, not Prime Minister de Maizière. Meckel's SPD-East was agitating for complete denuclearization and withdrawal of all outside forces from Germany. Reflecting a year later, Meckel admitted to Elizabeth Pond that the Americans considered him "more Soviet than the Soviets," but explained that he had just been trying hard to address Soviet security concerns. The West Germans also noted, with raised eyebrows, that Meckel and his top aide (and old friend from the West German peace movement) Carlchristian von Braunmühl were appointing relatives to ministry posts and had insisted on sending a new East German ambassador to the United States even as the GDR was on the verge of extinction. See Elizabeth Pond, *Beyond the Wall: Germany's Road to Unification* (Washington, D.C.: Brookings Institution, 1993), p. 220, and the harsh portrait of Meckel's ministry in "Wer ist Teltschik?," *Der Spiegel*, August 6, 1990, p. 56. For more insight into East German attitudes, see Ulrich Albrecht, *Die Abwicklung der DDR: die 2 + 4 Verhandlungen, ein Insider-Bericht* (Opladen: Westdeutscher Verlag, 1992), pp. 93–94. For the West German Chancellery's annoyance with Meckel, see Bonn 21593, "Chancellery Views on Issues Related to German Unity," 11 Jul 90; for the American view, see Rice to Scowcroft, "Your Meeting with GDR Foreign Minister Meckel, July 13," 12 Jul 90.

11. The best primary source on the negotiation of the treaty working out the circumstances of political union is the account of the chief West German negotiator (with a contribution from his East German counterpart), Wolfgang Schäuble, *Der Vertrag: Wie ich über die deutsche Einheit verhandelte*, ed. Dirk Koch and Klaus Wirtgen (Stuttgart: Deutsche Verlags Anstalt, 1991), pp. 101–264.

12. Zelikow interview with Chernyayev, Moscow, January 1994. Chernyayev also thought that, if there had not been a coup, Gorbachev might have been forced to resign during December 1990. For Gorbachev's comment to Bush at their September meeting in Helsinki, see the excerpt from the Soviet memcon quoted in Anatoly Chernyayev, *Shest' let s Gorbachevym: po dnevnikovym zapisyam* (Moscow: Progress Publishers, 1993), p. 358.

13. Teltschik, *329 Tage*, p. 310.

14. The account that follows is based on Teltschik, *329 Tage*, p. 307; EUR paper, "Limiting German Manpower Levels: The U.S. Perspective," n.d. but apparently written

during the second week of July (copy in Zoellick's office files includes Zoellick's annotations about Bartholomew's views); and Zelikow's July 12 notes about the debriefing on the Baker-Genscher and Scowcroft-Blackwill-Teltschik consultations in Houston. Baker arranged to have the NSC staff confer with Defense Department officials to arrive at the Americans' preferred troop number, which he could pass along to Genscher, with nothing written down. American preferences dovetailed with the range being considered in Bonn, though the working-level analyses leaned, like those of the West German Defense Ministry, more toward the upper end—380,000–400,000.

15. Teltschik, *329 Tage*, pp. 312–313. Although we did not review records of Meckel's meeting with Baker, Meckel and Scowcroft had disagreed about the future of nuclear weapons, the presence of allied troops in Berlin, and the inclusion of eastern Germany in NATO. See Zelikow's notes of meeting between Meckel and Scowcroft, 13 Jul 90.

16. See Bonn 21593, "Chancellery Views on Issues Related to German Unity," 11 Jul 90; Teltschik, *329 Tage*, pp. 312, 315.

17. Teltschik, *329 Tage*, pp. 316–317; for another eyewitness account, see Theo Waigel and Manfred Schell, *Tage, die Deutschland und die Welt veränderten: Vom Mauerfall zum Kaukasus, Die deutsche Währungsunion* (Munich: Bruckmann, 1994), p. 28.

18. The discussion that follows is based on Falin, *Politische Erinnerungen*, p. 494. Chernyayev confirms Falin's last-minute efforts to turn Gorbachev around, but he says that by this time Falin and the Central Committee staff had little influence on the Soviet president. Zelikow interview with Chernyayev, Moscow, January 1994.

19. The account that follows is based on Zelikow interviews with Chernyayev, Moscow, January 1994, and Tarasenko, Providence, June 1993.

20. Teltschik, *329 Tage*, p. 319. Kvitsinsky later attached a good deal of importance to Wörner's trip. Kwizinskij, *Vor dem Sturm*, p. 51 (mistakenly dating the visit as occurring on June 14 instead of July 14).

21. Both the German and the Soviet notes of this meeting have, in effect, been published. They are consistent, and the account in the text draws on both. See Teltschik, *329 Tage*, pp. 319–324; Gorbachev, *Gody trudnykh reshenii*, pp. 223–233. Direct quotations from Gorbachev are from the Soviet memcon and are given as quotations in the original. See also Chernyayev, *Shest' let s Gorbachevym*, p. 358.

22. Waigel and Schell, *Tage, die Deutschland und die Welt veränderten*, pp. 31, 37.

23. Ibid., pp. 34–37.

24. The constant historical presence of the Second World War was felt on the German side, too. Press spokesman Hans Klein's book about this trip recounts or evokes anecdotes and episodes from the war on literally dozens of different occasions. See Hans Klein, *Es begann im Kaukasus: Der entscheidene Schritt in die Einheit Deutschlands* (Berlin: Ullstein, 1991).

25. Waigel and Schell, *Tage, die Deutschland und die Welt veränderten*, pp. 41–42.

26. On the Kohl-Gorbachev exchanges on this point, see Teltschik, *329 Tage*, pp. 337–338; and Pond, *Beyond the Wall*, p. 324 n. 26.

27. On this late night conversation, see Klein, *Es begann im Kaukasus*, pp. 234–235. Klein treats the passages in quotation marks as the chancellor's actual words. Participants in this discussion were Kohl, Genscher, Waigel, Teltschik, Klein, Kastrup, and Gert Haller from the Finance Ministry.

28. Gorbachev was joined by Shevardnadze, Sitaryan, Kvitsinsky, Soviet ambassador to the FRG Vladimir Terekhov, press spokesman Arkady Maslennikov, and an interpreter. Kohl was accompanied by Genscher, Waigel, Teltschik, Klein, Ambassador Blech, Kastrup, Haller, Walter Neuer from the Chancellery staff, and the interpreter.

29. On the following account of the meetings in the Caucasus, the best sources are Teltschik, 329 Tage, pp. 319–339; and Waigel and Schell, Tage, die Deutschland und die Welt veränderten, pp. 37–52; see also Klein, Es begann im Kaukasus.

30. Talking to the American chargé in Bonn, George Ward, at a July 19 reception, Teltschik recalled the Germans' surprise at the breakthrough in Moscow and commented on the lack of debate over major issues. Gorbachev's own dominance had seemed so complete that he appeared to be making policy at the table, brusquely overruling his subordinates. Bonn 22864, "Teltschik's Comments on Recent Kohl-Gorbachev Meeting," 23 Jul 90. Kastrup, briefing allied ambassadors at NATO, made similar points. It was remarkable, Kastrup commented, to see Gorbachev in action. See USNATO 4094, "FRG Political Director Kastrup Debriefs the NAC on Kohl-Gorbachev Meetings in the Soviet Union," 19 Jul 90.

31. The account that follows is drawn from Kohl statement from AP wire; Gorbachev remarks from FBIS translation of live TV broadcast on Moscow Television Service, 16 Jul 90.

32. Pond, Beyond the Wall, p. 223. As it dawned on American officials that journalists were forming this impression of U.S. incapacity (in part because the journalists did not know about some of the American efforts but also because many journalists simply did not understand the story), U.S. officials reacted with surprise and alarm. Zoellick and Ross then gave the press extensive background information on the subject in Paris. But journalists could detect the tone of defensiveness, and the first impression stuck. Pond commented later that, for a variety of reasons, "the assumption is now firmly embedded in conventional wisdom that the Bush administration did little to manage the end of the cold war and simply benefited from it as the apple fell into its lap." Pond found this journalistic impression odd, given the "standard German government view (but maverick American view) that the Bush administration did in fact act decisively in helping to shape events in Germany, and that the outcome would have been very different were this not the case." Ibid., pp. 153–154.

33. Albrecht, Die Abwicklung der DDR, p. 86; and see pp. 85–86, 118–21. Albrecht was a West Berlin academic recruited by the Social Democrat Meckel to head his planning staff. The thirty-eight-year-old former minister Meckel, who distrusted the old East German diplomatic bureaucracy, was also aided by Hans-Jochen Misselwitz and Carlchristian von Braunmühl, a psychotherapist who was the younger brother of a diplomat who had been one of Genscher's closest aides in the 1980s. Meckel and his team, strongly influenced by the West German peace movement and Egon Bahr, were skeptical of all the Two Plus Four "establishment" politicians and diplomats. These attitudes were reciprocated by the scorn the West German diplomats felt toward Meckel and his advisers. See Richard Kiessler and Frank Elbe, Ein runder Tisch mit scharfen Ecken: Der diplomatische Weg zur deutschen Einheit (Baden-Baden: Nomos, 1993), pp. 180, 189–201. Whatever the disagreements over substance, the East German Foreign Ministry under Meckel represented a minor party in a CDU-East–dominated government that was going out of existence. Nor did Meckel and his advisers exhibit notable persuasive or analytical skills to offset their weak power base. They were never taken seriously by any of the other governments involved in the Two Plus Four negotiations.

34. On the handling of the Polish question in Paris, see Albrecht, Die Abwicklung der DDR, pp. 109–115. On July 3 Mazowiecki had written to Kohl, reasserting the demand for preunification negotiation of a Polish-German treaty although he knew that Kohl had already rejected it. See Teltschik, 329 Tage, p. 296. The next day the Polish political director joined the other Two Plus Four officials in Berlin to press for new language modifying

the paragraphs covering borders, which had been agreed to in June. He was rebuffed. But the Polish diplomat thought that Poland might settle for a narrow treaty just covering borders, and dropping the more complicated economic issues between the two countries, if the treaty could be produced around the time of unification and ratified before the final settlement took effect. Kastrup told Seitz that only Bush would be able to persuade Kohl to accept this. Seitz to Baker, 4 Jul 90. The American leadership had other things on their mind and were not interested in reopening the border issue. On July 13, just before leaving with Kohl and Genscher for the USSR, Kastrup told Seitz that a Polish-German border treaty could be signed quickly after unification. The amount of time that would be needed could be measured in days, not months. Dufourcq told Seitz the same day that Sku-biszewski would go along with a Polish-German treaty signed *after* unification. Seitz to Zoellick, 13 Jul 90. The momentum of events, and perhaps the NATO summit, had apparently caused the Poles to settle during the second week of July for what they already had.

35. On the meetings in Paris, see Kiessler and Elbe, *Ein runder Tisch mit scharfen Ecken,* pp. 180–181; Eagleburger (Acting) to President Bush (for his evening reading), 18 Jul 90; State 253095, "Official-Informal" (draft detailed report on morning ministerial session prepared by EUR/CE note taker Andrew Goodman), 2 Aug 90; State 253099, "Official-Informal" (draft report on political directors' meeting), 2 Aug 90; and EUR/CE draft cable, "July 17 Two-plus-Four Ministerial in Paris, Afternoon Session with Polish Foreign Minister: Detailed Account," 3 Aug 90. Of the various briefing papers prepared for Baker, the most important is Zoellick to Baker, "Two-Plus-Four Ministerial, July 17, 1990, Paris," n.d. (probably July 15 or 16, 1990). On the Polish position going into the Paris meeting, see Warsaw 10940, "Skubiszewski Statement on 'Two-Plus-Four,'" 13 Jul 90; Warsaw 10942, "Poland and the German Question: Two Plus Four Plus One," 14 Jul 90; Bonn 22115, "FRG Views on Polish Border Issue," 16 Jul 90.

36. The following account is drawn from Memcon for meeting between Baker and Shevardnadze, Ambassador Curley's residence in Paris, July 18, 1990.

37. Shevardnadze is even more unequivocal in his memoirs. "Without the decisions passed by the NATO Council in London, membership of Germany in NATO would have been unacceptable to us." Shevardnadze, *Moi vybor,* p. 236.

38. See State 253097, "Official-Informal" (July 19 Two-Plus-Four Political Directors' Meeting: Detailed Account), 2 Aug 90; Bonn 22679, "July 19 Two-Plus-Four Political Directors' Meeting in Bonn: Briefing NATO Permreps," 20 Jul 90; Seitz to the Record, "Telephone Conversation with Dieter Kastrup, FRG Political Director, 7/26/90," 26 Jul 90; Bonn 23949, "Views of Genscher Advisor on Unification Issues," 1 Aug 90 (reporting on July 31 conversation with Elbe). See also London 14412, "Highlights of Legal Experts' Meeting on German Unification," 26 Jul 90.

39. Teltschik, *329 Tage,* p. 346.

40. Zelikow's notes from August 10 NATO ministerial; Teltschik, *329 Tage,* p. 350 (entry for August 22; the other call was on August 30).

41. A good analysis of the domestic politics surrounding the second state treaty was presented at the time in "Gebot der Schonung," *Der Spiegel,* July 16, 1990, pp. 18–20.

42. See Schäuble, *Der Vertrag.*

43. As an example of the difficulty presented by this issue, one of the many agreements the FRG did not assume from the GDR was an East German treaty which included provisions related to the GDR's restitution and indemnification of Jewish victims of the Holocaust. The apparent FRG decision to jettison these obligations caused a strong reaction among the world Jewish community, which was felt instantly in Washington.

After several discussions of the problem with Bonn, Baker called Genscher and explained that the issue "could cause a firestorm on the Hill against the [Two Plus Four] Final Settlement we are negotiating." Genscher undertook to find a solution. Baker to President Bush (for his evening reading), 30 Aug 90. Another problem for the United States arose from the hasty FRG decision not to apply the existing NATO status of forces agreement to U.S. forces in Berlin. The ultimate satisfactory resolution of both the Jewish claims and U.S. stationing issues are detailed later in this chapter.

44. See Schäuble, *Der Vertrag;* Konrad Jarausch, *The Rush to German Unity* (New York: Oxford University Press, 1994), pp. 169–175; Dobbins to Zoellick, "The Second FRG-GDR State Treaty," July 16, 1990; EmbBerlin 4671, "Outline of the Unification Treaty," 23 Jul 90; Bonn 23253, "Second State Treaty between the FRG and GDR: Interior Minister Schaeuble's Comments," 25 Jul 90.

45. Chernyayev, *Shest' let s Gorbachevym,* pp. 358–359.

46. Treaty between the Federal Republic of Germany and the Union of Soviet Socialist Republics on Good-Neighborliness, Partnership, and Co-Operation, signed in Bonn, November 9, 1990, reprinted in Jonathan Osmond, *German Reunification: A Reference Guide and Commentary* (Harlow, Essex: Longman, 1992), pp. 292–296.

47. The Germans initially considered signing the general treaty in October, to coincide with a planned Franco-Soviet agreement. But they realized that it might anger the Poles if, having promised to conclude the border treaty as soon as possible after unification, the Germans proved themselves able to conclude a treaty with Moscow weeks or months before they finished the treaty with Warsaw. So they signed the general treaty during Gorbachev's November visit, the same week in which they concluded their treaty with the Poles.

48. See CIA to State (George), "GDR Obligations to the USSR," 23 Feb 90; Bonn 18446, "An Outlook on Economic Relations between a United Germany and the Soviet Union," 14 Jun 90.

49. For the account that follows, see Teltschik, *329 Tage,* pp. 357–358.

50. For the general chronology of events, see Teltschik, *329 Tage,* pp. 348–358. On the sanguine West German estimates in July, see Bonn 23949, "Views of Genscher Advisor on Unification Issues," 1 Aug 90 (discussing July 31 meeting between chargé George Ward and Frank Elbe).

51. For the account that follows, see Teltschik, *329 Tage,* pp. 359–360.

52. These negotiations were concluded in Moscow on September 9 and resulted in the quick delivery of 255,000 tons of beef and 60,000 tons of butter. See Teltschik, *329 Tage,* p. 361.

53. By some strange coincidence DM 15 billion is the same sum then–East German premier Hans Modrow had pleaded for from Kohl about eight months earlier. Neither Gorbachev nor Kohl appears to have noticed the parallel. On the issues in the transition treaty negotiations, see also Waigel and Schell, *Tage, die Deutschland und die Welt verän derten,* pp. 52–56.

54. Teltschik, *329 Tage,* pp. 361–363; Bonn 28719, "Kohl and Gorbachev Agree on Amount of FRG-Soviet 'Transition' Treaty," 11 Sep 90. Bush and Kohl had spoken on September 5 and 6, principally about Persian Gulf crisis issues and the upcoming U.S. summit meeting with Gorbachev in Helsinki. Bush and Gorbachev met in Finland on September 9. Bush and Kohl talked again on September 11 and reported to each other on the results of their discussions. The Gulf conflict had dominated all these conversations.

55. See Bonn 31589, "FRG-Soviet Stationing/Withdrawal Treaty: Analysis," 4 Oct 90; Bonn 31573, "FRG-Soviet Treaty on Stationing and Withdrawal: A Synopsis," 4 Oct 90.

The Germans consulted with the American government in exhaustive detail about the progress of these negotiations.

56. Note for Baker, Seitz, Tutwiler, Ross, Dobbins, and Blackwill from Zoellick, "Article by Minister Genscher on U.S.-German Relations," 20 Jul 90.

57. See State 250137, "Working with the FRG on Bilateral Issues," 31 Jul 90; the State Department's European bureau maintained a constantly updated "Checklist of Bilateral Issues with Germany" to provide a running reference for the status of these questions. For background on specific issues, see Germany Task Force paper (DOD-State drafted), "Stationing Rights and the SOFA," 29 Mar 90; Germany Task Force paper (State-DOD drafted), "Berlin Garrison," 29 Mar 90; Joint Staff (J-5) information paper, "Military Liaison Missions (MLM)," 22 Feb 90; L-Young to Zoellick and Seitz, "Legal Options for Basing Rights and a SOFA in the FRG and Berlin," 18 Apr 90; Seitz to Zoellick, 1 Jun 90 attaching EUR/CE-Seymour through Dobbins to Seitz, "Checklist for U.S.-FRG Bilateral Agenda: Berlin and Other Four-Power Issues," 30 May 90; Seitz to Zoellick, "Action Plan for Berlin," 23 Jul 90. Several sets of intelligence issues also arose from the unification of Germany. These matters were addressed by a small interagency committee, co-chaired by William Working and Zelikow on the NSC staff, and including Dobbins and Peter Burleigh from State, Richard Haver from the office of the defense secretary, and representatives from the Joint Staff and the intelligence community. Gates supervised the process. The policies agreed to in this group were then discussed and settled satisfactorily with the relevant FRG officials. The British government was also consulted.

58. See Shostal through Dobbins to Seitz, "Pentagon Meeting on FRG and Berlin Stationing," 21 Jul 90. For the Pentagon perspective, see Weinrod (OSD/ISP) to Hadley, "Meeting with PDAS Dobbins on German Unification/Two-plus-Four Issues," 19 Jul 90.

59. For the discussion that follows, see Bonn 23949, "Views of Genscher Advisor on Unification Issues," 1 Aug 90; Bonn 25322, "Stationing of Forces in the FRG and Berlin," 14 Aug 90; Bonn 26037, "Stationing of Forces in the FRG and Berlin," 20 Aug 90.

60. See Dobbins (Acting) through Kimmitt to Baker, "Request for Signature: Letter to Genscher on Allied Troop Stationing in FRG and Berlin," 15 Aug 90. Baker signed the letter the same day.

61. See Bonn 26813, "Possible Movement in FRG Stationing Position," 24 Aug 90; draft EUR cable (actual message reference number unavailable), "Stationing Talks: Applicability of NATO-Related Agreements to Eastern Germany," 29 Aug 90; Dobbins to Zoellick, "August 23 One-Plus-Three Political Directors' Meeting," 27 Aug 90; Foulon to Zoellick, "Day One of Stationing Talks—Problems Emerge," 29 Aug 90; Bonn 27371, "FRG Stationing Talks: Still Far Apart after First Day of Talks," 29 Aug 90. Baker phoned Genscher on August 30. For Genscher's written reply responding to this call and resolving the key issue, see Genscher to Baker, 31 Aug 90 (the official copy was delivered by the FRG embassy on September 3). Genscher promised an "analogous extension" of the NATO SOFA to the former GDR in a cosmetic form that would allay Soviet concerns during the transition period but "ensure that when members of the forces of the Allies and their dependents travel to the present GDR, they essentially enjoy the same rights as in the Federal Republic of Germany." See also Bonn 24379, "Future Allied Presence in Berlin," 6 Aug 90.

62. See Bonn 28458, "Bonn Stationing Talks," 7 Sep 90 (from Ledsky); Zoellick to Baker, "German Stationing/SOFA and Bilateral Issues—Suggested Points to Mention to FM Genscher in Advance of Moscow," 9 Sep 90; Bonn 28652, "FRG Stationing Talks: September 10 Meetings of NATO SOFA and Supplementary Agreements Working Groups," 10 Sep 90; State 305304, "Status of the Bonn Stationing Negotiations," 11 Sep 90; Bonn 28789, "FRG Stationing Talks: September 11 Update," 12 Sep 90 (from Ledsky); Bonn 28790,

"FRG Stationing Talks: September 11 Plenary," 12 Sep 90; Bonn 28946, "FRG Stationing Talks: Request for Authorization to Agree to Presence Convention Extension," 12 Sep 90; Bonn 28949, "FRG Stationing Talks: September 12 Working Group Meeting on SOFA Extension Note," 12 Sep 90; Bonn 29871, "Revisions to Proposed FRG Note on the Termination of the Relations Convention and the Settlement Convention," 19 Sep 90.

63. See Zoellick to Baker, "German Stationing/SOFA and Bilateral Issues," 9 Sep 90; Baker letter to Genscher, 5 Sep 90 (apparently sent September 7); State 304186, "Briefing Paper on U.S.-FRG Issues for Two-Plus-Four Ministerial in Moscow," 8 Sep 90; Genscher to Baker, 25 Sep 90.

64. On these talks, see Kastrup to Seitz, 29 Aug 90. A controversy later flared up in Germany over whether Kastrup had erred in negotiating the final settlement by allowing the Soviets to immunize their occupation measures, including massive confiscations of property, from any later legal challenge. Kiessler and Elbe defend Kastrup against the charge in *Ein runder Tisch mit scharfen Ecken,* pp. 182–188. Their defense is supported by the negotiating record. The August 17 Soviet draft settlement did include a formal offer of immunity, but the idea of including this blanket protection in a treaty was rejected by both Kastrup and the U.S. government. The September 1 Soviet draft returned to this provision, and it was again opposed by both Bonn and Washington. The matter was thereupon settled by a letter from Genscher to the Four Power ministers repeating a June 15 joint Bundestag-Volkskammer declaration that the 1945–1949 expropriations were irreversible. This was a statement of fact. The question of compensation for the expropriations was reserved to the German parliament. There is no specific language establishing formal legal immunities.

65. These September talks were nominally chaired by the East Germans, but de Maizière, as the new foreign minister, asked his delegation head to yield the chairmanship to Kastrup. Elbe considered it quite fortunate that Meckel's "troop" did not run this crucial meeting. See Kiessler and Elbe, *Ein runder Tisch mit scharfen Ecken,* p. 203. The American delegation was led by Zoellick, joined by Seitz, Zelikow, Young, Koblitz, and EUR desk officer Andrew Goodman. The West German delegation was led by Kastrup and included Elbe, Peter Hartmann from the Chancellery staff, Christian Pauls, Klaus Scharioth, and Martin Ney. The Soviet delegation was led by Bondarenko and included Gennadi Shikhin, Valery Golovin, Valery Rogoshin, Vladimir Grinin, and Kiril Toropov. The British delegation was led by Weston, joined by Hillary Synnott, Jonathan Powell, and Michael Wood. The French delegation was led by Dufourcq, joined by Denis Gauer, Thierry Dana, and Marie-Reine d'Haussy. The East German team (reorganized after Meckel's departure) was led by Helmut Domke, joined by Ernst Krabatsch, Herbert Süss, Fritz Holzwarth, Thilo Steinbach, Max Wegricht, and Günter Hillmann. Unless otherwise cited, the discussion that follows is based on Zelikow's notes of the meetings; various annotated drafts and notes in Zoellick's office files; Moscow 31295, "Soviets Raise Three Points of Contention Regarding Two-Plus-Four Final Settlement," 6 Sep 90 (Kvitsinsky called in Matlock on September 6); and the State Department records of the September negotiations in East Berlin. Seitz to Baker, "September 3 One-plus-Three Political Directors' Meeting in Berlin: Detailed Account," 31 Jan 91; Seitz to Baker, "September 4–7 Two-plus-Four Political Directors' Meeting in Berlin: Detailed Account of September 4 Session," 31 Jan 91; Seitz to Baker, "September 4–7 Two-plus-Four Political Directors' Meeting in Berlin: Detailed Account of September 5 Session," 15 Mar 91; Seitz to Baker, "September 4–7 Two-plus-Four Political Directors' Meeting in Berlin: Detailed Account of September 6 Session," 15 Mar 91; Seitz to Baker, "September 4–7 Two-plus-Four Political Directors' Meeting in Berlin: Detailed Account of September 7 Session," 15 Mar 91.

66. Dobbins to Zoellick, "August 23 One-Plus-Three Political Directors' Meeting," 27 Aug 90 (attaching August 20 letter from Kastrup providing a further debriefing on the Genscher-Shevardnadze meetings in Moscow).

67. See article 3 of the Treaty on the Final Settlement with Respect to Germany, signed in Moscow, September 12, 1990; Memcon for meeting between Baker and Shevardnadze, Fisherman's Lodge, Irkutsk, 1 Aug 90 (the two ministers were joined only by Ross and Tarasenko); Eagleburger to President Bush (for his evening reading), 10 Aug 90 (on August 9 NATO agreement in CFE coordinating group); letter from Kastrup to Seitz, 20 Aug 90; Kiessler and Elbe, *Ein runder Tisch mit scharfen Ecken,* p. 203.

68. At the end of the Berlin negotiations, Elbe and his East German counterpart switched places at the delegation table. The American team noticed, and Zoellick joked about this visible coming together of the two Germanys. One of the old East German diplomats behind Elbe grumbled about his East German colleague that "I've always known where he really came from." Elbe retells the story in *Ein runder Tisch mit scharfen Ecken,* p. 204. The new East German delegation head, Helmut Domke, left no doubt where his sympathies lay. At the end of the session he gave all the delegates a numbered lithograph, prepared for the occasion. It was an austere painting of a waiting room, recognizable to East Germans as the place where they would have to wait interminably under the old regime in order to request permission to travel to the West. Domke thought it was an appropriate memento for a negotiation that would ensure no East German would ever be in this situation again.

69. For the account that follows, see Memcon of meeting between Baker and Shevard-nadze, Helsinki, 9 Sep 90. Only the U.S. government was still expressing concerns about the theoretical linkage of German troop reductions to Soviet troop withdrawals in the final settlement.

70. See Kiessler and Elbe, *Ein runder Tisch mit scharfen Ecken,* pp. 208–209 (on the September 10 meeting with Kvitsinsky); Seitz to Baker, "September 11 Two-plus-Four Political Directors Meeting in Moscow: Detailed Account," 15 Mar 91; Zoellick briefing paper for Baker, "German Final Settlement: Moscow Meeting Notes and Attachments," 9 Sep 90 (with Zoellick's annotations). A later version of this package, dated September 12, reflects the outcome of the last political directors' meeting. Delegations at the September 11 meeting were similar to those at the Berlin talks, except that Kvitsinsky headed the Soviet team instead of Bondarenko, and on the U.S. delegation Rice, who had been in Helsinki and was accompanying Baker, replaced Zelikow.

71. Kiessler and Elbe, *Ein runder Tisch mit scharfen Ecken,* p. 209; Zoellick to Baker, "German Final Settlement: Moscow Meeting Notes and Attachments," 12 Sep 90. Zoellick saw no way to compromise this opposition, except perhaps to accept a prohibition for only as long as Soviet troops remained in Germany. The Americans noted that the language extending the prohibition on movement of foreign troops beyond the accepted ban on "stationing" had not appeared in the Soviet draft settlements of August 17 or September 1. It showed up only in Berlin, in a draft provision that "contingents of troops [from Britain, America, and France] . . . will not cross a line corresponding to" the current borders of the GDR. Then the Soviets proposed adding that foreign troops will not be stationed in the former GDR "and they will not carry out any military activities there." The proposal was first debated on September 6.

72. See Seitz to Baker, "September 11 Two-plus-Four Political Directors' Meeting in Moscow: Detailed Account," 15 Mar 91, attached memcon pp. 10–16 (describing the eve-ning discussion of the issue). This account corrects the inaccurate version of the supposed

"British problem" reported by Pond, *Beyond the Wall*, pp. 324–325 n. 32, based on her interviews in the German Foreign Ministry.

73. Shevardnadze, *Moi vybor*, p. 246.

74. The account that follows is drawn from Kiessler and Elbe, *Ein runder Tisch mit scharfen Ecken*, pp. 210–212; a last-minute reference to the Baker-Genscher understanding was added early in the morning of September 12 to Zoellick's briefing paper on the subject for Baker. See "German Final Settlement: Moscow Meeting Notes and Attachments," 12 Sep 90 (last item in briefing points at Table 3). Although Elbe refers to Baker's being jet-lagged, Baker had been in Moscow for nearly two days, and had traveled there from Helsinki, not Washington.

75. See Shevardnadze, *Moi vybor*. p. 247; Kiessler and Elbe, *Ein runder Tisch mit scharfen Ecken*, p. 212.

76. Zelikow's notes of the meeting; Seitz to Baker, "September 4–7 Two-plus-Four Political Directors' Meeting in Berlin: Detailed Account of September 6 Session," 15 Mar 91, pp. 12–13 of attached memcon.

77. Agreed Minute to the Treaty on the Final Settlement with Respect to Germany, signed in Moscow, September 12, 1990. This provision thus went beyond even West German defense minister Stoltenberg's original February plan for extending NATO to the former GDR. Eastern Germany was not neutralized; it was not demilitarized; Bundeswehr units fully integrated into NATO would be stationed there freely after 1994; and foreign NATO forces could train and exercise (on a small scale, interpreted as fewer than 13,000 troops at a time) in eastern Germany. In a national emergency Germany could interpret "deployed" as needed under the circumstances. On the interpretation of defense provisions in the Final Settlement, see Hearings before the Senate Armed Services Committee, *Implications of Treaty on Final German Settlement for NATO Strategy and U.S. Military Presence in Europe*, 101st Cong., 2d sess., October 4, 1990 (testimony of James Dobbins, Stephen Hadley, and Major General John Sewall).

78. Account based on Rice's recollections of the meeting.

Epilogue

1. On the American military's departure from Berlin, see Stephen Kinzer, "The G.I.s' Legacy: Basketball and Sweet Memories," *New York Times*, September 27, 1994, p. A4. On the Soviet military's departure from Germany, see Claus J. Duisberg, "Der Abzug der russischen Truppen aus Deutschland," *Europa Archiv*, August 25, 1994, p. 16. The Ottawa understanding on U.S. and Soviet troops stationed on foreign soil was never incorporated into the CFE treaty and was overtaken by events.

2. See also the appraisal of Kohl's and Bush's roles in Robert D. Blackwill, "German Unification and American Diplomacy," *Aussenpolitik*, III/94, 211, 223–225.

3. Excerpt from interview with Lothar de Maizière in Ekkehard Kuhn, ed., *Gorbatschow und die deutsche Einheit: Aussagen der wichtigsten russischen und deutschen Beteiligten* (Bonn: Bouvier, 1993), p. 167.

Index

ik,